Psychology for the 21st Century

Jennie Brooks Jamison

Psychology for the 21st Century is meant to inform and educate teachers and students about a wide range of psychological theories and research investigating psychological processes, health, and mental health with an international minded approach. The materials provided are meant for information purposes and are not meant as medical advice or instructions. *Psychology for the 21st Century* is not to be used for self-diagnosis and treatment for any mental health, physical health, or general well-being concern. Please consult a licensed physician or other health care provider about all mental health, physical health, or well-being concerns and discuss anything of interest from this book with that person.

"International Baccalaureate" is a registered trademark of the International Baccalaureate Organization (IB). The material in this text has been developed independently of the IB, which was not involved with the production of this text and in no way endorses it.

© 2017 Wisdom Quest, LLC

ISBN-13: 9781530993345
ISBN-10: 10:1530993342

Printed in the United States of America

About the Author

Jennie Brooks Jamison has been teaching International Baccalaureate (IB) psychology since 1986 at St. Petersburg High School in Florida. Jennie leads workshops for both new and experienced IB psychology teachers and is a long time IB examiner.

Jennie actively practices Tai Chi, Yoga, and P90X, keeps an organic urban garden with her husband, volunteers with Big Cat Rescue in Tampa, hikes the Florida Everglades and the Blue Ridge Mountains whenever possible, and lives St. Petersburg, Florida.

Also by Jennie Brooks Jamison

Understanding Research Methods in Psychology: Second Edition (2013)

Abnormal Psychology: An International Perspective (2013)

Health Psychology: Where East Meets West in Perfect Balance (2012)

Levels of Analysis in Psychology (2010)

Table of Contents

How to choose material to teach:
I will not teach all of this to my own students! Sometimes there are many examples for topics and it is recommended that teachers choose based on their option choices when possible (such as with genes and behavior and then Social Cognitive Theory). I include a large amount of background material so it is available if you want it.

The chapter titles identify the level of thinking strategy (command terms) modeled for students. All chapters for biological, cognitive, and sociocultural approaches to behavior titled **knowledge and understanding** model describe and contain the background knowledge for required topics. Material selected for knowledge and understanding are from the IB syllabus under the column guidance.

Chapter titles using **analysis and evaluation** model explain (for analysis) and evaluate, discuss, contrast, or to what extent (for synthesis and evaluation). They contain applications of the topics for greater understanding, though students should know they can use background studies for testing.

The book is designed for students to develop the highest level of thinking skills.

*To IB teachers: The **human relationships option is not included** because it does not thread through the entire program as well as the other three. I recommend abnormal, health, or developmental for the most streamlined course. The page space was devoted to giving more depth for everything else.*

8

Preface

What can I give you to take home each day from a psychology class that will help you successfully navigate through a more complex and multicultural world? How can I use psychology to give you personal strength and hope for the future? Can I challenge you to think about the development of your own thinking?

Psychology is where we learn how to live and the knowledge should help everyone have a sense of control over the future. Psychology applies to all aspects of our lives, such as raising children, taking care of mental and physical health, understanding friends and family, getting the edge as an athlete, considering the best way to teach, avoiding blunders from misunderstanding other cultures, and succeeding in careers such as medicine, law, and business.

When considering how to set up a book for students studying modern psychology, I focused on creating a multicultural book highlighting practical topics useful for all psychology students. The principles of Jerome Bruner and Lev Vygotsky guide me, and both promote understanding the structure of a subject and learning in zones of development. Bruner's structure is the basis of my top-down component (culture as the main thread) and Vygotsky's zone of proximal development (ZPD) is the basis of my bottom-up component (knowledge to analysis to evaluation).

The age of testing is frustrating and often promotes classrooms focusing on memorizing what needs to go on a test and sometimes nothing else. Students are justified in saying, "I am not a test score!" How many times have I heard this complaint about the educational system's focus on standardized testing? I agree with Jerome Bruner (1977) that there is far too much emphasis on achievement testing over the intellectual atmosphere of the classroom. Education is most relevant when it prepares students *for the future,* and in the twenty-first century students must prepare to live in a multicultural society.

This is not suggesting that people forget their national heritage, and discussions about globalization in this book confirms the need for everyone to learn about their heritage and countries, but also learn about and respect others. This does not mean to accept everyone's beliefs and behavior, but promotes an attitude that all cultures have much to offer if we have a deep understanding of their practices and avoid stereotyping. The multicultural thinker knows the difference between celebrating culture and accepting atrocities, and knows better than to tolerate other's intolerances. Avoid the superficial thinking that comes from social media and extremists! In-depth knowledge and critical thought better serve you.

As Bruner believed, it is more beneficial for students to have an understanding of a subject than it is for them to see the material simply as facts. Facts come and go, but thinking never goes out of style. Investments in thinking are not easily demonstrated on objective tests, though focusing on thinking really does take care of what students need for testing.

The trick to teaching is to sample a range of topics without littering the table with too many. Students tend to manage large amounts of unrelated facts by compartmentalizing the information. They easily get lost in the vast amount of facts out there. This is why a top-down approach using culture to organize the course is valuable. Students approach the bottom-up components of the course with a fresh view.

I had two main challenges in writing this book. One was to break down important ideas without losing their complexity. The other was to provide enough depth. The typical introductory text is far too generalized for students to get an understanding of the material.

Making meaning of human behavior is not easy. Many things contribute to any one behavior. Do not be fooled by popular media that makes it *appear* that human behavior or answers to difficult life problems are simple.

School is *supposed* to be a challenging intellectual experience. However, school does not need to be overwhelming. The trick is to have some good organizing principles.School should push you beyond what you would do on your own, so students, in Vygotskian terms, are a head taller while in class than they are in normal life.

For my mother, Bernice Brooks

Chapter 1:
The 21st Century Student

Chapter Objectives

Students will:
1. Explain attributes of students preparing to live in the 21st century.
2. See how the book is organized for IB students so they can master required skills for their exams.
3. Get familiar with different thinking strategies (command terms in IB language) and understand they must regularly practice critical thinking skills.
4. Learn about a model that organizes the topics to learn both top-down thinking and bottom-up thinking.
5. Get oriented to research methods used to study human behavior, important ethical considerations, and their links to Theory of Knowledge.
6. Be introduced to approaches to teaching and learning and get acquainted with the concept "authentic learning."

1.1 Attributes of the 21st century student
Students in the twenty-first century:

1. *Think globally and are preparing to live in a multicultural world.* Psychology theories and research originated in the US and Europe and were tested on western samples, often college students (Berry, 2013; Berry, et al., 2011; Triandis, 2007, 2002, 1994; Matsumoto & Juang, 2008). We should not downplay the importance of the original theory and the classic studies verifying these theories as they provide a point of departure, but students must understand that psychological topics are incomplete unless they apply to all (Triandis, 2012; 2002). If students stop learning about a topic with an original western view, they risk adopting **ethnocentric** views, something Berry (2013) calls the **dumping** of western psychology on the rest of the world, which overwhelms contributions from other groups to understanding behavior. Do not assume that others share your attitudes, beliefs, or even use words such as depression to mean the same thing!

2. *Are flexible thinkers, able to use many thinking strategies.* Students should study psychology not just for knowledge, but for analysis and evaluation. Students should use a combination of bottom-up and top-down strategies to become the best thinkers possible. This book combines the two approaches. The top-down part of this book uses culture as an organizing principle filtering down into everything else, because culture affects gene expression and neural networks, cognition, and all social behavior and social cognition. The bottom-up part of this book has students learn important knowledge, then demonstrate analysis and evaluation, all the while keeping culture in mind. Every student can benefit

from understanding different ways to think, called command terms in International Baccalaureate Program (IB) language.

3. *Take responsibility for learning.* The IB organization has a list of learner attributes, called the Learner Profile, that apply to all students who recognize that facts change quickly but good critical thinking never goes out of style, especially since they are preparing to interact with people from other cultures. Learners should be knowledgeable, open-minded, good thinkers, principled, reflective, good communicators, balanced, inquirers, caring and respectful of others, and willing to take risks. The **TED talk "The power of belief"** helps you understand that it takes time to develop these attributes and master critical thinking.

4. *Take responsibility for their health.* We know enough about gene expression and neuroplasticity to conclude that people can and should make positive health choices. Just because much of the wear and tear of poor diet, sleep, and stress management habits has not shown up in adolescents, it does not mean they are healthy. In reality, millions of young people are already on the road to poor health, and educators see more students now with health problems that usually did not begin until someone was much older! Education, awareness, and personal responsibility for health choices are critical for educating students in the 21st Century. Health Psychology is an important area of study for everyone. The book provides many opportunities for students to learn they have control over much of what happens to them. Genes are not destiny!

Watch the **TED talk "The power of belief"** to help you understand that it takes time to develop anything you want to do. It is worth making an effort because you will find out why people do what they do in psychology! Used under license with megapixl.com.

1.2: For IB students: Organization of the IB syllabus

The IB psychology syllabus is a modern view of psychology using three approaches to behavior (ATB) for learning. This focus assumes that all human behavior is a combination of biological, cognitive, and sociocultural factors interacting in complex ways.

Each approach to behavior is divided into three sections. AO means **assessment objective**, outlined in the IB psychology syllabus.

1. AO1 topics are basic knowledge, the tools needed for analysis and evaluation with AO2 and AO3 topics.

2. AO2 topics require analysis and application, building on basic knowledge.

3. AO3 topics require synthesis and evaluation, building further on knowledge, analysis, and application.

The syllabus is organized around basic knowledge, then application/analysis and synthesis/evaluation. The idea is that knowledge flows into analysis and application, which then flows into synthesis and evaluation.

Thinking: Regurgitate is not an IB command term!

Avoid making sample model answers using the different command terms and then passing them around to everyone in class. Students using the 'model answer' approach do not learn anything. They memorize and regurgitate on tests, which is the lowest level of thinking. Do not go online and look for model answers, or worse, buy them from people claiming to guarantee high marks if you

can take their model answers to the test. This is not learning! These people are promoting memorizing and their own profit! Is it ethical for someone to sell you model answers to a test? What if examiners are familiar with the model answers? It seems like plagiarism so be careful.

Each assessment level is assigned a group of **command terms** illustrating different thinking strategies, each set matching the goals of the assessment level.

Using different thinking strategies (command terms for IB) effectively

Students must practice using the different thinking strategies (command terms). Critical thinking is not easy but can be mastered with repeated practice. One strategy is to study a topic and then decide what you could say about it when using all the other types of strategies. Practice your own thinking as no one can do it for you.

Over time, students will develop flexibility of thinking by showing they can switch strategies while still using the same material.

When writing, it is important to make it clear which type of thinking is used (command terms for IB students). Students might introduce a topic by, for example, saying they will explain a topic by giving details and reasons. Then students should use these words a few more times in the essay, directing the examiner's attention to the explicit use of the thinking. A table of many thinking strategies (command terms) follows. If studying the IB course, the definitions are in the syllabus. Students can look up the words as a way to get started.

The structure of the IB thinking strategies (command terms) is useful for all students. I do not see the word regurgitate on this list so avoid it!

Inquiry, collaboration, and communication
Try using command terms effectively in regular group discussions. For each testing topic, pretend you must describe it, explain it, etc. For example, what are the important details that for a good description? It is not *all* of them, just the most important ones. We always study more than needed for tests so you can learn. Then go into depth with the important details so it is different from an outline. Also decide which details are important from background material to include when describing a testing topic.

This activity is new so be a good risk-taker and have patience to develop the skill.

The goal is not to create a model answer for all to memorize but for students to streamline study skills. Over time students will spend less time studying because they are more efficient! This takes teamwork. Image source: pixabay.com

Knowledge and comprehension thinking (AO1 level command terms for IB)	Analysis and application thinking (AO2 level command terms for IB)	Synthesis and evaluation thinking (AO3 level command terms for IB)	Taking action (AO4 level command terms for IB): These are for the IA as they must take action
Describe	Comment	Contrast	Design
Identify	Explain	Discuss	Investigate
Outline	Suggest	Evaluate	Predict
		To what extent?	

This book highlights internationalism and culture. As such, it is designed to demonstrate how culture affects all aspects of human behavior, including gene expression and neural activity, cognition, and social behavior and social cognition. The point is to keep internationalism in the back of your mind as you take the course. The model below demonstrates how to do this.

The three approaches to behavior (ATB) are interactive and multidirectional. This **multidirectional model** demonstrates a way to envision and organize the course material.

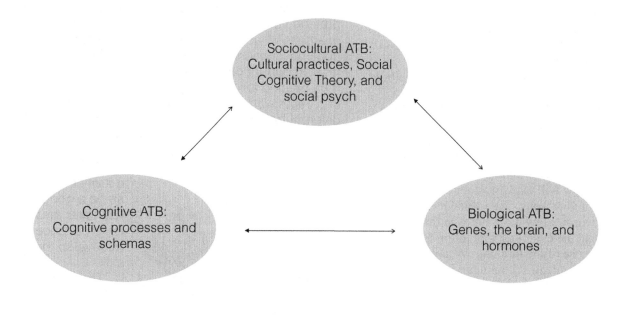

Multidirectional Model

Multidirectional means that each approach to behavior affects the others. Cultural practices are in the top box because they moderate all aspects of human behavior, including social behavior, cognitions, and even genes and neural networks. However, the biological and cognitive approaches to behavior can affect each other and also filters up into the sociocultural ATB for processing. Many examples of multidirectional processing are in the book and examples follow.

1. When studying **eyewitness memory** students will read that memory can be faulty, stress hormones damage memory, and that culture, through own-race bias, affects the process. The cognitive aspects of faulty eyewitness memory have more meaning when taking all parts of the model into account.
2. Some groups have greater genetic risks for **depression** but cultural values of **collectivism** provide a buffer against the actual expression of depression **schemas**.
3. fMRI studies show that people growing up with values of **individualism** and **collectivism** show clear neural differences when considering their view of the self as **independent** or **interdependent**.
4. **Evolutionary needs** for adaptation helped create social behavior such as **conformity** or cognitive processes such as **language**, increasing chances for survival. However, conformity and language are ultimately filtered through our cultural lens.
5. **Schemas** can activate biological processes, such as in **depression**, and contribute to **stereotypes**.

You can see how behavior is created through many different pathways ways using a multidirectional way.

Use of this model increases critical thought. Students can draw it into their essays, referring to it throughout as a way to organize thoughts. The model is demonstrated throughout the book but students can make their own when it is not explicitly included as there is not room in the book to draw a model for each topic!

1.3: Research methods: Quick reference

Research methods and ethics are a primary source of critical thinking in psychology. It is recommended that students get an overview now and then refer back to these pages each time they learn a new piece of research. Chapters 35-37 give more depth.

Each research method is valuable and is selected based on what the researcher wants to know. An introduction to the different research methods follows. There are two general categories of research methods.

1. **Quantitative Research Methods**: Researchers using quantitative methods seek objective knowledge and gather and analyze data with numbers.

2. **Qualitative Research Methods**: Researchers use methods to find meaning and context about people and do not quantify, or use numbers, to gather and analyze data. Qualitative researchers write descriptive reports revealing important themes showing the richness of people's unique situations.

Inquiry, collaboration, and communication

The best critical thinking is woven into essays. Avoid the strategy of describing a study and then tacking something memorized from these pages onto the end.

Practice top-down thinking by studying some theory and then raising an issue, such as what evidence would you want to see about it? Read about the different methods and think about which (or which combination) would be best and even compare with what a researcher used.

Brainstorm how ethics might affect studying the theory before reading the study. Reflect on the ethical rules in a small group as the you read together. Then make a specific judgment (evaluation) rather than simply saying that a study raises ethical concerns or that a study is unethical.

Try reading some original research because often specific strengths and limitations are discussed with the conclusions. The ATL boxes throughout the book also direct your attention to other critical thought, such as tolerating uncertainty or alternative explanations.

Nothing is hard if the teacher helps students flesh it out by helping with critical reading and providing an environment where students can safely learn to take some risks.

Avoid the stress and confusion this person has by taking the time to reflect on methods and ethics at the beginning of the course. Used with license from megapixl.com.

Quantitive methods: Experiment

Why is it used?	Experiments are the only method finding the cause of behavior.

How is it used?	1. Experiments compare at least two groups or conditions, manipulates at least one independent variable (IV) and measures at least one dependent variable (DV), seeks maximum control over variables, uses random assignment to groups or conditions, and analyzes data with both descriptive and inferential statistics. **True experiments** are tightly controlled, take place in a lab setting, and have a manipulated IV. 2. Ethical considerations include informed consent, the use of deception, benefits versus risks to participants, potential harm, participant rights to withdraw and have access to results, and the use of inducements.
Quasi-experiments	Quasi-experiments do not have a manipulated IV and compare naturally occurring traits, for example the males versus the females, and do not use random assignment to groups or conditions.
Field experiments	Data are gathered in a natural setting instead of a lab. An IV is manipulated and a DV is measured but there is less control over extraneous variables. Confounding variables, such as people walking through the parking lot where researchers might collect data, can interfere with the study. Advantages include researching behavior in the real world setting and providing triangulation for lab experiments.
Natural experiments	Sometimes naturally occurring circumstances allow a researcher to investigate a topic that was not planned but where an IV and DV can be identified (Coolican, 2014). One example was the chance to study behavior when a town just got television. The natural experiment by Tannis Williams (1986) in a Canadian town she called "Notel" is a favorite. Williams did not plan the IV but it and the DVs were identifiable. She studied behavior before television and then after it arrived and concluded that creativity and reading fluency dropped and aggression increased.
Strengths and limitations of experiments	Strengths: 1. Control is the greatest strength. Look to see that the sample is well defined, that all variables that might influence the study outcome are controlled, and that participants are randomly allocated to conditions. Students will have much to say about control when writing. True experiments are the most controlled of the experiment types. 2. Experiments are the only research method showing cause and effect. Weaknesses: 1. Poor control is the greatest weakness. Look to see what controls are used. Quasi, field, and natural experiments have less control than true experiments, so this is a weakness. These experiments are valuable, but must be interpreted with less control in mind. 2. Ethics can be a problem. By their nature, participants are sometimes exposed to conditions that might pose some potential harm. Some experiments studied in this book are contentious, because people are stressed in some conditions or deceived. 3. Experimenter bias can influence the study. 4. Low ecological validity is NOT a weaknesses, so avoid this superficial judgment. Experiments are supposed to be artificial because they test theories and not the real world. Triangulation can help with this concern.

Quantitative methods: Correlation studies

Why is it used?	**Correlation** is really a statistic used to analyze data, often from **questionnaires**, a research method used to gather data about human characteristics. Questionnaires are used in genetic research or can ask for attitudes or beliefs. Correlation studies examine relationships, or the extent to which two variables occur together and how they occur together. Correlation never implies causation. Go ahead and call this research *correlation studies*.
How is it used?	Researchers gather data, such as the hours someone watches TV and level of creativity. Results are plotted on a graph and researchers look for the straightness of the line appearing on the graph. The straighter the line is, the stronger the correlation. Correlations can be positive, negative, or show no relationship. Ethical concerns include informed consent, and participant rights to withdraw and have access to results.
Strengths and limitations of correlation studies	Strengths: 1. Correlation can be used when it is unethical to run an experiment. For example, it is unethical to force someone to use Facebook for long periods of time to see if they get depressed. Instead, we correlate depression symptoms with time spent on Facebook and the number of "likes" people have. 2. The research question might ask for a relationship, and it is quite valuable for this. Remember that each method serves a purpose. Weaknesses: 1. Correlation studies never imply causation, no matter how many replications exist. 2. The pathway for the correlation is hard to know. For example, if someone finds a correlation between watching TV and violence, does it mean that TV brings out violence in people or that violent people watch more TV?

Quantitative methods: Surveys

Why is it used?	Surveys aim to make statistical inferences about a larger population, and, for example, might survey a random sample of University of Florida students, and then make conclusions (or inferences) about all the students based on the sample. Surveys are not the same as questionnaires, which usually concentrate on one behavior. Surveys contain a broad range of goals and are useful for evaluating large scale campaigns, such as national health campaigns.

How is it used?	Generally, survey researchers set a series of goals and then write questions for each goal. Surveys are given to random samples of participants. Data are analyzed with correlations or descriptive statistics such as mean and standard deviation. Ethical concerns include informed consent and confidentiality.
Strengths and limitations of surveys	Strengths: 1. Many objectives can be studied at the same time. 2. Surveys use random samples that can be generalized to a larger target population, so they are very useful for finding, for example, how much problem drinking occurs on a college campus and if efforts to reduce it work. Limitations: 1. Ethics are a concern because many surveys are sent out via email and it is impossible to know who filled it out or if the consent form was understood. 2. Social desirability can bias participant answers. 3. Question writing must be correct. One example is the problem with double-barreled questions asking for more than one thing. Which one is the participant answering?

Qualitative method: Interview

Why is it used?	The purpose of an interview is to ask questions to get someone's point of view. Semi-structured interviews are popular with qualitative researchers where the researcher has specific topics to ask but does so in a conversational way so participants can give their personal perspective.
How is it used?	Semi-structured interviews can be one-on-one or use focus groups, and can use narratives, a story that sparks conversation from the participant. Ethical concerns include informed consent, confidentiality, and potential harm to both the participant and researcher. These ethical concerns also apply to observation and case studies. Data is usually analyzed with inductive content analysis, specifically IPA, which reveals important themes.

Strengths and limitations of interviews	Strengths (Coolican, 2004, Neuman, 2006): 1. This is the good way to get someone's point of view, especially if you want to probe deeply into their answers, something a questionnaire does not allow. 2. A natural conversation provides a rich account of a person's situation. 3. People are more likely to give a detailed response if they are relaxed, and may open up the most during an interview using focus groups. 4. Interviews using vignettes allow people to tell their story. Limitations (Coolican, 2004, Neuman, 2006). 1. Reliability can be poor and it is hard to compare data from one study to the next because each interviewer might use different questions. 2. Focus group interviews can create extreme responses, called the polarization effect. 3. Narrative vignettes pose challenges when researcher code responses because of their personal nature.

Qualitative method: Observation

Why is it used?	Observation is the best choice for studying behavior in natural settings.
How is it used?	Observations are either overt, where participants know they are being studied, or overt, where they do not know about the study. Researchers set goals, gain access to an observation site, and write detailed observations, called thick descriptions. Data are analyzed with inductive content analysis, such as Grounded Theory, which reveals important themes.
Strengths and limitations of observations	Strengths: 1. They are high in ecological validity, but only if the researcher knows his or her presence has not affected the study. 2. Detailed accounts of behavior are possible in a natural setting. 3. Covert observations reduce participant expectancy. Limitations: 1. Ethics is a problem for covert observations because of the deception. 2. Overt studies might increase participant expectancy.

Qualitative method: Case Study

Why is it used?	Case studies examine an individual or group within their unique situation. Case studies can follow progress in therapy or examine relationships in corporations. The goal is to get a complete view of behavior and many sources are used, such as interviews, observations, or documentation such as emails and letters. Case studies concentrate on unique traits of individuals or groups
How is it used?	Case studies are intrinsic or instrumental. Instrumental cases are the most important, as they examine how individual or group experiences fit with larger theory. Intrinsic studies are unusual or interesting but rarely apply to a larger group.
Strengths and limitations of case studies	Strengths: 1)They are the best choice for giving detailed descriptions of an event, organization, or the progress of a patient in therapy. 2)Cases focus on context. 3)They often use multiple sources of data, such as interviewing and observing. Limitations: 1)Researcher bias can be a problem. 2)The researcher must be well trained because multiple methods are often used to collect data, such as interviewing and observing.

Theory of Knowledge (TOK) Link for the IB Student: Knowledge Framework

Methods used to produce knowledge is one of the 5 interacting components of the knowledge framework related to areas of knowledge (AOK). Since research methods is a main source of critical thought for psychology, this aspect of TOK is a good link throughout your study of psychology. TOK can be found in everything we do in psychology, so it is important to narrow down a few things so students are not overwhelmed but have something to bring to their TOK discussions.

Some things related to creating knowledge that students can look for as we learn about psychology include:

1. What are the assumptions of each research method? Each assumes that something can be known and shared about behavior, but each also places limitations on what is known.
2. What ethical constraints are placed on research? To what extent is our knowledge limited by ethical constraints?
3. When researchers create models, how well do they really predict behavior? Cognitive ATB is full of examples, such as memory models and the Theory of Planned Behavior.
4. What do we know about someone when we report a statistic about them? Might it vary depending on the choices researchers make about which statistics to use when evaluating data? This is a sophisticated question, so hold judgement until you have studied chapter 35 and 36. For example, the different levels of measurement used with experiments tell you varying things about people.
5. Replication is a defining feature of science. To what extent have psychologists been able to replicate studies? Appendix #5 covers this issue.
6. One interesting area of knowledge (AOK) is indigenous knowledge. Indigenous Psychology (IP) is making a huge contribution to shared knowledge. Stay open-minded and understand that a global psychology includes IP knowledge using different methods. Enjoy learning about other cultures and their contributions.
7. Look up and scrutinize some of the questionnaires used in studies for language biases and operational definitions of concepts. Questionnaires used to measure where someone falls on a cultural dimension is a good choice. Checklists used to diagnose mental disorders is another good choice. What are their strengths and limitations?

1.4: Ethics in psychological research: Quick reference

Decisions about ethics are part of both quantitative and qualitative research and this chart details important considerations. The researcher's ultimate responsibility is to weigh the potential benefits versus potential risks for any study. **Risks versus benefits** should be highlighted by students as an approach to learning: **Thinking skills** (reflection and critical thought), and is critical as an approach to teaching: **Conceptual understanding** (a big idea for research skills).

Ethics issue	Summary
Informed consent	Informed consent forms are the most important tool for researchers. They should include what participants are expected to do, any potential risks they might encounter, that a participant's identity will remain confidential, any limits to confidentiality, that participants have the right to withdraw from the study and remove their data, how the data will be used, and how to contact researchers with more questions.
Confidentiality	This must be guaranteed and outlined in the informed consent form. If there are any limits to confidentiality, these must be clearly stated in the consent form.
Potential harm	All potential risks should be outlined in the informed consent form. For example, someone in an experiment about mental illness treatments must know they could be randomly assigned to a placebo group or perhaps a no treatment group and understand what this might mean for their condition. If there is any potential harm, researchers must make a clear consideration of the benefit versus the risk, and can inflict no lasting harm. If a study poses too much risk, then do not do it. It all comes down to risk versus benefit.
Use of inducements	An inducement is something given to participants, such as money or medical care, for participating in a study. Inducements should never be so much that someone would participate in the study just to get them. For example, one neuroplasticity experiment reviewed in this book paid participants $500 for being blindfolded for 5 days to see neuroplastic changes in the visual cortex. Deciding what is an appropriate inducement is challenging.
Use of deception	Deception cannot be used unless there is no other way to get the data, the risk for harm is not great, and participants are debriefed as soon as possible, hopefully right after their participation. The use of deception is a violation of the rule to get informed consent, and should not be done without careful consideration. Some of the older social psychology experiments used deception and students might consider if they would be allowed today.
Use of animals	The American Psychological Association says animals can be used in research that benefits humans but the benefits must be great, animals must be treated humanely, and given medical care. This might include humanely euthanizing the animals. Students might reflect on the material in chapter 10 about the use of animals in research because a consideration of their ethical use includes deciding if they are good models for humans.

Ethics issue	Summary
Ethics in genetics research	Examples of ethical considerations that come with conducting genetic research follow (see http://genomics.energy.gov and Farah, 2008). 1. Privacy and confidentiality: These should be clearly stated in the informed consent, including the use of the findings in future studies using the same database of participants. The informed consent is the best place to outline who has access to information and if the information can be used in future studies. 2. Fairness in how genetic research is used: For example, to what extent should insurance companies, employers, courts, schools, adoption agencies, and the military have access? What limits are appropriate? 3. How might this information be used in court cases to decide the extent to which someone is responsible for their behavior? 4. How might genetic information stigmatize people or cause psychological problems from knowing genetic differences? Might people be treated differently or face discrimination? Might knowing about a genetic risk become self-fulfilling and cause someone to give up?

The ethical guidelines from both international and national sources have much in common. They all emphasize the need for informed consent. Stemming from getting consent is respecting the dignity and ability for one to make choices about what happens to them, so deception and potential harm must be carefully justified if they are part of the study at all. Benefits must also outweigh risks. Students might examine the website http://psychology-resources.org/ and click on "explore the world of psychology," standards, then ethics. Students can compare international ethical standards with those of many countries. This helps students understand the international nature of research and ethics.

1.6: Approaches to teaching and learning

The IB Organization focuses on the intellectual environment of the classroom and these practices are a fundamental part of all lessons.

The text boxes in this book is where to find application of approaches to teaching and learning. Designing a course involves more than going over material and teachers and students should use these strategies as they go through the course.

Approaches to teaching

Teaching practices will promote:

1. Inquiry
2. Conceptual understanding
3. Reflect both local situations and global awareness

> **IB Learner Profile:**
> **Always working in the background**
> Teachers will see references to profile characteristics throughout the book, such as being open-minded, knowledgeable, balanced, and caring. Being a good thinker doubles as an approach to learning.
>
> Collaboration allows students to practice being a communicator, so group discussion is encouraged and frequently recommended.
>
> You may have noticed that some of the command terms double with the learner profile, such as being reflective, which is part of the definition of the command term discussion.
>
> It is safe to say that the learner profile, the approaches to teaching and learning, and what students must do to meet the demands of the command terms overlap.

4. Teamwork and collaboration
5. The needs of all students
6. Feedback from assessments

Approaches to learning

Learning takes place in these categories:

1. Thinking skills (effective use of IB command terms, among other things)
2. Communication skills
3. Social skills
4. Self-management skills
5. Research skills

Authentic learning

The 21st century student is well aware of global issues confronting them as they become adults and this is a chance to tackle some of interest while studying the course topics. **Authentic learning** is a chance to learn by doing, and students can ponder real problems faced both locally and globally and suggest strategies (Lombardi, 2007).

Even a few authentic learning activities can enrich the course and make students feel more connected to the material. This book includes many chances to authentically learn, and taking the time to use some of them is worth it.

> **Authentic learning article**
> Teachers and perhaps even students should read the article titled "Authentic learning for the 21st Century: an overview" by Marilyn Lombardi. Google the title to read the article.

Chapter 2
Time at the Starting Gate: Studying Autism to get interested in the Approaches to Behavior

---

Chapter objectives

Students will:
1. Learn about autism, an interesting topic to get interested in the levels of analysis.
2. Explain the importance of culture in shaping human behavior.

Humans evolved to live in cultures, cultures that required the evolution of a complex biologically based language and cognitive abilities for development (Matsumoto, 2008; Tomasello, 2004).

Complex human behavior takes place within all three approaches to behavior, biological, cognitive, and sociocultural, and involves social interaction and language use. If someone does not fully participate in human culture, it is an opportunity to investigate why all three ATB are important. The study of **autism** is one such opportunity.

Psychologists often study people with particular deficits to figure out what is supposed to happen, and it may be hard to visualize how important culture is to shaping human behavior until you meet people who struggle to live within it. The multidirectional model illustrates how the three approaches to behavior interrelate when studying autism.

Start the class with Temple's website and TED Talk

Visit Temple's website at www.templegrandin.com and watch her TED Talk titled "The world needs all kinds of minds." The DSM-5 defines autism differently now as a broad spectrum. This means some autistic people participate in some aspects of culture, such as focusing on and excelling in a technical job, and others are very impaired and might never use language. The most impaired people are the ones fully outside of culture and can be seen in the recommended films.

What all autistic persons have in common is problems with social interaction and communication, part of a definition of culture and the deficits defined as abnormal in the DSM-5.

Many autistics make great contributions and this must be appreciated but how do their lives fit with Matsumoto's definition of culture? Culture is defined in the top box on the next page and is detailed in the next chapter. This should help students think about culture.

Sociocultural:
Culture is learned and is defined as a "unique meaning and information system, shared by a group and transmitted across generations, that allows the group to meet basic needs of survival, pursue happiness and well-being, and derive meaning from life" (Matsumoto & Juang, 2008, p. 12). People with Autism have trouble with social interaction and understanding other's minds.

Cognitive:
People with Autism have trouble understanding other's minds, meaning they lack an intact theory of mind. People with Autism can have language, but cognitions are inflexible and not tuned into others. They have damaged theories of mind.

Biological:
People with Autism have, for example, can have damage to the social centers of the brain. There is no one clear picture of damage that applies to all. Possibly over 100 genes are implicated as pathways to Autism.

What is Autism?

Autistic persons have persistent problems with shared social communication and interaction (American Psychiatric Association, 2013). They are not very interested in relationships with other humans and many autistic persons never develop language. Even high functioning autistics have delays in language development and have trouble understanding the intentions of others in social relationships and do not understand expected cultural norms. Autistic persons have limited and rigid interests, such as extensive detailed knowledge of electrical equipment or the weather. Their impairment is obviously outside of normal functioning.

The case of Temple Grandin

Temple Grandin's case is a useful example. She is a high functioning autistic so do not think that all autistics are like her. Temple is an associate professor at Colorado State University with a specialty in cattle management. Temple's language development was delayed until between ages three and four, which is early for most autistics. It was frustrating for Temple that she could not communicate with words. Instead, she screamed or made noises. Temple developed a squeeze machine to help manage her anxieties and later this machine was adapted to calm animals in slaughter houses. Temple was lucky that someone recognized her talents and helped her develop a life around a career.

Temple refers to other humans as ISPs, or interesting sociological phenomena (Grandin, 1999). She openly admits that autistic people are socially inept. Other humans are too complicated and Temple avoids complex social relationships. Temple believes it is more productive to help autistics organize their lives around a career rather than try to improve their social skills. Temple did not even realize that humans communicated emotions through their eyes until she read Simon Baron-Cohen's book about mind blindness.

Temple has a clear rule system with four categories to guide social behavior. The first is 'really bad things', such as murder. The second is 'courtesy rules' such as table manners. The third is 'illegal but not bad', such as illegal parking, though Temple says taking a handicapped parking space is especially a problem because it also infringes on courtesy rules. The last is 'sins of the system', such as going to jail for using illegal drugs.

Anytime Temple faces a social situation, these four categories guide her behavior. Temple is celibate because the rules about social relationships are so complex and emotional that she fears that she might commit a sin of the system. Temple thinks jobs are so important for autistic people that they should never jeopardize them by committing a sin of the system in a social relationship with a colleague. Temple says that autistic people must learn sets of rules and follow them exactly. Navigating social relationships is hard, but if an autistic person wants to date and marry, they should do it outside of work with someone who shares career interests. Autistic people rarely marry and have children. An autistic person would have trouble enculturating, or transmitting culture, to the next generation. Autistics need the assistance of other people who are concerned about their welfare to give them cues about how to behave in a world they have trouble understanding.

Temple thinks in sets of pictures similar to a series of Internet pages stored in her long-term memory. Temple scrolls through these 'web pages' for clues relating to her rigid categories before deciding what to do. Temple says she can pass simple theory of mind tests requiring someone to view a situation as another might. Temple has trouble passing complex mind reading tests. In addition, she has trouble thinking on

---

Thinking skills: Introducing social cognition
People with autism struggle with **social cognition**, something important for human culture. Social cognition means "the process by which people think about and make sense of other people, themselves, and social situations (Fiske, 2004, p. 122). Social cognition is always working in the background and is a motivating factor behind this section's opening statement for studying humans living in cultures.

Studying people with autism is valuable to understand how most people spend their time—being social. It influences a great deal of what we study in the cognitive ATB, such as decision making, schema formation, and stereotyping. It comes up again in the sociocultural ATB with stereotyping and realizing what motivates people to identify with an in-group or model other's behavior. Social cognition is described in the SCATB.

The term **theory of mind** (ToM) is a related concept, meaning people have the intention to understand other's minds. People with autism also have trouble with mind reading tests, discussed in detail in the developmental chapters.

Work to transfer this knowledge to other IB topics, meaning to draw relationships between ideas.

Films about autism
I use two films for this section. One is "The Impact of Disorders and Trauma on the Social Brain." The other is "Rage for Order: Autism."

The films introduce some people with Autism so you can see what their lives are like. In addition, we can learn a great deal about the purpose of human culture, and get an introduction to some cognitive and biological concepts.

If these are not available, any films about autism will be helpful for students to get a sense of what their lives are like.

her feet when faced with new social situations where there is no available 'web page'. Many autistics cannot pass mind reading tests at all. By age four, most children consistently pass mind reading tests and use information for social purposes.

Someone without autism does not create rigid categories that fit every social situation. People receive and process cues from individuals, the group, the situation, and the larger cultural expectations before deciding what to do. They respond one way in a specific context and then differently in another, unlike people with autism.

Autistic people often exist outside of the human cultural context. Autistics are intelligent and are capable of learning detailed physical information but lack the symbolic mental representations needed to process other's social behavior (Pinker, 2002). For example, an autistic may know detailed information about electrical equipment or the weather, but the information is not used to navigate through human social relationships. Rather, it is recited.

The social learning process in autistics is damaged. Attempts at social learning in autistics do not meet the demands of human culture. For example, many autistics imitate in odd ways, such as echoing another's speech instead of trying to make sense of it (Pinker, 2002). The poor social functioning in autistics is caused by damage to the social brain. This damage often starts early in fetal development. An essential feature of our evolved human culture is that we think about what others are thinking, and adjust behavior accordingly to what we think others are thinking (Matsumoto, 2008). For example, when meeting someone new, you automatically start evaluating the other person. Are they nice or smart? Do they seem to like you? In addition, you manage impressions about yourself for the benefit of the other person's same judgments about you. Humans instinctively read other's intentions when they meet up with someone in a social situation and make appropriate changes as needed. We do not scroll through a series of pictures in our minds before deciding what to do; we automatically behave in give and take social relationships that are tied to language. Think of all the social negotiations that go on with a simple task such as manufacturing clothing on a large scale. If humans could not work together each individual would make their own clothing, including growing and weaving.

Temple Grandin and a source for more information about autism

Photo by Rosalie Winard
Curtsey of T. Grandin

It is hard to think about the importance of culture to behavior because we are living in the midst of it, but culture is the most important aspect of human life. The IB mission and learner profile direct students to increase intercultural understanding and become internationally minded, so structuring a course around culture makes sense.

In the next chapter we explore important topics about culture, including culture and cultural norms, etics and emics, and the dimensions of culture.

All three important for the sociocultural approach to behavior. Culture and cultural norms and emics/etics are background knowledge and cultural dimensions are a testing topic, and they are interrelated and offer an elegant way to organize the course. You may not realize it yet but culture evolved to help humans survive and it affects all aspects of behavior, such as cognitions, social behavior, and biological mechanisms such as gene expression and neural networks.

Chapter 3
Describing Culture and the Cultural Tools for Studying Human Behavior

---

Chapter objectives

Students will:
1. Practice using thinking strategies related to knowledge and understanding, with describe modeled. Describe does not mean to memorize and regurgitate. Rather it means to pick out the most important points and use them in a detailed account.
2. Describe human culture.
3. Describe important differences between animals and humans.
4. Describe human subjective culture, a productive way to think about human culture.
5. Describe the importance of etics and emics in psychology research.
6. Describe the importance of cultural dimensions in psychology research.

Start the class with some useful sociocultural topics

Three topics from the sociocultural approach to behavior are worth studying first. Culture/cultural norms defines human culture as distinct from animals, introducing students to the world of human subjective culture. Etics/emics and cultural dimensions are research tools for comparing cultures. Cultural dimensions are directly tested on exams and the other two are background material.

3.1: Culture and cultural norms

Describing culture

Describe means to give a detailed account. The most important details are that humans live in the world of subjective culture where we make meaning out of everything and transmit cultural practices to children. Language is the reason humans have subjective culture, and this is very different from animal social groups. A formal definition is next but don't memorize it. Rather, consider what is important to take away from it.

    Culture is learned and is "a unique meaning and information system, shared by a group and transmitted across generations, that allows the group to meet basic needs of survival, pursue happiness and well-being, and derive meaning from life" (Matsumoto & Juang, 2008, p. 12). This definition helps develop the book's theme, that humans evolved to participate in culture and this participation required the evolution of complex cognitive abilities rooted in language.

Weddings, birthdays, the meaning of laws, whether or not to make you own decisions or look to the group for help, and even popular names for children are examples of human culture (human subjective culture), so pretty much everything humans do shows our culture.

Linking culture and language

Human culture is learned and shared (Heider, 2003). Culture is not genetically inherited. Language ability is innate, but we learn the specific language(s) we speak. Babies adopted from birth by parents from a different culture do not spontaneously make language sounds their biological parents speak. Instead, they make the sounds of the language they hear each day.

To share cultural practices we must have some way of communicating and making meaning with children (Heider, 2003). This is done mostly through language as children are **enculturated**. *Human culture requires complex language so its practices and their meanings can be shared.*

To enter human culture, children must learn from other humans. **Narratives**, a special type of story that helps children understand cultural norms, are the primary way that children learn about their culture (Bruner, 1990). Because *enculturation takes place primarily through narratives*, it is unlikely that children can enter human culture without other humans.

You might want to read the few studies about feral and abused children that point to this conclusion. Students are fascinated with cases such as Genie and feral children, but the cases need some context. Perhaps children can *survive* without other humans, if, for example, they are taken care of by dogs, but children do not develop language and understand human culture without other people

Let's consider the difference between animals and humans. What do you do each day and what do you talk about? You might go to school or a job, play a team sport, or go on a vacation. Animals do not do any of these things unless humans involve them for a human purpose. Most human talk is symbolic, such as getting a job or considering colleges. In contrast, animals live in the world of objects. Research suggesting that animals have basic language abilities train them with tasks using objects rather than abstractions. Animal training to use sign language requires operant conditioning, something not necessary for children to develop language.

Kanzi with his word board. He now lives on a preserve in Iowa.
Photo by Elizabeth Cleaveland
Used with permission of from the Ape Cognition and Conservation Center, apeinitiative.org.

Kanzi, a Bonobo, is an interesting case and should be discussed. Kanzi can follow some abstract commands and even ask for something abstract. Watch the Youtube videos about him and speculate about the extent to which he makes meaning out of what he learns.

How are your relationships different? Human talk takes place mainly through special stories called **narratives**, which involve *making meaning* about something. It is unlikely that you get together with friends and talk about an object, such as a table, but if you do, the conversation is directed at its symbolic value, such as a treasured antique and people tend to tell stories about these sorts of things. You talk about the difficulty of a test, share some new gossip, or talk about future careers, all things requiring people to make meaning. Cultural differences become important because the meaning of what people do and talk about varies.

Human children have plenty of time to acquire culture. Of all the living species, human children are dependent on adults for the longest amount of time (Heider, 2003). While animals come into the world with genetically programmed behaviors, human babies come into the world with a large amount of genetically programmed *potentials* that have to be shaped by culture, such as language. Human babies are *unfinished* at birth. Babies should come into the world with the instructions "some assembly required" (Kalat, 2007)!

Human culture is different from animal social groups (Matsumoto & Juang, 2008). Human cultures are complex, differentiated (can be modified or changed), and institutionalized (Matsumoto, 2008). Humans have grammatical language, a theory of other's minds, a need to enhance the self, complex social relationships, mathematics, art, sports, hobbies, schools, space exploration, and organized war. Humans play varying roles, such as parent, brother, business owner, and soccer goalie.

Films about animal behavior
Students can watch the PBS Nature DVD titled *Chimpanzees* that includes a part about Kanzi. YouTube has many segments about Kanzi and I show *An Ape of Genius* parts 1 & 2. Students might consider the similarities and differences between humans and animals. Do Bonobos have subjective culture?

Norms for each role vary and are communicated to children as they are **enculturated**. Future generations benefit from one generation's improvements and continue them. Consider all that goes into food production. We may take it for granted, but only humans working together with other humans can mechanize food production, send food to all parts of the world, and sell it in stores. Animals do not have the symbolic thinking and language required to have complex, differentiated, and institutionalized lives. If you celebrate your dog's birthday, it is because you want it—the dog has no conception of a birthday. Dogs do not create doggie designer clothing, decide between buying organic or non-organic food, or get together to design better housing or educational systems.

One goal for the future is educating students so they respect other cultures (Matsumoto, 2008). Teaching about ethnocentrism and cultural relativism is a key component to respecting others.

Ethnocentrism and cultural relativism

Ethnocentrism and **cultural relativism** remind us that other cultures *make meaning* in different ways. (Hank Davis, personal communication, December, 2007).

If we fail to recognize the role of **enculturation** in making us who we are, we increase the risk of becoming ethnocentric (Hank Davis, personal communication, December 2007). Ethnocentric people treat their own culture as if it was the model by which all cultures should be judged. The reason the Tabassum interview about depression in Pakistani immigrants to the UK is selected for the topic etics/emics in the next section is because it reminds us to be careful about assuming a word's definition is similar from one culture to another. The study illustrates the problem of assuming depression means the same thing across cultures.

Cultural relativism can help minimize ethnocentrism as long as students understand that relativism does not mean to accept everything or think that all cultural practices are correct. We do not want to become *extremists* about cultural relativism (Tavris & Wade, 2001). It just means that others *can* be right and judgment must be made without ethnocentrism.

Ethnocentrism and cultural relativism represent extremes of thinking and neither show good critical judgment.

Subjective culture: A good way to separate humans and animals

Triandis (1994) uses the term **subjective culture** to describe how people categorize the human-made aspects of their lives, and this includes things such as what happens at a wedding and the meaning of a stop sign when driving. Subjective culture includes language, attitudes, beliefs, categories (**schemas**), norms, roles, and values guiding behavior. One's **language** is the most obvious aspect of someone's subjective culture.

The word subjective means that categories are arbitrary but important to people living under different circumstances. These categories are valued and then shared with others. Subjective culture is transmitted to children through enculturation, making up the expected cultural norms learned early in life. Learning about subjective culture helps students understand how different human culture is from the world of animals, even intelligent Bonobos such as Kanzi.

Everyone creates categories, but what goes into those categories varies between cultures (Triandis, 1994), such as expected gender roles or the values that make up cultural dimensions (such as individualism or collectivism), another topic in this chapter.

For example, two of the many types of norms that are categories guiding behavior are next (Triandis, 1994).

1. *Mores*, an accepted set of behaviors, such as how a wedding should be conducted.
2. *Roles* are a special kind of norm describing how people should act in a social situation. For example, there are gender and parental roles.

Children learn about subjective culture from parents, peers, and institutions (Triandis, 2002).

For example, people in individualist cultures are more likely to value independence and evaluate the self through personal performance (Triandis, 1994). People from collectivist cultures value interdependence and evaluate the self through creating harmonious relationships with others. These norms affect a wide range of behavior, including how someone conforms or values time.

Thinking skills: Tolerate Uncertainty

Kanzi's case helps create boundaries between animal social groups and human culture. What does Kanzi's case mean? Kanzi recognizes commands, such as "put the coke into the jelly jar," but this command and most of his skills involve objects. Kanzi may be a rare case of a chimpanzee learning some interactions without operant conditioning, but if I asked you to pour coke into the jelly jar you might ask why. Kanzi's skills are the result of interacting with humans rather than with other chimps in the wild. Human culture requires **collaboration**, something not seen between chimpanzees in research (Tomasello, 2004).

1. Do other Bonobos have similar skills? Does it matter if there are others? How many cases would you want to see?
2. Consider how Kanzi was trained and how his abilities are similar and different from human language development.
3. What other questions need answering?

Because subjective culture revolves around social behavior, it is largely missing from the daily lives of people with autism. Kanzi the Bonobo does not have subjective culture, even if he does extraordinary things.

Etics and emics is next. The Tabassum interview study illustrates the proper use of etics and emics in research and demonstrates a group's subjective culture, their categories and attitudes toward depression. Use the Tabassum study as research evidence for both topics.

CAS idea: Support Kanzi's home,

Check out apeinitiative.org to see where Kanzi and the other Bonobos now live. The YouTube videos are older and Kanzi is now in a preserve. Students might raise money to support Kanzi and the other Bonobos and help out with ideas for projects such as designing a play gym for them. Bonobos are endangered and need your help.

Nicole Scott is the Research Coordinator and would love to hear from you. She is willing to Skype with anyone interested in learning about the preserve or discussing a CAS project.

3.2: Etics and emics

Describe means to give a detailed account. Next is important aspects of etics and emics. As in all sections in this book using describe, students should collaborate and decide on the most important details. Over time you will get better at doing this so you do not have to be told.

Etics and **emics** are research tools. Etics are used to compare cultures and emics are used to describe cultures (Triandis, 2002). Making meaningful comparisons between cultures can be tricky and requires the proper use of both etics and emics.

Etics are universal behaviors and emics are culture-specific behaviors. Historically, researchers started cross-cultural research with an etic description in mind, such as a western view of **depression**. The behaviors defining the category 'major depression' are useful to the researcher but may be different from emic descriptions of 'depression' within a different culture. If paying attention, researchers quickly realize the original etic description does not apply and then collects data about the emic characteristics of a group to avoid **ethnocentrism**. Emic descriptions may include the word 'depression' but can be used quite differently.

> **Thinking skills/conceptual understanding: Drawing relationships between ideas**
> Etics and emics come up frequently in this course. For example, when studying abnormal psychology the proper use of etics and emics has given the DSM-5 a more meaningful description of anorexia that is a better fit across cultures. Older definitions that required people to have a fear of getting fat did not apply to everyone and prevented accurate diagnoses.

Two researchers studied later in this course who are examples of people highly sensitive to distinctions between emics and etics are Paul Ekman, who studied emotions, and Michael Cole, who studied memory and intelligence. This is one reason why their work is still so valuable. Modern psychologists want make valid comparisons across cultures but also want to value emic expressions of behavior.

Studying depression: An example of using etics and emics

Let's start with an interview study showing why it is important to take emic descriptions of **depression** into account and then we'll look at John Berry's comments about using emics and etics properly in research.

What are the differences between the **emics** of depression and the western **etic** definitions used to evaluate and treat depression in ethnic populations living within western cultures?

The **aim of the interview study** was to compare emic definitions of depression from Pakistanis living in the United Kingdom with the etic descriptions used by western psychiatrists (Tabassum, Macaskill, & Ahmad, 2000).

First and second generation Pakistani men and women were participants. All lived in a poor UK urban setting. Interviews took place in participant's homes in English, Urdu, Punjabi, or a combination of the languages.

Procedures are next. The interviews asked about the perception of causes for mental disorder, family perception and reaction to mental disorder, and the community status of people with mental disorder. The researchers experienced some difficulties translating the questions because the Pakistani culture had some different schemas for mental disorder.

The Pakistani have definitions for the word depression that are different from Western views. This study is useful for abnormal psych with the topics normality/abnormality and clinical biases in diagnosis: culture Used with license from megapixl.com.

Results showed emic descriptions of mental disorder using *physical* symptoms, and 63% viewed *aggression as a main symptom* of abnormality. Pakistan is a **collectivist** culture emphasizing politeness in social behavior. Aggressive displays are viewed as abnormal and are more important to the Pakistani than the emotional symptoms of abnormality valued in the West. Some of the other identified causes of mental disorder were similar to those from western models, with 63% identifying stress as one factor.

Some participants used the terms 'anxiety' and 'depression' but the words in Urdu had different meanings.

Twenty-five percent of the participants attributed mental disorders to supernatural causes and 35% believed in faith healers.

Most males thought a general practitioner (GP) should be consulted for treatment. Fewer females identified a GP as the first person to consult, but there may be cultural barriers to these women getting help from doctors. These difficulties include language barriers, that most of the doctors are males, and many Muslim women have difficulty with hospitalization because of the Purdah.

Many believed families should cope with mental health problems and hospitalization was a last resort.

The interviewer was known to be a doctor, so social desirability possibly interfered with the responses, and this is one limitation of the study.

The study successfully identified barriers women face in getting mental health treatment and differences between emic and etic approaches to understanding mental disorder.

One **conclusion** was that doctors may need more training to understand cross-cultural views of abnormality.

John Berry: Use etics and emics correctly in research

Berry (1969) was the first to apply **etics** and **emics** to cultural research in psychology. Berry asked how psychologists could make cross-cultural comparisons without a specific research strategy.

Etics are pan-cultural groups of continuums and every culture falls onto these continuums in some way (Hank Davis, personal communication, June, 2008). Examples of etics are marriage, kinship principles, views about intelligence, time orientation and all the other dimensions of culture, the education of children, and stress. *When we compare cultures we use etics* (Triandis, 2002). The categories of **subjective culture**, such as expected gender role behavior, can be compared as etics.

Examples of emics are specific definitions of marriage and kinship rules, what is valued in educating children, monochronic or polychronic time orientation, and how stress is experienced.

Describing a culture requires a knowledge of emics (Triandis, 2002). Aspects of **subjective culture**, such as how a group defines abnormal behavior is an example. These are **schemas** and all cultures have them for what is considered normal or abnormal.

A research strategy was needed as psychologists struggled with the problem of how to study cultures so they could be

---

Thinking skills/conceptual understanding: Universalism

Universalism versus **relativism** is studied as background material in the sociocultural ATB, but students should reflect on it's meaning early in the course and why it is important to consider culture—both your culture and other cultures. Students will learn a great deal about other cultures from reading this book.

The goal is to create a global psychology, a universalist position, meaning "basic processes are common to our species, while their development and expression are culturally shaped" (Berry, 2013, p. 55). A complete psychology will eventually include research from all over the world using **etics** and **emics** to study cultures.

Without understanding culture, universalism, and etics/emics, students can get stuck in the rut of thinking that psychology theories formed and studied in the West automatically apply to all. If a topic lacks cross-cultural verification, then the research is incomplete.

understood from the point of view of the native cultures (Berry, 1969).

Berry designed a three-step process outlining the proper use of emics and etics so even a western researcher could fairly study people from nonwestern cultures.

An emic approach studies humans from within their system and the researcher *discovers* cultural practices. In contrast, an etic approach studies cultures from the outside and researchers collect data that fits into *preexisting categories* assumed to be universal. Ideally, psychologists should describe both emics specific to a group and etics that make comparisons between cultures possible.

Historically, psychologists studied other cultures using emics from their own culture (called imposed etics) assumed to be useful. However, these etics were not always meaningful to those studied.

Berry's 3 steps for creating universal categories

Step 1	Step 2	Step 3
Psychologists might have to start cross-cultural research with an imposed etic but cannot assume it is true. Researchers must be open to changing the original (imposed) etic with new information from creating descriptions of behavior in other cultures. The goal is to create a meaningful emic description of behavior that will also fit into a useful universal category. The interview about the meaning of abnormality and depression shows us that describing meaningful emics will require us to alter an imposed etic (that depression is shown through emotions such as sadness).	Researchers next create new categories that reflect what is observed in another culture. Berry called these new etics the *derived* etics, which are more useful for making comparisons between two groups.	Finally, derived etic categories are applied to new research settings, modified again with new data, and then more new etic categories are created. It is only when all groups for comparison have been studied this way that we have real *universals* for comparison.

Both Paul Ekman and Michael Cole (researchers reviewed later in this book, Ekman under universalism and Cole under culture and cognition) approached other cultures with imposed etics, realized they had to change those etics with emic descriptions, and created new methods for meaningful comparisons between cultures. Tabassum's research is also valuable for finding future variables that are real comparisons between cultures. Students studying abnormal psychology should know that the DSM-5 category for anorexia is changed from DSM-IV to reflect the proper use of etics and emics for more accurate diagnoses.

3.3: Cultural Dimensions
The nuts and bolts of cultural dimensions
Describe means to give a detailed account. Next is the important aspects of cultural dimensions.

Communication and social skills: Class activities

Have fun when studying cultural dimensions.

1. Get a copy of Hofstede's book *Exploring Cultures*. Use the activity "What do you see" to orient students to the importance to learning about cultural dimensions. This is fun and promotes communicating.
2. Next we read the section in this chapter about the nuts and bolts of cultural dimensions.
3. Students next go online to Hofstede's website at geert-hofstede.com to read descriptions of some of the dimensions Hofstede studied. Look up many of the countries because students gain valuable knowledge about why stereotypes people have about others are incorrect. Small groups can brainstorm comparisons and contrasts.
4. I use the activity "What do you feel" next from *Exploring Cultures*.
5. Students then know we are leaving nation profiles to work with the dimensions at the individual level.
6. We read theory by Triandis and the supporting study about culture and compliance, another sociocultural topic, by Petrova, Cialdini, & Sills (2007).
7. Time orientation and the self-dimension of independent self and interdependent self are detailed in chapter 20.

Dimensions of culture describe the values of a group, such as if people value independence or if instead they should follow the group's expectations. Cultural dimensions are **etics**, research tools used to compare cultures. For example, we might not know how the foot-in-the-door compliance technique (our sample study) differs cross-culturally without correlating it with individualism and collectivism.

Harry Triandis, Edward T. Hall, and Geert Hofstede are three important contributors to the dimensions of culture (Hank Davis, personal communication, June, 2008).

Hofstede and Hofstede (2005) define a dimension of culture as "an aspect of culture that can be measured relative to other cultures" (p. 23). The dimensions represent values important to groups living together. They emerged as researchers considered how to accurately study behavior cross-culturally.

Research skills: Inventing research tools

Researchers have to invent new ways to study behavior. Cultural dimensions evolved over time to help compare cultures meaningfully.

The dimensions are **continuums**, such as individualism-collectivism. Everyone falls somewhere on the continuums for each dimension with just a few at one extreme or the other.

The dimensions of culture can be studied at either the group level (defined as country), or the individual level. *The distinction is important.* Individualism and collectivism tend to be opposite poles when studied at the country level but people have access to both ends of the poles according to the context of the situation when studied at the individual level (Triandis & Gelfand, 2012).

Hofstede studied the dimensions at the country level and this is what students will see when they visit his website. It is fun and often a student's first experience with the dimensions, but just remember that Hofstede's results are tendencies describing a country as a whole and may not apply to individuals.

Avoid **stereotyping** people by over identifying them with a country level dimension of culture. Students really want to know how individuals behave, so Triandis and Hall are good theories to learn. Many studies now show how individuals behave according to the continuums at the individual level, such as compliance to a request, academic achievement, stress management, health habits, in-group identity, conformity, attributions, emotions, and language use.

The dimensions of culture are abstract so *do not oversimplify* them. Details of cultural dimensions follow.

1. *The dimensions of culture are etics,* or universal behaviors. A dimension of culture must be backed up with research showing it really is universal, also relating cultural dimensions to the topic of **universalism**.

2. *Any etic can be a dimension of culture.* Examples include but are not limited to the following. Individualism-collectivism is the most studied dimension. The first five were identified by Hofstede (2005).

   A. **Individualism versus Collectivism**
   B. **Masculinity versus Femininity**
   C. **Power Distance**
   D. **Uncertainty Avoidance**
   E. **Long and short term orientation**
   F. **Time Orientation: Monochronic versus Polychronic**
   G. **Tight versus loose cultures**
   H. **High context versus low context**
   I. **Independent self versus interdependent self** (the self dimension)

Thinking skills/conceptual understanding: Individualism-collectivism:

1. They are abstractions.
2. Do not oversimplify people's behavior by stereotyping them as one or the other after reading Hofstede's country level profiles.
3. Avoid stereotyping by understanding that everyone has access to both ends of the continuum. People go back and forth based on the context of a situation.
4. The I-C dimension can be overused (Berry, Poortinga, Breugelmans, Chasiotis, & Sam, 2011). Avoid assuming a behavior is explained by individualism or collectivism unless the study explicitly gathers data to show it. Check to see if the study used the dimensions to collect and analyze data.

---

3. *The dimensions of culture were originally ecological level studies,* meaning they were categories used to study groups such as countries rather than individuals. Avoid the **ecological fallacy**. Individuals living in a country cannot be assumed to behave the same way as the national profile. However, people in cultural groups do have *tendencies* to behave as more one than the other.

4. *Where a country falls on the dimensions of culture can change.* Is the world becoming more individualistic? There are many implications for behavior if this is true. For example, aggression may increase in traditionally collectivist cultures if people become more individualistic. In collectivistic countries, an individual's behavior is constrained by the group (called tight cultures) far more than it is in individualistic cultures.

Next is an example chart showing some of Hofstede's nation characteristics. Remember, it is fun to go on the website and look at all the countries, but it is incorrect to apply these nation characteristics to individuals. The next topic is how Harry Triandis described cultural dimensions for individuals.

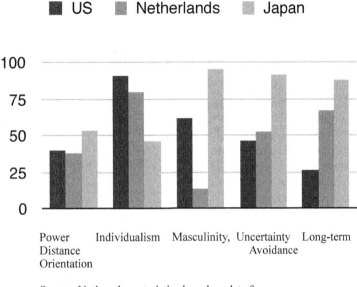

US ■ **Netherlands** ■ **Japan** ■

Power Distance Orientation	Individualism	Masculinity,	Uncertainty Avoidance	Long-term

Source: Nation characteristics based on data from
www.geerthofstede.com/countries.

Triandis on the I-C dimension and individual behavior

Avoid **stereotyping** individuals as strictly individualist or collectivist (Triandis, 1996). Although a group has tendencies toward one or the other, many variations become obvious if a study is properly designed.

Individualism and collectivism generally describe everyone, but *no one is completely individualistic or collectivist.* Instead, think about people as combinations of the two poles.

Individualism_____Collectivism

Characteristics of collectivism:
1. Collectivists are concerned with a group's values and people follow group expectations. Correct behavior is determined by group goals.
2. The 'self' includes characteristics of the larger group. The self is interdependent.
3. In-group norms establish expected behavior. People from collectivist societies are enculturated and socialized to enjoy fulfilling their duty to the group.

Characteristics of individualism:
1. Individualists are concerned with personal goals that may be different from the goals of a larger group.
2. The "self" is independent.
3. People are not expected to follow in-group norms. Instead, meeting one's obligations to an in-group depends on the rewards or disadvantages it brings to the person.

To make further distinctions, numerous types of collectivism and individualism exist. For example, Japanese collectivism is different from other groups. This is illustrated by gender differences in how the Japanese express their collectivism. For example, it is more acceptable for men to comment to other men than to women about politics. Additionally, the Japanese traditionally have a greater difference between their public and private behavior than other people. Private behavior considered immoral by an individualist was not considered immoral in Japan unless knowledge about it became public and tarnished the reputation of the group. Shame is more important to the Japanese and guilt is more important to people in individualistic cultures.

Triandis (1996) eventually decided the characteristics of both collectivism and individualism could be seen as a mix in everyone. *"One way of thinking about these constructs is that we are all collectivists but some of us are also individualists"* (p. 37). Children are dependent on adults and essentially collectivists. Some people are encouraged to act as individuals when growing up and receive rewards for independent behavior. In other places, children are socialized to closely follow the guidelines of the group and receive rewards for doing their duties. A few extreme individualists and collectivists exist, but most people are a combination, with an emphasis toward one side.

> **Thinking skills: Understanding the self**
> One way to categorize how people view the 'self' is through the continuum **independent self-interdependent self**. This is probably another cultural dimension and is described in chapter 21 about evaluating cultural dimensions. Individualism-collectivism is probably correlated with the independent-interdependent self.

Research about individualism-collectivism and compliance

The aim of this correlation study was to strengthen the research on one of the commitment/consistency **compliance techniques**, the **foot-in-the-door** strategy, because early compliance research used only western samples (Petrova, Cialdini, & Sills, 2007). Whether or not you realize it, you have been the victim of the foot-in-the-door either with advertising or on a personal level.

Students will find learning about compliance useful for the knowledge and understanding section for the sociocultural topic **Social Identity Theory** as it is an example of in-group behavior.

Compliance is "yielding to social pressure in one's public behavior, even though one's private beliefs may not have changed" (Matsumoto, 2008, p. 369).

One compliance technique is **commitment/consistency** (Cialdini & Sagan, 2005). Humans want consistency and are more likely to comply with a request if they have already committed to a similar request. Professionals use a variety of strategies to get someone to comply to a request consistent with a previous commitment. The foot-in-the-door strategy is one example where a person makes a small request that will surely be granted. The initial request is followed by a greater request. To remain consistent, the second request will likely be granted.

Evidence was needed to see if cultural differences in compliance were related to personal levels of individualism and collectivism (Petrova, et al., 2007).

Researchers proposed three hypotheses. First, participants who agreed to the first request would comply more frequently to the second request. Second, compliance would be greater in the US students than the Asian students. Third, individualism and collectivism would account for the compliance differences.

All participants attended Arizona State University and surveys were in English. **Variables** to be correlated were complying with a request, being an individualist, or being a collectivist.

Procedures are next. Emails requested that students take an online survey containing questions on numerous topics, such as education and career goals, and consulting family members in decision-making.

One month after the first request, participants received a second email asking them to fill out another online survey related to the first one.

Once someone has their foot in the door it may be hard to get it out. This is a common technique used in advertising. Can you find examples of this technique in ads for items you buy?

Next time you want someone to do something, get your foot in the door with a small request they will surely agree to and then follow it up with the real thing you want. It just might work! Used with license from megapixl.com.

Results showed that 10.2% of the Asian sample and 8% of the US sample complied with the first request. Although a smaller percentage of US students complied with the first request, 21.6% responded to the second request. In contrast, only 9.9% of the Asian students complied with the second request.

The authors **concluded** that, "Although both cultures' participants were more likely to comply with a request if they had chosen to comply with a similar request one month earlier, this tendency was more pronounced among US participants than among Asian participants" (p. 15). In addition, individualism is correlated with compliance to a second request after a first request. Research shows Asian persons are more likely to comply with requests if the request is perceived as expected in-group behavior, which might explain the differences.

The researchers believe strengths of this study include its measurement of behavior in a natural setting and the ability to use surveys for both groups in English.

Differences between the samples were not large, one study limitation. Possibly Asian students attending US universities have more characteristics of individualist cultures than Asian students living in Asia. Correlations show relationships and never imply causes so interpret the results correctly.

Using email as a way to collect data has strengths and limitations. It is easy to distribute email surveys and participants remain anonymous. However, it is impossible to verify who fills out the surveys. Last, participants cannot ask immediate questions about the informed consent forms unless they are present with researchers. This could be an ethical concern for the study.

Communicating and conceptual understanding: Advertising activity and highest levels of critical thought

1. Compliance techniques are all around us. The class could find examples of retailers and **advertisers** using the foot-in-the-door technique and brainstorm how it is used in everyday relationships.
2. Just because a behavior is different cross-culturally it is not necessarily attributed to a dimension of culture. The study has to correlate behavior to the dimensions or divide participants into groups based on testing them as falling at one end of a dimension.
3. Replication is important for validity. Students might explore the extent to which compliance has been correlated to a dimension. A large body of research explores compliance techniques, but it could still be incomplete unless the cultural studies have more than just Petrova's study.

Moving into studying the biological approach to behavior

One reason to study culture, etics and emics, and cultural dimensions first is because the brain, neural networks, and genes unfold within cultures. Students will see many references to these topics in the biological APB and also in all the other chapters. It helps to know what they mean and strengthens the course's internationalism.

Chapter 4
The Biological Approach to Behavior: The brain and behavior: Knowledge and Understanding

Chapter objectives

Students will:
1. Practice knowledge and comprehension thinking strategies, with describe (detailed account) modeled.
2. Describe the nervous system, neural networks, and neural transmission.
3. Describe the organization of the brain into various lobes.
4. Describe neuroplasticity.
5. Describe techniques used to study the brain, such as electrical activity, structural imaging, and functional imaging.

This chapter demonstrates the thinking strategy describe (command term for IB). It is background material for analysis and evaluation in the next chapter about the brain and behavior. Brain parts and processes come up throughout the book so you will know what they mean.

The nuts and bolts about brain structures, brain processes, and techniques needed to study them are needed to understand why, for example, someone has a mental illness, how a child develops language, or how someone responds to emotions on other's faces. Biology works behind the scenes to help create behavior, which is what you want to learn about and the reason you signed up for a psychology course. We stay focused on the people part of biology in this course, so do not worry that the biological information in a psychology course is too hard!

Brain films
You might start this material with the films *The Behaving Brain* and *The Responsive Brain* available to stream from the series Discovering Psychology through www.learner.org. This site has many films to use throughout the course. Students can watch them at home if needed.

4.1: Nuts and bolts of the brain: The nervous system, neural networks, and neural transmission

Depression and children's language development are examples to get students interested in studying the brain.

People diagnosed with **depression** have many symptoms such as sadness and hopelessness, low interest and pleasure in activities, weight loss or gain, trouble sleeping, fatigue, feelings of worthlessness and guilt, reduced ability to think and concentrate, and sometimes suicidal thoughts (American Psychiatric Association, 2013). These symptoms are listed in the DSM-5, a western classification system for mental illness, so keep in mind for future discussions about culture and behavior that people from different cultures can have other symptoms or ways to express distress. However, on a biological level, depression is often associated with lowered amounts of the neurotransmitter **serotonin**, so understanding the nervous system and neural transmission are points of departure for studying mental illness. Watch Robert Sapolsky's **Youtube** lectures about depression to get started!

As a second example, children come into the world with evolved potentials for **language** (Kuhl, 2010). Language has a biological basis but children must develop the language(s) they will speak as they interact with their cultures. Kuhl refers to newborns as children of the world because they can perceive sounds from all languages. Between 10 and 12 months children become children of culture, meaning their perceptual abilities are pruned so they can focus on the sounds of the languages they will speak. Perceptual pruning of excess neurons is made possible by **neuroplasticity**, the brain's ability to reorganize itself in response to experience. Language is also a good behavior to use for **Evolutionary Psychology**, one evolutionary explanation of behavior.

> **Conceptual understanding: Making good generalizations**
> Practice making useful generalizations, such as *the brain is a product of its environmental history over the lifespan.* Good generalizations help students organize material. It takes practice to avoid over or under-generalizing, but the point of the course is to learn to think. **Under-generalizing** is when students fail to see important connections between ideas. **Over-generalization** is when students draw too many relationships that make no sense. Getting a balance takes time.
>
> I suggest reading about a topic, sitting back and reflecting, and then practicing making a good generalization. It will help with organizing the course material without memorizing.

Layout of the nervous system, neural networks, and neural transmission

Just how does the nervous system and neural transmission work? Describe means to give a detailed account, so the important details follow.

Think of the **nervous system** as the biology CEO in charge of helping people have thoughts and movements. This is incredible because even something simple such as jumping away from a car that might hit you or feeling happy or sad is controlled by the nervous system. Detailing the nervous system is a good place to start a study of biology because it is where behavior comes from. It is made up of the brain, spinal cord, sensory organs, and all the nerves connecting these organs to the rest of the body (InnerBody, 2014). A **nerve** is a bundle of many neurons and a **neuron** is a single nerve cell (Gray & Bjorklund, 2014). The nervous system interacts with all other systems in the body and is divided into the **central nervous system** and the **peripheral nervous system**. The central nervous system is the brain and the spinal cord (Gray & Bjorklund, 2014). The peripheral nervous system is the connecting nerves spreading out from the brain and spinal cord to the rest of the body to sensory organs, muscles, and glands. We are not conscious of most of what goes on in the nervous system as it automatically controls our functions, which is a good thing because it would interfere with humans thinking about their social lives!

The brain is a **neural network**, a series of billions of webbed interconnections transmitting signals. Studying neural transmission helps us see how synaptic connections are formed to create the network.

Neural transmission is an important function of the nervous system (See figure below). The brain contains billions of neurons continually talking to other neurons by relaying chemical or electrical signals. Generally, neural transmission is a process that takes place at **synapses**, the junction between neurons. Neural transmission allows for the communication between neurons, releasing a **neurotransmitter** such as serotonin from one neuron that binds to **receptors** of another neuron. Neurotransmitters are chemical messengers. Let's look into the process of neural transmission a little deeper.

Chemical signals are important for this course, so this is the focus of the lesson. **Neurons** are the smallest unit of the nervous system and look different from other cells in your body. Neurons are shaped like trees, with branches called **dendrites** that receive messages from other neurons. The process follows.

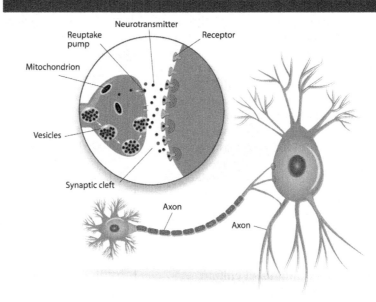

STRUCTURE OF A TYPICAL CHEMICAL SYNAPSE

Neural transmission. Neurotransmitters must cross the synapse for neurons to communicate.
Used with license from shutterstock.com.

1. Neurons fire when enough stimulation occurs to reach a threshold to create an **action potential**. The action potential goes down the trunk of dendrites, called **axons**, which end at the root of the neuron, called **axon terminals**. The axon terminal's membrane that touches one side of the synapse is the **presynaptic membrane**. The neuron on the other side of the synapse is the **postsynaptic membrane**.

2. The pre and postsynaptic membranes do not touch, so there must be some way for one neuron to talk to another. Chemicals called **neurotransmitters** are stored in small sacs at the end of axon terminals and they do the talking.

3. The action potential activates the neurotransmitter to be released from the sacs, cross the synapse, and bind to the receptors of another neuron.

4. The concepts **excitatory synapse** and **inhibitory synapse** help us understand how the brain manages all these communications. Communication between neurons can be excitatory, meaning it creates more action potentials on the other side of the synapse. Communication can also be inhibitory, which decreases action potentials. Thousands of excitatory and inhibitory communication can happen at the same time, and this is important to know because the actual amount of action potentials created is the result of a total effect of excitatory and inhibitory communication (Gray & Bjorklund, 2014). This balance affects how the brain communicates messages and ultimately creates behavior, so it is best if all circuits work the way they are intended. Some neurotransmitters are excitatory, such as **serotonin**, and some are inhibitory, such as GABA.

5. After neurotransmitters bind with receptors on the postsynaptic neuron, some neurotransmitters are left in the synapse that must be removed (Gazzaniga, Ivry, & Mangun, 2014). **Reuptake** is one way, where some remaining neurotransmitter is absorbed back into presynaptic receptors. Reuptake is

important for this course because it is how **Prozac** works, and it blocks the reuptake of serotonin. Prozac is part of a class of antidepressants called selective serotonin reuptake inhibitors (SSRI). It is thought that increasing serotonin at synapses improves mood and lessens depressive symptoms.

Neurotransmitters are chemical messengers that jump across synapses and affect the production of action potentials. Each type of neurotransmitter consists of molecules with similar characteristics (Gazzaniga, et al., 2014).

Serotonin is part of a group of neurotransmitters along with dopamine and norepinephrine called **monoamines**, meaning each is synthesized from a single amino acid. Serotonin is synthesized from **tryptophan**. Serotonin depletion is related to depression, so let's look at it more closely. Our bodies do not produce tryptophan and we must get it from foods such as milk, meat, and vegetables, so it is important to make healthy food choices (Somer, 1999). "No other neurotransmitter is as strongly linked to your diet as serotonin" (p. 14). So keep in mind that the environment interacts with our biology, an important concept that will come up frequently in this course.

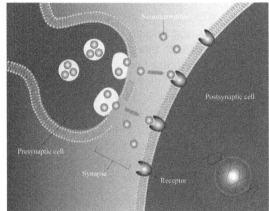

Here is a closer look at neurotransmitters crossing the synapse. This is something students must understand. People diagnosed with depression have too little serotonin in the synapses.
Used under license with megapixl.com.

Besides dietary problems, serotonin depletion can occur because of genetics. One genetic pathway to depression is having the ss alleles of the **serotonin transporter gene**. These people have transcriptional inefficiency, so there is not enough serotonin promoted to the brain (Caspi, et al., 2010, 2003). Remember this because it will come up again in the biological ATB, once with the topic of neurotransmitters and their effect on behavior and with the topic of genes and behavior. This gene is related to depression (abnormal), alcoholism (health) and attachment (developmental).

Serotonin is synthesized both in neurons in the central nervous system and in cells located in the gut. Contrary to popular belief, most serotonin is not located in the brain. Roughly 80% of serotonin is produced in the gut and helps the GI tract operate smoothly. Serotonin cannot pass through the blood-brain barrier, so what is used in the brain is produced there. Serotonin is linked to a large range of behaviors seen by clinicians besides depression, including antisocial behavior, autism, anxiety, addictions, sleep and appetite problems, and eating disorders.

Other neurotransmitters students might study are amino acids, such as g-aminobutyric acid (GABA), which is related to anxiety. Neurons can fire too easily and often without proper amounts of GABA.

Two last terms to know about neural transmission are **agonist** and **antagonist**. Agonists increase activity and antagonists decrease activity.

Agonists are chemicals that influence neural transmission by imitating the action of neurotransmitters at the postsynaptic receptor

> **Thinking skills: Drawing relationships between ideas**
> Neurotransmission details are in this chapter, but the information will be used in chapter 5 with the topic neurotransmitter effects on behavior and again in chapter 9 with the topic genes and behavior.
> **Serotonin** is an example neurotransmitter for this book and it frequently comes up in research. Understanding depression in the abnormal psychology section requires students to think about serotonin.

by either blocking reuptake or increasing their release (Gazzaniga, et al., 2014). **Prozac** is an agonist drug, increasing serotonin at synapses. Antagonists are chemicals that influence neural transmission by reducing the action of a neurotransmitter at the postsynaptic neuron (Gazzaniga, et al., 2014). Drugs reducing dopamine for people diagnosed with schizophrenia are antagonist chemicals.

4.2: The important parts of the human brain
A tour of the brain: How the nervous system is organized

Describe means to give a detailed account. The important details about the human brain follow.

The brain is part of the nervous system. **Morphology** is the biological study of the form and structure of an organism and this section includes subcortical and cortical brain structures and examples of why it is important to know about them. Learning about brain parts does not have to be tedious and boring because in a psychology class there is always the opportunity to apply what you learn to analyzing your's and other's behavior.

The human brain is small at birth and its immaturity allows it to grow as children develop within their cultures, so even when studying the brain it is important to remember that culture shapes all aspects of development. The human brain doubles in weight by age two and continues to grow into adulthood, so it takes a long time to mature.

The brain is kind of ugly but it is possibly the final frontier for science. Researchers are just starting to flesh out how it develops within cultural contexts. Scientists already know what the brain parts are, but this is different from knowing everything about how they work (Gray & Bjorklund, 2014). Avoid oversimplification and have some awe for the work that goes into researching the brain.

The brain is organized in a hierarchical way so its function is an interactive process between cortical (the higher regions), and subcortical (the lower regions) of the brain. The higher regions are used for planning and motivation and the lower regions refine and turn those plans into behavior (Gray & Bjorklund, 2014). Our tour of the brain starts with the higher brain regions.

Cortical brain structure: The higher functions

The cerebral cortex consists of two symmetrical hemispheres and the surface is made up of folded layers of neurons so more can be packed inside your head. The cerebral cortex is then divided further into four cortexes (lobes) making up the **cerebral cortex**.

The four lobes are the **frontal lobe**, the **parietal lobe**, the **temporal lobe**, and the **occipital lobe**. Some textbooks list the **limbic lobe** as a fifth lobe, and we will use this language because the limbic system is important for topics studied in this course. The limbic system is part of the subcortical brain so we will talk about it there.

Think of the **frontal lobe** as the brain's director, serving an executive function. This is the part of the human brain that differs most from animals. This executive function is responsible for **cognitive control**, the ability to select cognitions from a large variety of choices and is required for goal directed behavior and decision-making (Gazzaniga, et al., 2014). Although the frontal lobe is usually highlighted in discussions of cognitive control, it does not work alone but oversees connections with other brain regions, thus making complex behavior possible. The frontal lobe takes a long time to mature and the cerebral cortex has a major growth spurt during adolescence. It makes sense that the human frontal lobe takes a long time to mature within cultures because if the brain was intact early in life, as was once thought, it would be hard to learn. Instead, the brain constantly grows new neurons and connections to adapt to anything you learn or prunes off excess neurons that are not needed. The undeveloped frontal cortex may be a good explanation for why teenagers sometimes have poor self-control, make bad decisions, and engage in risky behavior (Sabbagh, 2006). Another example is learning the **language** or languages spoken in your culture that requires neuronal pruning for the refinement of sound perception during the first year of life that ends with the remarkable ability to speak full grammatical languages (Kuhl, 2010).

There is a general flow of information between all the lobes allowing the cerebral cortex to function as a whole (Gray & Bjorklund, 2014). The brain is set up hierarchically, meaning to be arranged in order of rank, and the higher regions are in constant communication with lower regions.

Subcortical brain structure: Lower brain functions

Subcortical brain regions are the more primitive brain parts and are shared with animals. The term subcortical means the lower regions are located under the cerebral cortex. We'll start at the bottom where the spinal cord becomes the **brainstem** as it enters the brain and work up to the top of the subcortical structures.

There are three parts of the brainstem, the **medulla**, **pons**, and **midbrain**. The medulla and pons help regulate breathing and heart rate so you do not have to think about it, organizes reflexes, and helps with balance. The midbrain is related to movement.

The **thalamus** is on top of the brainstem and generally acts as a relay station connecting other brain parts and helping keep the brain aroused.

The **cerebellum** is important because it helps coordinate movement sequences. The **basal ganglia** manages slow deliberate movement. Both manage sensory information.

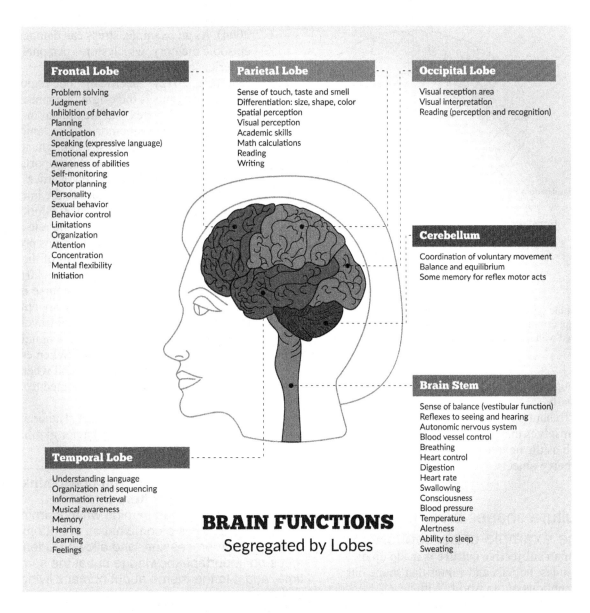

Main brain cortexes (lobes) along with other important brain parts
Used with license from shutterstock.com.

The most important subcortical structure for this class is the **limbic system**, referred to as the **limbic lobe**. It is an evolutionarily older part of the brain and contains the amygdala, the hippocampus, and the hypothalamus.

The **amygdala** regulates basic drives and some emotions. It is intact at birth because, for example, it is related to fears, and animals and humans must have a developed fear response right away to survive. This is adaptive for people and animals. The amygdala is referred to in many places in this book. One place is studying why Prozac helps people lessen **depression**. One experiment about **neuroplasticity** shows that the amygdala is less active after taking Prozac, so fears are calmed (Tao, 2012). The amygdala is also involved for processing emotional memories, such as when studying **flashbulb memory**.

The **hippocampus** is related to memory and emotion. Unfortunately, stress hormones affect the hippocampus, and prolonged stress can even kill off cells in the hippocampus (Sapolsky, 2004). As an example, stress can damage episodic memory, which stores personally experienced memories (Sternberg & Sternberg, 2012). Specifically, one region of the hippocampus is the origin of connections to the cerebral cortex that are crucial in consolidating these memories (Gazzaniga, et al., 2014). Even a word list you might study can be affected by stress, so it is important to manage stress to be an efficient learner.

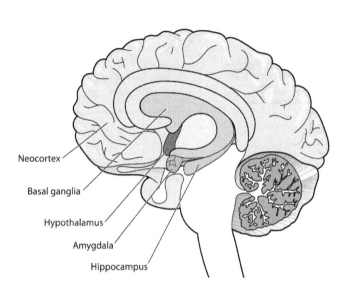

Limbic system: Pay close attention to the amygdala and hippocampus as both come up often in this book. Used with license from megapixel.com

The **hypothalamus** regulates the internal environment of the body (Gray & Bjorklund, 2014). For example, it controls the release of certain hormones. The hypothalamus produces hormones that control a large part of the endocrine system (Gazzaniga, et al., 2014). One hormone of interest to this course is **leptin**, responsible for regulating appetite. Leptin is produced in fat cells and travels through the bloodstream to give a signal to the hypothalamus that you are full. When enough fat is stored, leptin levels drop and when enough fat is lost, leptin levels rise, signaling you to eat. Leptin is an important hormone related to **obesity**.

To sum up, the brain is divided into higher and lower structures that constantly interact. The brain parts themselves may be boring, but they are more interesting when studied with specific behavior in mind, such as the next topic about how people perceive objects.

Culture shapes brain function: The example of perception

Human **subjective culture** is made up of attitudes, beliefs, and values that shape our perceptions of the world. With new knowledge about **neuroplasticity**, culture and the brain cannot be thought of as separate (Ambady & Freeman, 2014). The brain changes quickly in response to environmental demands, so it makes sense that cultural values shape brain structures used during

Thinking skills: Practice Top-down thinking with the culture thread
Keep the culture thread in mind when learning about the brain. It is a combination of bottom-up and top-down processing, and allows students to focus on important knowledge but at the same time, add it to the theme about humans living in cultures.

I will point out some opportunities as we go through the course.

cognitions.

The field of **cultural neuroscience** is new, and aims to study the interaction between culture and biology.

This section focuses on research about how the one's perception of objects varies depending on whether someone lives in a culture valuing collective or individualist practices, linking this section to the study of **cultural dimensions**. It also describes how emotion perception differs cross-culturally.

Studies of object perception are one example. One classic quasi-experiment using a framed-line test

---

Try the Framed-Line Test (FLT)

This is similar to the FLT used in the Kitayama experiment described below. The box is 1 inch in length and the line is 1/4 inch long or 25% of the length of the box.

Directions: The class should try both study conditions (the independent variable), absolute or relative. In a different size boxes from the one above provided by the teacher, draw the line absolutely (1/4 inch), or relatively (25% of the box). Students cannot use a ruler to help and must use their judgment.

Kitayama used Japanese and US participants and you may not be able to replicate the results, but the exercise is a good way to try out study procedures.

---

aimed to see how culture shaped perception. **Procedures** involved Japanese and US participants looking at a square with a line hanging from the top that did not touch the bottom of the square (Kitayama, Duffy, Kawamura, & Larsen, 2003). Then they were asked to draw in squares of a different size under two different conditions, an absolute drawing where the line was to be exactly as it was in the figure and a relative drawing, where the line was to be the same proportion. The FLT is an important tool to gather data because it asks participants to either ignore contextual information (the absolute condition) or use contextual information (the relative condition). The box and line are not social cues. **Results** showed Japanese participants did better with the relative condition that required them to focus on content and US participants did better with the absolute drawing that downplayed context.

Hedden and colleagues used fMRI in a correlation study that **aimed to see** which parts of the brain were used during the FLT, believing context was the reason for the differences (as cited in Ambady & Freeman, 2014). Relative perception involves looking at the context of the drawing and absolute perception does not use context. **Results** showed cultural differences in brain

Inquiry: Challenge assumptions
The 21st century student is interested in understanding other cultures and is educated about the reasons for behavior and cognitive differences.

activation. When in a task condition different from their cultural values, both groups had more brain activity in the frontal and parietal regions related to attention. The authors correlated the findings with collectivism or individualism. So, for Japanese participants, the brain activation was greatest when in the absolute condition, without context, which is valued in **collectivist** groups. For US participants, it was the opposite. Brain activation was greatest in the relative task, where context was needed. Context is not as important to **individualistic** groups. The authors **concluded** that our brains seem to work harder when we do a task that is not consistent with the way our sensory processes develop within our cultures.

Culture shapes brain function: The example of emotion perception

Understanding the intentions of others (having a theory of mind) is critical for survival, a topic detailed further under natural selection and developmental psychology. Someone's facial expression gives signals of what to do within cultures (Ambady & Freeman, 2014).

One study about culture and **emotion** by Chiao and colleagues showed Japanese and US participants pictures of fearful, happy, and neutral Japanese and US faces (as cited in Ambady & Freeman, 2014). In both groups, **amygdala** activity was stronger for the same group faces showing fear, as US participants responded more to US faces and Japanese participants responded more to Japanese faces. Fear signals from the faces of one's **in-group** may have great value for communicating danger and in getting help from other in-group members. It is an adaptive response. The in-group is studied with **Social Identity** in the sociocultural ATB.

What should students take away from learning about culture, object perception, and emotion perception? Do not assume that people in other cultures think the same and it follows that neuroplastic changes throughout the lifespan have created differences in the way the brain is organized that affect behavior.

4.3: Techniques used to study the brain

Describe means to give a detailed account. Next is important details about technologies to study the brain.

Each technique is selected based on what someone wants to know. Each has advantages and disadvantages.

1. Studies of electrical activity, such as EEG, ERP, MEG and TMS.
2. Structural imaging, such as MRI
3. Functional imaging, such as fMRI

Techniques to study electrical activity

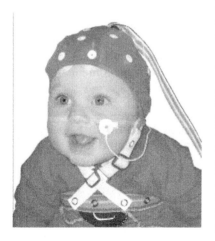

Baby wearing the ERP cap.
Source, Kuhl, P. (2010).
Curtsey of P. Kuhl

Electrical activity is a noninvasive way to study the brain and a good choice for studying language development in babies and small children, sleep stages, and neuroplasticity.

Electroencephalogram (EEG) uses electrodes glued to the scalp to measure electrical activity of the cells where the electrodes are glued (Kalat, 2007). Research about sleep stages shows EEG readings for each of the five sleep stages. For example, we know someone is asleep during stage 2 when a burst of sleep spindles appear on the EEG recording. Tissue from the scalp and skull are passive conductors of electrical current and the EEG gives a constant recording of general brain activity (Gazzaniga, et al., 2014). Although EEG is useful for understanding general brain activity, such as in studying sleep stages, it is not good for studying the brain when a researcher wants to know which brain regions are activated during cognitive tasks.

Event-related potential (ERP) uses EEG and is a good way to measure changes in brain activity as someone responds to stimuli (Gray & Bjorklund, 2014). For example, ERP is used to study language processing in babies (Kuhl, 2010). ERPs show electrical activity timed to a particular stimulus, such as babies hearing words from a language different from the one their parents speak. The goal is to see how the EEG readings fluctuate right after the stimulus to see if the brain responds differently. ERP provides good temporal resolution, is noiseless, and allows researchers to study people without the ability to use language in a study, such as a baby. The brief change in electrical activity is event-related, which explains its name.

Magnetoencephalography (MEG) uses sensors within a MEG helmet to record the small magnetic fields produced by electrical currents in the brain (Gazzaniga, et al., 2014, Kuhl, 2010). "MEG allows precise localization of the neural currents responsible for the sources of the magnetic fields" (Kuhl, 2010, p. 713) and has allowed researchers to study sound discrimination in babies. Babies cannot talk so researchers must rely on brain activity to tell if a baby hears a sound as it registers in the brain. MEG is noiseless and has good spatial and temporal resolution (Kuhl, 2010).

Transcranial magnetic stimulation (TMS) is a way to study localized functions in the brain (Gray & Bjorklund, 2014). An electrical current passes through a well-insulated copper coil and produces a magnetic field that is put over a specific place on the head. The magnetic current passes into the skull and an electrical current is created in the neurons just beneath the skull where the TMS is placed. The neurons are temporarily stimulated and can be used for a variety of studies. TMS produces "temporary lesions" (Gazzaniga, et al., 2014), far less invasive than making permanent lesions in an animal or studying brain damaged people. Researchers can see the role of a specific parts of the cerebral cortex to behavior. TMS affects only areas of the brain just under surface of the skull, including the cerebral cortex (Gray & Bjorklund, 2014). TMS may be useful one day as a treatment for psychiatric disorders such as depression (Horvath, Perez, Forrow, Frengi, & Pascual-Leone, 2013). TMS is generally considered safe but some has potential side effects such as headaches. TMS is loud, so earplugs must be worn. Most studies use a TMS coil that looks like a figure eight, which produces high spatial resolution.

A picture of Alvaro Pascual-Leone holding a TMS coil to a study participant's head is in the next chapter under the section neuroplasticity. Be sure to watch the film about his experiment!

Structural imaging

Structural images measure physical properties in the brain (Gazzaniga, et al., 2014).

Magnetic Resonance Imaging (MRI) shows high resolution images of brain tissue (Gazzaniga, et al., 2014). MRI works by acting on the magnetic properties of the atoms in the brain, in particular hydrogen.

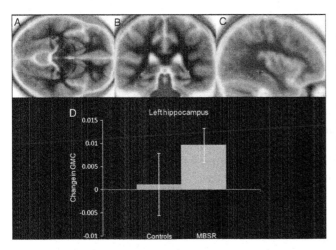

This is what an MRI scan look like. MRI shows that gray matter in the left hippocampus increases after meditation (MSBR group) as compared to controls.

Source: Holzel, B. K., Carmody, J., Vangel, M., Cbngleton, C., Yerrametti, S. M., Gard, T. , & Lazar, S. W. (2011). Mindfulness practice leads to increases in regional brain gray matter density. *Psychiatry Research: Neuroimaging,* 191, 36-43. Used with permission.

A hydrogen atom proton moves constantly, producing a small magnetic field that is not strong enough to align the protons in any particular way. The MRI machine creates a much stronger magnetic field, so when someone enters the scanner, their protons become oriented to the direction of the magnetic field. Next, radio waves pass through the magnetized regions and the protons absorb the energy. The radio waves make these protons give off a signal the MRI machine senses. The MRI then makes a three-dimensional picture of brain structure that can be viewed from many angles. MRI is useful for studies when a researcher wants to study something structural about the brain.

Functional imaging

Some great advances in studying the brain come from the ability to see how it functions when someone does a task. **Functional imaging** (fMRI) measures "metabolic changes correlated with neural activity" (Gazzaniga, et al., 2014, p. 105), and is different from just seeing brain structure with MRI or its electrical activity with EEG. The next chapter has a section about **neuroplasticity** that includes an fMRI experiment demonstrating how Prozac affects the adolescent brain to reduce **depression**. The figure below shows fMRI scans demonstrating how Broca's area develops differently when someone learns a second language early or later in life.

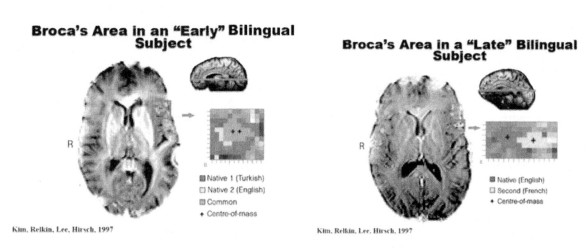

fMRI shows how Broca's area develops differently when someone learns a second language early or later in life. Teachers can use 'The Mind' series about language to see Joy Hirsch explain these fMRI readings in more detail. Source: Kim, K.H., Relkin, N.R., Lee, K., & Hirsch, J. (1997). Distinct cortical areas associated with native and second languages. *Nature*, 171-4.
Curtsey of J. Hirsch

fMRI creates a magnetic field around someone's brain, causing hemoglobin carrying oxygen to give off radio waves measuring the amount of blood used in even deep brain regions (Gray & Bjorklund, 2014). The image shows a blood oxygen level-dependent effect, or **BOLD effect**. *Blood flow increases when a brain region is active*. Blood releases oxygen to active neurons faster than to inactive neurons. (Gazzaniga, et al., 2014). Participants in fMRI studies can watch a computer screen inside the scanner and talk to researchers through a microphone as they do a study task (Gray & Bjorklund, 2014). Researchers use a control condition and compare it with the BOLD areas image during a task to identify brain areas with the greatest increase of activity to decide which brain areas are active.

4.4: Neuroplasticity

Description of neuroplasticity: The important details

Neuroplasticity refers to "the brain's ability to reorganize itself in response to the environment throughout the lifespan. Neuroplasticity allows neurons in the brain to compensate for injury or disease and to adjust their activities in response to new situations or changes in their environment" (www.medterms.com).

Neuroplasticity is necessary for having an interactive approaches to behavior view of psychology. Experiences are powerful modifiers of our brains. Some factors causing neuroplasticity are pre- and postnatal experiences, stimulating environments, sex hormones, diet, genetics, drugs, brain injury, and stress (Kolb & Robinson, 2011; Kolb, Gibb, & Robinson, 2004).

The important details of neuroplasticity follow.

1. *The assumption underlying neuroplasticity is that as behavior changes there must also be a corresponding change in the neural circuitry that produces behavior* (Kolb, et al., 2004). Neuroplasticity occurs over the entire lifespan, though the brain is most plastic early in development.

2. *Neuroplasticity is the normal state of the nervous system and its mechanisms that suppress or enhance the brain are adaptive* (Pascual-Leone, 2009). Neuroplasticity makes everything possible from mastering the violin, adapting to blindness after one loses sight, learning to use a computer, or responding to Prozac too treat depression.

3. *Individual neurons are very specialized and must interact with others to affect behavior* (Pascual-Leone, 2009). Neuroplastic change is made possible when individual neurons are engaged with others through neural networks. Neuroplasticity is probably one of evolution's great accomplishments to help us survive environmental demands.

4. Kolb and Robinson (2011) outline eight principles of neuroplasticity, but it is enough for students to understand just a few. These help students avoid oversimplification when evaluating research.

A. *Neuroplastic changes are time-dependent.* Neuroplastic changes in the brain differ over the space of a few day but then are not necessarily permanent. Do not assume changes are permanent, especially when interpreting lab experiments run over short periods of time.

B. *Neuroplastic changes might happen just at certain ages.* Many assume that young brains are always better at making neuroplastic changes than older brains but this is not always true. For example, different types of neuroplastic changes depend on age, which Kolb found in his experiments about rats living in enriched environments.

C. *Not all neuroplastic changes are good.* For example, brain changes to the prefrontal neurons from drug and alcohol abuse might be the cause of bad behavior in addicts.

Chapter 5
The Biological Approach to Behavior: Analysis and Evaluation: The Brain and Behavior

Chapter objectives

Students will:
1. Practice thinking strategies related to analyzing and application as well as synthesis and evaluation. Explain and evaluate are modeled.
2. Explain neuroplasticity and evaluate research on its importance to understanding the effects enriched environments on the brain, what happens to the visual cortex after blindness, and how Prozac alters the brain.
3. Explain localization of function in the brain and evaluate research related to understanding bilingualism, including a whistled language.
4. Evaluate contributions of technology to understanding brain function and behavior as applied to childhood obesity, lie detection in court, and court cases about pain.
5. Explain how neurotransmitters and their effect on behavior, evaluating the body of evidence.

5.1: Neuroplasticity

Research demonstrates that the environment is a cause of neuroplastic changes to the brain, part of an explanation. An evaluation of **neuroplasticity** research includes a judgment (appraisal) that large body of research shows it is a fundamental concept for modern psychology.

We start with animal research showing the mechanisms of neuroplasticity because we cannot cut open human brains. These same mechanisms are assumed to work the same way in humans, though human neuroplasticity research just uses technology such as fMRI or TMS to see changes.

Explain means to give a detailed account including reasons and causes. Enriched environments are a cause of positive neuroplastic changes. Animal models might be useful might be useful for explaining the mechanisms of neuroplasticity, though this is a complicated issue that must be carefully considered.

Early experiments aimed to see if stimulating environments affected the growth of neurons in rats and one place to look for neuroplastic change was at the synapses between neurons (Kolb, 1999).

One experiment **aimed to compare** rats placed in enriched environments for three months beginning at weaning or as young adults with those of similar ages raised in standard cages. Enriched or standard cages was the **independent variable**. Rats housed in enriched environments at both ages showed better performance on a variety of behavioral tasks than the control rats living in standard cages. **Results** showed that both age groups housed in enriched environments showed a large increase in the length and density of dendrites in cortical pyramidal neurons in comparison with rats raised in the standard cages.

In another experiment testing prenatal experience on neuroplasticity, pregnant rat mothers were housed in enriched environments and compared to control rats in standard cages (**the IV**). **Results** showed that their babies had increases in synaptic space on cortical neurons as adults. It is possible that hormonal changes in the mother were passed onto the babies through the placenta and these hormones gave messages to genes that caused the growth (Kolb, Gibb & Robinson, 2004).

Dietary supplements also cause neuroplastic changes in rats (Kolb & Robinson, 2011). For example, experiments using rats found that perinatal choline supplements enhanced spacial navigation, increased nerve growth factor in the hippocampus, and increased dentritic growth in the hippocampus and cerebral cortex.

Thinking skills: Ethics in research

Using animals in experiments comes with special ethical considerations. In these experiments rats were humanely euthanized and their brains were examined for neuroplastic changes so scientists could demonstrate the mechanisms. The American Psychological Association allows animals to be used as subjects and even euthanized in research only as long as the research is of great benefit to science and the animals are treated humanely. However, just because the research meets basic APA ethical standards does not automatically mean animals are useful as models for understanding humans. This is a complicated issue, further discussed in chapter 10 about the role of animal research in understanding human behavior. Can their use be defended? Researchers often write that animals are useful for understanding the mechanisms of something, and are not fully generalizable to humans. Something to consider!

Some higher level critical thinking: Tolerate uncertainty because of ethics and research challenges in studying neuroplasticity

Rats, mice, and primates are subjects in experiments where scientists compare specific brain damage to normal brains under varying conditions as human brains cannot be damaged in the lab. We should not assume that human brains are plastic in exactly the same way as rat brains (Kolb, 1999). However, some generalizations from rat experiments probably apply to humans.

Measuring neuroplasticity in the lab is challenging (Kolb, et al., 2004). It involves deciding if synaptic changes have occurred between neurons. As the human brain contains roughly 100 billion neurons and each neuron makes about several thousand synapses, it is not easy to study. Scanning the brain for changes takes too much time. A better technique stains a random subset of neurons so that cell bodies and dendritic trees are visible. Researchers can estimate the number of synapses on the dendritic surface at a given time.

The substance **BrdU** is one way to stain (mark) new neurons (Gould & Gross, 2002). BrdU is used because it is

Your brain is getting some good exercise with the topic neuroplasticity, and the classroom is the stimulating environment. This is the kind of thinking that can create positive neuroplasticity in your brain. Every time you learn something new, the brain changes.
Source: pixabay.com

absorbed by cells undergoing DNA synthesis. Research using BrdU marking shows that neurons grow even in higher species, such as in the prefrontal cortexes of monkeys.

Studying neurogenesis in labs *does not prove anything*. There are some frustrating limitations to this research. For example, BrdU is toxic and researchers must monitor the dosage. Because it enters cells during protein synthesis, BrdU has the potential to cause mutations. Ethical guidelines allow animals to be put at more risk than humans if the research is of great scientific value to humans. How can we validate neurogenesis and neuroplasticity in humans? Is there a safe level for humans in research or are we limited to inferring brain changes from animal experiments? Another concern is that lab conditions might keep new neurons from surviving as long as they would in a natural environment. It is possible that lab studies have underestimated the amount of neuron growth in animals.

Next is two examples of neuroplasticity in humans.

Neuroplasticity in humans: Recruitment of the visual cortex after blindness

What happens when someone loses their sight? An explanation of **neuroplasticity** in humans shows that the environment (the blindness) causes neuroplastic changes in the visual cortex. For example, it can be argued that blind people have greater tactile (touch) abilities than sighted people and it is because the occipital visual cortex is recruited for non-visual processing after blindness.

The **aim of the experiment** was to figure out the mechanisms involved (Merabet et al., 2008). Were **visual cortex** changes made possible because we already have existing neural networks that spark into action when needed? This may be a good example of mother nature taking care of us. If so, then the visual cortex cross-over from processing sight to tactile stimuli could be the unmasking of already existing neural connections not in use before blindness that help blind people adapt. The authors thought it was a better explanation than the brain creating completely new neural connections.

This existing neural cross-over mechanism was predicted and the researchers aimed to show that even in sighted people, blindness for a short time (5 days) would unmask the existing but unused neural connections.

An entertaining neuroplasticity researcher and a great film!
As of the writing of this book, this film segment about the neuroplasticity of the visual cortex is available through http://www.chedd-angier.com/frontiers/season13.html#2. The segment is in the middle portion of the film, all of which is quite good.

If a DVD can be found or the segment accessed from the above site, students can see a simulation of visual cortex recruitment experiments in a Scientific American Frontiers film *Changing your Mind*. Alvaro Pascual-Leone is part of Merabet's research team and is featured in the film along with one of the participants from the earliest experiment on this topic from 2002, Michelle. Alan Alda hosts the series, so it is funny and popular. Although this is just one of the segments, neuroplasticity across a number of behaviors is reviewed in the rest of the film. The segment is still relevant, and is just when the research was done.

I show the film before reading about the experiment to prime students. They are typically very concerned about the ethics of this study so it is a good lesson about informed consent, risk, and inducements.

Participants all had normal sight. They stayed in the hospital for five days and were randomly assigned to the sighted group or the non-sighted group, the **independent variable**. The non-sighted group was suddenly and completely deprived of sight with a blindfold. Blindfolds contained photographic paper to make sure no one peeked. The sighted group wore blindfolds just for the training and testing but it was off the rest of the time. All participants had five days of intensive tactile (touch) stimulation with four to six hours of Braille reading and two more of tactile games such as dominos.

Some of the participants from both groups had fMRI scans on day 1, 3, 5 and then 24 hours after the blindfolds were removed for the non-sighted group.

fMRI **results** showed that the visual cortex was not activated during tactile stimulation (the index finger used to read Braille was rubbed) on day 1, 3 or 24 hours after blindfold removal in both groups. However, by day 5, the visual cortex was activated for the tactile stimulation in the blindfold group but not the sighted group.

The other participants from both groups underwent a process using a **transcranial magnetic stimulation coil** (TMS) that temporarily shut down the part of the brain it was placed near. In this study, the visual cortex of the non-sighted group was zapped by the TMS coil after the five days and it lessened the sensitivity of the Braille reading, giving further evidence that the visual cortex was recruited for tactile processing. In comparison, **results** showed that the sighted group zapped by the coil had little effect on tactile sensitivity because their brains had not rewired.

Be assured that everyone's brain in the non-sighted group went back to normal by 24 hours after the study. As you might guess, an extensive informed consent form outlined what participants were expected to do, potential risks, and inducements for participation, which in this case was $500 for the week.

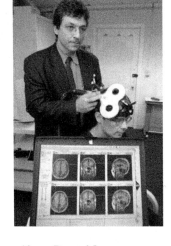

Alvaro Pascual-Leone holding a TMS coil. Curtsey of A. Pascual-Leone

---

Thinking skills: Ethics
What is a fair inducement for being in such an experiment? Would you participate for $500? Is it too much for a college student? Would college students do this just for the money?

Inducements cannot be so great that someone would be in the study just to get them. The TMS coil is not without side effects, which can be mild, such as headaches, but can include more severe effects in rare cases.

The authors **concluded** that sudden short term blindness while getting tactile use training caused neuroplastic crossover changes. The researchers believe these neural connection become much stronger for blind people over time to help them adapt to what they must do.

Neuroplasticity in humans: Prozac normalizes the brain

It can be argued that **Prozac** causes neuroplastic changes that lessen depression, so researchers want to know how it works.

An experiment using **fMRI aimed to** investigate the brains of twenty-one healthy adolescents and nineteen adolescents diagnosed with depression aged eleven to eighteen and compare their brains to normal participants to see changes made after taking Prozac (Tao et al., 2012). The **independent variable** was having a diagnosis of depression and taking Prozac or not.

The study lasted for eight weeks. **Procedures** are next. Participants watched fearful faces while fMRI scans were collected at the start and the end of the study. After the baseline scans, the adolescents with depression took Prozac for eight weeks.

Results include the following. Baseline fMRI readings showed that adolescents with depression had higher brain activation in the frontal, temporal, and limbic cortexes. After eight weeks, the brain scans of adolescents with depression looked the same as the brains of healthy adolescents. These three brain regions were no longer hyperactive. In addition, the **amygdala**, a brain region associated with emotions, showed heightened activity as participants with depression looked at the fearful faces. Amygdala activity returned to the level shown in healthy participants after eight weeks on Prozac.

Inquiry: Class activities

1. Google "neuroscience for kids: language" to learn about Broca and Wernicke and their patients.
2. Next Google "neuroscience for kids: hemispheres" to learn about split-brain patients.
3. Kagan's comments are a good place to practice critical thinking. They give good reasons to challenge the classic localization view that strict localization is valid.
4. Notice that fMRI has helped us understand the brain a great deal since Broca and Wernicke's time. Review fMRI.
5. The whistling language experiment is a good experiment to help students understand that the brain is not as localized as once thought. Watch the **YouTube video** about it, and just type in whistling language. The best one is about 10 minutes long.
6. Read the whistling language experiment and the Hull and Vaid meta-analysis. Bilingualism studies support abandoning a strict localization view.

5.3: Localization of brain function

Explanation of localization: The brain is generally localized for language

Explain means to give a detailed account including reasons and causes. This section includes important details as well as good reasons for believing the brain is generally localized for language, though it is not completely localized. The concept **neuroplasticity** allows the brain to be modified with experience.

Language is the focus of this section because a large amount of localization research is about it. In addition, language is the fundamental cognitive process allowing people to live in cultures, so it is important to understand some neuroscience related to it.

Two key details of localization follow.

Inquiry: Practice discovering more key details

Start with the two key details about localization, but add something from each of the other sections about split-brain patients and reasons the classic localization theory is outdated.

---

1. The brain is generally localized for language in the left hemisphere but modern research shows that it is not as localized as once believed.
2. The right hemisphere plays more of a supportive role in language than originally thought from studying people with abnormal brains, so strict localization is invalid.

This section starts with details of split-brain cases and a summary of the classic localization view. Next is details of the pitfalls of believing in strict localization and then studies giving reasons why the right hemisphere gets involved more often than you might think.

Split-brain cases and the localization issue

Split-brain cases are intriguing but must be considered with care. Ninety-six percent of split-brain patients produce speech from the left-hemisphere (Gazzaniga, et al., 2014). These cases, along with imaging studies, help scientists understand that language is primarily localized in the left hemisphere. However, there are also some split-brain cases where the right hemisphere also produces language, and scientists conclude that the right hemisphere can develop language as well, an example of incredible

neuroplasticity. For example, some patients could name the object "spoon" shown to the left field, and "cow" to the right field, but did not know if the objects were the same. They did not start out being able to do this with the right field, with one patient taking 10 years to develop the skill. This is part of the evidence for a modern understanding of localization— the right hemisphere plays a greater role in language than once thought and the brain is not strictly localized.

One finding about split-brain patients is that the left hemisphere retains the ability to make causal attributions about the world after surgery and is dominant for problem-solving as demonstrated in an experiment by Gazzaniga and LeDoux (as cited in Gazzaniga, et al., 2014). The left hemisphere

---

Conceptual understanding: Generalizing from research
Researchers often study people with abnormalities so they can learn the mechanisms for something, such as how memory works. They openly admit that these cases are hard to generalize, a mistake made by Broca and Wernicke. This same thing happens with much of the animal research.

---

can be called **the interpreter**. Participants were shown two pictures at the same time to the left and right field. Then they choose from a group of pictures the one best matching each picture. The original pictures were of a chicken claw to the left field and a snow scene to the right field. The best choice was a picture of the chicken for the claw and a shovel for the scow scene. However, one participant selected shovel for the claw and when asked, said the shovel would be needed to pick up chicken droppings. The participant's left field knew nothing about the snow, so context was used based on what it did know. The interpreter did a good job of filling in an answer!

When evaluating split-brain cases it is important to remember that these patients have chronic epileptic seizures and therefore have abnormal brains even before their operations, so there are some limitations to using them as evidence (Gazzaniga,et al., 2014). The cases with little to no cognitive impairment were analyzed and applied to understanding localization the most, so conclusions are stronger than if scientists used the most abnormal brains. Students must also ask if the operations really severed all brain connections, and the early cases are hard to verify because all we have to rely upon is operation case notes. Studies using MRIs are the best for discovering if some fibers stayed connected. Split-brain cases do help scientists understand localization but it is also important to evaluate them. Look to see if split-brain cases use MRI or raise some questions about them.

Thinking skills: Historical versus modern research
Broca and Wernicke are interesting, but should be considered historical.

How do you know which studies are historical? Sometimes older studies are fine as long as they have stood the test of time. Sometimes older research is just when the research was done. However, scientists had limited ways of studying the brain during Broca's and Wernicke's time, so they cannot be used as good evidence about how the brain works.

Classic localizationist view

Broca and **Wernicke** are researchers frequently cited on exams but keep in mind that psychologists have learned a tremendous amount about localization and language since then. Recent research has modified the early **classic localizationist view**. A complete evaluation of historical cases requires students to know their limitations.

Paul Broca did an autopsy on the brain of a man in the 19th century who could speak only the word "tan" a few years before his death. He found damage to the area we now call Broca's area (Gazzaniga, et al., 2014). The patient had Broca's **aphasia**, meaning difficulty with language production and comprehension after some type of neurological damage. Broca decided language was localized in the left hemisphere because of "Tan" and similar patients. Researchers have recently challenged the conclusion that Broca's area is alone responsible for speech problems, citing, for example, that many patients have lesions in Broca's area but do not have aphasia. Since Broca never dissected Tan's brain, he could not see if anything else was damaged, and new MRI studies show Tan also had damage in the basal ganglia and insular cortex.

Carl Wernicke has a similar story. Wernicke's aphasia, when the patient has problems with language comprehension, really only happens when there is damage to Wernicke's area and damage to, for example, the white matter connecting the temporal lobe language centers to other parts of the brain.

Resist the urge to find single causes of behavior and believe in strict localization

The urge to find a single cause for behavior contributes to the attractiveness of localization theories (Kagan, 2007). Some sensory functions are localized to specific neural regions. But abstract human cognitive processing is possible only with the coordination of many smaller brain regions. "The error in the argument for localization is the assumption that if a select area of the brain is reliably activated by an event or task, then the psychological process being engaged by the event is probably localized in the same area" (p. 362). For example, damage to a specific part of the brain may make a person unable to comprehend language but it does not mean that language comprehension is localized in the damaged area. The specific damage is just disruption in one part of the total process. Language comprehension requires "an intact basal membrane, an auditory nerve, several brain stem nuclei, a thalamus, parts of the frontal lobe," *and* **Wernicke's area** (p. 363). Damage to Wernicke's area is not enough to explain language comprehension problems.

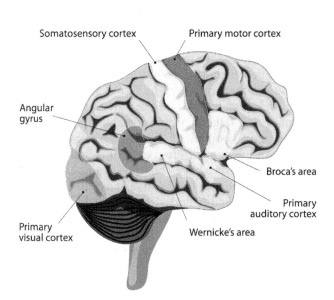

Broca's and Wernicke's area
Used with license from megapixel.com.

Popular culture has contributed to the common reductionist view of localization. Left-brain/right-brain explanations for behavior are oversimplified and part of popular culture (Kalat, 2007). The modern research on localization does not support a *strict* division. You may have taken a test to see if you are left or right-brained. Persons typically claim that they are "right-brained," for example, simply from performing poorly on a logic test or well on a creativity test. Without a brain scan it is impossible to know if you are mainly "right brained."

Modern studies about localization: The whistled language

An explanation and evaluation of localization should include some modern research. It can be argued that environmental conditions shaped the brains of people living under particular geographical constraints. An explanation and evaluation is next.

Shepherds in the Canary Islands use a **whistled language** called *Silbo Gomero* to communicate with other shepherds over long distances. Silbo is a rare language that is endangered in our modern world (Carrerias, Lopez, Rivero, & Corina, 2005). Silbo whistlers provided a chance to study how the brain adapts to environmental demands. The authors believe "that areas of the brain normally associated with spoken-language function are also activated in proficient whistlers, but not in controls, when they are listening to Silbo Gomero" (p. 31).

This study is a quasi-experiment, with participants either skilled Silbo users or not, one of the **independent variables**, with the other the two tasks, passive or active listening.

Silbo reduces the total range of the Spanish language   phonemes, the sounds that are different from each other, to two, along with four consonants. Silbo "words" change Spanish words into whistles that range from low to high pitch and differ in melody. Silbo whistlers use *context* to figure out the *meaning* of the whistles. *The demands of the environment shaped the way the shepherds communicated in their culture and their brains adapted.*

The left temporal and inferior frontal lobes of the brain are not limited to the processing of spoken language as one might think. They are also activated when deaf persons process visual sign language and when people process non-linguistic acoustic symbols.

The **aim of the study** was to see if the whistled language was also processed in the left temporal and inferior frontal lobes and to see if the brains of Silbo users differed from the brains of non-Silbo users.

Procedures are next. Silbadores, users of Silbo, and non-users had their brains scanned with **fMRI** while completing two tasks. The first task was a baseline scan. Both groups listened passively to Silbo and Spanish sentences that were compared to digitally reversed Silbo sentences. In the second task both groups paid attention to Silbo and Spanish sentences that were mixed with silent periods.

A Silboradore from the Canary Islands. Make sure to watch the YouTube show to see how the whistled language is passed on to children.
Source: Carrerias, et al., (2005)
Used with permission

Results showed that the brains of skilled Silbo whistlers in both tasks used parts of the left hemisphere associated with speech production. In addition, the brain scans of Silbo users showed an activation of the right-hemisphere superior-midtemporal region when using both Spanish and Silbo. It is interesting that the right hemisphere is involved to some degree, because this is something found in other bilingual research.

The authors **conclude**, "Silbo modulates cortical activity in the Silbadores and not in the controls" (p. 31). How are the brain changes in Silbo users explained? Silbo uses pitch and melody that are distinct from spoken language. But at the same time the sounds are a way to communicate. Even if the whistled sounds are unusual, the left hemisphere responds to them *because* they are used as a language.

An evaluation of this study includes the judgment that it is part of a growing body of research showing how the brain is not as localized as once thought and a strength is that it uses normal people. The use of fMRI shows the brain regions involved, but remember that fMRI has both strengths and limitations.

Modern research about localization: Bilingualism, neuroplasticity, and localization

Further explanation and evaluation about localization includes another piece of modern research. It can be argued that the brains of **bilingual** persons are different from the brains of monolingual persons, and acquiring a second language early in life makes a difference.

Neuroplasticity explains the differences. Acquiring two languages on or before age 6 stimulates more and different neural pathways than in children who speak just one language and in people who acquire a second language after age 6 (Hull & Vaid, 2006).

This study is a **meta-analysis**, a type of correlation study. A description and evaluation of meta-analysis research is included at the end of this section, but generally, a meta-analysis looks for *themes* in a large body of studies on the same topic that use different designs. Little differences in study design make comparisons confusing without meta-analysis research.

Hull and Vaid examined 23 studies of normal monolingual and bilingual participants. The **aim of the study** was to see if and under what conditions second language experience affected brain development.

It was believed that the left hemisphere was dominant for language but they were convinced the right hemisphere supported the left. They identified four hypotheses to explain possible right hemisphere involvement.

One is that bilinguals use more of the right brain.

The second is that skilled bilinguals are more right brain lateralized than monolinguals.

The third is that the closer in time two languages are acquired, the more similar the brain localization, so learning a second language before age 6 seems critical.

The fourth is that the early stages of learning a second language depends largely on contextual cues, which are localized in the right hemisphere. The left hemisphere becomes dominant as the person becomes more skilled with the second language and it is processed in a way similar to the first.

Would results of the meta-analysis support any of the four?

Two key **results** of the meta-analysis are listed below, but early experience seems the most important aspect relating to brain localization.

1. Monolinguals and bilinguals who learned their second language after age 6 showed the most left hemisphere dominance, supporting the second hypothesis.
2. Early bilinguals were bi-lateral, supporting the first hypothesis.

Science has come a long way since Broca and Wernicke's research in our understanding of localization. More research needs to clarify these findings (A limitation until more is done), but a judgment (an appraisal) suggests there is some evidence that left hemispheric dominance even in monolinguals is not absolute.

What is a meta-analysis?

Meta-analyses make sense of a wide range of studies on a topic by correlating patterns (Coolican, 2004). Let's say someone wants to study bilingualism. There may be many studies investigating the topic. After conducting a literature search it might seem impossible to make useful generalizations about bilingualism because of the large number and because the studies are *not fully comparable*. They use a variety of samples, tasks, and designs. At best, generalizations made in texts are usually based on a selective number of available studies. How can psychologists make clearer statements about the entire body of research on a topic? This is where a meta-analysis is helpful.

Meta-analysis organizes hundreds of studies in such a way to make them comparable. Researchers conducting meta-analyses create new data by sorting studies into categories. The new study, the meta-analysis, uses the data in such a way that an individual study becomes similar to an individual's response in a single study. Researchers statistically analyze the effect sizes of the studies in the meta-analysis to draw conclusions. Calculating the size of the effect tells the researchers something about the strength of the conclusions. For example, Hull and Vaid (2006) found strength primarily for hypothesis about the age of learning a second language. This would be a strength of their study.

5.4: The contribution of technology in understanding brain function and behavior

Evaluate means to make a judgment (appraisal). Technology has revolutionized our understanding of the human brain but we must recognize that technology is not perfect, so it has both strengths and limitations. Ethical concerns about accuracy and privacy come up any time technology is used to study the brain.

Technology is appealing, but if not accurate it can negatively influence data interpretation and place study participants at unnecessary risk. Privacy of the scans must be addressed in the informed consent form, such as how the information will be used.

Review the different technologies in the section about techniques used to study the brain in the previous chapter and note the advantages and disadvantages. This section includes an evaluation of EEG to investigate sleep stages, event-related potential (ERP) to investigate language development, and fMRI for studying obesity and lie detection.

The choice for using a particular technology to study the brain and behavior depends on two things.

1. Some technologies are not appropriate for certain populations.
2. A technology is selected depending on what someone wants to know. fMRI is often a choice because researchers want to see the function of the brain during a task. ERP measures neural activity in milliseconds and is a good choice for studying language development.

Next is examples of EEG and fMRI technologies, along with their strengths and limitations.

Evaluation of the contributions of EEG and event-related potentials (ERP): Important strengths and limitations

EEG is a good choice for showing general brain activity for behaviors such as sleep stages and **ERP** is a good choice because it directly measures neural activity and picks up the rapid brain activity associated with human speech. Chapter 8 contains evaluations of natural selection, and these include research about **language** development in babies. fMRI is not a good choice for this type of research because it does not directly measure neural activity and BOLD measurements are delayed over several seconds.

Strengths and limitations of EEG and ERP are next.

A strengths of EEG follows.
EEG is useful for understanding general brain activity, such as in studying sleep stages.

A limitation of EEG follows.
EEG is not good for studying the brain when a researcher wants to know which brain regions are activated during cognitive tasks.

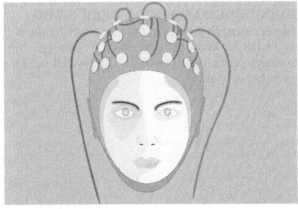

EEG studies use this cap where electrodes measure electrical activity in the brain.
Used with license from megapixl.com.

Strengths of ERP follow (Kuhl & Gaxiola, 2008).

1. It is a good choice for studying babies because they do not need to speak.
2. It has high temporal (time) resolution of milliseconds, which means it is good for rapid human speech.
3. It is noninvasive and inexpensive.
4. It is noiseless, which is good for babies who might be afraid of a noisy fMRI machine, plus researchers would have to cover a child's ears while at the same time giving babies a sound stimulus.

Limitations of ERP follow (Kuhl & Gaxiola, 2008).
1. It has low spatial resolution. However this is not the goal of studies on infant speech perception. If someone wants to see the function of the brain they should use fMRI.
2. It is sensitive to movement, but not as much as fMRI.

> **Using studies more than once: A demonstration of good generalizing**
> It may seem like a lot of trouble to flip over to another chapter to read the Kuhl experiment, but in the long run it saves time. This is because one piece of research can serve multiple topics and it is easier than my coming up with new studies each time a topic is explored! The book is designed for students to reuse studies when applicable.

Research evidence that ERP contributes to research about children's language development

It can be argued that ERP has made great contributions to our understanding of children's language development, and this is important to do when evaluating.

The section in chapter 8 about natural selection contains one of these. Patricia Kuhl used ERP to measure neural activity in babies as they acquired language sounds. Her aim was to show that babies from English speaking homes could acquire the sounds of Mandarin in the sensitive period when the brain prunes its ability to hear sounds other than those spoken in the native language. ERP measurements showed distinct neural activity for English and Mandarin sounds.

Research evidence: EEG contributes greatly to what we know about the importance of a good night sleep

Sleep research is a good topic for studying the contributions of **EEG**. When evaluating the use of EEG and what we know about sleep needs coming from this data, we can make a judgment (appraisal) that research leads to the conclusion that we all need a good night sleep to be healthy, safe, and have good memory consolidation.

Class activities about sleep research

I teach the topic in a wider context so students have a reason to care about sleep stages. Teach stages of sleep. Students will not be happy to learn they need 9.25 hours of sleep each night for optimal health and school performance, but it plants the idea that sleep is worth studying.

1. Students can study dreams in more depth and can investigate Carskadon's article about sleep and adolescent behavior. The film *What are dreams?* from NOVA answers questions students have about dreams and reviews some basic sleep research.
2. Two films are helpful in getting students to understand the importance of sleep. One is *Inside the teenage brain* from Frontline and the other is *The sleep famine* from Films for the Humanities and Sciences.
3. I have students do the **sleep challenge**, located in Appendix 1. For the IB student, this is a good exercise in **self-management** and can be used for **CAS**.

The importance of a good night of sleep

Getting a proper night sleep can be challenging for 21st Century students who might argue they cannot do all they want and still sleep. However, learning about sleep might persuade students to become better self-managers and use better time management to do well in school, participate in important activities, and stay healthy. People must sleep long enough to go through all the stages four to five times a night. There is no way to sleep less, remain healthy, and perform your best in school.

Sleep is critical for reducing stress, increasing immunity, improving memory and decision-making, and repairing muscle, among the many other things that happen during quality sleep. It is well documented by researchers such as Mary Carskadon that adolescents need 9.25 hours of sleep each night for optimal school performance (Frontline, 1999).

Surveys show teens average about 7.5 hours of sleep each night, with about a quarter of teenagers getting 6.5 hours or less (Frontline, 1999). The problem could be increasing in the age of Facebook and other social media.

Adolescents face plenty of obstacles to sleep, such as school start time, jobs, and, social media. In addition, hormonal changes beginning at puberty push teen circadian rhythms forward at night (Harvard Mental Health Letter, July, 2005). Many sleep-deprived adolescents use the weekends to catch up on sleep. It may seem like a good strategy but makes it hard to start the school week. The brain gets a signal that nighttime is from 2 a.m. until 1 p.m. the next day, a sleep cycle that is hard to reset on Sunday night.

Wolfson and Carskadon (1998) report sleep habits and grades from the Sleep Habits Survey using 3120 high school students in Rhode Island, US. Between ages 13 and 19, the amount of sleep decreased by as much as 50 minutes each night. Adolescents describing themselves as struggling academically reported sleeping an average of 25 minutes less each night then those reporting good grades. In addition, students with bad grades report that they go to bed later on weekend nights than those with good grades.

Understanding sleep stages is a good place to start so everyone understands what is supposed to happen while sleeping. We know about sleep stages because of EEG.

Sleep stages

Humans cycle through five sleep stages each night four to five times, with REM sleep (rapid-eye-movement) called the fifth stage in this book. These stages take place within a 24 hour **circadian rhythm** system, a biological clock naturally regulating waking and sleep.

Sleep is a drive and we become sleepier the longer we stay awake. Even if someone thinks it is possible to beat the sleep-wake cycle, the drive still takes over quickly and is the master of us. The figure above shows the stages measured by **EEG**.

A description of sleep stages follows along with information about REM and non-REM dreaming (National Sleep Foundation, 2014; Gray & Bjorklund, 2014; Walcutt, 2015). As you go from awake to

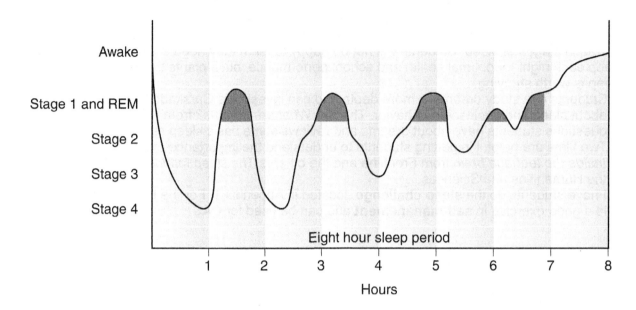

Sleep stages. These stages are known because of changes in EEG.
Used with license from megapixl.com.

stage 4 sleep, brain waves are slower in frequency but gain amplitude, meaning they are more vertical with REM resembling the awake state (Gray & Bjorklund, 2014).

When awake and not attending to anything, an **EEG** records **alpha waves**. When awake and attentive, EEG records **beta waves**.

3. Stage 1 is light sleep, when you are just starting to fall asleep. Eyes move slowly and you can easily be awakened. These are periods of dreaminess similar to day dreaming as you drop off to sleep.
4. Stage 2 involves slower brain waves and eye movement stops. Body temperature drops and you are less aware of surroundings. EEGs show a burst of waves indicating someone is now asleep.
5. Stage 3 is the transition into deep sleep, the most restorative sleep, when EEG starts to record slow brain waves called **delta waves**. Muscles relax and blood supplies to them increase. Hormones such as growth hormone are released.
6. Stage four is the deepest restorative sleep, called **delta sleep**, when EEG also measures delta waves. You do not stay here for the entire night and instead come back to lighter sleep until REM starts and then the process repeats four to five times before waking. Stages 2-4 are called **non-REM sleep**.
7. **REM sleep** involves rapid breathing and eyes dart around rapidly. REM starts about 90 minutes into sleep and gets longer as the number of sleep cycles progress. Arms and legs are paralyzed to keep you from getting up and acting out dreams. EEG records **beta waves** similar to those of someone awake and attentive. People have more dreams in REM and report them regularly in sleep studies.
8. REM dreams are called **true dreams**, meaning you think the action is real and not imaginary. True dreams appear a story and the longer someone is in REM, the more elaborate the action. Content analysis of REM dreams show that objects and people make up most of the dreaming. Non-REM dreams tend to be less dramatic and more similar to thoughts, such as thinking about a test. Dreaming during non-REM happens about half of the time in dream studies.

A proper night sleep might improve your memory, health, and driving

Finding practical applications for what scientists know about sleep stages through EEG helps us make a judgment about its usefulness. Adolescents may think they can have good memories, stay healthy, and drive responsibly without adequate sleep, but the research does not support that view.

Perhaps we evolved the need for sleep, a time when people are not aware of their surroundings so that incoming sensory signals could stop for a while so the brain could make sense of everything (Stickgold & Ellenbogen, 2008). Other processes happening during sleep, such as immune system regulation and the release of growth hormones, may also have evolved to happen during a time of sleep's inactivity. Scientists have much to learn about the details, but we know many things happen at night that directly affect us.

A large body of research shows sleep is important for cognitive tasks such as **memory** and **verbal skills**.

1. Sleep strengthens and enhances memories, particularly emotional memories, as if the time asleep allows us to decide which memories to retain and in what detail (Stickgold & Ellenbogen, 2008).
2. Sleep is the time to rehearse the most difficult aspects of a task and solve problems (Stickgold & Ellenbogen, 2008).
3. Experiments using EEG show that sleep is required for both children and adults to perform well on tasks requiring declarative memory, the factual memories (Wilhelm, Diekelmann, & Born, 2008).

Research also shows proper sleep in critical for health (Carskadon, 2004).

1. Sleep loss is related to lowered **immunity**.
2. Sleep deprivation is related to **obesity**.
3. The normal pattern of **cortisol** release is altered after sleep deprivation, disrupting the regulation of cortisol, an important stress hormone. The natural cycle of cortisol levels is lower at night and then rises again by morning when you wake.

Is this you driving to school in the morning? Used with license from megapixl.com.

Driving when sleep deprived is dangerous (Carskadon, 2004).

1. Sleep loss for one night or two hours each night for a week gives people the same risk for crashes as someone who is intoxicated.
2. Many drivers in charge of mass transportation, such as train drivers and aviation pilots, report falling asleep, particularly at night and when experiencing jet lag after flying long distances.

An evaluation of fMRI: Strengths and limitations
It is important to reflect on strengths and limitations of **fMRI** because its use is considered revolutionary and is used so frequently. There is always more to the story than what is reported in general textbooks and on websites.

Strengths of fMRI follow.

1. fMRI scans have higher spatial resolutions of 2 to 3 cubic millimeters, greater than PET images with a spatial resolution of 6 to 9 cubic millimeters (Dobbs, 2005).
2. fMRI does not require the use of radioactive injections and is safer than PET imaging (Gazzaniga, et al., 2014). As the same individual can be repeatedly tested in an fMRI study, scientists can get a complete analysis on an individual. In contrast, participants in PET studies can only have 12 to 16 radioactive injections.

3. Localizing brain activity during a task is easier with fMRI (Gazzaniga, et al., 2014). Data can be collected all in one session. Localizing brain function is not as precise when PET images are averaged after multiple testing days.
4. The temporal resolution, or the time it takes to complete measurements, is faster with fMRI scans (Gazzaniga, et al., 2014). It takes about an hour for a PET scan to complete a picture of the brain. It takes an fMRI scan only 1 to 2 minutes to scan most of the brain (Dobbs, 2005).

Limitations of fMRI follow.

1. There is concern about fMRI accuracy (Dobbs, 2005). fMRI measures blood flow changes during a cognitive task rather than having a brain part actually light up (Gray & Bjorklund, 2014). fMRI provides correlations between cognitive tasks and brain activity, not statements about causation (Gazzaniga, et al., 2014).
2. Blood flow is an indirect way to view neuron activity (Bookheimer, 2002). Blood flow in the brain is fairly slow, starting about 2 seconds after neural activity starts and hits the highest point between 5-7 seconds. The image is recorded more slowly than actual neural activity.
3. Quality fMRI readings can be limited by non-task related cognitions during experiments that might cause the same brain activation (Bennett & Miller, 2010).
4. fMRI scans collect data in voxels, a combination of volume and pixels (Dobbs, 2005). Each voxel contains thousands of neurons, so for the image to light up, thousands or even millions of neurons must light up in order for the scan to perceive them. Perhaps "an entire stadium had to shout to be heard" (p. 2).
5. Some neurons important to a cognitive task may not draw as much blood as other neurons or may use little blood because they are more efficient (Dobbs, 2005). In both cases, the scan might not detect important neuron activity.

The important thing to take away from studying strengths and limitations is to avoid jumping on the bandwagon that fMRI provides the answers to everything! Its contributions are great but require good thinkers to keep its limitations in the back of their mind. Examples of fMRI about obesity and lie detection are worth thinking through for a balanced evaluation.

Research using fMRI: Food advertising and childhood obesity

It can be argued that one contribution of fMRI is to identify children who need help resisting advertising. When evaluating fMRI this is an example where using the technology is a strength.

> **Youtube video**
> Watch the video about this study called *Food advertising's impact on obese children.*

Students want to know the effects of **advertising** on behavior, particularly children. If Amanda Bruce and her colleagues are right, obese children either should not have exposure to advertising or should be taught cognitive-control strategies to resist them. Keep in mind the strengths and limitations of using fMRI as you read.

Food and drink companies spend about $10 billion each year in advertisements directed at children in the US each year, and the majority of these ads are for unhealthy foods (Bruce, et al., 2013). A growing body of research using fMRI shows that advertising activates reward areas in the **limbic system** and cognitive control areas in the **prefrontal cortex**. This study uses fMRI to see how these brain regions are active while children look at both food and nonfood logos.

The **aim of the experiment** was to compare active brain regions when children looked at food and nonfood logos, the **independent variable** (Bruce, et al., 2013). The hypothesis was that normal weight children would show more brain activation in cognitive control regions and obese children would show more activation in reward regions.

Ten normal weight and ten obese children aged 10-14 were in the sample.

Procedures are next. First the children and their parents filled out questionnaires, some of them about self-control. For example, one question was "Do you generally say or do things without stopping to think?" to see if the children scored high or low on impulsiveness (Bruce, et al., 2013, p. 760).

While in the fMRI scanner, children looked at 60 pairs of food logos, nonfood logos, and blurred images. The table below is an example of the pairing. Actual logos were used in the study.

Food logo	Nonfood logo	Control slide
McDonald's	Nike	Blurred slide

Results follow.

1. Obese children scored higher on impulsiveness.
2. Obese children showed greater activation in reward centers in the limbic system when looking at food logos.
3. Normal weight children showed greater activation in cognitive control centers when looking at food logos.
4. The brain activation was not as great when looking at nonfood logos or blurred pictures.

The authors **concluded** that obese children might benefit from training in cognitive and self control. Learning to delay gratification is one strategy, as Body Mass Index (BMI) and delayed gratification were negatively correlated in the study, meaning that as delayed gratification went up, BMI went down.

The study has limitations. The small sample size means the study must be replicated with other participants. Second, researchers needed to match the food and nonfood logos for familiarity, so they might not have tested all the right ones that are important to a specific child or even the logos rated as the happiest by a different test group of children. As a result, the study may have underestimated the effect of advertising on the brain.

It cannot be assumed that unactivated brain areas meant they were not working. However, the researchers controlled for fMRI limitations by measuring impulsiveness with questionnaires that then matched activated brain regions in obese children. This experiment has both strengths and limitations but when evaluating, a judgment can be made that fMRI is effectively used here as long as students understand that fMRI is not without limitations.

Research using fMRI: Lie detection in court cases

It can be argued that studying **fMRI** as applied in court cases helps us understand limitations of **lie detection** technology. An evaluation must include that there may be more limitations than strengths when bringing fMRI evidence into the courtroom. People might think using fMRI to catch a liar is a good thing, but what are lawyers really bringing to court?

When making judgments about the contributions of technology, it is helpful to consider test cases where technology is applied outside of the lab. Are fMRI scans reliable and valid for use as court evidence of someone lying or telling the truth?

Neuroimaging should be used in courts as evidence *if it is accurate* (Jones, Marois, Farah, & Greely, 2013). The wedding of neuroscience and the law is called **neurolaw** and could help courts in many ways.

Ways neuroimaging might help courts
It might increase juror confidence in scientific evidence.
It might tell us the level of someone's responsibility for their actions.
It could help judges make unbiased sentencing decisions.
It could reveal a person's mental state at the time of a crime.
It might reveal if memories are accurate.
It could help us know if someone is telling the truth or lying.

To be found guilty in a US court, someone must have been in a "legally culpable state of mind" (p. 17628), meaning the person acted with intention. US courts assume people are responsible but make exceptions in some cases, and this is one place technology might help answer difficult questions. For example, one man killed his wife in a violent rage and then neuroimaging found a cyst on his prefrontal cortex. The jury decided he had reduced self-control.

Technology must be accurate, such as how well fMRI can show someone's current mental state. We really have more questions than answers. For example, can it show if a person really is in as much pain as claimed so courts do not rely on self-reports? How might we use the scans and stay ethical, given the issue of privacy concerns about mind-reading people's emotions and thoughts?

So far, no method of **lie detection** has been shown to have high accuracy (Farah, Hutchinson, Phelps, & Wagner, 2014). Older lie detection methods measured changes in emotion and were flawed. fMRI is more appealing because it measures physiological changes in the brain that are

> **Thinking skills: Avoid assuming fMRI can tell us all we want to know!**
> Although fMRI is valuable for teaching us about advertising effects on the brain, is it useful for court cases? Perhaps fMRI really cannot detect lies accurately or we do not know enough about how it works. Technology in court is new and the Frye standard requires that evidence should generally be accepted by the public. If fMRI does not accurately detect lies then it should not be used.

correlated with the cognitions related to lying, possibly even pinpointing actual deception in the brain.

The public, including lawyers wanting to help their clients, find neuroimaging appealing, but its use requires everyone to be well educated about its advantages and limitations. Technology's appeal for the lay public is in contrast to two questions neuroscientists have about it (Farah, et al., 2014).

1. Do fMRI scans pick up consistent brain regions when someone lies?
2. What are these regions?

The answers require knowledge about how lie detection experiments are designed. In most studies using fMRI, participants are told to lie and then tell the truth in different experimental trials. The scans for the truth and lie conditions are then compared to scans from a baseline condition. Greater brain activation between lie and truth conditions are assumed to be correlates of deception. Prefrontal cortex, anterior cingulate cortex, and parietal cortex regions are areas consistently activated. Are these regions found consistently enough for high reliability and are these regions the only ones involved?

Data in these studies are collected on groups rather than individuals, which becomes important for considering how valid fMRI is for any individual testimony.

Conclusions are different between studies. For example, no particular brain region is active across all the studies. The reason for the variability could simply be because each study uses different tasks. There are still many questions to answer and two of these follow (Farah, Hutchinson, Phelps, & Wagner, 2014).

1. To what extent are lab experiment findings the result of confounding variables?
2. How well do lab studies about deception on groups generalize to individuals?

The answers to these questions are complicated, and this discussion points out a few things for the class to consider when evaluating the contribution of fMRI for lie detection.

Might the same brain activity thought to correlate with deceptive cognitions be caused by other cognitions a participant uses during the experiment? There really is no way to know at this time, so general cognitive activity might confound (interfere with) experiment results. For example, it is not known if the cognition needed to do a simple task creates the brain activation interpreted to be a lie. There may be too much risk of confusing truths and lies.

Most lie detection research is done by averaging data on groups, so it might not generalize well to studying lies in individuals. Another concern is generalizing lab studies using healthy and educated college students as participants to criminals getting scanned for court evidence. A large number of criminals qualify for psychiatric disorders such as antisocial personality, so deception is part of their character. Deception usually does not show up on BOLD patterns of the prefrontal cortex when criminals are scanned.

Would you agree to get a brain scan for court? It is a fairly new type of evidence that might become commonplace one day. But are the scans accurate? How might they be most useful? Might students go to the principal's office for a scan to test for honesty one day? Norms might change.
Used with license from megapixl.com.

Lying in lab experiments differs from the lies told by people who appear in court. Participants in lab studies lie on tasks without personal meaning. Real life lying is personal and rehearsed. Might rehearsal or heightened emotion change the brain activation seen in scans? Evidence shows that practice can lessen prefrontal cortex activation. This occurs because people do not need to exert as much executive control to recall the lie over time. One study showed that memorized lies showed less BOLD activity than an unpracticed lie.

Even small behaviors can interfere with the study and reduce scan accuracy, such as making small toe or finger movements that cannot be seen by researchers. It might be easy for someone in a trial to develop a countermeasure if asked to take a scan.

As of 2014, three attempts were made to use fMRI lie detection in courts and judges in all three cases rejected the evidence (Farah, et al., 2014). One case involved testimonies about employment discrimination. It was rejected because the use of fMRI violated the Frye standard, which required that evidence presented be generally accepted by society, and the Daubert standard, which required judges to act as gate-keepers for scientific evidence and not just allow neuroscience evidence to be admitted simply because it seems scientific.

Communicating: Technology debate activity

1. Look up No Lie MRI and Millennium Magnetic Technologies on the Internet and evaluate their accuracy claims (These companies come and go, so students might have to search for them). What role might this company and similar others have for future use in courts?
2. Consider the pros and cons of using neuroimaging as mind-reading. What privacy concerns arise? How might we balance the privacy rights of individuals with the right of the courts to investigate and try crimes?
3. Follow more attempts to bring fMRI into court. One article reported in *Nature* is "Science in court: head case" by Virginia Hughes. Google the title. See if you can find more recent cases using scans as evidence.

Another attempt to use fMRI lie detection was a murder case where the accused person used the company **No Lie MRI** to scan him. The court refused to accept the evidence, claiming experts in the field did not agree with the interpretation from No Lie MRI employees. The rise of private companies promising to deliver scanning accuracy needs further scrutiny. These companies make claims that fMRI is accurate, but is this true?

Neuroimaging might be beneficial but each use of it may require different policies (Farah, et al., 2014). More research should be conducted, refining lab studies so results from the body of research is useful to situations to which fMRI is applied. Since privacy concerns are great with fMRI use in courts, effort must go into considering when and how neuroimaging should be allowed.

5.5: Neurotransmitters and their effect on behavior: Depression and alcoholism

Detailed descriptions of neurotransmitters and neurotransmission are in the previous chapter. The purpose of this section is to evaluate research showing how neurotransmission effects behavior.

This section should not be too hard because we reuse material in chapter 7 about genes and behavior related to depression and alcoholism.

Neurotransmission and depression

First, neurotransmission affects depressed mood. The role of the **serotonin transporter gene** in **depression** has received a great deal of attention.

People with the ss alleles of the serotonin transporter gene have **transcriptional inefficiency** and this means that their brains do not have enough serotonin (Caspi, et al., 2010). This is a clear example of how neurotransmission affects behavior.

Caspi's research has about 40 independent replications, so an evaluation should include that it has a strong research base. On the other hand, the research is correlation, so having transcriptional inefficiency that comes from having the ss allele is not a direct cause depression. Animal experiments do show cause but students must consider how well the animals act as models for humans.

Neurotransmission and alcoholism

The l allele (long version) of the **serotonin transporter gene** (5-HTT) is correlated with **low response to alcohol** (LR), a topic studied in depth in chapter 7.

The l allele causes a faster reuptake of serotonin at synapses, meaning serotonin empties faster (Schuckit, 2008a). Low levels of serotonin at synapses may contribute to someone drinking large amounts of alcohol to feel its effects (Schuckit, 2008b). LR is the most studied and verified genetic risk for alcoholism (Schuckit, 2013), so a judgment must include conclude that it has a strong research base. This research is also correlation and cannot be interpreted to show the l allele is a cause of alcoholism.

Chapter 6
Biological Approach to Behavior: Genetics and Behavior: Knowledge and Understanding

Chapter objectives

Students will:
1. Practice thinking strategies (command terms) related to knowledge and understanding, with describe modeled.
2. Describe the make-up of human genome, the nature of the gene, and gene expression.
3. Describe the use of correlations in studying human behavior and genetics.
4. Describe epigenetics, factors that affect gene expression.
5. Describe natural selection: The survival of the fittest.

This material is needed to analyze and evaluate topics about genetics and behavior in the next chapter. Students may need to include some of these details in essays about genetics as all analysis and evaluation should include relevant detail.

6.1: Gene basics
The nature of the gene, gene regulation, and gene expression

Describe means to give a detailed account. Next is the important details about genes that everyone should know.

All human **phenotypes**, our observable characteristics and traits, are affected by genes, but our genes must interact with the environment as they develop (Moore, 2013). It is incorrect to ask if a behavior is the result of nature versus nurture. Rather, human behavior comes from the complex interplay of nature *and* nurture.

Chromosomes are found in cell nuclei, which contain **chromatin**, consisting of **DNA** and **histones**, a protein acting as a spool for DNA to wind around so it fits into cells (Moore, 2013, Carey, 2003). DNA is a spiral ladder of **nucleotide** chains that are pairs of the chemicals adenine, thymine, guanine, and cytosine (letters A, T, G, and C) that come in varying sequences (Lahey, 2008). The genetic code is carried in the sequences of nucleotides. **Genes** *are portions of DNA sequences that direct protein synthesis and produce cell structures— this is how we get behavior.* DNA strands are coiled around **histones**, which must unravel for genes to express. The unraveling is an example of how genes can interact with the environment. When DNA is coiled around histones, the gene is silent and does not affect behavior, but if unraveled, is available to interact with other factors and then can express and affect behavior (Moore, 2013).

Most human DNA is the same. Human diversity is partly because some genes are different from one another, either in multiple versions or in a single variation (Lahey, 2008). When a stretch of DNA comes in multiple versions, it is called a **polymorphism**. Single nucleotide polymorphisms (SNPs) are chains of DNA that differ in just one letter, the single variation. An **allele** is a variation of a gene and can be either an SNP or a polymorphism. One polymorphism studied in this course is the three variations of the **serotonin transporter gene**, ll, sl, and ss alleles. The two short alleles (ss) heighten one's reactivity to stress and increases the risk for **depression**.

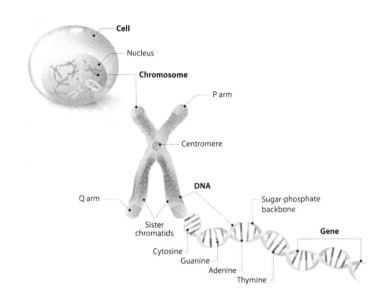

DNA
Used with license from megapixl.com.

Why should we care about these technicalities? Genes cannot affect behavior unless they are expressed. This means that just having a gene is not enough. To affect behavior, genes must become templates, or master patterns, for proteins (Higgins, E, 2008). DNA turns into proteins in two ways, through **transcription** and **translation**. Scientists have known since the 1960s that "genes are contained in DNA molecules, that the genetic code is transcribed into RNA and then translated into a **protein**, and that this process is often regulated by environmental stimuli" (APA, 2000, p. 380).

Two proteins of interest to psychologists are the **serotonin transporter protein**, related to the reuptake of serotonin in synapses and the behavior **depression**, and the **glucocorticoid receptor protein**, related to reacting to fear and feeling **stress** (Moore, 2013). Both aid **neurotransmission**, studied earlier in this book. Just do not think these proteins are a direct path to depression or stress behaviors, because they have to interact with non-genetic factors to affect behavior.

Transcription and translation are what students should know because *this is where we have some control*. Perhaps we can learn to be more effective parents, choose better diets, limit exposure to pesticides, and reduce stress so that stress hormones, pesticides, or lack of nutrients do not interfere with normal gene expression.

Transcription means that the genetic code is transferred from DNA to intermediate molecules of mRNA, or messenger RNA (Lahey, 2008). Messenger RNA codes for amino acids that determine which proteins appear in the cells. These proteins make up the structure of behavior and are translated, meaning the message on the mRNA is read so the end product of protein synthesis can occur. Although all cells contain the same genes, different cells use the genes differently (Higgins, E., 2008). This is why neural cells differ from, for example, liver cells.

6.2: Correlations are used in human genetic research

Scientists cannot *directly* study genes and how they combine with other genes and the environment the way you might wish. Scientists instead rely on statistical models using **correlations** to analyze data about the behavioral effects of genes in humans (APA, 2000). It is correct to say that correlations are "statistical relationships" and not the cause and effect results from genetic experiments sometimes done on animals. Animal experiments may be used as models for understanding human behavior, but cannot be assumed to be so. Evaluate each animal study case by case.

Scientists have to use the correlation method because it is unethical to alter genes in humans to study their effects. Tolerate uncertainty when studying animal genetic research and practice asking questions about their usefulness for understanding humans.

6.3: Epigenetics: Factors that affect gene expression
A detailed account of epigenetics

Describe means to give a detailed account and next is important details about epigenetic and examples of how it works in obesity and stress.

Each person has an entire lifetime of experiences that alters genes, so having a particular gene is not as important as knowing what the gene was made to do after interacting with the environment (Moore, 2013).

Epigenetics means that factors beyond genes, including diet, stress, lack of exercise, or living with an abusive parent, get inside genes and alter their expression.

Let's now review some important ideas about gene expression so you can understand how genes interact with the environment to influence behavior.

Many people incorrectly think that genes are a direct cause of most complex human behavior. There are about 25,000 genes in the human genome, much fewer than expected. Cells are similar, and signals from the environment make a nose different from a tooth or increase the risk that someone has depression or acts violently. Scientists have identified about 3 million **polymorphisms**, or variations of our genes, that probably explains behavior differences. However, having a particular polymorphism does not guarantee that someone gets a disorder or has a health problem because *genes cannot affect behavior unless they are expressed.*

Genes can be switched on and off by epigenesis.

Epigenesis takes place in several ways and two important for this course are **histone modification** and **DNA methylation** (Australian Academy of Science, 2006). In everyday language, histone modification and DNA methylation allow outside factors to get inside genes and alter their expression.

> **Films for epigenetics**
> *Epigenetics: How food upsets our genes* and *Ghost in your genes* are two good films to use. I bought my copies from Amazon. After seeing these films everyone started drinking green tea or bought a new water bottle!
>
> The one about how food upsets our genes explains the **Dutch Hunger Winter** study where people starved during the WWII Nazi food blockade had epigenetic changes leading to greater health and mental health problems. This study is a good example of epigenetic research.

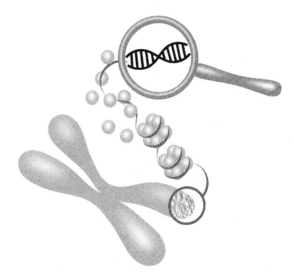

Epigenetics: Pretend you are looking through a magnifying class at DNA to see histones unraveling. This is what has to happen for a gene to affect behavior. Used under license from megapixel.com.

Histone modification can take place in many ways. DNA strands are long and must be tightly coiled around protein groups called **histones** to fit inside cells. One type of histone modification happens when stress hormones signal histones to unravel, meaning a gene is expressed that might have remained silent. Someone growing up in an abusive home might express genes related to aggression because of chronic stress.

Normal DNA methylation silences genes (Moore, 2013; Australian Academy of Science, 2006). Methylation means that methyl tags get attached to the bases (most commonly cytosine) from which DNA is made. Some genes should remain silent, meaning the transcription process cannot occur. Methylation happens independently with some sections of chromatin silenced and some not silenced, so it is not simply one sweeping process.

Abnormal methylation, however, can silence, or inactivate, genes that should be expressed. One example relates to cancer, such as abnormal methylation that inactivates genes to fight tumors. Another example is detailed under the next heading about rat babies with abnormally silenced genes that should have produced the right amount of glucocorticoid receptors (GR), giving them heightened stress responses.

> **Thinking skills: Gene expression**
> Epigenesis is just one way genes interact with the environment. Genes affect behavior through many pathways. Two other paths to be studied in this class are **gene-environment correlation** with **depression** and **insecure attachment**, and **endophenotypes** with **alcoholism.**
> To simplify: If you feel overwhelmed by studying genetics, genes related to any behavior do not work alone, except in rare cases. If I explain the pathways clearly enough, then you can appreciate the many things people can do to lower their risk of a health or mental health problem.

Children can inherit epigenome changes from parents, so an awareness that your behavior can affect future generations is important. **Folate**, a B vitamin, is one nutrient necessary for normal methylation. Green vegetables and oranges are two foods containing folate.

An example of epigenetic research: Obesity

Diet is an important epigenetic factor for obesity. The **aim of the experiment** was to show that a pregnant mother's poor **diet** has epigenetic effects on offspring increasing their risk of obesity (Vucetic, Kimmel, Totoki, Hollenbeck, & Reyes, 2010). Eating good foods and the right amount of food is required to remain at an ideal weight.

Procedures involved one group of mouse mothers eating a high-fat diet during pregnancy and the period of milk production and another group eating a normal diet. The normal or high-fat diet was the **independent variable. Results** showed that the mothers eating the high-fat diet showed a preference for high-fat and sugary foods as compared to control mice. Mice eating high-fat diets also showed clear changes in gene expression, such as an up-regulation of the **dopamine** reuptake transporter (DAT) gene. **Up-regulation** means that cells, in response to external stimuli, make more receptors. Dopamine reuptake is how dopamine is emptied from synapses so the mouse brains emptied of dopamine faster than normal. When dopamine is depleted, people want to do something to make more dopamine. This is similar to what happens to drug addicts and alcoholics. Drugs and alcohol flood the brain with dopamine, and the brain tries to compensate. People end up needing more drugs and alcohol to feel normal. High fat and sugary foods are addictive and make similar changes in dopamine activity.

These changes are passed on to offspring, so children inherit their parent's epigenome (Vucetic, et al., 2010). Mouse babies showed epigenetic changes similar to the changes in their mothers and showed a preference for high-fat and sugary foods. Up-regulation of DAT was just one of those changes.

One lesson to take from this experiment is that science is showing how important diet is to health. It is hard to change one's diet, especially for teenagers receiving constant fast food advertising and sometimes little money to spend, but you see what can happen.

Another example of epigenetics: The stress response in rat and human babies

The lab of Michael Meany gives us great insight into how maternal care (in rats) affects stress responses throughout the lifespan of their young. A large body of research supports the conclusion that mothering behavior makes epigenetic changes to genes and influences behavior (Moore, 2013).

The **aim of the experiment** was to investigate the behavior of rat mothers (either high-LG or low-LG, the **independent variable**, with LG standing for licking and grooming) and its effects on stress reactivity in offspring. Weaver predicted that the failure to be groomed as a baby produced epigenetic changes causing lifelong heightened stress reactivity (as cited in Moore, 2013). **Results** showed that rat babies with high-LG mothers had different (abnormal) DNA methylation than babies from low-LG mothers. Babies with low-LG mothers produced fewer glucocorticoid receptors (GR) in the hippocampus within one to six days after birth, demonstrating epigenetic silencing of genes related to proteins coding for GR production. To make sure this was just from being licked and groomed (from the environment), a different group of baby rats were placed with non-biological mothers right after birth, and the results were the same. The GR changes were seen in all baby rats with low-LG mothering and lasted the entire lifespan.

This is the way a normal rat mom handles her baby. Used under license from Megapixel.com.

The authors **concluded** that the body of experimental research on rats may serve as a model for understanding epigenetic changes in human babies.

When studying humans, babies whose mothers were depressed during their 2nd trimester of pregnancy had abnormal methlyation in the gene encoding for **serotonin** receptors (Devlin, Brain, Austin, & Oberlander, 2010). Abnormal methylation results in serotonin reuptake inefficiency, meaning the proteins regulating how much serotonin is available at synapses between neurons do not work properly, often providing too little serotonin, something correlated with **depression**. A baby's brain could be programmed even before they are born to have a greater risk for stress reactivity throughout life and possibly depression. About 15% of mothers have mood disorders sometime during their pregnancy, and a third of them take antidepressants, both large risk factors for the child because they reprogram the developing brain.

6.4: Natural selection: Survival of the fittest

Describe means to give a detailed account. Detailed knowledge about natural selection follows.

An evolutionary explanation of behavior is a modern view of **natural selection**. **Evolutionary Psychology** (EP) is the explanation used in this book, and is important because it explains the evolution of human cognitive processes. Students should study EP because the course focuses on humans living together in cultures, which requires complex cognitive processes such as **language**, the example behavior. In addition, **social cognition** is an important topic for all psychology courses, and requires language. Language, as well as our complex cultures and social cognition, evolved for survival needs and makes humans distinct from animals.

Natural Selection: Survival of the fittest

The first task is to understand Charles Darwin's natural selection. **Survival of the fittest** is the foundation of natural selection. It means obstacles in the environment are imposed on reproduction, such as predators and food supplies, and organisms must adapt and overcome these obstacles to survive (Gray & Bjorklund,

2014). **Adaptation** means changing according to circumstances. Any inherited trait helping an organism to reproduce is selected and passed on to the next generation, because evolution is all about reproducing and increasing fitness to survive. The purpose of evolution is to ensure that genes spread and survive (Baron-Cohen, 1995). Individuals reproducing more than others spread more genes around.

Evolution does not have a goal to improve an organism because survival of genes is the main goal (Baron-Cohen, 1995). Over time, the evolution of adaptive mental processes in humans increases the fitness of the group so the group reproduces more and spreads more genes to offspring.

Darwin did not know about genes, though he thought something must pass through eggs and sperm, but natural selection is a good framework for understanding evolution as we pass on our genes to the next group (Gray & Bjorklund, 2014). The genes getting passed on to the next generation are the ones that improve chances for survival.

Natural selection depends on two types of genetic variability. One is the natural reshuffling of genes during reproduction and the other is mutations, errors in DNA replication (Gray & Bjorklund, 2014). Most mutations are selected out because they are harmful, but sometimes they help people survive.

People believe many myths about natural selection that are not true. One is that people decide to evolve particular traits. This is not true because adaption is about spreading genes and has nothing to do with any notion that an organism should be improved. Even cultural evolution, such as creating clothing to protect us from the weather or conforming to group norms, is constrained by adaptations to the environment and in the end, helps to spread genes. Another myth is that humans are the most evolved group (Gray & Bjorklund, 2014), more than chimpanzees, tigers, or any other organism. The truth is that each species is fully evolved for what is needed for survival.

Four key details sum up the main points about natural selection (Gray & Bjorklund, 2014).

1. The goal of evolution is to spread genes to the next generation, so all traits that increase offspring are selected.
2. The members of any generation have variations in their traits.
3. All individuals with traits that increase offspring will survive more than those with traits that will not increase offspring.

CAS idea:
A logical extension from learning about genes: Health and GMOs
Everything is interconnected and students should be educated about **genetically modified organisms** (GMO). Many foods consumed in the US are genetically modified. The class might investigate what it means to genetically modify foods. Keep an open mind and become knowledgeable about the risks and benefits of GMOs. Make an informed opinion based on evidence, and this means evidence from scientific research, not simply an opinion from someone's blog (unless they are a very credible source and cite their evidence from scientific research) or from Twitter. Read the real research. Your decisions to consume or not consume GMOs should come from reflecting on scientific evidence.
  CAS ideas:
1. Trace the food sources of your school district or favorite restaurants. Where does the food come from, what is in it, and does it contain GMOs? Educate others of your findings.
2. Grow your own food organically.
3. Become educated about what organic really means.
4. Get involved with local farming. Visit a farm, talk to farmers, and even intern with a farm. In my area, the Tampa, FL Sweetwater Farm takes interns and has summer programs.

Chapter 7
Biological Approach to Behavior: Genetics and Behavior: Analysis and Evaluation

Chapter Objectives

Students will:
1. Practice thinking strategies (command terms) relevant to analysis and application as well as synthesis and evaluation, with explain and evaluate modeled.
2. Explain genetic similarity and evaluate research about alcoholism and bullying.
3. Explain how researchers correlate genetics and behavior, and evaluate research related to depression, insecure attachment, and alcoholism.
4. Explain Evolutionary Psychology (EP) assumptions and evaluate research related to language and the theory of mind.
5. Study the examples most related to their IB option area(s) for testing, but could learn about all the examples for deeper knowledge about genes and behavior. Follow this same advice throughout the book as more examples are included than are needed.

Genes are rarely the determining factor for behavior, something comforting to know. Although popular media makes it sound as if genes are a direct line to behavior the research shows otherwise. This means we are not prisoners of our genes. Carefully read the material about genetics in the previous chapter before starting. By the end of this chapter students should feel empowered that they have some control over what happens to them.

The section about EP is a chance to study behaviors humans evolved to live together in cultures. It helps us understand children and language development, and for students interested in developmental psychology, theory of mind is required.

7.1: Genetic similarity: Twin and adoption studies

Explain means to give a detailed account including reasons and causes. Next is important details about genetic similarity and reasons it is useful for studying behavior. Evaluate means to make a judgment (an appraisal), and strengths and limitations of twin and adoption studies are highlighted.

Genetic research methods are selected based on what someone wants to know. Twin and adoption studies have a specific goal, which is *to estimate the importance of genes to behavior.*

This section explains research methods investigating **genetic similarity**, which can also be called **genetic inheritance** or **relatedness**. Researchers study genetic similarity to understand the importance of genes to behavior. The rule is simple— the greater the genetic similarity (relatedness), the greater the genetic influence.

The reality of studying genes and behavior is that scientists can only observe **phenotypes** in family members (Carey, 2003). It would be nice if scientists could directly study **genotypes**, but they cannot, and must rely on observable traits between people. The family unit is a good place to study genetic similarity, but you will not learn much from correlating traits in the typical family as an estimate of **heritability** (Carey, 2003).

> **Thinking skills: Use of correlations**
> Students must tolerate uncertainty because twin and adoptions studies use correlation statistics to analyze data and they do not shed light on particular genes and behavior.
> Correlations show relationships and never causation. Successful evaluations of twin and adoption studies include how data is gathered and analyzed.

The reason is that trait similarities within ordinary families can be accounted for by any of the following three factors, "shared genes, shared environments, and some combination of shared environments and genes" (Carey, 2003, p. 297).

Instead, twin and adoption methods allow scientists to flesh out the general contribution of genes to a phenotype and are better parts of a family unit for estimating the heritability of a trait.

Explanation of twin studies

Key details and reasons follow. Some evaluative remarks are included that are important for making a judgment.

1. Comparisons between monozygotic (MZ), or identical twins, and dizygotic (DZ), or fraternal twins are useful for scientists.
2. MZ twins come from a single fertilized egg and start with the same genes (Carey, 2003). However, some of the cells separate and develop differently as the original cell divides many times. Any trait differences between MZ twins are due to environmental factors.
3. DZ twins come from different eggs that are separately fertilized (Carey, 2003). DZ twins share 50% of their genes, the same way as in all brothers and sisters, so differences in traits are a combination of genes and the environment.

Twins can help us find out if genetics is a reason for behavior.
Used with license from megapixl.com.

4. Twin research is valuable for scientists because if genes are important for a trait, then MZ twins would have more similarity for it than DZ twins. If both twins develop a trait, it is said they are **concordant** for that trait and genes are important. If just one twin develops the trait, it is said they are **discordant** for that trait, and genes are not as important.

5. Carey (2003) uses the term "**equal environments assumption**" (p. 298) to describe the main assumption of twin research. It means that environments are not supposed to make either DZ or MZ twins more similar.
6. As a result, twin research controls for environmental influences and allows scientists to estimate the influence of genes. Twin studies also help us see then how much of the variability in traits must be left for environmental factors.
7. Criticisms of twin studies include that they often use very small samples. Another is that MZ twins usually have a more similar environment than DZ twins, as parents tend to dress MZ twins alike, for example. The greater shared environment could confound results.

Thinking skills: Use Important terms correctly

1. **Phenotype:** A phenotype is an observable trait, such as a having a low response to alcohol, symptoms of depression or obesity.
2. **Genotype:** A genotype is a person's genetic make-up.
3. **Heritability:** Twin and adoption studies give us heritability statistics, but this does not mean we can tell from these statistics if a phenotype is really inherited (Moore, 2013). This sounds confusing, but heritability statistics only apply to differences seen within the group studied. Results cannot be generalized or compared with anyone outside the studied population (Moore, 2013). Avoid over-interpreting the results of twin and adoption studies. They just tell us if genes play a role, but cannot show exactly what role. *In the end, it is not all that useful to know the results of twin and adoption studies unless we also understand the studies investigating the contribution of genes and the environment to behavior* (Moore, 2013). If you wish to know specific genetic and environmental factors contributing to a behavior, then the next section about genes and behavior will be of more help. One such example is through gene-environment correlation studies about behaviors such as depression, reviewed in the section 7.2.

Explanation of adoption studies

Key details and reasons follow. Some evaluative remarks are included that are helpful in making a judgement.

1. Adoption studies assume that if parents adopt a child who is not genetically related to them, then any similarity in traits must be related to environmental factors (Carey, 2003).
2. On the other hand, any similarity in traits between a child adopted at birth and the biological parents must be because of genes.
3. The point of running an adoption study is to control for the effects of genes, so if the adopted child has high similarity of a trait from the biological parent that does not exist in the adoptive parents, it is considered evidence for genetic influence. However, adoption studies also then show how much of the variability in traits is due to environmental factors. It may be easier to separate the effects of genes and the environment in adoption studies than it is in twin studies.
4. Two criticisms of adoption studies are selective placement and screening.
A. First, adoption research assumes there is no selective placement for the child, so if the placement was selective it can confound the study. Selective placement means a child is adopted by parents who share traits with their biological parents, such as being of the same race (Carey, 2003). This is something adoption agencies sometimes do, and it is hard to know if selective placement influences the trait development in the adopted child, but it could.

B. Adoptive parents are often screened to make sure they are not impoverished and do not have mental illnesses, addictions, or criminal records (Carey, 2003). Researchers must interpret this screening correctly, and realize that screening is done to make sure a trait is not there in the adoptive parents. For example, adoptive parents are unlikely to be allowed to adopt a child if they are criminals or have mental illnesses.

Adoption research: Alcoholism

An evaluation adoption research requires students to make a judgment about its ability to explain behavior.

Both twin and adoption studies point to a genetic influence for alcoholism for both males and females (Heath, 1995). One notable adoption study was conducted by Cadoret and colleagues in the US using a sample from Iowa (as cited in Heath, 1995). Two early pioneering adoption studies from Denmark and Sweden reported higher genetic risks for children adopted away from biological parents with alcohol problems, but neither interviewed the adopted parents. Would a study including interviews find the same thing?

The US has laws protecting the privacy of biological parents so it is quite an undertaking to run an adoption study in the US. The Iowa adoption study was one of the first.

The **aim of the study** was to see if children adopted away from biological parents with alcohol or antisocial problems would have higher rates of alcoholism than the general public (Cadoret, Yates, Troughton, Woolworth, & Stewart, 1995). For the **procedures**, 95 males adopted at birth were studied until adulthood. Two pathways were hypothesized to lead to alcoholism. One was that males adopted away from biological parents with alcohol problems would have higher rates of alcoholism than the general public. The other was that males adopted away from biological parents with anti-social behavior would have higher rates of alcoholism than the general public (antisocial behavior gives people a risk for alcoholism). Data included interviews with adoptive parents, psychiatric testing of adoptive parents, and testing the adopted children for alcohol problems into adulthood.

Results showed correlations that supported both hypotheses. Biological parents with alcohol problems was correlated to adopted children's risk as adults. In addition, biological parents with anti-social behavior was also correlated to adopted children's risk of problem drinking as adults.

The authors **concluded** that two genetic pathways contributed to alcoholism in adopted males. An evaluation of adoption studies includes the strengths that they control environmental factors and are a starting point in explaining genetic risks for alcoholism. However, limitations include the difficulty of getting samples for ethical reasons, design problems of early pioneering studies that never interviewed the adoptive parents, and that adoption studies tell us nothing about how genes interact with the environment. Adoption studies are a starting point to consider genetic risks for alcoholism.

Thinking and inquiry: Tolerate uncertainty

Even if a body of twin and adoption studies point to genetic risks for alcoholism, the earliest research used samples from European ancestry and do not generalize well to all (Heath, 1995).

Furthermore, twin and adoption studies are really a starting point to consider genetic influences and we should look to studies about gene-environment interaction to build on the results (Heath, 1995).

Students will be interested in Marc Schuckit's research in the section about genes and behavior to build on this adoption study.

Twin research: Being bullied has both genetic and environmental influences

Anti-bullying programs should target both genetic and environmental influences to children who are chronic **bullying** victims. Twin studies untangle some general genetic and environmental contributions. An evaluation requires students to make a judgment about their ability to explain behavior.

The aims of the correlation study follow (Bowes, et al., 2013).

1. How are chronically bullied children different from non-bullied children at age 12, both in mental health and academic success?
2. What are some genetic and environmental influences in children who are chronic victims of bullies?

Both MZ and DZ twins and their families from the UK were participants. Interviews took place when children were 5, 7, 10, and 12 years old.

Procedures involved interviews asking mothers, for example, if either twin was bullied during primary school and later in secondary school. If yes, mothers and children were asked to tell what happened. Answers were coded into categories such as 'repeated harmful acts' and 'whether there was a difference in the power between children.'

Children with bullying in both primary and secondary school were considered chronic victims.

Results included the following.

Bullying will not likely end until we target all of its sources. Twin studies may help us help those most at risk. Are these findings similar or different from what you thought about people who get bullied?
Used with license from megapixl.com.

1. Correlations between MZ twins were higher for chronic bullying than DZ twins, suggesting that genetics made a contribution to being chronically bullied. Chronically bullied children had higher rates of mental health problems and lower academic performance.
2. Early adjustment problems and lower intelligence were identified as important genetic contributions.
3. Family environmental factors, such as maltreatment, low socioeconomic status, and lack of support for the mothers also contributed to a child becoming a chronic bullying victim.

The authors **concluded** that bullying programs need to consider both genetic and family influences to be most effective. One goal of bullying programs might be to focus on children likely to be victims, aiming to make them more resilient to both genetic and family contributions to the problem.

7.2: Genes and behavior: Correlating genes with the environment

Explain means to give a detailed account with reasons and causes. This section details different ways to correlate genes with the environment and reasons these studies are important. Evaluate means to make a judgment (appraisal) and it is important to take into account strengths and limitations of this type of research, including if the research stands the test of time.

Gene-environment correlation (GxE) and **endophenotypes** are two ways to show the correlation studies between genes and behavior and are the two examples in this section.

There has been a shift away from using twin and adoption methods (Caspi & Moffitt, 2006). Newer research aims to identify specific genes related to behavior. Twin and adoption studies are still useful, and the previous research about alcoholism and bullying demonstrates this. However, they do not provide all the information about genes and behaviors modern scientists want to understand. GxE correlations and endophenotypes allow scientists to see the importance of a polymorphism to behavior.

Explanation of gene-environment correlations to study depression
Key details follow, including reasons the method is valuable.

1. **Gene-environment correlations** (GxE) show how a *genetic risk can make one sensitive to the environment.*
2. GxE studies investigate the effect of genes on behavior that might not be seen unless the study is designed to see the different environments in which genes express.

Application of GxE: Depression and the serotonin transporter gene
It can be argued that short alleles of the serotonin transporter gene increase one's sensitivity to stress, which then increases the risk for **depression**. Evaluate means to make a judgment (appraisal) based on evidence. Is there enough evidence to support this claim?

One lesson to learn from this class is that genes can make someone more sensitive to stressful life events (Zimmerman, et al., 2011). This should help students understand they are in control over much of what happens to them in life because without the stress it is unlikely the gene will express.

Studying depression helps us consider how genes influence behavior. The answer is tricky. Genes are the basis of behavior and are important, but are rarely the determining factor in complex behavior. There are some rare instances when a gene directly affects behavior but for the most part genes must interact with the environment in some way.

It might be helpful to think about genes this way — *genes cannot affect behavior unless they are expressed.* Students should come away from this section understanding that we cannot change our genes, so we must pay attention to environmental factors, such as stress levels and diets, or our genes might nip us on our heels one day!

This is a good place to use the multidirectional model from chapter one. Many factors interacting in complicated ways from all three approaches to behavior contribute to depression, so this section tries to flesh out how genes work with the environment to produce mental disorder.

Everyday sadness is different from depression. They can't just snap out of it. Having the ss alleles of the 5-HTT gene is not a good predictor of getting depression. It has to interact with the environment, and in Caspi's study stressful life events were the trigger.
Used with license from megapixl.com.

Sociocultural:
1. *Stressful events*
2. *Culture and gene expression.* East Asian samples carry higher rates of the ss allele of 5-HTT but show less depression than Caucasian samples. It is thought that people living in traditional collectivist cultures (dimensions of culture) have a buffer against stress.

Cognitive:
Depressive schemas, which vary by culture. Some cultures do not even value individual feelings or use the same words to describe depression as in western cultures.

Biological:
1. Serotonin transporter gene (5-HTT) and depression
2. Gene-culture coevolution, the biological basis for the dimension of culture individualism-collectivism.

When studying genetic affects on **depression**, it is important to remember that genes affect behavior but do not work alone.

People commonly blame their personality, depression, or health problems on genes. Popular media and outdated scientific theory are responsible for creating the widely held public belief that genes directly cause behavior. *We must become better consumers of media and ask good questions about scientific research.* Genes are not a direct cause of most complex human behavior. The old phrase "nature versus nurture" deserves a proper burial. Modern psychologists study interactions between nature *and* nurture. Studying genes and depression is a model for educating the public about the "falsehood of genetic (and environmental) determinism" (Caspi, Hariri, Holmes, Uher, & Moffitt, 2010, p.11).

Knowing that genes do not directly determine complex behavior inspires hope that we can make effective life changes and helps us understand that life events shape behavior (Peele & DeGrandpre, 1995). "Americans are increasingly likely to attribute their own—and other's—behavior to innate biological causes" (p.1). The article is aptly titled "My genes made me do it." Demands for clear causes of behavior rest on incorrect assumptions about the ways genes affect behavior. "The quest for genetic explanations of why we do what we do more accurately reflects the desire for hard certainties about frightening societal problems than the true complexities of human affairs" (p.1).

The human genome contains about 25,000 genes and scientists have identified several million **polymorphisms** of them, which are probably responsible for physical and mental health problems.

Polymorphisms interact with the environment and other genes to affect behavior. It takes years to study just one polymorphism, so have some awe for the process. Knowledge is steadily progressing and the goals are to prevent mental and physical illness by making people more resilient to environmental stressors and develop effective treatments. People with specific polymorphisms can be matched to prevention programs or even particular drug treatments.

Caspi used **gene X environment correlation** (GxE) methods, *and showed that genes make one sensitive to the environment and express differently in different environments.* People exposed to similar environments have different responses, so genes are important and scientists can show how they interact with environmental factors and affect behavior (Caspi, et al., 2010).

Human genetic studies about 5-HTT and depression: Illustration of GxE correlation

One gene, the **serotonin transporter gene** (5-HTT), stands out in research about genetic risks for **depression**. Avshalom Caspi's work was pivotal and now used as a model for studying other polymorphisms and behavior. Just remember that 5-HTT is not the only gene related to depression, but is one well studied and a good place to start learning about genes and behavior.

Certain polymorphisms of 5-HTT, specifically the ss alleles, *heighten one's reactivity to stress, and reactivity to stress is correlated with higher rates of depression* (Caspi, et al., 2003). The gene alone is not a reliable predictor of depression, so it must be studied as it unfolds in the environment. The pathway is illustrated below.

ss alleles of 5-HTT ⟶ reactivity to stress ⟶ risk for depression

Everyone experiences stressors. Why do some people respond with depression? Let's create a **risk model**. A risk model means that with each added stressor, someone's chances of having a mental illness increases. For example, the risk rises if someone has the ss alleles. Add a life stressor, such as losing a job, and the risk increases. The risk increases as the number of stressful events grow. Each person has a different risk model. The risk for depression goes down if a person has two long alleles, even in the presence of stress. Possessing two long alleles is correlated with **resilience** to depression.

Genetic vulnerability for reacting to stress is related to a polymorphism in the **promoter** region of 5-HTT (Caspi, et al., 2003) Promoters are near the genes they regulate and assist in gene transcription, part of the process of gene expression, making sure that normal amounts of serotonin are in the brain. People with the s allele have **transcriptional inefficiency**, meaning that proper amounts of serotonin are not in the brain. The serotonin transporter system is important because low levels of the neurotransmitter **serotonin** are correlated to depression, so genes affect **neurotransmission** that then affect behavior.

> ### Thinking and conceptual understanding
>
> Caspi claims to have 40 independent replications. **Replication** means that others conduct studies using similar methods and attempt to find the same thing.
>
> It seems an easy thing to do, but we need to consider some recent attacks on replication in psychology and challenges to this view. See appendix #5 for things to consider when evaluating claims that a study is replicated.
>
>
>
> Scientists hope for replication, a defining feature of science. Source: pixabay.com

The **aim of the study** was to see the correlation between genetic type, having one short and one long allele (s/l heterozygotes), two short alleles (s/s homozygotes) or two long alleles (l/l homozygotes) of 5-

HTT, with responses on questionnaires about stressful life events and questionnaires diagnosing depression (Caspi, et al., 2003).

The sample used 847 Caucasians from a random sample of New Zealanders, all twenty-six years old.

Procedures follow. Participants were placed into one of three groups based on having one short and one long allele (sl), two short alleles (ss), or two long alleles (ll) of the serotonin transporter gene. They filled out a life history survey with questions about life events such as employment, health, and relationships. No difference was found in the amount of stressors from participants in the three groups. Another questionnaire found that 17% of all participants qualified for a major depression diagnosis using DSM-IV.

Data were analyzed with correlations between depression symptoms, genotype, stressful events, and their interactions. **Results** follow.

1. Participants with the ss alleles had a greater risk of depression after four or more stressful events over a period of five years.
2. Participants with the ll alleles and the same number of stressful events had a much lower risk.
3. Reports of low stress environments predicted lower rates of depression regardless of genotype.

The authors **concluded** that the gene 5-HTT affects depression greatly, but only as it interacts with stressful environments.

Correlations do not show cause and effect, but the study is part of a large body of research. About forty independently run studies show that the s allele influences the way people react to stress, giving them more risk for depression so the conclusion is strong (Caspi, et al., 2010). Some studies did not replicate the findings, but several researchers have identified them as having poor study designs.

Animal genetic experiments about 5-HTT and depression

The **aim of animal experiments** is to support the claim that the ss alleles make people more sensitive and reactive to the environment and then have a greater risk for depression.

Rhesus monkeys have the same 5-HTT polymorphisms as humans (Caspi, et al., 2010). Experiments using monkeys support conclusions of human studies and often use the **procedure** where some baby Rhesus monkeys are taken from their mothers and raised with peers and some stay with their mothers. Clear patterns of behavior emerged. **Results** show that monkeys with the l allele of 5-HTT protested their situation less. In addition, they showed effective coping skills appropriate for monkeys. Monkeys with the s allele showed more anxiety and had decreased amounts of serotonin in their spinal fluid as compared to monkeys with the short allele raised under normal living conditions (Caspi, et al., 2003).

Is it ethical to place baby monkeys under stress in experiments? The American Psychological Association has rules about using animals in research stating the benefits of the research must outweigh the risk to the animal, meaning there must be a good reason for running the study. In addition, animals must be treated humanely, kept as free of pain as possible, and receive medical care.

Are rhesus monkeys good enough models for humans for their use to be ethical? Used under license from megapixl.com.

Thinking skills: What is the value of animal research?
Consider the usefulness of animal research for learning about human behavior.
1. What criteria should be used to decide if animal research is beneficial to learning about humans?
2. Do the benefits to humans outweigh the risks to the animals? The benefits should be great.
3. Chapter 10 about the value of animals in research to understand human behavior includes a discussion about using monkeys to study depression.

Culture, gene expression and depression: A biological basis for the individualism-collectivism dimension

Culture affects gene expression so we should include culture in our study of depression and genes.

Gene-culture coevolution is a new theory explaining human behavior as interactions between "two complementary evolution processes, cultural and genetic evolution" (Chiao & Blizinsky, 2010, p. 529). Cultural values create the environments in which genes express and this is why this topic is so important to study. We cannot assume that genes express the same way in different environments.

Culture affects everyone's self-construal, or the way we view the self. The **dimensions of culture** are **etics**, or universal sets of continuums reflecting the values of a group that guide self-construal. Everyone falls somewhere on the continuum. **Individualism-collectivism** is one dimension of culture studied with gene expression. Groups high on individualism value independence and self-expression. Groups high on collectivism value conformity and relationship harmony.

Genes also affect behavior, with the **serotonin transporter gene** and **depression** as one example. East Asians have higher rates of the s risk alleles, and 70-80% carry at least one short allele of 5-HTT. In contrast, 40-45% of Caucasian samples of Western Europe origin carry at least one short allele.

Although East Asian cultures have a higher genetic risk, they have a lower prevalence of depression.

Gene-culture co-evolution explains that collective cultural values provide buffers from stress in groups with more genetic vulnerabilities to illness. Collectivism fine-tunes the environment so genetic vulnerabilities are not as damaging to groups.

The authors gathered evidence about the frequency of the short and long alleles of 5-HTT and depression prevalence from 124 studies. Twenty-nine countries representing a mixture of individualism and collectivism values were evaluated.

The authors show a correlation for the first time between the values of individualism-collectivism and expression of the serotonin transporter gene. The field of **cultural neuroscience** is rapidly developing and needs more investigation.

Explanation of gene-environment correlations to studying genetic risks for insecure attachment

Chapter 33 about **developmental psychology** includes a section about attachment theory. Research about a GxE correlation study about genetic risks for **insecure attachment** is reviewed there.

Attachment is a required developmental psychology topic and can be used as example research for this section.

Explanation of endophenotypes to study alcoholism

Key details follow, including reasons the method is valuable.

1. One way to study how genes affect behavior is through **endophenotypes** (Schuckit, 2008a). It means to take a behavior one wants to study and relate it to a **phenotype** that is related to a **polymorphism**.
2. Let's use alcoholism as an example. Genes account for 40-60% of the factors contributing to alcoholism (Schuckit, 2013). When genes interact with the environment the risk for alcoholism increases. A phenotype is an observable physical characteristic, such as a low response to alcohol, which is an intermediate factor correlated with a polymorphism. This diagram shows the pathway. The relationship is not direct from the gene to a behavior!

Behavior (alcoholism)⟶ Phenotype (low response to alcohol)⟶l allele of serotonin
transporter gene

3. Schuckit (2008a) identified four phenotypes correlated with alcoholism.
A. Low response to alcohol (LR), the example in this chapter
B. Facial flushing
C. Personality characteristics such as impulsiveness
D. Psychiatric disorders such as major depression, PTSD, panic disorder, antisocial personality disorder, and schizophrenia

Endophenotype research: Low response to alcohol

The phenotype **low response to alcohol** (LR) is correlated with a higher risk for alcoholism (Schuckit, 2008a, 2008b). Evaluate means to make a judgment (appraisal) based on evidence. Is there enough evidence to support this claim? The **aim of the study** was to see the correlation between the LR phenotype and the l allele of the serotonin transporter gene.

Many alcoholics report that it takes great amounts alcohol for them to feel its effects. Schuckit (2008a) hypothesized, "if individuals drink more for effects and more alcohol is required to achieve the feelings they want, then they are more likely to drink more heavily per occasion" (p. 3). Therefore, these drinkers spend more time with heavy drinking peers and run a higher risk of developing a high tolerance to alcohol. The drinking behavior with peers increases the risk of alcoholism.

Data were collected during the **procedures** in three ways and analyzed with correlations.
1. Questionnaires that ask people about drinking habits and response to alcohol
2. Genotyping
3. Observations of people's cognitive and motor abilities at different levels of alcohol consumption

Film reviewing LR research
Marc Schuckit is featured in the film *The Hijacked Brain*. This film is older, but still relevant as research by people such as Schuckit stands the test of time. It helps students understand addictions, part of health psychology.

Results show that the l allele (long version) of the **serotonin transporter gene** (5-HTT) is correlated with LR. The l allele causes a faster reuptake of serotonin at synapses, meaning serotonin empties faster (Schuckit, 2008a). Schuckit **concluded** that low levels of serotonin at synapses may contribute to someone drinking large amounts of alcohol to feel its effects (Schuckit, 2008b).

Low response to alcohol (LR) research stands the test of time

Research about LR has taken place for over 30 years, and is the most studied and verified of all the phenotypes identified for alcoholism (Schuckit, 2013).

Research conclusions about LR over time follow (Schuckit, 2013).
1. LR can be demonstrated early, when someone starts his or her drinking career.
2. LR is a reliable predictor of future risk for developing problem drinking and alcohol use disorder.
3. LR is 40% to 60% related to a genetic risk.
4. Having a lowered sensitivity to alcohol is related to faster serotonin reuptake.
5. Environmental factors such as drinking with peers and being reactive to stress heighten the risk that someone will develop problem drinking.

Thirty years of research has verified that LR early in life is clearly related to developing problem drinking later in life (Schuckit, Smith, & Kalmijn, 2014).

For example, the **aim of one correlation study** was to show that LR behavior early in life predicted greater risk of alcohol use later in life. One of the five hypotheses was that men testing as LR at the start of the study would be predicted to have greater incidence of alcohol use disorder later in life.

Participants were men in San Diego studied from about age 20 to age 50. For the **procedures**, data included interviews, such as men's reports of how much they drank along with how much was needed to feel intoxicated.

Results showed a strong correlation between LR at age 20 and the development of alcohol use disorder later in life.

Thinking skills: Research standing the test of time!
Good critical thinkers look to see if research results hold up over time. When research is newer, texts should identify it as such, along with tentative conclusions. LR research is one of the many topics in this book that stands the test of time.

Caspi's depression research also stands the test of time.

7.3: Evolutionary explanations of behavior: Evolutionary Psychology (EP)

Start this section with a TED Talk
Start this section with the **TED Talk** from Patricia Kuhl titled "The linguistic genius of babies." Language is a potential we come into the world with that develops as we learn about our culture. Since EP is about the evolution of human cognitive processes this is a great example.

Having a working behavior on the floor when learning about a new theory is helpful.

Explain means to give a detailed account with reasons and causes. Next is details about the assumptions of EP and reasons it makes sense as an explanation for the evolution of human cognitive processes. Evaluate means to make a judgment (appraisal) based on evidence. Students should make judgments about EP as an explanation for the evolution of the cognitive processes that define us as humans. Is there enough support for EP from studying **language** and **theory of mind**?

Since Darwin's time many have contributed new ideas about how the brain evolved (Gazzaniga, Ivry, & Mangun, 2009). One such contribution comes from **Evolutionary Psychology** (EP), a modern view of **natural selection**, claiming all evolved cognitive processes contribute to human survival.

"The mind is a set of information-processing machines that were designed by natural selection to solve adaptive problems faced by our hunter-gatherer ancestors" (Cosmides & Tooby, 1997, p. 1). Humans evolved different brain regions and neural connections for the

---

Thinking skills: No evolution theory is proven
EPs believe the many challenges humans face, such as raising children and communicating, pushed humans to adapt by developing cognitive abilities such as language. But can researchers correlate cognitive abilities with these environmental challenges?

It is impossible (Buller, 2009). To correlate the environmental demands with an evolved trait, the trait must be compared in different species with a common ancestor. If the different species have different traits, perhaps environmental factors that might have prompted the different adaptations can be correlated with the trait. Our closest relative, the chimpanzee, does not have a complex language system or sophisticated cognitive processes. However, the common relative we shared with them is extinct, so it is impossible to know if they evolved differently from the common ancestor.

Although not proven, plenty of research from Pat Kuhl, Janet Werker, and Simon Baron-Cohen (theory of mind) supports EP.

different adaptive problems faced (Baron-Cohen, 1995).

EP's assumptions follow (Cosmides & Tooby, 1997). These are important details.

Evolutionary Psychology (EP) assumptions

The brain is a system with circuits to create behavior that best fits with one's environment.

Natural selection designed these circuits to solve problems faced by our ancestors. These circuits are not designed to solve *any* problem, just *adaptive* problems. Adaptive problems are the ones that keep coming up in evolutionary history. Solutions to these problems must affect *reproduction* in some way, which is the basis of natural selection. **Language** is an example of a good solution to evolutionary problems related to communication and raising children.

"Different neural circuits are specialized for solving different adaptive problems" (p. 8). For example, babies come into the world with evolved circuits that allow them to pay attention to faces. Even 10 minute old babies pay attention to faces. Babies have innate hypotheses about a number of things in their world, such as objects, a theory of mind, and physical causality. Life is difficult for those missing these hypotheses.

Natural selection took a long time to design brain circuitry, so our modern minds are similar to ancient minds. Our minds did not evolve in modern societies. Rather, our brain lived most of its evolutionary existence in hunter-gatherer societies. For about 10 million years, natural selection shaped the brain with neural circuitry that solved adaptive problems.

Some reasons EP is important are next. Think of the many problems humans came across in their environments, such as creating social groups so people could live together, attracting mates, raising children, and navigating territory (Matsumoto & Juang, 2008). These needs are biologically based and have social consequences. **Culture** offered a solution, a way to survive. "Culture is a solution to the problem of individual's adaptations to their contexts to address their social motives and biological needs" (p. 8).

An evolutionary point of view still allows for individual differences (Baron-Cohen, 1995). There are just some evolutionary universals we all need to survive. Through natural selection humans evolved cognitive processes to solve these problems. *Transmitting practices to the next generation was probably the greatest adaptive problem for humans*. A brain-based **language** was an excellent solution.

Darwin wrote that children developed language so rapidly that a biological predisposition to it must exist (Gazzaniga, Iet al., 2009).

Next, let's look at some evidence to support EP, including language development, the theory of mind, and social intelligence, which are all related. All three are tools for **enculturation**.

This baby comes equipped with evolved potentials to learn the language(s) he or she will speak and stays busy listening to other humans. Language solved an adaptive problem of needing to transmit practices to the next generation. This baby also comes equipped with skills that will turn into a theory of mind. Source: pixabay.com.

Evidence for making a judgment about EP: Some theory about language development

Babies come into the world with evolved potentials to help them learn their culture's language (Kuhl, 2000). "What is innate regarding language is not a universal grammar and phonetics, but innate learning

---

Thinking skills: This section also includes the information about language enculturation

Language is learned and shared (Heider, 2003). It is the primary way children are enculturated.

Children come into the world as universal language listeners and can hear the sounds of all languages. Language surrounds children in everyday life as they are enculturated. By the time babies are 11 months, they hear the sounds of the language(s) they will speak. This change is accompanied by neuroplastic changes in the brain. This transformation takes place through enculturation, and Janet Werker's BA-DA experiment is evidence it has occurred. Enculturation is a required topic for the sociocultural ATB and **language enculturation** can be used as an example.

---

biases and strategies that place constraints on perception and learning" (p. 11856). Babies discover the rules of the language used by their cultures from evolved and built-in perceptual abilities. The brain has great **neuroplasticity** for language in early life.

The process of language learning follows (Kuhl, 2000).

1. *Infants have an innate ability to perceive the basic units of all languages.* Young babies are '**citizens of the world.**' New babies hear and respond to the phonemes, the sounds of speech, of *all* languages. Infants do not understand the meaning of the sounds but have an innate ability to discriminate between them.

2. *Babies use learning strategies that map language rules.* A child's perceptual abilities change so they become '**culture-bound listeners.**' By nine months, babies can detect the legal pattern of sounds for their culture's language. For example, the sound combination "zw" and "vl" is legal in Dutch but not in English. By nine months, babies learning English pay attention to English longer and Dutch babies pay attention to Dutch longer. Babies do not know what words mean, but have a "perceptual sleeve" that words fit into as a child learns them.

Language films

1. *To Talk*, part of the *Baby Human* series, is available from Amazon. Both Patricia Kuhl and Janet Werker are featured.
2. Kuhl is interviewed in the film *TV in the Baby Bottle*, and discusses how TV hampers a child's language learning. It is available from Films for the Humanities and Sciences. This film is also important for chapter 17 about cognition in the digital world.

---

3. ***Motherese*, or *parentese*, a universal way of talking to babies, is beneficial.** Motherese helps babies discriminate speech sounds. Infant-directed language exaggerates the sounds babies must learn and helps them form categories through repeating words in stereotyped sentences, such as "See the _____" and "Where is the _____?" that highlight ways to use new words.

4. *There is a critical period for language related to one's language experience.* The ability to learn language later in life may be constrained by the initial mapping involved in learning one's native language. It is easiest to learn a second language when both are heard during the time when innate perceptual abilities are tuning into the sounds of language and then acting as magnets for other related sounds.

Research evidence for an evolved language ability: Janet Werker's Ba-Da experiment

A classic quasi-experiment demonstrated that children's speech perception reorganized by the end of the first year of life, moving children from universal language listeners to language specific listeners (Werker

& Lalonde, 1988). This experiment supports EP and Kuhl's theories, showing that babies come into the world ready to hear any language and it unfolds within cultures as babies tune into the sounds of the language they will speak.

English and Hindi language sounds were used in the study. Adult English speakers can hear two categories of phonemes, or sounds (ba vs da). Adult Hindi speakers can hear three categories, (ba vs. da and da vs. Da). English speaking adults cannot hear the Hindi Da as it is not a sound used in English.

The **aims of the experiment** were to see what babies could hear and at what age developmental changes occurred.

A group of infants aged 6 to 8 months and a group aged 11 to 13 months participated in the experiment. Age and the language sounds were the **independent variables**. The age when a child could no longer hear the difference between the sounds was the **dependent variable**.

Procedures are next. The study used a "head turn method" to know when babies heard a sound change or could not hear it. All the babies were conditioned to turn their heads away from a researcher to a box with a toy animal clapping symbols when a sound category changed. The animal box was the reinforcer for a correct head turn.

Babies heard random pairings of the sounds ba, da, and Da.

Results showed that babies 6-8 months discriminated between all the sounds, even though some of these babies were from English speaking families and had never heard Hindi spoken. This finding is consistent with theory suggesting that babies come into the world as universal listeners able to hear all language sounds. Babies 11-13 months from English speaking families could no longer hear the Hindi Da sound and did not turn their head toward the animal box when the sounds changed from ba or da to Da.

The researchers **concluded** this was evidence that a baby's brain reorganizes during the first year of life and become language-specific listeners, ready to pay attention to the sounds from the words they will speak.

This experiment is now part of a large body of work that has **observer, time**, and **space triangulation**, meaning it has been tested by many researchers over time and across cultures. It stands the test of time.

Research evidence for an evolved language ability: Social interaction, learning Mandarin as a second language, and a baby's brain

This experiment **aimed to show** that social interaction was required for developing language potentials (Kuhl & Gaxiola, 2008).

Remember that nine months is during the critical period for perceptual pruning of sounds, as 8-month olds can still hear the sounds of all languages but 11-month olds just hear the sounds of their native language. Would the babies be able to also discriminate Mandarin sounds at 11 months even though they did not hear it from their parents? For this study, the **independent variable** was interaction directly with an adult, through audio-only, or through television. Change in the ERP readings was the **dependent variable**.

Procedures follow. Infants heard Mandarin during 12, 25-minute sessions where a Mandarin speaking researcher played with the children and read stories. A control group of English speaking babies had the same sessions but in English. Two other groups heard Mandarin or English stories and games through audio-only teaching or through the television.

There is no substitute for a caregiver reading to and directly interacting with a child.
Used with license from megapixl.com.

Children were tested with Mandarin words that differed from English words while wearing caps measuring **event-related potentials** (ERP).

Results showed that children learning Mandarin through direct social interaction learned the most sounds as evidenced by ERPs. Children learning Mandarin through the television or audio-only teaching learned no more than controls who did not hear any Mandarin. The learning though direct contact was intact even after 30 days when the babies did not hear any more adults speaking Mandarin.

These findings have been replicated across other languages and samples, so it has strong support. The lesson here is that there is no substitute for face-to-face social contact with adults when learning language.

> **Thinking skills: Does TV help babies learn language?**
> This Mandarin study is the one Kuhl presents in the film, *TV in the Baby Bottle*. Students might look into the issue more and consider if babies can learn language from TV and if babies and toddlers should watch any TV.

Theory of mind: Evidence for EP

How often do you think about what someone else is thinking? Thinking about other's thoughts probably takes up the majority of your time. It is extremely useful to know something about your parent, teacher, or friend's thoughts before you say or do something.

It was an evolutionary breakthrough for humans to develop the ability to reliably guess what another, especially a possible rival, was thinking (Baron-Cohen, 1995). If we are going to study humans living together in cultures, then it is important to know something about the evolution of "mind reading," which is not to be confused with psychic abilities. Mind reading, or having a **theory of mind** (ToM), evolved as part of human **social intelligence**, defined as "the ability to process information about the behavior of others and to react adaptively" (Baron-Cohen, 1995, p. 13).

Many other aspects of studying humans such as a child's cognitive development is tied in some way to the ToM.

ToM is defined as "the ability to represent and infer unobservable mental states such as desires, intention, and beliefs from the self and others" (Gazzaniga, Ivry, & Mangun, 2002, p. 676). Only humans have fully developed ToMs. Chimpanzees have some aspects of it (Call & Tomasello, 2008). Chimpanzees have knowledge and perception of others and can understand some intentions. However, chimpanzees fail at 'false belief' tests, where they have to understand that someone else has beliefs different from theirs and that someone can believe something different. So chimpanzees have not evolved all aspects of the fully developed human ToM. Human children master false belief problems by age four. People with **autism** have trouble with false belief tests. Without a fully developed ToM, people with autism have trouble with social relationships.

The ToM is brain based. **fMRI** evidence shows that the right temporo-junction (RTJP) is active when humans decode the intentions of others (Saxe & Wexler, 2005). What makes the RTJP special? It was recruited specifically when study participants made **attributions** (how people explain the cause of something) of other's mental states. RTJP activity was the most active in conditions where participants made sense of inconsistent information about others. *The brain has a specific function devoted to the ToM and is probably a fundamental aspect of human social cognition.*

So much of what humans do is directed at being social. As stated at the beginning of this book, *humans evolved to live in cultures*. Humans evolved complex cognitive abilities to be social and these social lives take place within cultures.

Evidence for EP: Human social intelligence

The evolution of the human brain required a social environment (Baron-Cohen, 1995). Social intelligence was a primary adaptive problem driving the human brain's evolution of cognitive skills.

Social behavior is complex. Remember how hard it was for Temple Grandin, a high functioning autistic person, to manage social interactions? The most adaptive way to manage social behavior was to develop a mechanism allowing humans to decode the intentions of others, the ToM.

Mind reading is universal and people in all cultures have a ToM (Baron-Cohen, 1995). Humans are born with innate *skills* that form the basis of mind reading, consistent with EP assumption #1. Three of the skills are the **intentionality detector** (ID), the **eye-direction detector** (ED), the **shared-attention mechanism** (SAM). Each becomes available to children at specific times in development. All four are assumed to be evolutionarily advantageous to humans and fit with EP assumption #4. We are not conscious of these processes because the mechanisms probably require large amounts of neural circuitry, as EP assumption #3 suggests.

Age and mechanism	Description of process
Phase 1: ID and EDD, ages birth to 9 months (Baron-Cohen, 1995)	The ID helps infants read motion and sound signals important to their needs. The EDD relates to the visual system. It helps infants to recognize someone's eyes and know if these eyes are looking at them, giving babies the ability to understanding other's perceptions. Experiments support the existence of EDD in 3 year olds. Children were shown two sets of photographs. Each set showed a face looking at them and one looking away. One of the pictures in each pair only showed the eyes looking at the child, with the entire face of the one photograph slightly turned. The other photograph in the pair showed both the nose and eyes aimed at the child. Regardless of which cue the children received, they knew which photograph was looking at them. Animals also know if something is looking at them. To survive, animals must know if a predator is watching them. So animals and children share some basic abilities but children go on to rapidly pass anything a chimp does.
Phase 2: SAM, ages 9-18 months (Baron-Cohen, 1995)	SAM shows children the relationship between 3 important things—an agent, the self, and an object/other agent. For example, "Mom sees (and I see) the flower." Mom is the agent seeing an object, the flower, and the "I see" is the child's self. This is an amazing skill and is required for high-level social interaction where the baby infers that they are sharing a perception with another, seeing the same thing. The EDD, the visual system, is frequently used by SAM. SAM requires perceptual information to work correctly and, for example, if someone says, "look at that flower", we use our visual system to attend to the correct object. In addition, SAM can get perceptual input from the needs identified by the ID.
Babies still do not understand certain things and a full command of ToM continues to develop, but you see the ToM is a good example of an evolved potential for humans to have sophisticated cognitive processing.	The full ToM might need a system for understanding the full range of mental states of others. While the ID, EDD, and SAM are building blocks to the ToM, there are still mental states that young babies do not understand. These include guessing, pretending, imagining, deceiving, and understanding false beliefs. Later in development children understand there are many mental states and that people can relate to each other. Baron-Cohen gives the following example. "The statement 'Snow White *thought* the woman selling apples was a kind person' can be true, while 'Snow White *thought* her wicked stepmother was a kind person' may be false" (p. 53), even if they are the same person. Snow White is a complicated story and children have to *develop* the ability to understand it.

A complex relationship probably exists between language and the TOM, and *they may have helped each other develop* (Baron-Cohen, 1995). The ToM and language evolved, but they do *not arrive intact in a baby*. Instead, **natural selection** gave us the *ability to learn* (Pinker, 1994).

Chapter 8
The Biological Level of Analysis: Hormones: Knowledge and Understanding

---

Chapter Objectives

Students will:
1. Practice using thinking strategies related to knowledge and understanding, with describe modeled.
2. Describe hormones.
3. Describe pheromones.

This is a short chapter because there are just two topics. Background material follows that is needed to study hormones and behavior in the next chapter.

8.1: Hormones: Key details

Describe means to give a detailed account. The key details of hormones follow.

1. "**Hormones** are the body's chemical messengers" (MedlinePlus, 2012, p. 1). Many hormones affect behavior and some of these are secreted by the endocrine glands and some are secreted by organs you might not think of as related to hormones, such as the intestines or the brain (Gray, 2011). Leptin, a hormone related to obesity, is and example and is produced by fat tissue in the digestive organs.
2. Hormones travel to specific target tissues through the bloodstream and affect behavior.
3. Hormones and neurotransmitters have a common evolutionary origin (Gray, 2011). Both are ways to send messages. They can act differently because neurotransmitters transmit messages by way of synapses and hormones transmit messages by way of the bloodstream. Sometimes a chemical can act as both a hormone and a neurotransmitter, such as **epinephrine**, produced by the adrenal cortex.
4. Hormones cooperate with neurotransmitters. An example of this cooperation is between the hormone cortisol and the neurotransmitter/hormone epinephrine, also known as adrenaline, explained in section 9.2 in the next chapter.
5. Hormones affect behavior in a number of ways. As examples, hormones affect mood and contribute to depressed symptoms. Hormones affect sexual reproduction or prepare people for puberty or parenting.

Stress hormones signal to run from an attacker. Last, hormones affect appetite and relate to obesity. Hormones affect behavior temporarily or permanently (Gray, 2011). Stress hormones can have short-term effects on the brain and cause students to forget what they stayed up all night studying, or it can have a long term effect of killing brain cells in the hippocampus.

6. Even small amounts of hormone can greatly affect behavior so it is very serious when someone does not produce the right amount. You do not want too much or too little of any hormone.

Leptin, a hormone regulating appetite and **cortisol**, an important human stress hormone, are the examples highlighted in the next chapter.

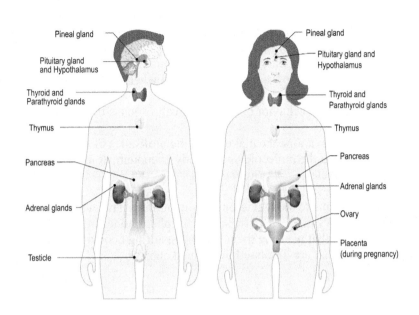

ENDOCRINE SYSTEM

Endocrine system
Used with license from megapixl.com

8.2: Pheromones: Key details

Describe means to give a detailed account. Key details of **pheromones** follow (Wyatt, 2015).

1. Pheromones are "chemical signals that have evolved for communication with other members of the same species" (p. 1).
2. Pheromones are signals that are common for all males or females of a species and are not specific to individuals. Smelling a pheromone cannot identify an individual in a species.
3. Pheromones bring out a particular stereotyped reaction (called a releaser effect) or a developmental effect (called a primer effect). The stereotyped reaction can happen even when it is not appropriate, something seen when studying pheromones in insects. Some pheromones produce both effects, such as in mice when pheromones signal aggressive behavior, mate attraction, and also stimulates puberty in females.
4. Responses to pheromones are innate and are generally not influenced by learning. Sometimes experience affects the action of pheromones but this is subtle, such as when a moth that has mated is not affected by the female pheromones of other moths.
5. Pheromones exist in all animals, including mammals.
6. Pheromones are involved in many behaviors, such as mate attraction and choice, following the trail of another animal, and in some species is part of parent-child interaction.
7. Smell is important for detecting pheromones. In the past it was believed that animals had a structure called the **vomeronasal** (VNO) that contain receptors specific to picking up particular pheromones and nothing else (Doty, 2014) The VNO was believed to be separate from the olfactory receptors that evolved to sense pheromones, with each receptor responding to just one pheromone. But this conclusion has come under criticism as it has been shown that the VNO in mice also has receptors

similar to those in the general olfactory system, so it is not clear that the VNO is specific to pheromones even in animals.

8. The human VNO is small and much harder to locate in human adults (Kalat, 2007). Might it be something from our evolutionary history? And does it affect behavior in a meaningful way?

Three steps for identifying pheromones are important because if we want to make an argument that humans have them, scientists must follow this process and demonstrate it (Wyatt, 2015). All animals have pheromones but identifying them in humans is controversial because of the difficulties in conducting the research and the many alternative explanations for study results.

The three steps follow and should be used when trying to identify human pheromones (Wyatt, 2015).

1. Find a specific behavior or physiological response that is mediated by a specific chemical within a species.
2. Isolate and examine the make-up of the molecules of that chemical.
3. Confirm that the molecule under study is enough, at natural concentrations in humans, to produce an effect (the releaser or primer effect).

So far attempts to study pheromones in humans have not followed these steps and the claims are inconclusive (Wyatt, 2015). The search for pheromones in humans is worth pursuing because it seems common sense that we have them and the resulting behavior is intriguing, but the debate is unresolved for many reasons that are discussed in the next chapter.

Watch the TED Talk by Tristram Wyatt:
The smelly mystery of the human pheromone

This is an excellent TED Talk by the same T. Wyatt referenced above. This will help students understand that there is a great deal we still need to learn about human pheromones.

Chapter 9
Biological Approach to behavior: Hormones: analysis and evaluation

Chapter objectives

Students will:
1. Practice thinking strategies (command terms) related to analysis and application as well as synthesis and evaluation, with explain and evaluate modeled.
2. Explain how leptin affects obesity and evaluate research linking leptin and obesity.
3. Evaluate leptin therapy as an obesity treatment.
4. Explain how cortisol activates the stress response and evaluate research linking cortisol, stress, and immunity.
5. Explain how cortisol can alter gene expression.
6. See that leptin and cortisol apply to studying the IB abnormal, health, and developmental options.
7. Evaluate human pheromone research related to attraction, mother-child interaction, and alcohol consumption.

Two **hormones** of interest to a 21st Century global community are **leptin** and **cortisol**. Leptin is important because of increasing global **obesity**, called "globesity" by the World Health Organization. Cortisol, an important stress hormone, is important because stress levels can be high in our 24/7 world and can even alter gene expression and the brain.

Students may assume that **pheromones** exist in humans, especially if they read popular media about the effect of scents. However, the research is more flimsy than you might expect. It is a valuable thinking exercise by challenging assumptions and reflecting on strengths and limitations of the research.

9.1: Hormones: Let's start with a good film about leptin and work from there

---

Class activities for hormones: Have fun with it

Learn about hormone details from the previous chapter.
1. Study **leptin**, related to health psychology. Show the film segment "Deconstructing Obesity" where Jeff Friedman explains the mechanisms of leptin and shows the ob mice. A free copy is available as part of a 4-part lecture series, "The science of fat" from www.biointeractive.org. This series is also available for streaming. Although it is from 2004, it is not outdated. Its purpose is to explain how leptin works. The other lectures are equally excellent. Ronald Evans discusses the role **culture** plays in obesity with a case of the Pima Indians. The case study on humans is a good opportunity to learn about the case study method. The Knight experiment with mice illustrates how we study the actual mechanisms of leptin in a lab setting and is a good place to discuss the ethics of animal studies.
2. Study **cortisol**, related to the health and abnormal options. Start with the National Geographic film, *Stress: Portrait of a Killer* featuring Robert Sapolsky. I also teach mindfulness-meditation to students from the beginning of this unit and with the health option. Developing the patience to sit quietly takes time so we start meditating right away. I selected cortisol's effects on immunity as the example for this chapter because it applies to student lives. Students get some insight into why they might get so many colds! Material about how hormones altering genes uses cortisol as an example and can be cross-referenced to the research about genes and behavior in chapter 7. Cortisol is also needed for health problems and traumas (developmental).

Hormones and obesity: The ob gene and leptin

Explain means to give a detailed account including reasons and causes. It can be argued that leptin deficiency is one cause of obesity, and next is important details useful for making the argument along with reasons leptin is worthy of continued research. Evaluate means to make a judgment (appraisal) using evidence, and it is clear from studying the topic that we still have much to learn about leptin and when it can be used as an obesity treatment.

Friedman (2011, 2009) discovered and named the ob gene (obesity gene) in 1995. The **ob gene** regulates the production of **leptin**, a peptide hormone produced from fat cells that regulates appetite. About 8% of obesity is related to mutations of the ob gene. *This is a rare instance when genes are a direct cause of behavior.* OB gene mutation cases are rare because a person failing to produce any hormone would not have much chance of survival (Friedman, 2011). These rare ob mutation cases are a way for psychologists to isolate the role of leptin in obesity in research.

Thinking skills: Use the terms correctly

1. **Leptin deficiency** is when someone does not produce leptin.
2. **Leptin resistance** is when someone has plenty of leptin, but the brain has lost its sensitivity to it.
3. **Leptin sensitivity** is when people have normal levels of leptin and the brain responds to its signals.

Why do you think some people are obese? Is it lack of willpower? Is it modern sedentary lifestyles? These questions are important because many people think willpower and lifestyle are the main reasons (Howard Hughes Medical Institute, 2005). Friedman (2011, 2009) has a new perspective. About 8% of obese people have a mutation of the ob gene, a direct path to obesity. These people are **leptin deficient** and do not produce any leptin.

Low leptin levels signal hunger. People with the ob gene mutation eat huge amounts of food and can become morbidly obese. *Leptin treatment is very effective in these cases.* Friedman (2011) reported a case of a 3-year old obese child who ate up to 1300 calories at one sitting, which is about half of what an adult should eat in one day! The child rapidly slimmed down after leptin replacement therapy and ate in the normal range for her age, 180 calories at a meal. Leptin's role in obesity is supported by animal research. Friedman refers to a mouse knock-out experiment, meaning that mice are genetically engineered to lack the expression of the ob gene. Mice that do not express the ob gene and lack leptin are obese and inactive as compared to control mice, even when living under the same conditions. These ob mice can effectively be treated with leptin replacement injections.

What about the other 92% of obese people? Their obesity involves more complex interactions between the environment and genes. Friedman says the problem is complicated because so many obese people are **leptin resistant**, meaning they have *high levels of leptin but somehow do not respond correctly to fullness signals.* These people have plenty of leptin so something must be wrong with the signal to stop eating.

An explanation of how leptin affects appetite

Leptin comes from body fat, circulates in the bloodstream, and sends messages to the brain to regulate hunger (Knight, et al., 2010). It is a natural biological system that balances energy intake and energy use. One's body should sense that there is either enough or not enough body fat, triggering hunger or fullness to stabilize it. When fat mass falls, leptin levels fall and appetite increases until we have enough body fat again (Friedman, 2011). When fat mass increases, leptin levels also increase, and we are no longer hungry.

Dieting is hard. If a dieter restricts food and loses body fat, then the body does not produce enough leptin, and the hunger signal is triggered so more body fat can be produced. The hunger signal is a basic drive, a natural response to body fat loss and hard to resist. Friedman (Howard Hughes Medical Institute, 2005) compared it to the urge to breathe after holding one's breath for a long time. You just have to breathe! The same thing happens to dieters. You just cannot resist food!

Lean people with normal levels of leptin who also eat the right amounts of a balanced diet have high leptin levels and get a signal to stop eating when full. Most people stay within a normal weight range because they are **leptin sensitive**, meaning they get the right signals from leptin. Obese people either are leptin deficient (8% with the ob gene mutation) or are frequently leptin resistant (92%). Scientists need

This is how leptin works.
Source: Friedman, J. M. (2009). Obesity: causes and control of excess body fat. *Nature,* 459, 340-342. Curtsey of J. Friedman

to learn more about treating leptin resistance because it is a stumbling block for dieters. People with the ob gene mutation and some but not all people with leptin resistance respond to leptin injections.

Research about leptin and obesity: Case study of a human with the ob gene mutation

Rare extreme cases are useful because they help scientists understand a biological mechanism and ultimately to understand normal behavior (O'Rahilly, 2002). Cases of people with the ob gene mutation who are leptin deficient and do not produce leptin fall into this category.

Case study is a useful research method. First, cases further our understanding of a biological system early in its discovery, such as verifying Friedman's early theory about leptin and appetite. Second, cases clarify our understanding of possible treatments, such as how leptin replacement therapy might help. There are few cases of ob gene mutations, perhaps just four or five, but scientists have learned much from them.

The **aim of the study** was to report a case about a child with a naturally occurring **ob gene mutation** (Gibson, 2004). The child is the fourth reported case. The first two were Pakistani cousins living in the United Kingdom. The third case was from a Turkish family. All three previous cases benefited from leptin replacement therapy.

The patient was of normal weight at birth to Pakistani parents living in Canada. At birth the baby's weight scored in the 50th percentile of the normal range. Right after birth the patient had problems with breastfeeding and started drinking formula. The baby was insatiable and fed ravenously on the formula. At three months the baby weighed in the 95th percentile for normal baby weight. The child continued to gain weight rapidly and by five years old weighed 64 kg (140.8 pounds) with a body mass index of 43.4.

The doctors used leptin replacement therapy because of its success in treating similar cases and got informed consent from both the parents and child. The child's body produced no leptin on its own and testing confirmed the ob gene mutation. The family came from the same region of Pakistan as the two cousins living in the UK, though they were not related over the past four generations.

Results showed that the child lost weight just two weeks after starting leptin injections. The child's body mass index dropped to 24.2 over two years of leptin replacement. Overall body fat decreased from 53.4% to 38.1%. The patient grew normally over the two years and continued to slim down to a better weight for her age that was sustained over the course of treatment.

Research about leptin and obesity: A second case study showing a different pathway to leptin deficiency and obesity.

The **aim of this case study** was to examine a different and rare case that shows a newly discovered genetic pathway to leptin deficiency and obesity (Wabitsch, et al. 2015).

This boy was the first child of two normal weight Pakistani parents who were cousins. The child was in the normal weight range at birth but weighed 33.7 kg by age 2.6, in the 99th percentile of weight for that age group. The boy was extremely hungry all the time, was morbidly obese, and quickly ate 680 calories during the test breakfast given to him by researchers.

This boy was different from Gibson's case because he had plenty of leptin. However, this boy had a "mutation in the gene encoding leptin receptor" (p. 51), making leptin inactive. This means the boy had plenty of leptin but did not send signals that he was full.

Results showed that the boy responded well to leptin replacement therapy. Although this type of leptin deficiency is rare,

---

Thinking skills: Making effective evaluations
An effective evaluation of leptin cases includes two things. One is that the human research uses the case study method, so it does not show causation.

The other is that the more we research the topic, the more complicated knowing the path to obesity becomes. This is consistent with what we know about genetic research in general. Scientists are expanding what is known about genetic contributions to behavior rather than narrowing them down, making it more complicated but more realistic!

the researchers advise doctors to test extremely obese children for this problem to at least rule it out as a cause.

Now we are ready to discuss what happens in more typical obesity cases. The next section explores the causes of leptin resistance, where people have plenty of active leptin but do not get the signal they are full.

Causes of leptin resistance: An explanation supported by research

People probably have to eat their way to leptin resistance. This conclusion is supported by research such as the following experiment.

The **aim of the experiment** was to understand the causes of leptin resistance in humans, though mice would have to be used as subjects because of the experimental conditions (Knight, 2010). Researchers wanted to decide which of two theories about the development of leptin resistance were valid. It was assumed that research using mice was useful for drawing conclusions about humans.

One theory claims obese people have high plasma leptin levels that cause leptin insensitivity in neuron receptors. If this is true, then leptin itself is a path to obesity, stimulating a protein that inhibits leptin signaling. The other theory is that eating too much fat over time is a direct path to leptin resistance. This means large amounts of fat bombard neurons, damaging normal leptin signals or causing stress and inflammation in some way. People must eat large amounts of fatty foods over time to become leptin resistant if the second theory is true.

Ob mouse and a normal mouse: The ob mouse was genetically engineered to lack the expression of leptin. Jeff Friedman explains more about these mice in the film "Deconstructing obesity."
Curtsey of J. Friedman

Procedures follow. Knight made a leptin infusion pump to keep blood leptin levels of ob gene mutated mice similar to the levels in normal control mice for the entire experiment. The ob gene mutation means that the body does not produce leptin, so the ob mice were normalized with the leptin pumps. The wild mice already produced enough leptin so the pump use kept leptin levels the same in both conditions. Researchers started the pumps for both groups at age four weeks and randomly assigned the mice to either have a high fat diet or a low fat diet for twenty weeks. The high or low fat diet was the **independent variable**. The **dependent variable** was developing leptin resistance.

Results showed that both groups of mice became obese but control mice on the high fat diet developed leptin resistance. Ob gene mice on a high fat diet or a low fat diet had normal leptin levels. Knight **concluded** that the results support the second theory.

A judgment about leptin resistance includes that this type of research is done using animals and may not fully represent all the factors involved in human obesity. However, the use of animals does allow researchers to isolate factors they could not if using humans, and one goal of running the experiment was to discover more about the mechanisms of leptin resistance.

Using leptin therapy to treat human obesity: What does the research show?

Making a judgment about leptin as an obesity therapy is complicated because it works for some people but not all. There is still much to know but it still can be argued that leptin therapy can be useful to treat some obesity cases.

"In the spirit of science, leptin has proven to be unpredictable and truly fascinating—a system worth exploring and understanding" (Friedman & Mantzoros, 2015, p. 1). Leptin can be effective in treating obesity when used in high doses by altering appetite and activating several brain areas for some people,

---

Thinking skills: Reflecting on obese mice

Scientists study ob (obesity gene) mice as models for understanding leptin's role in obesity. There are some mice with a naturally occurring ob mutation that become morbidly obese because they do not produce leptin (Lutz & Woods, 2012). Sometimes researchers use the mice with the natural mutation and other times the mice are knockouts, meaning they are genetically modified to lack the expression of ob. Is the benefit worth the harm to the animals if we create knockouts? It might be hard for researchers to just use the naturally occurring ob mutations.

Obesity is a growing global problem with significant health costs, so if mice are good models, then should they be used? The answer is not easy.

Chapter 10 raises the questions about whether animals are good models for humans in research. Get a balanced view of the benefits and risks and if the mice are good models before making a decision.

---

but is not the standard treatment for obesity as was hoped. Leptin is most effective with the most extreme cases of obesity (Friedman, 2014).

Tolerate uncertainty, as it shows good critical thought. Although there is still a lot to know about leptin, some interesting research shows how leptin can help treat obesity.

For example, people who diet or are leptin resistant are less active and very hungry compared with leptin sensitive people (Kissileff, et al., 2012). One experiment used ten participants who were treated with leptin or a placebo while they were on a weight-sustaining liquid diet in a hospital setting. Results showed that participants felt fuller and perceived they had eaten more, suggesting they were getting better leptin signals of satiation as compared to participants taking placebo injections. This was the first study to demonstrate that leptin resistant people could have similar effects from taking leptin as those completely leptin deficient. Mice research supports this conclusion. Leptin injections in ob mice increased their activity and lowered food seeking behavior (Ribeiro, et al., 2011).

For another research example, people with leptin deficiency give food a high 'liking' rating as a reward on self-report questionnaires, but after leptin injections the liking rating is reduced even before they lose weight (Domingos, Vaynshteyn, Sordillo, & Friedman, 2014). This finding has been replicated in mice, though the mice cannot give a subjective liking rating for food. Researchers did observe less preference for sugary foods in mice after leptin injections.

Questions needing answering to fully understand leptin and obesity follow (Friedman, 2014). Students might consider these unanswered questions limitations of our current understanding, though on any given day this could change and we know more or clarify something.

1. It is still not fully understood how leptin is sent to the central nervous system.
2. We need to find out what regulates leptin gene expression.
3. Scientists are still not exactly sure how we "decide to eat or not eat" (p. T6). Eating is part of a complex motivational system and leptin is part of it, but the entire process is still not clear.

9.2: Explanation of the hormone cortisol: The stress response

Explain means to give a detailed account with reasons and causes. It can be argued that cortisol is the result of activation of the HPA axis and chronic high levels negatively affect health. Next is details about cortisol and reasons it affects the stress response. There is a great deal of research showing cortisol activates the stress response and one example study shows this is an experiment, so a judgment includes that there is a body of research showing this. This book cannot cover all the other studies verifying the conclusion, but is a good example from Sheldon Cohen, someone famous for his research on the topic.

Cortisol is the most important glucocorticoid, a steroid hormone produced by the adrenal cortex and released in response to stress. The word steroid describes the structure of five groups of hormones that also include testosterone and estrogen (Sapolsky, 2004).

Cortisol acts in a similar way to **epinephrine**, which acts as a neurotransmitter and a hormone. Epinephrine acts within seconds of someone perceiving a stressor and cortisol backs up this action after minutes and hours (Sapolsky, 2004).

Thinking skills: Cortisol, trauma and development
An application of the hormone cortisol to human behavior is found in chapter 32 about trauma and development. This is not just for students learning about developmental psychology but for all because you might have to answer an exam question about how hormones affect human behavior.

Epinephrine helps control the sympathetic nervous system, part of the autonomic nervous system, which has the job of maintaining homeostasis in the body (Advameg, 2015). The autonomic nervous system produces epinephrine right away in response to a stressor while cortisol takes longer to produce, perhaps hours to fully kick in, showing how a hormone cooperates with a chemical such as epinephrine.

Epinephrine affects most body tissue, such as increasing heart rate and respiration and contracting muscles, allowing you to spring into action, the **fight or flight syndrome** (Advameg, 2015). Cortisol also affects the body, and shuts down immunity and reproduction, for example, so all of your energy is channelled into handling the stressor (Sapolsky, 2004).

Stressors are "anything that throws your body out of allostatic balance and the stress response is your body's attempt to restore allostasis" (Sapolsky, 2004, p. 8). Allostasis means returning to stability.

STRESS RESPONSE SYSTEM

Hypothalamus
CRH
Pituitary gland
ACTH
Adrenal gland
The hypothalamus responds to level of cortisol

CRH - Corticotropin-releasing hormone
ACTH - Adrenocorticotropic hormone

Cortisol
To immune system

The HPA axis. This is what happens behind the scenes when you feel stress. Used under license from megapixl.com

Allostasis is a modern view of **homeostasis**, which means remaining to stability, and involves more than a single homeostatic function, such as turning off cortisol production after a stressful event. Allostasis seems better for our modern approach to psychology, because it refers to "the brain coordinating body-wide changes, often including changes in behavior" (Sapolsky, 2004, p. 8). Allostasis can include many interacting biological, cognitive, and sociocultural factors.

Researchers know how the general stress response works. Any perceived stressor activates a cascade of events stimulating the **HPA Axis** and ending with cortisol production. You have to perceive something to be a stressor first because the adrenal cortex does not think on its own (Sapolsky, 2004)!

HPA Axis refers to the hypothalamus, pituitary gland, and adrenal cortex (Kalat, 2007). Stressors, such as teacher announcing a test or someone accidentally stepping out in front of a bus, activate the hypothalamus. The hypothalamus sends a message to the pituitary gland to produce ACTH, a hormone, which sends a message to the adrenal glands to produce **cortisol**. Cortisol is often used as a stress measurement by researchers.

Why do we need cortisol? Some cortisol is necessary to respond to emergencies, such as accidentally stepping out in front of a bus and jumping away. Moderate amounts of cortisol are adaptive (Sapolsky, 2004). The problem is that we do not spend much time jumping out from in front of buses. Most human stressors are man-made, such as worrying about school. Humans frequently have the stress response turned on most of the time, and scientists know that chronic activation of the HPA axis is linked to health problems, such as damaged immunity, increased risk of heart disease and mental illness, and damage to telomeres, which protect chromosomes from damage as they divide.

Next is information about stress effects on immunity and an experiment showing the effects of cortisol on it, a useful application of the topic that helps students make an evaluation.

An explanation of how cortisol and stress affects immunity

It can be argued that chronic stress lowers immunity and increases the risk of disease. Sapolsky (2004) has some ideas about the connection. What follows is a detailed account of the immune system with reasons it can be damaged by stress.

The **immune system** fights off invaders, such as viruses and bacteria. It identifies foreign substances in the body and creates memories of those substances so that antibodies can fight off future invaders.

Lymphocytes are immune system cells affected by stress hormones. **T cells** and **B cells** (the white blood cells) are two types of lymphocytes. T cells migrate from bone marrow and mature in the thymus and B cells stay in the bone marrow to mature. T cells are responsible for cell-mediated immunity and spring into action when a virus or bacteria invade the body, sending out an alarm that causes killer cells to grow, attack, and kill the invader. B cells play a different role, called antibody-related immunity. Once the T cells have signaled the alarm, the T cells send a message to B cells to grow, seek, and bind to the infectious substance and create a memory of these substances for future immune resistance.

Stress hormones interfere with immunity in many ways.

1. Stress hormones block the creation of new lymphocytes.
2. Stress hormones interfere with the release of lymphocytes into circulation.
3. New lymphocytes do not remain long in circulation in the presence of stress hormones.
4. New antibodies have difficulty forming in the presence of stress hormones.
5. Stress hormones make it difficult for lymphocytes to communicate correctly.

Sapolsky *speculates* about how stress hormones suppress immunity. When faced with a stressor, immunity is enhanced, probably to help you prepare to fight off a crisis. But after one hour, the presence of stress hormones has the opposite effect. Now immunity is suppressed. The body must have some way of bringing the heightened immunity back into balance. This works well for the example of accidentally stepping out in front of a bus. The crisis is over quickly and you avoid getting smashed. However, after an hour of heightened stress response related rises in immune activation, stress hormones seem to have the opposite effect.

Self-management: Meditate as a class activity.

The 21st century student can use meditation as a way to manage stress. Students studying the health option for the IB exam will find this material useful for thinking about the section on health promotion and might practice meditation as they study that material as authentic learning.

My students practice Mindfulness-meditation to reduce stress, and we start at the beginning of the junior year and carry it through the course under the banner of mindful learning.

Mindfulness meditation is a program developed by Jon Kabat-Zinn. IB students can meditate for **CAS**.

The stress system should reset itself quickly after fleeing the bus. But since most human stress is man-made, stress can last longer than an hour. Stressing over tests, telling the story about jumping away from a bus, or taking care of someone with a long-term illness all last longer than an hour. Now the immune system is over-worked and the result is immune suppression. Sapolsky (2004) says that what goes up must come down, and over-working the immune system plunges it even below normal baselines.

Whatever the pathway is between stress and disease, the two are linked and this is why everyone should learn to cope with stress and be better self-managers.

Research supporting the argument that stress hormones increase one's risk for the common cold

An evaluation of cortisol's effect on behavior should include research support. A classic experiment shows that chronic stress increases the risk of catching the **common cold** (Cohen et al., 1998). The **aim of the experiment** was to see if particular types of stressors increased the risk of catching a cold. This experiment grouped data into those with lesser or greater stress to see who was most susceptible.

The sample consisted of 125 men and 151 women ranging in age from 18 to 55. All participants were paid $800.

Experiment **procedures** follow.

1. Participants were interviewed about their social networks, education, diet, and health practices after getting a check-up to make sure they were healthy.
2. Life stress interviews asked about employment, relationships, finances, social networks, health practices, personality, and housing, among other things.
3. Participants were quarantined.
4. Everyone was given nasal drops with a low infectious dose of two cold viruses.
5. The quarantine lasted for 5 days after exposure and participants were required to stay at least 3 feet away from others when interacting. During this time participants were tested for cold symptoms and evidence of having the virus.
6. The quarantine ended but the study lasted for 28 days to see if anyone developed a cold.

Would you agree to catch a cold for $800?
Used with license from megapixl.com.

Cohen used 8 different controls to make sure that nothing confounded (meaning interfered) the experiment. For example, factors such as age, gender, and education level were controlled.

Results included the following.

1. Stressors lasting one month or longer are more important than short-term stressors.
2. The longer the stressor lasted, the greater the risk of illness.
3. Relationship difficulties and job problems contribute the most to stress.
4. The risk for catching colds is related to higher levels of **stress hormones**.

Ethics in research:Use of inducements

Is $800 a fair inducement for participation? Does this meet the APA ethics standards outlined in chapter 1?

Would you agree to be exposed to a cold virus for $800? Would you do it just for the money?

Hormones can alter gene expression: An explanation of how cortisol and sex hormones do this

Cortisol can alter genes and learning about it gives us a good reason to learn to manage stress. This section contains important details about hormones affecting gene expression and reasons this knowledge is valuable.

Genes are altered after long-term stress. This is because glucocorticoid receptors are activated (Walker, 2001).

Genes cannot affect behavior unless they are expressed, so for example, having the ss alleles of 5-HTT, the **serotonin transporter gene**, will not cause depression, but having the genetic predisposition *and* chronic stress can alter the **transcription process** of genes.

"Cells, including neurons, contain receptors for many hormones, including glucocorticoids" (Walker, 2001, p. 202). Once the hormone binds to the receptor, it triggers the transcription process, and then the gene is expressed and someone then has a higher risk of depression. When no stress hormone is around, the receptor has no influence on the transcription process.

The ss alleles of 5-HTT give people greater reactivity to stress and they are more likely to have depression, but only in the presence of stressful events. Chapter 7 evaluates research on the serotonin transporter gene in the section about genetics and behavior, so you can see how the process works. The gene influences how much the neurotransmitter serotonin is produced in the brain.

The lesson here is that certain genetic predispositions can make a person more sensitive to the environment. When someone is more sensitive to stress, the transcription process regulating gene expression starts because the HPA axis is frequently activated. This relationship between hormones and genes can spell trouble for certain people. It raises the question of whether we should all get genotyped so people at risk can get preventive stress management training. This involves many ethical issues, such as people's right to privacy and what might be done with the information, but is worth considering.

> **Communication skills: Ethics and genetic testing**
> The class might debate the pros and cons of genetic testing. For example, on one hand people with greater risk can learn to manage stress effectively. On the other hand, it raises privacy issues and may be a self-fulfilling prophesy, because having certain alleles does not guarantee developing a disorder.

Sex hormones estrogen and **testosterone** also influence gene expression and do so by moving into target cells by **passive diffusion** and binding to receptors (Walker, 2001). Passive diffusion means to transport a substance across a membrane without expending energy. It is spontaneous movement of a substance from a concentrated area to a less concentrated one. Adolescence is a particularly vulnerable time for the expression of psychiatric disorders because changes in gonadal hormones can affect otherwise silent genes. This helps answer the question of why many people have their first episodes of mental illness starting after puberty.

9.3: Pheromones: Do humans have them?

This section starts with two experiments so we have something on the floor as examples to evaluate.

Research about human pheromones, attraction, and mother-baby interaction: Classic research and challenges to the conclusions

Can humans use their sense of smell to detect critical information related to **attraction** from secretions from the armpit? Can human babies can identify their mothers by smelling breast pads used by breastfeeding women?

Two classic experiments examined these research questions and are often cited as evidence that humans have pheromones (Russell, 1976).

Attraction research

The **aim of the experiment** was to show that human **attraction** is influenced by pheromones.

The sample was 16 male and 13 female college students who wore a t-shirt for 24 hours and did not use deodorant for that time (Russell, 1976).

Procedures involved participants smelling t-shirts, one that was their own, one from an unknown male, and one from an unknown female (the **independent variable**). The task was to identify which shirt was their own, which was from the male, and which was from the female.

Results showed that 13 males 9 females correctly identified the shirts.

Russell **concluded** that humans have a system for processing pheromones that affects attraction.

> **Thinking skills: Challenge your assumptions**
> It is commonly believed that humans have pheromones and it seems to make sense, but this conclusion has had difficulty standing up in research.
>
> This does not mean the search for human pheromones is unworthy of continued investigation. However, it needs to start with an understanding of the research issues involved in studying the topic, including how scientists should identify pheromones (noted in the previous chapter) and alternative explanations for results of commonly cited studies.
>
> **Advertisements** for perfume may be part of the reason people believe humans have pheromones. The class might look at some of the claims from the perfume industry and see how they stand up to the science of pheromones.

Mother-baby interaction research

In another experiment 10 breast feeding mothers and their babies were participants (Russell, 1976). The **aim of the study** was to show that **mother-baby interaction** was guided by pheromones and that human response to pheromones started early. **Procedures** involved babies smelling their mother's breast pad, a clean one, one from a stranger, and one soaked with cow's milk (the **independent variable**).

Results showed that babies could not tell their mother's breast pad until they were 6 weeks old, and then 6 of the 10 babies got it right. Familiarity was measured by the baby showing a more intense sucking than they used when exposed to the other pads.

Russell **concluded** from the results that humans have a system for processing pheromones, it starts young, and affects mother-infant interaction.

Alternative explanations for Russell's findings?

Russell's conclusions have been challenged, particularly the smelling of t-shirts by college students in the attraction study.

Alternative explanations could account for Russell's findings. Since male sweat has a stronger smell than female sweat, participants could have decided to rate all the stronger and less pleasant smells as male and the weaker and more pleasant smells as female (Doty, 2014). So the findings might be because participants are aware that male sweat is stronger and less pleasant. Doty set out to test this idea in a series of experiments. The **aim of the experiments** was to show that social conditioning might be the reason for judging a smell as male or female.

Procedures follow. Male and female armpit sweat was collected on gauze pads and given to male and female participants in sniff bottles (Doty, 2014). Participants were instructed in all the studies that they were to tell which smells were male or female by smelling the bottles. The instructions included that some of the smells were female and some male and some in combinations (**independent variable**).

In reality, one study used the sweat just from males, one study used the sweat just from females, and in another the sweat was from both males and females. In all the studies participants rated the intensity and pleasantness of the smells.

Results from all the experiments follow.

1. When the smells were from both males and females, about half the participants got the male and female smells correct. All participants rated the strongest smells male and both the weaker and the neutral (some bottles contained no sweat) smells as female.
2. When the smells were just female or female, participants said the strongest smells were male and the weaker or neutral smells were female.
3. No differences were found between male and female smell ratings when all the smells were equally incubated.

Do you think you can tell if a t-shirt has been worn by a male or a female by its smell?
Source: pixabay.com.

Doty **concluded** that smell identification could easily have occurred from social conditioning. If armpit smell was a real attraction mechanism, then ratings of pleasant smells by men should be primarily assigned to females and vise versa. In addition to social conditioning, males tend to eat more meat than women, so diet could **confound** the study.

It is inconclusive that smell is related to attraction. Other researchers have also challenged Russell's conclusions, suggesting that smells are not necessarily related to attraction as evidenced by the fact that there is no difference in how male and female smells are rated when they are incubated in the same amounts.

Research about human pheromones: How about this? Might males drink more alcohol when exposed to the smell of fertile females?

Students interested in health behavior and **problem drinking** might find this study interesting. This was the first research to investigate the idea that males drink more alcohol when exposed to **pheromones** from fertile females (Tan & Goldman, 2015).

This research is presented in great detail to show students just how hard it is to design a credible study about human pheromones.

The **aim of the correlation study** was to see if decisions about drinking and sex can be cued unconsciously from pheromones.

There is a short window of time when females get pregnant, about 3% of the time they try, and it is assumed that humans must have evolved ways to encourage mating during the short time each month women are fertile (Tan & Goldman, 2015). Research shows that alcohol use is one way to encourage sex.

Cues given by female primates when they are fertile are much stronger than cues given by human females. However, humans do give off *some* cues that might influence behavior. Human female cues include changes in scent, skin tone, and voice pitch.

> **Thinking skills: Ethics in research**
> This study uses deception. Rules regarding deception include that it must be the only way to gather data, it cannot be harmful to participants, and everyone must be debriefed after participation or as soon as possible. The general rule is that the benefit to science must outweigh the risk to the participant. Does this study meet these requirements?

Designing the study was quite challenging because there was so much to control. These challenges should be carefully considered when evaluating strengths and limitations of the study and two are noted next.

1. Females providing t-shirts for males to smell could not use deodorant, perfume or contraceptives, showered with unscented soap, avoided food with strong smells such as garlic, avoided smoking and drinking alcohol, and even washed sheets in unscented detergent during the time they wore the t-shirts. **Snowball sampling** was used to recruit the females, meaning one woman was recruited and she recommended the next, and so on. The researchers did not have full control over who was selected but this might have been the only way to get any participants.
2. For the t-shirts to be effective for the study, they had to be used within one week after the women submitted them. Researchers hoped for a large supply and offered $10 per shirt but in the end, just 30 from 14 women were provided. There was no way to verify compliance with the conditions of the study.

The **procedures** started with telling the male participants the study was about consumer preferences. The female researchers were using contraceptives so as not to interfere with the real study topic, which was to see male behavior in reaction to pheromones from the sample providing the t-shirts.

The males were first primed with a t-shirt (either from a time when the female was fertile or not fertile) and then were told they were rating a laundry detergent used for washing (the deception). Participants were instructed to take three deep breaths from the t-shirt in a bag and rate how much the liked the smell and if they would buy the detergent.

Next the males spent time tasting a variety of beverages and rating their preferences. These included soft drinks, coffee, sparkling water, and a variety of "beers" that were really non-alcoholic. This was done to prevent actual effects of using alcohol on participants and most did not realize the beer was non-alcoholic. Those who thought it was non-alcoholic had their data withdrawn at the end of the study. The amount of "beer" consumed was recorded.

The males next went into another room that was arranged for a critical part of the study, which was to see female approach behavior, as it was predicted that those who drank the most beer after smelling the t-shirts would show more female approach behavior. Five chairs were placed in a row with a female's purse hanging on a chair at one end of the line and a female sweater hanging on a chair on the opposite end. The available seats in the middle were open for sitting and it was noted if the males sat closest to where they thought a female might be.

The males were debriefed right after their participation.

Results follow.

> **Thinking and communicating: Debating the study's credibility**
>
> All research about pheromones can be challenging to conduct and the class might debate the credibility of the study designs and conclusions.
>
> Do alternative explanations explain the results better? How might pheromones in humans differ from pheromones in animals, if in fact students agree that scientists have reliable established that humans have pheromones?
>
> The next section outlines some issues about researching human pheromones that will help the evaluation.

1. Men exposed to the t-shirts with scents from fertile females drank significantly more of the "beer" than those exposed to the t-shirts from non-fertile females.
2. Males exposed to the t-shirts with scents from fertile females sat closer to the seats where women were expected to sit.

The authors **concluded** that they discovered a new pathway to human alcohol use involving unconscious signaling from pheromones.

The authors noted that study results must be viewed with caution because replication was needed. Consider how hard it might be to replicate any study about female pheromones, given the challenges of participant recruitment and the details that must be followed to get credible t-shirts. Another study limitation might be confounding beer drinking with general thirst.

Some things to consider when evaluating human pheromone research

Many alternative explanations and confounding variables exist for pheromone research results. Next is some issues to consider (Wyatt, 2015).

1. Human pheromones are assumed to exist but for the most part have not been verified using the study guidelines outlined in the previous chapter.
2. One reasons to think we may verify human pheromones in the future is that if other mammals have them then it makes sense that humans also have them. Animals and humans develop more glands that give off odors at puberty, and although humans and the highest apes (bonobos, chimps, and gorillas) do not use odors as much for communication as lower animals, humans might use odor for some subtle communication.
3. Avoid concluding that research where participants smell t-shirts means pheromones are being smelled. Humans can smell other non-pheromone body odors. The research is inconsistent on this issue. Be careful about "**Pheromone Parties**" if you hear about them because they most likely involve individual smells and not pheromones!
4. **Culture** could confound conclusions about pheromones because reactions to smells are part of **enculturation**.
5. Armpit sweat is not the only place researchers should look for pheromones. For example, some people from Northeast Asia have a genetic variation that makes them produce little of the odors found in armpits. This is certainly not evidence for an evolved trait for armpit smell accounting for attraction!

Researchers assume that the **steroids** androsterone, androstenol, androstadienone, and estratetraenol are the human pheromones. There are many reasons researchers assume this (Doty, 2014).

1. These steroids are externally secreted.
2. They have a musk smell that has been reinforced throughout folk takes as important for attraction.

However, these steroids are not necessarily reliable for predicting the existence for human pheromones affecting behavior for several reasons (Doty, 2014).

1. These steroids are actually low in armpit sweat and many people cannot smell them.
2. It is not logical to conclude that just because these steroids exist in sweat that they communicate as a pheromone.

In conclusion, there is much to consider when evaluating if humans have pheromones. It is important to withhold judgment and tolerate uncertainty when considering human pheromones.

Chapter 10
Biological Approach to Behavior: The Role of Animal Research in Understanding Human Behavior: Analysis and Evaluation

Chapter objectives

Students will:
1. Practice thinking strategies (command terms) related to analysis and application, as well as synthesis and evaluation, with explain and evaluate demonstrated.
2. Explain the important differences between human and animal brains and evaluate research investigating these differences.
3. Make a judgment about (evaluate) the value of animal models in research.
4. Find this material useful when evaluating research using animals because if there are meaningful brain differences and animals are not useful models, then it is ethically contentious to use them in studies. The material in this chapter is directly tested only for IB students taking the HL course but is useful for all students.

10.1 Comparison between human and animal brains

Explain means to give a detailed account with reasons and causes. Learning about the differences between human and animal brains helps students appreciate the special nature of human **language** and **social cognition** and how humans evolved to live and collaborate within complex cultures. Next is details comparing animal and human brains along with experiments demonstrating reasons to believe the human brain is special.

Frontal lobe and **language center** differences are two examples.

Explanation of frontal lobe differences: Key details

Basics about the cerebral cortex and **frontal lobes** are detailed in chapter 4, so review it if needed. Key details about the frontal lobe follow.

1. The size and degree of folding on the cerebral cortex is what is most different between species (Kalat, 2007).
2. The **prefrontal cortex** is the front portion of the frontal lobe. "In general, the larger a species' cerebral cortex, the higher percentage of it is devoted to the prefrontal cortex" (Kalat, 2007, p. 100).
3. All mammals have a prefrontal cortex, but it has become enlarged the most during human evolution (Gazzaniga, et al., 2014). The expansion is greatest in the **white matter**, brain tissue containing nerve fibers surrounded by myelin that acts as insulation.
4. Cognitions unique to humans may be possible because of *more brain connections* rather than because the human brain has more neurons (Gazzaniga, et al., 2014).

Cat   Dog   Rhesus monkey   Human

The human prefrontal cortex takes a long time to develop so it makes sense that both white matter and cognitive control also

Prefrontal cortex for four species
Source: www.thebrain.mcgill.ca
Used with permission.

take a long time to develop in humans (Gazzaniga, et al., 2014). We must grow and learn throughout our lifespan and the human frontal cortex has a lot to integrate! Even consider what Kanzi the Bonobo (chapter 3) could learn, so he needed a larger cortex than monkeys, though Kanzi's prefrontal cortex is not as enlarged as human brains.

Research supporting prefrontal lobe enlargement in humans

The human **prefrontal cortex** is enlarged compared to animals.

Modern research supports the conclusion that the human prefrontal cortex is enlarged compared to other species (Passingham & Smaers, 2014). Scientists did not alway agree in the past, with some claiming the human prefrontal cortex was not enlarged. This is a reminder that it can take many years to sort out how to conduct research so a correct conclusion can be made. Prefrontal cortex researchers have used different definitions and measurements when conducting studies, accounting for the different conclusions in the past.

The **aim of the study** was to clarify the measurement and comparison problems in the existing body of studies and concludes the human prefrontal really is enlarged, *especially in areas where the most connections are made.*

The **study gathered data** through making measurements to compare human and animal brain areas. Do not call this an experiment or correlation study!

Consider the tough decisions to be made before testing the hypothesis that the human prefrontal cortex is enlarged in comparison to other species. Which non-human species should be used for the comparison? Which brain areas should be used as a reference point to show the prefrontal cortex is enlarged?

> **Thinking: An evolving science**
> Animals are used and the APA has specific rules that students should know. But with new knowledge, might it be time to reflect on our approach to research? Science grows with new research that should not be ignored. Saying only PETA members are against animals in research is irrelevant and clouds the science that should be used for reasoning.

Procedures are next. The authors selected a section of the **visual cortex** called the striate cortex as a reference point because it was a consistent point of input across species used in the study (Passingham & Smaers, 2014). They also used association areas of the brain as a second comparison point. This is different from other studies comparing the prefrontal cortex across species to the entire brain size, which did not show any significant difference.

It is hard to compare human brains to all other primates and monkeys, because primate brain parts can be easily seem in MRI scans and the brain parts of monkeys are not easy to see. To manage the problem, *the authors compared humans to primates and then primates to monkeys*. The earlier studies failing to show brain differences between species had compared humans to all primates and monkeys.

Results follow.

1. There are three grades of **prefrontal cortex** enlargement. The human prefrontal cortex is larger than the chimpanzee and the chimpanzee prefrontal cortex was larger than monkeys and gibbon. The prefrontal cortex of both humans and primates is more enlarged than anticipated.
2. Other parts of the cortex, such as the **motor cortex**, are also enlarged in humans compared to primates. This explains why humans are more goal-directed than animals, because the prefrontal cortex has many connections to the motor cortex. Association areas were found enlarged in humans, which are three and a half times bigger than in primates. It supports the conclusion that cognitive abilities unique to humans are possible because of more connections rather than just size differences.

The authors **concluded** that there is evidence for an enlarged human prefrontal cortex. Data for this study were measured by brain tissue rather than the number of cells. The authors do not know if their findings would stand up if measured the other way, and an effective evaluation should include this concern. This is something for future research to discover, though an enlarged human prefrontal cortex is a widely held belief at this time.

Explanation of language center differences

There are good reasons to believe that human language centers are unique.

Humans are unique because we have evolved a grammatical **language** different from animal communications (Rilling & Stout, 2014). Although Bonobos such as Kanzi seems fairly sophisticated, human are the only species that uses rules to combine a huge number symbols into a limitless number of meanings. Humans also have unique ways of **making and using tools** and **social learning** that require a language.

Human tool making and use is collaborative and furthers human culture.

Chimpanzees imitate when using tools, but the result is typically just what they observe. Humans imitate not just by producing the end product of a task, but even over-imitate steps that might not even get someone to the end product just to see what happens!

The human brain has tripled in size and has had many changes to its organization over the last 2.5 million years of evolution. When defending the argument that human language centers are different from animals we must find something about the human brain that is different from animals.

> **Thinking skills: Natural Selection at work**
> How did the language centers in the human brain evolve differently from that of animals (Rilling & Stout, 2014)? **Natural selection** is believed to be at work if we can find a characteristic of the human brain that is not part of primate brains. It would mean that human trait evolved after humans and primates separated from a common ancestor about 5-7 million years ago. Did Rilling and Stout find the evidence?

One thing to say about the human brain is that more of the cerebral cortex is used for conceptual processing and more of animal brains are used for perceptual processing. Conceptual processing requires language. So just what is unique about the neural circuits in the language centers of human brains?

Broca's area is one place to look. Humans use Broca's area 44 (BA44) to process language (Rilling & Stout, 2014). The human Broca's area processes syntax and has wider cortical **minicolumns** as compared with a similar part of the chimpanzee brain. Larger minicolumns *allow the human brain to have more connections*. This difference is important because brain differences between humans and animals have much to do with greater connections. Minicolumns differences in the brain related to motor or visual function are not different between chimps and humans, *so the language difference is special*. Animals actually use several parts of Broca's area when communicating with animal calls (BA44, BA45, and BA6) and they do not have all the connections.

In addition, Macaque monkeys have an area called macaque F5, which contain **mirror neurons** located in the same brain area as BA44 in humans (Rilling & Stout, 2014). Mirror neurons help monkeys process the actions of others. Human Broca's area BA44 also processes mirror neurons, but the human Broca's area also organizes speech and other language actions. Monkey calls are not processed in a brain part equivalent to Broca's area, and instead they have emotional expressions rather than something under cognitive control. Monkey calls are processed instead by the **limbic system**.

Wernicke's area is another place to look. Human brains have differences in Wernicke's area as compared with monkeys and chimpanzees relating to processing sound (Rilling & Stout, 2014). The human Wernicke's area has wider minicolumns in the **planum temporale**, and they are wider in the left hemisphere.

White matter connections are different, specifically the **arcuate fasciculus**, a bundle of axons helping communication from Wernicke's to Broca's area (Rilling & Stout, 2014). White matter plays a role in nerve signaling and organizes communication between cortexes and the frontal lobe. Macaque monkeys and chimpanzees have an arcuate fasciculus but *humans have a huge projection from it that expanded during evolution* that transmits words from Wernicke's area to Broca's area (Rilling & Stout, 2014). Animals do not have this projection.

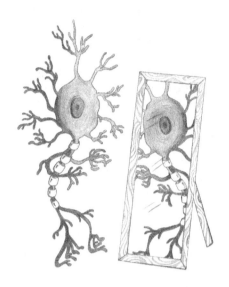

Is this the real way mirror neurons work? Mirror neurons function differently in humans and animals and is one reason language is special and unique in humans. Used with license from megapixl.com.

Summing up the language center differences: Humans and primates

Humans	Chimps and monkeys
Broca's area (BA44): processes human language Remember: It is all about having more brain connections and humans have many more!	BA 44, BA45, BA6 for processing animal calls F5 is in same position as human BA44, but contains mirror neurons to process actions Calls processed in limbic system and not in BA
Wernicke's area (WA): humans have wider minicolumns, especially in left hemisphere	Minicolumns are not as wide in areas similar to Wernicke's area

Humans	Chimps and monkeys
White matter in arcuate fasciculus differs, which allows communication from Wernicke's area to Broca's area

Huge projection from the arcuate fasciculus processes words and from WA to BA | Have an arcuate fasciculus similar to humans but lacks the projection |

Students can make a judgment based on this evidence and would be correct in saying that as we currently understand it, language centers in the human brain are different and special from that of animal brains.

10.2: The value of animal models in research

Evaluate means to make a judgment (appraisal) supported by evidence. Is there enough evidence to support the conclusion that animals are good models for humans or that it is ethical to use animals in research about humans?

Good judgments requires students to consider the differences between human and animal brains and decide if animals are similar enough to justify their use and possible suffering in studies. Other concerns are incorrect reporting and interpretation of results if the animal models used to learn about humans do not generalize well (Preuss & Robert, 2014).

We have already studied some animal research, such as monkey experiments related to the serotonin transporter gene and depression, mice experiments to study leptin and obesity, and rat experiments to study the mechanisms of neuroplasticity. We also studied how the prefrontal cortex and language centers differ between humans and animals.

Just because animals are used in psychological research does not automatically mean it is a good thing. Animals may or may not have enough value when generalizing to humans for their use to be ethical. Withhold judgment until you have reviewed the evidence and carefully considered the issues in depth.

> **Thinking skills: Challenge assumptions**
> Challenge your assumptions about animals and research and withhold judgment until you have weighed the evidence.
> Many students automatically think animals are relevant for studying humans simply because they are used so often and introductory texts discuss animal research as accepted.
> This is not about someone being a PETA member and loving animals. Rather it is about the science.

Ethical considerations for using animals in research

An evaluation must include ethical considerations about using animals in studies. Research that might cause animals to suffer requires scientists to weigh the benefits of the research to humans versus the risks to the animals (Gray & Bjorklund, 2014). **Benefits versus risks** must be considered each time a study is proposed and if the benefits are not great enough then the risk is unjustified. This is in addition to considerations of the extent to which animals are useful models for humans.

Weighing the pros and cons of using model animals in studies

What is it like to be a mouse or a monkey in a study?

The 21st century student is caring and knowledgeable and should get educated on this aspect of animal research. It is a good debate for the class.

Review new research that helps answer questions about an animal's experience in a study. Neuroimaging allows us to see differences between physical pain and the psychological pain considered suffering (Farah, 2010). For example, the anterior cingulate cortex lights up in both humans and animals when experiencing **psychological aspects of pain** such as its intensity and duration. Animal studies must be well justified if they are to be used at all. Google Martha Farah because she has many free articles on her website.

Scientists claim to learn about basic biological mechanisms of human behavior from animal models, but can this claim be validated? Although great advances in imaging technology have helped scientists study human and primate brains, invasive techniques are still used with certain types of animals used as models for humans (Preuss & Robert, 2014).

Invasive techniques include causing brain lesions to see the effects on behavior, placing animals under great stress, or genetically engineering them to lack the expression of a gene, called **knockouts**. Just a small number of species are subjects in invasive research and we must ask good questions about their use. Mice, rats, and lower level monkeys are the species most often used, making up the **model-organism paradigm** (MOP) (Preuss & Robert, 2014).

Using MOP animals may not seem a big concern at first glance because general psychology texts usually discuss using them as the accepted way, but further scrutiny shows the answer is more complicated.

Using model animals has advantages (Preuss & Robert, 2014).

1. *Their use standardizes research and increases internal validity.* For example, research about the **prefrontal cortex** or **neuroplasticity** needs to use similar experimental animal subjects. MOP animals were originally selected because they had certain characteristics, such as quickly maturing rats. Over time the animals were domesticated and promoted, at least in the minds of researchers, as typical animals able to represent all species. Eventually MOP animals became quality controlled, bred for lab use, and sanctioned by institutions funding research.

2. *It is practical to use MOP animals* because they are lab-friendly in many ways, such as being inexpensive and manageable, making observations easier.

Rhesus monkeys and rats are two common MOP animals.
Used under license of Megapixel.com.

Using animal models also has limitations (Preuss & Robert, 2014).

1. *Increasing internal validity does not mean that study results using these standardized animals produces good external validity.* This means study results may not generalize well.
2. *We must question the assumption that study findings from using MOP animals are useful for understanding other species.* It is easy to ignore differences between all species unless we look closely. Modern evolution theory does not support the older Darwinian linear view of a continuity between all species. Darwin incorrectly thought that some species were more advanced because they had been subject to more selection over time, making humans the most advanced but basically similar to animals (Preuss, 2009). Modern evolution theory believes each species has a unique evolutionary history.
3. *It used to be acceptable to generalize between species.* However, advances in imaging technology show more differences in animal and human brains than before.

Even with these criticisms, many researchers still hold the view that MOP animal study results are generalizable.

What if a researcher wanted to use an animal model for studying the human prefrontal cortex? If you use a rat, for example, its brain has to get an inflated status to qualify as anything close to the human or even primate prefrontal cortex (Preuss & Robert, 2014). The rat frontal lobe areas are connected to subcortical areas in the **limbic system** that are related to emotion and automatic processing. The human prefrontal cortex processes language and is highly connected to other brain areas. *So the rat frontal lobe areas are not really functionally similar to areas researchers link to humans.* If scientists call this area in rats 'prefrontal' data might be distorted.

Do you see the problem? The rats make are easy to study but there are many questions about their suitability as human models.

Evaluation: Are monkeys good models for studying human depression?

Mice are popular models for understanding human **depression**, but the research requires the mice to be subjected to stress and it does not realistically resemble how humans develop depression within a social context (Xu, et al., 2015).

How about using macaque monkeys, one of the MOP animals, to study depression development in natural animal groups? The **aim of the observation study** was to see how depression developed in monkeys in a natural setting.

There is a naturally occurring depression in monkeys, as we studied with the topic genetic influences on behavior. Monkeys have the same alleles as humans for the serotonin transporter gene, ss, sl, and ll (Caspi et al., 2010).

Procedures follow. This study used all female monkeys, some with naturally occurring depression, some that had been socially isolated as part of the study, and some healthy monkeys (Xu, et al., 2015). All lived in a free enclosure environment similar to natural monkey groups. Observations were made for eight days, looking for symptoms of monkey depression such as slumped posture and lessened social interaction.

Thinking skills: Idea for further investigation
Carol Shivley at Wake Forest University uses primates to research many topics. She is one author of the Xu (2015) study and is featured in the film *Stress; Portrait of a Killer*, where her research on obesity with monkeys is reviewed. The film is wonderful and should be shown when studying hormones or obesity.

Perhaps this study and any of Shivley's research using monkeys in natural environments are worth using as test cases to see when animals are good models for humans.

Results showed that depression developed in similar ways as it does in humans. For example, the monkey group competed for scarce resources, something natural in monkey and human life. The social hierarchy in the monkey group that was also thought to contribute to depression.

The authors **concluded** that this was more evidence that genetic contributions to depression predispose one to depression. Also, the study had more ecological validity because it used natural social context to study depression. They also think it is a more ethical approach to isolating factors leading to depression than using mice. *Do you agree?*

Another evaluation: Are mice useful for studying alcoholism?

This information is not from one specific study but is from a review of research using animals to learn about alcoholism. "Overall, the DNA sequences of humans and other organisms (such as primates, rodents, and even fruit flies) are rather similar" (Phillips, 2002, p. 202).

Phillips (2002) gives an example of using mice to study **alcoholism**, claiming there is enough similarity to use the animals.

One genetic risk for alcoholism in humans is dopamine D2 receptor gene (called DRD2). **Dopamine** is a **neurotransmitter** regulating the pleasure and reward systems.

Mice have a region on chromosome 9 for dopamine (called Drd2) similar to the place on human chromosome 11 where DRD2 is found. This gene in mice and humans can interfere with the ability to have control over drinking.

Knockout mice, meaning they are genetically engineered to lack the expression of a gene, are useful in understanding the role of the gene because when Drd2 is not expressed, the mice drink far less alcohol than normal litter mates.

Phillips admits that human drinking cannot be exactly replicated in animals, but mouse models may give us some idea of how the gene appears to be a switch for voluntary control over drinking. Human problem drinking is different because it takes place in a social context, such as with heavy drinking peer groups as we learned when studying Marc Schuckit's research in chapter 7. Creating social stress in animals can mimic some of the human social context for drinking, but it never is exactly the same thing (Phillips, 2002).

What do you think? It is worth raising and genetically altering the mice for this type of study and putting the animals under stress?

Extension of our animal discussion: CAS idea and class activity:
Animals and the planet's health: ZooCollege.com

How do we want to think about our relationship with animals? The 21st century student thinks globally and acts locally, and is aware of the issues related to the planet's health and the role of animals. One of those issues is the problem of losing top predators and its effect on the ecosystem. How we think about our relationship with animals is a crucial decision for the planet's future. Are animals for research, our entertainment, or do they have a job to do in the wild? Some ways to get involved include the following.

1. Get informed. What role do animals play in protecting the planet's health? Do you know much about the consequences of losing our top predators?
2. Specifically consider for example, the role big cats such as tigers, lions, leopards, jaguars, cougars, servals, bobcats, and all the other wildcats play as our top predators.
3. Learn about the big cats. Carole Baskin of Big Cat Rescue (BCR) in Tampa, Florida is generously allowing all students access to ZooCollege.com. This is the training site for all BCR workers. You may use the site for **free with the pass code zoofree**. All training and tests are available for learning about big cats and how keepers care for them.
4. What big cats live in your area and are they endangered? The IB student is concerned about global issues but takes local action. What might you do to get involved to help these majestic big cats that are so needed for a stable ecosystem?
5. Can you educate others, raise money, or become active in protecting them?
6. The cats pictured below all live at BCR and their stories might get you interested in the issues. Read a little about them and then log onto bigcatrescue.org for more details.

All photos are curtsey of C. Baskin of Big Cat Rescue.

Meet the cats at Big Cat Rescue

Andre was used as a prop when he was a cub. People could pay to hold him and get their photo taken. Read about what really happens in this abusive practice at bigcatrescue.org. Luckily for Andre, someone who knew him as a cub rescued him and sent him to BCR. Now he is the goofiest tiger at BCR and loves to "talk" to his keepers and tour guests. Andre enjoys playing in his pool and living among grass and trees.

Reise the cougar lived in a tiny cage with a concrete floor with no toys to play with in a now defunct "sanctuary" in South Florida. Now she plays in grass and rolls in the dirt, batting her balls around her enclosure for fun.

Kali's owner had all the good intentions in the world but when life got in the way could not afford to take care of her. Tigers cost $10,000 a year just to feed!

Chapter 11
The Cognitive
Approach to Behavior:
Cognitive Processing:
Knowledge and
Understanding

Chapter objectives

Students will:
1. Practice thinking strategies (command terms) relevant to knowledge and understanding with describe modeled.
2. Participate in activities to start the cognitive ATB
3. Describe the computer analogy of the mind as an information processing system.
4. Describe the cultural approach to studying cognition and practice some top-down processing using the culture thread.
5. Describe background concepts related to the Multi-store Model of Memory.
6. Describe background concepts related to Working Memory.
7. Describe the Levels of Processing Model (LOP), useful for evaluating the reliability of eyewitness memory in the next chapter and useful for learning how to study.
8. Describe schema theory and schema formation.
9. Describe top-down and bottom-up processing, concepts relevant to understanding schema.
10. Describe stereotyping, which often drive our schemas about expected behavior.
11. Describe the two systems model of thinking, a dual processing model.
12. Describe heuristics, including representativeness, availability, affect heuristic, and anchoring-adjustment.
13. Describe the Theory of Planned Behavior Model of thinking and decision-making.

11.1: Activities to start the cognitive ATB
Improving our memory
Divide the class into two groups. Both groups will listen to a passage and recall as much of it as possible. This activity is from an experiment by Bransford and Johnson (1972).

"A newspaper is better than a magazine/ A seashore is a better place than the street/ At first it is better to run than to walk/ You may have to try several times/ It takes some skill but it's easy to learn/ Even young children can enjoy it/ Once successful, complications are minimal/ Birds seldom get too close/ Rain, however, soaks in very fast/ Too many people doing the same thing can also cause problems/ One needs lots of room/ If there are no complications, it can be very peaceful/ A rock will serve as an anchor/ If things break loose from it, however, you will not get a second chance (p. 722).

You have 5 minutes to write down everything you remember.

The difference between the two groups, the independent variable, is that one group gets a direction first. One group is told before starting that directions are for making and flying a kite. The other groups gets no direction.

Compare how many steps each group recalls.

The group with the direction probably recalled more items and this was what Bransford and Johnson found. It is because the direction provided a category, a **schema**, that helps encoding and storage. If you were in the group with the direction, you probably retrieved the information more easily. The group without a direction had no meaningful way to encode and store the information, so it makes sense that they retrieved fewer items.

We are always hoping to improve our memories and cognitive psychologists have put much effort into figuring out how it all works. Part of this chapter is devoted to these memory models. Which model is best and helps you understand how your memory works? Try to withhold judgment until you have studied this chapter and the next.

The history of cognitive psychology: An exercise in understanding B. F. Skinner and reactions to his work

> **Inquiry and collaboration: Activity to start cognitive psychology: Have fun with Skinner!**
>
> Skinner is one of the historical theorists fun to role-play with students. I tell students they will interview me playing Skinner for a few days. They can ask anything they wish and learn about his principles.
>
> This is a chance for students to practice asking good questions and think critically about Skinner's principles. We cover everything from Walden Two to the superstitious pigeons to verbal behavior to education. Students are easily taken in by Skinner's presence and must carefully consider what he is saying.
>
> It might take a few days for students to figure out what is wrong with Skinner's principles, but it is a valuable experience for developing thinking skills. Students should understand some of the flaws leading to the cognitive revolution that got a spark in the 1950s in the US.

11.2: The importance of taking a cultural approach to studying cognition

All cognitions flow through a cultural lens, and examples are the **theory of planned behavior**, **heuristics**, **selective attention**, **schema**, **eyewitness memory**, **flashbulb memories**, **stereotyping** and **cognitive dissonance**. Keep this idea in the back of your mind and look for cross-cultural research demonstrating the view that culture is a lens through which our cognitions flow. However, not all cognition has been verified cross-culturally, such as the cognitive bias **illusory correlation**. Either it is not an **etic** or it has not yet been well studied. Students might consider how important **subjective culture** is to studying cognition. If cognitions are filtered through cultural lenses that contain schemas, then categories for norms are created that are important to a group.

The view that culture and cognition are closely related has been around a long time (Berry et al., 2011; Matsumoto & Juang, 2008). Many believe culture is cognition, because culture is really a set of representations and schemas about the world (Matsumoto & Juang, 2008). Hofstede (2001) even thought of culture as mental software, with programs for each group.

The description of culture used in this book helps us understand the view that culture is cognition. If culture is a system of knowledge, then people actively construct information about the world that allows them to live in

Culture is the lens with which we view the world. Our thoughts filter through our cultural values.
Used with license from shutterstock.com.

cultures (Matsumoto & Juang, 2008). This knowledge is passed on to children through **enculturation**. Some cognitions even evolved so humans could live in cultures, such as **language** and the **Theory of Mind** (ToM), reviewed in chapter 7 about natural selection.

The different cognitive processes, such as perception, language, memory, and attention, developed as people constructed knowledge within their cultural groups. So it is helpful for the 21st century student to think globally when studying cognitions. We do not want to ignore classic theory and research, but must extend it to see how it applies to everyone.

It has been argued that we should think about cognition as **contextualized cognition**, a term used by Michael Cole to explain why cultures appear so different when using cognitive processes everyone has, such as memory (Berry, et al., 2011). Cole thought people showed differences in cognition because of the situation or the context of their lives, and would perform well at routine tasks required by their cultures. This does not mean

Conceptual understanding
Increase critical thought by showing you can keep an idea in the back of your mind as you study specific material. There is much to learn in the cognitive ATB, just remember what Triandis said, that research is incomplete unless it is studied cross-culturally. It is fun to learn classic theory and research but discussions, evaluations, and all the other higher order thinking strategies (command terms) require a bigger picture!

we must abandon the search for universals, a topic studied in with the sociocultural ATB, because people have much in common. There are plenty of universals about human cognition, but we must include cross-cultural research to see what is universal and what is contextualized.

Learn important knowledge from the bottom-up, but keep in mind that culture may influence any cognition and the 21st century student is open-minded enough to appreciate the interaction.

11.3: Cognition and the computer analogy of the mind as an information processing system

Students need details about the mind as an information processing system to use as building blocks for studying memory and decision making.

Cognitive psychologists view the mind as an information processor similar to a computer. Information processing involves inout, processing, and output.

No one theory exists for information processing (Gray & Bjorklund, 2014). However, cognitive psychologists use a set of assumptions to understand the mind as an information processor.

1. Mental processing in the mind can be studied scientifically.
2. Behavior is the result of information processing. The steps of information processing follow.
   a. Information is acquired from the world around us.
   b. The information is stored.
   c. Stored information is represented in the mind.
   d. Internal representations direct behavior.
3. There is a limit to what can be cognitively processed because people have limited mental storage space and time to spend on it (Gray & Bjorklund, 2014).

Next students study three memory models, and all three take the view that the mind is similar to a computer with input and output.

Use the term correctly: Define cognition
Cognition refers to the mental processes for understanding and gaining knowledge about the world. These processes include attention, memory, language, decision-making, perception and mental representations of knowledge such as spatial (mental) rotation.

The computer is a useful analogy for the human mind with its input, processing, and output.
Used with license from shutterstock.com.

11.4: The Multi-store Model of Memory

The important details about the **Multi-store Model of Memory** follow.

The Multi-store Model of memory has three distinct levels of memory making up its structure, a **sensory register**, a **short-term store**, and a **long-term store** (Atkinson & Shiffrin, 1968). Memory also includes another dimension, our **control processes**. This means that memories can be modified and restructured as desired by people to a large extent with strategies such as mnemonics or through schemas.

The structure of memory and its control processes are always interacting. Details of each structural part of the model follow. This model is a good example of the analogy of the mind as a computer because it accounts for input, processing, and output.

Sensory register

A **sensory register** is where the external stimuli comes first before it can go into short and long term stores or can decay and be forgotten as new stimuli quickly replaces it (Atkinson & Shiffrin, 1968). It has been shown that a visual stimulus leaves a trace that decays within several hundred milliseconds unless it moves to the short-term or long-term stores.

The sensory register has been demonstrated in research (Sperling, 1960). How much can be remembered from a quick visual stimuli? This was tested in seven experiments where participants were exposed to a series of letters for 50 milliseconds and then asked for either a partial list of the letters or the whole list (the **independent variable**). For example, some of the letters included the following from a set of about 500 letter groupings. These include RNF, KLB, and YNX.

Results showed that participants recalled about 4 items, that partial recall was greater than whole recall, and that delays in the time between exposure caused less recall. Sperling provided evidence for the sensory register but in real life most people are unaware of all the stimuli they receive, partially because they are not asked to recall it. Stimuli in the sensory register is quickly forgotten unless it moves quickly to the short-term store.

Multi-Store Model of Memory

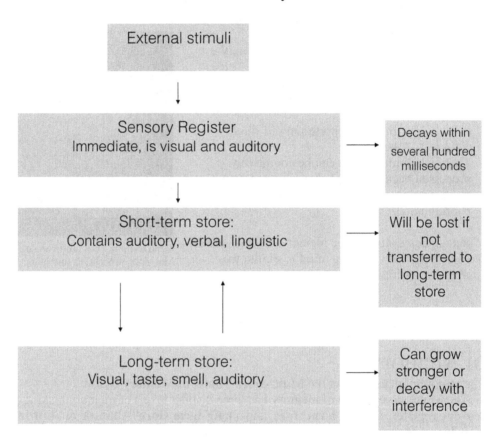

Based on Atkinson & Shiffrin (1968)

Short-term store

The **short-term store** holds information for a short time, perhaps 15-30 seconds, and then it is either lost or it is rehearsed and transferred to the long-term store (Atkinson & Shiffrin, 1968). The short and long-term stores *are distinct*, and some evidence for this is cases of people with damage to the **hippocampus**. These people remember everything from the

> **Thinking skills: How good is this evidence?**
> Students may know something about **H. M.**, a man who had parts of his brain removed to help stop seizures in 1953, including much of the hippocampus. H.M. cannot form new long term memories. Is this evidence for a distinct short and long-term store? This case is detailed in the next chapter evaluating the memory models.

past up until the point where the damage occurs and then are unable to add information to long-term memory. They have access to short term memory but cannot transfer it to long-term.

Other evidence comes from a 1959 experiment by Peterson and Peterson (as cited in Atkinson & Shriffin, 1968). Participants heard a set of trigrams (a group of 3 letters) and recalled them after intervals of 3, 6, 9, 12, 15, and 18 seconds (the **independent variable**). To prevent rehearsal, participants counted backward by three's from a specific number until asked to recall the trigrams. Researchers assumed that counting backward kept participants from rehearsing the trigrams. **Results** showed that they were remembered for about 15 seconds. It was concluded that his was evidence for the short-term store and its limits.

What can be held in the short-term store has been studied by many researchers such as George Miller (1956). Try this test. Can you recall these 21 numbers (Sternberg & Sternberg, 2012)?

$$101001000100001000100$$

You might need to rehearse and chunk them into smaller groups. Chunking is an automatic strategy since Miller (1956) found that people generally could recall 7 items, plus or minus 2.

Transferring memories from short-term stores to long-term stores depends on our **control processes** (Atkinson & Shiffrin, 1968). Evidence for using control processes for transfer comes from experiments where participants repeat a series of numbers. Some of the numbers appeared in a particular sequences every few trials, and it is assumed these were more easily recalled because of **rehearsal**, and this transferred the numbers to long-term memory.

Long-term store

The **long-term store** contains memories from all sensory processes, such as seeing, hearing, tasting, and smelling (Atkinson & Shiffrin, 1968). No one knows for sure how much material can be held in the long-term store and it might be infinite, but it is proposed that if something from short-term memory is successfully transferred to the long-term store, then it can be retrieved.

The term **permastore** describes the lasting nature of long-term memory. For example, research shows that people who took college level math courses above calculus could recall their high school algebra material even after 50 years (Bahrick & Hall, 1991). Participants in the study who did not take college math courses did not recall high school math more than chance. Interesting and going against popular belief, taking the SAT had no effect on high school math recall later in life, so it appears actually taking math courses helped rehearse the material enough for it to become a permastore.

We can forget things in long-term memory because of **decay** and **interference**. Interference may be out of someone's control processes and this has been demonstrated in research where participants have longer and longer lists of items to remember. The addition of newer items could interfere with recalling others as the trials become more difficult or the person may be using ineffective searches.

11.5: Working Memory

Describe means to give a detailed account. The important details about Working Memory follow.

Working Memory is the most accepted modern memory model (Sternberg & Sternberg, 2012). Working-memory is a newer model with a different approach to short- and long-term storage (Baddeley, 2009). WorkingMemory contains the most recently activated parts of long-term memory, those we are conscious of. Long-term memories move to temporary storage in working-memory so they can be used in short-term memory.

The key details of Alan Baddeley's **Working Memory** model follow (Baddeley, 2009). It is a more complex view of memory and suggests there are many parts involved in working memory.

1. The **visiospatial sketchpad** holds visual and spatial information in temporary storage.
2. The **phonological loop** holds speech-like information in temporary storage.
3. The **central executive** plays a critical role because it acts as a coordinator, "An attentional controller" (p. 53) deciding what to process and how to do it.
4. The **subsidiary slave systems** performs other cognitive tasks such as perception.
5. The last part is the **episodic buffer**, a **limited-capacity system** able to hold approximately four chunks of memory. It links the other parts and is responsible for "allowing various subcomponents of working memory to interact with long-term memory" (p. 53). It allows us to make sense of everything held in the other parts. It binds information in the visiospatial sketchpad and the phonological loop and anything else in long-term memory needed to help make the information relevant. The episodic buffer allows us to think.

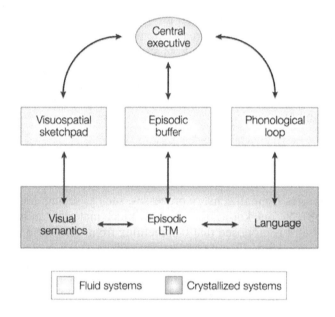

Working-memory model. Source: Baddeley, A. (2003).
Working-memory: Looking back and looking forward.
Nature Reviews and Neuroscience, 4, 829-839.
Curtsey of A. Baddeley

11.6: Levels of Processing memory model

Levels of Processing memory model (LOP) is not required for IB students, but it is included in this book for three reasons. First, LOP is a reason for faulty **eyewitness memory** and is referenced in chapter 14. Second, LOP is an important memory model and is very useful for students such as in learning how to study, an application included in this section. Third, LOP is a challenge to the Multi-store memory model and working memory in that it claims memory should be considered a continuous process where depth of processing is the key. IB students can use LOP to help evaluate the other two memory models.

Details of levels of processing model

The key details of the Craik and Lockhart's **levels of processing model** (LOP) follow (Sternberg & Sternberg, 2012).

1. Remembering does not occur in three distinct memory stores, such as Atkinson and Shriffrin's sensory store, short-term store, and long-term store, but instead varies depending on the depth of encoding.
2. The depth of processing is a continuum of encoding, such as **physical or perceptual level**, **phonological level**, and **semantic level**. The physical or perceptual level is shallow processing and the semantic level is the deepest level.
3. There could be an infinite numbers of depths, but it is enough to know these three.
4. The way something is encoded is the key to the level of processing.

Examples of Level of Processing depths for the word *dog*

Physical/Perceptual: Shallow processing	Phonological	Semantic: Deep processing
Processing: What does the word look like? Example: DOG: Is the word in capital letters?	Processing: Sounds related to the word, such as a rhyme Example: DOG: Does it rhyme with hog?	Processing: What does the word mean? Example: DOG: Is this an animal? What are some common behaviors of a dog?

Classic research for Levels of Processing

The aim of the experiment was to demonstrate that the depth of processing was more important to remembering than the time taken for processing (Craik & Tulving, 1975). **Procedures** involved participants performing one of two tasks (the **independent variable**). One was a non-semantic task where participants saw a word and made a decision about how it fit with a pattern of vowels (V) and consonants (C). They saw combinations of Vs and Cs, such as CCVVC or VCCCV, and then judged if words such as *brain* fit the combinations. This was a hard task because participants were told to respond quickly. The other was a semantic processing task where participants decided if a word fit into a sentence where a word was left out, such as "the man threw the ball to the _____ (child)" (p. 280). Some words were appropriate and some were not, so participants had to consider the meaning of each sentence and the sample word. The semantic processing group was also told to respond rapidly.

    Results showed that participants in the deep semantic processing task showed the most correct responses, even though the non-semantic group took longer to finish their assignment. The authors concluded that the most accurate recall comes from depth of processing rather than having a longer time to do a task.

LOP has been modified over time

The basic LOP framework stands the test of time after many decades, but some changes have been made (Lockhart, 2002; Ekuni, Vaz, & Bueno, 2011). Two additions are important.

1. **Transfer-appropriate processing** means to use the level of processing that best fits a task. For example, someone assigned a phonological task should get a cue using a rhyme so the retrieval environment matches the encoding environment.

2. **Robust encoding** clarifies how transfer-appropriate processing fits with the original LOP model. Lockhart (2002) maintains that deep levels of processing is still the best encoding method, even if transfer-appropriate processing can work, because retrieval environments are never exactly the same as the encoding environment. Robust encoding means that the more deeply encoded something is, the more it responds to a variety of cues when recall is necessary. For example, studying with deep processing creates semantic networks so that any type of encoding is easy to retrieve.

Applications of LOP: Eyewitness memory and study habits

It can be argued that levels of processing explains why **eyewitnesses memory** is so full of mistakes. This is reviewed in chapter 14 about the reliability of memory.

It can also be argued that good **note taking** and a study strategy called the **spacing effect** produce deeper levels of processing and greater learning. This is evidence that helps us make the judgment that LOP is valuable.

Levels of processing has a clear application to education because it helps students understand the best way to study (Marsh & Butler, 2013). LOP enhances learning "to the extent that the processes engaged during initial learning match the processes required for the critical task" (p. 301). Students who must demonstrate higher level thinking should process topics at a deep level, the correct application of **robust encoding** to get the most out of **appropriate-transfer**.

Note taking is one application. The quality of encoding when taking notes is critical for recall (Marsh & Butler, 2013). Conclusions that quality note taking promotes greater depth of processing follow.

1. *The quantity and quality of notes matter.* Complete and precise notes are better than vague notes for deep processing. To help students learn to take notes, teachers should give cues about what to write. Cued note takers recalled more information than uncued note takers in studies.
2. *Quality note taking helps students see the 'big picture.'* Quality note takers do not recall more items but they recall the most important information.
3. *Good note taking promotes transfer.* The best notes summarize important points for later review. Students who summarize important points when taking notes recall more than students who take notes without summarizing.

Self-management: Apply what you learn!

Your class might develop a note taking system for deep processing. Next, figure out the correct spacing effect for remembering what you learn for tests and put a plan into action to correctly apply it.

Challenge yourself to stop procrastinating. You might find you have more free time after using spacing effects.

Another application spaces practice for test preparation, called the **spacing effect**. This means students study a little over time with delays in between. Conclusions that spacing practice is the best way to prepare for tests follow.

1. *Procrastination does not help learning in the long run.* The 'procrastination scallop' describes how students avoid regular studying but cram right before a test. This habit gets reinforced because it works fairly well in the short-term but gives the false impression that material has been learned for the long-term.
2. *The spacing effect has research support for long-term learning.* Research shows the best spacing interval is 10%-20% of the desired retention interval. For example, to remember material after 5 days, students need to study over a period of 12-24 hours. Spacing a student's studies over 1-2 years is needed for learning to still be intact after 10 years.
3. *Deep processing works every time!* Applying the spacing effect means studying repeatedly after delays. This allows students to find new ideas and meaning when studying, which promotes deep processing.

11.7: Schema theory formation, priming, and activation

Descriptions of schemas and scripts

Describe means to give a detailed account, and important details of schema follow. This section is long because schema comes up so often when studying psychology.

Schemas are organizational framework in the mind that forms as someone grows up in their culture. Schemas categorize objects, events, and human practices in meaningful ways. Schemas help us make sense of old and new experiences, and gives us a way to rapidly process information (Gureckis & Gladstone, 2010).

Conceptual understanding
Schemas and scripts are categories of one's **subjective culture**, a term used by Harry Triandis. Categories influence one's beliefs and attitudes and subjective culture is reviewed in chapter 3.

Schemas have slots for many different types of information and a set of relational structures to organize them (Gureckis & Gladstone, 2010). Schemas help us make predictions about the world and we automatically fill-in those slots based on prior experiences. For example, if you are invited to a birthday party, you have a schema about what is supposed to happen. If you do not receive information about the particular plans for it, you fill the slots based on existing schemas about what to expect.

Schemas are useful because people must have a way to organize the world. On the other hand, there are two downsides to schemas. One is that we have a **limited capacity** for storing memories and we use schemas during **encoding**, so they can affect their retrieval (Gureckis & Gladstone, 2010). The other is that schemas can lead to **stereotyping**, so it is important to learn how schemas affect thinking.

Schema theory and research spans all the approaches to behavior. Schemas are biologically based. The brain is set up to categorize and these categories change as a child interacts with others. Culture determines the contents of schemas and they become representations in the mind that guide behavior.

Scripts are a special type of schema about events, such as the script for what happens at a

Children learn a birthday party script quickly. How many scripts for different events in your life can you list?
Used with license from megapixl.com.

birthday party (Gray & Bjorklund, 2014). We have thousands of scripts and some examples are what happens at a restaurant, at school, and how to celebrate holidays. Scripts are knowledge about situations we have faced over time and inform us about what is supposed to happen in the future (Schank, 2010). **Cultural scripts** are one type, the information everyone knows within a cultural group, such as how to plan a holiday celebration. **Idiosyncratic scripts** are another type, the knowledge specific to your personal situations, such as what is explained to others so they can understand, for example, what happened to you on a vacation. Every aspect of the world is hard to comprehend without scripts. Even children without language know basic scripts, such as a bedtime routine, and are confused if the script is violated.

Differing scripts are the main reason for misunderstandings between people (Schank, 2010). People have different scripts based on their cultural experiences and they do not always match!

Classic research demonstrating schemas: Frederick Bartlett

Bartlett (1932) was the first to show that schemas affect how people process information. The **aim of the study** was to demonstrate the **reconstructive nature of memory**, showing that people actively remembered objects, scenes, or events according to prior experiences.

Procedures are next. Bartlett's experiment used a **serial reproduction** format, where college students in the UK read a Native American Indian legend called *'War of the Ghosts'* and recalled it immediately afterwards and then at different intervals, such as days or months later.

Results showed that participants distorted the story, and Bartlett believed this was because they had preexisting schema that did not match the legend's use of Native American Indian cultural norms. Participants used one of three **distortions** when recalling the legend.

> **Class activities**
> Try the War of the Ghosts story in class. The story can be found online. Did your class find the same thing? Also try priming other routine activities similar to the Bower study below. How are scripts used?

1. **Assimilation**, where a participant changed the story to fit in with what was more familiar from the student's culture, such as changing obligations to spirits with obligations to parents
2. **Leveling**, where the legend was shortened because some of the material was not considered important
3. **Sharpening**, where the legend's details were put into different order to match the participant's schema

Classic research demonstrating scripts

A series of studies shows that people organize knowledge around hundreds of routine activities, that it is fairly easy to activate **scripts**, and that people use them to fill in gaps (Bower, Black & Turner, 1979). These were not experiments and the **aim of the studies** was to demonstrate the use of scripts.

One of these studies identified norms for scripts for a variety of scenes. **Results** for the "visiting a doctor" script follows. The first line, 'visiting a doctor,' primes the use of a script.

<u>**"Visiting a doctor**</u>
Enter office
Check in with receptionist
Sit down
Wait
Look at other people
Read magazine
Name called
Follow nurse
Enter exam room
Undress
Sit on table
Talk to nurse
Nurse tests
Wait
Doctor enters
Doctor greets
Talk to doctor about problem
Doctor asks questions
Doctor examines
Get dressed
Get medicine
Make another appointment
Leave office" (p. 182)

Another study in this series **aimed to show** that people will retrieve previously used scripts to fill in gaps in a story that were not part of the story to make it complete (Bower, et al., 1979). The researchers expected that the surface memories of the actions in the original story would fade quickly, requiring someone to use a script to fill gaps. This study does not have a control group so it is not an experiment.

Procedures are next. Eighteen participants first read a story unrelated to the experiment as a warm-up activity. Next, everyone read 9 scripts, each containing 20 actions, in random order, including visiting health professionals, shopping, and attending a party. For example, one of the scripts follows.

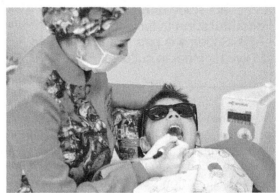

The Dentist
"Bill had a toothache. It seemed like forever before he finally arrived at the dentist's office. Bill looked around at the various dental posters on the wall. Finally the dental hygienist checked and x-rayed his teeth. He wondered what the dentist was doing. The dentist said Bill had a lot of cavities. As soon as he'd made another appointment, he left the dentist's office" (p. 190).

A script immediately comes to mind when seeing a picture of a dentist and patient.
Source: pixabay.com.

Next, participants were distracted by recalling and writing the warm-up story. Last, participants were given one minute to recall each script correctly, with the story titles used as primes for the scripts.

As an example, the text used for scoring scripts for visiting a health professional followed the norm script listed above. Each story had a general script gathered from other students.

Results showed that participants used stated script actions the most, followed by unstated script actions that fit a general script. Although participants used the stated script actions the most, they filled in gaps with unstated script actions.

The authors **concluded** that people filled in gaps with scripts for actions when primed with a script title.

Formation of schemas

The formation of schemas is explained by combining all three approaches to behavior. This includes **limited capacity theory** from the cognitive ATB, the need to learn **cultural norms** during **enculturation** from the sociocultural ATB, both which are **adaptive**, coming from the biological ATB. *Schemas are important for how we adapt and survive, transmit culture to children, and manage the limited capacity of memory processing.*

Limited capacity refers to how "working memory holds only the most recently activated, or conscious, portion of long-term memory, and it moves these activated elements into and out of brief, temporary memory storage" (Dosher, as cited in Sternberg & Sternberg, 2012, p. 203). The **episodic buffer** is the part of **Working Memory** responsible for limited capacity. It provides temporary storage for integrated episodes, or scenes, and acts as a buffer between the other components of Working Memory (Baddeley, 2000, Baddeley, 2002). The episodic buffer has a limited capacity because there would be far too much of a cognitive demand to make the entire working memory system access to a large amount of information stored in long-term memory (Baddeley, 2000). People access memories held in the episodic buffer through our conscious awareness and the episodic buffer helps create new mental representations for problem solving.

The schemas that help us organize mental representations held in working memory serve adaptation and enculturation needs.

Combining the sociocultural and biological ATB, Konner (2007) proposed that humans have a built-in mechanism called the **Cultural Acquisition Device** (CAD).

> **Thinking skills: Schema relates to the sociocultural ATB**
> Students study **universalism** and **enculturation** in the sociocultural ATB. Schema is part of our ability to live together in cultures.

People have universal processes (parts of the CAD), such as language, attachments, and complex cognitions that are developed as children reach ages 5-7 allowing for **enculturation** to take place over many years. **Schemas** are one component of the CAD, part of the symbolic processes necessary for enculturation. Konner calls it "cultural schematization" (p. 94). Other parts of the CAD include social learning such as modeling, and emotional enculturation, such as attachment. The CAD provides a framework for understanding how children grow and develop within all cultures.

Konner gives an example of how cultures actively build schemas about expected behavior from people living in the highlands of New Guinea. Common practice is to give all goods and services to one respected man who is trusted to distribute them fairly. Children growing up with this belief form schemas about how goods should be distributed and their attitudes reflect this cultural practice. It is different from attitudes about how goods and services should be distributed in other cultures, but it is adaptive for their group.

Next is an example of schema formation about **mental illness**. This example involves people in a cultural group paying attention to specific behaviors, perhaps what is available to conscious awareness from the episodic buffer. It also illustrates the values of a group used for enculturation, one reason we must understand and respect other cultures.

Examples of how schemas are easily primed and activated also include **gender role behavior, eyewitness memory**, and **aggression**, reviewed in the next chapter about evaluating schemas.

Schema formation: An example showing why people living in different cultures have different beliefs about mental illness

All cultures have schemas about diagnosing **mental illness**, and although there are some universal aspects to them, the details vary. All diagnostic systems, including dominant psychiatric manuals such as the DSM are really schematic categories.

Schemas are created in cultural groups based on how the group thinks about and experiences behaviors (Castillo, 1997). Schemas **reify** a belief into something real for the group. Reifying "occurs when people are collectively projecting onto an object a level of reality the object does not actually possess" (p. 19). The way a behavior is thought of in a cultural group is real to them, even if it is not real in reality. The group then treats a set of behaviors as real mental illnesses. Reification is the concept that gives us an international perspective on behavior because it shows how societies come to label anything as important. Do not assume that others outside of your culture share the same schemas.

How do schemas form about mental illness? A behavior is noticed by a cultural group and is interpreted as a mental illness within a cultural definition.

This is why it is sometimes hard to diagnose **depression** outside of western cultures (Castillo, 1997). In the United States, a set of behaviors are classified as 'major depression' in the DSM-5. This diagnosis is based on how **stress** is expressed in the US through emotion, representing schemas for abnormality in the US. It is ethnocentric to look at behavior in a different culture and say, "This is simply how someone experiences depression in another culture" because our own views are schematic. **Etics** and **emics** help us understand why. Stress is an etic, something common to all cultures, however, different experiences in expressing stress are emics. For example, the word depression means something different to the Pakistani. An interview study about the emics of depression in Pakistani ethnic groups living in the U.K is detailed in chapter 3. As another example, in China, schemas about expressing stress are more often experienced as bodily symptoms such as fatigue. Although the Chinese Classification of Mental Disorders (CCMD) has a schematic category called 'depressive episode,' the diagnosis is not used as frequently. The depressive symptoms experienced in the West are as not important to Chinese schemas, and little attention is paid to them (Castillo, 1997).

11.8: Top-down and bottom-up processing: Concepts related to schema

Describe means to give a detailed account. Next is important details about **bottom-up processing** and **top-down processing**, two concepts related to studying **schema**.

Bottom-up processing: Important details

Bottom-up processing refers to data-driven theories about **perception** that start with the eyes taking in stimuli (Sternberg & Sternberg, 2012). The process moves upward as the mind pieces together details, piecing together individual elements and working into a whole.

The key details of bottom-up processing follow (Sternberg& Sternberg, 2012).

1. It starts with the eyes taking in stimuli, called data-driven or sensory-driven.
2. It focuses on details and works upward.
3. It pieces together individual elements and works toward wholeness.
4. Perception of sensory information directs cognition.
5. It is the opposite of top-down processing.

One theory of bottom-up processing is James Gibson's **Direct Perception Theory**. Perceptions must have a way to become connected to the mind (Sternberg & Sternberg, 2012). Direct Perception Theory suggests that a stimulus input is all we need to perceive the environment, a suggestion that all knowledge comes from the senses (Gibson & Gibson, 1955). It is a bottom-up theory because perception starts with the

Train tracks are a good example of judging distance through direct perception. The tracks are perceived to get farther away because they converge in the distance.
Source: Pixabay.com

stimulus and then builds up in the mind to the image one sees. We do not need higher level thinking to direct the process. There is enough contextual evidence from what we sense in the environment to make perceptual judgments (Sternberg & Sternberg, 2012).

The railroad track picture is a good example of what Gibson meant by sensory stimuli containing all we need to create perceptions. Seeing the tracks converge helps you perceive distance. The train track is the direct stimulus and all that is needed. Similar stimuli, such as texture, can also imply distance. Look at photograph of rocks, where texture on them in the foreground imply its closeness. Rocks appear in the distance because the textures not easily seen, implying they are far away. Texture also fades in photographs of a mountain range, implying a perception of distance. Find other photographs to see how this works.

Classic research demonstrating Direct Perception Theory

The **aim of the experiment** was to demonstrate how a stimulus item directly creates a mental perception of an object that then can be identified as distinct from other similar objects (Gibson & Gibson, 1955).

Procedures are next. Participants were shown a picture of a critical four-coil scribble embedded in a group of 12 nonsense scribbles completely different from the critical scribble. They were told that four coils in a separate picture of 17 scribbles were the same as the critical one.

Participants were supposed to pick the correct matches (the **dependent variable**).

Results showed that after repeated trials (the **independent variable**), participants were able to identify the similar ones accurately. It was concluded that perceptual learning occurred. The stimulus started out as indistinguishable from the other similar coils but later became familiar enough for participants to select the correct matches.

Were the verbal descriptions evidence that higher thinking was used to create the perceptions? The authors said no, because the item descriptions were the result of the perception and evidence that participants created relationships between items in the learning process. Instead, this was evidence of thinking moving upward to wholeness.

Top-down processing: Important details

Top-down processing is when people construct a mental perception of a stimulus and it affects cognition from the top (Sternberg & Sternberg, 2012). Top-down theories are constructionist approaches to understanding **perception**. Top-down processing depends on one's expectancies and schemas, so perception is influenced by experiences and memories.

The key details of top-down processing follow.

1. It is a constructionist approach to perception learning.
2. It depends on one experiences and expectancies.
3. **Schemas** can direct top-down processing.
4. It is **intelligent perception** because one uses higher-order thinking to create perceptions.
5. It is the opposite of bottom-up processing.

> **Self-management: Mindfulness meditation improves both bottom-up and top-down processing**
>
> Students in the 21st century should practice **mindfulness meditation** (MM) to calm the mind, one way to take responsibility for health. It also improves learning.
>
> MM aids top-down processing by improving attentional processing (van den Hurk, Giommi, Barendregt, & Gielen, 2010). It makes attention tasks more efficient with fewer errors.
>
> MM aids bottom-up processing by creating smaller and even no reaction time between the time someone receives two different stimuli, such as sound and visual signals.

Even if bottom-up theories explain some of our perceptual learning, many favor top-down processing (Sternberg & Sternberg, 2012) Two of those reasons follow.

1. Bottom-up theories ignore **context effects**, meaning the effect of our surroundings on what we perceive. See Palmer (1975) under research demonstrating top-down processing for details.
2. The **word-superiority effect** suggests that perceiving a letter from an intact word is easier to perceive than a letter in a string of nonsense letters, again suggesting the importance of context.

Two examples of top-down processing are when we make sense of **ambiguous figures** and the **Stroop Effect**.

Examples of Ambiguous figures. How does previous schemas or experiences affect what you see first? The first is the duck/rabbit from J. Jastrow and the other is the young/old woman from E. G. Boring.

The **Stroop Effect** tests interference with visual attention, when our minds automatically attend to one aspect of a task to the detriment of another task (Stroop, 1935). The Stroop Effect is an example of top-down processing because people have training in word recognition more than color recognition, so our attention automatically goes to the words. Prior experience affects attention.

Stroop in action
Google 'images for the Stroop Effect' to see a variety of Stroop tests. Try them and see what happens.

Research demonstrating top-down processing

Can you think about a giraffe or a microscope without seeing them within a background of related objects (Bar, 2004)? Scenes we are normally exposed to in our environments make it easier to correctly perceive objects related to them, and this is demonstrated in research.

The **aim of one experiment** was to show the effects of visual scenes on object perception (Palmer, 1975).

Procedures are next. Participants saw 24 pairs of slides. One slide contained one object, a loaf of bread, a mailbox, or a drum. The second set of slides provided either context for the objects, incorrect context, or no context (was blank), the **independent variable**. For example, a contextual scene for the loaf of bread was a kitchen counter, containing objects such as toaster, cutting board, knife, spatula, and a sponge. Participants saw variations of context and objects in the different conditions. Participants saw the contextual slides for 2 seconds and the object slides for less than a second. The task was to identify the object and rate their confidence that they were correct.

An additional condition measured the effects of visual sensory information on object recognition. This was done by pairing an object with an inappropriate scene, but where the object looked similar to an object that really fit the scene. For example, a mailbox has the same basic shape as a ATBf of bread, but when paired with the kitchen scene, does not match. However, participants were given such a short time to see the object that they relied on sensory information, the shape, to make a decision.

Results showed that participants seeing an appropriate context identified objects correctly the most followed by the no context condition or the inappropriate context. Confidence ratings were highest for the appropriate condition followed by no context and inappropriate context. The same pattern was found for sensory information.

The authors **concluded** that context was important to object perception. Even object perception with just sensory information was context driven. This is evidence for context as an important part of top-down processing.

The **hippocampus** is one brain part related to the need for context when perceiving objects (Bar, 2004). Research shows the hippocampus receives input from many sources, but favors associative relationships over items input by themselves.

Top-down and bottom-up processing at work: Males and females use different cognitive processing for mental rotation tasks and it might have developed in part because of schemas

Gender, math, and schema is a topic evaluated in the next chapter so this is worth considering.

It can be argued that males use bottom-up processing and females use top-down processing to solve **mental rotation tasks**. It might also be argued that the reason males and females developed these differences was because of **stereotyping**, which can give people **schemas** about how they should perform.

There are no differences in most mathematical tasks between males and females, but there are robust differences on mental rotation tasks. Mental rotation tasks require visuospatial skills, and may be a reason more men are represented in careers such as engineering and architecture.

The **aim of the experiment** was to use fMRI to see brain activity in males and

> **Class activity**
> Google Vandenberg **mental rotations** tests and have the class take them. What do you notice? See if each student can figure out how he or she goes about solving the problem.
> Debrief the activity by asking students if they think these differences are at least in part because of schemas people have about male and female math performance.

females as they performed mental rotation tasks (Butler, et al., 2006). Would any brain activation differences point to differences in how males and females used different kinds of mental processing when tackling the mental rotation tasks?

Procedures involved males and females deciding if pairs of figures were the same or different on two tasks (the **independent variable**). The mental rotation figures on the next page are some of the pairs. In one task, participants were told to mentally rotate each figure in the pairs, because they were either the same and just rotated differently or they really were different. A second task was used as a control where participants were told not to mentally rotate the figures, as they were either the same or mirror images of each other and not rotated.

fMRI **results** for the women when asked to mentally rotate the figures follow.

1. They used more conscious effortful thinking related to top-down processing.
2. This involved more activity in the right dorsal medial prefrontal cortex.
3. Prefrontal cortex activation implies great effort in both decision-making and in spatial working memory.

fMRI **results** for the men when asked to mentally rotate showed:

1. They use more bottom-up processing emphasizing automatic sensorimotor activity and effortlessness automatic thinking.
2. This involved more brain activity in the primary sensory cortexes, basal ganglia, and postcentral gyri.
3. Deactivation of the parieto-insular vestibular cortex, which is related to effective unconscious processing.

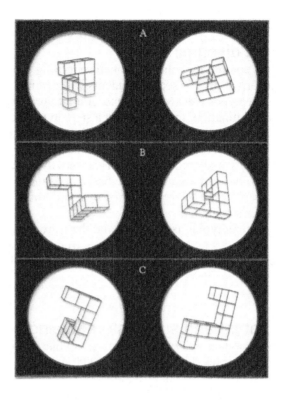

Some of the mental rotation figure pairs used in the study.
Source: Shepard, R. N. & Metzler, J. (1971). Mental rotation of three-dimensional objects. *Science*, 171, 701-703.
Used with permission from AAAS.

A: Figures are the same but with a rotation in the plane
B: Figures are the same but with a rotation in depth
C : Mirror-image figures rotated in depth

You might want to know why males and females have these differences. fMRI pointed to men using a large-scale network in their brains to do mental rotation tasks and women did not.

How these differences came about is up for debate, with contributions from genes, hormones, **stereotypes**, schooling, and child-rearing.

Thinking skills: Avoiding extreme positions

Avoid extreme positions by claiming top-down processing is better than bottom-up processing. Consider how both can be useful.

I do favor top-down processing when teaching, and the ability to **thread** ideas through a course requires it. Practice starting with a general idea, such as *'culture affects biology, cognition, and social behavior'* or *'the brain is a product of its environmental history over the lifespan'* and find examples from all over the course of them. It helps with getting 'lost in the trees.' This practice seems to promote **deep processing** as learned with the LOP model rather than shallow processing.

11.9: Stereotyping

Describe means to give a detailed account. Next is details about **stereotypes** and their formation, which can lead to the **schemas** that guide behavior. Knowledge about stereotyping is useful for the evaluation in the next chapter about schemas as a main reason females are poorly represented in mathematics, engineering, and computer science fields.

We like to think of ourselves as having good judgment, but people process large amounts of information each day and automatically simplify it. The result is that people are at risk for errors predisposing us to have one viewpoint over another.

Stereotyping is universal and not necessarily a direct cause of prejudice and discrimination

It is commonly believed that **stereotyping** is a direct cause of prejudice and discrimination, but this is incorrect. In this section students will distinguish two types of stereotypes and learn how both are formed.

Stereotypes *can* switch on and turn into prejudice and discrimination, though having a stereotype does not directly lead to either (Aronson, Wilson, & Akert., 2007). Stereotypes are most often just ways to simplify and organize the world. Stereotypes are *adaptive*, as long as they are based on some real experiences and are supported by some truths about other's behavior.

Stereotyping is universal and there are many similarities in the way that people from different cultures stereotype (Matsumoto & Juang, 2008).

> **Thinking skills: Stereotyping is also a topic for the sociocultural ATB**
> Students will use stereotyping as a required topic in the sociocultural ATB (chapter 19). The details here are necessary to thinking about their role in creating schemas.

Blatant and subtle stereotyping

Stereotypes are *cognitive* inter-group biases and are different from prejudice, which are *emotional* inter-group biases (Fiske & Taylor, 2008; Aronson, 2007). Discrimination is the behavior that comes from prejudice (Aronson, et al., 2007).

Fiske & Taylor (2008) divide stereotyping into two types, **blatant stereotyping** and **subtle stereotyping**.

The difference between blatant stereotyping and subtle stereotyping is linked to the **dual-processing approach**, a model useful for thinking about **social cognition**. This means processing can be seen on a continuum from automatic to controlled processing. People have access to both sides and can learn to have more conscious controlled thoughts. Blatant stereotyping is primarily controlled and conscious while subtle stereotyping is primarily automatic and unconscious (Fiske & Taylor, 2008). This same model is useful to represent the **two systems model of thinking**.

Dual Processing Model

Automatic ————————————————————— Conscious Controlled
Processing   Processing

The formation of blatant stereotypes happens when people identify with their **in-group** using controlled conscious social thinking. **Social identity theory**, studied in the sociocultural ATB, is blatant stereotyping, demonstrating the circumstances in which people give their allegiance to the in-group. We have biases toward an in-group and biases against out-groups (Matsumoto & Juang, 2008). Taken to the extreme, identifying with an in-group can lead to intense competition and **aggression**. Blatant in-group biases take place in response to inter-group threats to one's values and economic resources (Fiske & Taylor, 2008).

In contrast, subtle forms of stereotyping come from interpersonal conflicts. Subtle stereotyping challenges our notions that all stereotypes reflect deliberate prejudice and seem to be a main reason that females, for example, are poorly represented in mathematics, engineering, and computer science jobs.

The *difference* between automatic and controlled stereotyping matters a great deal when we think about how it *affects behavior*. People are more likely to be held responsible for their actions when they come from controlled conscious processing than they are if behavior comes from automatic and unintentional processing. For example, one effect of subtle stereotyping on behavior reviewed in this section is about gender stereotypes and their effects on female's mathematics abilities. Parents and teachers do not intend to negatively affect behavior, even if stereotyping has great consequence for the girls. In contrast, identifying with an in-group is controlled and conscious blatant stereotyping. **Infrahumanization** studies, reviewed in the Sociocultural ATB about social identity theory, highlights how far consciously identifying with an in-group can go.

The formation of subtle stereotypes

Many factors contribute to subtle stereotype formation. These factors work together and in reality cannot be separated. *Awareness may prevent the worst effects of subtle stereotyping.* The important details follow.

1. Subtle stereotypes form automatically and unintentionally, occur mostly in *ambiguous* and *ambivalent* situations, and stem from inner conflict (Fiske & Taylor, 2008). People like to think of themselves as not holding or acting on stereotypes, but research shows they do, even if it is accidental and automatic.

2. Everyday cognitive processing, such as selective attention, attributions, and schemas contribute to the automatic nature of subtle stereotyping (Matsumoto & Juang, 2008). **Attributions** contribute to the formation of stereotypes and reinforce them. "Stereotypes are dispositional attributions— negative ones" (Aronson, Wilson, & Akert, 2007, p. 436). Our cognitive processes are efficient. **Schemas** describe how we form categories to organize objects and social relationships (Matsumoto & Juang, 2008). "As a specific type of schema, stereotypes are beliefs about the characteristics of group members and theories about why those attributes go together" (Fiske, 2004, p. 399). We grow up viewing the world through **cultural filters** reflecting **enculturation**. Although stereotypes are often based on some truth about a group, many are incorrect and

> **Thinking skills: Drawing relationships between ideas**
> Consider how so many concepts studied in the course are related. Drawing relationships between ideas is an important critical thinking skill. The class can figure out where to draw relationships throughout the course. The class might create diagrams showing how concepts are related, both within and between each ATB.

are learned through others and the media rather than direct experience. Schemas are too easily accessible and automatic, creating **category confusion** (Fiske & Taylor, 2008). This is when people create general categories, such as gender or race, far faster than they can name individual identities. It is easy to confuse one individual with another from the same category. This may be a factor contributing to problems with **eyewitness memory**.

3. The rapidness of automatic categorizing and interpreting ambiguous situations cause stereotypes to form (Fiske & Taylor, 2008). Ambiguity is present in most social situations, so we are stuck with making interpretations. The result of interpretations can be problematic.

Correlation research about gender stereotypes in education: One effect of subtle stereotyping on behavior

Females are underrepresented in some fields of science and engineering and seems related to mathematics performance. There is a large body of research suggesting that subtle stereotyping heavily influences female perceptions of their mathematical abilities and performance.

These gender stereotypes are not intentional but come from automatic processing and interpreting of ambiguous information. However, the consequences are great.

Children internalize stereotyped messages from parents about mathematics abilities (Herbert & Stipek, 2005). Males outnumber girls in advanced mathematics courses and enter financially profitable careers requiring advanced mathematics skills at a higher rate. *Competency beliefs* may a reason for this difference and the **aim of this correlation study** was to investigate this possibility.

Procedures are next. Males and females between kindergarten and first grade as compared to the fifth grade were in the sample and data were gathered through interviews and achievement test scores. Hypotheses follow.

1. Boys would rate their mathematical abilities higher than girls starting in the first grade but would not perform better than the girls on achievement tests.
2. Parent and teacher ratings of verbal abilities would favor the girls and ratings of mathematics abilities would favor the boys.
3. Parent and teacher ratings of abilities would predict the children's own ratings.

Children rated their mathematics and verbal abilities during kindergarten or the first grade and then again in the third and fifth grade. Trained interviewers administered the questionnaire and children responded to questions such as "How good are you at learning new numbers?" and "How good are you at reading compared to all the students in your class?"

> **Thinking skills: Gender differences in behavior**
> Stereotyping is one good place to consider gender differences. Gender role behavior can be based on stereotypes that affect the self-concept and form schemas for accepted behavior.
>
> The Herbert and Stipek study and the research by Williams and Best under the next heading are a point of departure for considering why people have gender role stereotypes.
>
> The Williams and Best study might challenge your assumptions because research shows gender stereotyping is universal.

Parents rated their child's mathematical and verbal abilities and teachers predicted the children's mathematics and verbal skills for the next school year.

Last, children took mathematics and verbal achievement tests in kindergarten and again in third and fifth grade.

Results included the following.

1. Boys rated their mathematics abilities higher than the girls starting in the third grade even though performance on achievement tests was similar.
2. Teachers, but not parents, rated girls' verbal skills as higher. Parents, but not teachers, rated boy's mathematics abilities higher than girls.
3. Parent ratings of mathematics performance by the fifth grade were correlated with their own children's self-ratings. Parental lower ratings of math performance emerged during the third grade, *the same time as it emerged in the children.* Teacher ratings overall were more consistent with actual test scores than those of parents.

Culture and stereotyping

Gender **stereotypes** are the basis for differences in how males and females view their self-concept and roles (Williams & Best, 1994). The **aim of the correlation study** was to the question, do people all over the world use similar gender stereotypes and to what extent does someone's self-concept reflect these stereotypes?

Procedures are next. Participants in over 30 countries thought about 300 adjectives describing people and checked the ones they associated with men or women, or which words described both men and women.

Male-associated		Female-associated	
Adventurous	Capable	Affectionate	Complicated
Determined	Enterprising	Dreamy	Excitable
Humorous	Inventive	Forgiving	Fussy
Opinionated	Rational	Kind	Sophisticated
Realistic	Serious	Patient	Sensitive
Unscrupulous	Tough	Talkative	Worrying

Sample words from Williams & Best (1994)

Results showed high similarity across cultures for the words associated with men or women. The researchers next categorized the adjective selections according to strength, favorability, and activity. Words connected with men were linked to strength and activity, and were judged more favorable.

The extent to which these stereotypes affected the self-concept was tested by asking university students to think about the 300 adjectives and to check the ones describing the self and the ideal self (the person you want to become).

Results showed that across culture, the self and ideal self of men were mostly related to masculine words and the self and ideal self-concepts of women were mostly related to feminine words. In addition, both males and females across cultures described the ideal self using more masculine words.

In **conclusion**, there is no support for cultural differences in gender stereotyping or in how the stereotypes affect one's self-concept. Gender stereotypes and affects on the self-concept appear pancultural (universal).

11.10 The two systems model of thinking

Describe means to give a detailed account. Next is details about the **two systems model of thinking**, introduced earlier in this chapter as the dual processing model under the topic stereotyping.

For a class activity, make a judgment about these two situations below, first about breakups of long distance relationships, and then for happiness ratings about our lives. How do you know if you are making a good judgment? We like to think we make good decisions but do we really?

142

Activity: Make a judgment
"What proportion of long-distance relationships break up within a year" (Kahneman & Frederick, 2002, p. 53)?

This seems pretty simple at first glance but in reality, most people answer the question as if it were asked differently, "Do instances of swift breakups of long-distance relationships come readily to mind" (p. 53)?

People answering the question the second way are using the availability heuristic. It is automatically processed and can be modified and corrected if it is considered in-depth but often people fail to do this. This is an interesting thinking concern and is a good place to start thinking about the two systems model of thinking. People tend to substitute a target attribute with a heuristic attribute, something that easily comes to one's mind, especially if you know some instances where couples either broke up quickly or stayed together.

Try this one. **How happy are you with your life? How many dates have you had recently?** When college students are asked this there is no correlation between the two answers unless the dating question comes first. This is probably because if you have to think about dating first it evokes a mood, and answers to the second question might be influenced by having romance on one's mind. This again is the availability heuristic and is first automatically processed.

As you learn about System 1 and System 2 processing, consider how each affected your judgment.

Since many people hold the belief that they can make better judgments if they just think about a problem more, it is important to see how this might be done (Newell, 2013). The two systems model is a way to visualize how someone might think more about a problem before making a decision. Tolerate uncertainty because the two systems model is still controversial and needs more research. One problem is that researchers do not all use the same language when describing "thinking." Although it appears they are all talking about the same thing, it cannot be assumed.

For the student in an introductory psychology course, the model simplifies (hopefully does not oversimplify) thinking processes. For the purposes of this course, let's assume the model is useful yet recognize it might be refined in the future. Some researchers have called this model the dual processing model and it is useful for showing us how people may make judgments (Fiske & Taylor, 2008; Kahneman & Frederick, 2002). One way to represent this model follows and as we have already seen, it distinguishes the thinking related to subtle and blatant stereotyping.

Dual Processing: A way to envision the two systems model

System 1
Automatic ——————————————————— Conscious Controlled
Processing   Processing

The dual processing model is a continuum with two sides (automatic, intuitive processing) and (analytic, reflective, under conscious control). People have access to both ends of the continuum (Kahneman & Frederick, 2002).

Dual processing models are envisioned in many ways and one useful for thinking about decision-making divides it into two general processes, **System 1** and **System 2** (Kahneman & Frederick, 2002). System is a useful label for the processing because they differ according to speed, controllability, and the types of content one thinks about.

Characteristics of Systems 1 & 2

	System 1	System 2
Controllability	Automatic, intuitive, effortless	Analytic, reflective, under conscious control, takes effort, applies rules
Speed	Fast	Slow
Content used with each system,	Emotional content, when first making attributions, concrete and specific	Neutral content, abstractions

Based on Kahneman & Tversky, 2002

The dual processing model is assumed to work by having System 1 first quickly and automatically processing intuitive answers when someone makes a judgment (Kahneman & Frederick, 2002). System 2 oversees System 1, acting as quality control, and can agree with the judgment or correct it. What people call intuitive judgments are those from System 1 that System 2 endorses. Systems 1 and 2 are influenced by many factors and several follow.

1. Mood
2. The amount of time someone has to consider the evidence
3. Features of the task

Researchers assume the two systems can operate at the same time and that most often, even after deliberation, the original judgment is retained.

The study of **heuristics** and other **thinking biases** illustrate the two systems at work and help us consider two questions.

1. Why does System 1 makes errors?
2. Why does System 2 not always catch and correct these errors?

These questions are addressed in the next chapter that includes an evaluation of thinking and decision making. Heuristics help us answer these questions.

11.11: Decision making and heuristics

Describe means to give a detailed account. Next is important details about heuristics, one decision-making strategy.

Decision-making is a cognitive process where people choose a belief or action from a wide range of possibilities. Psychologists study how these choices are made, and know heuristics are often useful but can lead to big judgment errors.

We like to think our decisions are the result of careful attention to all available information, but there is so much information out there that no one can effectively process all of it. Instead, we use filters to sort through and select what seems important from all the incoming stimuli (Sternberg & Sternberg, 2012). Research shows we use heuristics and have biases that make decisions less certain than we might like, but it is probably impossible to avoid them.

A **heuristic** is a cognitive bias, a mental shortcut that makes decisions easier because they allow us to use fewer pieces of information (Sternberg & Sternberg, 2012). The concept **natural assessment** explains how heuristics work (Kahneman & Frederick, 2002). The activity about judging the proportion of long-distance relationship breakups is a good example. The target attribute is to judge the number of breakups. However, people instead use a natural assessment (a heuristic judgment) to make a decision where we think of the instances of the problem that come to mind, such as the instances of breakups. It is far easier to call up information related to similar instances of something you already know.

Three types of heuristics follow (Tversky & Kahneman, 1974).

1. **Representativeness**
2. **Availability** (including **affect heuristics**)
3. **Anchoring and adjustment**

Activity: Think about how the availability heuristic rules your judgments!
Have the class consider several instances when the availability heuristic seemed a good shortcut but relying on available information actually clouded judgment.

For example, we hear so much about terrible plane crashes that it makes us fear planes more than cars, even though people are more likely to be in a car crash!

Source: based on a related activity from Sternberg & Sternberg (2012).

Representative heuristic

Representativeness refers to judgments about the probability that something might occur (Tversky & Kahneman, 1974). Examples follow.

1. If one object belongs to a class of objects.
2. If an event stems from a particular process.
3. The probability that a process will result in an event.

Using representative heuristics to make judgments means someone decides if one object stands for a larger class or process.

Next is an example description of a person to illustrate how it works (Tversky & Kahneman, 1974).

"Steve is shy, but can be helpful. Steve is not all that interested in people or the reality of life. Steve likes order and pays attention to detail."

What if you were asked to decide the probability that Steve belonged to a particular occupation, such as librarian, engineer, salesman, pilot, teacher, or farmer?

People are likely to use a representative heuristic and think of how well Steve represents people in these professions by considering his similarity.

A representative heuristic can lead to mistakes in judgment because it fails to take into account "prior probability of outcomes" (p. 185). A correct judgment takes into account the base-rate frequency of the occupations, meaning that there are many more farmers and teachers than librarians. However, a representative heuristic does not take base-rate frequency into account and instead, stereotypes are relied on to make a judgment.

The **aim of one experiment** was to test the use of the representative heuristics (Tversky & Kahneman, 1974). For the **procedures**, participants were given a description of a person and then asked the probability that the person was either a lawyer or an engineer. One group was told the sample was 70% engineers and 30% lawyers and the other group was told the opposite, that 30% were engineers and 70% were lawyers, the **independent variable**. If participants used base-rate estimates then the first group would give a higher chance to the person being an engineer and the second group would give the higher chance to the lawyer. **Results** showed that participants in both groups used representative heuristics and instead gave the person an equal chance of being in either profession.

Failure to take into account base-rates is one of the many errors using a representative heuristic brings to decision making.

Availability heuristic

Decisions using the **availability heuristic** are made based on what someone can recall as important similar instances of something. You probably used an availability heuristic to answer the question about long-distance romance breakups.

The availability heuristic is a useful shortcut because the instance of a larger class of items is easier and faster to recall than instances of what happens less frequently (Tversky & Kahneman, 1974). For example, answer this question.

"What is the risk that a middle-aged person might have a heart attack?"

It may be easier to think of people who have had a heart attack than the people who have not and is a good example of using the availability heuristic, just as it is easier to think of relationship break-ups rather than those lasting a long time.

The frequency that something occurred is just one cognitive bias leading to the availability heuristic. Other biases can cause incorrect judgments and two examples follow.

1. The **illusory correlation**
2. Retrievability

The **illusory correlation** is when people expect two things to be related even when they are not, described in chapter 13 about reliability of cognitive processes. **Retrievability** means that the information most easily retrieved will be judged more important (Tversky & Kahneman, 1974). For example, when asked to judge if a list contains more male or female names, people are more likely to say males if the listed names contain more famous males. So familiarity with the names becomes a cue to use the availability heuristic because they are easy to retrieve.

Next is an activity leading into the upcoming topic about the **affect heuristic**.

Class activity
Divide the class into two groups and assign one group a time pressure and the other no time pressure. Next, both groups should rate each on a scale of 1 (high benefit & low risk)-7 (low benefit & high risk)

Alcoholic beverages	Chemical plants	Space exploration
Eating red meat	Food preservatives	Roller Skates
Texting while driving	Cigarettes	Bicycles
Cell phones	Surfing	Eating fast food
Air travel	Explosives	Genetically modified food
Water fluoridation	Motorcycles	(GMOs)
Backpacking		

Based on and including items from:
Finucane, Alhakami, Slovic, & Johnson, 2000

Affect heuristic is related to availability, but the difference is that affect heuristics are made in response to an **emotion** (Newell, 2013). **Affect** is defined for use with the affect heuristic as "a specific quality of goodness or badness experienced as a feeling state" (Slovic, Finucane, Peters, & MacGregor, 2004, p. 312). If you were in the group with a time pressure in the above activity, it is likely you used an affect heuristic the make your decisions because it is more efficient than thinking through the actual risks and benefits. Conclusions about risk versus benefit for each item likely differs depending on whether or not you had a time pressure.

Plenty of research evidence points to the conclusion that situations requiring someone to make a decision automatically causes an emotional (affective) evaluation (Kahneman & Frederick, 2002).

By definition, an affect heuristic means that positive and negative emotions become attached to the images we hold in our minds that guide decision making (Finucane, Peters, & Slovic, 2003). An affect heuristic helps integrate information for making judgments and helps people set priorities. Mental images of stimuli that go into making a decision bring up emotions that influence our perceptions, and these perceptions sway final decisions. For example, decisions about risk automatically bring up an emotion reactions that influence judgment.

The pathway for using an affect heuristic follows (Finucane, et al., 2003).

Thinking skills: We will use this again
Emotion and cognitive processes comes up later in the cognitive ATP, so the affect heuristic is important to know. Research supports the concept and is evaluated in the chapter about emotion and cognitive processing.

It is useful here because it is part of a body of research supporting the widespread use of heuristics in making judgments, and this conclusion is evaluated in the next chapter.

1. Each person has distinct characteristics that they bring to any decision.
2. These characteristics influence what is salient (most noticeable) about the stimuli for making a decision.
3. Differences in the way people react to stimuli result in each person "mapping" stimuli in unique ways.
4. Each person has an "affective pool" of judgment stimuli held as mental images and each is marked with varying degrees of emotion.
5. People consult this affective pool when deciding something.
6. Affective impressions of stimuli are easily *available* and are one cue for decision making, often times more efficient (in the person's mind at least) than going through a lengthier process of evaluating all aspects of a problem.

7. The affect heuristic is a mental short-cut because it is easier to assess and seems more efficient for making judgments.

Anchoring and adjustment heuristic

The **anchoring and adjustment** heuristic is where judgments and decisions are made based on a reference point, called the end-anchor. Adjustments made to reach a final decision are usually biased toward the anchor and incorrect (Tversky & Kahneman, 1974).

Try this problem.

"How many (Florida, or substitute your state, region, or country) schools have International Baccalaureate programs?"

The class might be divided into groups and the teacher can give each group a different anchor, an arbitrary number. Students then decide if the number of schools with an IB program is smaller or larger than the anchor and then guess how many.

Research using this format has shown that the anchor had a great effect on someone's answer and that the adjustments from the anchor were insufficient to produce a correct answer.

11.12: Theory of planned behavior

Describe means to give a detailed account. The **theory of planned behavior** is one decision making model that has many relevant applications such as making **health decisions** about **smoking, exercising,** using **alcohol,** eating **junk food,** practicing **safe sex,** exclusive **breast-feeding,** and even **texting** while driving.

Important details of the theory of planned behavior follow.

The theory of planned behavior gives us a framework for understanding and predicting someone's decisions (Ajzen, 2012). It is well supported and has been applied successfully to judgments made about a variety of behaviors, such as deciding to exercise, eat healthy foods, donate blood, conserve energy, or use alcohol and drugs. The theory is also important for understanding what must happen to change someone's behavior.

The theory of planned behavior builds on an earlier model called the theory of reasoned action and is better because it includes someone's level of perceived control. This is the belief someone has that he or she can start and carry through with their intentions. Perceived control is similar to Bandura's **self-efficacy** (part of Social Cognitive Theory), also important for health promotion. A model of the theory of planned action follows.

Theory of Planned Behavior

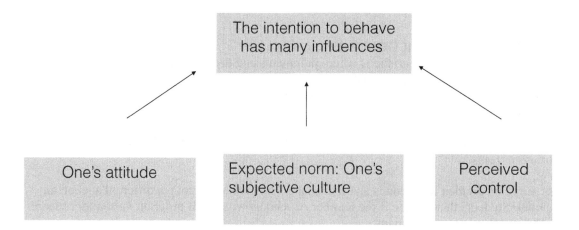

Here is how the model works. Let's say someone has an intention to exercise. Their attitude toward it, the expected norm, and the level of perceived control come together determine to an outcome.

An **attitude** is formed from a variety of beliefs people hold about the behavior and the expected outcome (Ajzen, 2012). A belief might be that people should follow through with a doctor's orders to start a walking program to lose weight, expecting an outcome of becoming healthier.

An **expected norm** is the belief that the larger group promotes the behavior. Norms are a good application of **subjective culture** because groups have **schemas** for expected behavior and these are categories someone consults when making a decision. Ajzen (2012) noted that subjective culture had much to do with how interpersonal relationships guided behavior and cited Harry Triandis, a theorist detailed starting in chapter 3, as important. If the larger group values and rewards people for taking care of their health, then this value is likely to influence someone's decision to exercise.

Perceived control is an important part of the model because there are so many internal and external factors either helping or hindering ones intentions (Ajzen, 2012). These factors follow.

1. Correct information
2. Mental and physical skills required for the task
3. Social support
4. Emotions
5. Having barriers or no barriers to getting started

> **Thinking skills: Drawing relationships**
> Students interested in **health psychology** can use the theory of planned behavior as a health promotion model.
> The chapters about health psychology also includes the **Health Belief Model** and **Social Cognitive Theory**, but students can use the theory of planned behavior instead of or in addition to them.

When considering exercise, these factors might include the following.

1. Knowledge about how to train at the gym to achieve the best results
2. An absence of physical limitations or a way to compensate for them
3. Family and friends encourage exercise and perhaps someone will become a workout buddy
4. Overcoming fears, especially if someone started to exercise before and quit
5. Having or not having the money to join a gym and perhaps hiring a personal trainer

Perceived control is much indebted to the concept **self-efficacy** (Ajzen, 2012). High perceived control affects one's perseverance to tackle even difficult tasks. The task can seem intimidating if someone must lose a great deal of weight, so perceived control must be addressed for success.

All parts of the model are assumed to be under one's cognitive control, making up a belief system about their intentions that is easily accessed in memory (Ajzen, 2012). Beliefs guide all parts of the model and we must acknowledge that they can change. When someone changes their beliefs, they might stop exercising, so cognition is a driving force of the model.

The model assumes that intentions guide behavior but perceived control might moderate the intentions (Ajzen, 2012). For example, a doctor might advise someone to exercise and eat a balance diet and the person might have good intentions, but may also have a financial barrier to joining a gym, hiring a personal trainer, or buying organic foods.

Avoid misunderstandings of the theory. Sometimes people think the theory of planned action describes a fully rational and objective person who considers all information with an unbiased mind (Ajzen, 2012). This is not so because someone could have beliefs that rest on faulty knowledge or are unrealistic. Regardless of how someone gets a belief or if it is faulty, the model still predicts behavior. People also do not consciously consider every aspect of their beliefs every time they do something. The deepest conscious processing about an intention concerns the most important decisions, especially if they have great consequence. For example, following medical advice to exercise to lose weight might require deep processing. Everyday behaviors such as taking a multivitamin each day do not require deep processing.

CAS or a class activity: Authentic learning: Self-management and health

To make the **theory of planned behavior** relevant to everyday life, students might pick an intended behavior and follow through with a self-management project to achieve it.

Ideas include better study habits (the section on LOP can guide you), getting enough sleep, starting a stress reduction program (such as meditation, Tai Chi, or yoga), exercising, eating less junk food, putting the cell phone away while driving, saving money for a specific goal, or improving the way one trains to enhance sport performance. The class can think of other things as well. It is recommended that the behaviors are things that can be managed with a little effort and are not embarrassing to anyone.

As you study the model, consider how each part contributes to current behavior and your intentions to change.

List the attitudes, norms, and perceived control that influence the behavior. Next set a time frame for making the change, and target the aspects of the model you think are most likely to influence success.

If, for example, you want to make some progress after 30 days, log what you do to meet the challenge, noting the attitudes, norms, and perceived control important to success of lack of success each day.

If someone sees a lack of success early on, what might be done to overcome barriers? Sometimes being aware of barriers and learning about your topic, such as the way people should exercise or what one should eat to be healthy, can help strengthen attitudes and intentions. Are there ways to get past any norms against your progress?

Document progress. How did you do and how helpful was the model?

Chapter 12
The Cognitive Approach to Behavior: Cognitive Processing : Analysis and Evaluation

---

Chapter objectives

Students will:
1. Practice thinking strategies (command terms) related to analysis and application as well as synthesis and evaluation, with explain, contrast, and evaluate demonstrated.
2. Evaluate the Multi-store Model of memory.
3. Evaluate Working Memory, including the example of how cell phones and driving do not mix.
4. Contrast the Multi-store Model of memory and Working Memory.
5. Evaluate schema theory, using the example that schemas explain faulty eyewitness memory.
6. Evaluate schema theory, with the example that gender schema is the reason girls are poorly represented in math, engineering, and computer science fields.
7. Evaluate schema theory, with the example that schemas activate aggressive behavior.
8. Explain and evaluate heuristics, an example of factors affecting thinking and decision making.
9. Evaluate the theory of planned behavior.

**Note: Cognitive processes count as behaviors (you are remembering or making a decision) and can be supported with the background research. For a richer evaluation, this chapter extends the links between processes and specific behaviors, increasing critical thought, giving more support for TOK discussions about the relevance of psychology models in predicting behavior, and giving some great Extended Essay ideas.

12.2 Evaluate the Multi-store Model of Memory

Evaluate means to make a judgment (appraisal) using evidence. Although there is evidence for all three memory stores, this model has been challenged by the more comprehensive and complex Working Memory model. Working Memory proposes that there is more to memory than what can be described by the Multi-store Model and the classic research supporting it. In addition, research challenges the conclusion that the **serial position effect**, cited as evidence for different memory stores, is universal.

First let's look at two classic experiments and a biological case study cited as evidence for the distinct parts of the Multi-store Model of memory.

Classic research evidence: The serial position effect (recency-primacy)

One classic demonstration of distinct short and long term memory stores comes from an experiment about the **serial position effect** on free recall (Murdock, 1962). The **aim of the experiment** was to provide the existence of separate long and short term stores.

Procedures are next. Six groups of participants were read 80 different word lists, with each group having a different number of words per list and a different amount of time to hear the words. The word lists and time are the **independent variables**. For example, one group had 30 words presented at 1 second intervals and another had 15 words at 2 second intervals.

It was predicted that participants would recall more words at the beginning or end of the word list (a **recency-primacy effect**), creating a U shaped graph with fewer words recalled from the middle of the list.

Results showed that all groups demonstrated a primacy effect for the first 3-4 words and a recency effect for the last 8 words. This has been **concluded** to be evidence for separate long and short term memory stores.

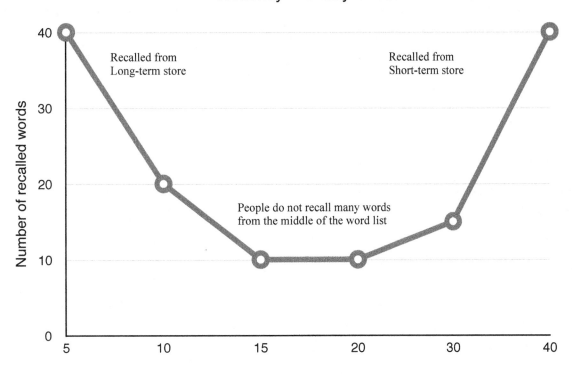

The classic U shaped graph: Similar to findings of
Murdock (1962)

More classic research evidence: Recency-primacy effect exists even after presentation and delay variables are added

Further evidence for both long and short-term stores comes from two experiments where the presentation time and delay were introduced as variables (Glanzer & Cunitz, 1966). The hypothesis was that words recalled from the beginning of a list comes from the long-term store and words recalled from the end of a list come the short-term store, even with different presentation times and delays.

The **aim of one experiment** was to show that words recalled through long-term storage from the beginning of the U curve would still demonstrate a long-term store, even with different presentation rates of the words. **Procedures** involved participants hearing 8 lists of 20 words that varied, for example, in presentation (3, 6, and 9 second intervals), the **independent variable**. Each list had the same number of words. Participants wrote down as many words as they could recall for 2 minutes after each list.

Results showed that participants still were storing words in long-term memory even after different presentation rate, demonstrating that long-term memory still stored words even after longer intervals. The primacy effect is strong.

The **aim of a second experiment** was to show that words recalled from the end of a word list demonstrated short-term stores, with the independent variable of time delays as evidence for this. Participants were shown fifteen 15 word lists for 1 second and then a delay of 2 seconds before the next word, the **independent variable**. After the researcher got to the last word, a number from 0-9 (the delay of 10 or 30 seconds) was shown and participants counted out loud from that number to prevent recall until told to write as many words as they could recall.

> **Thinking skills: Class activity**
> Try this out on yourselves. Come up with two lists of common words, 20-30 for each list, and see what can be recalled. Try more word lists with time delays and counting backwards as in the Glanzer experiment to see what you find.

Results showed that even a 10 second delay was enough to influence the number of words participants could recall from the end of the word list and 30 seconds removed the recency effect. This is because participants could only hold information in short-term memory for a brief time.

The authors **concluded** that these experiments were evidence for two distinct memory stores.

Research support: The case of H. M.

H.M. suffered from severe seizures and finally decided to have some pretty radical surgery to stop them (Adelson, 2005). In 1953 H.M. had most of his hippocampus and amygdala removed along with much of the surrounding cortex. H.M. had long-term memories of much of his childhood but could not create any new long-term memories, even though his short-term memory was learning new things all the time.

This case shows how important the hippocampus is to memory and it supports the distinction between long- and short-term stores in the Multi-store Model of memory.

H.M. liked to work crossword puzzles so his

> **Film**
> As of the writing of this book the Scientific American Frontiers film *Don't Forget* is still available. One segment is about people who have short-term memories and cannot create new long-term memories. The other segments are also quite good. The film is available from www.pbs.org.

doctors designed them to see if he could learn new information about people from far in the past, which he did by learning new facts about well-known people he knew about from before 1953.

One of H.M.'s doctors laughs when he says that H.M. still does not know him, even though they have worked together for many years. This is because H.M. cannot store any new long-term memories.

The serial position effect may not be universal: Formal schooling and culture challenge conclusions about the distinct stores

A good evaluation considers counterclaims. Challenges to the conclusion that the serial position effect is evidence of distinct stores comes from cross-cultural research about the effects of **formal schooling** and

culture on memory. These studies may be decades old but they are not out of date. It is just when they did the research. The conclusions are still defended and recommended by Michael Cole (personal communication with Michael Cole, 5/19/16).

Might formal schooling be the reason someone demonstrates a primacy or recency effect? The **aim of one quasi-experiment** was to see if formal schooling, age, or culture caused the primacy and recency effects (Wagner, 1973).

Urban Mexican children and adults with formal education were compared to rural children and adults, some with formal education and others without it (Wagner, 1973). Word pairs (animals and objects) were shown over 14 trials and participants were asked to recall which animals were paired with the objects.

Results showed all groups with formal education showed a primacy effect. Participants without formal education had no primacy effect greater than middle-position recall, yet had a recency effect. Groups with formal schooling showed improved primacy

Animals and object pairings
Wagner, 1973
Examples of the pairings:
fish-boot   frog-picture   bird-ladder
spider-bell   shrimp-bottle   scorpion-flower pot

effect with age, perhaps because formal schooling aids people in learning the memory control processes such as clustering and rehearsal.

It was **concluded** that rural unschooled children do not use verbal rehearsal needed to transfer items into long-term memory as assumed in the Atkinson and Shiffrin model, leading to the conclusion that the *reason for the primacy effect may have more to do with formal schooling rather than distinct memory stores.*

A similar finding came from an experiment **aiming to compare** a serial recall task with Mexican children living in cities and receiving formal schooling according across four age groups, with participants ranging from ages 7-21 (Wagner, 1975). These results were compared with previous results from US participants. Participants saw the same animal-object pairings but half were in a labeling condition where they were to name the animal or object. **Results** showed no difference between the formally schooled Mexican participants and the US participants. The increased use of verbal labeling improved the recency effect in all age groups but weakened the primacy effect in participants over 10. Again, Wagner **concluded** that *formal schooling evened the playing field for showing a primacy effect.*

What about culture? Does **culture** influence primacy and recency effects? One finding from extensive study of

Thinking: Avoiding oversimplification
No research is complete unless it is examined cross-culturally, so students should avoid oversimplification and go beyond what is in standard texts for a global perspective.
The sociocultural ATB topic culture and cognitive processes details more of Cole's work with the Kpelle.

memory in the **Kpelle** in Africa is that although US school children show a clear U pattern for serial recall, the Kpelle graph is rather flat as they do not show a primacy or recency effect (Cole & Gay, 1972). This difference is explained not through schooling but because Kpelle children are **enculturated** to approach organizing information to be remembered differently.

Strengths of the Multi-store Model of memory

1. Much research about memory comes from this early model and we have learned a great deal using this as a starting point.
2. Research has verified its components, such as Sperling, Peterson, Murdock, and Glanzer.
3. It may explain the recency-primacy effect.
4. Biological case studies such as H.M. are used as evidence for the model.

Limitations of the Multi-store Model of memory

1. It is simple and perhaps ignores some of the complexities of remembering. It is a linear model with distinct limitations for each part.
2. It has been challenged by Working Memory and Levels of Processing models that envision memory as more complex and continuous instead of consisting of distinct parts.
3. Its focus on rehearsal as the main way to remember may be oversimplified.
4. Cross-cultural research about the effects of formal schooling and cultural values challenges the universality of the serial position effect, something that has been heavily cited as evidence for distinct memory stores.

12.2: Evaluate Working Memory

Evaluate means to make a judgment (appraisal) using evidence. **Working memory** is well supported, with *each part of the model carefully tested.* Two examples from this large body of research are next followed by an application to everyday life about using cell phones when driving and cultural testing.

Working memory challenges the Multi-store Memory model's view of the short-term, suggesting it is better to think of memory having a "controlling executive system responsible for coordinating and monitoring the many and complex subroutines that are responsible for both acquiring new material and retrieving old" (Baddeley & Hitch, 1974, p. 47).

Evidence for the visuospatial sketchpad

One way to show that working memory is made up of specialized parts is to run experiments using a **dual task format**. If successful, these experiments show that short-term memory for visuospatial information is aided by a specialized part of working memory, the **visuospatial sketchpad** (Logie, Zucco, & Baddeley, 1990).

The **aim of the experiment** was to show that the short-term storage of visual-spatial information relies on the visuospatial sketchpad (Logie, et al., 1990).

Procedures are next. Experiment participants received two *primary tasks,* the **independent variable**. Participants in the first group completed a visual span task where they saw patterns of squares presented two at a time until the screen was full. The task was to identify where the incorrect square was during the second and third trials as compared with the first. The other group saw a letter span task where a random sequence of letters appeared on a screen one at a time and participants were to recall the order of the letters.

Each primary task had a *secondary task* going on at the same time and the conditions varied so that each primary task was tested with each secondary task, another **independent variable**. One was mental arithmetic and the other was to name an arrangement of squares on a screen as filled or unfilled squares.

Next participants completed the primary tasks with each secondary task to see under which conditions the primary tasks were impaired.

Results showed that primary tasks had less impairment from the secondary tasks using the same parts of working memory. Conversely, the primary tasks were most impaired when the secondary task used a different part of working memory (for example, the letter span task being most impaired by the secondary mental arithmetic task).

The most important practical application to take away from the Logie experiment is to do one task at a time or at least do not do another task at the same time that interferes with Working Memory. This is a challenge for students wanting to task-switch.
Source: pixabay.com.

This study was also run using a repeated measures design to control for subject variables and showed the same thing, something important to making a judgment about the quality of the research. The authors **concluded** these study results were evidence for a separate visuospatial sketchpad, as well as evidence that working memory is aided by different slave systems.

Evidence for the phonological loop

An experiment investigating the **phonological loop** is one example of how well Working Memory is researched, providing more evidence that memory is not just a simple system with distinct parts.

Rehearsal is important to for encoding information into memory, and one experiment used articulary suppression, meaning to interfere with rehearsal, to test the importance of the phonological loop (Papagno, Valentine, & Baddeley, 1991). The **aim of the study** was to show that articulatory suppression interfered with learning new foreign language vocabulary but did not impair learning word pairs for the native language. For **procedures,** participants were native Italian speakers who learned Italian word pairs in one condition (such as cavallo-libro) and Italian-Russian word pairs (such as rosa-svieti) in another condition, the **independent variable**. The suppression (interference) was the familiar native words being paired with the new Russian words which were to be remembered. **Results** showed that the visual and auditory presentation of the word pairs interfered with learning the new foreign language vocabulary but not native words. The authors **concluded** that the phonological loop was essential to Working Memory. This study was replicated with English speakers.

> **Activity: The loop at work**
> Learn this list while constantly repeating the word *twenty* silently, *school, giraffe, sushi, rainfall, coffee, truck, television, flag, building, mountain, kayak, airplane, lunch, holiday.*
>
> This is hard because the word twenty interferes with rehearsal and the words are not stored.

Evaluation of working memory: Cell phones and driving do not mix

It helps to have a real life example of using memory on the floor to see how strong the argument is that working memory is a credible model. Working memory is clearly a problem when people drive and talk on cell phones at the same time, and there is evidence for this conclusion.

It can be argued that **cell phone** use while driving is not safe and we know this because trying to two things at once violates the limited capacity of Working Memory. The **central executive** is disrupted when attention is divided (Baddeley, 2009). Researchers have known this for a long time, illustrated with three studies between 1997 and 2013 studying cognitive disruptions when driving.

One study **aimed to see** the link between cell phone use and accidents. Participants were 699 drivers with cell phones who had been in accidents where no one was hurt but there was property damage (Redelmeier & Tibshirani, 1997). Phone bills were analyzed from a 14-month period for each person.

> **Thinking skills and self-management: Challenging beliefs**
> Research shows people cannot use cell phones and drive responsibly, even if they think they can. Look into this topic more if you do not believe it. Even hand-free devices do not help. Be **open-minded** to the possibility that people are not always the best judges of their behavior. For IB students, open-mindedness is part of the **Learner Profile**.

Results showed the risk for an accident was four times higher when using a cell phone. The risk was the same regardless of age or experience. Calls placed the closest to the accidents, within five minutes, created the most risk. Hand-free units installed in some of the cars did not reduce the risk.

A series of experiments examined if participants would be accurate at recognizing objects they fixated on while in a driving simulator (Strayer & Drews, 2007). This study **aimed to see** if participants could recall objects presented where the driver's eyes were looking in a single or double-task condition, the **independent variable**. The single-task condition involved just driving. The double-task condition involved driving and talking to a research assistant on a cell phone. **Results** showed that even when a driver's eyes were fixated on an object shown through the simulator, they recalled fewer of them when also talking on a cell phone. The authors call this **inattention-blindness**, something people do not recognize in themselves. Working Memory's limited capacity does not allow us to attend to all the things we wish we could. Even talking to a passenger is safer than talking on the phone. Another experiment in the series assigned some participants to talk on the phone and some to talk with a friend seated in the front seat while driving 8

miles of highway with instructions to find a particular rest stop. **Results** showed that 88% of drivers with a friend found the rest stop and just 50% of drivers on the phone found it. Passengers seemed to help the drivers by adjusting their conversations to what was happening on the road.

A Center for Disease Control (2013) study builds on the first two **aiming to investigate** the problems of **texting** and **emailing** while driving. In the US each day, about 9 people are killed and 1,153 people are hurt in car accidents involving a distracted driver. The CDC identified three types of distractions.

1. Visual, where people take their eyes off the road
2. Manual, where people takes their hands off the wheel
3. Cognitive, where someone's mind is not on driving

We cannot pay attention to driving while using cell phones, even if we want to think we can.
Used with license from megapixl.com.

Approximately 31% of drivers surveyed reported texting and emailing while driving. Texting is a cognitive distraction and takes one's mind off the road for longer periods of time than other distractions. The CDC maintains there is no safe way to text and email while driving because they are huge distractors.

Working memory has reinterpreted the recency effect

A well defended judgment includes asking if an older theory might be better explained as a function of Working Memory. Might the Atkinson-Shiffrin model be oversimplified?

Two reasons to doubt the conclusion that the **recency effect** reflects a distinct short-term store follow (Baddeley & Hitch, 1993).

1. Evidence shows the existence of a long-term recency effect that questions the simplified idea that recency is a result of short-term memory.
2. Interference activities do not seem to impair the recency effect.

Recency might really be a temporary retrieval strategy from **implicit memory**, and this idea better fits the working memory model that short- and long-term memories are linked.

Alternative explanations: What to take away from working memory and recency

Alternative explanations should be noted when discussing, evaluating, and contrasting these two memory models.

Avoid oversimplifying memory, which is probably the greatest weakness of the Atkinson-Shiffrin model. Consider the Baddeley and Hitch reinterpretation given that working memory is the most used memory model today.

Implicit memories are long-term memories that guide behavior without us having to consciously think about them. Implicit memories can easily be **primed**, meaning an experience you have can easily reactivate an implicit memory and put it into working memory.

One of the many lines of reasoning behind this reinterpretation of recency comes from critiquing the way older recency experiments are conducted. They used immediate free recall where participants were told to recall the last items on a list first. One experiment by Baddeley and Hitch in 1977 showing problems of older research gave participants a list of nonsense syllables (as cited in Baddeley & Hitch, 1993). Free recall words were given to participants either visually or auditorily. At the same time, each group did a digit-span task given in the opposite modality (meaning the visual group had the digit-span test auditorily and vise versa). Since both tasks are assumed to be in short-term memory, an interference task should wipe-out the recency effect. This did not happen. Other supporting experiments show a lack of the recency effect if participants are told to recall the items in the middle first.

It is concluded that a specific retrieval strategy is involved with showing a short-term recency effect.

What about long-term recency? There is evidence that long-term recency is not affected when study participants are told to either recall items from the first, middle, or last sections first, but is it noted that more research must be done to clarify this result. Working Memory is an interesting and more complex reinterpretation of recency.

Is working memory valid cross-culturally?

Some studies compare working memory across culture but it is not a large body of research. The existing studies show that Working Memory seems to generally function the same way across cultures. Two brief examples follow.

One experiment compared adolescents in Russia and Kyrgyzstan using a spatial working memory test (Ismatullina, Voronin, Shelemetieva, & Malykh, 2014). Since Working Memory is important for a variety of reasoning abilities it was important to see if culture might cause participants to use different strategies affecting working memory. Although these two cultures are very different, results showed no cultural differences in spatial working memory.

Another example is an experiment comparing Canadian and Chinese participants as they solved complex subtraction and multiplication problems (Imbo & LeFevre, 2010). Would participants show cultural differences in the uses of phonological and visuospatial working memory? Results showed both groups relied on phonological and visuospatial working memory to solve problems, even though Chinese participants were more accurate in both subtraction and multiplication.

Strengths of Working Memory

1. It is the most accepted model of memory in modern psychology because it explains a wider range of tasks involved in reasoning, comprehending language, and learning (Sternberg & Sternberg, 2012; Baddeley & Hitch, 1976).
2. It has more real-life applications, such as texting and driving.
3. It gives good reasons to believe short-term memory is not a separate system.
4. It provides a more complex view of the recency effect.
5. It has cross-cultural validation, though it is not a large body of research.

Limitations of Working Memory

1. It explains short-term memory but does not give a full account of the long-term component that is linked to short-term remembering.

12.4 Contrast the Multi-store Model of memory and Working memory

Contrast means to account for the differences between two items. The best contrasts refer to both throughout an essay rather than a paragraph about one and then a paragraph about the other. Next is a chart showing important contrasts between the two memory models.

Contrasts between Working Memory (WM) and the Multi-store Model of memory

Topic	Working Memory (WM)	Multi-store Model of Memory
General definition of short-term memory	WM is a newer way to envision the part of short-term memory that someone is actively using. It is your active memory, part of long-term memory that had been activated for use.	Working memory is another way to say short-term memory and it is separate and distinct from long-term memory.
The relationship between short-and long-term memory	WM is part of long-term memory, nesting inside it. WM is just the activated parts of long-term memory for use. Short-term memory is part of WM, and just contains the briefer and fleeting parts of one's memory.	Short-term memory is separate and distinct from long-term memory
Differences in how information moves between short- and long-term memory	Items stay in long-term memory yet WM can activate parts of long-term storage when needed. Remember that WM nests inside long-term memory. WM then moves what needs to go into short-term memory for immediate use.	There is movement from the short-term store to the long-term store and then back but never at the same time (no double sided arrows!). The movement is constrained by the distinction in the model between the short- and long-term stores.
The main emphasis of the models	The emphasis is on activation of information for use and the distinction between short- and long-term memory.	Each component of the memory model is separate and distinct.
Interpretation of the Recency Effect	Recency is reinterpreted as implicit memory that is primed and activated into working memory.	Recency is part of the evidence for distinct memory stores.
Cultural relevance: Is the model universal?	A small body of research validates working memory across cultures.	The serial position effect may not be universal, something cited as evidence for distinct memory stores.

Based on Sternberg & Sternberg (2012) with some additions

12.4: Evaluation of schema theory: Do schemas account for faulty eyewitness memory?

Evaluate means to make a judgment (appraisal) using evidence. It can be argued that **scripts** are one reason for unreliable **eyewitness memory** and evidence supports the conclusion that schemas play some role.

Many variables have been studied to understand why eyewitness memories are unreliable, such as exposure time and arousal level, but what about witness expectation (Greenberg, Westcott, & Bailey, 1998)? Any event activates **scripts** for what is supposed to happen, and when memory for an event is hazy and perhaps a long time has passed, eyewitnesses fill in gaps with scripts. The scripts assist memory but can be distorted. Research shows people have **schemas** about the way a typical crime happens and these expectancies shape the scripts used when recalling what happened during a real crime.

The **aim of the experiment** was to see if scripts for a robbery would create gap-filling errors in memory when participants were asked questions about a robbery event they had seen.

The study had three **independent variables**.

1. Central (main) actions or peripheral (less important) actions removed from the slides
2. Rates of exposure, either 2 or 8 seconds
3. Retention rates, either 5 minutes or 1 week

Procedures are next. Participants watched 24 slides showing a 7-11 store robbery that followed a typical script. The order of events started with the robber entering and pretending to shop, approaching the cashier and demanding money, and then escaping. Slides contained both central and peripheral actions. Central actions included the robber approaching the counter and taking money. Peripheral actions included the cashier removing the money from the register and the robber putting it in his pocket.

Half the participants saw the robbery event with three central actions missing and half saw the slides with three peripheral slides missing. Half saw the slide for 2 seconds and half saw them for 8 seconds. Retention was measured by having half report what they saw after 5 minutes and half after 1 week.

Participants were all given a recognition test with 18 items measuring seen and unseen actions. All questions began with, "Did you see?"

Results showed that participants filled in the gaps in the slides with a common script for the order of events in a robbery.

1. Participants in the central action condition filled in gaps more often than those in the peripheral group, *demonstrating that the script was activated for the actions most likely to be part of people's scripts.*
2. Participants seeing the slides for 2 seconds had more errors than those seeing them for 8 seconds.
3. Participants taking the recognition test a week after seeing the event were more likely to give false answers than those asked after 5 minutes.

The authors **concluded** that scripts are gap-fillers for eyewitnesses and that people have scripts for robberies, even though just 10% of the participants had a personal experience with one. These results have practical applications, and police should question eyewitnesses right after a crime. Waiting to question witnesses means they not only omit important details but introduce details they do not see but know about from a script.

There are other reasons for faulty eyewitness memory, detailed in chapter 14 about evaluations of the reliability of cognitive processes, and students should cross-reference this before making a judgment. However, a judgment about schemas and eyewitness memory should include that it is supported by evidence.

12.5: Evaluation of schema theory: Gender schemas affect academic performance and career choice

Evaluate means to make a judgment (appraisal) using evidence. Gender is "a social category that organizes and shapes children's lives from birth" (Leaper, 2013, p. 326). This conclusion implies that **schemas**, categories used for organization, are important influences on behavior. A specific application to math performance and careers helps create a well developed judgement.

There is ample evidence to support the argument that **gender schema theory** is a primary reason girls are poorly represented in mathematics, engineering, and computer science fields. However, students must avoid thinking that schema is the *only reason* we see differences in academic and career choices, even if there is strong evidence to support this conclusion. Biological and Social Cognitive Theory are two other theories interacting with schemas.

Gender schema theory basics:

Many people theorize about gender schemas, but Sandra Bem is well known. Bem argues that children's **gender schemas** are automatically activated and primed, guiding gender role behavior. This theory is also useful for students studying **developmental psychology**.

Gender schemas are primed early in life and are activated any time someone considers maleness or femaleness about themselves and other things around them, such as hobbies, jobs, or clothing (Bem, 1998, 1981).

Schemas help provide the cognitive consistency children need (Bem, 1998). They are categories children form from observing what is valued by their cultures. Their formation is a constructive process and serves to organize the huge amount of information out there in the world, including evaluations of one's self-concept.

A gender schema is formed when children learn definitions of male and female from observing what is practiced within their culture and form categories of the opposing dimensions 'male' and 'female' based on these definitions (Bem, 1998). Children then use these gender schemas to organize and make sense of all new information about the world.

Once children constructs a gender schema, it primes them to search and sort information based on his or her gender schema (Bem, 1998). The gender schema is a reference point for deciding what is valued about being male or female. All words and even jobs get categorized according to gender schema. Words such as 'tender' or 'eagle' do not

> **Thinking skills: Gender schemas are pancultural**
>
> "Gender is a fundamental, culturally universal social category" (Kapadia & Gala, 2015, p. 319). Similarities in gender differences are found across cultures.
>
> As such, the categories represented in gender schemas reflect one's **subjective culture**. Culture and gender are terms full of values for a group, and are deeply rooted in behavior.
>
> Avoid falling into the trap of thinking the stereotypes found in gender schemas are easy to change or that the feminist movement has ended gender disparities.

necessarily imply feminine or masculine. In the same way, jobs, hobbies, and clothes get categorized. For example, why are dresses necessarily feminine? It is because this definition is valued by a cultural group. (Bem, 1998). The result is that a child applies these schemas to guide what they should do and evaluate their own adequacy as a person.

Bem does not believe gender has to be a category because it is not naturally more perceptible for children than other attributes of a person (Bem, 1998). Anything used as a category for schemas, such as a caste system in some cultures, is relevant only if given significance by the group. Bem promotes raising children free of gender schemas, which she called raising gender-aschematic children. If gender schemas are learned, then they can be unlearned.

Experiments support Bem's gender schema theory. The **aim of one experiment** was to examine gender schemas of 48 male and 48 female participants who were designated as sex typed or non-sex typed through the Bem Sex Role Inventory (Bem, 1981). **Procedures** involved participants seeing 61 randomly ordered words at 3-second intervals, including animal names, proper names, and clothing. Some of the words were feminine and some were masculine (the **independent variable**). After the word presentation, participants wrote down as many as they could recall. **Results** showed that both males and females recalled equal numbers of words, but the order in which the words were recalled differed according to who was designated as sex typed or non-sex typed. A sex-typed participant recalling a feminine word remembered a series of feminine words in clusters. The non-sex typed participants used different clustering. The results support the conclusion that sex-typed people are more likely to create categories based on gender. "As children learn the contents of their society's gender schema, they learn which attributes are to be linked with their own sex, and hence, with themselves" (Bem, 1998, p. 265).

Clothing is gender-typed and you might wonder how it got this way. All cultures have some similarities about which clothes are typed as feminine. Cultural norms for clothes are often harder for boys to cross. What do you think?
Source: pixabay.com.

Gender schema influences on academic performance

Hasn't the feminist movement taken care of any academic performance and resulting occupational differences between males and females? Common sense would conclude it has, but research suggests otherwise. We still have gender differences in academics, and it affects interests and skills needed for career success (Leaper, 2013). It is clearly documented that males and females tend to stay away from occupations that are different from their gender role expectations, and **gender schema** research helps us understand why.

At least in the US, females have lower high school dropout rates and get more bachelor's and master's degrees than males (Leaper, 2013). However, males get more doctoral, medical, and law degrees than females.

Differences also exist for specific subjects (Leaper, 2013). Girls are better at reading, writing, and standardized verbal tests through high school than boys. In contrast, boys are better in the physical sciences than girls, though at the high school level the gap narrows.

Gender differences exist in careers requiring the most mathematics, such as geoscience, engineering, economics, mathematics, computer science, and physical sciences (Ceci, Ginther, Kahn & Williams, 2014).

> **Thinking skills: Gender stereotyping is pancultural**
> There is great cross-cultural similarity in the words associated with maleness and femaleness. In the previous chapter under the section about stereotyping, students saw the words consistently labeled male or female. These stereotypes are part of gender schemas and influence behavior.

Differences in science show up at the college level (Leaper, 2013). Males get far more degrees in physics (78%), computer science (78%), and engineering (80%). Females may get an equal amount of doctoral degrees in life sciences, but they get few doctoral degrees in mathematics (27%), physics (just 15%), computer science (20%), and engineering (18%).

This is puzzling because females excel more in reading and writing, the gender gap has closed for general mathematics, and some females have high level math abilities. It seems as if people with both math and verbal abilities should have more job choices. However, females are still underrepresented in certain fields (Leaper, 2013). We therefore must evaluate research showing why women who may have a wider range of abilities than men still choose careers reflecting gender-typed values.

Theories suggesting that biological advantages, such as the hormone testosterone that might give males the edge in spatial skills, are hard to support (Leaper, 2013). Biological theories also fails to explain why there are fewer gender differences in the middle group of math skills but why there are bigger gaps in science and math careers.

Gender differences in beliefs about math skills and jobs in particular show up in kindergarten and increase into college (Ceci, et al., 2014). Research over a number of decades suggests that gender stereotypes about specific school subjects influence someone's academic self-concept and the occupations associated with these subjects (Leaper, 2013). This is where gender schema theory is helpful.

Schemas are categories in our minds useful for interpreting social situations (Valian, 2009). Schemas include **stereotypes** and all the rules needed to navigate the social world. We need social schemas because they provide valuable information about people and their social groupings. However, schemas, like stereotypes, tend to *oversimplify*, and this is where people make mistakes. Gender schemas are hypotheses (proposed explanations) about maleness and femaleness that people have a tendency to share.

There is ample evidence from research conducted over a number of decades to show that gender schemas "skew perceptions and evaluations of men and women, causing them to overrate men and underrate women" (Valian, 2009, p. 32). Gender schemas therefore are judgments about people's abilities and value that influence behavior.

When reading the following studies, try to think of relevant ethical considerations that should be applied and brainstorm ways to work them into essays so ethics (and any other research method critique) is not just tacked on to the end of an essay.

Research evidence: Gender schemas influence competence and social evaluations in gender-typed occupations

Women may not pick academic majors related to male gender-typed jobs because of messages that they will not be as competent as men in those jobs. Remember from studying Bem's theory that gender schemas are primed from early in life anytime someone considers maleness and femaleness about themselves or other things in the world (Bem, 1998, 1981).

An example experiment from the body of research on this topic shows how schemas become activated when judging women's competence for a male-typed job (Heilman, Wallen, Fuchs, & Tamkins, 2004).

Gender stereotypes both describe differences between males and females and prescribe social norms for acceptable behavior. Even when women preform well in a male-typed job they still get gender biased evaluations and social penalties.

The **aim of this experiment** was to show the reactions to men and women in male-typed jobs when both clearly had preformed well. The study had two hypotheses.

> **Thinking skills: Gender schema research stands the test of time**
> Four decades of research demonstrates how gender schemas affect behavior.
>
> Gender schemas are a problem because they include **stereotypes** learned early and are automatically activated when decisions are made (Kapadia & Gala, 2015). Even when someone is older and thinks a stereotype is inaccurate and not helpful, automatically activated stereotypes are still likely to influence behavior because it is hard to get rid of over-learned stereotypes. In addition, the process of **socialization** constantly bombards people with gender stereotypes.

1. Women would be judged less competent and less achievement-oriented when descriptions of their performance were ambiguous rather than clearly stated.
2. Women would be judged less likable and more hostile than men when information about their success on the job was clearly stated and not ambiguous.

Procedures are next. Participants read a job description about a Vice President in an aircraft company responsible for sales and training executives, and understanding tasks such as assembling engines and using fuel tanks were important for success. Each participant rated a male and female employee, counterbalanced so half rated the male first and the other half the female first. A third employee, a male was also rated but was done so last and not used in the results. The purpose of the third dummy employee was to help with the male gender-typing of the job.

The **independent variables** were whether the raters were male or female and whether the judgment was based on a clear evaluation or an ambiguous evaluation.

The two evaluation statements used in the experiment follow.

Clear evaluation statement "Andrea (James) has recently undergone the company-wide annual performance review and she (he) received consistently high evaluations. She (he) has been designated as a "stellar performer" based on sales volume, number of new client accounts, and actual dollars earned. Her (his) performance is in the top 5% of all employees at her (his) level" (p. 418).	**Ambiguous evaluation statement** "Andrea (James) has undergone the company-wide performance review and she (he) was evaluated very highly by all reviewers. She (he) was highly praised for her (his) sales volume figures, number of new client accounts, and actual dollars earned. She (he) has been identified as one of a small group of rising stars. Her (his) performance is in the top 5% of all the company VPs" (p. 418).

Results supported both hypotheses.

1. Women were rated less competent and achievement-oriented in the ambiguous condition. Women were not judged equal to men until their performance was clearly stated.
2. Women were rated as less likable and more hostile when their performance was clearly stated but not when performance was ambiguous.

It was **concluded** that women must perform extremely well and this must be clearly stated for them to be judged as competent as men. However, being judged competent has a social consequence for women as less likable and more hostile.

Note that both male and female participants judged the employees the same way, so even females used stereotyped norms as a basis for their judgments. There are penalties for violating accepted social norms and these rules are in our gender schemas.

Research evidence: Field-specific ability beliefs (FAB) and stereotypes about gender and ability work together to influence women to stay away from STEM (science, technology, engineering, math) fields

Can you quickly name 10 women who are well-known and noted for their brilliance (Meyer, Cimpian, & Leslie, 2015)? This task can be challenging and people seem to quickly run out of names or have to stop and really think.

The stereotype that 'femaleness' is not associated with innate brilliance is widespread in our culture, well documented, and has great consequences (Meyer, et al., 2015). One consequence is that females are not as likely to choose academic subjects needed to enter careers that are assumed to require innate brilliance. The assumption that innate brilliance is required for some careers is called the **field-specific ability belief** (FAB).

Remember that gender schemas are primed early in life and are activated anytime someone considers maleness or femaleness about themselves or other things (Bem, 1998; 1981). FABs about jobs having male characteristics such as innate brilliance work along with stereotypes about gender and is one reason women stay away from **STEM careers** (Meyer, et al., 2015).

The pathway for FAB contribution to gender gaps in STEM fields follows (Meyer, et al., 2015).

FABS + Stereotypes that men have more raw = Gender gaps in STEM fields
                           intellectual abilities

The **aim of one correlation study** was to see if people in the general public held FABs and if these were correlated to women's rates of entering STEM careers (Meyer, et al., 2015). Research already shows that academics hold FABs and these are correlated to women's underrepresentation in STEM careers. If the general public also holds FABs, then it could influence female's choices for school subjects even more, especially when paired with general stereotypes about differences in male and female intellectual abilities.

The main prediction was that the beliefs of the general public will predict female representation in a career. This means that if a career is believed to require innate brilliance, there will be fewer females in it.

Participants took the survey online. Surveys asked questions about beliefs about a variety of subjects that included STEM courses, participant's exposure to these subjects in school, and estimations of the number of females in each academic field.

Examples of the questions testing participant beliefs (Meyer, et al., 2015, p. 6).

1. "Being a top scholar of [field] requires a special aptitude that just can't be taught."
2. "With the right amount of effort and dedication, anyone can become a top scholar in [field]."
3. "To succeed in [field] you have to be a special type of person; not just anyone can be successful in it."

Results supported the prediction. Correlations showed that females were less represented in fields in which participants believed innate brilliance was required.

The authors **concluded** that FABs were an important factor in how females were represented across academic subjects, as FABs were usually paired with stereotypes that females lacked the same intellectual abilities as males. FABs are important and point to where effort should be made to change stereotypes and beliefs.

Research evidence: Altering stereotypes increases girls' sense of belonging and interest in computer science and engineering

The popular **Mattel doll Barbie** became a source of controversy when a book was released in 2010 along with the new 'Computer Engineer Barbie,' with Barbie saying she only wrote software and needed the help of two men to fix computers.

This was not the only controversy for Barbie. Also in 2010, Mattel wanted girls to vote for the next Barbie theme (Cheryan, Master, & Meltzoff, 2015). The choices were computer engineer, architect, news anchor, surgeon, or environmentalist. Both computer engineer Barbie and news anchor Barbie were released, computer engineer Barbie because of the campaign from female engineers and technology specialists, and news anchor Barbie because she was the most popular all around with the girls.

However you judge these Barbies and others that have been controversial, they may symbolize a long-standing problem—women equal men in non-STEM fields but are still underrepresented in careers related to mathematics, engineering, and science (Cheryan, et al., 2015). We cannot just assume that women are not interested in STEM fields because they have caught up in other careers they were not previously choosing. Perhaps we must ask what has happened for females to catch up with males in non-STEM careers but still lag behind in computer science and engineering.

There is enough evidence to make a judgment that "stereotypes of the field act as educational gatekeepers, constraining who enters the field, and that interventions to broaden cultural representation of these fields can help to draw more diversity into them" (Cheryan, et al., 2015, p. 2).

Recall that gender schemas are primed

> **Inquiry activity: Toy and job stereotypes**
> What role might toys have in creating stereotypes about male and female jobs?
>
> In 1992, Teen Talk Barbie had a chip allowing her to say four things, one of which was "math is tough." The chip was removed after outcries, but the doll may have already done some damage.
>
> The class might do some research about toys and academic/job stereotypes and draw some tentative conclusions. Not all toys promote stereotypes, so watch going into this activity with a specific outcome in mind. Look specifically at STEM job related toys versus other occupations.
>
> **Youtube** has the Teen Talk Barbie video. Also look at the most recent Barbie advertisements, including Youtube, where Barbie let's girls be what they want to be and also the ones showing the new Barbie body types. What role might Barbie and other toys play?
>
> How might you design a study to find out?
>
>
>
> Are these toys as innocent as they look? This topic relates to **developmental psychology** when we ask the question of how gender-typed toy choice is created. What role does gender schema play?
> Source: pixabay.com

from early in life anytime someone considers maleness and femaleness about themselves or other things in the world (Bem, 1998, 1981). Boys and girls have stereotypes about math abilities in elementary school and research clearly links these stereotypes to lower math performance in girls (Cheryan, et al., 2015). Because these stereotypes start so early in life, they contribute to girls failing to choose academic subjects necessary for computer science and engineering from the start.

Well-defended judgments should include details about the content of computer science and engineering stereotypes and how they lead to women failing to choose STEM jobs.

Stereotypes are found in three places, the people who take these jobs, the work environment, and the values linked with the jobs (Cheryan, et al., 2015). When these combine with stereotypes about male and females differences in ability, it is a main contributor to female participation in these careers. Next is a model of the pathway.

Stereotypes: The job culture
1. People are socially isolated, geeky males with glasses.
2. Work is not a helping occupation and with little chance for collaboration
3. Job values are masculine, such as playing video games, and requires genius

Result:
Females are less likely to choose careers in computer science and engineering

Stereotypes: Ability differences

Boys are better suited for math because they have more innate ability

Source: Based on Cheryan, et al., 2015

Well-defended judgments also include the three main sources of gender stereotypes about computer science and engineering and how research shows these stereotypes can be altered. This table summarizes these sources and research providing evidence stereotypes can change (Cheryan, et al., 2015).

Media	Narrow characterizations of people in the careers	Environment: Cues gained from setting and objects
Source: Movies, for example, portray computer scientists and engineers as male, White or Asian, and without social skills. High school students say media influences them more than any other source.	Source: Computer and engineering websites may include a female who is supposed to be a role model for girls, but includes stereotypes for the field, such as she enjoys working independently (interpreted as social isolation). This suggests to girls that they must fit a stereotype to be successful.	Source: Environments in which the work is to be done can be male stereotyped. Objects in rooms are cues to what is expected.

Media	Narrow characterizations of people in the careers	Environment: Cues gained from setting and objects
Ways to change stereotype: Research results: Girls read one of two news articles, one with stereotypes and one saying the roles are becoming more diverse. The group with the more diverse message said they said they were more interested in computers and engineering than girls reading stereotyped content.	**Ways to change the stereotype**: Research results: Girls interacted with people posing as computer scientists. All told participants they were college juniors majoring in computer science, but half were stereotyped for the field and the others were not. For example, stereotypes included shirts saying "I code therefore I am" and reports about playing video games for fun. The non-stereotyped people said they liked to be with friends and wore clothing without computer phrases. Girls interacting with the non-stereotyped people said they were more interested in computer science.	**Ways to change the stereotype**: Research results: Girls who entered a computer science classroom with non-stereotyped objects, such as nature posters, general interest books, and water bottles reported more interest in computer science than girls who entered a computer science room with stereotyped objects, such as Star Trek posters and piles of soda cans.

The authors conclude it is not necessary to "de-geek" computer science and engineering occupations. Instead, show girls they do not necessarily have to fit the stereotype to be part of the field. You may wonder if it is fair to tell girls they do not have to fit a stereotype when they will see plenty of it in those careers and must manage situations with those people. However, consider that these stereotypes are not always the case, and it might open the door for diversity in these professions.

Perhaps the only way for women to be equally represented in all the STEM careers is to change the stereotypes within gender schemas. Females do seem to need interventions to get past long established gender stereotypes. The next section explains why.

Wait a minute: Aren't gender schemas hard to change?

The opinions and research presented above can't be so easy to achieve! The challenge is that children create their gender identities from gender schemas, which are made up of categories that are already evident by 14 months (Kapadia & Gala, 2015). Young children have cognitions about male and female early, and clearly show gender stereotypes in their behavior by age 3. This increases until age 5-7, when children develop some degree of gender flexibility that grows until age 11. However, developing some gender flexibility is not enough to override the strong stereotypes learned early that are activated any time children consider maleness and femaleness about themselves or others, including things. Stereotypes therefore develop when children are too young to have the cognitive abilities to consider them carefully.

Research even demonstrates that girls have stronger cognitions for gender than boys (Kapadia & Gala, 2015). By 18 months, girls show preferences for girl-typed toys and can match faces and voices of girl-typed toys as well as boy-typed toys. Boys cannot do this even by 24 months. By 24 months the girls could correctly select toys to match gender-typed tasks.

To sum up the problem, stereotypes are learned young and are automatically activated when decisions are made (Kapadia & Gala, 2015). Even when someone is older and thinks a stereotype is inaccurate and not helpful, automatically activated stereotypes are still likely to determine behavior because it is hard to get rid of the over-learned stereotypes. In addition, the process of **socialization** constantly bombards people with gender stereotypes.

It is therefore understandable why it may take monumental efforts to change the contents of gender schemas that drive many females away from STEM careers.

Thinking skills: Make good generalizations and enjoy your learning through in-depth study

The best critical thinkers understand that conclusions such as "boys are better than girls at math" are superficial and overgeneralized. Certain aspects of behavior may be different, and sweeping generalizations are not helpful. An example of a good generalization is "boys and girls have similar cognitive abilities related to math, but there are robust differences in some skills, such as spatial rotation tasks that need examination."

Students develop an appreciation for the nuances of behavior differences when a topic is studied in depth. It is more interesting and helps students avoid thinking fallacies.

My recommendation is to never end your study of a topic with a general text.

12.6 Evaluate schema theory: Gender schemas and aggression

Evaluate means to make a judgment (appraisal) using evidence. Children learn gender **stereotypes** early and research shows that by age 5, boys use direct forms of **aggression** and girls use indirect forms (Leaper, 2013). This material is also relevant for **developmental psychology** when considering how boys might be socialized to choose male-typed toys.

Schema is not the only explanation of aggression, but there is compelling evidence that schema plays an important role. Remember from studying genetics that genes are not really a reliable predictor of actual behavior, and generally can contribute only to a risk. Genes are not a direct path to why someone is aggressive so schema theory should be carefully considered as a better reason for the actual start of aggression. Be sure to review the material from Social Cognitive Theory in the sociocultural ATP because Bandura thinks modeling and self-efficacy are greater predictors of behavior than schema. Students must weight the evidence and make a judgment that can be supported.

One model shows how aggression stereotypes are reflected in gender schemas that influence behavior. This is the **Integrated Gender-Linked Model of Aggression Subtypes** (Ostrov & Godleski, 2010). The model combines two earlier models into something more streamlined and explains how beliefs about gender-congruent behavior held in schemas become automatic behavior. This components of this newer model have been researched and supported over four decades, and demonstrates the influence of gender schemas on aggression.

The model has 6 parts. Gender schema is part of each step.

Step #1: Encoding
Gender related peer experiences are encoded into memory and are available as cues for what to do whenever a child is in an ambiguous situation and they feel provoked. The encoded cues are most often consistent with a child's gender schema.

Step #2: Interpretation

Cues about what to do in a provoking social situation are interpreted and directly influenced by gender schemas. For example, if a girl feels slighted by a group of other girls, and the situation is ambiguous in any way, she is likely to feel distressed and interpret the girl's slights as hostile if other experiences with girls are similar and her gender schemas tell her this is what girls do when they are aggressive.

Step #3: Clarify goals

Gender schema is important when children clarify their goals for possible action when provoked. Goals most appropriate for their gender are likely to be considered first.

Step #4: Considering how to respond

This is when a child considers possible responses (not to use aggression, use physical aggression, or use relational aggression). The choice is based on experience and gender schema. Schemas are particularly influenced by self-construals (independent for boys or interdependent for girls) affecting which responses are most judged most important.

Step #5: Deciding what to do

Children are most likely to choose the behavior consistent with their gender in-group. However, when a child evaluates a behavior option that is outside their gender schema, the behavior is less likely to be used.

Step #6: Either uses aggression or not

During and after its use, the child stores information about the usefulness of the behavior. Since the behavior is usually consistent with stereotypes held within the gender schema, over time it becomes automatic without a conscious effort to think through the steps.

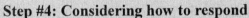

Integrated Gender-linked Model of Aggression Subtypes
Source: Based on Ostrov & Godleski (2010).

Research evidence: Aggression subtypes model is supported

Aggression, toy selection, and playmate choice are the most identified sex-typed behaviors. The **aim of the correlation study** was to investigate the relationship between children who passed a gender-labeling task and these three behaviors (Fagot, Leinbach, & Hagan, 1986). This study supports the overall idea of the Integrated Gender-Linked Model of Aggression Subtypes that beliefs about gender-congruent behavior are part of gender schemas, and these schemas influence aggression.

For the **procedures**, children looked at a series of pictures and said if it was "boy" or "girl." Children who passed this test were assumed to be able to apply these labels to themselves. Some children passed and others did not, and all were participants.

It was predicted that children who passed the gender-labeling test would choose gender stereotyped toys and playmates, and that boys would show aggression but girls would not.

Children were then filmed while playing and observers coded their behaviors related to aggression, toy selection, and playmate choice.

Results confirmed the prediction for both aggression and playmate choice. Correlations about aggression were striking. Aggression scores for girls who passed the gender-labeling test were far lower than girls who did not pass it. This suggests that once a girl learns gender-typed labels, she changes her behavior. Boys who did not pass the gender-labeling test had fairly similar aggression scores to the boys who did pass it because boys do not have to change their behavior once they have an intact gender schema.

The authors **concluded** that children start learning gender schemas from birth, and once they can verbalize the gender-typed labels, their behavior is consistent with the schemas.

Research evidence to support step #4 of the Integrated Gender-linked Model of Aggression Subtypes

A body of research spanning four decades supports this part of the model, suggesting that gender schemas influence the possible responses to aggression as being appropriate or inappropriate for one's gender.

Rather than picking one particular study as an example, next is a summary of research conclusions supporting step #4 of the model.

Thinking skills: Important background information to understand this section
Self-construals (the way one views the self) develop during the **enculturation** process, turning into **schemas** about what to do in any situation. Part of the enculturation process for self-construals includes the categories of **independent self** (unique and autonomous) or **interdependent self** (connected and relational), one **cultural dimension**. Research shows boys are enculturated toward a tendency for an independent self-construal and girls to an interdependent self-construal (Ostrov & Godleski, 2010; Rose & Rudolph, 2006; Cross & Madson, 1997)). Both self-construals affect which responses to stress and conflict in relationships are considered.

The self dimension (a **cultural dimension**) is detailed more in chapter 20 and enculturation is detailed in chapters 22 and 23.

Overall, males tend to use direct aggression and females tend to use indirect use aggression, and their responses to conflict reflect self-construals deeply engrained in gender schemas (Cross & Madson, 1997).

1. Girls with an interdependent self-construal are less likely to respond to conflict in a way that might threaten a relationship.

2. Girls have different representations of aggression in their minds than boys, can view direct physical aggression as a failure to control emotions.

3. Indirect aggression is used more often, is more subtle, and includes talking behind someone's back, telling secrets, and excluding other girls from groups.

4. Indirect aggression is "well suited to the needs and goals of individuals with an interdependent self-construal because it can protect existing relationships from the target's feelings of resentment, revenge, or both" (p. 22).

> **Thinking skills: Gender schemas give us the same problem again**
> Gender schemas are a problem because they include stereotypes learned early and are automatically activated when decisions are made (Kapadia & Gala, 2015). Even when someone is older and thinks a stereotype is inaccurate and not helpful, automatically activated stereotypes are still likely to influence behavior because it is hard to get rid of over-learned stereotypes.

5. Females use more indirect aggression as they get older when their social groups and networks increase. Females are well-known for spreading rumors and excluding others.

Criticisms of schema theory

Albert Bandura is an important critic of schema theory and a good choice for considering limitations since students must study modeling and self-efficacy in the sociocultural ATP. A discussion of Bandura's criticisms can be found in chapter 19 and generally, Bandura says cognitive theories downplay the contributions of environmental factors. Bandura claims that children model early and also self-regulate by age 4, and neither requires the child to have gender constancy.

Students interested in **developmental psychology** might use both gender schema theory and Bandura's Social Cognitive Theory of gender.

12.7: Explain and evaluate theories of thinking and decision-making

Explain includes giving reasons and causes. Heuristics are reasons people sometimes make poor decisions and experiments provide causal evidence of this. However, heuristics can also be helpful.

It was once assumed that decision making was a conscious, deliberate, and controlled thinking (System 2) using based probability reasoning (Newell, 2013). **Bayes's theorem** is one example of deliberate thinking for finding out what we do not know from the information we do know. When reading the medical decision making research, understand that medical students are taught to use Baysian reasoning. However, research shows they use heuristics instead in many instances and this can lead to perfectly good judgments.

> **Class activity**
> Students can look up Bayes's theorem and work through a problem using it. How much of real life decision making is done this way?

The assumption that people use more deliberate reasoning just is not the reality of decision making! We instead use mental shortcuts, leading some early theorists to call humans "cognitive cripples" (Newell, 2013, p. 606). When Tversky and Kahneman published some early work on heuristics, they did not mean to paint a picture of humans as poor decision makers, but instead showed how the process really worked—we used heuristics much of the time because of so much uncertainty. So the study of heuristics makes up a great deal of decision making. People can be System 2 thinkers, but it takes more effort.

Evaluate means to make a judgment (appraisal) using evidence. There is ample evidence to show that **heuristics** influence decision making, and we are often not aware of how often they are used, evidence for the **System 1-System 2** continuum.

Heuristics influence many areas of decision making, and when making an evaluation, students should consider classic research as well as research investigating their use in daily life, such as judging **food intake/calories** and **medical decision making**.

It is impossible to examine research from all the types of heuristics, so this is a sample of what is out there.

Classic research evidence: The anchoring and adjustment heuristic

One example of an **anchoring and adjustment** experiment follows. The **aim of the experiment** was to investigate the judgment problem of insufficient adjustment (Tversky & Kahneman, 1974).

For **procedures**, participants judged the percent of African countries in the United Nations. The **independent variable** was either the larger or smaller anchor. The anchor was selected from a number between 0-100 selected by spinning a wheel as everyone watched. For example, one group got the anchor number 10 and the other 65. Participants first judged if the number of African nations in the United Nations was greater or less than the anchor and then estimated it as a percentage.

Results showed that the group with the smaller anchor number estimated 25% and the group with the larger anchor number estimated 45%, demonstrating the influence of anchors on decision making.

Research evidence: Judgments about how much food someone eats: Application of the anchoring and adjustment heuristic

One application of the anchoring and adjustment heuristic is related to **health psychology**. The **anchoring and adjustment heuristic** provides one reason people have trouble sticking to diets. Anchors play a role in making poor decisions about how many calories or how much food is consumed. **Portion size** seems to matter when making food intake judgments.

Why do people eat more food when served a large portion and less when served a small portion? The **aim of one experiment** was to see if the presence of an anchor caused someone to estimate how much they would eat (Marchiori, Papies, & Klein, 2014).

Procedures are next. Participants were randomly assigned to one of two anchor groups or a non-anchor group, the **independent variable**. The anchor groups visualized large or small portions of food and estimated how much they would eat. Half of the participants in both anchor groups were told the imagined portion size was randomly chosen and should not influence their estimate of what they would eat. Estimations from both anchor groups were compared to a group that did not visualize portion sizes and just judged how much food they would eat.

Results showed that those who imagined large portions estimated they would eat more and those imagining smaller portions estimated they would eat less. The group without any anchor estimated the least amount. The warning that the portion size imagined should have no effect on their answers did nothing to change the estimates of anyone in either anchor groups.

The researchers **concluded** that the anchoring and adjustment heuristic was a good explanation for the poor judgment used when estimating food intake relative to portion size.

We seem to be terrible judges of the amount we eat and it is likely because of anchoring and adjustment. Apparently if we imagine the smaller portion of cookies we will estimate eating a smaller amount. But who wants just a small portion of cookies! Used with license from megapixl.com.

More research evidence: The calorie illusion: Application of the anchoring and adjustment heuristic

The negative **calorie illusion** lurks in the background of people's judgments when counting calories. This means people underestimate the calorie count of unhealthy foods when they are paired with a healthy food (Forwood, Ahern, Hollands, Fletcher, & Marteau, 2013).

How might we explain the negative calorie illusion? Some research concludes it is because of an averaging effect, where the healthy and unhealthy foods are seen together and then averaged, so the **aim of the experiment** was to clarify if the cause was really averaging or if it was because of the **anchoring and adjustment heuristic**.

The authors hypothesized that participants did not average the calories but used the anchor meal to make a judgment, failing to make the needed adjustment.

Procedures are next. Participants were assigned to one of 4 groups, the **independent variable**. All the anchor meals were listed as having 500 calories.

> **Class activity**
> These two food intake judgment experiments are easy to replicate in class. Teachers do not need to deceive students acting as study participants! This is because the tendency is to think our judgments are good and to automatically use an anchor.
> If you find different results, consider if it is not because of prior learning. The use of System 2 thinking should help people make better judgements.

1. Participants saw a main meal (an anchor) followed by a test meal by itself.
2. Participants saw a main meal (an anchor) followed by a test meal that included a small healthy side dish.
3. Participants saw a main meal (an anchor) including a small healthy side dish and then saw a test meal.
4. Participants saw a main (an anchor) that included a small healthy side dish and then saw a test meal with a small healthy side dish.

Results showed that group #3 judged the meal to have the fewest calories (600). The other groups were higher, with #1 judging 674 calories, #2 judging 638 calories, and group #4 judging 639.

The authors **concluded** that the anchor caused the variations in calorie judgment.

Classic research evidence: Availability heuristic

The **aim of one experiment** about the **availability heuristic** was to demonstrate what happens when we are unable to conduct a complete mental search for all real instances of something and instead must create a rule based on the instances of something that are similar and available to us (Tversky & Kahneman, 1973).

Procedures are next. This experiment used the problem of figuring out if a letter, for example R, was more likely to be the first or third letter of in words. In reality, just 8 letters appear more frequently in the third position in words, the letters, D, X, Z, K, L, N, R, and V. This study used 3 of these letters.

Participants were instructed to judge, for example:

If the letter R is more likely to be in _____ *the first position (in words).*
_____ *the third position (in words).*

Next everyone was asked to estimate a ratio of these two values of the larger to the smaller, or _____ *:1.*

Groups were varied by the position they saw first and the letters to create different conditions (the **independent variable**) for the experiment.

Results showed that of 152 participants, 105 thought the letter R (or other selected letters) was most often seen in the first position. In fact, all 5 of the most common letters studied (excluding X and Z) were judged to be more likely in the first position.

This same result was also found in repeated measures studies, so the authors **concluded** that the evidence was solid.

Research evidence: Judgments about medical diagnoses can be influenced by the availability and anchoring/adjustment heuristics

Many students want to go into a **medical profession**, so this is a good chance to learn something about the heuristics used in medical diagnoses. It can be argued that medical professionals use heuristics when making decisions and that much of the time they are helpful although sometimes heuristics hinder correct diagnosis and treatment.

Medical professionals use a variety of heuristics when making diagnoses, and without them there is so much information to sift through that decision making would be impossible (Vickrey, Samuels, & Ropper, 2010). However, this does not mean that the use of a heuristic automatically results in poor decisions. Physicians should learn about heuristics because they are not aware they use them, especially when they are trained in medical school to use **System 2 reasoning**.

The research on medical diagnosis and heuristics consists of experiments, surveys, correlation studies, and case studies. Just do not assume that this **method triangulation** automatically demonstrates a large body of research. The authors all noted the need for more research about of the role of heuristics in medical decisions.

Two example studies are reviewed next so you can get an idea of what is published.

The **aim of one survey study** was to show how the availability heuristic is used in medical decision-making. Physicians were asked if they ever had a situation where a patient was negatively affected because they did not get a blood transfusion when they might have had one (Vickrey, et al., 2010). They were also asked to estimate the actual risk of negative effects from not getting a transfusion. **Results** showed that overwhelmingly, physicians who had the personal experience with a patient estimated the risk of negative effects much higher than the actual risk. Their estimations were also much higher than doctors who had not had the personal experience. This is an example of the **availability heuristic** and medical decisions.

The **anchoring and adjustment heuristic** can also create biases because physicians tend to judge an initial diagnosis from either extreme, 0% or 100%, and fail to adjust enough when given more details (Vickrey, et al., 2010).

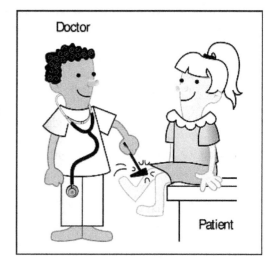

Doctors use heuristics more often than you might think when making a diagnosis. To what extent is it a good thing or a problem?
Source: pixabay.com.

The **aim of one experiment** was to see if Internal Medicine residents making diagnoses would be different if exposed to an **anchor** (Phang, Ravani, Schaefer, Wright, & McLaughlin, 2015). Case summaries were created with target diagnoses, some loaded with information about the patient and some with fewer details. One of the conditions provided a high or low anchor for the target condition hypothyroidism. These conditions were tested as follows.

1. High anchor condition: Participants rated their agreement with the statement "In females under the age of 30 with weight loss of > 10% the prevalence of hypothyroidism is > 95%" (p. e74).
2. Low anchor condition: Participants rated their agreement with the statement "In females under the age of 30 with weight loss > 10% the prevalence of hypothyroidism is <0.000001%" (p. e74).

Results showed that doctors made the most correct diagnoses when they received the patient summary with the most information and also with the high anchor.

Medical schools tend to perceive heuristics as damaging to a doctor's thinking but this is not necessarily true. Doctors receive training in probability reasoning but somehow still switch to using heuristics when making a diagnosis. Why do they do this? It is hard to know but the authors believe the limitations of **working memory** play a role. Heuristics allow decisions to be made with less effort and people lack the necessary information for **System 2** thinking. Heuristics may even lead to better diagnoses because of the limitations of working memory!

Conclusions about thinking and decision making: Strengths and limitations

Strengths	Limitations
Heuristics can help us make good decisions so avoid thinking they always lead to errors.	Some critics say the labels "availability," "representativeness," or "anchor" are simplistic and fail to show underlying mechanisms involved in making a decision (Newell, 2013).
There is ample evidence to support the conclusion that we use heuristics in decision making and they do not always lead to poor decisions.	As stated in the last chapter under the section about System 1 and System 2 thinking, it remains to be seen if this continues to be a useful framework.
Research about heuristics shows that it is successful in offering us a **coherence approach** to thinking focusing on general rules and a **correspondence approach** showing it has real life applications (Newell, 2013). It is a nice combination of both theory and application.	
The dual processing approach (System 1 and System 2 thinking) is widely used and helps us understand humans as "activated actors" with access to both automatic thinking and conscious controlled processing (Fiske & Taylor, 2008).	

12.8: Evaluate the Theory of Planned Behavior

Evaluate means to make a judgment (appraisal) using evidence. The **theory of planned behavior** (TPB) has been studied over many decades as applied to many behaviors, especially **health psychology**.

Explain includes giving reasons. These strength and limitations are the reasons the theory has some value yet may still have some weaknesses.

Strengths	Limitations
Research over time suggests that the theory of planned behavior is a good predictor of intentions. For example, a meta-analysis (a correlation study examining the results of a large number of studies) showed the theory of planned behavior was a good predictor of health intentions, especially addictions (Godin & Kok, 1996). Perceived control adds to the theory's predictive ability and researchers have known about this for a long time.	The research is mostly correlation and this never implies a cause and effect relationship. Be careful when interpreting study results. Therefore, the TPB lacks **method triangulation**, or validation from studies using other research methods.
It has **time triangulation** and **observer triangulation**.	Perceived control was added to the earlier theory of reasoned action to create the theory of planned behavior, and this change relied on the concept **self-efficacy**. It could be argued that the concept perceived control relies too heavily on **Social Cognitive Theory's** concept self efficacy. Social Cognitive Theory could be a more comprehensive theory. Bandura (2004) points out that other health promotion models are very similar to his theory and are just different ways to describe self-efficacy or outcome expectations. In addition, Bandura feels Social Cognitive Theory offers the best ideas for educating people about managing their health. It does little good to predict behavior if there is not a clear path to changing it.
It is a revision of the earlier **theory of reasoned action** and stands up better in research because perceived control is added to the model.	How well does the theory explain actual behavior? This is one criticism from Bandura and worth considering because the research focuses more on intentions, though intentions and actual behavior are considered closely linked. Social Cognitive Theory has been tested with success for changing actual behavior. Ajzen (2015) knows that many studies about the theory of planned behavior limit their goals to studying intention, but there are some targeting actual behavior. Increasing **fish consumption** and **breastfeeding** are two examples but the studies have conflicting results.
It has cross-cultural relevance, meaning it has **space triangulation.**	It is not as good a predictor of getting medical screenings (Godin & Kok, 1996).

Research evidence: TBP and addictions

The **theory of planned behavior** has been shown effective in predicting intentions to treat **addictions**.

The **aim of one correlation study** was to show that the theory of planned behavior was useful for predicting who would complete substance abuse treatment (Zemore & Ajzen, 2014). Predicting who is at risk for failing to complete treatment is critical because drop-out rates are so high, averaging about 40%. Participants were part of an outpatient treatment program in California who answered a number of surveys measuring all parts of the theory of planned behavior as well as treatment motivation. **Results** showed that intentions to finish treatment were correlated the most to attitudes and perceived control. The authors note that this was a fairly small sample and want to see other similar research. However, these findings fit in with a larger body of research about applying the theory of planned behavior to addictions that has been conducted over decades.

**Sample survey questions
(Zemore & Ajzen, 2014, p. 178)**
1. I plan to complete my treatment program. (intention)
2. I will complete my treatment program. (intention)
3. If I wanted to, I could easily complete my treatment program. (perceived control)
4. It is up to me whether I complete my treatment program. (perceived control).
5. Most of my friends and class mates drink alcohol. (subjective norm)

Research evidence: TPB and eating healthier food

The **theory of planned behavior** seems a good predictor of intentions to eat healthier diets.

The **aim of one correlation study** was to investigate how the cognitive aspects of the theory of planned action were related to someone's intention to eat less **junk food** (Ajzen & Sheikh, 2013). Survey questions in the gray box above were used with the words "fast food" substituted for alcohol-related words. **Results** showed that the intention to eat less junk food was predicted by attitudes toward food.

Many correlations studies investigate how the theory of planned behavior influences intentions to limit **sugar-sweetened beverages**. One example found that intentions to cut down were influenced by norms in teenagers and attitudes in their parents (Riebl, et al., 2016). The authors concluded that although it is helpful for parents to encourage less consumption, other people important to adolescents should also encourage it as norms are important to teens.

What about actually changing behavior beyond having an intention to do so? **The aim of another correlation study** was to test *both intentions and behavior* to see if the theory of planned behavior was a good predictor of the intentions to increase **fish consumption** and the *actual behavior* of eating more (Verbeke & Vackier, 2005).

This study had many hypotheses and two of interest follow.

Reducing soda consumption can be hard. Can following the Theory of Planned Behavior help?
Source: pixabay.com.

1. Attitude, norms, and perceived control will be positively correlated to the intention to eat fish.
2. One's intention to eat more fish and perceived control will be positively correlated to *eating more fish* (the behavior).

Data were collected with surveys. For example, questions about attitude asked about beliefs toward eating fish and participants rated their attitude on scales such as good versus bad, beneficial versus harmful, and pleasant versus unpleasant. Questions about norms asked for example, the extent to which people and institutions thought it was a good idea for the person to eat fish. Perceived control questions included " I can make many different meals with fish" (p. 81). Participants were also asked about their consumption.

Results supported both hypotheses. The most important finding was that the habit to eat fish was influenced by perceived control and this then predicted higher intentions and actually eating more fish.

The sample was from the coastal area of West Flanders where many people fish for a living, so this location probably influenced the habit of eating more fish.

Next let's move on to studies conducted in different parts of the world to see the cultural relevance of the theory of planned behavior.

The Theory of Planned Behavior can help you make the healthy choice to eat more fish. Look into the source of your fish for the healthiest choices. Source: pixabay.com.

Class activity

After reading about research and seeing sample survey questions asked to participants, the class might design their own surveys for behaviors important to students at your school. Students can practice correlating the different parts of the theory of planned behavior to the answers.

Topics might be rated to exercising, eating healthy foods, or getting enough sleep. There are plenty of other ideas as well.

Get informed consent from all participants and for ethical reasons, choose a topic that will not embarrass anyone. Model the sample questions included in this section.

Research evidence: Culture and TPB: Smoking in China

Smoking is a health problem in China. China is the largest maker of cigarettes, about a third of the world's smokers live there, and studies show a growing prevalence of adolescent smoking (Guo, et al., 2007). The **aim of this correlation study** was to compare the TPB and the **theory of reasoned action** with the hypothesis that both could predict smoking in Chinese adolescents but that one would be superior.

Surveys were given to adolescents in school in seven different cities. Data were collected at a baseline and then after one year.

At baseline, students were asked if they intended to smoke any time during the next year. Actual smoking behavior was measured after one year.

Results are next.

1. Attitudes and norms were influenced by intentions, which is consistent with the theory of reasoned action. This may be beneficial for predicting behavior in adolescents with low perceived control.
2. Perceived control was influenced by intentions, which is consistent with the TPB. More of the adolescents had a profile where perceived control interacted with attitudes and norms, and is a greater predictor of smoking in more participants.

The authors **concluded** that the TPB was the best theory for predicting smoking behavior in Chinese adolescents. One limitation of the study was the use of self-reports, which are hard to verify.

This study provides **space triangulation** for the TPB.

Research evidence: TPB and the breastfeeding in Malaysian women

Malaysia has adopted the World Health Organization's recommendations that women exclusively use breastfeeding for babies from birth to 6 months and continue until the child is about 2 (Tengku, Tengku, Muda, & Bakar, 2016). Breastfeeding has increased but is not yet exclusive, so the **aim of this correlation study** is to see if the TPB is a good predictor of intentions to do so.

Two of the hypotheses follow. *This is a study where intentions and actual behavior is examined.*

1. The women's attitude, perceptions of norms, and perceived control would predict intentions.
2. The women's perceived control (including difficulties with breastfeeding) would predict the exclusiveness of breastfeeding behavior.

Surveys included questions related to all aspects of the TPB model. For example, women answered questions about attitude such as "Breastfeeding my infants with breast milk only for 6 months is possible" (p. 51).

Results showed that the TPB was helpful in predicting intentions and behavior in these women, with perceived control as the greatest factor. However, most participants had low intention to breastfeed but then used it after getting social support. Therefore, *TPB was not as successful in predicting actual behavior*. The biggest factor in actual behavior seemed to be support provided after birth so women could learn to overcome difficulties.

The authors **conclude** that the TPB helps to assess intentions in this sample but the key to actual behavior rested on social support and education.

This study provides more **space triangulation** for the conclusion that TPB is a good predictor of intentions. However, *it questions if the TPB actually affects behavior*. This is an interesting study in light of Bandura's claim that the **Social Cognitive Theory** is a better predictor of actual self-management behavior.

Conclusions about the TPB

The research body is extensive and shows that TPB is valuable for predicting intentions for a variety of behaviors. It is also useful for explaining behavior across cultures. However, there are still some limitations of the model, including that it is unclear if it is valuable for predicting actual behavior. Pay attention to the use of correlations and evaluate this research method carefully as the body of research lacks **method triangulation**.

CAS and Self-management: What might it take for people to make healthy choices?
One insight for students to take away is that establishing a habit of healthy behavior might be vital for an intention to translate into behavior. There are many ways students can establish a habit, and one idea is for the behavior to become a norm and to increase perceived control through education and increasing access to healthy choices.

IB students might tackle this issue for **CAS**. For example, learning to cook is a good activity, especially if you learn to cook meals culturally relevant for you. Just doing this might get you away from fast food and start a new habit.

When reading all these studies note that different parts of the model seem important for different behaviors and age groups. This might help when targeting behaviors for change.

Texting while driving seems correlated with attitude, so this is a place to start with changing that behavior (Bazaragan-Hejazi, et al., 2016).

Chapter 13
The Cognitive Approach
Behavior: The Reliability
of Cognitive Processes:
Knowledge and
Understanding

Chapter Objectives

Students will:
1. Practice thinking strategies related to knowledge and understanding, with describe modeled.
2. Describe schema processing.
3. Describe confirmation bias, an example of a cognitive bias influencing thinking and decision-making, with illusory correlation as an example.
4. Describe cognitive dissonance, an example of a cognitive bias influencing thinking and decision-making.
5. Describe selective attention, an example of a cognitive bias in thinking and decision-making.

This chapter contains the background information helpful to explain and evaluate the reliability of cognitive processes in chapter 14.

13.1: Schema processing
Details about schema processing are detailed in chapter 11. Chapter 12 used **eyewitness memory** as an example for evaluating the claim that these memories are the result of schema. This is useful background reading before students tackle the evaluation of the body of research on the topic in chapter 14.

Bartlett's *War of the Ghosts* study can also be used as an example of the schema processing related to the reconstructive nature of memory.

13.2: Confirmation biases: They influence thinking and decision-making

Describe means to give a detailed account. Next is important details about **confirmation biases** useful as background knowledge to evaluate the reliability of thinking and decision making in the next chapter.

The mind automatically tries to simplify decision-making and we do not always recognize how often biases affect judgment. It is natural to use these and knowledge of them might help us consider their influence on judgment. The **illusory correlation** is one example where we think categories go together that really do not (Sternberg & Sternberg, 2012). The illusory correlation is incorrect cause and effect thinking.

Two other biases are the **overconfidence bias** and **hindsight bias**. Overconfidence is when poor decisions are made because people believe they have more skills or knowledge than they really do (Sternberg & Sternberg, 2012). Hindsight bias means people think after the fact that they should have been able to predict an outcome (Sternberg & Sternberg, 2012).

We like to think of ourselves as having good judgment, but people process large amounts of information each day and automatically simplify it. The result is that people are at risk for **cognitive biases**, the errors making us more likely to have one viewpoint over another.

Confirmation biases are "the seeking or interpreting of evidence in ways that are partial to existing beliefs, expectations, or a hypothesis in mind" (Nickerson, 1998, p. 175). It may be the biggest reason for misunderstandings.

There is a difference between *impartially* considering evidence and *case-building*, where evidence is gathered to fit with a particular case someone wants to make. Sometimes people consciously build a case, such as lawyers defending a client, but in most instances, case-building is automatic and unintentional.

Since confirmation biases are unintentional and automatic, they can contribute to subtle **stereotyping**.

People use confirmation biases even when they have no particular stake in a decision and do not need a specific motivation to defend a belief (Nickerson, 1998).

A body of evidence supports confirmation biases, with experiments investigating the following (Nickerson, 1998).

1. Seeing patterns in data based on what someone is looking for, such as the **illusory correlation**
2. Favoring specific evidence to support existing beliefs
3. Looking only for positive evidence and ignoring negative findings

What is the first thing that comes to mind when you see this picture of a medical professional? Make a list of jobs and write down the first thing that comes to mind about the people doing these jobs. Then read the Hamilton & Rose study on the next page. Source: pixabay.com.

Research support: The illusory correlation

An **illusory correlation** happens "when we expect two things to be related, and we fool ourselves into believing that they are—even when they are actually unrelated" (Aronson, Wilson, & White, 2007, p. 433). Illusory correlations can lead to **stereotyping**, so it is important to have more controlled conscious thinking about them to avoid unintended consequences.

The illusory correlation was supported in an experiment **aiming to show** the strength of stereotypes even when information contradicted them (Hamilton & Rose, 1980). It was predicted that participants would link stereotypes with occupations even when other information was presented.

Procedures are next. Participants read cards with 24 statements about a person who belonged to one of three occupational groups. Each statement identified an occupation and two traits for someone. Some traits were stereotypes for the occupation and others were not, the **independent variable**. For example, one card read, "Doug, an accountant, is timid and thoughtful" (Hamilton & Rose, 1980, p. 835). Participants next filled out a questionnaire judging the number of times the traits described members of each occupation.

Results showed that participants judged a connection between occupations and stereotypes, even though the cards contained different traits. The authors **concluded** that participants confirmed their stereotypes, even when the other information was available.

Other research investigated the cognitive mechanisms for the illusory correlation and found it happened during the "encoding of serially presented stimulus items" (Hamilton, Dugan, & Trolier, 1985, p. 5).

Thinking skills: Practice top-down thinking
Here is another chance to consider the problem that some research conducted in the West fails to have cross-cultural verification. Without it, conclusions are tentative at best.

The illusory correlation is confirmed in western samples but I cannot find anything about it being studied with nonwestern samples. Until that is done, the research on the illusory correlation is incomplete. Email me if anyone finds some. I asked David Matsumoto and he did not know of any either (Anne T., personal assistant to Dr. Matsumoto, personal communication, 3/16/15).

13.3: Cognitive dissonance: It influences thinking and decision-making

Cognitive dissonance is the psychological tension people feel from holding inconsistent beliefs (Festinger, 1957), such as eating fast food or smoking even though it is well documented that both increase the risk for many medical conditions.

People like to keep their attitudes and opinions internally consistent (Festinger, 1957). Generally this is so, as we have consistency between attitudes and behavior much of the time.

It gets our attention when attitudes and behavior are inconsistent. Festinger used the example of smoking. Many parents even tell their children not to smoke when they do it! People have many ways of rationalizing that smoking is not so bad (Festinger, 1957). For example, they can say smoking is better than the weight they might gain after quitting, that people cannot avoid every danger in life, or that the pleasure of smoking outweighs the risks. Rationalizing helps us maintain consistency between beliefs and behavior.

Smokers have cognitive dissonance as they manage the tension between continuing to smoke and knowledge that it is a health risk. Source: pixabay.com

People are not always good at rationalizing to explain inconsistencies to themselves, and these failures cause cognitive dissonance, the resulting psychological tension.

Tension makes people want to reduce dissonance and regain cognitive consistency, which Festinger called **cognitive consonance**. People go to great lengths to reduce dissonance, even avoiding situations that increase the tension. The important point is that the pressure to have consonance and the need to reduce dissonance is great.

Dissonance can come from many sources and is an everyday thing, such as cultural beliefs, and life experience.

Key details of cognitive dissonance (Festinger, 1957)

People prefer to have attitudes and opinions internally consistent and it works most of the time.

Key details of cognitive dissonance (Festinger, 1957)
When attitudes and behavior are not consistent, it gets our attention. People rationalize to maintain consistency.
People are not always good at rationalizing and these failures cause cognitive dissonance, which results in psychological tension.
Tensions makes people feel uncomfortable, and we go to great lengths to reduce dissonance and regain cognitive consistency, called cognitive consonance.
The important point to remember is the pressure to have consonance and the need to reduce dissonance is great.
Strategies to reduce tension include: A. Changing one's attitude, and then for example, the person stops smoking. B. Changing the environment, such as hanging around with other smokers so their behavior does not stand out as unusual. C. Adding new information that allows the person to maintain their behavior without tension. For example, someone might actively seeking out information that many people have smoked all their lives with no health problems and highlight it as important.

Cognitive dissonance is well supported, and one classic study is next.

Research evidence: A classic experiment demonstrating cognitive dissonance

Festinger and Carlsmith (1959) supported cognitive dissonance theory in an experiment about forced compliance. The **aim of the experiment** was to show that a person's private opinion will change to reduce dissonance when it conflicts with what they are forced to do.

The hypothesis was that participants given smaller rewards would show greater changes in their private opinion than participants given greater rewards.

Procedures are next. Stanford University students were asked to do simple tasks for an hour, such as turning pegs on a board a quarter turn clockwise and then going back and turning each another quarter turn or putting 12 spools into a tray, emptying it, and then putting them in again. Researchers timed participants with a stopwatch and took notes to make it appear the tasks were important. As you might imagine, the tasks were boring and participants had negative attitudes toward them, showing dissonance between what they thought about the task and the fact they were doing it anyway.

The **independent variable** was whether a participant was paid $1 or $20 to tell another student waiting in the office (really a confederate) that the task was interesting.

Thinking: Ethics in research
Is the deception in this study justified? Apply the rules from the ethics quick reference in chapter 1.

Results showed that most all participants were willing to tell the confederates the tasks were fun, but when interviewed after the study, there was a clear difference in private opinion change between the groups. As predicted, participants paid just $1 changed their private opinion more to reduce dissonance than those getting $20, who had a reason to enjoy the tasks and experienced less dissonance.

Research evidence: Smokers rationalize more than non-smokers

The **aim of a correlation study** was to compare beliefs about **smoking** between smokers and nonsmokers (Johnson, 1968).

The study had two hypotheses.

1. Nonsmokers and former smokers are less likely to agree with rationalizations used to reduce cognitive dissonance than smokers.
2. Smokers who say they intend to quit would agree with fewer rationalizations to reduce dissonance and maintain smoking than smokers.

Questionnaires were given to participants with retesting after 15 months. The questionnaires had 127 statements that could be used as rationalizations to continue smoking. Participant answers were coded as agreeing or disagreeing with the statements.

Example statements follow.

1. "It is stupid to stop smoking" (p. 260).
2. "That many old people have smoked for long periods of time and have not developed lung cancer is reasonably clear evidence that lung cancer is not caused by smoking" (p. 260).
3. "The statistics which demonstrate a relationship between smoking and health hazards are misleading" (p. 260.

> **Thinking skills: Ethics in research**
> Correlation studies using questionnaires are used to avoid placing participants in experimental conditions which might cause them to do something potentially damaging that they do not already do. Researchers want to assess dissonance reduction but do not want to promote smoking.

Results supported both hypotheses. Smokers agreed with more statements that could help them reduce dissonance and keep smoking on both the original and the 15 month retest questionnaires. Smokers intending to quit were more like former smokers in their answers and they agreed with fewer statements.

Findings about smoking and dissonance are consistent over time, suggesting people reduce dissonance to continue smoking.

The **aim of one newer experiment** was to investigate if dissonance reduction was different in smokers immediately after dissonance was felt and then after time passed (Kneer, Glock, & Rieger, 2012). **Results** showed that smoker's first ratings of their health risks were higher than their second ratings. Researchers **concluded** dissonance reduction was immediate, but after time defensiveness and suppression affected information processing.

What does this mean? Health information is probably effective for nonsmokers because it confirms beliefs that smoking is bad for one's health. However, health information given to smokers likely results in immediate dissonance and then in less information processing over time, so different strategies are needed if the goal of public health officials is to end smoking.

Research evidence: Culture affects cognitive dissonance

Research shows the importance of **culture** in how dissonance starts and is reduced (Hoshino-Browne, et al., 2005).

Dissonance is part of human nature and everyone experiences it. However, people in individualistic and collectivistic cultures have different ways of viewing the self. People in **individualistic cultures** tend to have **independent self-construals** where an individual's view of the self is most valued. People from **collectivistic cultures** have **interdependent self-construals**, where the larger in-group determines to value of the self. When dissonance occurs across cultures, it is reduced according to view of the self.

The **aim of this quasi-experiment** was to show how independent and interdependent views of the self were used to reduce dissonance.

The hypothesis was that European Canadians would rationalize decisions because making a poor choice would threaten the independent self. Asian Canadians would rationalize decisions for close friends because making a poor choice for a valued in-group member threatened their interdependent self.

Procedures are next. Everyone was told they were part of a study about decision-making so university officials could choose the best new menu items for the student cafeteria. Then everyone was randomly assigned to either the self or friend condition (the **independent variable**).

All looked through 25 Chinese food menu items and choose 10 based on their own or a friend's preferences. Next participants rank ordered their 10 choices based on their own preferences or a friend's. Then all were given 2 gift coupons for the 5th and 6th choices and asked to choose one for themselves and one for a friend. The researcher left the room for about 10 minutes and upon returning, asked participants to examine the menu items again, this time with longer descriptions and prices, and rank ordered them a second time with a different rating scale. The differences between the first and second ratings created dissonance.

Thinking skills: Practice top-down processing

This is a chance to use the culture thread. Remember Triandis said a theory is not relevant unless it applies to all. Dissonance is studied across cultures and resolving psychological tension depends on values about the self that differ between individualistic and collectivistic cultures studied in chapter 3, linking this topic to **cultural dimensions** (the self dimension). This shows how the self dimension is used in research, a topic for the sociocultural ATB.

It seems cognitive dissonance is pancultural.

Results showed that European Canadian students rationalized their second ratings most when they made decisions for themselves and Asian Canadians rationalized their second rating most when making choices for a friend, supporting the hypothesis. These cultural differences in how dissonance starts and is reduced was replicated in other studies.

Dissonance is supported by a strong body of research that includes cross-cultural evidence. It would be interesting to see if the results of the study using Canadian-Asians were similar if tested in groups never living in the West.

13.4: Selective attention

Next is important details about **selective attention**, which is a **cognitive bias** because we are not always aware of how often we focus on a limited amount of things and filter out other things that could be important.

Attention is a cognitive process where people must concentrate on a particular aspect of information to actively process it. We must filter and sift through all that is out there to make sense of the world, ignoring some things and attending to others. Suppose you want to do math homework at your house but there are also many people talking and a dog is barking. Selective attention abilities allows you to filter out the people talking and the barking dog and just concentrate on the math problems. Attention gives us an efficient way to use limited mental capacities.

Attention does four main things for our cognitive processing (Sternberg & Sternberg, 2012).

It detects signals and allows us to be vigilant. For example, when driving you must pay attention to signs and traffic.

> Attention does four main things for our cognitive processing (Sternberg & Sternberg, 2012).

It searches for important things. For example, you can find something even when many distractors are around, such as finding lost jewelry in a cluttered room.

It selectively attends to what is needed. Paying attention to some stimuli and ignoring others is required to do homework in a noisy house.

It divides attention between more than one task when needed. It is possible to divide our cognitive abilities so we can attend to more than one thing at a time, such as talking on the phone and doing household chores at the same time.

Selective attention seems constantly at work. It is well illustrated by what Colin Cherry called the **cocktail party problem**, where someone must pay attention to one conversation when there are also many other conversations you can hear, such as being in a noisy classroom where many groups are thinking through a project or at an actual party (as cited in Sternberg & Sternberg, 2012). Cherry studied the cocktail party problem in the lab by presenting different conversations to each ear of participants. One ear was the conversation the participant was to shadow (or repeat) while the other ear heard something else. With great concentration, participants were able to sift out the differences and pay attention to one of them, by focusing on the pitch and rhythm of the speech, the loudness, and location of the sound.

Many theories of selective attention are around, but Ulric Neisser does a good job of summing up a two process theory of selection attention (as cited in Sternberg & Sternberg, 2012). The two processes follow and are part of the **System 1 and 2 model of thinking**.

1. *Automatic pre-attention processing*. We automatically notice basic sensory data, such as speech sounds, though these do not convey meaning. It gets our attention!
2. **Controlled attention**. This part of our attention takes effort and uses other cognitive processes such as Working Memory so we can remember what we attend to, a topic fully developed in chapter 12. Controlled processing allows us to make a clear mental representation of the object of attention.

Class activity: Selective attention
Try a shadowing experiment the way Colin Cherry used it. Have one person read a book passage into one ear and the participant must shadow it, or say the same thing. At the same time, have another person say something else into the other ear, such as a math equation. How well does the participant selectively attend to the book passage?

Source: Based on a related activity in Sternberg & Sternberg (2012).

Chapter 14
The Cognitive Approach to Behavior: Reliability of Cognitive Processes: Analysis and Evaluation

Chapter objectives

Students will:
1. Practice thinking strategies (command terms) related to analysis and application as well as synthesis and evaluation, with explain and evaluate demonstrated.
2. Explain and evaluate reconstructive memory. Eyewitness memory is the example, which can be influenced by schemas.
3. Explain and evaluate biases in thinking and decision making, with heuristics, cognitive biases, cognitive dissonance, the illusory correlation, and selective attention as examples.

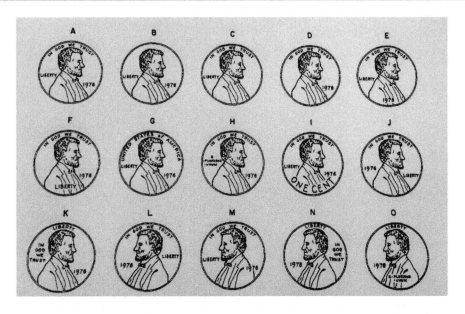

Penny line-up: Try the penny line-up before starting this chapter. You might say you know a penny when you see one. Which one is correct? Decide without looking at a penny. The wrong penny can easily be sent to jail. Now get out a real penny and see which one is correct. How many people in your class identified the right penny or sent the wrong one to jail? This illustrates a common problem in eyewitness memory where someone is sure they know who is responsible. But do they? Source: Nickerson, R. S. & Adams, J. A. (1979). Long-term memory for a common object. *Cognitive Psychology,* 11, 287-307.
Curtsey of R. Nickerson

This is a brief note to students as a reminder that the Bartlett *War of the Ghosts study* is an example of reconstructive memory. Bartlett is evidence of cultural **schemas** interfering with recall.

14.1: Reconstructive memory: The example of eyewitness memory

Introduction to studying the reliability of memory

Explain means to give a detailed account including reasons and causes. **Eyewitness memory** is a popular example of reconstructive memory, and *the reasons and causes for its unreliability come from schemas, memory encoding and retrieval problems, and stress hormones.*

Numerous eyewitness experiments are detailed so the class can see the depth of the research base. There are also many good reasons that eyewitness memory is a problem in courts and why people have misconceptions about the limitations of their memory.

Evaluate means to make a judgment (appraisal) based on evidence. Evidence from all three approaches to behavior support the conclusion that memory is more unreliable than we would like to admit and that eyewitness memory is faulty. Since Loftus started studying eyewitness memory, a large body of research has confirmed its unreliability. The research in this sections includes the following.

1. Cognitive ATB classic experiments from Loftus and her colleagues
2. Sociocultural ATB research about own-race bias
3. Cognitive ATB research about the encoding, storage, and retrieval of memories
4. Biological ATB research showing how stress hormones affect memory consolidation

This is a good place to use the multi-directional model because the ATBs interact and influence each other in the study of eyewitness memory.

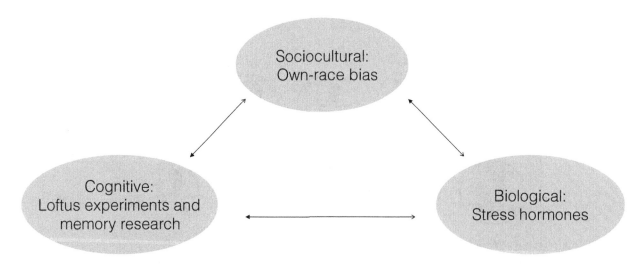

People have two misconceptions about their memories. One is that memories are exact. Another is that memories are not influenced by outside information. Research shows that memories are not just reconstructive, but are *constructive* (Sternberg & Sternberg, 2012). The constructive nature of memory means that any time we recall something, we must build those memories, and many things can interfere with the process, such as preexisting **schemas**.

The consequences of faulty eyewitness memory

There are many good reasons for the conclusion that faulty eyewitness memory is a problem in court cases.

James Newsome and Calvin C. Johnson served long jail sentences for crimes they did not commit (Wrightsman, Green, Nietzel, & Fortune, 2002). Eyewitnesses identified Newsome as the person who shot and killed a Chicago grocer, even though the fingerprints of a known killer out on parole at the time were left at the crime scene that did not match Newsome's fingerprints. Later the real killer was identified and Newsome released. Johnson had a similar experience. He spent 16 years in prison for a rape he did not commit. The victim selected Johnson from a photographic lineup two weeks after the attack and the jury convicted him, even though forensic tests were presented at the trial showing Johnson was not the right suspect. Johnson was released after DNA testing showed he could not be responsible. Faulty witness memory was responsible for the injustices.

> **Loftus films**
> Two video ideas:
> 1. DVD: Classic Studies in Psychology
> 2. TED Talk with Loftus: How reliable is your memory?
>
> The first is available through Films for the Humanities and Sciences. Eyewitness memory is one of the segments and the film also includes segments about attachment and the Bobo experiments. The demonstrations are detailed and very useful for clarifying the aim, IV, DV, procedures, and results.

Jurors value eyewitnesses, even though research shows eyewitness memories are unreliable. In addition, jurors place great value on the expressed confidence level of eyewitnesses, which is also faulty.

Elizabeth Loftus is a leading figure in studying **eyewitness memory**. Her experiments demonstrate that memory is easily distorted with even the simple change of a word during questioning.

Cognitive ATB: Classic experiments from Elizabeth Loftus

Three experiment variables have been tested to show the reconstructive nature of eyewitness memory and its unreliability.

1. The phrasing of a question
2. Information supplied after an event
3. Repetition of misleading information about an event

Experiment variable #1: Phrasing of a question

Details of experiments investigating the phrasing of a question follow and they show causation, important for an explanation.

The **aim of one experiment** was to show that the phrasing of a question affected someone's speed judgment after viewing a film of a crash (Loftus and Palmer, 1974). Some words used in eyewitness questioning seem more suggestible.

For **procedures**, 45 students watched seven films about a car accident. After each film, participants filled out a questionnaire that included a critical question asking them to estimate the speed of the car. Participants were assigned to get different verbs and were asked how fast the cars were going when they *hit, smashed, collided, bumped,* or *contacted* the other cars, the **independent variable**. Speed estimation is the **dependent variable**.

Results follow.

Verb	Mean speed estimate
Contact	31.8
Hit	34
Bump	38.1
Collide	39.3
Smash	40.5

Source: Loftus & Palmer (1974)

The authors **concluded** that the wording of a question affected memory, but wanted more data to confirm that using different words caused different representations in people's minds making the accident seem more severe. For example, the word 'smash' might make someone think the accident was worse than the word 'contact,' causing them to think about it more carefully.

The **aim of a second experiment** was also to show that the phrasing of a question affected memory. For **procedures**, participants watched a film of an accident and then filled out a questionnaire. The critical question asked how fast the car was going when either *hit* or *smashed* into the other car, the **independent variable**. Then a week later, participants filled out another questionnaire and the critical question asked if they saw any broken glass during the accident. In actuality, there was no broken glass in the film, but **results** showed the following. Broken glass was assumed to imply that it was a bad accident. A control group did not hear the words hit or smash.

Response	Smashed	Hit	Control group
Yes	16	7	6
No	34	43	44

Source: Loftus & Palmer (1974)

This is more evidence for an evaluation that the wording of a question influences the reliability of memory. Eyewitnesses have information from seeing the accident and then information after the accident. Both information sources become integrated and people have trouble telling the difference between them, ending up with one memory about the accident.

Experiment variable #2: Information supplied after an event

Details of experiments investigating the second variable follow. These experiments show causation, important for an explanation.

A series of experiments **aimed to show** that information supplied after an event affects the reliability of memory for the event (Loftus, Miller, & Burns, 1978). Would consistent, misleading, or irrelevant information given after an event have an influence? Does it matter if the information is given right after the event or right before a final testing about the event?

One experiment tested 195 participants who saw 30 slides. For **procedures**, half saw a Datsun at a stop sign and the other saw the same car at a yield sign, the **independent variable**. After seeing the slides, everyone filled out a questionnaire about the accident, but half of the participants in the stop sign condition filled out a questionnaire containing a critical question, "Did another car pass the Datsun while it was stopped at a stop sign?" (p. 22). Half of the other group had the same question but it said yield sign instead of stop sign. So half of the participants in each group had consistent information and half had misleading (inconsistent) information.

A 20 minute filler activity distracted participants so they would not rehearse the slides. Then everyone saw a series of slides consisting of pairs of pictures. Participants chose which of the two pictures in each pair they had seen before. The critical pair showed the original slide of the Datsun either stopped at the

Source: Loftus, et al., (1978)
Curtsey of E. Loftus

stop sign or yield sign. In actuality, participants saw just the one slide, and the goal was to see if they could recognize it from the critical pair.

Results follow.

Percentage of time participants identified
the original slide correctly

Consistent information	Inconsistent information
75%	41%

Source: Loftus, et al., (1978)

The next experiment **aimed to show** that misleading information given to a participant right before a final recognition test affected memory more than misleading information given right after the event.

For **procedures**, participants saw the same slides of the Datsun cars. The study varied retention time and either had immediate or delayed questionnaires.

1. After seeing the slides, the researchers varied the retention time before having the recognition test, the independent variable, 20 minutes after seeing the original slides, 1 day, 2 days, or 1 week later.
2. Each retention group, half of the participants filled out the questionnaire either immediately after seeing the slides or just before the recognition test.
3. As a control, some participants saw the slides, filled out the questionnaire right after seeing them, and then immediately took the recognition test.

Results show that memory is unreliable after receiving misleading information and it is the most unreliable when the information is received just before the final recognition test.

Experiment variable #3: Repetition of misleading information after an event

A series of experiments demonstrated that repeated misleading claims are more damaging to memory than misleading claims that are heard just once (Foster, Huthwaite, Yesberg, Garry, & Loftus, 2012). These studies are experiments and show causation, important for an explanation.

The **aim of one of these experiments** was to see if "repeating misleading claims changes the way people report details about a witnessed event and if the number of eyewitnesses repeating these misleading claims matters" (p. 321).

Procedures are next. The study used a misinformation model where 64 participants witnessed an event, read a misleading account of the event, and then were tested to see if they recalled the original event correctly.

Participants watched a film of Eric the electrician stealing items from a house when he was working. Participants watched one of two films that were the same except for eight critical items.

Next, participants read three witness reports. Several **independent variables** were used. Each report had a control and a misleading version. The misleading report incorrectly described four of the critical items. The reports were then varied by source and repetition.

To vary source (two independent variables):

1. Half of the participants were told the three reports were from three different people.
2. Half were told the reports were from the same witness.

To vary repetition (two more independent variables):

1. Half read two control reports and one misleading report.

2. Half read three misleading reports.

Last, participants took a recognition test. Would they recall the correct items (the **dependent variable**)?

Results showed that people's memories were *most unreliable when the misleading claims were repeated*. It did not matter if the claims came from one person or three. The authors feel the number of sources needs further investigation.

Repetition matters, and is important because a repeated claim becomes familiar and true for someone. In the real world, jurors hear many witnesses, and if incorrect information is repeated, it makes the jurors more likely to believe it. "Roughly 10% of DNA exonerees have been convicted because at least three eyewitnesses were mistaken" (Foster, et al., 2012, p. 325).

Evaluating the Loftus experiments

An evaluation of the Loftus research is that it is strong and well studied.

The evidence showing eyewitness memory is strong but does not end with the research from Loftus and her colleagues. Other factors contribute to unreliability, such as culture, memory processes of encoding, storage, and retrieval, and stress, demonstrating that factors from all approaches to behavior contribute to the problem.

Strengths of the Loftus experiments	Limitation of the Loftus experiments
Its use of tightly controlled experiments is good. Avoid saying the studies are artificial and lack **ecological validity**. This is a superficial criticism because experiments are supposed to be artificial and each individual study are designed in such a way as to have low ecological validity on purpose. Of course psychologists want to eventually generalize their findings and this happens after a large body of research is conducted that showing various types of **triangulation**, such as method and observer triangulation.	Is the research ethical? Was there any deception? If so, was it justified and did the benefits to science outweigh the risk to participants?
It is high in observer and time triangulation.	

TOK Link: For the IB student

This is a good place to consider the importance of **triangulation** in evaluating psychological research.

What does it mean to create a body of research? Should it include some or all the types of triangulation detailed in chapter 36? Do not forget the need for space triangulation and what Harry Triandis said about research being incomplete unless it includes cross-cultural verification.

Psychological research never proves anything beyond a doubt but might triangulation make the body of research stronger? As students read on they will see research from all approaches to behavior. How strong does this make the body of eyewitness memory research?

Cognitive ATB: Role of memory processes: encoding, storage, and retrieval

We like to think memories are reliable, but research suggests otherwise. Evidence for evaluating the reliability of cognitive processing includes considering how memory processing contributes to the problem.

Encoding, **storage**, and **retrieval** are three important memory processes (Sternberg & Sternberg, 2012).

Information can only be transferred and stored if it is first encoded. Research shows people mainly use **acoustic encoding** (word sounds) when storing information into short-term memory but use **semantic encoding** (the meaning the words) for transfer and storage from short-term into long-term memory. Long-term memories are most important for eyewitness testimony because they must recall information days, weeks, or months after an event. Research about semantic encoding shows that participants in experiments cluster words into categories for storage when faced with having to remember long lists of words presented in random order (Bousfield, as cited in Sternberg & Sternberg, 2012). Participants in this experiment put the words back in order with categories, showing they used semantic encoding.

The **levels of processing model** also suggests people recall more when semantic encoding is used. The LOP model suggests that recall depends on the depth of processing, defined as the level of semantic encoding used (Craik & Tulving, 1975). A series of experiments demonstrated this by creating three groups assigned to remember a list of words. One group used shallow processing by answering simple questions, such as "Is the word in capital letters" (p. 272)? Another group used intermediate processing through rhyming. The deep processing group created categories for the words by fitting the word into a sentence. Participants in the deep processing condition recalled the most words.

It might seem that semantic encoding takes care of ensuring memories transferred into long-term memory are accurate and easy to retrieve. However, **interference** hinders retrieval (Sternberg & Sternberg, 2012).

Two types of interference are retroactive and proactive (Sternberg & Sternberg, 2012). **Retroactive interference** means new information received after an event or task influences memory before someone must recall it. **Proactive interference** means information from the past affects learning new information accurately. Bartlett's **War of the Ghost** study is a good example of proactive interference, with **schemas** hindering how someone processes new information. The **recency effect** and **primacy effect** are variables related to interference (Sternberg & Sternberg, 2012). Recency effect means people remember words near the end of a list more easily and primacy means people remember words near the beginning of a list (at least in western samples as we learned before). Proactive interference can hinder recency effects and retroactive can hinder primacy effects more.

Thinking skills and class discussion
Loftus showed that **retroactive interference** damages eyewitness memory. Use the term correctly when evaluating Loftus to improve the sophistication of your essays. Cross-reference this reference to **schemas** to the section about them and Bartlett's study.

Consider how the **recency-primacy** effects might be a problem for eyewitnesses recalling an event.

Investigate if people can be trained to give better eyewitness testimony. A number of original studies have been published on the subject.

Sociocultural ATB: Own-race bias affects eyewitness memory

Own-race bias (ORB) affects eyewitness memory and a **quasi-field experiment aimed** to test the idea that people are best at remembering faces from people of their own race (Wright, Boyd, & Tredoux, 2001). This field experiment increases the **method triangulation** of experimental evidence showing eyewitness memory is unreliable.

Procedures are next. Participants were 201 black and white persons at shopping centers in Cape Town, South Africa and Bristol, England. Males and females between the ages of 10-50 were approached by four confederates, one black and one white, at each location. The confederates asked one of four questions, such as "Excuse me, do you have the time"? Three minutes later a researcher debriefed each participant about the nature of the study and asked if they agreed to participate further. All agreed.

The witnesses completed three tasks for the study. First, they identified photographs in a sequential lineup where the photographs were shown all at once. Second, participants selected a photograph of the suspect in a forced-choice lineup from the entire group. Third, participants rated their confidence level for selecting photographs.

Photographs of the confederates wearing different clothing from those worn when at the shopping center were mixed in with nine filler photographs in the lineups.

Results confirmed that ORB affects eyewitness memory. Thirty percent of the witnesses correctly selected the confederate in the sequential lineup, and they were more likely to do this if the witness and the confederate were of the same race. Sixty-three percent of the witnesses selected the confederate in the forced-choice lineup, and again, they were more likely to do so when the confederate was of the same race. There were significant differences between the identifications made between the own-race conditions and different-race conditions. Unfortunately, between 40 and 70% of the identifications were incorrect in both lineups. In addition, a correlation was found between high confidence levels and selecting someone of the same race.

How can the results of ORB studies help jurors? It is hard to know. Jurors believe eyewitness memories are accurate. One tactic might be to warn jurors about ORB.

Theories explaining ORB vary. One is a contact theory. People may be more likely to recall faces from their own race because they are experts at examining these faces. We know that ORB lessens when people have more contact with others. *Perhaps a positive consequence of living in a global society is a lessening of ORB.*

This field experiment tested a more varied sample than lab experiments that typically use college students. The authors know the study has limitations. It is impossible to control all variables that might influence a field study's outcome. Only one kind of situation was tested, a simple question from a stranger. Ethics prevent researchers from staging situations more similar to those eyewitnesses typically experience. Finally, the study used deception, but each participant was debriefed within three minutes of participation and the conditions of the study were non-threatening.

Biological ATB: Stress hormones can damage memory consolidation

It is well documented that **stress hormones** can damage memory consolidation (Sapolsky, 2004), so it is worth reviewing how this process helps in evaluating the reliability of eyewitness memory.

It would be unethical to expose participants to the severe stressors that occur during real eyewitness experiences, so information about the brain and eyewitness memory comes from related research.

Sapolsky (2004) explains, "Short-term stressors of mild to moderate severity enhance cognition, while major or prolonged stressors are disruptive" (p. 204).

Two important brain areas related to memory are the **cortex** and the **hippocampus**. Sapolsky uses a computer analogy to explain how they work. The cortex is the hard drive, where memories are stored. The hippocampus is a keyboard, which allows people to input and access memories in the hard drive.

Thinking skills: Drawing relationships
Hormones are part of the biological ATP and are important for **health psychology** (the health problem stress) and abnormal psychology (people with depression have higher levels of cortisol).

This material also requires students to apply what they know about the **brain**, such as the hippocampus, neural networks, and neurotransmitters.

Memories are stored in **neural networks**, meaning patterns of excitation of many neurons, within the cortex and hippocampus. To learn and store a memory, strengthening of neural networks must occur. Here is another application for **neuroplasticity**. The brain

A   B

C   D

E   F

G

Now that you have learned about eyewitness memory, try the **dollar bill line-up**. Examine these without looking at a dollar. Which is the correct dollar bill, if any? We think we know a dollar when we see one, but do we? If you are not from the US, students can photoshop a bill from your country's currency or use the dollar if familiar enough with it. Now get out a dollar bill to see if any of these are correct. Did more people have the correct answer this time? Created by Ann Martin, St. Petersburg High School IB student, Class of 2017. Used with permission.

changes any time you learn something new. Strengthening of neural networks occur when **neurotransmitters** cross the **synapses** between neurons (Sapolsky, 2004). **Glutamate** is probably the most excitatory of all the neurotransmitters and is the one used more than others in the cortex and the hippocampus. For most neural communications, it only takes a small amount of excitation for a little bit of neural network strengthening to occur, but glutamate works differently. A little bit is not enough. When a large amount of glutamate is released, the excitation, or strengthening process really takes off, and learning occurs.

If this is how learning occurs, what happens when stress hormones are added?

Sapolsky thinks people are most likely to remember events with *emotional* significance. However, when emotions are involved, so are stress hormones.

During a stressful situation, the sympathetic nervous system activates and pours epinephrine and norepinephrine into one's bloodstream. When the sympathetic nervous system activates it also signals the hippocampus into a more alert state, heightening memory consolidation. In addition, the sympathetic nervous system stimulates memory by increasing the amount of glucose in the bloodstream, which increases the amount of blood going to the brain. So during a mild to moderate stressor, cognition is enhanced. This is why people can easily recall the events from a favorite band's concert.

What happens to memories after a really shocking event? Why are these memories often unreliable?

Too many **glucocorticoids** damage the neural network strengthening process (Sapolsky, 2004). The hippocampus has two different receptors for glucocorticoids, a high-affinity receptor and a low-affinity receptor. Glucocorticoids are better at attaching to high-affinity receptors and will do this first because these receptors enhance learning. So when stress is mild to moderate, these receptors are filled first. However, if a large amount of glucocorticoids flood the brain at once, they also find their way to the low-affinity receptors, which decrease learning. In addition, during great stressors, the **amygdala**, part of the emotional brain, sends messages that activate the hippocampus and further contributes to damaged memories. If this is not enough, large amounts of glucocorticoids weaken neural networks and interfere with **neurogenesis**.

Concluding statements about reconstructive memory

A multidirectional model is well suited to considering all the factors interacting when someone must reconstruct a memory. The evidence goes against common knowledge that eyewitness memory is reliable, challenging assumptions of our cognitive processing.

This conclusion is similar to what is found in research about selective attention and the other cognitive biases, as well as when we use heuristics and anchors when making decisions.

14.2: Biases in thinking and decision-making

Heuristics

Reuse the material about **availability heuristic** and the **anchoring and adjustment heuristic** from earlier chapters. An evaluation of heuristics is that there is strong evidence that they can bias thinking, though they do not always lead to poor decision making.

Cognitive Biases

Reuse the material in the last chapter as evidence that **cognitive dissonance**, the **illusory correlation**, and **selective attention** have strong evidence as cognitive biases that can affect decision making. However, it must be noted that research about the illusory correlation it still incomplete as it has not been verified cross-culturally.

Chapter 15
Cognitive Approach to Behavior: Emotion and Cognition: Knowledge and Understanding

15.1: Flashbulb memories

Describe means to give a detailed account. Key details about FB memories follow.

1. **Flashbulb memories** (FB) are "distinctly vivid, precise, concrete, long-lasting memories of the personal circumstances surrounding people's discovery of shocking events" (Finkenauer, et al., 1998, p. 191). People have FB memories but their accuracy is questioned and the quest to find a special mechanism for them has been difficult.

2. FB memories are **autobiographical memories** involving the personal memories of the *context* in which someone hears the news (Hirst & Phelps, 2016). This is called the "reception context." Autobiographical memories are related to the self. FB memories are different from **event memories**, or the facts about an incident, such as how many planes were involved in the 9/11 attacks. Most FB memories also differ from **first-hand memories** that come with direct experience, such as having to run out of the World Trade Center to survive as opposed to someone learning about the attacks from television news. These distinctions are important when considering the merit of arguments about FB memory models, their accuracy, and the special nature of FB memories in the next chapter.

3. Time is assumed by the public and even criminal investigators to affect the forgetting curve for FB memories less than it does with other memories. This idea has been challenged and is discussed in the next chapter.

4. Culture affects FB memories (Wang & Aydin, 2009). Information transmission varies by culture and it may affect an individual's reception context for events, which then affects what is socially shared.

5. Three mechanisms of FB memories are **etics,** importance, the experience of intense emotion, and post-event social sharing (Kulkofsky et al., 2011; Wang & Aydin, 2009).

6. FB memories also have **emic** features (Kulkofsky et al., 2011; Wang & Aydin, 2009). For example, people living in cultures valuing a person's individuality and self-expression report more intense emotions, more reflection, and more social sharing about FB memories than people in cultures that do not value individuality and self-expression.

7. Finkenauer's **Emotional-Integrative Model** of FB Memories is the most current and supported of the FB theories. This does not mean it is without critics, and we will explore these issues in the next chapter, such as operational definitions making it hard to verify what is necessary and sufficient for actually producing a FB memory.

8. There is no clear agreement if FB memories are accurate or represent a special type of memory distinct from everyday memories.

9. The **amygdala** is active when creating FB memories in people who are closest to the event, such as people in Manhattan who actually witnessed the 9/11 attacks as opposed to people who saw it through media (Phelps & Sharot, 2008). This is support for the conclusion that the amygdala is important for consolidating emotional memories.

10. The **hippocampus** does not play as much of a role in the retention of emotional memories such as FB memories as it does for neutral memories (Phelps & Sharot, 2008).

15.3: The affect heuristic: How emotion affects decision-making

The **affect heuristic** is described in chapter 11 under the topic **availability heuristic**. Students already study heuristics so they might select this material to use again for this section.

Chapter 16
Cognitive Approach to Behavior: Emotion and Cognition: Synthesis and Evaluation

---

16.1: The influence of emotion on cognitive processing: Discuss and assess the merit of flashbulb memories

Flashbulb memories fit in with the theme of humans living together in cultures

I recall when I heard about the September 11th attacks. I was teaching an IB psychology class when another teacher came in the room and said to turn on the television. We were confronted with planes crashing into the World Trade Center. At first I was in shock because it did not seem real. It took a little while to piece together the news, as the reporters were speculating about it, but then the news took on a terrible reality. Just typing this brings back the sadness and the total silence of my students (very unusual!).

If you recall the September 11th attacks, the assassination of a world leader, hearing the news about the death of a loved one, survived a natural disaster, or witnessed a crime, you might have flashbulb memories.

Flashbulb memories (FB) make up much of important storytelling that goes on within **cultures** so we must know if they are a special kind of memory with specific mechanisms and if they are accurate. *People assume that any highly vivid and emotional memory is accurate, especially if someone has high* *confidence in them* (Phelps & Sharot, 2008). This is especially a problem in the legal system. Does this lay (public) view of emotional memory stack up to research?

FB memory research spans all three approaches to behavior. It involves the cognitive process memory, the brain is active, and culture acts as a mediator, a good application of the multidirectional model.

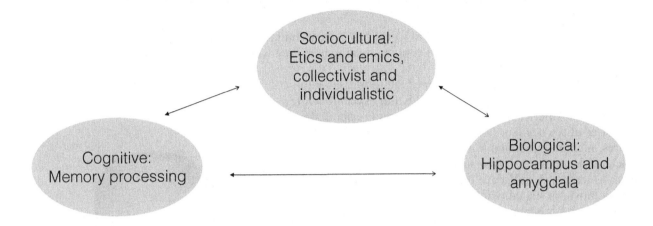

Differing viewpoints about FB memories
FB memory research can be grouped into several research lines.
1. One research line investigates models of FB memories, such as Finkenauer's **Emotional Integrative Model of FB memories**, the most current and supported of the models. Being current and supported does not mean the model is without critics.
2. A second investigates the reliability of FB memories, and there is no agreement that they are accurate or a special class of memories distinct from everyday memories.
3. A third investigates the biology behind FB memories, examining the **hippocampus** and **amygdala**.

This topic is a good chance to use thinking strategies discuss and to what extent, because it is a topic without clear agreement and students need to use good critical thinking.

Discuss means to give a considered and balanced view supported by evidence. A balanced view is demonstrated by doing three things.
1. Supporting a model over other options, including some criticisms of the most supported one because all models assume FB memories are more accurate than other memories and require special mechanisms
2. Looking at a sample of research, with one group of studies supporting the view that FB memories are special memories, even if they are always accurate, and another group of studies supporting the view that they are not a special type of memory
3. Noting the importance of amygdala activation in people who were closest to the event, such as people in Manhattan during the 9/11 attacks having the most accurate FB memories

To what extent is a good thinking strategy for this topic in addition to discuss because after getting a balanced view we can decide which opinions have merit. "To what extent" means to consider the merits of an argument that are supported by evidence. Does the Emotional Integrative Model have merit? Does the claim that FB memories are accurate, special, and distinct from everyday memories have merit? Does the conclusion that the amygdala is important for consolidating emotional memory have merit?

Let's start with models claiming FB memories are distinct and special. Then evidence about the special nature of FB memories is discussed. Last, research on the amygdala is discussed.

Flashbulb memory models: The Emotional Integrative Model has the most support but still has critics

The idea that vivid memories are hard to forget has been around for a long time. FB memories date back to 1899 when F. W. Colegrove asked people to recall where they were when President Lincoln was shot (Neisser & Hyman, 2000).

Roger Brown and James Kulik coined the term flashbulb memory in their 1977 study. Brown and Kulik asked 40 white and 40 black Americans to answer a questionnaire about their memories of the death or failed assassinations of nine historical figures, including JFK and Martin Luther King, and the shocking death of a personal acquaintance. They predicted black Americans would have greater FB memories for the leaders most associated with civil rights, which was believed to be of higher consequence. The hypothesis was confirmed. Be aware that Brown and Kulik simply asked people for a FB memory and did not investigate their claim that the memories were accurate over time (Hirst & Phelps, 2016).

We like to think our flashbulb memories are real but what is the merit of the evidence? Used with license from megapixl.com.

The **photographic theory of flashbulb memories** became the first theory of FB memories. Brown and Kulik (1977) believed FB memories were strong because they elicited a "Now Print!" neurophysiological mechanism. Surprise, consequentiality, and rehearsal strategies were important to registering FB memories in the brain. If the news is a shock and is of great consequence to the individual, then it likely compels frequent rehearsal. The event is "on a person's mind" and is the subject of conversations.

Much has happened in FB memory research since Brown and Kulik's time and their theory has been challenged and replaced by Finkenauer's Emotional-Integrative Model.

According to Olivier Luminet (personal communications, January, 2009 and May, 2016), *the Emotional-Integrative Model is the most current and supported of the FB memory theories.*

Finkenauer's **Emotional-Integrative Model of flashbulb memories** distinguishes the different components of emotions (Finkenauer, et al., 1998).

Finkenauer believes emotions are not just subjective feelings or states of arousal. They are more complex and involve information processing, response, and regulatory components. Each component is important to creating a FB memory.

The Emotional-Integrative Model has 5 steps and takes into account the complex nature of memories. The key is that it contains both *direct* and *indirect pathways* from the actual event to FB memories.

Step	Process
Step #1	An appraisal of novelty leads to surprise, which *directly* affects the FB memory.

Step	Process
Step #2	If one appraises the event as novel and the event also has personal significance a person experiences an intense subjective emotion. The subjective emotions affect FB memories in two ways. First, the subjective emotions, along with surprise, contribute *directly* to the FB memory. Second, the emotions trigger rehearsal, the next step.
Step #3	The intensity of one's emotional state and the FB memory trigger rehearsal of the event. Rehearsal takes place through narrating and listening to media accounts. Rehearsal has an *indirect* but important affect on the FB memory.
Step #4	The entire process is mediated by previously existing person characteristics, such as knowledge of the event, attitudes, and values.
Step #5	The end product is the FB memory of the event.

The Emotional-Integrative Model was first tested after Belgian King Baudouin unexpectedly died of a heart attack in 1993 and **aimed to examine** the model's components as compared to other theories (Finkenauer, et al., 1998). The death affected the Belgium people because he was successful at unifying a country that was divided by culture and language. Participants were French-speaking Belgium persons. **Procedures** involved collecting data through a questionnaire 7 to 8 months after the death. The questionnaire asked about the different factors thought to contribute to FB memories, such as where and what a person was doing when the news arrived, memory of the event, rehearsal of the event, subjective emotions, surprise level, novelty level, importance level, and level of sympathy.

Results showed that the Emotional-Integrative Model was supported over the others used for comparison. For example, Brown and Kulik's model was not supported because there was no evidence that importance and subjective emotions directly determined the FB memory, things important to that model.

Finkenauer's model has been refined with continued research. It uses the same 5 steps, but it has been discovered that people **do not need both a direct *and* an indirect pathway** activated to have a FB memory (Luminet & Curci, 2009). They could have either. The refined model also includes **social identity**, a topic studied under the sociocultural ATB. This model has now been considered and tested over time and has more support, giving it some merit.

This refinement was found in a quasi-experiment where participants were placed into the US group and the non-US group (Luminet & Curci, 2009). The non-US group included people from Belgium, Italy, Romania, and the Netherlands.

> **Try Finkenauer's model on yourself**
> Form small groups and test the model by thinking of possible FB memories each person may have and run it through the 5 steps. Does the model make sense? For example, Do you have a FB memory about Michael Jackson's death?
>
>
>
> Image used with license from megapixl.com.

The **aims of the study** were to compare the Emotional Integrative model to 3 other models and see if **social identity** affected any of the paths leading to FB memories (direct and indirect pathways). Everyone filled out questionnaires about FB memories, event memories, importance, novelty, intensity of emotions, and rehearsal.

Results showed that that both groups formed FB memories and again, the Emotional Integrative model was supported over other models because the pathways in the 5 steps were important. Direct pathways of surprise and novelty seem most important for people when their social identity is salient (most visible) for the event, and in this case a threat to the American social identity was a direct pathway to a FB memory. For the non-US group, the indirect pathway of rehearsal led to the FB memory. When reconsidering the study about the King of Belgium, it was determined that the threat to the Belgium social identity made it seem the direct pathway was required.

It appears the model has some merit over other models.

Culture and FB memories: An etic?

The Emotional-Integrative Model was originally tested on a Western European sample so cross-cultural research was needed to see how it worked for everyone.

A quasi-experiment on flashbulb and event memories about the September 11th attacks used participants from 6 countries (Curci & Luminet, 2006).

The study **aimed to show** that people had FB memories, and that they varied cross-culturally.

Procedures used a **test-retest design**, typical of flashbulb memory research, was used where participants were tested right after the event and then after a longer time. Data were first collected an average of 21 days after the attacks and then again 524 days later.

The sample was from the US, Belgium, Italy, the Netherlands, Japan, and Romania.

The authors had several hypotheses.

1. US participants were expected to have the greatest flashbulb memory consistency (remember this is not testing accuracy) and event consistency.
2. Dutch, Italians, and Belgium participants were also expected to have high levels of flashbulb memory consistency and event consistency.
3. The Japanese and Romanian participants were expected to the lowest levels of flashbulb memories and event consistencies. Participants from Japan were assumed to have different cultural rules about social sharing which would affect reporting memories. The Romanians had the least access to mass media that might affect rehearsal.

Data were collected with questionnaires asking about event memory, social sharing, novelty, importance to the person, and watching media reports.

Results follow.

1. US participants had the highest level of flashbulb memory attributes and were more accurate for event memory. The Dutch and Italians had the next highest level of flashbulb memory attributes and accuracy of events.
2. US and European participants scored higher on most variables affecting flashbulb memories. The Romanians did not report rehearsing the event through media stories. The Japanese reported the fewest emotional variables. It can be assumed that culture affects social sharing.

Do these results add to the merit of the Emotional-Integrative Model?

All participants had consistent FB memories of the September 11th attacks. However, the *direct and indirect pathways work differently across culture*. Both direct and indirect pathways were involved in the memories of US and Western European participants. Differences were seen in the Romanian and Japanese samples. The indirect pathway had the least effect on Romanians (they had limited access to media). The direct pathways had the least effect on the Japanese (remember they reported the fewest emotional variables). Japan is a **collectivist** culture and the public sharing of emotional events is not as accepted.

Some aspects of FB memories seem universal and are **etics** (Kulkofsky et al., 2011, Wang & Aydin, 2009). These are the importance of the event, experiencing intense emotion, and post-event rehearsal through social sharing. However, there are emic aspects to FB as well. Culture affects personal importance (even though national importance is universal), emotionality and surprise level (Kulkofsky, et al., 2011). People living in countries valuing a person's individuality and self-expression report more intense emotion (Wang & Aydin, 2009). FB memories factors are shown the least in Chinese samples and this might be because of collective values (Kulkofsky, et al., 2011).

Cultural research helps give the model more merit.

Are FB memories accurate and are they special memories distinct from everyday memories?

A sample of the research is included so students get an idea of the differing viewpoints because it is impossible to detail all of the arguments. To simplify but hopefully avoid oversimplification, there are arguments on both sides. Some claim FB memories are special and distinct from everyday memories and other say they are not. This is a place to tolerate uncertainty because a particular conclusion is not clear. This section gives a balanced view for our discussion and continuing assessment of merit.

Conceptual understanding: Refining models and considering criticisms

The Emotional-Integrative model has some merit because it has been compared to other models, it has been tested over time, and has been refined to fit research findings. It is becoming a more complete model, with **social identity** added.

The culture and FB memory research further tested and supported the model. The class might discuss how these refinements might explain the emic features of FB memories.

However, Finkenauer has critics. For example, the **test-retest design** measures consistency of memories rather than accuracy (Hirst & Phelps, 2016). For FB memories to be a special type of memory, they must be more accurate than everyday memories. This is difficult to show for those wanting to support a model.

Someone can have consistently inaccurate autobiographical memories! It has been argued that people may recall FB memories better than everyday memories, but the decline is equal, and once there is an inaccuracy it tends to be the memory repeated to others, called **time-slice confusion**, meaning confusing the first memory with the second to third time someone hears about an incident (Hirst & Phelps, 2016). Just think of all the different news and social media that come with any incident. What was the real context memory?

Another concern for all FB memory models is having necessary and sufficient paths to a FB memory. Look at the Finkenauer steps. What is necessary and/or sufficient (Hirst & Phelps, 2016)? This task is harder than it might appear. Finkenauer recently revised the model so that direct *and* indirect pathways are not necessary. It is suggested that surprise or personal significance are not necessary or sufficient either.

The argument that FB memories are special, distinct, and perhaps accurate

The claim that FB memories are special and distinct rests on the ability to show they are accurate and long lasting (Talarico & Rubin, 2007). Older theories even claimed FB memories required a special mechanism, such as Brown and Kulik's "Now Print!" mechanism, something that has not stood up to testing. Next is two experiments with different findings.

One experiment **aimed to show** that FB memories are a special type of autobiographical memory and that they are accurate (Curci, Lanciano, Maddalena, Maddalena, & Sartori, 2015). The event was the resignation of Pope Benedict XVI. Catholic Italians were compared to those who did not attend church or were not Catholics. For **procedures**, participants filled out questionnaires and **results** showed that the Catholics were most concerned about the resignation and had the strongest and accurate FB memories. So there is some evidence giving merit to the claim that FB memories can be accurate. However, this is balanced with a somewhat opposing view that also has some merit.

The **aim of another experiment** was to show that FB memories were a special type of memory but were not all that accurate (Talarico & Rubin, 2007). For **procedures**, Duke University students were tested the day after 9/11 for their memory of the attacks and then were assigned to one of three follow-up conditions of 1, 6, or 32 weeks afterwards. Participants filled out questionnaires at the baseline time and at the follow-up asking about memories of the attack and also important events happening the days before it. **Results** shows FB memories were distinct from everyday memories with greater emotion, more rehearsal, more confidence in the accuracy, and more recollection. It was **concluded** that FB memories are special. However, the accuracy of both types of memories were poor over time.

Does either argument have enough merit for the conclusion that FB memories are special memories and accurate to say "to a great extent?" Probably not because there are some research issues to be resolved. For example, operationally defining terms in research is critical to the outcome. FB memories are usually defined as consistent rather than accurate, so this must be resolved (Hirst & Phelps, 2016).

Some claim there is nothing special or accurate about FB memories

"Memories become flashbulbs primarily through the significance that is attached to them *afterwards*" (Neisser & Harsch, 2000, p. 70). The term "benchmark" is a better description of the memories than the term "flashbulb" memory.

The problems of eyewitness memory are the same as those of FB memories because they are often wrong from the start or are easily altered over time. Pondering the events, talking about them over and over with others (narrating), and hearing media reports are responsible for the vividness of the memories.

The researchers were concerned about how FB memory study results were interpreted by researchers. The **aim of the experiment** was to investigate memories of the Challenger crash that call into question the reliability of FB memories. For **procedures**, participants filled out a questionnaire about their recollections of the Challenger crash within 24 hours of the crash and then again 3 years later.

Results showed more discrepancies than expected as well as high confidence levels that the memories were correct. Interviews were

I think I have a FB memory about the Challenger crash. I was student teaching at the time and watching the launch on TV. But do I really?
Source: pixabay.com.

conducted with some of the participants to clarify the results. Of interest to the researchers was the surprise and disbelief that some participants showed about the discrepancies between their two sets of data.

This line of research may reduce the merit of FB memory theories. However, this study has criticisms, such as the failure to compare the FB memories with everyday memories or compare the FB memories at different points in time to see when they became mistaken, so students should consider if this study helps or hinders the merits of FB memory (Talarico as cited in Law, 2011).

The amygdala is important to consolidating emotional memories

Two parts of the limbic system are important for our continued discussion about FB memory. The **amygdala** helps process emotion and the near-by **hippocampus** helps form episodic memories and aids their storage and retrieval (Phelps & Sharot, 2008). Plenty of research shows the amygdala helps with storage of emotion arousing events so they can be better recalled.

We should say something about how emotion influences **memory encoding** because it seems important to retrieving FB memories. Emotion influences attention and perception. When someone is in an emotionally charged situation, attention and perception resources are usually limited. Emotions are linked to our visual cortices, which enhance perception and attention to the situation. In effect, there is an attention-and perception-narrowing around what is emotional and this might result in greater memory.

But how does the brain process these narrowed memories?

fMRI studies show that the brain processes neutral stimuli and highly emotional stimuli differently. When participants look at neutral scenes, a part of the hippocampus called the parahippocampus is activated during subjective recall of the scenes. The parahippocampus is important for perceiving complex details of a scene.

In contrast, fMRI studies show that when participants look at emotional scenes and have a strong subjective feeling when retrieving these memories, the amygdala is activated and the hippocampus is deactivated. Research on the 9/11 attacks find that the intensity of subjective recall by those closest to the World Trade Center is accompanied by the greatest activation of the amygdala and the least activation of the hippocampus compared to participants without first-hand memories.

At first researchers were surprised that the hippocampus was not involved in highly emotional memories. The hippocampus helps with **complex scene details** but this was not the way thing worked with the highly emotional subjective memories recalled by people with FB memories.

A closer look at the amygdala is needed. What does it do that matters for recalling vivid emotional memories?

One job of the amygdala is to work with the narrowed and enhanced attention and perception process to encode emotion-linked items and the details related to them. However, with the hippocampus less activated, fewer *complex* details may get encoded.

Another job of the amygdala is to strengthen the retention of emotionally arousing events. If an item is properly encoded, then the memories have a better chance of being recalled. It is known however, that when the amygdala pairs up with attention narrowing the complexities of a scene might not get properly encoded. The person thinks they recall the whole scene correctly but really just gets the gist of it all, a general overview with missing complexity.

Someone with high confidence in a FB memory may really just have the gist of it. Learning about the brain's role in vivid emotional memories helps us avoid assuming they are accurate.

Conclusions about FB memories

A considered and balanced view of theory and research leaves us with the conclusion that FM memory models and claims of accuracy have some merit but still have many challenges to meet before having great merit.

Look for future research to investigate the weaknesses of current research, such as operational definitions of memory (consistency versus accuracy) and the need to identify sufficient and/or necessary paths to FB memories.

16.2: The influence of emotion on cognitive processing: Discuss the affect heuristic and decision making

Should I smoke, eat GMO foods, fear terrorists, text while driving, or backpack?

Conceptual understanding: Define affect heuristic

The **affect heuristic** is a "faint whisper of emotion" when someone has a sense of goodness or badness about something (Slovic, Finucane, Peters, & MacGregor, 2004, p. 312). Affect heuristics allow us to make decisions rapidly, automatically, and unconsciously.

Affect heuristics are examples of **System 1 thinking**.

Discuss means to give a considered and balanced view supported by evidence. Next is a reflection (consideration) on how people are most likely to use an **affect heuristic** when making judgments (decisions-making) about risk.

We like to think we are rational and analytic when **judging benefits versus risks**, such as whether or not to smoke, fear terrorists, go on a backpacking trip, text while driving, or eat genetically modified foods. Rational and analytic decision making uses **System 2 thinking** that is slow and requires effort and conscious thought. However, research shows that we are not likely to be analytic and rational much of the time.

We are more likely to use heuristics to make judgments as you learned in chapter 11, and much of these rely on affect (emotion).

A reflection on the affect heuristic starts with a little bit of its history, moves into considering supporting research, and then shows practical applications.

Let's get some examples to consider. If you did not recreate the affect heuristic experiment from chapter 11 in your class here it is again.

Class activity

Divide the class into two groups and assign one group a time pressure and the other no time pressure. Next, both groups should rate each on a scale of 1 (high benefit & low risk)-7 (low benefit & high risk)

Alcoholic beverages	Chemical plants	Space exploration
Eating red meat	Food preservatives	Roller Skates
Texting while driving	Cigarettes	Bicycles
Cell phones	Surfing	Eating fast food
Air travel	Explosives	Genetically modified food
Water fluoridation	Motorcycles	(GMOs)
Backpacking		

Based on and including items from:
Finucane, Alhakami, Slovic, & Johnson, 2000

Students with the time pressure likely used an affect heuristic to judge. We so often must make a decision quickly and the time pressure group mimicked this. People ride bicycles frequently, and unconsciously and automatically assess risk before doing it. If someone likes biking, then the risk if often thought to be low, even if biking really has many risks.

Decision making researchers realized that affect (emotion) played a large part in making judgments a long time ago. Early support came from the work of Zajonic in 1980 when he claimed that affect was usually the first response, and this automatic response influenced decisions (as cited in Finucane, Alhakami, Slovic, & Johnson, 2000). For example, we do not just see a car, but see a beautiful or ugly car, and this is because our affect (emotion) labels everything we perceive.

People use affect heuristics when making decisions because images in our minds are tagged with positive or negative emotions (Finucane, et al., 2000). When faced with making a judgment, people consult this "affective pool" that contains a lifetime of positive and negatives tags for everything encountered. Affect is just as important for making judgments as availability and anchoring. People just do not always have time to stop and make fully rational choices where they weight the pros and cons of a variety of choices. Affect heuristics are more efficient and quick, helping people navigate through an uncertain and often dangerous world (Slovic, et al., 2004). Much of the time the affect heuristic is adaptive and helps us make good decisions.

Research support for affect heuristics: Judging risk

People make judgements every day about whether or not to engage in activities. Risk and benefit are separate things, and for example, backpacking can have the high benefit of enjoyment and a high risk of getting injured, yet people still go backpacking. This is an example of what is meant when researchers say there is a positive correlation in everyday life between risk and benefit, with people doing things that have high risk and high enjoyment and avoiding things with low risk and low enjoyment (such as cleaning your room).

However, there is an inverse relationship when making judgments about risk and benefit *in people's minds*, meaning if the risk is thought to be high, then it is judged to have low benefit and vise versa (Finucane, et al., 2000). The backpacking example illustrates this.

This inverse relationship cannot simply be explained by cognitions because there is a tendency for people to judge activities they like (tagged with positive affect) with high benefit and low risk and judge disliked activities (tagged with negative affect) as low in benefit and high in risk.

The **aim of this experiment** was to show that the affect heuristic comes before people make judgments and was the reason for the inverse relationship seen between risk and benefit (Finucane, et al., 2000).

Procedures are next. This study used time pressure as a way to bring up the affect pools

Backpacking is fun and has benefits but also has risks. How might you use the affect heuristic when deciding to do an activity such as this one?
Source: pixabay.com.

people use to make judgments. Participants were randomly assigned to the time pressure group or the no time pressure group, the **independent variable**. Participants judged 23 activities common for Australians and rated then on a scale of not at all risky (or beneficial) to very risky (or beneficial).

The activities were shown on a computer screen one at a time. Example activities were food preservatives, cigarettes, swimming pools, and motorcycles. Participants in the time pressure group had 5.2 seconds to consider each item and then saw a screen that said time was up and to click on the scale. The no time pressure group took as long as they liked to make a judgment.

Results showed that participants in the time pressure condition rated the activities faster and the inverse relationship was stronger, showing more extremes between risk and benefit.

The authors **concluded** that the affect heuristic was activated more with a time pressure and accounted for the stronger inverse relationships between risk and benefit.

More research evidence for affect heuristics: Judging risk of nuclear power, natural gas, and using food preservatives

This **aim of the experiment** was to show that raising or lowering the favorability of something by providing different types of information would change the someone's affect when making a judgment (Finucane, et al., 2000).

If the affect heuristic theory is correct, then giving someone favorable information should make the judged risk or benefit lower and vise versa. Hypotheses follow.

1. When information shows the benefit is high, judgment of risk is low.
2. When information shows benefit is low, judgment of risk is high.
3. When information shows risk is high, benefit judgment is low.
4. When information shows risk is low, benefit judgment is high.

For **procedures**, participants all filled out questionnaires about perceived risks and benefits of nuclear energy, natural gas, or the use of food preservatives. Next everyone was then randomly assigned to read information about these showing they had great benefit, low benefit, high risk, or low risk, the independent variables.

Results confirmed the hypotheses. The information activated affect and participant judgments were in line with the favorability rating as compared with baseline risk judgments in the first questionnaires.

Chapter 17
Cognitive Approach to Behavior: Cognitive Processing in the Digital World

---

Chapter objectives

Students will (this is the HL extension for IB students but SL students can benefit):
1. Practice thinking strategies (command terms) related to synthesis and evaluation with discuss modeled
2. Discuss positive effects on cognition, such as enhanced mental rotation skills and visual working memory
3. Discuss negative effects on cognition, such as decreased attention and lowered memory
4. Identify and discuss the research methods used to study cognitive processing/digital world
5. Reflect on the newest digital natives

It is hard to be objective about how the digital world affects cognition because we are living in the midst of it. For adolescents, it is a social norm to text, use Google searches, spend time on social media, and play video games, so it is even harder to be objective than it is for adults.

Let's start with an activity to see how much time you spend on Facebook and other social media, talking and texting with cell phones, watching television, and playing video games. Go back to chapter 11 under the section **Theory of Planned Behavior** and find the box with the CAS/class activity for self-management. Create a questionnaire about technology use. How many hours are spent on each device or popular site? What are the perceived effects? Include how much sleep someone gets each night and how he or she feels throughout the next day, including any anxiety when being away from the cell phone. This data is a good place to start a discussion.

If the class decides to take action, then everyone can set a goal according to the Theory of Planned Behavior.

How much time do you spend with electronic devices? Do you know how they might affect you? Keep an open mind and get the facts. The effects are not all bad!
Used with license from megapixl.com.

Discuss means to give a considered and balanced view supported by research. The goal of this chapter is to reflect on both the good and the bad. No one suggests giving up the Internet, cell phones, and video games, but you may get some perspective on how it all affects you.

Reflecting on technology use and cognition is complicated because the same device can have both good and bad effects. How do we create a balance to get the good effects and minimize the risks? How can we study the effects and remain ethical? Benefits must outweigh risks, so the class can brainstorm ethics with each piece of research to keep critical thought at the center of this lesson.

TED Talk: Daphne Bavelier: Your brain on video games
This TED Talk stimulates great conversation about judging research. Bavelier outlines myths people have about video games and then explains experiment results about topics such as attention and mental rotation. She emphasizes that the benefits come from moderate use of the games rather than binge playing and that scientists face many challenges when creating games to help people with particular problems.

   A large body of research exists and newer studies correct some of the earlier design flaws. One example is participant expectancy. The experiment about video games improving visual working memory attempts to correct the problem. Boot, Blakeley, & Simons (2011) is one source for learning about research methods limitations related to this topic. A discussion about research methods includes an awareness of these and some resolutions.

17.1 Positive effects of video games: Mental rotation and visual working memory

Both of these positive effects come from playing video games, so we must watch attacking them as a waste of time. Surveys show that 99% of boys and 94% of girls play video games, but boys play more of the first person action shooter games that have the most benefits (Baily, West, & Anderson, 2011).

This section gives an overview of video game research findings and then details two example studies. We can review just a few examples for this course, but overall, action video games enhance mental rotation, selective attention, visual working memory, visual spatial processing, problem-solving, flexibility of task-switching, and faster processing of information.

Experiments usually compare participants without video game experience, called naive gamers, to participants with experience (Granic, Lobel, & Engels, 2014).

Overview of some video game benefits

Cognition	Description
Knowledge representation in our memory: Mental rotation (Granic, et al., 2014) **Mental representation is listed as cognitive processing in chapter 7 of Sternberg & Sternberg (2012)**	Action ("shooter") games have the greatest benefit, and these are usually violent. Positive effects are not found from playing other types of video games. Benefits may be because of the demands to make quick decisions within a three-dimensional space requiring focused attention. Improvements in spatial skills are similar to taking formal school courses and may be a good way to increase success in STEM fields. fMRI shows that the brain region controlling attention was less active in experienced gamers, leading researchers to conclude that playing the games caused more efficient attention and ability to filter out what is irrelevant. Experiments are used to study this topic.

Cognition	Description

Problem-solving (Granic, et al., 2014)	Video games allow people to explore a wide range of solutions to problems. The best games have open-ended problems. Players do not need to read a manual to find solutions but instead use trial and error. Adolescents with higher problem-solving skills on video games also have higher grades.
	   Strategic video games, such as role-playing games, have the most benefit, more than racing and fighting games.
	   Correlations are most often used to study and cannot show causation.

Visual working memory (Blacker, Curby, Klobusicky, & Chein, 2014; McDermott, Bavelier, & Green, 2014)	AVGP (action video game players) have an advantage over inexperienced players in visual working memory capacity after training, with some precision improvements.
	   This advantage for AVGPs was not found for long-term memory.
	   These findings come from experiments.

Research support #1: Action video games may help girls get better mental rotation skills needed for STEM careers

Much discussion was given to the reasons females did not perform as well in the math courses keeping them from entering STEM fields earlier in this book. Could this problem be reversed by having girls play action video games when they are young? Plenty of research shows that mental rotation skills, a high level spatial skill, can be learned and that training is long-lasting and transfers to different tasks (Uttal, et al., 2013). Closing the gender gap and keeping college students in STEM fields are important. Boys play action video games far more than girls and the trick is to get girls to use them (Feng, Spence, & Pratt, 2007).

One experiment demonstrates how first person action games can benefit girls (Feng, et al., 2007). The **aim of the study** was to see if 10 hours of action video game playing changed mental rotation skills (the **dependent variable**) of males and females more than a non-action game.

All 20 participants had no gaming experience before the study. Same-gender pairs were created and then one of the pair was assigned to the action game group and the other assigned to the non-action game group, the **independent variable**.

The **procedure** involved testing both groups for mental rotation skills before and after playing the games. The action game group played 10 hours of Medal Of Honor: Pacific Assault. This is a first person shooter game and participants must pay close attention and make quick decisions. The other group played 10 hours of Ballance, a puzzle game where the object was to guide a ball through obstacles.

Getting girls to play action video games may help them get the mental rotation skills needed for STEM fields. How can we get the benefits of gaming without its negative effects? How can we be ethical when studying this topic?
Used with license from megapixl.com.

Results showed that males and females in both groups showed improvement but the difference was significant only in the action game condition. In addition, the improvement was greatest for females playing Medal of Honor.

The authors **concluded** that action video games can improve mental rotation skills in females and might be a strategy to improve women's participation in STEM fields.

Research support #2: Visual working memory improves

Visual **working memory** (VWM) is theorized to have limited capacity, but what if playing video games can improve its capacity and/or encoding precision (Blacker, Curby, Klobusicky, & Chein, 2014)?

The **aim of the experiment** was to see if action video game training caused improvements in VWM capacity and encoding precision.

Male college students were randomly assigned to one of two training groups, one playing the first person shooter action video games Call of Duty: Modern Warfare and Call of Duty: Black Ops or a control group playing The Sims, a strategy game where the player takes on the role of a character and makes decisions. The two groups are the **independent variable** conditions.

For the **procedures**, participants trained with the games for 30 hours spread over 30 days. After the 30 days, VWM was tested with several tasks, and one was a change detection task similar to the colored circles you saw in Bavelier's TED Talk. Participants saw 32 trials of a blank screen, and for each trial were told to remember groups of colored squares, then saw another blank screen, and last had a test where the groups of squares were the same as before except that one was a different color. Participants pressed a key to indicate the two pictures were the same or different.

In response to criticisms that video games studies were inaccurate because of design flaws such as failing to control for participant expectancy, *this study was the first to ask participants if they expected to get better or worse during the training.* No differences were found between the groups. Everyone in the sample, both experienced and naive gamers, should have the same expectancy for making progress (Boot, et al., 2011).

Results showed that participants in the action video game training condition had significantly improved VWM capacity and encoding precision than the control group (Blacker, et al., 2014). It was not known if the action games directly enhanced VWM or if it improved via improved selection attention.

17.2: Negative effects of video games, cell phones, and computer use: Attention and memory

Many negative effects are demonstrated in studies, including increased aggressive cognition and lowered attention and memory. Next is a table summarizing some of the concerns about digital use and then two studies are detailed.

Cognition	Description
Aggressive cognition (Carnagey & Anderson, 2005)	Participants playing video games where violence is rewarded have more aggressive cognitions than those playing nonviolent games or when violence is punished. The aggressive cognitions then cause more aggressive behavior. This was found through experiments.
Executive function: Control over attention (Baily, et al., 2011)	Executive function means someone has controlled attention. Correlation studies show that video games are related to impulsiveness, hyperactivity, and disruptions when someone uses their cognitive control (such as in a Stroop test).

Memory (Sparrow, Liu, & Wegner, 2011; Wood, et al., 2011)	People who know they can use Google to search for information have poorer memory for that information than those who do not expect to be able to use Google searches.
	    Students multitasking with technologies remember less from class instruction then those not using technology.
	    These results are found through experiments.

Cognition	Description
Attention (Thornton, Faires, Robbins, & Rollins, 2014)	Talking and texting on cell phones distracts attention when walking, driving, working, having social interactions, and learning complex tasks. Just having a cell phone near-by is enough to cause the problems because people feel a constant need to attend to it. It takes longer for students to complete a reading task with the same performance on tests when they have cell phones with them. This is studied with experiments.
Attention: Task-switching (Wallace, 2016)	Different from multitasking (works well when doing a well practiced and less complex activity), task switching is done with complex tasks. Task switching means to change attention between tasks, such as typing a paper, answering a text on a cell phone, going back to the paper, and then going online to a social media site. All tasks use different schemas and efficiency drops each time someone switches. We might think we do well at task switching but research does not support this idea.

Research support #1: The mere presence of a cell phone disrupts attention on complex tasks

The **aim of the experiment** was to see if the presence of a cell phone was a disruption for simple tasks requiring lower levels of attention and complex tasks demanding greater attention (Thornton, et al., 2014).

For the **procedures**, participants were tested in pairs and were seated at different tables where they could not see each other. As the researcher gave instructions, she put a cell phone and stopwatch on the corner of one table. The other participant had a small notebook the size of a cell phone at the same place at their table. She later picked up the stopwatch when giving instructions but left the cell phone. Having a cell phone or not on the table and the simple or complex tasks were the **independent variables**.

One of the two tasks is described next. It was a digit cancellation task where participants looked at a page of numbers. In the simple task, participants were given a target number and then told to cross off all instances of that number as it appeared (2: 3824… where the 2 is crossed off). In the complex task participants were given a target number and told to cross off the numbers together in the list that equaled that number (3: 32161830… where the first 2 and 1 were crossed out and then 3 and 0 were crossed out).

Results showed that performance was worse on the harder tasks for participants with phones on their table.

The authors **conclude** that even if a cell phone is not being used, its presence is an attention distractor. This experiment was done again using the student's own cell phones with one class having their cell phones with them during the testing and another class without cell phones. Cell phones do not affect simple tasks, but do affect demanding tasks, supporting the conclusion that perhaps cell phones should not be around when people must do something complicated.

The full text article is recommended for class discussion as people often demand to have their phones!

Could this innocent looking device cause such problems with high level learning? Be open-minded and look into the facts. Used with license from megapixl.com.

Research support #2: Memory suffers when students use digital media in class

Technology use during classroom lectures is now the norm and researchers want to know if it improves learning. People seem to perceive that it does. The **aim of the experiment** was to compare off-task multitasking using digital technologies with controls using pen and paper or word processing only when learning real-time classroom lecture material (Wood, et al., 2011).

One hypothesis was that learning would be lower in participants assigned to a multitasking condition as compared with a non-multitasking condition.

For **procedures**, participants were randomly assigned to one of seven conditions, the **independent variable**. These were:

1. Off-task multitasking with Facebook
2. Off-task multitasking by texting with a cellphone
3. Off-task multitasking with MSN messaging
4. Off-task multitasking by emailing
5. Natural technology use with no multitasking (a control where participants used any technology they wished or none if they wished)
6. Word-processing only with no multitasking
7. Pen and paper only with no multitasking

Participants were students in a research methods class who attended three lectures about topics required for that class. All of the off-task multitaskers stayed in contact with research assistants during the lectures who all used standardized messages. At the end of each lecture participants took a test about the lecture material and the scores on the three tests were the **dependent variable**.

Results supported the hypothesis. Memory for class material was lower in all of the off-task multitasking conditions than for participants using pen and paper or minimal technology. In addition, those using no technology performed the best, and this included participants choosing to use no technology in the natural technology condition. It should be noted that multitaskers showed no memory improvement over the three lectures, so practice at multitasking does not make someone a better student.

Contrary to perceptions, research shows that using pen and paper is the best memory strategy. The class might try a natural experiment where students use different technologies and see how your results compare to Wood, et al., (2011). Source: pixabay.com

The authors **concluded** that technology can have a negative impact on classroom learning. This finding is contrary to perceptions that it is helpful. This study can provide a foundation for future research that should investigate, for example, technology use under more controlled conditions. This study was run in a natural setting and although steps were taken to ensure participants stuck to the assigned condition, it cannot be known if the rules were completely followed.

17.3: Reflecting on the newest digital natives

At 3, Kalani already loves to play games on her mother's cell phone, and quickly becomes mesmerized. Kalani's mom does not like her to play with the phone very often because Kalani does not want to give it back. She might scream and become uncooperative until she is busy doing something else. Phone games are a limited treat.

Even with limited screen time, Kalani has had early exposure to television, computers, and cell phones. She is part of a generation that might be called generation iPad, digital natives even more comfortable using technology than today's high school students. The class might look at some **YouTube** videos such as "A magazine is an iPad that does not work" and "Generation iPad" from ABC news, among others. How is your life as a millennial different from today's young children? How old were you when you first used a computer or a cell phone? Might the youngest digital natives think differently as they develop?

The American Academy of Pediatrics (2016) advises that parents create screen-free zones at home, especially in bedrooms and during meals. Children under 2 should have no screen time and should learn from humans rather than the television or computer. Children and adolescents should limit screen time to about two hours each day. Do you think parents take this advice? Why or why not? How did your use as a younger child fit the recommendations?

The American Academy of Pediatrics might reconsider its position to allow about an hour a day for children under two (Reddy, 2015). The class can read the article and discuss the reasons. Students should also revisit research by Patricia Kuhl from chapter 7 and watch the recommended film "A baby in the TV bottle" for a balanced view.

Kalani quickly is mesmerized by phone games. Her mother limits her use and this fits with advice from the American Academy of Pediatrics. We have not yet fully studied children this age. Might Kalani process information differently?
Used with permission

Why care about the effects of an online life? Children's technology use increased about 20% between 2004 and 2009, logging more than 7.5 hours each day (Wallace, 2016). Children are now media multitaskers, using more than one technology at once, such as watching television, using a computer, and texting all at the same time, so the actual total time each day might be over 10 hours. At the same time, daily print media use dropped over the same five year period from 43 to 38 minutes. We must consider what changes to cognition might happen with the earlier and increased use and if it is a good thing.

Thinking skills, inquiry, and collaboration

Students can observe children's use of technology and then work in groups to draw some conclusions about their attention, problem-solving, and language skills. Come up with behaviors to observe. Students can observe children in a natural setting without permission as long as they do not introduce anything new into the environment. However, students should get parent permission if observing children they know.

Students might also brainstorm how to conduct ethical research about using violent video games to help girls increase spatial skills. Can the benefits of a study outweigh the risks? In preparation for this discussion, students should read about video games and aggression, which researchers do not want to promote, and review the material about schemas, girls, and math earlier in this book about evaluating schema theory.

Chapter 18
The Sociocultural Approach to behavior: The Individual and the Group: Knowledge and Understanding

---

Chapter objectives

Students will:
1. Practice thinking strategies about knowledge and comprehension, with outline and describe modeled.
2. Outline the need to highlight the cultural in sociocultural: Internationalism in psychology.
3. Describe in-groups and out-groups, concepts needed for Social Identity Theory.
4. Describe conformity.
5. Describe compliance techniques.
6. Describe Zimbardo's Stanford Prison experiment
7. Describe modeling (social/cultural learning) and self-efficacy, key concepts for Bandura's Social Cognitive Theory.
8. Describe socialization.
9. Describe social cognition.
10. Describe stereotyping.

18.1: Highlighting the cultural in sociocultural: Let's focus on internationalism

Outline means to give a brief summary. Next is a summary of points highlighting the need to focus on culture when studying of all sociocultural topics. Students should be able to summarize what is important about how social psychology got its start and how it is now interrelated with cross-cultural psychology and cultural psychology research.

Psychology theories and research started in the US and Europe and were tested on western samples, often college students (Berry, 2013; Berry, et al., 2011; Triandis, 2007, 2002, 1994; Matsumoto & Juang, 2008). This includes social psychology topics such as Social Identity Theory, conformity, stereotyping, and compliance. We should not downplay the importance of the original theory and the classic studies verifying these theories as they provide a point of departure for studying the topics.

However, students must understand that psychological topics are incomplete unless they apply to all, and this is the main reason for taking a cultural point of view (Triandis, 2012; 2002). If students stop learning about a topic with an original western view, they risk adopting **ethnocentric** views of the world, something Berry (2013) calls **dumping** of western psychology on the rest of the world, which overwhelms contributions from other groups to understanding behavior.

It then becomes important to consider how well original theories and studies generalize to other cultures. It may seem a daunting task, but each topic in this chapter provides a piece of the puzzle needed for an international perspective by reviewing classic theories and studies and then research showing how the topic applies to other cultures.

The first lesson to learn is that *cross-cultural psychology and cultural psychology are really a series of research tools used to see when and in what way western theories apply to all.*

Students might wonder if the terms **cultural psychology** and **cross-cultural psychology** are the same thing. They are not, and both are needed for a balanced view of behavior. Cross-cultural psychologists view culture as something "outside of the person," an **etic** approach searching for meaningful universals (Triandis, 2007). Cultural psychologists view culture as something "inside of the person," an **emic** approach leading to the study of **indigenous psychology**, an insiders view coming from within cultures. Cross-cultural psychologists examine content and cultural psychologists examine context, but in the end, a complete study of behavior requires both.

Thinking skills: Promoting internationalism
This is not simply for IB students, but for all students preparing to live in the 21st century. The first part of the **IB mission** statement speaks to us all, "IB aims to develop inquiring, knowledgeable and caring young people who help to create a better and more peaceful world through **intercultural understanding** and respect."

The key to getting an international view may be to keep the culture thread in mind when studying any topic.

Image used with license from megapixl.com.

Chapter 3 includes topics from the sociocultural ATB so students already understand culture and cultural norms, etics and emics, and cultural dimensions. It is helpful as a framework for studying the topics in this chapter and the rest of psychology. Students can avoid oversimplification and take an international approach to the entire course by recognizing that someone's biology, cognition, and social influence unfolds within a cultural context.

18.2: Social Identity Theory Basics: In-groups and out-groups

Thinking skills and reflection
The phrase 'shared social category' relates to **subjective culture** studied when defining culture in chapter 3. When a category is valued by a group it becomes a cultural norm. Categories are also studied with **schema**. Students can make a list of all their in-groups to see these shared social categories, many of which can have high emotional meaning.

This section gives key details about **Social Identity Theory**, including the concepts **in-groups** and **out-groups**.

Social identity refers to people belonging to larger groups. Social Identity Theory (SIT) and **Social Categorization Theory** (SCT) originated in the UK to explain how an individual's self is intertwined with group behavior and intergroup interaction (Hogg, Terry, & White, 1995). Henri Tajfel did the early work on SIT in the 1950s examining perceptions, cognitions, and belief systems related to discrimination. In the 1980s, John Turner created SCT, which enhanced SIT. Both propose, "Group behaviors derive from cognitive representations of the self in terms of membership in a **shared social category**, in which, in effect, there is no psychological separation between self and the group as a whole" (Yuki, 2003, p. 166).

All social psychology concepts are **etics** with **emic** features, so a complete study of SIT starts with the original theory and ends with its cross-cultural applications, showing it is an etic with emic characteristics. The model below shows the path.

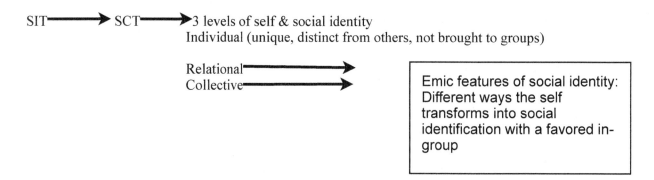

The pathway showing how SIT evolved into a culturally relevant theory.

Tajfel theorized that people improve their self-concept via their self-esteem by belonging to a group (Hogg, Terry, & White, 1995). When someone belongs to a group, it is automatically seen as a favored **in-group**. Outsiders are viewed as unfavored **out-groups**. Tajfel's original SIT focused on *enhancing one's self-esteem by creating categories of in-groups and out-groups.*

According to SIT, people belong to many groups, such as nations, sport teams, and families, and each group varies in importance to one's self-concept (Hogg, et al., 1995). Each group is represented in one's mind as a **schema** telling us what to think, feel, and do. In specific contexts, a particular social identity with a group becomes the most salient (striking, noticeable) way of self-regulating behavior. Once the proper social identity for a particular context is identified, those behaviors become **stereotypes** of the in-group and the **norm**. The behaviors of out-groups are stereotypes of what others are like, and these stereotypes can spark fierce competition and even discrimination.

Identifying with an in-group is natural but creates cognitive categories of "us" and "them" that enhance the self but sharpen distinctions between in-groups and out-groups (Fiske, 2004). Research shows that people receiving a short-term threat automatically stereotype and stigmatize out-groups. Categorizing and self-enhancement are

---

Thinking skills: Core motives
We might not want to think of ourselves as aligning with a favored in-group and even conforming to a group, but the research suggests that we do. This stems from our **core motives**, such as belonging, controlling, enhancing the self, and trusting.

Social psychology studies " how the thoughts, feelings, and behaviors of individuals are influenced by the actual, imagined, or implied presence of other human beings" (Fiske, 2004, p. 4).

Our core motives help us survive, and the need to belong to an **in-group** is strong. A large body of research on SIT, conformity, and compliance demonstrate this and shows that people will sometimes do things they think they would never do because of belonging to a favored in-group. Research about SIT, conformity, compliance, and how quickly we align with an in-group are examples in this book.

subjective beliefs that are not necessarily true but give *meaning* to an in-group (Hogg, et, al., 1995). The in-group is always favored. Identification with sport teams is a good example of an in-group seen as different from the other team, the out-group. Perhaps the highly competitive nature of sports and even aggression is caused by social identity.

SIT is well studied and has cultural relevance, a topic that is evaluated in the next chapter. Just remember that intergroup conflict does not happen unless people see themselves as members of separate groups (Fiske & Taylor, 2008).

18.3: Conformity to in-group norms

Next is key details about conformity to in-group norms that necessarily to use on exams but helps us understand the power of in-groups and out-groups and get a historical perspective. This section has a great deal of detail so students get the full picture of how in-groups behave and can see that conforming to in-groups is a behavior seen cross-culturally.

Although people may deny their tendency to conform, the research shows otherwise. Humans are social creatures and belonging needs are strong. Zimbardo (2007) warns that the worst abuses that humans commit against other humans "are not the consequences of exotic forms of influence, such as hypnosis, psychotropic drugs, or brainwashing, but rather the systematic manipulation of the most mundane aspects of human nature over time in confining settings" (p. 259). **Self-serving biases** make us believe we are not vulnerable to social influence. Zimbardo warns that simply because we hold self-serving biases, we tend to underestimate **situational** influences on behavior. The tendency is to focus on **dispositions**, meaning that something inside of the person, such as their personality, is considered the reason for their behavior.

Conformity research investigates a particular kind of social influence, how a majority influences individual behavior. Conformity serves two purposes (Aronson, et al., 2007). It is a way to get information from others to interpret ambiguous situations. We conform in simple ways after finding out what others are doing, such as how to address a professor. It also serves the normative purpose of satisfying the need to belong to a group. These two purposes fit in with the idea that humans evolved to interact with others in cultural groups.

Thinking Skills: The self-serving bias
The **self-serving bias** (SSB) is an attribution error. Making an attribution means to assign cause for something. The SSB means that people are more likely to attribute success to themselves (internal attributions) and blame failures on the situation (external attributions) (Aronson, et al., 2007). The self-serving bias is an **etic**, so it is seen in all cultures.

People use a self-serving bias for two reasons related to core motives. First, self-serving attributions protect one's self-worth when it is threatened. Second, people want to enhance the self, feel a sense of control, and make good impressions. See how the core motives are important again?

Solomon Asch's classic conformity experiment

The classic experiment demonstrating conformity is next. The **aim of the experiment** was to show that people are likely to conform to group norms, even going against their personal judgment of something that is obviously true (Asch, 1956).

The **procedure** involved 7-9 participants gathering in a classroom for what they thought was a visual discrimination experiment. The task was to match a standard line with one of three other lines. All but one participant, called the critical subject, had been prompted to give an incorrect response on certain trials. The individual who was not prompted heard the others give incorrect answers that clearly contradicted his own observation. Would the critical subject, who was put in the position of being a minority of one against a wrong and unanimous majority, conform to the incorrect answers?

Everyone's answer was said out loud and in order so the critical subject was the next to last to answer. The role of the experimenter was to impartially administer the tasks, and though aware of disagreement between participants, continued on with the study as if nothing was odd.

Results showed that some participants conformed more than others, but of the approximately 100 participants, 75% conformed to the majority on at least one of the critical trials. Some participants conformed on all the trials!

The Asch experiment used deception so it is important to ask if the benefits of the study outweigh the risks to participants to justify dispensing with informed consent. Another ethical concern was keep individual responses confidential because it took place in a group.

Between the original study in 1955 and 1994, there were 94 experiments using Asch's procedure and 39 modifications of the original model, with 17 of these testing conformity cross-culturally (Fiske, 2004). The study of conformity did not end in 1994.

One research question of importance was how conformity as defined and studied in the West applied cross-culturally. Do others conform and in the same way?

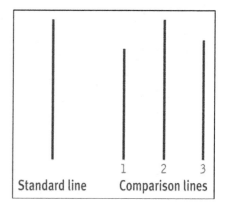

Standard line   Comparison lines

Lines similar to those used in the Asch experiment.

The real participant in the Asch experiment leans in and shows disbelief at the answers of the others!
Source: Asch, S. E. (1955). Opinions and social pressure. *Scientific American,* 193 (5), 31-35. Used with permission.

Conformity to in-groups is pancultural

It should be no surprise to students to see **dimensions of culture** again as we describe culture and conformity because individualism and collectivism are important reasons for behavior. **Individualism** and **collectivism** occur in degrees, and influence conformity in many ways such as with the cultural dimension of **tightness versus looseness** (Triandis, 1995).

People from tight cultures conform more to an in-group than people form loose cultures. Japan is an example of a tight culture, though modern Japan is not as tight as it was historically. The US is a loose culture (people in the US still conform but do it a little differently than people in tight cultures).

Triandis (1994) tells a story about something that happened when he was in Japan in 1990. "I read an account in the English language *Japan Times* about a starling event. A teacher slammed a heavy door on the head of a student who was two minutes late for class, killing her" (p. 159). Triandis was intrigued that there were varied opinions in public discussions about the killing. Some of the opinions showed an understanding of the teacher's attempts to train students to be on time.

Another story from Triandis (1995) told about a 13 year-old Japanese student, Yuhei Komada, who was **bullied** by classmates. Yuhei endured bullying from the group and was later found suffocated in a closet. Triandis was not sure if Yuhei did anything to start the bullying, but remarked that the bullying, called *ijime,* happened when someone did not fit into the **in-group**. How was Yuhei different? He did not use the Japanese dialect of the community, his father was educated in Tokyo, and his family had only lived in the community for 17 years.

Both stories are about people conforming to in-group norms. Historically, when the Japanese were a very tight culture, Japanese samurai were even allowed to kill people of a lesser rank if they thought their behavior deviated from expected norms.

Japanese children are protected when they identify with an in-group. In tight cultures people are expected behave as other's behave. Conforming shields people from making social judgments that bring criticism and have unfortunate effects on one's social position (Triandis, 1994).

Tightness requires homogeneous groups where the rules are clear. In contrast, in less homogeneous cultures, the norms are not always so clear or enforced.

The Japanese are more likely to conform to an **in-group's norm** expectations than they are to **out-groups**, so the way they conform is a little different from people in other cultures (Aronson, et al., 2007).

It then makes sense that some of the Asch replications found Japanese participants unwilling to conform to the opinions of strangers. The Matsuda experiment reviewed next details why.

Matsuda shows how culture affects conformity: This is also a chance to learn something about Japanese culture

Cross-cultural experiments had often found less conformity in Japanese samples than Asch found in the American samples (Matsuda, 1985).

Matsuda believed these experiments were flawed because they did not take into account the importance of Japanese **in-groups**. He designed an experiment with the **aim to study** in-groups specific to Japanese culture and how participants conformed to each, believing a properly designed study would demonstrate that Japanese persons *do* conform.

Matsuda identified three different types of Japanese relationships. The Japanese select appropriate behavior based on the kind of relationship they have with a group and these relationships affect the level of conformity in an experiment.

Categories of Japanese in-groups

Type of group	Definition
Uchi	Uchi relationships are the most intimate of the three.
Seken	Seken is an intermediate level of intimacy.
Soto	Soto relationships are when there are few ties between people.
Amae, something that confounds studying Japanese relationships	Amae applies to uchi relationships and is a "mutual understanding among members that allows moderate deviation" (Matsuda, 1985, p. 86). Amae permits a Japanese person to feel less pressure to conform to another. Amae does not allow the person to fully deviate. However, a person can carefully compare their view to that of others and decide on an appropriate range of deviation. Amae does not exist in seken relationships so there is little room for deviation to those groups. As Soto relationships are not important, people are generally indifferent to the other's opinions.

Matsuda hypothesized that the most conformity took place in seken relationships. Conformity to uchi relationships would come next. He expected the least conformity from soto relationships.

Conformity was operationalized as a change in judgment to the group view with the change occurring from an initial correct choice. This is a modification of Asch's procedure.

Procedures are next. Seven groups of Japanese females were formed based on the three intimacy levels of uchi, seken, and soto, the **independent variable**. The uchi groups were made up of females selecting each other as important in-group members. Having a group of females give self-presentations to the others created the moderate intimacy seken groups. The soto groups were not given any instructions to get to know each other.

Each participant sat in front of a computer and could not see each other's answers. They saw a figure on the screen and compared it to three others. Participants rated how close the figure was to the other three, with answers ranging from 0-5. After all four team members completed the task, each was told the mean response of the group. Seventeen trials were conducted, and for all but three, participants were given the correct mean of the group. The three trials used for the experiment gave an incorrect mean. Next everyone was asked to confirm their answers. They could change their answer or keep their original answer. Responses were anonymous.

These Japanese schoolgirls might be an uchi relationship. The level of conformity depends on the level of intimacy.
Source: pixabay.com

Results showed that conformity was high, especially in uchi groups, and the degree of conformity was greater than expected, especially since the conditions of the experiment made it easy to avoid conforming. The girl's responses were anonymous and there was no face-to-face interaction.

This is an important study because it showed the Japanese conform but *only in specific contexts*. Matsuda's conclusions fit in with a larger body of evidence showing that **context** is an important determinant of behavior.

The study has limitations. First, the sample used all females. Females may conform more than males. Second, Matsuda's experiment is a modification of Asch's original so it is not completely comparable.

Takano challenges the belief that the Japanese conform more than others

Many believe that the Japanese conform because they are part of a **collectivist culture**, but this generalization is not entirely true and the **aim of the experiment** was to investigate this. (Takano & Sogon, 2008).

Concluding that the Japanese are more collectivist because of conformity research is misleading (Takano & Sogon, 2008). For example, previous research concluding the Japanese conform confounds conformity with the kind of discipline used in different sport club groups. **Procedures** in one experiment created groups based on association with a sport club. There are two kinds of sport clubs in Japan, informal clubs (doukoukai) and formal sport clubs (taikukai). The discipline in formal clubs is strict and vertical. The discipline in informal clubs is looser.

To control for discipline and avoid confounding the experiment, groups were created from only informal *non-sport* clubs. The study used a *strict replication of Asch's experiment* so that the results could be weighed against the original findings.

Results showed less conformity in non-sport clubs than previous reports from studies creating groups using sport clubs. The percentage of conformity was similar to those found in American samples.

18.5: Compliance techniques: Creating in-group behavior

Class activity: Advertising
Students can look up examples of how advertisers use each compliance technique. They can start with the things they buy the most. Include advertising to children. Do you see how advertisers create in-group compliance?

Compliance techniques were first described in chapter 3 because the correlation study about the foot-in-the-door is also an example of research demonstrating **individualism-collectivism**. Review that material before starting this section.

What is compliance and what are some common techniques?

Compliance is "yielding to social pressure in one's public behavior, even though one's private beliefs may not have changed" (Matsumoto, 2008, p. 369).

Compliance techniques are used both professionally, in sales and fundraising, and in everyday life (Cialdini & Sagarin, 2005).

Compliance techniques socially evolved. The **evolution** of social influences ties social psychology to the biological approach to behavior. Compliance professionals who use the techniques successfully prosper and survive, passing their success to the next generation.

Many compliance techniques have been identified and studied (Cialdini & Sagarin, 2005).

Compliance techniques (Cialdini & Sagarin, 2005)

Compliance technique	Description
Reciprocity	**Reciprocity**. People are more likely to comply with requests from someone who has already done them a favor. Reciprocity served an evolutionary purpose. People could give away things and then get something back because another person is likely to return the favor. The **door-in-the-face** concession is one example where an extreme request is made, refused, and then the person makes a less demanding request—the real request.
Friendship/liking	People are more likely to comply with requests from those they like. The point of this strategy is to get others to like you first. Tupperware is a company with success at using the friendship-liking strategy. Attractiveness, similarity, such as wearing the same types of clothing, giving compliments, having a previous relationship with a person, and using a similar type of communication are factors that increase the intensity of the friendship-liking strategy.
Authority	Requests from legitimate authority figures are more likely to be followed. Sales professionals benefit from describing themselves as experts in a field.

Compliance technique	Description
Commitment/ consistency	Humans want consistency and are more likely to comply with a request if they have already committed to a similar request. Professionals use a variety of strategies that capitalize on getting a person to comply to a request that is consistent with a previous commitment. A. **Foot-in-the-door** techniques involve a person making a small request that will surely be granted. The initial request is followed by a greater request. To remain consistent, the second request will likely be granted. B. **Bait-and-switch procedures** are sales strategies where one item is advertised but when a person arrives at the store, the item is no longer available. However, other items are available, but often at a greater price. C. **Low-ball techniques** are part of sales pitches where an item is offered at a low price, but when the customer agrees to buy it, suddenly there is some reason, perhaps a calculation error, that interferes with the initial low price. The person is likely to agree to buy the item because of the initial commitment.
Scarcity	People are more likely to try to get an item if it is perceived as scarce because scarce items are more attractive. We lose a sense of freedom if an item is unavailable so it is best to get it when obtainable. The psychological reactance theory explains that when people perceive a freedom as limited, such as the ability to acquire a good, it becomes more desirable. The **limited number** and **deadline technique** are two sales strategies that use the scarcity principle.

Classic research about compliance

One experiment about compliance tests reciprocity with the **door-in-the-face** technique (Cialdini et al., 1975).

How can we increase the chance that someone complies with a request? One way is to make an extreme request that will surely be rejected and then follow it with a smaller one, the real request. This tactic works because someone feels pressure to match a requestor's concession.

Two assumptions are made about the success of the door-in-the-face technique. First, the target must reject the extreme request, showing they have taken a position on the request. The concession from the researcher then places pressure on the target to also make a concession. Second, the target must realize the researcher has made a concession.

The **aim of experiment** was to demonstrate that someone "who followed a refused initial request with a smaller request would obtain more agreement to the smaller request than a person who made only the smaller request" (p.208).

The sample consisted of 72 participants walking on university sidewalks during the day. For **procedures**, psychology students made one of three requests to participants, the **independent variable**.

1. *Rejection-moderation condition.* Participants were asked to serve as counselors to juvenile delinquents for two years. When participants refused the extreme request they were asked to chaperone a group from the juvenile detention center to the zoo for two hours.

2. *Smaller request only control*. Participants were asked to chaperone the group from the juvenile detention center to the zoo for two hours.
3. *Exposure control*. Participants were asked to comply with either request.

Results showed that no one agreed to the extreme request and there was significantly greater agreement to the smaller request when someone had heard the extreme one. This experiment is part of a larger body of research on the door-in-the-face technique, which is extended to include other variables to ensure the two assumptions outlined above are demonstrated in experiments.

Cross-cultural research: Compliance is correlated with individualism-collectivism

The correlation study about commitment/consistency using the **foot-in-the-door** technique is detailed in chapter 3 about **cultural dimensions**.

18.6: Zimbardo's Stanford Prison Experiment: The power of the situation makes people quick to identify with an in-group

Zimbardo (2007) uses the Stanford Prison Experiment (SPE) to show the power of the situation. This is also not really for use on exams but is good background. Zimbardo believes that most people, even social scientists, underestimate the influence of the situation on behavior. We often deny how easily and quickly one's character can be transformed if placed in a particular situation. At least in the West, we minimize the role situations play in creating and maintaining the conditions under which evil acts are committed. "People and situations are usually in a state of dynamic tension. Although you probably think of yourself as having a consistent personality across time and space that is likely not to be true" (p. 8). Zimbardo challenges the view that most of us have of ourselves.

The Stanford Prison Experiment took place in 1971 and the **aim of the study** was to show the power of the situation. It is still relevant for understanding why the power of the situation makes people quick to identify with an **in-group**.

Procedures are next. Researchers took 24 healthy male participants, primarily white middle class college students, and randomly assigned them to be guards or prisoners. Participants did not know each other before the study that took place in the basement of the Stanford University Psychology Department. A mock prison was created with cells, solitary confinement rooms, and an exercise yard. Both guards and prisoners were given clothing that identified the role they were assigned that included khaki pants and mirror sunglasses for the guards, and smocks and an ankle lock for the prisoners. Participants were paid $15 for each day of the study. The guards had a brief orientation and were told to keep order, prevent escapes, that the prisoners should feel helpless, and that there was to be no violence against the prisoners.

The study started with the surprise public arrest of the prisoners by real police, which was the only deception used in the study. They were processed and placed in the mock prison, remaining there 24 hours a day while the guards worked 8 hour shifts.

Film and class activity
The film *Quiet Rage* is powerful. Reading about the SPE is not the same as seeing it in action. The film prompts good class discussion about the power of the situation.
Zimbardo's website, www.lucifereffect.com contains valuable resources for considering why people commit atrocities and materials about resisting influence. Have the class spend time looking through the website.

The researchers were surprised that the assigned roles overtook the participants so quickly. **Results** showed that prisoners experienced a loss of personal identity, arbitrary control from the guards, and were deprived of adequate sleep and privacy. They reacted with disbelief, rebellion, and then passiveness. Half of the prisoners were released early because they developed emotional and cognitive disorders. These disorders disappeared after the participants resumed their normal lives. The guards quickly assumed their roles in the mock prison. Some of the guards took the power of establishing and enforcing rules too far and became abusive, especially during the hours when they thought they were not being observed. Though the study was originally designed to last for 2 weeks, Zimbardo ended it after 6 days.

The biggest **conclusion** of the SPE is that situations are significant.

The ethics of the SPE

Avoid taking the extreme position that the SPE was unethical because there is much to consider. Zimbardo feels it was unethical in some respects but ethical in others.

Arguments that it was unethical follow.

1. The study caused human suffering. Several of the prisoners showed severe stress.
2. The guards suffered because they realized what they did to the prisoners. The abuse to the prisoners put them under greater stress than those participating in Milgram's experiment.

> **Thinking skills: Ethics is the sociocultural ATB**
> Students should reflect on the ethics of many social psychology studies. Zimbardo's comments may help you understand that deciding if a study is ethical is complicated, but in the end, the benefits must outweigh the risks. Would this study be allowed today?

3. The informed consent form contained nothing about the surprise arrests.
4. The researchers should have ended the study before they did. Zimbardo says he was conflicted over his dual roles of an investigator with research goals and someone who was to uphold ethical principles. Zimbardo said that neither he nor the ethics committee had any idea that the participants would take on their roles so quickly.

Arguments that it was ethical follow.

1. All participants signed an informed consent form stating they knew their privacy would be invaded, the food would be minimal, some of their civil rights would be infringed upon, and they might be harassed.
2. The surprise arrests were the only deceptive part of the study. All other conditions were disclosed.
3. The mock prison was open for outsiders to inspect. Parents could visit, decide their son was suffering, and remove him from the study. However, no parent removed his or her son.
4. There was extensive debriefing.
5. There were some positive outcomes for the participants. Benefits must outweigh the risks to participants. Although Zimbardo was not sure the gains of the study outweighed the immediate suffering of participants, he argued that there were longer-term gains expressed by participants. Many said that it was a valuable learning experience.

18.7 Social Cognitive Theory: Modeling (social/cultural learning) and self-efficacy

Describe means to give a detailed account. Next is important details about **Social Cognitive Theory** needed to evaluate it in the next chapter.

Social Cognitive Theory explains how culture is transmitted to children, how cognition mediates reinforcement, and how **modeling** and **self-efficacy** predict behavior.

Bandura may be the most cited researcher in the history of psychology. Social Cognitive Theory explains many behaviors such as depression, phobias, eating disorders, education, aggression and delinquency, moral behavior, gender roles and identity, health behavior, sport performance, careers and organizational behavior, culture and behavior, language use, and terrorism.

Social Cognitive Theory Basics

- **Modeling** and **self-efficacy** are key concepts. Modeling means to observe the actions of another person and use the observations as a guide for future behavior (Bandura, 1977). Self-efficacy is the belief that one is capable of starting and carrying through with an action.
- Social Cognitive Theory explains how people grow and change in all cultures (Bandura, 2002).Modeling and self-efficacy develop as children grow up within cultures.
- Modeling takes place through four processes—attention, retention, reproduction, and motivation.
- The **anticipation of reinforcement** is mediated by **outcome expectancies**, which means people have strong beliefs of what will happen in the future, such as believing that drinking lessens stress and will help them make friends. Both expectations are incorrect but can lead to problem drinking.
- Self-efficacy explains which behaviors are actually performed within cultures.
- Self-efficacy is the greatest predictor of behavior, more than **schemas** and **genes**.
- We are all agents of our own behavior and the word agency means to influence one's personal life. This is done by anticipating reinforcement from our own experiences and from the group and deciding which ones work best, so we act as agents both personally and through the collective group.
- Personal agency is when someone guides his or her own individual actions, such as slipping on icy steps and being more careful in the future.
- Collective agency means that people achieve some goals in groups, such as educating children. Students learn by modeling teachers with high self-efficacy and through schools where leaders have high expectations and standards.
- The degree to which groups use personal or collective agency varies by culture. The degrees are sometimes measured with a **dimension of culture**, such as **individualism** or **collectivism**. Self-efficacy is the key to all successful behavior and is incorrectly believed to apply only to individualistic cultures.
- Social Cognitive Theory is a simple and elegant theory explaining a wide variety of behaviors.

The nuts and bolts of modeling

Modeling was the focus of Bandura's earliest research. Modeling means to observe the actions of another person, form an idea of how one should behave, and use the ideas as a guide for future behavior (Bandura, 1977) The Bobo experiments demonstrate modeling and are included in the next chapter about evaluating Social Cognitive Theory.

Modeling occurs through four processes, **attention**, **retention**, **reproduction**, and **motivation**. We will use the Bobo experiments as an example for thinking through the steps.

Modeling process	Description
Attention	Children pay attention to a model. In the Bobo experiment in this book about modeling and aggression, the models were an adult live model, a film of an adult model, or a film of a cartoon character model. The children attended to how the models verbally and physically behaved toward the Bobo doll.
Retention	Children retain the observations for later use. Retention, or *learning*, was measured by asking the children to repeat the scenes they observed. Both male and female children demonstrated what they saw.
Reproduction	Children's behavior in spontaneous play tested the reproduction of what the children observed. Children learn behaviors that are not necessarily reproduced unless the behaviors receive reinforcement. While both male and female children showed that they retained the same behaviors, boys reproduced the aggressive behaviors in spontaneous play far more often than the girls.
Motivation	The motivation is the *anticipated consequences* for reproducing the modeled behaviors. Boys receive rewards more often for using aggression than girls. This is the explanation for why boys produce the aggression.

Learning starts in young children through **imitating** adult behavior, and success depends on the model's quick reactions. If children do not have reinforcement available to them, their ability to imitate quickly declines (Bandura, 1977). Children without symbolic **language** cannot easily store information cognitively for later use and instead rely on trial and error.

Children become capable of **delayed imitation** as they develop language and cognitively develop (Bandura, 1977). This is the start of *modeling*. Children use verbal symbols to store observed behavior. *Language is the primary way that children model once they have representational thought.* Social learning occurs rapidly once children are able to store and creatively use modeled behavior through verbal symbols.

The motivation for a behavior can be influenced in a couple of ways.

1. **Vicarious reinforcement**. This means to see something happen to another person and learn from their successes and failures. The Bobo experiments demonstrate vicarious reinforcement. A model rewarded for a behavior is more effective than modeling without a reward. Second, if a model goes unpunished for an undesirable behavior, it increases similar acts in the observer. This explains **phobias**. Monkeys with no prior fear of snakes can develop a fear after viewing a video of monkeys showing fear of snakes (Zinbarg & Mineka, 2000). Girls can mode the low efficacy of female **math** models (Bandura, 1997). In humans, vicarious reinforcement depends on specific factors, including the severity of the consequences and model's success in justifying their behavior (Bandura, 1977).
2. **Self-regulation**. Self-regulation means that we act as our own agents of behavior and do not always need an external source of reinforcement (Bandura, 1977). Self-regulation is the motivation for much human behavior. Children may start off needing reinforcement but eventually become self-regulators and use self-appraisals to judge the quality of those behaviors. Each new behavior is judged against previous behavior. Think of all the behavior humans self-regulate, such as school or sport performance, gender role expectations, what is gained in an aggressive act, or even how terrorists judge the value of a mission.

Self-efficacy

Self-efficacy, the belief that one is capable of starting and carrying through a required action, is as an important motivator of behavior. Research demonstrating causes and treatments of alcoholism and people's health behavior demonstrate self-efficacy in the next chapter when evaluating Social Cognitive Theory.

High perceived self-efficacy to follow through on a behavior is linked to both prosocial behaviors and antisocial behaviors. For example, one purpose of schools is to promote high self-efficacy for achievement through **teacher models with high self-efficacy** for their own understanding of a subject. In another example, criminals can have high efficacy in their ability to follow through with an antisocial aggressive act.

Teachers with high self-efficacy for their subject are models promoting achievement. Source: pixabay.com.

Gender and culture affect self-efficacy that than affects the anticipation of reinforcement. *This is a powerful generalization explaining many behaviors, such as gender-linked behavior, academics, many mental illnesses, health behavior, and aggression.*

Moral disengagement

Moral disengagement explains when people abandon a moral belief. We often wonder why people can do things that seem to go against their basic morals, and students can apply this as one theory explaining **terrorism**.

A terrorism activity is part of the appendices. Students should know something about terrorism other than what they hear from popular media because it seems to be increasing. The lesson is an application of Social Cognitive Theory as well as many social psychology concepts, such as Social Identity Theory and conformity.

18.8: Socialization

Socialization is "the process by which we internalize and learn the rules and patterns of the society in which we live" (Matsumoto & Juang, 2008, p. 60). Describe means to give a detailed account and the key details follow.

Key details of socialization
Socalization refers to all the things people need to learn to live in a society, meaning children observe and talk (mostly through narratives) with others, and see the situations and contexts in which something happens, such as traditions followed to celebrate a holiday or expected study habits for school (Matsumoto & Juang, 2008).
Socialization (and enculturation) starts the day as someone is born. Children are socialized (and enculturated) by parents, other important people, and institutions such as schools (Matsumoto & Juang, 2008).
Language is the primary way adults socialize and enculturate children, demonstrated in the study of narratives and socialization.

Key details of socialization

Peggy Miller's **discourse model of socialization** is a good approach to studying socialization. The model focuses on how "children are socialized into systems of meaning" (Miller, Fung, & Koven, 2007, p. 597). This is done through repeated **narratives** between parents and children, which are the building blocks of socialization. A narrative is a special story helping children understand what is expected in a culture. *Children cannot become enculturated unless there is a socialization process in place so they can learn what is important to do.* Miller's model focuses on these repeated narratives.

The key parts of Peggy Miller's discourse model of socialization are next (Miller, et al., 2007).

1. Children participate regularly each day in narratives with adults, with the end goal of understanding culture (becoming enculturated).
2. Stories socialize children from the day they are born, drawing them into local practices they must understand. These stories launch children onto the path to adulthood.
3. Children's stories might seem unimportant at first glance, but are the building blocks of socialization.
4. Parents from different cultures use storytelling for different cultural ends, so socialization via stories is culturally specialized from the day a child is born.

The following research is an application of Miller's model. It can be argued that storytelling (narration) is the most important vehicle for socializing children.

Research evidence: Storytelling is the key to socializing children

It can be argued that children's storytelling, mostly through narratives, is the main vehicle for socialization.

A large body of research supports Miller's model (Miller, et al., 2007). The **aim of one study** shows that narratives socialize children because they teach expected behavior for a culture, particularly moral behavior meant to improve children as they develop.

The **procedures** used **ethnography**, observations studies of cultural practices, to show differences in how Taiwanese and European American parents use narratives to instruct children in moral and social practices.

Results showed that parents in Taiwan used stories with 2 years old children to highlight their mistakes, and most of these stories took place right after the child's misbehavior. Taiwanese parents took every chance to correct children by pointing out specific problems with their behavior. Narratives were full of a child's incorrect behavior as the main point of the story and the endings aimed to teach children what they should have done.

Activity: Interview children

One way to understand the importance of narratives for socialization is to interview children and see for yourself.

Divide the class into 3 groups, and interview children at age 3, age 5, and age 7. Brainstorm questions about daily life and cultural norms to ask the children and then compare the answers across the age groups. Students should be able to see children's greater socialization at each point. This activity also illustrates cognitive development, described next with the theories of **Lev Vygotsky** and **Jerome Bruner**.

In contrast, European American parents rarely used narratives to call attention to a child's past misbehavior. They used stories to entertain children or raise their self-esteem.

These storytelling differences also reflect larger cultural values for each group. Taiwanese parents used narratives to teach Confucian goals of self-improvement and respecting teaching and listening. The European American parents focused on an individual's self-esteem, consistent with individualism values.

Socialization research about storytelling is a good place to learn something about language development theories

It is hard to understand human socialization (and **enculturation**) unless it is grounded in developmental theories of **language**, something students of **developmental psychology** need to know anyway.

Children's talk, and particularly narratives, aids human cognitive development, making socialization and enculturation just two of the many benefits of children's language development. It can be argued that language is the most fundamental of the cognitive processes and that all the other human cognitive processes, such as memory, attention, and decision making, cannot develop without it.

Consider an example from my own life that is common in a child's socialization. My brother John told me his 3-year-old daughter Lauren was a math genius. His belief was based on Lauren's ability to count to 50. I asked to interview her. We were having supper and Lauren was sitting in her high chair. I asked Lauren what she did that day. Here is our exchange.

"I am getting married."
"Who are you marrying?"
"Dustin." (a boy from her daycare)
"Does Dustin have a job?"
"Yes."
"What is his job?"
"It is his job to get spanked."
"How much does that pay?"
"About 40 cents."
"Is that a lot of money?"
"Yes."
"What can you buy with 40 cents?"
"Oh, a house."

> **Thinking skills: Socialization develops as language develops**
> *Language is the primary vehicle for* **socialization** *and* **enculturation**, so students should know something about Lev Vygotsky and Jerome Bruner.
> Studying **developmental psychology** requires students to know some well supported language theories for the play topic. The socialization section is a good place to do this because children cannot be socialized and enculturated without it! Vygotsky and Bruner are very useful for the developmental chapters.

John could not stop laughing. Lauren was not a math genius, at least in the way he thought. She did not know what it meant to have 40 of something. But Lauren was figuring out what it *meant* to have a job or get married, things she heard adults regularly discuss. Lauren was becoming **socialized** and **enculturated**, and was doing this through stories. Many of Lauren's stories were close to meeting the requirements of **narratives**.

Children's stories are funny and often very simple, but these stories are important for development (Miller, et al., 2007).

Culture is transmitted to children (enculturated) through repeated interactions with family members that are mediated by narratives and other communication . Narratives assist children in learning about **cultural norms (subjective culture)** and the content of narratives is specialized for the demands of particular cultures.

A large body of research shows that narratives define who we are as people *throughout the lifespan*. Parents narrate to children before they can produce speech, much of the interaction between parents and children contain narratives, most children's "talk" is narrative, and narrations are still important in later life.

This section starts with theories and research from **LevVygotsky**, as he built a framework for thinking about the importance of language to a child's development and socialization. Next is theory and research from **Jerome Bruner**, building on Vygotsky and including a discussion of narratives.

If you are studying developmental psychology, pay attention to Vygotsky and Bruner because you will need this to consider topics such as play and cognitive development.

Lev Vygotsky: Language and cognitive development

Vygotsky studied the process by which elementary thinking (recall) in children becomes internalized abstract thought. He considers language the most important cognitive process in humans. Vygotsky shows how other cognitive processes such as memory, attention, problem solving, and perception, are dependent on language. Vygotsky's theory is interactionist, meaning children develop with the help of parents, teachers, competent older children, and play. The interactions with others take place within a child's cultural context.

Vygotsky's research methods were "pilot studies," uncontrolled demonstrations that he called experiments in his writings. Many others have tested Vygotsky's theories using both experimental and non-experimental methods.

Vygotsky (1934) rejected the idea that animals had language. Human thought is clearly tied to language and animal thought is not tied to their communications. Animal abilities are limited without the technical aid of language.

Language and thought are separate in early development. Sometime during the second year, language and thought follow separate paths. There are pre-linguistic and pre-thought behaviors in the actions of babies. When thought and language come together as the child develops, thought becomes verbal and speech rational. At this point a child moves into symbolic thought and far beyond animal development.

Vygotsky criticizes Piaget's emphasis on **egocentric speech** as a sign of their maturation level, when it appeared children talked to themselves. In a pilot study, Vygotsky repeated Piagetian tasks but made them more difficult to show that Piaget was incorrect. When the tasks were hard, 'egocentric' speech doubled in children. In the same tasks without obstacles, 'egocentric' speech occurred less. If Piaget was correct, then the level of egocentric speech should remain constant. Jerome Bruner agreed, finding that **narration** increases when children solve novel problems. Self talk assists problem solving and cognitive development.

Vygotsky's demonstrations led him to theorize that egocentric speech was an intermediate phase leading to inner (abstract) speech. Vygotsky renamed egocentric speech **externalized speech**, suggesting it was socially motivated (used for **socialization**). Notice how children talk out loud when playing or doing a task, as if they have to say it out loud. Older children and adults sometimes talk out loud, but it is done less often and only during a difficult task or a novel situation. The use of externalized speech simply represents a time in a child's development when thought and speech are still unifying.

Language development is responsible for a child's general cognitive development. This means a child's ability to think abstractly and use the other cognitive processes depends on language. Vygotsky (1978) believed all development depends on the social environment, and especially what happens within the **zone of proximal development (ZPD)**.

Vygotsky thought development and learning were two different things. Learning is mastering a task. Development has more to do with a child's overall abilities. Learning should be paired with a child's developmental level because it awakens the developmental process.

Model of the Zone of Proximal Development

Things outside of a child's ability
The zone of proximal development: Things a child can do with help from an adult of more capable peer and is where learning occurs
Things a child can do on his or her own

The zone of proximal development is in the middle and the goal is to raise children to the top. Once a child reaches the top of the zone, a new zone of development is created. New ZPDs are constantly created.

The ZPD is "the difference between the actual developmental level as determined by independent problem solving and the level of potential development as determined through problem solving under adult guidance or in collaboration with more capable peers" (Vygotsky, 1978, p. 86). The ZPD creates the environment for symbolic thought. Think of the ZPD this way. On their own, children can only achieve so much. This is the actual developmental level. With the help of an adult or more capable peer, a child rises to the top of their developmental zone. Tutoring raises a child to the upper limits of his or her capabilities. Teachers are important in the ZPD process because they bring students up to the top of their zone of development.

This parent is helping her child move to a higher zone of development.
Used with license from megapixl.com.

Play moves children through the zones of development. In play, children act more maturely than they do in normal life. During play immediate perception does not constrain behavior. Something new and abstract happens when a child enters an imaginary world. Meaning is the most important thing when playing. What goes unnoticed in real life become openly noticed as rules for behavior. Vygotsky studied two sisters in one of his pilot demonstrations. The **aim of the study** was to show that play helped children achieve a higher zone of development. He asked these real life sisters to play being sisters. **Results** showed that in real life, the 'sister' behaviors go unnoticed. In play, both girls are concerned with showing their 'sisterhood'. The girls are explicit about the rules associated with being sisters, such as who the leader is, how they dress, and how they treat each other differently than others. In the sister game, the girls understood more about their sibling relationship as opposed to other relationships. *Real play is socially and culturally motivated and contributes to development.* Children use language in play to make sense of the world.

Animals are not building blocks for humans. The key difference is that human thought is tied to language. Vygotsky (1934) said Wolfgang Kohler's ape studies only show animals performing actions. Sultan the ape needed all the objects in view to use them. Animals only perform actions to complete tasks. Children in similar situations act *and* speak, and do so increasingly and persistently when a task becomes more difficult. When children are faced with complicated problems, action, speech, and perception are aimed at the same task. Animal problem solving lacks this unity.

Lucy can already read and is helping Kalani. A more capable peer can help raise a child to a higher zone of development.
Used with permission

Vygotsky demonstrated the unity of action, speech, and perception by giving children a task so complicated that they could not use tools to solve it. No adults were available to help. Children had to use *thought*. Children's externalized speech increased dramatically as they worked on the task.

Vygotsky makes similar distinctions between animal perception, attention, memory, and problem solving and human abilities.

Animal problem solving is completely determined by perception and not thinking. Animals are unable to modify their perceptual field. Humans can change their perceptual field at will. If students are asked to think about something happening in another country, they easily shift their perception. It was once thought that human perception was simply a continuation of animal perception. This idea comes from early experiments on 2 year-old children showing that they described different elements of problems separately. Vygotsky changed the study procedures to allow children without full command of language to pantomime their answers, and they understood more than early studies showed. Young children could see the picture as whole when language was removed. It is only later, when language is more developed, that children can use it to describe entire problems. Vygotsky shows that humans have a unique perceptual ability to see the world as a whole, with meaning as well as form.

Vygotsky claims human attention works in a similar way. Humans direct their attention in a dynamic way to different perceptual fields with the aid of language.

Evidence supports these differences between human and animal abilities. For example, recent research supports Vygotsky's view that attention differs between animals and humans.

Animals communicate but it is different from human language (Moll & Tomasello, 2007). Researchers make clear distinctions between chimp to chimp cooperative communication, chimp to human cooperative communication, and human to human cooperative communication. Think about human communication, even something as simple as pointing to a rainbow and saying, "Look at that beautiful rainbow." Children even hear stories about a pot of gold at the end of a rainbow. The stories require **shared attention**, where the parent points out the rainbow and the child looks. The parent and child talk about its beauty and they admire it together.

Chimps communicate, and even gesture to other chimps, such as in play, but never have

> ### Film about play, language, and the ZPD
> Show the film *Play: A Vygotskian Approach*, available from The film is available from www.davidsonfilmstore.com/Play.htm. It is funny and clearly explains Vygotsky.
>
> Discussions about real play and destructive play are helpful after the film and students might even conduct their own observations about children's play in natural settings.

been observed to *point out* something to another chimp (Moll & Tomasello, 2007). They lack the abstract shared attention. However, chimp abilities are greater when they interact with humans. Chimps use humans as tools and point to objects they want. But the chimp's understanding of pointing is missing something and that is the shared attention that humans routinely use early in life. Human cooperative communication is on an entirely different level. Even 14 month-old human babies understand the abstract pointing gesture. In studies where an adult infers (by pointing) that they prefer one of several containers, the babies make the correct selection. This behavior is the beginning of the human **theory of mind**. Human infants can communicate cooperatively "to simply share interest in things and inform others of things" (p. 7).

When a child acquires verbal skills, memory is freed from recall and becomes a synthesis of past and present that is directed at purposeful goals (Vygotsky, 1978). Children with language construct memory and this construction is socially and culturally motivated. Vygotsky used simple examples of tying a knot or marking one's place so as not to forget. These are artificial call symbols of human culture.

Jerome Bruner: language and cognitive development
Bruner's theory builds on what we know from Vygotsky and aims to further explain how language and storytelling promote cognitive development.

Bruner introduced the **language acquisition support system** (LASS) as a theory explaining how children move from innate prelinguistic skills to making meaning within the cultural context of a child's daily life. Human development has a biological basis, but the interaction between a caregiver and child activates this biology.

Research on Bruner's theories has method, observer, time, and space **triangulation**. Experimental evidence exists for the theory, but over time Bruner preferred non-experimental methods. The natural setting, though uncontrolled, is the only place where one sees the real interactions between adult and child.

The LASS means parents act as **scaffolds**, meaning supportive frameworks, for child development. Scaffold is similar to Vygotsky's ZPD.

The terms culture, intersubjectivity and intentions are needed for understanding how the LASS works.

Bruner (1996) situates language and development in a cultural context. Bruner believes the human mind evolved in the context of a symbolic culture shared by others. Language makes understanding the rules of one's culture possible. "Culture, then, though itself man-made, both forms and makes possible the workings of a distinctively human mind. On this view, learning and thinking are always dependent upon the utilization of cultural resources" (p. 4).

Intersubjectivity and intentions go together. **Intersubjectivity** means that there is interplay between adults and children long before children have actual language. It is a natural "dance," a give and take relationship, where one has an intention to connect to the other and decode what the other person intends to convey (a theory of mind). This all takes place at a symbolic level. Intersubjective experiences are part of daily human relationships throughout the lifespan. Intentions are uniquely human and probably have a biological base, as it appears that babies come into the world with innate **schemas** to figure out the intentions of others. Babies have prelinguistic behaviors that can be seen in **play** such as **peek-a-boo**.

> **Peek-a-boo is significant for the topic socialization and for developmental psychology**
> Bruner's famous observation study about peek-a-boo is part of socializing children and is reviewed in chapter 32 under the developmental topic of play benefits.

Animals cannot read sophisticated intentions from others. Of course a mother cat teaches her kittens how to use a litter box, but this teaching is innately wired into cat behavior. It is not a cognitive intention coming from a sophisticated brain that is considering all the possibilities for a child. No cat mother considers raising one from the litter to be a cat president! Animals do not have the brainpower or language to even consider this idea. In contrast, *human scaffolds spend much of their time making the world manageable for children.* **Cognitive development** largely depends on language and occurs in 3 phases.

3 phases of cognitive development (Bruner, 1996)

The first is the **enactive** phase. Babies have **skills** helping them manipulate objects. These skills are functionally the equivalent of language and develop from an innate set of action patterns hardwired into the brain at birth. Examples of these building blocks are grasping, sucking, and looking.

Babies quickly move into the second **ikonic** phase. The ikonic phase takes place from about 2-5 years of age when children learn actual language but still think in images rather than in symbols.

The third phase is called **symbolic** where the child now internalizes symbolic abstractions and has full command of language. Children of 6-7 years of age should have symbolic thought.

The outcome of development depends on the way that children are instructed. For example, language develops in a sociocultural context where performance feedback is important. An observation study shows this process (Bruner, 1983). A mother and baby played peek-a-boo to demonstrate the **intersubjective** experience between the mother and child. The mother initiates the game and the baby responds with babbling and eye contact at the appropriate times when language is used between adults. This type of interaction helps the baby learn how to do things with words. As you might guess, play is important to the entire intersubjective experience between adults and babies. Development moves rapidly during play because children use imagination to create problem-solving strategies without real world consequences.

Narratives help children master language and show they understand the values of their culture. Narratives, or particular types of stories, are the most frequently used type of human communication. "All narrative environments are specialized for cultural needs." (Bruner, 1990, p. 84).

One difference between animals and humans is the use of narration (Engel, 1995). Animals live in the world of objects. Humans live in a double world because we know objects but also have a second level of inner cognitive experience where we try to understand life. Stories create a child's sense of self and are where children integrate affect, cognition, and action. Not all stories are narratives. Bruner's criteria for identifying narratives from other types of talk follow (Engel, 1995). "A narrative:

1. Must have a sequence.
2. Must have a plot that conveys meaning.
3. Must have a high point, a tension that meets some kind of resolution.
4. Remains a narrative whether it is true or untrue.
5. Makes distinctions between the usual and the unusual.
6. Directs attention to personal and subjective experience." (p. 70-71).

Narratives make up most human talk and research shows that children narrative more when they must make sense out of something unusual. Joan Lucariello ran an experiment with 4 and 5 year-olds (as cited in Bruner, 1990). The **aim of the experiment** was to see what kinds of things started narratives. For **procedures**, children were divided into two groups and heard either a story about typical events at a birthday party or about a visit from a child's cousin who had come to play, the **independent variable**. Some of the stories violated accepted cultural **norms**, such as the birthday girl pouring water over the candles instead of blowing them out or that she was unhappy that day. Lucariello then asked the children questions about the stories. **Results** showed that the unusual stories sparked the most narration because the children tried to make sense of them. For example, one child tried to explain the unhappy birthday girl by suggesting that she did not have the right dress to wear. When directly asked questions about why things went as usual in the typical stories, the children had little to say and even shrugged as if it were unclear why the researcher asked about it. Even a slightly unusual story about the

Families socialize and enculturate children by passing down stories (narrating) to help them learn what to do.
Used with license from
megapixl.com.

cousin coming over to play received four times more elaboration in narratives than the typical story. Children talk more about why things are different rather than why they are normal.

Bruner (1990) describes an observation study giving experiments **method triangulation**. The **aim of the study** was to document changes in Emily's narrations over time as she developed. Emily's bedtime stories were observed and recorded from ages 18 to 36 months. A baby brother was born in the family during this time, replacing Emily as the center of attention and taking her room. Emily made great strides in language development during this time as she made sense of these events. **Results** showed an increase in Emily's use of terms such as "and then" and "because" to explain events. In addition, Emily moved from simple statements of Sunday morning breakfasts such as "Daddy did make some cornbread for Emmy have" (p. 91) to social **scripts** that had explanatory value such as "Tomorrow when we wake up from bed, first me and Daddy and Mommy, you, eat breakfast eat breakfast, like we usually do, and then we're going to play, and then soon as Daddy comes, Carl's going to come over and play awhile." (p. 93). By age 3, Emily was figuring out what happens in human culture.

> **Thinking skills: Pulling it together**
> Do you see how storytelling is key to socializing children and in promoting cognitive development? Humans must have a basic tool for socializing and enculturating children, and storytelling fits the requirement! It is a good opportunity to learn something about language, the most fundamental of all the cognitive processes and something often missing from courses. Narrating is an **etic**, found in all cultures.

18.9: Social cognition

Describe means to give a detailed account. Key details follow. **Social cognition** is "the process by which people think about and make sense of other people, themselves, and social situations (Fiske, 2004, p. 122).

Humans are always trying to make sense of everything around them so social cognition is always working in the background. Our **core motives** to understand, feel a sense of control, and to trust others are fundamental to driving our desire to understanding ourselves and others.

When trying to understand someone else, several things happen and it is a wonder we get it right so much of the time (Fiske, 2004)!

1. We might be accurate or inaccurate. This is because much of our decision making relies on mental shortcuts called **heuristics**. Context can affect our accuracy in understanding others. For example, you might accurately judge someone's behavior at school but do not have enough information to be accurate outside of school. Another factor is our failure to sample enough situations to be accurate and instead rely on what we know about others closest to us as examples (representative heuristic).
2. We might actively work at using conscious controlled thinking and this can be hard when available information is sparse or there is little time. Automatic thinking often takes over.

Social cognition is involved in many topics studied in this course and include the following.

1. The use of **heuristics**
2. Using **schemas** to make judgments about others, which can often lead to **stereotyping**
3. Cognitive biases such as the **illusory correlation**
4. How people think about their in-groups and out-groups

Consider **Bruner** again because his language development theory includes **intersubjectivity**, the decoding of other's intentions, so we use social cognition from birth. It takes about 5 years for a child to have a fully developed **theory of mind** (ToM), so we must practice social cognition. ToM is part of the evolutionary explanation of behavior in the biological ATB and is a required topic for developmental psychology. The ToM illustrates social cognition at work and is so important for human interaction that it is an involved potential we must learn to use as we are **socialized** and **enculturated**.

18.10 Stereotypes

Stereotypes were first detailed in chapter 11 because stereotypes often make up one's schemas. One way stereotyping is related to the sociocultural ATB is the blatant stereotyping used in **Social Identity Theory**. Identifying with an in-group is conscious and controlled stereotyping, the blatant kind.

The best way to bring stereotyping into essays about Social Identity Theory is to clearly label the favoring of an in-group as blatant stereotyping. Conflict with other groups requires the blatant stereotyping of favoring an in-group and seeing others as part of out-groups.

Chapter 19
The Sociocultural Approach to behavior: The Individual and the Group: Analysis and Evaluation

---

Chapter objectives

Students will:
1. Practice thinking strategies (command terms) related to analysis and application as well as synthesis and evaluation, with explain, discuss, and evaluate modeled.
2. Discuss Social Identity Theory
3. Evaluate Social Cognitive Theory
4. Explain stereotyping.

19.1 Discuss Social Identity Theory (SIT)

Discuss means to give a considered and balanced view supported by evidence. Social Identity Theory is well studied and has developed from the original theory by Tajfel into a theory with cultural relevance.

Discussing SIT involves tracing its development from Tajfel classic studies to it's cultural relevance through Yuki's research.

Classic SIT research by Tajfel

A reflection (consideration) starts with the classic early research demonstrating the basic processes of social identity.

The **aim of this series of experiments** was to show that in-group favoritism was a regular

> **Thinking skills: Reinterpreting old research and a terrorism application**
> Think back to the beginning of the course when you learned about **subjective culture** as a useful way to define human culture. Categorizing is an important part of one's subjective culture (Triandis & Gelfand, 2012). "Members of each culture have unique ways of categorizing experience" (p. 5). Who is part of an in-group is one of these categories. It has been suggested that early research by Asch, Zimbardo, and Milgram be reinterpreted according to social identity (M. Sageman, personal communication, 2015). Many atrocities, such as **terrorist acts**, may be explained by social identity and might be a good topic for the class to explore, an activity located in Appendix 2.

feature of intergroup interaction (Tajfel & Turner, 1986). Researchers had assumed that only great conflict would produce intense in-group favoritism, but Tajfel and Turner hypothesized that even a minimal in-group association would produce in-group favoritism and out-group discrimination.

Participants in numerous experiments were children and adults randomly assigned to membership in one of two distinct groups with a trivial difference (**the IV**). For the **procedures**, participants made decisions about how to divide up money to others. Everyone was anonymous and identified only by a code and knowledge of the group assigned. Participants knew their own group membership but there was no demand that money be awarded to anyone in either group. There was no social interaction between participants or staged hostility, so there was no particular link between group members other than a broad group membership category. "These groups are purely cognitive, and can be referred to as minimal" (Tajfel & Turner, 1986, p. 14).

Results showed in-groups were favored in all of the studies, and identifying with the in-group was more important than profit gaining in the decision-making.

The development of modern Social Identity Theory

As social identity research developed, *the emphasis on self-esteem declined in favor of theories emphasizing the cognitive component of categorization* (Fiske & Taylor, 2008). This is an important consideration and the change helped the theory evolve.

Social Categorization Theory (SCT) enhanced SIT and changed the focus from self-esteem to how categories determine group behavior (Hogg, Terry, & White, 1995). People create categories to fulfill belonging needs, which magnify similarities an in-group and an out-group (Fiske, 2004). Individuals see their in-group as more varied than they really are and out-groups as more similar to each other than they really are. This promotes belonging but increases out-group **stereotyping**. Unfortunately, threats to self-concept and belonging can lead to stereotyping and discrimination, even by otherwise well-meaning people.

Belonging to an in-group requires group members to share mental representations of the defining features of a group (Hogg, Terry, & White, 1995). A group's defining features are norms for group behavior in a specific context.

Identity with an in-group might explain sport aggression. Used with license from megapixl.com.

Creating categories requires **depersonalization**. When depersonalizing, the self is defined by the group category more than the individual self. For example, **aggression** at a sport event is depersonalized as a team behavior: high levels of emotional competition with another team (the out-group) are the norm. Depersonalizing is a way to change one's view of the self in a particular context to maintain one's belief of normal behavior (Hogg, Terry, & White, 1995).

Stereotyping and discrimination are best thought of as in-group preferences rather than out-group disfavor (Fiske, 2004). People prefer in-groups because they enhance our chances of survival. Any out-group threatening the well being of the in-group is likely to be stigmatized.

SIT/SCT should be studied with a cultural context in mind

When discussing, it is important to consider how well a theory applies to other cultures. SIT has been modified to do this, so the theory and research are strong and balanced.

All cultures must meet individual self-interest needs and group social identity needs (Brewer & Yuki, 2007). Both **individualistic** and **collectivist** cultures satisfy these needs but differ in *how* they do it.

Persons from individualistic and collectivist cultures have fundamentally different meanings of in-groups, so it is clear that *culture shapes and modifies social identity.*

Social identity is **universal**, an **etic**. Individuals need a way to buffer the difficulties of survival, and the evolution of complex human group living meets this need (Brewer & Yuki, 2007). It makes sense that the most important parts of human biology and cognition were directed at living in social groups. Even though social identity is an etic, *"the locus and content of social identity are clearly culturally defined and regulated"* (p. 307). The categories of **individualism** and **collectivism** are the most used way to collect and organize modern data about social identity and culture. Cross-cultural research provides valuable information about how to interpret another's in-group and out-group behavior.

SIT/SCT and culture: Making the theories relevant for everyone
SIT and SCT explain how in-groups shape representations of the individual self, but the self has different meanings in **individualist** and **collectivist** cultures (Brewer and Yuki, 2007).

The early research on social identity is from the West. *A cross-cultural view shows that the original SIT/SCT explanations are too simplistic.* Group cognitions defining one's social identity vary and the self really exists on three levels.

Three levels of social identity

Level	Description
Individual level	The self is unique.
Relational level	The self exists in a harmonious relationship with others.
Collective level	The self fits into depersonalized categories of groups with symbolic value to the person. Obligations to close interpersonal relationships are not required for membership in a collective group. *SIT and SCT explain the social self in the third level, far more appropriate to defining social identity in individualist cultures.*

Social identity in collectivist cultures is **relational**, and harmony and cooperation are valued. Relational social identities are **personalized** rather than **depersonalized**, tied to behaviors maintaining in-group harmony and cooperation. Relational group thinking is consistent with what we know about the Japanese **interdependent self** (Yuki, Maddox, Brewer, and Takemura, 2005), a topic detailed in chapters 3, 20, and 21.

Every culture has **emic** features of social identity, but generally, collectivistic cultures have relational social identities rather than categorical social identities. Research shows that both individualistic and collectivist participants refer to their social identity through in-groups.

Cross-cultural experiments demonstrating relational social identity
Quasi-experiments demonstrate differences in social identity through testing the trusting of in-groups and out-groups (Yuki, et al., 2005).

The **aim of one experiment** was to show that everyone values in-groups and makes distinctions between in-groups and out-groups, but just do it differently (Yuki, et al., 2005).

Trust is operationally defined as "an expectation of beneficent treatment from others in uncertain or risky situations" (p. 50). US and Japanese university students were compared in three types of depersonalized trust scenarios (the **independent variable**) *before* the participants knew how the other person had acted.

1. One scenario used someone from an in-group.
2. The second used someone defined as an out-group member, with a suggestion for a potential, though not actual, connection between the out-group member and the participant through an acquaintance.
3. The third was an out-group member with no potential connection to the participant.

It was predicted that both US and Japanese participants would trust the in-group member the most and would trust those in out-groups the least. In addition, differences in why the groups were accepted would be explained by culture. US participants were predicted to use categories and Japanese participants were predicted to use relational needs as the primary basis for deciding trust.

> **Thinking skills: Ethics in experiments**
> Yuki's experiment used deception. Consider if the benefits outweigh the risks to participants. Subjects must be debriefed immediately after participation.

Participants were 171 Ohio State University students and 199 Japanese university students. For the **procedures**, participants decided whether to trust an unknown person based on minimal information in different scenarios using the three in-groups and out-groups defined above. The three scenarios were about asking someone to watch luggage in an airport, allowing someone to borrow money at a restaurant, and buying concert tickets online from an individual.

Results confirmed the hypotheses that both US and Japanese participants trusted the unknown person from the in-group significantly more than they trusted either out-group person. Differences were found in trusting the potentially connected and the unconnected out-group member. The Japanese sample trusted the out-group member if that person had a potential connection to them. In contrast, the US sample did not trust either out-group member, even if the person had a potential connection.

This experiment was replicated using a real money allocation game and had similar findings.

An application of SIT: In-groups, out-groups, and justifying aggression
An example behavior is good for support a discussion. Does the theory support real life situations?

It is comforting to categorize others into in-groups and out-groups (Fiske & Taylor, 2008). Categorization relieves uncertainty about others and situations. However, if these categories take on a reality, strained group relations and even atrocities such as dehumanization and infrahumanization are possible.

You may have studied **dehumanization** and violence. History is full of examples of propaganda that denies an enemy *full human status* (Castano & Giner-Sorolla, 2006). One example comes from Nazi Germany. One survivor of a concentration camp noted that degrading the prisoners was a necessity for the system to work. Someone operating the gas chamber would be severely distressed if they did not rationalize that the people were not really human. Dehumanization is one way that troops get mentally prepared to kill the enemy because most soldiers would never kill anyone in civilian life. Dehumanization can increase aggression and requires reduced empathy for the victim so it is possible to disengage from the victim.

Infrahumanization, which means that a victim is given a *less than human status,* is one consequence of dehumanizing (Fiske & Taylor, 2008). Although most people do not directly participate in killings, research shows they will participate in infrahumanization. Studies on infrahumanization show people will justify the atrocities of their in-group members, particularly if the out-group has an emotional meaning for the in-group. Primary emotions, such as anger and happiness are still attributed to the victims, but the more subtle secondary emotions, such as love, hope, and humiliation are withheld (Castano & Giner-Sorolla, 2006).

The **aim of one experiment** showed the conditions under which infrahumanization occured. The authors "hypothesized that when individuals are presented with reminders of violence against the out-group for which their own in-group is held responsible, they infrahumanize the victim more than when such reminders are not included or than when such reminders merely present the fact of large-scale death without in-group responsibility" (p. 806).

One experiment randomly assigned 68 University of Kent at Canterbury (UK) students to two conditions, the accidental killing condition and the in-group responsibility condition, the **independent variable**. Participants read a story about humans encountering aliens called the Gs. The story ending depended on the assigned group. One group's story ending was that 10,000 aliens died as a result of an accident. The other group's story was that 10,000 aliens were attacked and killed by the soldiers and that few of the military group died. Participants reported their perceptions of how the aliens felt. **Results** showed that the in-group responsibility condition had a significantly stronger infrahumanization than the accidental killing group. This experiment was replicated using a real historical situation about the treatment of Aborigines in Australia.

Another replication studied white Americans of European decent from New York. The stories were about Native Americans. The results supported the research conducted in the UK.

Awareness of this rather negative human behavior is the start of creating effective public policy. The need to belong to an in-group will probably not go away so coming up with strategies to defuse violence are not simple.

19.2: Evaluate Social Cognitive Theory

Do not try and study all of this! IB teachers should choose the topics that match their options and of course anything else of interest to the class.

Evaluate means to make a judgment (appraisal) using evidence. Social Cognitive Theory is well supported and applies to a wide variety of behaviors. It is a strong theory tested in experiments, the only way to demonstrate causation. Bandura is sometimes said to have a limitation of ethics, but looking deeply into the concern shows it is a superficial criticism. For example, the Bobo experiments use a specific type of sample. In addition, self-efficacy and phobia experiments aim to raise everyone's self-efficacy and all aspects of the experiments are designed to protect participants. Some of the research is conducted using correlations to avoid affecting someone's self-efficacy level, such as in the example study about problem-drinking.

We will sample the wide range of research and touch on topics studied under health, developmental, and abnormal psychology. We evaluate a Bobo experiment about **aggression**, research about **problem drinking** relevant for health psychology, **gender role and identity** development for developmental psychology, and then reflect on an experiment about raising the self-efficacy of people diagnosed with **phobias** for abnormal psychology.

The health psychology chapter 29 includes many more research examples from Social Cognitive Theory. Bandura was very interested in health research and has some strong opinions backed by research. These include **alcoholism** and **obesity** treatments as well as **self-management strategies to promote health**. The obesity experiment called "cookie paradise" is a favorite and if interested, turn to chapter 31and read it. This is an experiment with plenty of ethical considerations to resolve before running the study.

Modeling research: Bobo experiment about learning versus performance

The Bobo studies are a series of experiments from the 1960s showing how normal children model aggression. Each Bobo experiment has a specific aim to test a particular aspect of modeling. Bandura believes there is too much emphasis on the biology of aggression (Bandura, 2001). "People possess the biological potential for aggression, but the answer to the cultural variation in aggressiveness lies more in ideology than in biology" (p. 20).

One experiment **aimed to show** *the difference between learning aggression and actually performing it* (Bandura, 1973).

The experiment examined "the hypothesis that reinforcements administered to a model influence the performance but not the acquisition" of behavior (Bandura, 1965, p. 589). This Bobo experiment confirms that children only perform what they learn in the presence of reinforcement. The experiment fits into a larger body of research that includes observations from cultural psychologists and anthropologists.

Experiment participants were 33 boys and 33 girls from the Stanford Nursery School. Participants were randomly assigned to one of three groups, a model rewarded for using aggression, a model punished for using aggression, or model with no consequences (the **independent variable**).

Procedures are next. Children were tested individually. The female experimenter told the children she had some work to do before going to the 'surprise playroom,' but that the child could watch a television show while waiting. The film showed a man ordering the Bobo doll to move. When the Bobo doll did not move, the model used four *novel* physical and verbal types of aggression against it. One example was that the model "pummeled it on the head with a mallet. Each response was accompanied by the verbalization, "Sockeroo...stay down" (p. 590-591). In the first condition the model was rewarded with verbal praise and food treats for showing aggression to the Bobo doll. In the second condition the model was punished with a scolding for showing aggression to the Bobo doll. In the third condition, a model received no consequences.

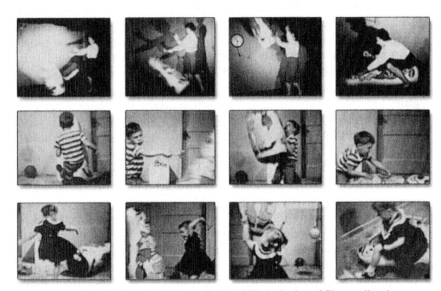

Data were gathered through observation. It is a mistake to think of the Bobo experiments as observation studies. Observation was a technique used to gather the experimental data.

To test for *performance*, observers watched as the children were brought into the 'surprise playroom' right after they saw the model. The room contained a variety of toys, including anything used by the model against the Bobo doll. Each child spent 10 minutes in the playroom

Source: Bandura, A, Ross, D., & Ross, S. A. (1963). Imitation of film-mediated aggressive models. *Journal of Abnormal and Social Psychology,* 66 (1), 3-11. Curtsey of A. Bandura

with the Bobo doll and toys and did whatever they wished during the time. Observers recorded behavior every five seconds.

To test for *learning*, the experimenter next entered the room with juice and booklets of stickers. The children were instructed that for each modeled verbal and physical behavior they demonstrated, they would receive a sticker and juice.

Results showed the performance of modeled aggression was different from the learning. Children seeing a model rewarded or receiving no consequences modeled more aggression than those seeing the model punished. Boys modeled aggression more than girls in all three conditions. There was especially a difference when the model was punished. Interestingly, boys performed a large amount of aggression even when the model was punished. However, gender differences disappeared when the children were asked to show what they learned. When given a positive incentive to show aggression, both males and females demonstrated what they learned.

Two **conclusions** were made from the results.

1. Learned behaviors are modeled only when they receive reinforcement.
2. The models acted as *disinhibitors* for the boys far more than the girls, reflecting the differences in reinforcement that males and females receive for aggression throughout their lives from models.

Critical thought: Studying aggression in a lab experiment

The Bobo experiments are tightly controlled lab experiments. Critics complain the experiments are too artificial and lack ecological validity. Ecological validity is the extent to which the conditions of the investigation can be generalized outside of the study. Are these criticisms valid?

Experiments are too often criticized for investigating exactly what people wish to know, the cause of behavior (Bandura, 1973). Experiments pinpoint specific causes. Cause cannot be known from naturalistic observations or correlations. Lab conditions hold one variable constant while others are manipulated. Criticisms that experiments are artificial reflect a misunderstanding of how knowledge advances. "Experiments are not intended to duplicate events as they occur in real life, and they would lose their value if they did" (p. 63). Theories are tested in the lab, not real life. As a funny example, Bandura points out that airline travelers do not rely on actual flights to determine the safety of new airplane designs. New airplanes are first tested in labs. Once a cause is established in a lab, it can be tested in the field. Results of lab experiments should be consistent with other types of research. This idea applies to interpreting all tightly controlled experiments. Look to see if the experiment has **method triangulation**. If so, then its lack of ecological validity is no longer a problem.

Thinking skills: The value of experiments

Students often wonder why researchers choose experiments and often incorrectly evaluate the method. Bandura is clear on the value!

Experiments serve a clear purpose and this is a good place to consider it.

Others have concerns about the novel behaviors used by the models, saying the novel behaviors are different from what the children know.

The experimental design *deliberately* used novel behaviors. Novel behaviors act as *controls* for previous learning. Prior aggressive behavior would *confound* the experiment. Criticisms that the novel behaviors taught to children do not reflect their real life aggression are superficial. The intent was to see if the child modeled the model's behaviors. The novel behaviors may not reflect what the children do in real life but testing real life was not the purpose of the experiment. The experiment meant to predict the conditions under which someone would perform aggression. Again, experiments must be artificial to test a theory. No one should make a claim based on the results of one experiment. Alone, an experiment lacks ecological validity. Poor ecological validity is not as much of a problem the study is placed within a larger body of research.

Bandura (1973) is critical of using **animals in research**. Human experiments are necessary because the determinants of behavior are *not the same across species*. Research in health promotion is a good example, because stress is an important variable. Human stressors are largely tied to perceptions, so animal research cannot measure the human mental experience (Bandura, 1997). This adds to our understanding of issues related to using animals as models for humans from chapter 10.

Ethics and Bobo

Two ethical considerations are *potential harm* and *removing adverse effects*. Critics claim the children were harmed because they were exposed to novel forms of aggression they did not already know and the children might continue to perform the aggression. Here are some things to consider when evaluating. The sample used normal children, not delinquents or those at risk for delinquency. The parents were likely to act as inhibitors of aggression. Even if children learned aggression, did they perform it? There is no evidence that the children continued to use the aggressive behaviors modeled in the experiments. Avoid an automatic response that the Bobo experiments are unethical.

Self-efficacy and aggression

Children do not just model aggression because **self-efficacy** must be high for someone to follow through with a behavior. For ethical reasons, it is hard to study aggression and self-efficacy in experiments so the conclusions here are based on correlation studies.

Children have beliefs about their ability to carry out either prosocial or antisocial acts (Bandura, 1997). *Self-efficacy influences beliefs about whether to behave prosocially or antisocially.* High self-efficacy for prosocial behavior results in the use of peaceful means to achieve goals. In contrast, some children have high self-efficacy to use aggression to get what they want and believe they can successfully carry out these acts. These children are more likely to use aggression with peers. Children with low self-efficacy to ability to carry out an aggressive act are unlikely to use aggression.

Peer groups support a child's sense of self-efficacy (Bandura, 1997). Children have a greater risk for using aggression in peer groups when they have high self-efficacy beliefs to use and carry out aggressive acts.

Peer groups form around similar beliefs and interests. Children with high self-efficacy to use aggression attract other children with the same beliefs. The peer group then reinforces each other's behavior. Where does the aggression start? Children model self-efficacy beliefs to start and carry out aggressive acts from parents. Parent models are more likely to use punishment and coercion to control children's behavior and are less likely to have positive interactions with their children. Power struggles

The peer group has a great effect on a child's self-efficacy to behave prosaically or with aggression. However, it all starts with parent models. Used with license from megapixel.com.

result where the parents either gives in or continues with the punishment until the child gives up. Children generalize their way of handling relationships to relationships outside of the family.

Self-efficacy and health behavior: Alcoholism
Social Cognitive Theory is well supported and two concepts are important.

Social Cognitive Theory: The start of problem drinking
The **anticipation of reinforcement** means to expect a pleasant reinforcement from the substance. One example is anticipating stress relief because of the **outcome expectancy** that alcohol helps people manage difficult situations.
Self-efficacy beliefs are judgments relating to one's ability to manage a situation, such as "I can say no if someone offers me a drink."

Many studies show that outcome expectancies and self-efficacy are probably the greatest predictors of the start of alcohol abuse. This section includes one study to help make the judgment that Social Cognitive Theory is well supported.

Research about risk factors for problem-drinking: Drinking refusal self-efficacy in college students
The **aim of a correlation study** was to understand the role of self-efficacy in college drinking, a big problem on college campuses (Young, Connor, Ricciardelli, & Saunders, 2006). Drinking remains a problem even though health promotion campaigns target it, especially **binge drinking**.

For the **procedures**, questionnaires were used to study **alcohol outcome expectancy** and **drinking refusal self-efficacy**. Alcohol outcome expectancies involve if-then statements about learning and reinforcement. An alcohol outcome expectancy might be "If I drink at the party, then everyone will think I am fun."

Drinking refusal self-efficacy is correlated with one's confidence to resist alcohol.

The sample consisted of 174 students from two Australian universities.

Students filled out two questionnaires, the Alcohol Expectancy Questionnaire (AEQ) and the Drinking Expectancy Profile (DEP).

The AEQ measures the number of outcome expectancies someone has for drinking. Participants agree or disagree with statements such as "I feel more creative after I've been drinking."

The DEP has questions about thoughts, feelings, and beliefs about the consequences of drinking. Questions include "I have more self-confidence when drinking" and "drinking makes me bad-tempered." It also measures refusal self-efficacy. Participants agree or disagree with statements about when they are most likely to drink including "when I am uptight" and "when I see others drinking."

Participants also reported the frequency of drinking (average number of drinking days each week), the amount consumed (volume, such as eight ounces), and filled out an alcohol dependence scale measuring the degree to which someone's drinking met the criteria for abuse or dependence using the DSM-IV criteria.

Data were analyzed with correlations. **Results** showed that positive drinking outcomes expectancies on the AEQ and DEP were correlated with the following.

1. Frequency of drinking
2. Quantity of drinking
3. Severity of someone's problem drinking

The authors **concluded** the study results could be helpful in designing both health promotion strategies and treatments. *What good does it do to educate people about the dangers of drinking if self-efficacy to refuse the drinks is low?* Colleges can raise self-efficacy by providing, for example, alcohol free tailgating sections at football games. Students see other people having fun without alcohol.

Gender roles: Judge how well the theory is supported

Thinking skills: Developmental psychology link

Gender identity and social roles is a required topic for **developmental psychology** so this is a good place to introduce a prominent theory. Is it a good theory? Bandura challenges that schema theory, cognitive development theory, and biological theories do not think environmental influences are important. Bandura takes a multidirectional approach that biology, cognitions, and the sociocultural environment all come together to create gender roles.

For an extra challenge and practice using **command terms**, follow along and consider the merits (to what extent) of the argument. You might even try contrasting this view with another if you would like a big mental challenge, such as gender schema theory, detailed in the cognitive ATB.

Social Cognitive Theory claims that we come into the world with biological predispositions related to being male or female, but these biological potentials do not dictate **gender role** behavior (Bussey & Bandura, 1999). Having male or female hormones, for example, does not guarantee particular behavior. Instead, modeling shapes biology and the resulting behavior can vary between cultures. Social Cognitive Theory explains how people grow and change within cultures, so it makes sense that modeling, outcomes expectations, and self-efficacy create different outcomes depending on which behaviors are valued and sanctioned as desirable within cultures.

This section contains the results of many experimental and correlation studies.

Social Cognitive Theory claims that gender roles and identity are explained by modeling, outcome expectations, and self-efficacy (Bussey & Bandura, 1999). This view is different from gender schema theory and cognitive developmental theory because factors other than cognitions are important.

Gender role development is socially influenced in three ways
(Bussey & Bandura, 1999)

Mechanism	Description: This list is not in the order they happen because the concepts weave together as children grow.
Modeling	**Modeling** takes place through parents, schools, peers, and media. When children have full use of language, adults routinely explain what is expected and then model these expectations. By age 4, children **self-regulate** their behavior as they **anticipate reinforcement** from models and apply what is reinforced by their culture. Specific gender-linked behavior is heavily sanctioned in most cultures so there is plenty for a child to observe. Remember the 4 steps of reinforcement (attention, retention, reproduction, and motivation) as they are at work in the background.
Outcome expectations	Children learn what is expected for future behavior (get their outcome expectations) from models. The expectations reflect the social and cultural norms that are maintained by social sanctions and taught as children are socialized and enculturated. Children learn which outcomes to model and apply to their own behavior as they **learn vicariously** and then **self-regulate**.
Self-efficacy	**Self-efficacy** is the motivation to put modeled gender role behavior into action. The *actual use of* any behavior depends on a child's level of **self-efficacy** to use it for achieving a goal. Bandura thought self-efficacy was the greatest predictor of behavior.

Let's see how these mechanism work.

Modeling allows children to learn the rules needed for creating new behavior. For example, experiments show that children can learn gender stereotypes from observing adult models.

Children pay attention to and model culturally sanctioned gender role behaviors and can see others achieve valued outcomes. For example, since boys in most western cultures are taught to follow gender roles more than girls, they pay attention to more same-sex models.

Children evaluate the outcomes they see others achieve and anticipate what they also might achieve. If **self-efficacy** is high and the child believes he can achieve a goal, he or she will do the same thing. *Just learning a stereotype does not account for actual behavior as children must have social sanctions and high self-efficacy as the motivations to reproduce it.* **A comprehensive theory must account for the motivation to behave.** But the way, gender schema contrasts the social cognitive view. Gender schema theory is concerned only with the child knowing the sex-linked behavior, with the motivation missing.

Criticisms that children do not always model same sex models in experiments are invalid because modeling in real life depends on how often a child sees a behavior, meaning they must see the behavior modeled repeatedly for it to be a **social norm**. When experiments are run where children see an increasing number of same-sex models displaying gender-linked behavior, they adopt the behavior these same-sex models.

Children create categories of themselves as male or female as they cognitively advance and master language (Bussey & Bandura, 1999). Labels of masculine and feminine categories help children notice gender as an important category. This process is seen as children learn vicariously through models and was noticed in children's comments as they participated in the Bobo experiments. For example, comments about a women being aggressive included, "That is not a way for ladies to behave" and "You should have seen what that girl did in there. She was acting like a man." In contrast, male aggressive behavior was admired and children said for example, "That man is a strong fighter... He is just like my dad."

By age 4 when children are developing more representational thought, they **self-regulate** gender roles, and do not have to rely solely on external social sanctions. Children have personal standards they start to judge behavior against and they act based on these. Children even act as teachers of others as they cognitively process gender standards. For example, 3-year-olds can watch behavior of another child who does not conform to norms and disapprove of a boy playing with a doll or girls with a truck, and even expect peers to have the same standards. But by age 4, children can apply these standards to regulating their own behavior. For example, self-standards can be seen in play experiments where children are left to play with toys not sanctioned for their sex. Boys might say they are "finished with these girl toys," fling them out of sight, or transform them into something masculine such as guns.

The adult is a model for a male child and this can become part of the child's self-regulated behavior, "This is what boys do!"
Used with license from mexapixl.com.

Parents play a huge role in modeling gender-linked behavior and self-efficacy to reach goals (Bussey & Bandura, 1999). Contrary to what parents claim, the research shows they create heavily gender-linked home environments. In addition, male and female parents differ in how they demand gender-typed behavior. Male parents demand and reward more male-typed behavior from their sons than mothers. Parents can also be inconsistent in the types of gender role behaviors they demand. For example, the same parent could focus on gender-typed clothing but ignore gender-related academic stereotypes. Complicating things is parental claims in self-reports that they require no gender differences between their children. However, observations show otherwise: actual behavior requirements are strongly gender-stereotyped.

People are **agents** of their behavior, meaning they self-regulate behavior (Bussey & Bandura, 1999). Self-efficacy is the greatest predictor of one's sense of agency to behave. Regardless of what is learned through modeling, *one has to hold the belief that he or she can follow through with achieving a goal to have the motivation to behave.*

There are two ways to increase a child's **self-efficacy**. One way is through modeling. The other is to persuade others that there is a way to achieve goals. Those with the strongest beliefs that they can achieve goals are most likely to master challenges. Research about career choice supports the idea that self-efficacy is a determinant of whether males and females will succeed at different careers. Since careers are so often gender-linked, self-efficacy is a key for success.

> **Thinking skills: The best theory to explain gender differences in occupations?**
> The topic of gender differences in mathematics and career choices was evaluated under the topic of schema. This was a convincing argument but is it a better one than Social Cognitive Theory?

It has been hard to change gender differences in mathematics performance and career choice as evidenced when we evaluated schema theory. A challenge to the conclusion that the reason is schemas comes from Social Cognitive Theory, where the reason for the differences is **self-efficacy**, something that has been known for a long time. For example, self-efficacy was found to be the most important reason for gender differences in mathematics problem solving, more than self-concept or even prior experience with the math problems (Pajares & Miller, 1994). Correlations also show large gender differences in people's perceived self-efficacy to master the college courses and job requirements of 20 male or female-typed jobs. Results showed males report high self-efficacy to achieve the education and duties of both male and female-typed jobs yet females report high self-efficacy for the female-typed jobs and lower self-efficacy for the male-typed jobs.

Treating anxiety: A research model to demonstrate how self-efficacy modifies biology in people with phobias

Bandura knows people can have biological tendencies for behavior, such as genes predisposing people to aggression, alcoholism, or anxiety, but claims modeling and self-efficacy are the greatest determinants of behavior. An evaluation includes a judgement of how well the research is designed to be ethical!

Experiments show that raising **self-efficacy** to cope with stressors modifies stress and neurotransmitters (Bandura, 1997, 1985).

The key to lowering physical stress reaction is to raise perceived coping self-efficacy (Bandura, 1997). Human stressors are mostly psychological, which presents challenges to designing ethical experiments. No one wants to create stress for study participants, such as with phobics who already have trouble managing stress.

Bandura designed a research model for scientists to ensure the experiments were ethical. The research model used participants with preexisting **phobias** who received mastery training to increase self-efficacy. Researchers created a series of conditions that varied the intensity of a stressor from low to high. Each level of intensity had a condition with and without guided mastery training through a **model** to increase a participant's sense of perceived coping self-efficacy. In addition, at each level of intensity, participants filled out a questionnaire about their perceived ability to cope. By the end of the experiment, everyone would be better able to manage their fears, even at high stress intensity.

Experiment: Raising self-efficacy to alter neurotransmission in phobics.

The **aim of the experiment** was to show that raising perceived coping self-efficacy through models would alter **neurotransmission** in participants with a **spider phobia** (Bandura, Taylor, Williams, Mefford, & Barchas, 1985).

Twelve women with severe a spider phobia were the participants. All were overly watchful and concerned, ruminated (thinking too much about something), and had nightmares about spiders.

For the **procedures**, the experiment included eighteen tasks of increasingly greater threatening interactions with a Wolf spider (**the IV**). For example, they would look down into a bowl containing the spider, then put their hand in the bowl, working up to letting it crawl on their hand and lap. Participants filled out a questionnaire at the start of the experiment rating themselves on a 10-point scale from low to high uncertainty that they could manage the task. As expected, participants rated their perceived coping self-efficacy as low, meaning they felt uncertain about managing the spider.

Are you afraid of this Wolf spider? If your fears are too great perhaps a model can help you learn to manage the spider correctly and calm the brain.
Used with license from megapixl.com.

Models were used to raise perceived coping self-efficacy to manage the tasks. The model went through all eighteen tasks, instructing participants on spider behavior and how to manage them, such as how to control the spider's movements as it walked across one's lap.

Blood samples and the self-efficacy questionnaire were taken throughout the study. **Results** follow.

1. Participants had high levels of epinephrine and norepinephrine on tasks for which had high uncertainty ratings. As the strength of their self-efficacy grew, levels of both **neurotransmitters** dropped.
2. Strengthening self-efficacy lowered all **neurotransmitters** measured, including dopamine, which was very high even when the women just thought about the spider.

The authors **concluded** that raising self-efficacy lowered neurotransmission in phobics. A control group getting no treatment was not used, but the authors said they were not testing self-efficacy as a treatment for spider phobias. Rather, they investigated the effects of raising self-efficacy on neurotransmission.

19.3: Explain stereotyping

Stereotype research has already been detailed in chapter 11 as leading to schemas and evaluated with Social Identity Theory so students should be able to make a judgment about the quality of research. Even subtle stereotyping is well researched and an example correlation study is in chapter 11.

This section focuses on explaining stereotyping. Explain means to give a detailed account with reasons and causes. Details are in chapter 11 so this section organizing the reasons and causes of stereotyping. This is best represented to students in the following table.

Reasons and causes for stereotyping

Reasons	Supporting information
Reason #1	**Social cognition** is the root of much stereotyping. We are always trying to understand others and often do not have sufficient information.
Reason #2: Relates to blatant stereotyping	Identification with a favored in-group (Social Identity theory) is a reason for blatant stereotyping (Fiske & Taylor, 2008). The stereotyping occurs in response to inter-group threats and has been shown to be a cause of prejudice against an out-group and infrahumanization in experiments, for example.
Reason #3: Relates to subtle stereotyping	The automatic nature of System 1 thinking works in the background for much of our decision making.
Reason #4: Relates to subtle stereotyping	Interpersonal conflict and ambiguous situations are reasons for subtle stereotyping (Fiske & Taylor, 2008).
Reason #5: Relates to subtle stereotyping	Everyday cognitive processing such as selective attention is a reason for subtle stereotyping (Fiske & Taylor, 2008).
Reason #6: Related to subtle stereotyping	Concept formation is designed for efficiency and this is a reason for subtle stereotyping (Aronson, WIlson, & Akert, 2007). We can end up automatically creating categories that are schemas driving behavior (Fiske, 2004).

These reasons came from research about stereotypes, so cite the subtle stereotyping correlation study about gender stereotypes in mathematics from chapter 11 and experiments from Tajfel and Yuki about the blatant stereotyping that happens when we identify with a favored in-group.

Chapter 20
The Sociocultural Approach to behavior: Cultural Origins of Behavior and Cognitions: Knowledge and Understanding

---

Chapter objectives

Students will:
1. Practice thinking strategies related to knowledge and understanding, with describe modeled.
2. Describe culture and cultural norms.
3. Describe cultural dimensions, with individualism-collectivism, time orientation, and the independent self-interdependent self (self-dimension) as examples.

20.1 Culture and cultural norms

Culture and **cultural norms** are described in chapter 3. Don't forget to review **subjective culture** because it is the best way to think about human cultural norms and it helps students understand differences between humans and animals.

20.2 Cultural dimensions

Cultural dimensions are detailed in chapter 3, with **individualism-collectivism** as an example. **Time orientation** is another cultural dimension popular with students and relevant for studying health psychology. Last is the self-dimension, made up of the **independent self** and **interdependent self**.

Cultural dimensions are **etics** and are research tools for making meaningful comparisons between cultures. The dimensions reflect the values of a group living together in a culture.

Time orientation: Key details

Edward T. Hall's *The Silent Language* (1959) shows how people's time use conveys a large range of social values. **Time orientation** is an etic and everyone falls somewhere on the continuum.

Polychronic_____Monochronic

    Time orientation spans two opposing ends of a continuum, **polychronic** and **monochronic**. Time orientation is important because it "is a cultural value as well as an organizing principle for relationships, **norms**, and expectations" (Jones & Brown, 2005, p. 307).

Monochronic, probably correlated with individualism, includes the following values.

Values of people with monochronic time orientation
People do one thing at a time and focus on time commitments
The culture is **low-context**. Context refers to the extent to which a culture believes the situation is important in determining behavior.
People think about deadlines and stick to plans.
People "put the job first". Time is a commodity that can be wasted. **Language** reflects time as a commodity, such as "don't waste time."
People respect property and respect privacy rules about disturbing others.
People emphasize promptness.
People focus on verbal language more than nonverbal language. The literal meaning of words is valued over the context of language use.

Polychronic, probably correlated with collectivism, includes the following values.

Values of people with polychronic time orientation
People do many things at once and are easily distracted.
The culture is **high-context**. The situation is used to explain behavior. Word meanings are dependent on the situation, so nuances such as inflection are used for understanding than literal meanings.
People have general goals and are not as concerned with deadlines. **Language** reflects this, such as "it will get done."
People put relationships first, and they readily borrow and lend.
Promptness is based on relationship factors. For example, polychronic persons may be on time for a respected grandmother but not for someone outside of the family.
People pay attention to nonverbal language.

Introduction to the self-dimension: Independent self and interdependent self

One's **self construal** (means the way someone views the self) controls social behavior, emotions, and thinking, and can even make neuroplastic changes to the brain. The self can be defined as "the idea or images that one has about oneself and how and why someone behaves as one does" (Matsumoto & Juang, p. 330). All social motivation seems linked to one's self, which can be seen in "all the statements made by a person, overtly or covertly, that include the words "I," "me," "mine," and "myself" (Triandis, 1989, p. 506).

The self is universal, an **etic**, but has **emic** features shaped by culture. One helpful way to envision these emic features is to use a self-dimension, **independent self** and **interdependent self** to describe self-construal across cultures. These self-construals develops in the **enculturation** process as we use our unique human **language** to talk about our culture and that of others (Matsumoto & Juang, 2008). Someone's self-construal then becomes a **self-schema**, the categories guiding behavior (Markus, 1977).

It might be hard to see how strongly the self regulates many aspects of behavior, so next are two examples related to routine thoughts someone might have.

Suppose you are in an experiment about categorization. How would you answer the question, which item goes with the cow? Is it the chicken or the grass?

Which item goes with the cow? Is it the chicken or the grass?
Source: (Nisbett & Masuda, 2006)
Curtsey of R. Nisbett

American children put the cow with the chicken, saying both are animals and Chinese children put the cow with the grass, saying cows eat grass (Nisbett & Masuda, 2006). Research shows that Americans classify according to a rule-based category system and East Asians categorize according to relationships. Both answers reflect something fundamental about someone's self-construal, such as how taking context into account influences categorizations in East Asians (Markus & Kitayama, 1991).

Next, suppose you are in a study investigating how people make **attributions**, meaning how people assign cause. How do you answer the question, "Why do people commit murders" (Nisbett & Masuda, 2006)?

Americans answer this question with internal attributions, meaning they say people commit murders because of some internal trait or characteristic of the person (Nisbett & Masuda, 2006). East Asians explain murders according to context, including historical factors. The answers show something basic about someone's self-construal (Markus & Kitayama, 1991).

The independent and interdependent self: Key details

Agency is a universal concept and means that people regulate their own behavior (Markus & Hamedani, 2007). Although everyone is an agent of their own behavior, the way in which it is done depends on the values of a cultural group.

People in the US experience agency in terms of an autonomous and **independent self** and show self-motivation and self-expression. In contrast, East Asians experience agency in terms of an **interdependent self**, which focuses on relational needs and harmony, and is achieved by adjusting the self to fit in with others.

Some aspects of the self are universal, such as a universal schema of one's body that is distinct from others and an awareness of dreams and the flow of thinking and emotions (Markus & Kitayama, 1991). However, many aspects of one's self-construal are culture specific and regulate thinking, emotions, and motivations. One example is the way people view relationships between the self and others. Everyone's self-construal falls someone on this dimension (continuum).

Independent Self ───────────────────────────── Interdependent Self

The **independent self** is a western self-construal, where people view the self as unique, autonomous, and individualist, using terms such as "realizing the self" to describe goals. The independent self is separate from others.

The **interdependent self** is relational, contextualized, and collective. Behavior depends largely on the thoughts and feelings of others in important groups. People are motivated to conform and fulfill obligations, and attributions are made based on context. Language reflects this definition. For example, the Japanese word for self, jibun, means, "One's share of the shared life space." This self-construal does not mean that some people merge their entire selves with others or have to always be with others. Individuals are still active agents of their own behavior but regulate themselves according to others.

Research supports the conclusion that independent and interdependent self-construals are **self-schemas** for organizing and experiencing the world (Markus & Kitayama, 1991).

One study about categorization is outlined above with responses to the cow, chickens and grass (Nisbett & Masuda, 2006).

In another experiment about the use of **attributions**, American and Indian Hindu

---

Thinking skills: The self-dimension and individualism-collectivism

The independent and interdependent self is related to the cultural dimension **individualism-collectivism**, and where someone falls on these continuums affects how they pay attention to information from the environment and decide what to label as important (Triandis, 1989). People in individualistic cultures tend to have independent self-construals, and they sample the private self more often. In contrast, people in collective cultures sample the collective self and monitor the self more often in relation to the group. When a group values these samplings, we can say that self-construal is an important aspect of **subjective culture**, a topic covered when describing culture in chapter 3.

---

participants thought up two prosocial behaviors and two deviant behaviors and wrote explanations for both (Markus & Kitayama, 1991). Researchers coded the answers according to how often participants made dispositional (internal) attributions and found that 40 percent of the American attributions were internal compared to 20 percent of the Hindu attributions.

Chapter 21
The Sociocultural Approach to Behavior: Cultural Origins of behavior and cognition: Synthesis and evaluation

Chapter objectives

Students will:
1. Practice thinking strategies (command terms) related to synthesis and evaluation, with evaluate and discuss modeled.
2. Evaluate cultural dimensions.
3. Discuss culture and its influence on behavior and cognition. Attention, perception, and memory are examples in this chapter. Conformity, Social Identity Theory, health beliefs, Theory of planned behavior, cognitive dissonance, compliance, and attachment are just some of the many examples of how culture influences behavior used in other chapters.

21.1: Evaluate cultural dimensions: A good way to classify culture

Students might find it easy to describe or even explain cultural dimensions, but evaluating is challenging. **Cultural dimensions** are abstract concepts used as research tools to compare cultures, and it is easy to have stereotypes about behavior if the topic is studied superficially. Many texts only give a generalized version of cultural dimensions but they are being used more often in research to understand behavior. The 21st century student makes well defended judgments about culture and behavior. So go into this section knowing that this is *an attempt to get at some of the core issues of using cultural dimensions to compare cultures.*

Evaluate means to make a judgment (appraisal) based on evidence. There is plenty of evidence to show that cultural dimensions are correlated with and/or the cause of behavior differences seen between cultures. However, a dimensional approach is just one way to compare cultures, so we will explore how cultural dimensions stack up against other approaches as a basis for making a judgment about its credibility and also explore its strengths and limitations.

Use research about compliance from chapter 3 (individualism-collectivism), and in this section

Triosity (time orientation related to health and academic performance) and health behavior (time orientation) as the main research support. The heading about culture and cognition includes some self-dimension research, and this can also be used in making a judgment.

Let's start with a concrete example: Comparing math performance

Suppose a researcher wants to compare **math performance** between two cultures, China and the US. We could report statistics about performance differences, but we really want to account for the differences. Could the differences be related to culture? And what about culture might be related to the differences? Might it be the values of **individualism or collectivism**? This pretend study is correlation because of **ethics**. It would be unethical to place children in experimental conditions where lower achievement or self-efficacy might occur.

 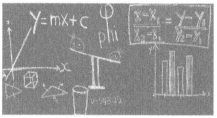 

A study comparing math performance between Chinese and US cultures requires a researcher to choose an approach to find out the aspects of culture that are related to performance in the quest to account for any differences. Choosing the individualism-collectivism dimension is one possible approach, and probably a good one given the way it was created from research by Harry Triandis about subjective culture along with its other strengths.
Pictures from: pixabay.com

To conduct the study we can give students a questionnaire categorizing them as falling more to individualism and collectivism. Then we can correlate math performance with either end of the dimension. Students can look up example questionnaires online.

The assumptions of taking a dimensional approach to comparing cultures

If we decide to use a **dimensional approach** and choose individualism-collectivism, there is an underlying assumption about using dimensions that students must understand. Taking a dimensional approach to classifying culture means the researcher compares cultures in studies according to how behavior fits on a dimension (a continuum), claiming that the dimension is the cause or is related to psychological factors that guide behavior.

The following model helps students think about a dimensional approach. It means that the practices and values of a culture lead to it falling on a particular dimension, such as individualism or collectivism. Having that tendency to behave as one more than the other affects the psyche that then guides behavior. In chapter 3 we learned that being from an individualistic or a collectivistic culture is related to the foot-in-the-door compliance technique (correlation). We will also learn in this chapter that having a polychronic time orientation causes someone to follow health advice less often (experiment). Researchers from both studies assumed that the values and practices of the cultural group led to people from that culture having a tendency to behave according to one end of the dimension.

Cultural environment ——→ Dimension ——→ The psyche guiding behavior

Based on Markus & Hamedani (2007)

Students must understand that cultural dimensions (one dimensional approach) is a prominent way to classify the dynamic interplay between the human psyche, culture, and behavior, but it is not the only approach (Markus & Hamedani, 2007).

The dimension **individualism-collectivism** is well known and is the most studied of the dimensions. Harry Triandis is the champion of individualism-collectivism. It offers "conceptual and explanatory parsimony" for comparing cultures and has the most data of all the dimensions (David Matsumoto, personal communication, March, 2015). **Time orientation** is also well supported, with some claiming that the way we organize time is the most central feature of being human. So right from the start it is suggested that cultural dimensions are a good way to think about culture and its relationship to behavior.

Inquiry and collaboration

Students might read the article from Scientific American Mind titled *Why math education in the US doesn't add up* about differences in the way math is taught across cultures. Is this because of culture (perhaps because of individualism-collectivism) or something else? It is hard to know because the researchers have not correlated their findings with a cultural dimension. Perhaps they should so we know a possible reason for the differences.

It is a chance for students to consider their own learning. Perhaps they can suggests ways to design ethical research investigating how cultural dimensions might account for these differences. Do not assume that a dimension explains differences unless research has specifically demonstrated it. Alternative explanations could account for the teaching differences but you see that the topic is not fully explored.

Article: Boaler, J. & Zoido, P. (2016, November/December). Why math education in the US doesn't add up. *Scientific American Mind, 27(6),* 18-19.

What if we choose a different approach? What about the independent-interdependent self?

We could choose the independent-interdependent self as an approach to comparing math performance between Chinese and US students. Researchers might find that self-construal (independent or interdependent) is related to math performance. However, students must understand that the self-dimension (in the end we will call it a dimension even though it started with some different assumptions) has more weaknesses than individualism-collectivism dimension.

Stacking up a dimensional approach to other choices to compare culture

It is worth knowing a little about other approaches to classifying cultures to avoid oversimplifying culture as just "falling on a dimension." There are really five approaches to studying "the dynamic interdependence between the psychological and the sociocultural" (Markus & Hamedani, 2007, p. 13).

Keep in mind that *these approaches are not mutually exclusive* and relate in many ways. The dimensional approach stands out because others ways of classifying behavior are very much related to it. Three of the approaches studied in this course follow.

Three approaches to classifying culture (Markus & Hamedani, 2007)

Approach	Description
Dimensional approaches	Dimensional approaches measure (quantify) differences, such as the cultural dimension individualism-collectivism first described in chapter 3. By the way, cultural dimensions are not the only dimensional approach. If you have ever heard of Schwartz's Basic Values, it is another one. It also has been studied, but not as much as individualism-collectivism. It is not necessary to learn about Schwartz, as the point is for students to avoid thinking individualism-collectivism and the other cultural dimensions described in chapter 3 are the only way researchers classify culture using dimensions.
Sociocultural Model: Our example can also be called a dimension even if it has some different assumptions	The sociocultural models approach focuses on the interacting self and cultural environment, which also is represented as a dimension, such as the **independent self-interdependent self**. This is related to individualism-collectivism, so remember these approaches are not mutually exclusive. Plenty of people call the self dimension a cultural dimension because it is so closely related to individualism-collectivism. It is not wrong to do this, though conceptually it is a bit different. The model looks a little different and we will use the self-dimension when studying culture and cognition. In this view, the self continually interacts with the shared meanings from the cultural environment to influence behavior. Cultural environment ⟷ The psyche (view of self) guiding behavior Based on Markus & Hamedani (2007)
Tool-kit approach	The tool-kit approach focuses on culture and cognition, such as Richard Nisbett's research about attention or categorization, reviewed in this chapter about cultural influences on behavior and cognition (attention and perception). This approach assumes that the meanings people have from cultural practices directly influence cognition and behavior. This approach is related to the independent and interdependent self, which is related to individualism-collectivism, so you can see all the relationships.

So cultural dimensions stack up well against other ways to classify culture and are even correlated with the other ways. Individualism-collectivism can be judged as the strongest of all the dimensions, part of your evaluation.

Evaluating time orientation: It is a well-supported dimension and helpful for making judgments about behavior

James Jones was leaving Trinidad after a year of researching time orientation. A local journalist threw him a party the night before his morning flight back to the US Jones had stopped wearing a watch while on the Island and still had some packing to do, so he asked someone at the party for the time and found it was 1:00. Jones automatically said it was time to leave. His announcement was not well received. Why did he want to leave when he was having fun? Jones decided to stay because he knew his host did not value his reasons for packing ahead of time and arriving at the airport on schedule. So Jones stayed at the party and managed to make the flight on time.

One style, polychronic or monochronic, is not more valuable than the other, and a mix is preferable and adaptive for living in a global society (Jones & Brown, 2005). Monochronic cultures value time and treat it as an asset. In contrast, polychronic cultures assign no natural value to time. Life in the present is valued and time follows the flow of daily life.

Present oriented cultures evolved out of necessity. Persons coping with oppressive social conditions found it adaptive to value the present over the future. Persons from monochronic cultures are future oriented because they see that what happens in the present directly determines the future. In contrast, those coping with difficult social conditions cannot reliably count on present behavior to determine the future because it is unpredictable.

A culture's time orientation affects individual behavior, such as children's socialization, and managing health, stress, and well-being.

Everyone has access to both ends of the continuum but that one or the other becomes a dominant *pattern* for a culture. One's **language** both reflects and supports a person's time orientation behavior. For example, in many African cultures the language does not recognize a strict difference between the past (zamani) and the present (sasa). In addition, the "future" is an abstract concept with less importance in an individual's life. The zamani-sasa is a cyclical continuum where ancestors are an active part of the present. The future depends on one's ancestors and may be part of an individual's awareness for only fleeting moments.

Research support: Time orientation, stress management, and mental health

Persons of African origin have a worldview characterized by five interrelating qualities, time, rhythm, improvisation, orality, and spirituality (**TRIOS**) (Jones & Brown, 2005). TRIOS is a questionnaire measuring these qualities. Present time orientation coordinates the TRIOS characteristics, "what matters is the life being lived, not the life being planned" (p. 315). *Context* is important to understanding TRIOSity. Present orientated persons have fewer psychological contextual constraints to manage. Persons high on past or future orientations are very constrained psychologically by past or future events. In contrast, presented oriented persons attach meaning to present oriented goals where the present has everything a person needs. Time orientation seems an important factor in managing daily lives.

Cultures high on TRIOSity are high-context language users. The meaning of words depends on knowledge of cultural practices. For example, the Trinidad word "mamaguy" allows words to mean their opposite. If someone says, "Your hair looks great," it means the opposite if the intent is to mamaguy another. Understanding is not simply a cognitive process in Trinidad and it is also an *emotional* process. The actual semantic context of words is not what gives language meaning. Someone familiar with the cultural meaning behind mamaguying knows to view the context, including inflections and important nonverbal cues. A cultural outsider is stripped of their power to harm others with a little mamaguying. Persons using high context languages regain personal power through this cultural practice.

Jones developed the TRIOS Scale and the **aim of the correlation study** was to show that TRIOSity existed more in African Americans and Africans than in white Americans, Asians, and Latinos. The sample consisted of 1415 participants. Female made up two-thirds of the sample. Approximately 40% were white, 21% were black, 19% were Latino, and 11% were Asian, with an average age of 20-21.

Results showed that African Americans scored the highest total and individual component TRIOS scores.

A body of correlation research supports TRIOS as a factor in experiencing stress and well-being. College students from Ghana, a largely white US university, and a largely black US university filled out the TRIOS Scale, and two stress scales, the CES-D Depression Scale, and the Positive and Negative Affect Scale (PANAS).

African American and African students both scored higher on TRIOS than white US students and similarly. High TRIOS scores were negatively correlated with stress and a **resilience** factor promoting well-being.

Research support: Time orientation and health beliefs

Brown and Segal (1996) researched time orientation and **health behavior**, specifically **hypertension** management. This study suggests culture is critical for predicting health behavior and demonstrates how the dimensions of culture are used as research tools.

The **aim of the quasi-experiment** was to see if differences in beliefs about hypertension and its treatment existed between White Americans and African Americans, the **independent variable.** Successfully managing hypertension requires future oriented thinking, so differences in time orientation affect following through with medical treatment plans.

> **Overlap with Health Psychology**
> Time orientation is a good choice for a cultural dimension if the class is going to study health psychology.
> The 21st century student understands how cultural values affect health.

Participants were measured on the first four factors of the **Health Belief Model**, the degree of poverty, and hypertension time orientation.

The Health Belief Model is one of the oldest health promotion models, and it focuses on social cognition and health behavior (Gurung, 2010). The model was created after surveys sponsored by the US Public Health Service showed people were not taking advantage of public health screenings.

The Health Belief Model consists of these factors relating to someone's perceptions about disease prevention and treatment (Hayden, 2009).

Health Belief Model: Each component influences the others
Perceived seriousness
Perceived susceptibility
Perceived benefits
Perceived barriers
Cues of action
Motivating factors, such as cultural practices
Self-efficacy, which may be the most important part because it predicts actual behavior

The Health Belief Model has had some success as a tool for conducting research about why people take or fail to take positive action for their health.

The sample consisted of 300 African and White Americans living in north and central Florida counties and the Southeast area referred to as the "stroke belt." All participants had hypertension for at least one year. Everyone was taking pharmaceutical medications.

Procedures are next. The Hypertension Temporal Orientation Scale questionnaire was developed by the researchers and administered through telephone interviews. The **dependent variables** for the study included the following.

1. Beliefs about a person's view of the severity of their hypertension
2. Beliefs about a person's susceptibility for experiencing the consequences of hypertension
3. Beliefs about the benefits of taking medication and/or home remedies
4. Beliefs about any barriers or costs involved to taking medication and/or home remedies

Results showed that African American participants were more present oriented than White Americans, particularly in response to questions about day-to-day hypertension management. African Americans were more likely to use home remedies and be noncompliant about taking pharmaceutical medications according to doctor's directions.

The authors **concluded** that health promotion campaigns and medical advice about treating hypertension on a day-to-day basis *must consider time orientation for success*. Health care providers should become educated about time orientation because it is the root of people's beliefs. It does not do any good to give someone directions about managing chronic health problems unless the advice is culturally relevant. For example, the most present oriented participants thought they were the least susceptible to long-term consequences of hypertension such as stroke and heart attack.

Cultural practices contribute to beliefs, as it is a norm to eat diets high in fat and calories in the "stroke belt." Perceived susceptibility and seriousness may be lower if a behavior is the norm, especially if the person has a polychronic time orientation.
Used with license from megapixl.com.

Strengths and limitations of a cultural dimension approach to classifying culture

A large body of research supports cultural dimensions, and individualism-collectivism is the most studied dimension.

Strengths follow.
1. *They provide a way to compare cultures*. They are a *dimensional approach* to studying the "dynamic interdependence between the psychological and the sociocultural" (Markus & Hamedani, 2007, p. 13). Dimensional approaches quantify differences between groups, so researchers using the dimensions of culture classify someone as, for example, individualist or collectivist for a study, and then make comparisons. Study participants might answer a questionnaire to see if they are more individualist or collectivistic, and then are placed into groups in a quasi-experiment.

2. *They are a parsimonious way to organize behavior*. Dimensions may reflect values and beliefs and can be described along continuums (Markus & Hamedani, 2007). Everyone falls somewhere on the continuum.

> **Thinking skills: Practice top-down thinking**
> **Subjective culture** has come up again, a good way to envision human **cultural norms**. Individualism-collectivism is a well developed theory with research to back it up, particularly at the individual level (as opposed to Hofstede's nation level) where people within cultures have access to both ends of the continuum based on the situation. The theory is flexible and accounts for a wide range of behavior. Concepts studied in this class relate so much! This is what is meant by threading.

3. *The individualism-collectivism dimension has the most data* and evolved as a research tool from studying **subjective culture**, so it has a clear scientific origin (Triandis & Gelfand, 2012). Individualism-collectivism was the most logical theme emerging from a vast amount of research on all the parts of subjective culture, such as categories, beliefs, and norms. A body of research demonstrates the great influence of individualism-collectivism on a variety of social and psychological experiences, such as attributions, self-concept, emotions, cognitions, and in-groups.

4. *They are **etics**, and as such are universal*. They are examples of the universal processes we share as

humans. Triandis was careful to develop a concept of subjective culture to include universal etics as well as emics, meaning what is understood from the inside of a culture. So the continuum individualism-collectivism is an example of the proper use of etics and emics (Triandis & Gelfand, 2012).

Weaknesses follow.
1. *Dimensions are not the only way to compare cultures.* The greatest problem with cultural dimensions, especially individualism-collectivism, is that they are overused. This is not a problem with the dimension approach itself, but it is an interpretation problem (Berry, et al., 2011). Any time someone sees a cultural difference they like to say it is because of individualism or collectivism. However, that conclusion is valid only if the researcher gathered data to show that the dimension is either correlated to a behavior that the dimensions caused the difference. Student must understand there are other meaningful ways to compare cultures.
2. *They tend to categorize behavior on the social level,* meaning they apply to groups (such as the nations research by Hofstede) and do not always accurately describe individuals. This is another interpretation error that can be avoided if students understand the difference between nation and individual level research. Avoid stereotyping by automatically applying the dimensions to individuals unless the research has made that specific application. Stick with Triandis, Hall, and Markus and Kitayama to study research aimed at individuals to avoid making interpretation mistakes.

Evaluation of the sociocultural models approach: The self-dimension
Independent self and interdependent self
The self-dimension is used when studying cognition and culture in this chapter and when studying **Social Identity Theory**. Since it has some assumptions a bit different from cultural dimensions it also has some of its own strengths and limitations, and it happens to have more weaknesses.

Strengths and limitations of the self-dimension
Strengths follow (Markus & Hamedani, 2007).

1. *It is a dynamic interplay* between what goes on in the minds of individuals, the psychological, and what goes on in the social world, the sociocultural.
2. *It is universal in the sense that everyone is a social being* and is either, for example independent or interdependent with the social world.
3. *Shared meaning is important* in the sociocultural model approach, consisting of culturally shared **schemas** between people living in a group.
4. *It focuses on agency,* the ability all humans have to self-regulate behavior in the context of our social world.
5. *It defines what to do and how to be* within cultures. "Doing" best describes the independent self and "being" best describes the interdependent self.
6. *Sociocultural models are well studied* and apply to many behaviors.

Weaknesses follow.
1. *The original theory of independent and interdependent self assumed that people from the US were individualistic and people from Japan were collectivistic* (Matsumoto & Juang, 2008). This is too simplistic and the result of incorrectly using the nation profiles to describe individual behavior. When individualism and collectivism are studied at the individual level, it is easy to see that no one person living in a culture falls to one side of the dimension, but rather have access to both ends based on context. As a result take care to avoid stereotyping others as falling into one end of the self-dimension

or the other just as you were warned with individualism-collectivism.

2. *Self-construal questionnaires make it hard for Asians to rate themselves* because many of the questions lack context (Matsumoto & Juang, 2008). For example, if Asians are asked to rate themselves, 'I am sociable,' they need context to do it. Again, this mistake comes from using the nation categories of dimensions as a basis for understanding culture.

3. *Indigenous psychology challenges* the notion that the continuum independent and interdependent self captures all the possibilities for people to envision the self (Bhawuk, 2008). Hindu Indians have a spiritual self that does not always fit on this continuum. See the chapter 24 about globalization effects for the argument.

Concluding evaluations about cultural dimensions

Cultural dimensions are very useful in comparing cultures as long as students do not see them as error-free and the only way to make comparisons. No research tool is error-free.

To sum up, students must avoid the following errors in thinking about cultural dimensions.

Error #1	Avoid stereotyping people based on the nation categories found from Hofstede's survey. As Triandis warned, individuals have access to both ends of the continuum and vary on where they fall based on the context of a situation. Hofstede was heavily criticized for using a nations approach, including many limitations of the IBM survey.
Error #2	Resist the urge to interpret all cultural differences as the result of a dimension, such as saying, "they must behave that way because they are from a collective culture."
Error #3	Watch failing to recognize that the many ways to classify culture are not mutually exclusive and are instead very related. For example, it is assumed that individualistic persons also have an independent self. Officially, the cultural dimension and sociocultural models approach have some different assumptions, but they are still quite similar and related. It is ok to call the independent-interdependent self a cultural dimension. Just remember it has a different underlying assumption.
Error #4	Watch failing to realize that the different cultural dimensions are not all equally well developed. The way Triandis used individualism-collectivism was well developed as a consistent theme emerging from studying subjective culture that could explain individual behavior (rather than a nation characteristic). The nation approach used by Hofstede is heavily criticized as not well developed.
Error #5	This next error is included because the independent and interdependent self is so often used as a dimension and closely related to individualism-collectivism. The independent and interdependent self, although used to describe a range of behavior, has some methodological criticisms stemming from the way it was envisioned from the start. Matsumoto is one critic (discussed under limitations). Indigenous psychology researchers are also critical of the model as a way to explain aspects of cultural effects on behavior. A discussion of this criticism is included in chapter 24 about the influence of globalization.

21.2: Culture and its influence on behavior and cognition

Discuss means to give a considered and balanced view with evidence. This section is a reflection (a consideration) on how culture affects cognition and behavior.

If culture is a system of shared values passed down to children through socialization and enculturation, then it follows that cognitions and the behaviors they guide differ between cultures. First is a consideration about culture and cognition and then students are reminded of all the research used in the book about culture and behavior.

Organizing ideas for considering cultural influences on behavior and cognition

There is substantial evidence for taking the position that culture affects the cognitions that guide behavior. Five assumptions are believed (Nisbett & Norenzayan, 2002).

1. There are some universals in cognitions. For example, babies are born with predispositions to develop a **theory of mind** and learn **language**.
2. Because there are some universal cognitions, there is not complete diversity between cultures. People have much in common. However, there are also many differences between people.
3. Cultures differ to great degree in basic problem-solving strategies.
4. People's cognitive processing is so closely tied to a group's cultural norms (subjective culture) that there seems little distinction between cognitive processing and cultural practices. The phrase "culture is cognition" is a good description. Chapter 11 started with this idea.

Schema helps us reflect on why there are many differences between cultures (Nisbett & Norenzayan, 2002). Schemas are built so people can "relate parts to each other and to the whole" (p. 5). For example, think of a holiday your family celebrates. The schema for celebrating Thanksgiving, if you live in the US, may involve getting together with specific people, watching football games, and cooking a turkey. Think through a few examples of schemas you have about celebrations, such as how to conduct a marriage ceremony or what happens at a religious celebration. Everything someone does is organized in schemas.

> **Thinking skills: Intersubjectivity, cultural schemas, and cognition**
> Remember the term intersubjectivity from studying Bruner? It allows for the interactions between adults and children so children can be socialized and enculturated.

Cultural schemas form during the **intersubjective** sharing of specific practices that give meaning to a group that start early as a child is **enculturated**. Cultural schemas then guide how people interpret all experiences throughout the lifespan. **Scripts**, the special type of schema about events in time that tell you what to do, how to do it, and with whom are particularly important to understanding differences in behavior and cognition. Cultural schemas are full of shared scripts with deep meaning for a group. The schemas make it possible to live together without constantly reinventing relationships and tasks.

There is also evidence that **language** differences influence cognition (Norenzayan, Choi, & Peng, 2007). This does not mean that the old Sapir-Whorf hypothesis is true because it was such an extreme view that language determines all thought. However, it has been shown that different languages make people attend to different things in their environment.

Culture is learned and shared (Heider, 2003). Adults share culture with children through language, the primary vehicle of enculturation. If you go back and review the description of culture in chapter 3 this idea will fall into place.

The rest of this section explores research demonstrating cultural influences on behavior and cognition in the following cognitive processes.

1. Attention and perception (holistic versus analytic thinking)
2. Memory

A toolkit approach to studying attention and perception: It starts with socialization

It is well documented that people can only attend to and perceive the things they pay attention to in their environment (Kitayama, Duffy, & Uchida, 2009). We learn what is important to attend to during the **socialization** process. Research shows that North Americans pay attention to focal objects,which are the main point of interest, the analytic reasoning. Asians in contrast pay attention to the broader context of objects, the holistic reasoning.

The **aim of one experiment** comparing attention in Japanese and North American participants (**the IV**) was to show differences in attention and perception (Nisbett & Masuda, 2003). For **procedures**, all participants saw a 20 second animated underwater scene twice and then reported what they saw. On the left is a still picture of the underwater scene. **Results** showed that North Americans mentioned the focal objects more often and Japanese participants said more about the entire context of the scene. Japanese participants talked about the whole scene 65% more often than North Americans and gave twice as many relationships between the fish and the context of the picture.

Next it was predicted that if one of the focal fish was shown to participants against a blank background or a novel background (**the IV**), the North Americans would recognize the focal fish more often and Japanese participants would be thrown off by the different context (Nisbett & Masuda, 2003). They were right.

Similar studies find the same difference, even showing that Caucasian Americans fix their eyes on the focal objects and Asian Americans have rapid eye movements between objects and the contextual background (Kitayama, et al., 2009). Differences in eye movements suggests that culture shapes cognition from the start of the socialization process.

Culture and attention: Still picture of the animated underwater scene.
Source: Nisbett & Masuda (2003).
Curtsey of R. Nisbett

The framed-line test: Culture influences perception

You probably tried the framed-line test when it was introduced under in chapter 4 with the biological ATB as a reminder that culture affects our biological processes. The framed-line test was the **perception** test given to participants demonstrating that culture affects perception and a reminder to use top-down processing throughout the course. Then the argument continued that brain differences shaped by culture that explained the results. Use this experiment again as an example of cultural influences on behavior and cognition.

Memory: It's all about context and meaning

Everyone uses memory processes and there are some universals, such as hindsight bias, where people change their minds after something happens (Matsumoto & Juang, 2008). On the other-hand, it has been shown that some African samples did not show recency/primacy effects the same way the **serial position effect** were demonstrated in western samples. It is unclear if schooling or enculturation creates these differences.

Memory skills are best shown when studied in meaningful contexts. Michael Cole's research on the Kpelle and Vai in Africa is an example of the effects of culture on **memory**, and people are often judged intelligent based for their ability to remember.

In the 1960s and 1970s, a series of experiments investigated two areas of cognitive abilities (Cole, 1996). One set of studies examined how the Kpelle and Vai in Africa performed on memory and intelligence tasks. The other set examined the effects of schooling on cognitive processing. Cole tells a great story about the challenges involved in gathering credible data. The process was full of unexpected findings and challenges to traditional research models. Getting past stereotypes was a major research design challenge.

In 1971 Cole tested a commonly believed idea that non-literate African tribal people used rote recall on memory tasks for which they had no emotional connection. Experiments using free recall tasks were a popular memory research format in the US. When given free recall tasks for familiar objects, US participants clustered the items into categories. Educated American adults used the clustering strategy increasingly with many trials. Small children do not perform well at clustering, even with many trials.

When Kpelle farmers in Africa took the same type of free recall test, they selected items representing familiar categories. However, there was no clear pattern of organization in how these they recalled the items. This finding was contrary to the popular stereotype that non-literate persons had tremendous memories. Even practice did not improve the Kpelle's memory. Cole did not want to report that Kpelle farmers had poor memories.

To remedy the problem, Cole designed experiments to make the free recall task culturally meaningful. Before running the studies, Cole first had to figure out how to present the objects to the Kpelle so that they *could* recall them.

How did Cole make the experimental tasks culturally relevant? The tasks had to relate to the context of daily Kpelle life. Otherwise, how could they recall the items? The decision was made to try narratives as the context for the free recall task. **Narrative interviews** are useful cross-cultural research tools because they allow people to tell stories about what is important to them.

> **Thinking skills: Internationalism**
> Do not assume that others think the same way you do or get educated in the same way. It helps avoid **ethnocentrism**.

The **aim of one experiment** was to show that memory depended on context. Free recall items were planted within two different stories (the **independent variable**) that made sense to the Kpelle about the bride wealth for a chief's daughter. In one story, different suitors offered clothes, food, tools, or utensils. In the second story a man kidnapped the girl who drops the same items along the way, but in no specific order by category.

Results showed that how the items were embedded into the stories affected the way in which they were recalled. Participants hearing the first story clustered the items. Those hearing the second story recalled the items according to the order they were presented in the story.

The lesson here is that *researchers cannot simply use the same task to test cognitive processing across cultures.*

More evidence about context, meaning, and memory: The effect of schooling on memory across cultures

People's memory and math skills depend a great deal on how they are schooled. We take it for granted that everyone experiences the same schooling, but this is not the case. Developmental psychology and cross-cultural research flourished in the 1960s with the goal to improve education in countries with low economic development (Cole, 1996). It was thought that giving children access to *formal education* would take them beyond their communities. This is in contrast to *fundamental education*, where children learn community traditions. Cole studied the impact of formal education on memory and math skills in Africa.

The formal education provided for the Africans was based on western schooling. What were the results? African students performed poorly. In 1963 Cole studied Kpelle students in Liberia to find out why.

Mathematics seemed harder for Kpelle students than US students. Cole aimed to show how making the material *culturally meaningful* to the lives of the Kpelle might improve mathematics performance. When observing classes, he noticed students were required to use rote memorization.

Cole was given three reasons for the poor performance. First, the children had perceptual problems that kept them from identifying geometrical shapes. Second, the children could not classify. Third, children used rote recall instead of thinking to come up with answers. When teachers used examples to teach in class and used similar items on tests, the students complained that these items were not covered in class.

Cole did not believe these claims.

Were Liberian students less able than students from the United States? To avoid such a gross generalization, Cole had to think creatively. He noted, for example, that the Kpelle showed high skill levels when trading in the marketplace. If people performed poorly in western traditional schooling tasks but performed well in settings important to their culture, then a new research strategy was needed.

Cole "needed to examine the circumstances in which Kpelle people encountered something recognizable as mathematics" (p. 74). Kpelle everyday activities were studied along with how Kpelle adults transmitted this knowledge to their children.

One complaint was that Kpelle students could not measure, so an obvious place to study Kpelle measurement was in the marketplace. Kpelle people measure rice in the marketplace differently than what is done in United States supermarkets. The Kpelle measured rice in several ways, such as *kopi*, a tin can measuring one dry pint, a *boke* or bucket, *tins* or tin cans, and bags. The relationship between these measurements was based on the common metric of the cup, but not as exact as western standards. How these measurements were used in the marketplace varied according to whether someone was buying or selling. Buying rice involved a kopi with the bottom pounded down to increase the volume and selling rice involved kopi that had a flat bottom to decrease the volume.

A quasi-experiment using Kpelle measurement was constructed. The **aim of the study** was to show that culture affected measurement ability. Participants were American and Kpelle adults and children. The **independent variable** was culture, being American or Kpelle. **Procedures** are next. "Each subject was presented with four mixing bowls of equal size holding different amounts of rice (1and 1/2 , 3, 4½, and 6 kopi), shown the tin to be used as the unit of measurement, and asked to estimate the number of tin cans (kopi) of rice in each bowl"(p. 76).

Results showed that the Kpelle could indeed measure and the adults were accurate. American adults overestimated the amounts of rice, up to 100% for the 6-can measurement. Both American and Kpelle children made estimating mistakes.

Buying and selling in an African market is different from shopping in the West. Cole found that measurement skills were good when the experimental tasks were *meaningful* to the Kpelle participants.
Source: pixabay.com.

Cole's experiment is an example of how making experimental tasks culturally relevant shows that people from all cultures have skills but those skills are just related to what is meaningful to everyday practice.

Formal schooling may affect Kpelle development but cultural *values* explain their behavior (Gay & Cole, 1996). Before formal schooling, Kpelle education was based on tribal culture with several fundamental values.

1. Learning was practical, such as how to build a house. Since **individualism** was downplayed, an individual's superior house building skills was frowned upon. Maintenance of the group was demanded, so Kpelle answers to questions reflected the knowledge of elders.
2. Children did not have to give reasons for answers, something valued in the West. Preserving the culture was primary, so just doing something was enough. Rarely did individuals justify actions if they maintained the culture.
3. Much of the education was *nonverbal*. Children learned through observation that was highly relevant but without the verbal link between the teacher's actions and the child's understanding of them. **Conformity** was expected. When Kpelle children entered formal school, they spent time learning English. Often there were no equivalent words in Kpelle that helped solve traditional western tests of memory and measurement.

The Kpelle experiments were replicated with Maya and Mestizo subjects in the Yucatan peninsula in the 1970s (Cole, 1996). The patterns were the same as those found with the Kpelle.

Culture and behavior: You have already read many examples
Some of the many examples about how culture influences behavior follow. This is a partial list because there are so many in the book.

1. Conformity
2. Compliance
3. Social Identity Theory
4. Health beliefs
5. Theory of planned behavior
6. Cognitive dissonance
7. Attachment and all other developmental topics
8. Depression, such as cultural differences in the expression of the serotonin transporter gene (gene-culture coevolution).

Chapter 22
Sociocultural Approach to Behavior: Cultural Influences on Individuals: Knowledge and Understanding

---

Chapter objectives

Students will:
1. Practice thinking skills (command terms) related to knowledge and understanding, with describe modeled.
2. Describe enculturation.
3. Describe universalism and relativism.
4. Describe etics and emics.
5. Describe factors underlying cultural change.

22.1: Enculturation

Culture is learned and shared (Heider, 2003). **Enculturation** is "the process by which youngsters learn and adopt the ways and manners of their culture" (Matsumoto & Juang, 2008, p. 60).

Enculturation works together with socialization but is different because it "refers to the products of socialization, the subjective, underlying, psychological processes of culture that become internalized through development" (Matsumoto & Juang, 2008, p. 60). Children are enculturated, for example, to have an **independent self** or **interdependent self** or to have a tendency toward **individualism** or **collectivism.**

Three types of enculturation are vertical, horizontal, and oblique (Berry, et al., 2011; Triandis, 2007).

1. *Vertical* means parents pass cultural values down to children.
2. *Horizontal* means peers exchange cultural values with each other.
3. *Oblique* means culture is passed on to others through social institutions such as schools, media, and religious organizations.

Three key details to help students describe enculturation are next.

Three key details about enculturation

Enculturation is different from socialization. Socialization is a process, the teachings used to raise children and enculturation is the product, the psyche housing what is learned through socialization (Matsumoto & Juang, 2008). There is nothing planned about enculturation as children are simply surrounded by culture (Berry, et al., 2011). In the end a person is competent in all aspects of their culture.

Enculturation is adaptive, and children learn behaviors that will help them survive in their cultures (Berry, et al., 2011).

Enculturation is unique to humans (Matsumoto & Juang, 2008). Children internalize what they learn through social cognition, which requires language and a theory of mind, where humans read the intentions of others, internalize the intentions through language, and then behave according to cultural norms (Matsumoto& Juang, 2008).

22.2: Universalism and relativism

This topic deepens your understanding of modern psychology because the 21st century student considers how psychological theory and research applies to everyone and how to avoid oversimplified and ethnocentric views. Being a good universalist means properly applying **etics** and **emics**, a topic used many times in this book. This topic is also important for studying **globalization** in chapter 24, for understanding mental health treatments in **abnormal psychology**, and attachment theory in **developmental psychology**.

There is much detail to go through when studying this topic, but it is a chance to learn about other cultures!

TOK Link for IB Students: Are Emotions Universal?

Are emotions universal? Emotion is one topic used to illustrate universalism and students should enjoy learning about Paul Ekman. Try the exercises to identify emotions as you read this section and consider Ekman's argument that they are universal. For a balanced view, can the argument that emotions are not universal be supported? Be careful because according to Ekman (2003) and Matsumoto and Juang (2008), we all have an innate facial affect program but what is displayed on the face is the result of cultural display rules reflecting schemas of a cultural group. Look into this more for class discussion. The etic is the 7 basic emotions and the emic expression of the etic is the cultural display rules. If something is a good universal for comparing cultures it does not imply that we are all the same because, for example, people express the innate basic emotions differently according to cultural norms.

How might modern psychologists create a global psychology? Avoid taking an extremist position. Perhaps we can combine universalism and relativism in some way for a balanced view.

Students must start their study with key details important for a clear description.

There are really three theoretical views about culture— absolutism, universalism, and relativism (Triandis, 2007). **Absolutism** means all human behavior is similar across cultures, so someone taking this view thinks culture is not important to shaping behavior. Absolutism is a historical position, but learning about it helps show where a balanced view lies. **Relativism** views behavior as unique in each culture. Avoiding ethnocentrism is critical for relativists and they do this by studying behavior "the way the natives see the world" (p. 67). Studies are conducted within a culture based on the values of a particular group. Comparisons with other cultures are avoided. **Indigenous psychology** evolved from relativism.

Universalism lies between absolutism and relativism and is the most balanced view (Triandis, 2007).

Universalism means that psychological processes are the same globally with culture shaping each process within groups. Universalists believe cultures can be compared, though they "are made cautiously and employ a wide variety of research methods and safeguards" (p. 67).

Universalism-relativism can be further broken down into a continuum ranging from extreme universalism to extreme relativism (Berry, et al., 2011).

Extreme universalism_____Moderate universalism_____Moderate relativism_____ Extreme
(absolutism)   relativism

Extreme positions are usually not productive. Defending the argument that culture is never important or that people can never be compared is hard. **Moderate universalism** uses the definition from Triandis where researchers properly use etics and emics to flesh out the shared processes and the unique expression of those processes. Moderate relativism means that psychological processes come from living in a specific sociocultural context, such as attending to different things in a photograph. For example, we learned from Richard Nisbett in the last chapter that some children are socialized to focus on context.

Most of the research reported in this book is the result of a moderate universalist approach, a view favored by many modern cross-cultural psychologists.

Process, competence, and performance are three psychological concepts important for understanding the universalist view (Berry, 2013).

1. *Processes* are shared by all, such as using memory, language, and creating categories.
2. *Competence* develops as one grows up within cultures, such an attitudes or values, which can be seen on where someone falls on cultural dimensions, and are based on the basic processes we all share.
3. *Performance* is the behavior based on what is acceptable within cultural norms, such as how people negotiate roles at work.

Universalism requires the proper use of **etics** and **emics** to sort out patterns related to process, competence, and performance, but in the end we should have a global psychology if all topics are studied with this approach.

Just because we might have a hard time generalizing from research conducted in the West, it does not mean we should get caught up in taking a relativist view (Triandis, 1994). People have much in common, so many universals are easily found. For example, universals exist in emotion and language. Other universals are found in social behaviors such as marriage ceremonies, athletic games, courtship, greetings, and educating children. The results of studies on western samples do not generalize well because we cannot assume the meaning and form of each universal is the same. This is why we need cultural psychology to show what differs, the emic expressions.

> **Thinking skills: Being a good universalist**
> John Berry showed us how to be good universalists and this is discussed under the topic about etics and emics in chapter 3.
>
> *Just because we might have a hard time generalizing from research conducted in the West, it does not mean we should get caught up in taking a relativist view* (Triandis, 1994).
>
> Avoid the oversimplification of saying that because there are some differences between people we should automatically become extreme relativists.

Every psychological process has both universal and culture specific parts (Triandis, 1994). Triandis gives an example about learning by citing an experiment using Japan and US participants. Both groups learned more and made fewer errors as the number of trials increased for a task. This is the universal part. However, there is also something culturally specific about learning related to getting rewards. US participants learned when they were rewarded and also when the experimenter was rewarded, but learned the most when they were personally rewarded. Japanese students also learned in both reward conditions, but learned just as much when the experimenter was rewarded as when they were. Individualism (US) and collectivism (Japanese) might explain the results. Japanese mothers reward their children by saying "I am happy" or "I am sad." Japanese children are **enculturated** to attend to the needs of others. In contrast, US children are enculturated to make judgments based on their own happiness or sadness.

Many examples of universalism are reviewed in this book, such as **social identity** and **stereotypes**. An example of moderate relativism is the **treatment of mental illness** in different cultures, detailed in chapter 27.

Emotion research is another example of universalism and is described next so students understand how a researcher arrives at a universal view.

Class activity about universalism: Emotions and mask drawing

Give each student two pieces of blank computer or construction paper. Each students should draw two masks, one for a celebration and one for war. These drawings can be elaborate and colored with markers and might even go up on the wall.

Emotions can be identified in the masks. Ask students to compare their masks and see if there are similarities. What types of universal emotions are used for celebration or war masks? Can you see some of Ekman's seven basic emotions in these masks?

Use Google images to see more examples of celebration and war masks.

Sample masks from Indonesia (first 2) and Africa (last 2). What emotions are conveyed through these masks? Used with license from megapixl.com.

Universalism: An example of how it works: Paul Ekman's study of emotions

Seven basic **emotions** are universal but cultural display rules account for variations in the actual expression of the emotions (Ekman, 2003). Everyone has an innate **facial affect program**, the biological aspect of emotions, which decodes and responds to emotional triggers, mainly from other faces, and particularly from the eyes. However, emotions are products of both the facial affect program *and* **cultural display rules** (Matsumoto & Juang, 2008).

Here is how it works. An emotional stimulus sends out two messages (Matsumoto & Juang, 2008). One message is sent to the universal facial affect program. This innate program contains the basic emotion themes and the resulting facial patterns stored in them. A second message is sent to the part of the brain that houses cultural information about which emotions are appropriate to display in which contexts. These display rules tell individuals to, for example, exaggerate, mask, or neutralize an emotion. Display rules are different in **individualistic** and **collectivist** cultures. The facial affect program dictates what emotions to show unless a cultural display rule tells the person to adjust it.

How Ekman (2003) discovered universal basic emotions and the cultural display rules that govern them is worth knowing. Everyone has **seven basic emotions** that are distinct and recognizable on the face, which are *happiness, anger, disgust, surprise, fear, contempt, and sadness.*

Ekman (2003) was not originally interested in human emotions. His first interest was hand movements, but many of life's important turning points are serendipitous, and Ekman was in the right place at the right time to receive a grant to study emotions.

In the beginning, Ekman did not believe that emotions were universal. Anthropologists at the time, such as Margaret Mead, believed emotions were socially acquired. Ekman started with this idea, well aware that Charles Darwin believed the opposite, that emotions were universal. Ekman originally speculated Darwin was wrong.

Ekman's first study examined five cultures, Chile, Argentina, Brazil, Japan, and the United States. Participants were shown photographs and asked to identify the emotion. Results showed great consistency, enough for Ekman to start believing emotions were universal. Ekman knew he needed more evidence because his first conclusions went against the prevailing view.

Next, Ekman studied Japanese cultural display rules. When alone, Japanese samples showed the same emotions as Americans. In public, the Japanese displayed just the emotions appropriate for particular contexts.

The next step was to study a group isolated from other cultures and the media. Ekman needed evidence to challenge the explanation that his Japanese and American participants had simply learned social cues from the media and exposure to other cultures.

Five of Ekman's 7 basic emotions: Happiness, surprise, fear, sadness, and anger.
Go to Google Images and type in Ekman's basic emotions to see some of the photos he took of emotions, including the original faces from New Guinea.

Source: pixabay.com

Ekman studied the Fore in Papua New Guinea. Ekman had already analyzed previous films of the Fore and used these in his new study. Ekman edited these films so the facial expression could be seen but nothing else to ensure participants could not get cues from the social context.

Gathering data in Papua New Guinea in the 1960s was challenging. Conditions were harsh and language barriers required translators. The Fore had no written language, so Ekman could not directly ask subjects to select a word from a list. "Instead, I asked them to make up a story about each facial expression. Tell me what is happening now, what happened before to make this person show this expression, and what is going to happen next" (Ekman, 2003, p. 7). Results showed similarity in the story content, but Ekman was unclear how to show that the stories corresponded with specific emotions. He suspected that data from the Fore was evidence for his universal emotions theory.

Ekman returned to New Guinea in 1968 and read stories to the Fore. Ekman asked them to select one of three pictures that most accurately described the emotion in a story. To control for experimenter bias and demand characteristics, Ekman showed one picture at a time. In addition, each picture was coded a certain way so the research did not have immediate access to its true label. "The results were clear-cut for happiness, anger, disgust, and sadness. Fear and surprise were not distinguished from each other......But fear and surprise were distinguished from anger, disgust and sadness" (Ekman, 2003, p.10). Ekman noted that fear and surprise were always distinguished in literate cultures. He was not sure how to account for this difference.

Ekman presented his findings in 1969 but many of his colleagues were still unconvinced because they truly believed behavior was attributed to nurture rather than nature, consistent with Behaviorism's influence in the US during that time. Now psychologists have accepted that emotions are universal and what varies is the cultural display.

Now that you have studied Ekman, try identifying the emotions on these varied faces.
Used under license from Megapixl.com.

Relativism: How can it be productively used?

Students should learn about indigenous psychology because it is needed for studying mental health treatments in **abnormal psychology** and attachment theory in **developmental psychology**. It is also an opportunity to learn about other cultures.

Some argue that behavior can only be understood from within cultures, called **indigenous psychology**, a reaction against Western dominated psychology (Berry, 2013). One can understand the view because there is such a contrast between mental illness diagnoses and treatments created in the West and what people need living in cultures with different backgrounds and values. It has even been argued that western psychology is really

Thinking skills
Your class might debate if it is ever useful to take an extremist relativist position. Some argue that we need different psychologies for each cultural region (Berry, et al., 2011). Others suggest indigenous psychology is most useful as an intermediate stage highlighting unmet needs of nonwestern groups, but that ultimately we need to use information from all cultural groups to create meaningful universals. Consider the debate as you read the example about the Maori of New Zealand, as well as the Baganda of Uganda reviewed under abnormal psychology for the topic of culture and diagnosis.

indigenous and unfortunately has become the standard for all.

Cross-cultural psychologists have attempted to remedy the Western dominance, but too often approached studying other cultures with an imposed etic that was never tested against emic characteristics.

So how might we think about indigenous psychology? It has made several important contributions.

Contributions of Indigenous Psychology (IP)
It studies local psychological concepts that are not similar to anything in the West (Berry , et al., 2011). One example is the Japanese word **amae**, meaning a mutual understanding that puts less pressure on people to conform. Amae applies mostly to uchi relationships, the most intimate ones in Japan. Matsuda (1985) used amae to study how the Japanese conform and this experiment is reviewed in chapter 18.
It takes into account local needs that are not studied in the West (Berry, et al., 2011), such as treating mental illnesses by local healers including important cultural contexts in which people live.
It can help create a global society by discovering culturally relevant behavior (the performance) showing common processes we all have (Berry, 2013).

Next is the case of **Maori of New Zealand**, useful for considering if a **relativist view** is necessary or if the healing practices are part of a helpful intermediate step highlighting unmet needs of nonwestern groups but in the end leading to the creation of meaningful universals.

Maori Indigenous mental health in New Zealand

Maori are Polynesian and are indigenous to New Zealand (Durie, 2009). They settled New Zealand around 1000 CE, about 800 years before the British arrived, and are about 15% of the current population. Similar to other indigenous groups, Maori have high rates of mental health problems.

Maori **health beliefs** are closely tied with the nature and the healing properties of plants, as well as an understanding of cultural norms. The people guarding this knowledge are called **tohunga**.

Maori traditional healing is different from modern western medicine in several ways.

1. It takes place within a cultural context. Avoid thinking of indigenous medicine as simply giving plant remedies and instead understand that plant use is embedded in deeply held cultural traditions.
2. Most treatments involve taking plant medicines. Leaves, bark, and berries are made into potions to swallow or apply externally, though using plants is not isolated from other cultural practices.
3. Healers have specialized knowledge about plants, massage (mirimiri), and incantations (karakia). This knowledge is combined with rituals, such as interpreting dreams, signs, and symbols, and goes far beyond folk knowledge of plants and symbols the average person might have.

Maori traditional culture is embedded in both relationships and nature. Indigenous psychology makes a great contribution that all can benefit from knowing.
Source: pixabay.com.

Healing takes place in three phases, assessment, spiritual reparation, and treatment. Each phase takes into account the different aspects of the person living within a cultural context.

1. *Assessment* means to find evidence for a breach of cultural expectations that has offended another. Maori assume the problems come from breakdowns in relationships due to unwise action or failure to meet cultural expectations.
2. *Incantation*, or karakia, makes up most of the second phase. Karakia are centuries old and give reassurance, protection, and restitution to the person. Modern healers sometimes use karakia based on Christian prayers with the same goals. Some places and people might be declared 'tapu,' traditionally meaning a place or person is safe or dangerous. Tapu in modern times means something is sacred. Infringing on tapu goes against cultural norms, and the result can be illness.
3. For *treatment*, healers restore balance between all the levels of the person—spiritual, cognitive, and family. All health problems are considered a lack of mental and physical balance.

Students studying abnormal psychology must answer questions about the effectiveness of treatments. How can we know if any western treatment or healing works? The answer is more complicated than it appears, but most students rely on western science as the standard for making judgments. This means westerners look for randomized experiments testing treatments, and if they do not exist, we judge the treatment ineffective. But is a western scientific approach always the best approach?

Traditional healing and western psychiatry are two different systems of knowledge, indigenous knowledge and scientific knowledge (Durie, 2009). Maori healers view individuals as part of a larger set of relationships that cannot be separated. Health and illness come from relationships, both with people and the natural world. Traditional healers become knowledgable and respected over long periods of time largely through oral traditions. They are older and considered wise, and *do not have to prove they are effective.*

This view clashes with western scientific knowledge where treatments mostly focus on individuals. Western science is empirical and based on skepticism. Experiments testing effectiveness are tightly controlled, artificial, and removed from the natural world and relationships. Samples are also tightly controlled and selected with certain characteristics so they do not bring confounding variables into the studies. The goal of experiments is to test treatments, so any treatment, such as Prozac or cognitive therapy, must be isolated from all other factors that might influence the person.

It is argued that we do not have to make a choice between traditional healing and western science, and both can be seen as unique and emerge from different cultural norms (Durie, 2009). Both can be respected and have strengths and limitations. "Importantly, the tools of one should not be used to analyze and understand the foundations of another, nor should it be concluded that a system of knowledge that cannot withstand scientific scrutiny, or alternately, a body of knowledge that is incapable of locating people within the natural world, lacks credibility" (p. 242).

Inquiry and collaboration: Approaches to research in the SCATB
Are Western style randomized experiments the best or only way to know if a treatment works? Consider this question when reading about Maori indigenous treatment.

Many western researchers dismiss traditional healers because they cannot be studied with objective controlled experiments. On the other hand, sometimes Maori have dismissed western treatments because the knowledge is created outside of a cultural context focusing on relationships.

Modern Maori healing does not always discount individual factors or biochemical factors as causes of mental illness. However, the values placed on interrelatedness creates values for effective treatment. Maori traditions call into question the exclusive use of western diagnostic systems such as the **DSM** because it can conflict with cultural values.

In New Zealand, Maori healing has reemerged and been integrated into the larger health system. For example, a mental health treatment center located within a larger western care facility is staffed with

Maori nurses and psychiatrists. It uses 'whaiori,' a guide for receiving and serving Maori with Maori views of the world. Facilities such as this one have resulted in more Maori seeking help.

TOK Link for IB Students: Systems of Knowledge

Systems of knowledge are important for TOK. Consider the questions about human sciences in the TOK guide by examining both western mental health treatments and traditional healing. Students can also discuss the question, "**Are methods of science useful for psychology?**" Avoid automatically assuming that they should be the required standard. This is a hard question and violates many people's schemas about knowledge creation.

Should western and traditional healing systems of knowledge remain separate, with indigenous knowledge specific to particular cultures? Evaluate Durie's view that both systems are unique and can be respected. Is this a credible relativist view and should we adopt this perspective? Can studying Maori healing help us understand a universalist view and Berry's opinion that indigenous psychology can help us create meaningful universals?

There are no right answers here, only well defended or poorly defended ones. Consider what psychology might be like if each culture group had a separate psychology with no overlap with others. Avoid the temptation to say that universalism fails to take into account emic expressions of a behavior.

Observations and interviews might even differ when studying indigenous cultures to give a clearer view of behavior

Avoid assuming that research methods developed in the West are adequate for studying all cultures. Constructing a global psychology rests on the ability to correctly learn about others.

Key details of **indigenous** research methods follow. These are general guidelines and each culture modifies them as needed to achieve their unique goals.

Four principles define indigenous research methods (Pe-Pua, 2006).

1. The relationship between the researcher and participants determines the quality of data.
2. Participants should be treated as equals.
3. Protecting participants from harm is more important than achieving a research goal.
4. Research methods should be the best one for the group studied and should be adapted to local cultural norms. The acceptance of a method does not justify its use.

Indigenous researchers use traditional methods when it makes sense, but develop new methods when they see behaviors that do not fit with existing theories and cannot be studied through existing methods.

One example for thinking through indigenous research methods is next.

Researchers have created new methods to study unique experiences of Filipinos. Can these experiences still be part of a good etic about mental health? Or should we be relativists?
Used with license from megapixl.com.

The Philippine experience

The development of indigenous psychology challenged the traditionally accepted role of both researchers and participants and that new methodologies were required to understand indigenous cultures (Pe-Pua, 2006).

This example illustrates the Filipino experience and is specific to them.

Avoid generalizing these methods as the way all other indigenous groups conduct research. Other cultural groups may use similar principles to guide research, but we are referring to indigenous methods from *within a culture*, so each culture might have a way to study people.

Filipino psychology began in the 1970s when new methods were needed to understand Filipino behavior from a native perspective (Pe-Pua, 2006). Western psychology misinterpreted Filipino behavior, and for example, called the use of indirect communication being dishonest. Rather, indirect communication was valued by Filipinos because it showed concern for others and avoided face loss.

A new form of observation research was designed. The topic was *pagkalaki*, generally meaning manhood, but with no clear translation into English. Western psychology had nothing similar to pagkalaki, so she went to a Filipino village with one research question, "What is the meaning of pagkalaki?" (p. 109) and no particular goal.

Over time culturally relevant methods uncovered ideas important for Filipinos that challenged US study conclusions. For example, American researchers thought the most important value for Filipino's was to maintain interpersonal relationships, a conclusion that did not show particular Filipino practices, even if it seemed generally descriptive of a collective culture. In contrast, these two terms better describe Filipinos.

1. *Kapwa*, or a shared identity, a core value for Filipinos
2. *Pakikipagkapwa*, treating another as kapwa

> **Research skills: Applying western research methods to other cultures**
> Filipino psychologists use western research methods with modifications when appropriate. However, sometimes these methods are invalid to explain cultural practices and values, and instead use indigenous methods to understand people from within the native culture. *Might there be times when cultures cannot be compared?*
> What do you think? This is also good for a **Theory of Knowledge** discussion.

The indigenous approach from within a culture is called *pakapa-kapa*, focusing on uncovering cultural practices. Indigenous observation and interviews are examples.

Several indigenous variations of **participant-observer observations** follow.

1. *Nakiktiugali* is a word meaning to adopt the practices of participants. Researchers immerse themselves into the culture while studying them and later can sit back at a distance to evaluate data.
2. *Pagdalaw-dalaw* means frequent visits, a common part of Filipino culture. It helps participants get comfortable with the researcher. One example comes from studying garbage scavengers. Researchers could not live at the dump sites and could not appear to be competing for scarce resources, so they just regularly visited and got to know the scavengers. After several visits, researchers realized they had violated a dress code and it was perceived as insulting for them to show up in the same tattered clothes as the scavengers, reminding scavengers of their low status. After finding this out, researchers changed the way they dressed to create better relationships with participants.

> **A note about the language**
> Don't get caught up in learning the Filipino words. They are hard to translate into other languages. Their use implies that the local research method cannot be understood in western terms. The methods may seem similar but the variations are particular to expected cultural norms for social sharing. The methods reflect Filipino **subjective culture**. Just enjoy learning something about a different culture.

3. *Panunuluyan* means to live at the research setting to be part of day-to-day life. Researchers live, eat, and sleep with a host while collecting data. It is seen by the participants as a way to show *kapwa*, the shared identity valued by Filipinos.

Two Filipino variations of **interviewing** follow.

1. *Pagtatanong-tanong* means to ask questions and *tanong-tanong* means to ask repeated questions. Filipinos spend much of their time talking and asking each other questions, so asking repeated questions is a way to be part of the group. It is not the same thing as an informal interview but rather the researcher and participant are equals where both ask the same number of questions and the participants help set goals. An example of using tanong-tanong was the research about manhood. The researcher could not interview men in a traditional way to avoid being perceived as seductive. Instead, she went to places men gathered and asked more general questions, letting the men participate.

2. *Ginabayang talakayan* is similar to focus groups but is really a collective discussion where participants share in creating questions and defining the direction of research.

Thinking skills and class activity: Cultural dimensions exercise
Look up the Philippines on Hofstede's website to see where they stand on the nation level scale **dimensions of culture**. Filipinos are characterized as low on individualism and high on power-distance. How does these scores compare with indigenous ideas? Do cultural theories such as cultural dimensions completely explain traditional cultural experiences? Draw some conclusions but remember what Triandis said, that individuals have access to both ends of the continuum and behave according to context. The nation profiles Hofstede created can easily become stereotypes! These issues are also related to where you stand on universalism versus relativism.

22.3: Emic and etic perspectives

To achieve a global psychology we must apply all theory and research to everyone, even modifying theory if needed, so we need to consider the proper use of etics and emics when studying behavior.

The proper use of etics and emics is required for meaningful conclusions to be made about understanding people both within their culture (**enculturation**) and when entering other cultures (**acculturation**). We do not want to risk ethnocentrism that could come from failing to make meaningful universals about people that involve both etics and emics. Review John Berry's steps for successfully studying people from other cultures in chapter 3. It is also hard to consider **globalization** effects without understanding how research should be conducted.

The 21st century student takes a global perspective when studying psychology and avoids extreme positions of both absolutism or relativism.

Many other topics in this book require the student to understand the proper use of etics and emics and examples follow.

1. The experience of depression symptoms in chapter 3 under etics and emics
2. Evaluating evidence demonstrating effects of globalization on individual attitudes and behavior, with emphasis on multiculturalism and indigenous psychology.
3. The role of culture in treating mental disorders.
3. An emic perspective was taken by Michael Cole as he developed culturally relevant ways to study memory in the Kpelle.
4. The proper use of etics and emics helped update the diagnosis of anorexia in the DSM-5.
5. Understanding attachment across cultures, such as research on the Efe from Africa in chapter 33

22.4: Factors underlying cultural change

Describe means to give a detailed account and the key details follow. These details are directly related to studying **acculturation** as the factors listed below require people to consider how they might change as a result of entering other cultures, both in the short-term and long-term. The list of factors below also are useful as a part of considering **globalization** effects on people, discussed in chapter 24.

Cultural change refers to what happens when as we move toward globalization, defined as "the compression of the world and the intensification of consciousness of the world as a whole" (Robertson as cited in Hong, Wan, No, & Chiu, 2007, p. 335). Many factors contribute to globalization, bringing formally isolated cultures into contact with others (Hong, et al., 2007).

Factors underlying cultural change	Description
International trade and investment	Some countries have benefited from this, such as China, but it has also contributed to greater differences between rich and poor. Sometimes local group knowledge and goods are exploited.
Rapid transportation and electronic communication	These have created a world where space and time have no meaning, as we can get somewhere fast and find out anything immediately from the Internet.
Migration	Migration alters the ethnic identity of both the people coming into a country and the people living in the host country. Some migrants are permanent residents and some are temporary, moving back to their original country after working for a short time. Even people moving back to their original countries have been exposed to cultural values that they bring home.
Travel	Business and recreational travel brings cultures together far more than you might expect. For example, Canada has a population of approximately 31 million but has about 50 million people visiting each year. The US has about 97 million people visiting each year just from air travel.
Educational opportunities	An example study in chapter 24 about globalization effects found that the view of one's self-concept changes to an individualistic orientation after moving to the city to attend western style universities, even within a country (Ma & Schoeneman, 1997). Students studying abroad might still be subject to selecting one of the acculturation strategies.

As a result, population movement and information sharing across national borders is growing (Hong, et al., 2007). Traditional cultural values are no longer isolated from Western ideas. One's **self-concept** can change, and this is one effect on behavior that is of concern, a topic to be explored as students study acculturation strategies and globalization effects on behavior later in this course.

What is important here is that students understand the factors that create the need to consider acculturation strategies and effects of globalization. We take for granted that these factors are commonplace, but what effect do they really have on people and what challenges do they bring to the entire discipline of psychology, a science largely theorized about and studied in the West as we work toward a global psychology?

Chapter 23
Sociocultural Approach to Behavior: Cultural Influences on Individuals: Synthesis and Evaluation

23.1: Discuss enculturation

Discuss means to give a considered and balanced view using evidence. This section is a critical reflection (consideration) of the role of enculturation for learning cultural norms.

Thinking skills
Review the topic **describing culture** from chapter 3 as a reminder of the complexities of human culture and how it differs from animal experience. The term **subjective culture** is important, because enculturation is about transferring values accepted by a group to children that become categories and schemas guiding behavior. For example, how to value the self (independent or interdependent), value time, or value personal or collective goals (individualism-collectivism) must be enculturated.

Our consideration starts with reflecting on that happens when someone is enculturated.

Key details about enculturation
Enculturation is different from socialization. Socialization is a process, the teachings used to raise children and enculturation is the product, the psyche housing what is learned through socialization (Matsumoto & Juang, 2008). There is nothing planned about enculturation as children are simply surrounded by culture (Berry, et al., 2011). In the end a person is competent in all aspects of their culture.
Enculturation is adaptive, and children learn behaviors that will help them survive in their cultures (Berry, et al., 2011).
Enculturation is unique to humans (Matsumoto & Juang, 2008). Children internalize what they learn through social cognition, which requires language and a theory of mind, where humans read the intentions of others, internalize the intentions through language, and then behave according to cultural norms (Matsumoto& Juang, 2008).
Enculturation takes a long time to develop. It takes practice, and family members, siblings and peers, and institutions assist children (Matsumoto & Juang, 2008).
Enculturation takes place through parents, peers, and institutions.
Enculturation ensures the continuity of cultural practices from one generation to the next (Triandis, 2007).

You might think that enculturation is hard to study because it is implicit, meaning it is implied and understood but not openly stated. Culture surrounds children and enculturation is subtle and unplanned. However, enculturation produces strong behaviors and cognitions that create **schemas** making up one's **subjective culture**, as well as related neuroplastic changes in the brain.

Enculturation is widely studied and our discussion uses three examples that all of us experience.

1. Child-rearing practices enculturate a sense of independence or interdependence.
2. Babies hearing language everyday start to discriminate the sounds of their language as they are enculturated.
3. Listening to music in everyday life creates children and adults who recognize and respond to specific music rhythms.

Research evidence: Child-rearing practices enculturate children have independent or interdependent self-construals

Enculturation is a general process of surrounding the child with culture, so the evidence to consider comes from **ethnography**, which means **observation research** about the specific cultural practices of a group. Reports of enculturation practices are part of a large body of ethnographies, which can be sampled by researchers to compare parenting across many cultures as children grow (Berry, et al., 2011).

These studies examined parent knowledge and values about the best way to raise children.

One argument supported by ethnographies is that a child's sleeping habits are important for enculturating behavior such as independence and self-direction (Berry, et al., 2011).

For example, parents in the Netherlands believe children should have regular sleep routines to prevent fussiness and increase health. In contrast American parents thought children should develop regular sleeping habits as they grew rather than have the habits highly regulated. As a result, Dutch children get more sleep than American children. In addition, Dutch children are observed to be quietly aroused when awake and American children actively alert. This may be because US parents talk to and touch their children more often. Dutch parents believe young children should have time alone so they will develop independence and learn to structure their time, an expected cultural norm in the Netherlands.

Another argument supported by ethnographies is that a parent's **independent self** or **interdependent self** is enculturated to children (Berry, et al., 2011).

Cultures emphasizing autonomy and self-direction had mothers focusing on these when parenting, and their children developed an independent self. In contrast, cultures valuing harmony and conformity had mothers focusing on these in raising children, and they produced children with an interdependent self. Preferences of the mother were passed to children and reflected larger cultural norms.

Research evidence: Language enculturation

This topic was introduced in the biological ATB in chapter 7 under the topic evolutionary explanations of behavior. Children come into the world with universal speech perception. Babies are surrounded by the **language** within their cultures, and by 11 months perceive the sounds of the language(s) they will speak. There are corresponding neuroplastic changes to the brain supporting the change. Janet Werker's BA-DA experiment is evidence of this enculturation process.

Music enculturation creates preferences and memory for music

Class activity: Music across culture

The class might listen to traditional and modern music from a variety of cultures. If the class has students from many cultures, have them bring in music from their cultures.

Teachers might do the tapping exercise in the Hannon and Trainer (2007) experiment to see how students spontaneously tap before reading the study. The class can then see how the tapping fits or does not fit with rhythms of the different music. The more musical students might be able to give some insight into the different meters across culture.

This is not simply an exercise in what people say they like, because the experiments focused on what is recognized about music according to categories we create as we listen to the everyday music of our culture.

How might living in a **multicultural society** influence music enculturation? Research suggests that people with significant exposure to more than one culture's music become **bimusical**, which is similar to **bilingualism** (Wong, Roy, & Margulis, 2009). In this experiment participants listening to both western and South Asian music had good recognition memory for the rhythm as opposed to those with exposure to just western or South Asian music. This may be an effect of **globalization**.

This section is long because there is much to consider and *we all love music*. We take it for granted that we recall certain tunes and have preferences, but have you considered that this is all a product of enculturation?

Both image sources: pixabay.com

Because a discussion must be supported by evidence, students might consider how they developed their preferences and memory for particular kinds of music. Research shows **music enculturation** starts early and has lasting effects.

Children are enculturated to speak a language, and music enculturation is a similar process where we respond to everyday music listening by tapping and dancing, and can recognize a wrong note, recall certain tunes, and feel the related emotions (Hannon & Trainer, 2007). These abilities have nothing to do with formal music training. Children are surrounded by music, and develop culture-specific knowledge of it. There are many universal aspects of music including pitch and rhythm that all children can identify early. However, there are many kinds of music with specific scales and rules regulating pitch and rhythm that children are enculturated to recognize and respond to as they develop.

Considering enculturation helps us understand what is universal about music development and what is culture specific.

Simple meter where the frequencies fall in small regular ratios is universally recognized (Hannon & Trainer, 2007). Babies respond more positively to simple rhythms than more complex ones and this seems the universal building block for enculturating children to culture-specific music systems because all cultures have music containing these simple intervals. However, someone's preference for music patterns is not simply because of a universal preference for the simple meter.

Research evidence: Adults lose the ability to process complex meter of music after enculturation

The **aim of one quasi-experiment** was to demonstrate that the way adults process music patterns come from music enculturation and not simply one's preference for music with a simple meter (Hannon & Trehub, 2005).

Meter is a repeated pattern of stresses giving music a beat (its rhythm). Meter is an internal representation (category) of music structure. North American adults asked to spontaneously tap with a rhythm create taps in clusters of 1:1 or 2:1 ratios. When they hear complex music, the rhythms are condensed to these simpler ratios. It is called simple ratios and is prominent in western music. Tapping ratio categories are assumed to be cognitive biases placing limits on the way the brain organizes rhythm.

Music rhythm in cultures such as South Asia, Africa, and the Middle East, however, is more complex, with clusters of short and long intervals with 2:3 ratios. People growing up hearing this music have no trouble with complex meter and tap and dance along with the music.

Does enculturation create cognitive biases for simple or complex meter?

The experiment compared babies and adults living in North America. It was predicted that adults would perform better on tasks using simple meter than tasks for complex meter. The **independent variables** were age and

---

Thinking skills: Think back to language development with the evolutionary explanation of behavior

Music has a similar developmental process to what Pat Kuhl said about babies coming into the world able to hear the sounds of all languages and developing a discrimination for the sounds they actually produce for the language(s) they will speak. Both are enculturated and come from hearing language and music in everyday life.

Music and language become **categories** that process information, part of **subjective culture**.

---

listening to simple or complex meter. Babies would show no difference on tasks for both simple and complex meter. Enculturation would be the reason for any differences between adults and babies.

For **procedures**, college students listened to folk-dance music from Serbia, Macedonia, and Bulgaria to get familiar with the music. Then they were tested with simplified versions of the melodies with just a piano and drum. The task was to identify if a simple or a complex meter, both with one note added, was a match or mismatch to the original music heard in the familiarization trial. Counterbalancing of the simple and complex tasks was used to avoid order effects, important to designing a well controlled experiment.

Next, babies aged 6.5 to 7.6 month listened to the same folk-dance music. Then they watched two television screens with a movie playing music with either a match or a mismatch to the original melodies. One group of babies saw the simple meter and the other saw the complex meter. Researchers recorded the amount of time the babies watched the match versus mismatched movies as evidence for being able to tell the difference.

Results showed that adults could identify the mismatch with simple meter better than complex meter. Babies showed no difference between the two conditions.

The authors **concluded** that a child's music perception is reorganized as they are enculturated.

For a balanced view, an alternative explanation for the results was suggested. Might infants just have a different way to process music meter? For example, babies process music serially and do not anticipate notes the way adults do. However, the researchers considered that more evidence supports the conclusion that enculturation transforms the infants abilities. For example, in a gradual process, babies become able to categorize rhythm (by 7 months) and then discriminate small changes in meter (by 9 months). This gradual process seems more consistent with what we know about enculturation for language.

Children are enculturated early to music, perhaps earlier than once thought.
Used with license from megapixl.com.

This experiment's conclusion is well supported. For example, the **aim of an experiment** was to show that enculturation was stronger in adults than children. 5th grade children and adults in the US listened to both simple and complex rhythms in novel western and Turkish classical music, the **independent variable** (Morrison, Demorest, & Stambaugh, 2008). They were tested by listening to longer versions of the same music and then had to pick one of several target music pieces matching the original. **Results** showed that both groups had better music memory for western music than Turkish music, with adults better with the complex western music than the children. The authors **concluded** that enculturation was the reason for the results, with adults more strongly enculturated than the children.

23.2: Discuss acculturation: Entering other cultures

Discuss means to give a considered and balanced view supported by evidence. Next is a critical reflection (consideration) of acculturation with evidence about triculturals, physical health (mainly obesity), and mental health. Acculturation stress is challenging to overcome, but research results can reveal possible solutions and also show how some people develop their own coping strategies.

Reflecting on what acculturation means

Acculturation is "the process of adapting to, and in many cases adopting, a different culture from the one in which a person was enculturated" (Matsumoto & Juang, 2008, p. 66). Acculturation can take place directly through immigration, for example, or indirectly, through media (Triandis, 2007). In contrast to enculturation, acculturation is the discontinuity of culture, and can be disruptive in some cases.

Acculturation is the idea used most frequently to understand the experience of ethnic groups living within larger cultures, and it affects a range of behaviors related to stress, mental and physical health, family conflict, and academic achievement (Sage Publications, n.d.).

Acculturation happens all over the world and does not just affect people moving from one culture to a new one. The new culture is also influenced by the people moving into it. The term **globalization** can "be seen as promoting some type of acculturation around the world by facilitating personal mobility across borders and the sharing of cultural values through music, electronic and print media, and education" (Sage Publications, n.d., 106-107).

Several acculturation models exist, but John Berry's model focusing on the individual is the example used in this section. Much of what we know about acculturation comes from his model, with Berry's term '**acculturation strategies**' now widely accepted (Yoon, 2013).

For a balanced view, critics suggest that Berry's model might make someone use a correspondence bias in explaining why people use a particular acculturation strategy. However, this criticism does not seem valid because Berry takes context into account, such as people fleeing political conflict or the amount of social support in settlement cultures.

The key details needed for a reflection about acculturation using Berry's model follow (Yoon, 2013; Berry et al., 2011; Berry, 1997, 2005; Berry & Sam, in press).

People can have two or more cultural identities, and really should be called *multicultural* rather than simply bicultural or even **tricultural** (J. Berry, personal communication, March 16, 2015). All multicultural identities follow the same general model, and the identities are either conflictual or compatible. Conflictual identities lead to **acculturation stress**.

John Berry's acculturation model

Parts of Berry's model	Description
Reasons people acculturate	People acculturate for reasons related to mobility, voluntariness, and permanence. Mobility means people immigrate to a new culture as opposed to having a group invade them and impose acculturation. Voluntariness varies from people choosing to immigrate who might want to integrate to refugees and indigenous people who are imposed upon. Permanence refers to how long someone stays in a new culture, from immigrants seeking to live somewhere forever versus a traveler or exchange student.
Berry focused on acculturation at the individual level	Berry theorized about acculturation at the individual level rather than the group level used in anthropology models. Berry examined **psychological acculturation** of individuals, such as stress and conflict.
Two questions one must answer when moving to a different culture	Two questions must be answered when a cultural group moves into a larger culture. A. The first is about cultural maintenance, "To what extent should one's original cultural identity be maintained?" B. The second is about contact and participation, "To what extent should one get involved with other cultural groups or live a life revolving around their original cultural group?"
4 acculturation strategies	1. **Assimilation** means the person wants to blend in and identify with the new culture. 2. **Separation** means the person plans to keep their identify tied to the original cultural group and avoids interacting with the new culture. 3. **Marginalization** means the person is not interested in staying identified with the original or new culture. 4. **Integration** means the person both retains the original culture and participates in the new one. Integrated people are **bicultural**.
The strategy choice affects the level of acculturative stress one feels	Integration causes the least amount of acculturative stress and marginalization causes the most.

Parts of Berry's model	Description
Integration works well in a multicultural society	Integration works best when a society is **multicultural**, meaning it values cultural diversity, has low levels of prejudice, and all cultural groups identify with a larger plural society. A newer term is **intercultural adaptation**, meaning how individuals develop positive relationships with many groups and develop multicultural beliefs.

Critically considering Berry's acculturation model: Tricultural research

Berry's model may describe the overall process of acculturation, but a balanced view is needed because there is still plenty to learn about multicultural identities. If we are going to be good **universalists**, then research must be conducted on the **emic** perspective of people with multiple identities to acculturate that then is integrated into a meaningful **etic** description of the concept multiculturalism.

The **aim of one questionnaire study** was to examine unique characteristics of tricultural identities in Jamaican immigrants in the US (Ferguson, Iturbide, & Gordon, 2013). Three dimensional (3D) acculturation identity means to internalize three cultures and triculturals may have higher levels of acculturative stress than biculturals who internalize two.

Jamaican immigrants make acculturation decisions based on Jamaican, African American, and the new US cultures. **Results** showed the following about 80 first generation Jamaican immigrants to the US (Ferguson, et al., 2013).

1. Fifty-one percent identified themselves as tricultural, 31% as bicultural, and 18% as monocultural.
2. Triculturals use the integration strategy for several reasons. The US promotes diversity more than some countries with many immigrants, such as Germany and France. Next, Immigrants may want new relationships because they are on the outside of both majority and minority cultural groups. Last, Jamaicans may have acculturated to some extent before coming to the US through remote acculturation via media.
3. Triculturals report more acculturative stress. Managing three identities is tough, and triculturals report greater amounts of mild depression and anxiety than biculturals.

In **conclusion**, it seems that more stress occurs when people manage more than two identities, making the concept multicultural more complex than it may seem on the surface. With all the information available on the Internet and international travel, education, business, and migration, there is much to know about how the factors underlying cultural change really affect people and we have not yet finished studying **multicultural identities**.

Thinking and collaboration

Describing culture from chapter 3 is important for thinking about acculturation. In particular, **subjective culture** helps students understand the complex nature of acculturation. People enter a culture full their own categories of values, beliefs, and dominant language(s). The class can even compare similarities and differences in subjective culture to see all the diversity just in one classroom. For example, who still eats traditional cultural foods at home and who knows how to cook them? This can prime students for reading research on the next pages.

Adapting one's original subjective culture to another is complex. John Berry describes the different strategies people use to acculturate. Understanding **social identity** and **cultural dimensions** is also useful as people test new in-groups/out-groups and as migrants often must learn about individualism. Considering acculturation also helps with the topic of **globalization** effects on individuals. Draw as many relationships as possible.

Acculturation and physical health: A well-documented problem for immigrants coming to western countries

There is a tremendous research base to consider in a discussion about **acculturation and physical health**. Sadly, acculturation is correlated with declining health for immigrants, especially when they come to western countries. For a balanced view we will consider some research suggesting that acculturated immigrants with higher incomes eat more vegetables, so acculturation does not always lead to poor health. However for many immigrants, health deteriorates with acculturation and some gender differences exist, at least in the Hispanic populations studied.

The section focuses on **dietary acculturation**, meaning that as immigrants acculturate, they tend to eat less culturally appropriate foods and more foods of the host cultures, particularly easily assessable foods, including fast foods, meat, and sugary foods. **Obesity**, **type 2 diabetes**, and **heart disease** are the health problems surfacing in the studies.

This discussion includes research about the following groups. The problem is not just seen when immigrants move to the US, so part of having a balanced view is to avoid oversimplifying the obesity issue as just a US problem.

1. Latinos acculturating to the US
2. The Chinese acculturating to the US
3. Filipinos acculturating to the US
4. Immigrants acculturating to Italy
5. Ghanaians acculturating to the UK
6. Gender differences in health and acculturation

A consideration must include research support so the task is now to go through a sample of the many studies available. This problem has been documented for decades and the sampling of research spans 2008 to 2016. *Both quantitative and qualitative research provide support, so students have a chance to integrate more qualitative research into the course.*

Dietary acculturation of Latinos, Chinese, and Filipinos living in the US

Correlations, interviews, and surveys are the primary research methods used to study **dietary acculturation** and all studies conclude that increased acculturation is most associated with decreased health because of dietary changes. The decline in health is worse for males than females, at least in Mexican samples.

The **aim of one interview study** was to find the reasons for becoming overweight among Latinos living in the US (Sussner, Lindsay, Greaney, & Peterson, 2008). The study used **focus groups and** revealed 7 themes.

1. Perceived food quality and availability
2. Food and eating practices
3. Breastfeeding practices
4. Beliefs about food and child feeding
5. Weight of mothers and children
6. Physical activity and sedentary lifestyles
7. Social isolation and support level

Thinking skills: Acculturation is a risk factor for obesity

Studying health psychology can include the health problem of **obesity**. It is something everyone should know something about because being overweight is on the rise globally, called globesity by the World Health Organization.

It seems **acculturation** is a risk factor for obesity.

Results included some interesting comments that can help us reflect on problems related to someone becoming acculturated. For example, many thought food was more widely available and of higher quality in their native land than in the US. One person commented that food in the US was often full of chemicals as compared to their country where "it's only water, earth, and the fruit has a nice smell even far away" and "In Puerto Rico… we had our own chickens and always had eggs and meat …. it's not so easy to get the vegetables here in the US" (p. 4). In addition, many of the mothers interviewed said exercise was promoted far more in their native country than in the US and they felt more socially isolated and pressured to spend more time working rather than spending time with family because "here (in the US) time is money" (p. 6).

Many factors contributed to less physical activity, such as spending more time watching television and using transportation to run errands rather than walking.

The authors **concluded** that these results should direct public health programs because low-income Latinos have the greatest prevalence of obesity in the US as compared with other ethnic groups.

Studies about Filipino and Chinese Americans have similar findings.

The **aim of one correlation study** was to show the relationship between acculturation and eating western foods (Vargas & Jurado, 2016). **Results** showed that bicultural Filipinos living in New Jersey reported a high acculturation to their native

Is everybody eating pizza and burgers after arriving in western countries? It is a stereotype that westerners, especially in the US, all eat fast food. Many do and many do not. How much fast food do students in your class eat? Do students whose families are closely tied with a particular culture still prepare those foods? Do the students know how to make these foods? Sounds like a **CAS** experience. A **film** titled *Understanding fat: Syndrome X and beyond* featuring Ronald Evans can be streamed from **Youtube**. One example is Mexican Pima Indians moving to the US.
Sources: pixabay.com and megapixel.com.

diet and a moderate western dietary acculturation. However, they still ate more calories and fat than they did in the Philippines and had increased BMIs and larger waistlines. For example, Filipinos still ate lots of rice, a carbohydrate staple in their traditional diets. It is theorized that Filipinos may suffer from **festival food syndrome**. This means immigrants who ate certain foods just at celebrations in their native countries now eat these foods more often in their new country. Festival foods are loaded with more fat and calories. So even Filipinos who have not acculturated to western diets may be eating too much of the foods high in fat and calories. The most acculturated Filipinos ate the most western food, consistent with findings from decades of research.

Focus group interviews with Chinese students attending US colleges also finds increases in BMI and weight gain when exposed to western foods (Wu & Smith, 2016). You do not have to be a permanent resident in a new country to be affected by acculturation. Students said they had little nutritional education, something colleges might want to include to prevent health risks.

CAS and/or class acculturation activity

Traditional foods, such as Indian, dim sum, tamales, and falafel are examples of foods from some of the cultural groups that move to western countries. *What better way is there to get to know a culture than to share food?* Perhaps the class can have an international food day and taste dishes from all the cultural groups in the class, and this includes regional American foods outside of pizza and hamburgers and European/other western foods. Traditional foods are not only linked to maintaining cultural roots, but have health benefits. Perhaps students can research and share the traditions and health benefits for their culture for eating certain foods. As the Ronald Evans film makes clear, some groups have higher genetic risks for certain diseases, and a traditional diet can be a buffer against developing the illnesses. Some of the author's students in the past have learned to cook traditional foods that might get lost as they become Americanized.
Source: pixabay.com.

Dietary acculturation in immigrant groups living in the UK and Italy

The **aim of an observation study** using food logs was to compare food habits with Ghanaians living in Ghana with those becoming acculturated to living in London (Gibson, Knight, Asante, Thomas, & Goff, 2016). Food logs including portion sizes were kept for 3 days. Participants reported height and weight and researchers calculated BMI from this information. **Results** showed that Ghanaians living in Ghana had diets lower in saturated fat and protein, and ate more traditional foods. Ghanaians living in London consumed more fats, meat, and proceeded foods. Traditional African diets reduce the risk of heart disease, and Africans have higher biological risk factors for heart disease and Type 2 diabetes. One reason for poor health in groups living in the UK and other western countries is the lack of cultural sensitivity in providing medical care, and this might include educating western medical practitioners in the ethnic diets of the people they are likely to see.

Similar findings come from immigrant groups living in Italy. A correlation study found that about half the sample was obese and most said they had gained weight after moving to Italy (Casali, Borsari, Marchesi, Borella, & Bargellini, 2015). The factors most associated with weight gain was being female, having less education, and coming from an African ethnic group. The culprit seems to be eating cheeses and snack foods and getting away from traditional diets.

Are there any solutions to the problems of dietary acculturation?

This research does not speak well for western diets, a topic students might want to look into a little more. To get a balanced view after reading some negative research, some survey findings suggest that higher incomes equal higher vegetable consumption (Lopez & Yamashita, 2015). Using Latino participants living in the US, it was found that Latinos with high acculturation *and* higher incomes also ate more vegetables. In contrast, highly acculturated Latinos (without the higher incomes) ate fewer vegetables.

Income seems a key factor in the health of acculturated immigrants. It is not the only factor, but this is something worth considering when we think about how to ease acculturative stress.

A last example: Interviews show that teens cope with acculturative stress

Korean adolescents face acculturative stress after moving to the US, and it is especially difficult because they often have generational conflicts with parents and grandparents (Kim, Suh, Kim, & Gopalan, 2012). When acculturating, many teens easily adopt more individualistic values while older generations maintain Confucianism and value family harmony and obligation. Negotiating a balance between the Korean and American self is a challenge. At school, Korean adolescents face discrimination, stereotyping, and difficulties with language. As a result, these teens can feel isolated and report depression and anxiety.

The **aim of the interview study** was to understand how Korean immigrant teens coped with the many stressors faced when acculturating.

Procedures involved using semi-structured interviews because it was the best way to get in-depth information and probe the meanings of life experiences. This was a **purposive sample**, a rigorous sampling method where participants are selected with specific characteristics. Criteria included that participants were in a US middle or high school, moved from South Korea, and had a Korean ethnic identity. Ethics were carefully considered, and the teens were assured that participation was voluntary and that results were confidential.

Korean peer groups were identified in interviews as a place to hang out and find support.
Source: pixabay.com.

The interviews were audiotaped and used 10 open-ended questions that allowed for probing and clarification. Some questions asked about reactions to stress and how the teens coped. Other questions asked about resources for coping with stress and overall happiness.

Data analysis looked for themes. This is a lengthy process where researchers first create a transcript merging audiotapes and field notes. Next, a coding system is designed to organize data. Last, data is compared and contrasted to look for a pattern in themes. Researchers checked with participants to make sure the themes were accurate, a step increasing the study's **credibility**.

Results showed three useful themes.

1. The most important theme was for Korean adolescents to participate in activities, such as clubs and volunteering that increased an overall sense of happiness. For example, some students with Taekwondo skills shared them with others and another taught violin lessons for free. Another teen visited elderly people in a nursing home, something reminding him of the time spent with his grandmother who still lived in South Korea.

2. Having social support from friends and family was the next important theme. Feeling connected with others was vital for happiness and stress reduction. For example, hanging out with other Korean students was noted as supportive.

3. Having positive emotions was the last theme. Even though participants had some negative emotions related to acculturative stress, a better coping strategy was to develop positive emotions. For example, one participant admitted that living int he US was difficult at times but staying focused on the positive reduced stress.

Sharing Taekwondo was one activity identified in interviews as important for staying connected with others.
Source: pixabay.com.

The authors **concluded** that culture played a large role in reducing stress, providing many opportunities for participants to identify with their culture and still interact with Americans. Ways to improve psychical and mental health of immigrants are better understood through these in-depth conservations between researcher and participant.

The authors would be interested in comparing coping strategies of adolescents still living in South Korea and then when living in the US. This is a direction for future research.

Chapter 24:
The Sociocultural Approach to Behavior:
The Influence of Globalization on Individual attitudes, Identities, and Behavior

Discuss means to offer a considered and balanced view based on evidence. This chapter takes a balanced view by exploring claims that globalization can affect individual identities, attitudes, and behavior in both positive and negative ways. However, the class should reflect on how adopting a global identity or an integrated acculturation strategy might ease the negative effects.

Many people's first thought about globalization is that it will lead to a world where everyone is the same, adopting the values and language of the dominant culture. This concern might be on people's minds the second they hear the word globalization. *We do not want to adopt a utopian view that we will live happily ever after as a global society.* However, research shows that globalization can lead to a richer multicultural society that does not destroy traditional cultural identities, attitudes, or behavior, so avoid automatically making a conclusion before weighing the evidence.

Globalization is defined as "the compression of the world and the intensification of consciousness of the world as a whole" (Robertson as cited in Hong, Wan, No, & Chiu, 2007, p. 335).

Review **acculturation**, **universalism**, **relativism**, **etics**, **self-efficacy**, **dimensions of culture**, **socialization**, and **enculturation** to help evaluate the effects of globalization on culture. Discussing globalization effects on identities, attitudes, and behavior involves considering the following three claims.

Three claims to evaluate when thinking about global effects
Globalization might lead to a homogenized society where everyone's identities, attitudes, and behavior are similar. It also might have a negative impact on the developing child.
Globalization might lead to a richer multicultural society, where people's identities, attitudes, and behavior reflect rich cultural differences but also find common ground. Remember that Harry Triandis says people have much in common!
We may need new research methods to properly study globalization influences. Developing new methodologies will enhance **indigenous psychology**, protecting and promoting traditional cultural practices for multicultural world where diversity flourishes (Bhawuk, 2008). There is evidence that enhancing indigenous psychology prevents researchers from applying **pseudo-etics,** those imposed etics Berry (1969) warned us against. New methodologies to study indigenous psychology should reduce negative effects of globalization on culture.

24.1: Does globalization lead to a homogenized society or child development problems?

Researchers arguing for the homogenized view believe western scientific, competitive, and individualistic values lead to the destruction of **indigenous cultures** (Hong, et al., 2007). For example, would people migrating from a nonwestern culture to the West or leaving a traditional village to live in a westernized city within their country adopt values of the new culture? At first glance, it seems impossible to avoid some effect.

A reflection about this issue is a chance to see the interaction between local and global influences.

Research supporting the homogenization view

One way to research the extent of homogenization is to study people's **self-concepts** and relate the findings to their exposure to individualistic culture (Ma & Schoeneman, 1997). The **aim of the correlation study** was to see the relationship between self-concept and exposure to individualism. It was predicted that participants living in traditional Kenyan culture (local) would have more social self-concepts and Kenyans exposed to individualistic values from working in cities or attending western-style universities (global) would have less social self-concepts. Adopting a less social self-concept might affect a wide range of behavior, the negative effects of globalization.

For **procedures**, American students living in Kenya and Kenyans living in traditional cultures or in cities filled out a questionnaire where they selected words that most described the self.

Results showed that American students and Kenyans living in the city reported just 12% and 17% of social words to describe the self. In contrast, Kenyans living in traditional cultures reported between 58% and 84%. Traditional Kenyans selected words representing social categories of kinship and work. Americans and Kenyans living in the cities selected nonsocial categories of self words.

The authors **concluded** that urbanization and education contributed to the nonsocial self-concepts common in individualistic cultures.

Changes in someone's self-construal could lead to local cultural destruction, although the particular effects are not documented in this study. Consider the **independent self** and **interdependent self** dimension already studied in this course. Research shows that self-construal affects cognition, attitude, and behavior, including values such as seeking harmonious relationships, so the effects on behavior could be great.

What about the developing child?

The impact of globalization on the developing child is worth considering and we may not know the full effects for many years. Children's development may be impacted in many ways and two examples follow (Thompson, 2012).

1. **Education:** Might children with access to computers gain knowledge about the West (global) that interferes with traditional cultures and languages (local)? Do all children have the same access and who should provide it? Are the skills required in school different because of globalization and how might this affect local cultures? Might learning goals change if students use technology and learn English, where English is a world currency, an entrance into other cultures? How might globalization affect children's thoughts about their current lives as well as expectations for their futures? In what ways are Indigenous groups responding?

2. **Health:** How might health services change as a result of globalization? Does it improve or hinder children's health?

These questions have no easy answers. Little research has explored globalization affects the developing child so we can only speculate about the long-term impact. One study showing changes in **socialization** (and possibly **enculturation**) of children as a result of globalization might spark class discussion.

The **aim of the correlation study** was to investigate Chinese rural (local) and urban (global) parental attitudes toward social change and reports from their adolescent children about parenting practices (Chen, Bian, Xin, Wang, & Silbereisen, 2010). For **procedures**, parents filled out a questionnaire about their perceptions of social change and their children filled out one about their perceptions of parenting practices. **Results** showed that urban parents are aware of more social changes then rural parents related to work opportunities and technology (product of global). Urban adolescents reported less controlling parents who encouraged independence. In addition, parents who perceived more job and technology opportunities were rated higher in using warmth and sensitivity to encourage their children to take advantage of them. The authors **concluded** that socialization practices may be changing in China.

Thinking and communication skills
Students might look into more examples of people's experiences where local and global influences interact, perhaps interviewing immigrants, students returning from study abroad, or people traveling extensively. How many people have abandoned their original cultural identities and behavior after exposure to another culture? Fundamentally you are asking if someone's **subjective culture** changes, and if so, what are the effects?

We learned in the last chapter that **acculturation** can contribute to behavior changes leading to some unfortunate consequences from **dietary acculturation**. This is an example where globalization might be making things worse for some people. Can how research results help us learn to reduce the problems of dietary acculturation?

Collaboration and inquiry
Students might brainstorm questions a researcher can investigate and the types of research methods best for answering them. Students can search the Internet for more information about children's health and education to get more information. There are no right answers, just well defended ones. Might more children grow up with global identities? See the end of this chapter for more about a global identity and global citizens.

Conclusions about possible negative effects

The questions raised in this section and the research shows that globalization presents many challenges. The studies are correlation, so they do not show that globalization caused anything. Students must reflect on what the correlations might mean.

When studying acculturation in chapter 23 you learned that many people have **acculturative stress** but find ways to cope. We must find ways to reduce negative consequences of globalization and increase well-being. The next section has some ideas.

24.2: Arguments that globalization can lead to a richer multicultural society
Principles for evaluating the multicultural view

Three principles used to evaluate the claim that globalization leads to a richer multicultural view
Many acculturation strategies promote multiculturalism. Integration and separation are the most likely **acculturation strategies** people use when introduced to a new culture, and they do not produce homogenization (Berry, 2008). Rather, integrated people adopt aspects of the new culture and keep their cultural heritage alive. Separated people resist the new culture and focus on intensifying their identities with their local culture.
Cultural diversity and multiculturalism are promoted when all cultural practices are respected, studied, and shared. One way to increase the likelihood that traditional cultures are valued and preserved is to create new research methodology to study and protect **indigenous cultures** (Bhawuk, 2008).
Marginalized people may benefit from globalization by adopting a new global identity (Kunst & Sam, 2013). Remember that marginalized people reject both the new culture and their original culture.

Each principle is addressed next.

Arguments for the richer multicultural view: Many acculturation strategies promote multiculturalism

Intercultural contact is the start of **acculturation** and **globalization** (Berry, 2013, 2008). Unfortunately, many people hold two beliefs about intercultural contact that are not necessarily true. One is that people moving into a new dominant culture change the most. Second, the original local cultural values and practices disappear as people assimilate into a dominant culture.

Learning about acculturation strategies should bring more critical thought to the issue. Many **acculturation strategies** are available and people do not simply assimilate into the new culture. They might integrate, separate, or become marginalized. Integration and separation include keeping one's original cultural values. Marginalized people may lose the most, because they do not participate in either their original

---

Research about trilinguals: The challenge of a multicultural identity

The Ferguson, et al. (2013) study in chapter 23 can be used for this section.

Managing a multicultural identity is challenging and the trilingual group uses the integration strategy to manage this new identity. They do not abandon their original cultural values. This is another example of local and global interaction.

The Kim et al. (2012) study in chapter 23 can also be used as it shows how Korean adolescents cope with acculturative stress.

culture or the new one. Perhaps globalization can help these people find a new identity. In the end, a richer multicultural identity might be the outcome for all, because even people from the dominant culture are exposed to new cultural practices through for example, restaurants and cultural events.

No one has to assimilate, but can keep their original culture while participating in aspects of other's cultures. There is no evidence that global development has led to complete homogenization and many nonwestern countries such as Taiwan and Japan have now become economically advanced because of the exposure (Bhawuk, 2008). Technology is probably the greatest factor in globalization but that does not automatically mean people abandon their cultures just by using it. "Using a cell phone does not make someone a low-context communicator, driving an automobile does not make someone an individualist, and culinary fusion is not ravaging ethnic cooking" (p. 306).

Go back and review acculturation research in chapter 23 to see examples of people acculturating. There are both pros and cons, but acculturation does not seem to lead to people completely losing their cultures Rather, it presents challenges that can be overcome.

Arguments for the richer multicultural view: Protect and enhance indigenous psychology: The traditional Indian identity (view of the self)

TOK Link: For IB students

Here is a chance to learn something about a culture that you might not know. It expands your understanding of people and helps with evaluations of concepts that are well studied and assumed to be **etics**.

The TOK class might discuss **knowledge creation** with this topic, such as using inductive methods to create new models for explaining behavior.

Research should come from theory, so it is important to develop **emic**-oriented theories (Bhawuk, 2008). Emic-oriented theories should take an inductive approach and start with culturally rich knowledge, perhaps using folk-wisdom or classic writings. The theory builds from this culturally rich knowledge.

One such approach uses the **Bhagavad-Gita**, a 700 verse classic about Hindu spirituality, to expand research about what is known about the **self-concept**. The goal is to create a model for studying **indigenous Indian psychology** that preserves traditional culture and avoids **pseudo-etics** related to the term self-concept.

Attempts to merge Indian and western psychology are new and should be encouraged. The Bhagavad-Gita has verses describing the self as closely tied to one's duties (Bhawuk, 2008). Indian culture believes people have different **social identities** from birth based on one's place in a **caste system**. Each caste is closely tied with one's duty to perform work. People gain perfection through hard work because one worships God by performing well in work. Serious social consequences exist for doing a poor job at one's work, so most people do their duty. However, a decision can be made about which of two paths to take about working that is related to the self-concept. Any time someone does a task or any action, they make a decision about the path to take.

Path #1 is the most common where people work to gain money, the fruits of their labor. Path #1 supports a *social self*, which is most related to the

Does the Hindu concept of self really fit onto the cultural dimension independent-interdependent self or into Bandura's theory of self-efficacy? Do we need to expand theory?
Source: pixabay.com.

self in well known theories. Path #2 is followed less often, and means detaching from work and not hoping for a specific outcome. Path #2 leads to liberation of the self from the physical and social world, leading to a *Real self* or *spiritual self.* Path #2 is said in the Bhagavad-Gita to be better than Path #1.

Knowing about the Indian spiritual self is what promotes multiculturalism in a global society.

This Indian indigenous view has consequences for two concepts about the self, **self-efficacy**, and the **independent self-interdependent self** (Bhawuk, 2008). Both are considered **etics** backed by a body of research.

Bandura claims that **self-efficacy** largely determines behavior, so it is important to consider if it applies to the spiritual self. Self-efficacy is the belief that one is capable of starting and carrying through with an action (Bandura, 1977). Self-efficacy is rooted in the concept **agency**, which means people influence their personal life circumstances (Bandura, 2002). Agents have an intention to act to achieve goals, and their self-efficacy level is the key to meeting those goals. People have both personal and collective agency, guiding some of their own behavior and meeting some goals through group membership. Bandura claimed that the degree to which people used personal and collective agency varied according to **individualism** and **collectivism**, so agency and self-efficacy have been studied with a cultural dimension. However, the entire theory of self-efficacy and agency implies a social self where the goals of an agent expand and move outward into the social world (Bhawuk, 2008).

Aum or om, is an important Hindu symbol representing Brahman, the almighty, the source of existence. The sound aum is said daily by Hindus and is thought of as pranava, meaning it is central to life and comes through our breath.

Aum is important to a Hindu spiritual self. Students practicing yoga say om but do you know what it means?
Sources: pixabay.com and about religion.com.

Is there a place for the spiritual self in Bandura's theory of self-efficacy? Nurturing an inner spiritual self implies getting rid of a social self and moving inward toward enlightenment. To do this, one must get rid of personal and collective agency to act as part of a social world and become one with the divine. *Understanding more about the spiritual self might expand the entire theory of self-efficacy.* Consider this: "It is perhaps easier for those from Asian cultures to visualize a scenario where one leads a harmonious life without setting life goals and being an agent in achieving them" (Bhawuk, 2008, p. 312).

A spiritual self also raises questions about the **independent self-interdependent self** dimension (Bhawuk, 2008). The self of western people is independent and the self of nonwestern people is interdependent, and this dimension is related to individualism and collectivism. Indians are collectivists and they generally have an interdependent self, but also have the capacity for a spiritual self, a metaphysical self called **atman** that goes beyond a social self. The atman is an independent self that becomes part of the divine Brahman, the supreme being. The atman has the potential to continue to grow infinitely as part of the divine. This cannot be accounted for with the current independent self-interdependent self continuum.

Arguments for the richer multicultural view: A global identity offers marginalized people a way to fit into a multicultural society

Evidence supports the conclusion that adopting a **global identity** can help marginalized people, showing one benefit of globalization. Global identity is a new type of identity, one effect of globalization on identity, attitudes, and behavior.

An online survey study **aimed to show** that there is an alternative to marginalization, the global identity (Kunst & Sam, 2013). The marginalization acculturation strategy does not have to be the only choice for people not wanting to keep their original culture or blend in with the new one. People are no longer required to think of themselves strictly in terms of their original culture or the new dominant one. People all over the world meet and share culture as part of a global community, and have the option to develop a global identity.

Global identities needed research support to see if it was a possibility for marginalized groups and if it might help reduce discrimination for all ethnic minorities. The authors gave several advantages of adopting a global identity.

1. Discrimination is less likely.
2. It offers an alternative to integration, which can be stressful because some people find it difficult to balance both the old and new culture.
3. It is helpful as a way to disengage from the discrimination threat.

A global identity offers more options for people. Avoid assuming that multicultural or global identities automatically threaten individual cultural values. This view is a stereotype that is not supported by research.
Source: pixabay.com.

The survey sample included three ethnic minority groups living in western multicultural societies, German-Turks, French-Maghrebis, and British-Pakistanis. These are the largest Muslim groups in their new countries.

Two of the hypotheses follow.

1. Participants scoring higher on marginalization will also score higher for a global identity than participants with low marginalization.
2. Marginalized participants scoring high for a global identity will show lower stress and higher life satisfaction than marginalized participants with a low global identity.

For **procedures**, a series of survey questions asked about discrimination, ethnic identity, stress, life satisfaction, and global identity.

Results confirmed both hypotheses, suggesting that adopting a global identity is a good strategy for making sense of the self. Global cultures celebrate differences between people and this may appeal to some otherwise marginalized people. Keep in mind that celebrating differences does not mean we should accept all behavior as appropriate and this could be dangerous to do, but it allows us to learn about and respect other cultures.

End with a TED Talk and discussion
Watch the Ted Talk titled "Global citizen" by Hugh Evans. What does the term global citizen mean? Do you think more young children will be global citizens in the future? On the other hand, might global citizenship have some negative impacts on traditional cultural values that are undesirable? This topic is controversial and should be explored with open-mindedness and an inquiring spirit. Withhold judgment until you get some facts and hear many opinions. There are no right answers, only well defended or poorly defended answers.

Activity is based on a TED Talk recommendation from Lee Parker during an IB Workshop Leaders discussion.

Chapter 25
Abnormal Psychology: Introduction & Factors influencing diagnosis

---

Chapter objectives

Students will:
1. Practice thinking strategies related to evaluation and synthesis, with discuss modeled.
2. Discuss key points for introducing abnormal psychology and review the multidirectional model for using the three approaches to behavior.
3. Discuss the concepts normal and abnormal, how their definitions have changed over time, and important issues driving discussions about normal and abnormal.
4. Discuss classification systems with the growth and changes in the DSM, ICD, and CCMD as examples.
5. Discuss validity and reliability of diagnosis.
6. Discuss the role of clinical biases in diagnosis, with gender and culture as examples.

25.1: Introduction: The future of global mental health

Discuss means to give a considered and balanced view supported by evidence. There is much to consider for studying abnormal psychology that go far beyond just knowing symptoms of mental disorders. Mental illness categories are all **schematic** and we are constantly seeking to improve our understanding the disorders. It is our task to reflect on the extent to which we have reduced mental health problems or if they are growing. If they are growing, why is this and

Why are prevalence rates of mental illnesses growing?
Start thinking about *why* prevalence of mental disorder is growing. Common sense suggests it should be lessening over time, especially in countries spending lots of money on medical services.

TED talks such as the two suggested in this chapter from Patel and Insel are places to start.

Avoid oversimplified answers. Reasons are tied up in diagnosis, definitions of abnormality, cultural relevance, and finances, just to give a few examples, so it is not an easy problem.

what can be done?

Our reflection starts with the idea that we have the power to significantly reduce mental illness. While there are no simple answers to why people get mental disorders and what to do about them, creating a sense of empowerment to bring well-being to all is the goal. For the IB student and anyone else wanting an international perspective on mental health, the IB mission focuses on **internationalism** and a **learner profile** that includes developing caring, knowledgeable, principled, and reflective people. Using a cross-cultural perspective is a clear path to stimulating intellectual growth, **intercultural understanding**, and compassion.

Let's consider the prevalence of mental illness on a global scale, and this can be included when answering test questions about **prevalence**. Over 450 million people worldwide have a mental illness (Torgovnick, 2012). Mental disorders account for more than 13% of global disease, consisting mainly of depression, substance use disorder, and schizophrenia. By 2030, mental illness is projected to become the second greatest health disease burden in middle-income countries and the third highest in low-income countries. Contrary to popular belief, people in rich countries do not always have access to mental health care. Nearly 50% of people living in rich countries with a diagnosed mental illness do not get treatment, and it escalates to 90% in low-income nations. People with mental health problems are less productive than they could be and have a greater risk of additional health problems.

Adolescent mental health prevalence is also a concern because untreated early mental disorder affects all aspects of development (Patel, Flisher, Hetrick, & McGorry, 2007). "At least one out of every four to five young people in the general population will suffer from at least one mental disorder in any given year" (p. 1303).

The current global scope is no improvement over a previous World Health Report (2001) warning, "One person in four will be affected by a mental disorder at some stage of life" (p.1). The World Health Organization (WHO) Director-General speculated that major depression was the leading cause of disability globally and had the potential to become a major cause of disease. The warnings may be a current reality.

With all that modern medicine offers to treat mental illness, why is the problem growing? Could the benefits of modernization and globalization also come with increased stress that contributes to mental disorder?

Watch Patel's TED Talk
The title is "Mental health for all by all."

Students will get an idea of how common and complex mental health problems are, along with an interesting idea about delivering treatment. This is a good introduction to the scope of modern mental health.

Most students do not realize how few people get treatment for mental health problems, even in rich countries.

You will not be left without hope. Mental health care advocate Vickram Patel suggests in a TED talk that mental health care can be delivered in ways that empower local communities (Torgovnick, 2012). Severe shortages of psychiatrists exist, with estimates of ratios as great as 1 to 200,000 people in some countries. Many do not have access to care even in rich countries. Patel suggests that more people can be trained to deliver basic mental health services, such as local nurses and other community health care providers. Patel gave the example of an Ugandan program where villagers were trained to give psychotherapy and 90% of people receiving the therapy improved. Somehow we can come together to promote well-being in our communities!

Stress, an interactive approach, and culture

Three themes have emerged in the field of abnormal psychology over the years that form a foundation for reflecting on mental disorders.

First, reducing **stress** lowers the risk of mental illness. Stress contributes to all mental illness, even the disorders students most associate with genetics, such as schizophrenia and autism. The genetic contribution to schizophrenia is about 50%, leaving room for other factors, such as stress. Twins are not

100% concordant for autism, so sociocultural factors must place stress on the developing brain. Understanding the role of stress in mental illness affects decisions about treatments and shifts the emphasis to creating health. Genetic contributions to substance use disorders are about 50%, and we now know that most genes related to mental illnesses, including depression and anorexia, can unfold in specific environments. We have control over the environment and can take action if educated.

Second, the many factors contributing to mental illness interact. The **multidirectional model** shows how some factors important for the course interact, hopefully reducing oversimplification.

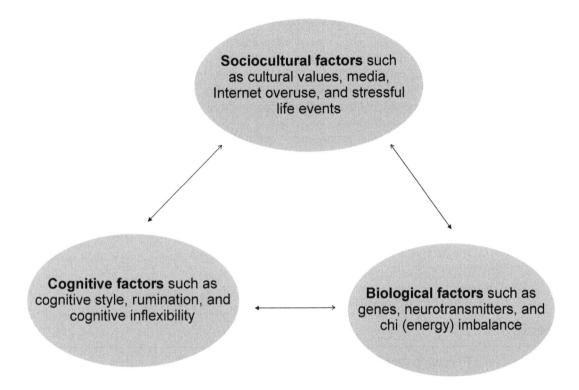

Third, an international view is recommended. All the material in this chapter is best organized under culture. *Otherwise, students run the risk of approaching mental illness with the frame of reference of their own cultures, looking at cultural differences as variations of the "real" way to view mental disorder.*

A more realistic approach focuses on **cognitive schemas**, or beliefs about a group's experiences with behavior (Castillo, 1997). Cognitive schemas **reify** beliefs into something real for the group. Reifying "occurs when people are collectively projecting onto an object a level of reality the object does not really possess" (p. 19). The way a behavior is thought of in a cultural group is real to them, even if it is not in actuality real. The brain adapts to the cultural schemas and the group treats a set of behaviors as real mental illnesses. Do not assume that others outside of your culture share similar schemas.

How do schemas about mental illness form? Specific behavior is noticed by a cultural group and is interpreted as a mental illness within a cultural definition (Castillo, 1997). The cultural definition becomes the reality. This is why, for example, the group of symptoms called "depression" in the West are not always accepted in other cultures.

Getting to the topics students really want to study

Students choose abnormal psychology because the want to study the causes and treatments of mental disorders. It is helpful to understand something about how disorders are classified and diagnosed first, so the rest of this chapter deals with those issues before we move on to the disorders.

25.2: Normality and abnormality

Normality and abnormality: The elements of abnormality

Discuss means to give a considered and balanced review supported by evidence. What follows are considerations about the terms normal and abnormal and why they are complex and have a controversial history, including why culture is critical to deciding if someone is abnormal.

There is no agreed upon definition of "**normality**" and "**abnormality**." Although some behaviors are clearly outside of accepted norms for any culture, such as schizophrenia and autism, others are debatable, such as the group of symptoms called depression.

When teaching it is important to avoid vagueness and oversimplification by using the elements of abnormality to distinguish the concepts and flesh out important issues.

The six **elements of abnormality** are useful for judging the difference between normal and abnormal behavior (Butcher, Mineka, & Hooley, 2007). One element may not be enough to make someone abnormal. The risk of abnormality increases with each addition of an element. Consider what each factor means and get some working examples for discussion. It is important to consider how many of the elements apply to someone's behavior. The more elements that apply, the greater the risk of abnormality.

Elements of abnormality (Butcher, et al., 2007)

Elements	Definition
Suffering	To have psychological pain and distress
Maladaptiveness	Failing to adapt, interfering with well-being, work, and relationships
Deviancy	Departing from usual or acceptable standards
Violation of the standards of society	Does not fit in with social and cultural norms
Social discomfort	After violating a norm, others around the person do not feel at ease
Irrationality and unpredictability	Illogical behavior others cannot predict

Class activity
For a class activity, students consider the meaning of each element and rank them in order of importance, noting that one is not necessarily enough to call someone abnormal or mentally ill. Have a discussion where students defend their responses and challenge each other, citing examples of disorders and cases such as Sherri Souza.

The case of Sherri Souza, whose spouse's return from military service in Iraq was postponed longer than expected for an extra tour of duty, is a good example (Horwitz, 2005). Sherri's symptoms included missing her husband, feeling anxiety for his safety, feeling anxiety over how her family would fare if he was killed or seriously injured, experiencing distress over late e-mails, and hiding in bed to wait for news.

Do Sherri's symptoms make her abnormal? Sherri described herself as depressed and was prescribed antidepressants. What do you think? *How many elements does Sherri have?* The answer is important and reflects your culture's **schemas** about normal and abnormal. The schemas of one's culture affect what is diagnosed as a mental illness, so the learning outcomes about normality and abnormality and validity and reliability of diagnosis are closely tied.

Allan Horwitz and Arthur Kleinman are two theorists highlighting concerns about defining normality and abnormality. Both worry that definitions of "abnormal" have expanded too much over time, with many consequences for people.

Schemas about normal and abnormal change over time, and affect diagnosing mental illness. The fifth edition of the Diagnostic and Statistical Manual for Mental Disorder (DSM-5) was released in 2013, illustrating a new chapter in thinking about normal and abnormal. Each edition of the DSM has refined, thrown out, and created new categories of mental disorder based on changing assumptions about normal and abnormal.

Overall, each DSM is more inclusive for many disorders, such as depression. This means that more people are considered abnormal and meet the diagnosis.

Some definitions of abnormal disappear or merge with other listed disorders with each manual, and previous abnormal behavior is now normal or must be reclassified as abnormal in a different way. For example, Aspergers' is no longer a disorder in DSM-5. Autism spectrum disorder is a new diagnosis meant to consolidate several DSM-IV disorders, including Aspergers. Whether it is a good development depends on whom you ask.

Allan Horwitz is concerned about changing definitions of abnormality

Serious mental illness needs diagnosis and treatment, but Horwitz believes some groups of symptoms have become *over-pathologized*, such as "depressive" symptoms, except when someone has severe depression with suicidal thoughts and/or psychotic symptoms (Horwitz, 2005). Horwitz raised questions a long time ago about the **validity** of the DSM-IV diagnosis for major depression and wondered if changing assumptions about "normality" and "abnormality" had turned everyday unhappiness into a disorder.

Thinking skills: Read Horwitz's article
Horwitz's article, *The Age of Depression*, is free on the Internet and is recommended for teachers because it details the evolution of the DSM from DSM-I to DSM-IV. Ambitious students can read it for more depth.

Reflecting on this concern involves understanding what went on that led to the removal of the bereavement exclusion from the DSM-5 category for major depression

The first two editions of DSM were context sensitive, meaning abnormality was diagnosed according to an individual's life situation. Horwitz examines the history of thinking about normal and abnormal using depression as an example. Early thought, including Freudian theory, distinguished depression *"without a cause,"* where the person was depressed even though everything in their life was fine, and depression *"with cause,"* meaning something happened to the person, such as a family death. The term,

bereavement exclusion comes from the distinction, meaning people grieving a loss were not treated for depression, but instead had depression-like symptoms "with cause." Only depression "without a cause" was considered abnormal. DSM I and II reflected the distinction. However, if abnormality was judged within the context of someone's life circumstances, it made diagnosis unreliable because it was too hard for everyone to talk about the same thing.

Students familiar with Rosenhan's (1973) observation study, where people posed as mentally ill to gain admission to hospitals, know that the failure of hospital personnel to distinguish normal from abnormal shook the psychiatric community. The controversy was one factor prompting the change to a symptom-based DSM in 1980. Rosenhan's study is free on the Internet and popular with students.

DSM III and IV focused on symptom lists all could agree upon to increase **reliability**, where people were considered abnormal, or depressed, if they had a certain number of the symptoms (Horwitz, 2005). No longer was a theory about causation based on life situations necessary. In addition, DSM-III changed the distinction between depression "with and without a cause," allowing a depression diagnosis one year after the death of a loved one. DSM-IV further shortened the time to two months.

> **Thinking skills: Class discussion & activity**
> Horwitz wonders about the trend toward inclusiveness. Consider the issue in a class discussion. Does including more people as depressed help people get needed treatment? Are more people inappropriately called abnormal? Did ordinary sadness become abnormal? Does it belittle the situation of people with serious mental illnesses? What societal factors contributed to the changes?

Arthur Kleinman's concerns about DSM-5 expansion of abnormality

Horwitz's arguments got a new twist when decisions about what to include in DSM-5 were being made. Kleinman (2012) is compassionate and insightful, and he wonders if the changes to diagnosing major depression in DSM-5 have gone too far. DSM-5 removes the bereavement exclusion, allowing someone with symptoms of grief from the death of a loved one, including sadness, disturbed sleep, loss of appetite, and feelings of deep loss, to be labeled abnormal and diagnosed as depression after the two-week symptom requirement.

Kleinman's article, *The Art of Medicine: Culture, Bereavement, and Psychiatry*, is free on the Internet and worth reading. Kleinman wonders if the changes to thinking about normal and abnormal will have profound consequences for people. Some of the questions raised int he article include the following. How long should someone grieve after the death of a close family member? Is grieving natural, helping people move forward? What would the world look like without grieving? Are cultural norms shifting to where feeling bad in any way is unacceptable? How important are unfortunate obstacles for maturing a person over the lifespan?

There is much to consider about defining normal and abnormal, and the psychiatric community struggles with changing social and cultural norms making up schemas of these two words. "Normal" and "abnormal" are more complicated than we may think at first glance. Source: pixabay.com

The authors of DSM-5 went ahead with the bereavement exclusion even in the face of Kleinman's challenge. It is a good discussion to consider its affect on how we think about normal and abnormal, and Kleinman's questions will be debated for many years as the authors of DSM-5 consider its future. The following questions are good for everyone to discuss, and a link to the Theory of Knowledge course for IB students.

DSM-5 supporters defend the bereavement exclusion, suggesting some people need a depression diagnosis when symptoms occur at the same time as an important loss (American Psychiatric Association, 2013). "When they occur together, the depressive symptoms and functional impairment tend to be more severe and the prognosis is worse compared with bereavement that is not accompanied by major depressive disorder" (p. 155).

Next is a discussion of culture and abnormality intended to place the elements of abnormality into an international context.

Culture affects our views of normal and abnormal

A person's cultural context is critical to considering "normality" and "abnormality" (Marsella & Yamada, 2007). Culture complicates thinking about normality and abnormality, but a diagnosis without it is incomplete (Marsella & Yamada, 2007).

Think back to the elements of abnormality and let's use **deviancy** as an example. Defining deviancy across culture is challenging because it involves understanding the balance between conformity and tolerance for deviancy (Yamada & Marsella, 2013). Some cultures require strict conformity to social norms and others permit a large amount of deviancy. Mental health professionals must know about norms related to conformity. Understanding the extent to which a culture has tendencies toward **individualism** or **collectivism** can help. This topic is further explained under the section about culture affecting diagnosis.

Understanding a person's cultural construction of reality helps us avoid calling them abnormal when they are not and conversely, helps us understand when someone is really abnormal and needs treatment. Otherwise, there is a risk of over or under-diagnosing people and giving destructive treatments, which are both ethical problems.

Almost every culture has its own system of diagnosis (Marsella & Yamada, 2007). The Chinese Classification of Mental Disorders (**CCMD-3**) is a good example of a nonwestern classification system, but it is not the only alternative to the **DSM-5** and the **ICD-10**. Other diagnostic systems, even the

CCMD, appear similar to western classification systems to some degree, but do not assume they are the same (Marsella & Yamada, 2007). For example, the meaning of the word depression is different for ethnic Pakistani living in the UK than it is for western psychiatrists, affecting diagnosis and treatment expectations (Tabassum, 2000). Pakistani views on abnormality are related to physical behaviors, such as aggression. Western views revolve around emotions. Misunderstandings are easy to imagine.

Avoid **decontextualizing** disorders (Marsella & Yamada, 2007). A disorder is not automatically similar for another culture. For example, **susto** is a way for some people in Mexican, Central American, and South American cultures to show distress (American Psychiatric Association, 2013). Susto's cause is the soul leaving the body during a stressful event. Symptoms include sleep difficulties, withdrawal, loss of appetite, and listlessness. Treatment for susto can include rituals using meditations, passing chicken eggs over the body, and herbs. The symptoms of susto are similar to western depression. Is susto a depressive disorder? *Do any similarities mean the disorder shares the same causes, expression and course as those in the West?* Absolutely not! "How can we separate a disorder from the very psyche in which it is construed and the very social context in which people respond to it" (Marsella & Yamada, 2007, p. 807-808)?

Evaluate research methods and ethics in abnormal psychology

The Tabassum interview study detailed in chapter 3 about **etics** and **emics** can be used when providing research about the concepts normal and abnormal. The Pakistani did not value emotional definitions of depression and instead thought aggression was a sign of abnormality.

An **interview** was a good method to discover the **emic** expressions of abnormality. Consider why this is so.

Over and under-diagnosis can be the consequences of failing to take culture into account and both are ethical problems.

25.3 Classification systems

Introduction to classification

The section about normal and abnormal leads directly into classification because if a group of behaviors are considered abnormal, then what is the best way to organize (classify) them so clinicians can use them? Go into this discussion remembering that all views of normal and abnormal and the resulting classification systems are **schematic**, the beliefs of a group that reflect **subjective culture**.

A discussion of classification systems includes considering what they are, examples of classification systems, and reasons for their use.

If a group of symptoms occur together and follow a particular course, then mental health professionals agree that these symptoms point to a specific mental disorder (Comer, 2013). The person receives a diagnosis from a predetermined category. These categories make up a **classification system.** Examples of classification systems follow:

1. Diagnostic and Statistical Manual of Mental Disorders (DSM-5)
2. International Classification of Disease (ICD-10)
3. Chinese Classification of Mental Disorders (CCMD-3)

Although the DSM-5 and ICD-10 are dominant, they are not necessarily accurate for everyone.

All classification systems have strengths and limitations. No classification system is "right" because they change over time and are not the only way to describe a person's symptoms.

Classifying disorders has advantages and disadvantages. On the positive side, health professionals can all talk about the same thing. In addition, researchers can study disorders more easily using participants fitting into a diagnostic category. On the negative side, a diagnosis based on a classification system can become a stigma or a label that prevents someone from taking personal action to improve their situation.

All manuals *evolve over time*. DSM-5 arrived in 2013 and the ICD-11 will be available by 2018. Although other cultures have similar diagnostic systems that developed in line with western manuals, such as the CCMD-3, the systems retain culture specific features useful for their populations.

Strategies to define cultural variations of mental disorders are moving forward. DSM-5 includes a new Cultural Formulation Interview (CFI) to make diagnosis based on a western classification system culturally relevant, an advance over previous manuals. However, DSM-5 says health providers *may use* the CFI to clarify cultural situations. Its use is not required.

Defining and classifying any mental disorder is challenging. Psychologists now understand that mental disorder results from the complex interplay between biology, cognitions, and sociocultural factors. In addition, no definite and clear distinction exists between mental health and mental disorder. DSM-IV (2000) even included the statement, "There is no assumption that each category of mental disorder is a complete discrete entity with absolute boundaries dividing it from other mental disorders or from no mental disorder" (p. xxxi). However, DSM-IV required health providers to use rigid diagnostic categories that were not always a clear fit.

DSM-5 still organizes mental illness into categories. Increasing **reliability** and stimulating research are its main purposes. DSM-5 does try to fix some DSM-IV limitations. One example is severity ratings for each disorder to provide some flexibility so real clinical cases have a chance to fit with diagnosis.

> **Practice top-down thinking**
> Students might study more than one classification system to get an international perspective. The DSM-5 and CCMD-3 are the main examples outlined here and used in the chapter about etiology (causes) of mental illness.
> All classification systems are **schemas** and as such are made up of a group's **subjective culture**.
> Schema is detailed in the cognitive approach to behavior, with mental illness and schemas as an example.

Next is an overview of what you will find in the DSM-5 and CCMD-3. The ICD is similar to the DSM as they evolved together. A brief history of the DSM is detailed in the next section about reliability and validity of diagnosis so students understand how it evolved into a reliable manual.

DSM-5

DSM-5 is a classification of disorders that imposes a **schema** on information gathered from clinical observations and scientific studies (APA, 2013). It is a reliable classification system providing a common language so everyone is talking about the same thing. DSM-5 is an evolving manual and subject to change with new research. Goals for DSM-5 were the same as those for the ICD-11.

DSM-5 contains 21 general categories with numerous disorders under each. Examples follow.

General category	Example disorders
Neurodevelopmental disorders	autism spectrum disorders, ADHD
Schizophrenic spectrum and other psychotic disorders	schizophrenia, schizoaffective disorder

General category	Example disorders
Bipolar and related disorders	bipolar I disorder, cyclothymic disorder
Depressive disorders	major depression
Anxiety disorders	specific phobia, agoraphobia, panic disorder, social anxiety disorder, generalized anxiety disorder
Obsessive-compulsive and related disorders	OCD, hoarding disorder
Trauma and stressor-related disorders	PTSD, reactive attachment disorder
Feeding and eating disorders	anorexia nervosa, bulimia nervosa, binge eating disorder
Substance-related and addictive disorders	alcohol use disorder
Personality disorders	antisocial personality disorder, narcissistic personality disorder

CCMD-3

The CCMD is a national classification system (Parker, Gladstone, & Chee, 2001). The first CCMD was published in 1979, CCMD-1 appeared in 1981, CCMD-2 in 1984, and CCMD-3 in 2001. CCMD-2 was revised for reliability with the DSM and the ICD manuals. The CCMD-3 is similar to the DSM but lists some disorders relevant to the Chinese, such as neurasthenia, Qi Kung disorder, and disorders due to witchcraft.

Next is a sample of the general categories in the CCMD-3 and example disorders. Most DSM disorders are included in the CCMD but can be organized differently. Disorders specific to the Chinese are grouped along with the western diagnoses.

General Category	Example disorders
Schizophrenia and other psychotic disorders	Schizophrenia
Mood disorders	Depressive episode, bipolar disorder

General Category	Example disorders
Hysteria, stress related disorders, neurosis	neurasthenia, phobias, obsession, mental disorders due to qi gong, mental disorders due to witchcraft, mental disorders related to culture
Physiological disorders related to psychological factors	anorexia nervosa

An important idea to take away from considering classification: Mental disorder manuals are schematic

DSM and ICD are western manuals and their classification categories are dominant rather than accurate (Marsella & Yamada, 2007). We must be careful about exporting western classification systems and assuming the disorders are **etics** because they do not necessarily describe norms guiding behavior in other cultures. Even if the DSM contains the Cultural Formulation Interview (CFI) to improve diagnosis, educating mental health providers about culture and behavior is crucial to its application.

Consider that Samoans have four categories for classifying mental illness (Marsella & Yamada, 2007).

1. "Ma'i o le mafaufau (physical brain abnormalities)
2. Ma'i aitu (spirit possession)
3. Ma'i valea (strange, severe, and stupid, improper behavior)
4. Excess emotion, such as Ma'i ita (anger, rage), Ma'i manatu (saddness, grief)" (p. 807).

To what extent do the Samoan categories fit with general DSM-5 classifications? Do we have to make them fit if they do not? Do not assume the **schema** for these categories is the same as the western manuals or the CCMD-3.

Uganda is another good example because 80% of healthcare needs in Uganda are handled by traditional healers who may not consult western manuals (Abbo, 2010). Four symptom classifications were identified from Abbo's interview study.

> **Thinking Skills: Evaluate classification systems: Exporting western diagnosis**
> Are we **DSMizing** the world? Consider the article *Are somatoform disorders changing with time?: The case of neurasthenia* (Sing & Kleinman, 2007). The article covered the increased rates of mental illness in China that mirrored pressures for the Chinese Classification of Mental Disorders (CCMD-3) to become similar to the DSM.
> John Berry's article *Achieving a Global Psychology* (2013) also discusses this concern and includes the terms etics and emics, a nice review for students.

1. Kazoole, acute mental disturbance
2. Kalogojjo, chronic mental illness with incoherent speech and talking to oneself
3. Eddalu, violent behavior related to psychosis
4. Ebirowoozo, depressive thoughts

How do these classifications fit in with the DSM or CCMD? Do they need to fit?

25.4: Validity and reliability of diagnosis
Can we end automatic reifying?

Discuss means to give a considered and balanced review supported by evidence. Thinking about how to balance reliability and validity is challenging and requires reflection.

Students often believe that mental disorders are real things. It is the biggest challenge for teaching abnormal psychology. *Reifying is automatic unless teachers make a big deal about it.* Reifying means to make an abstract idea real. Even the DSM-IV-TR (2000) warned, "A common misconception is that a classification system of mental disorders classifies people, when really what are being classified are disorders that people have" (p. xxxi). A more productive approach is to think about people "meeting the criteria for major depression" than to say, "the depressed person."

How would you know if this person qualifies for a depression diagnosis? Diagnosing people with mental disorders is full of clinical biases related to gender, culture, norms, and socioeconomic status. The current method of symptom checklists can be part of the problem because they are not objective measurements. We will explore gender and culture as part of clinical biases later in this chapter. Finding biological markers makes sense in light of diagnosing problems.
Source: pixabay.com

The following situations may help reduce reifying.

If a person reports symptoms such as blurry vision, itchy skin, cuts and sores healing slowly, increased thirst, frequent urination, and leg pain, a doctor thinks, "This person may have diabetes." The doctor sends the person for a blood test to verify if diabetes is the correct diagnosis. Physical disorders are "things" and have lab tests to verify the diagnoses.

Does it make sense to diagnose a fever by asking the patient to state how he or she feels? Would you take the person's temperature instead?

In contrast, if someone reports symptoms such as sadness, difficulty sleeping, feelings of worthlessness, decreased appetite and thoughts of suicide, a doctor thinks, "This person may have major depression." Blood testing biomarkers are still in early development. Questionnaires measuring subjective self-reports are currently used to make a diagnosis, and these lists represent **schemas** (reflecting **subjective culture**) that change over time. To complicate matters, some people may seem "crazy" but are really just expressing behavior that is part of their culture.

Setting the stage for discussing reliability and validity
Are diagnostic manuals **reliable** and **valid**?

The dominant manuals, the DSM-5 and the ICD-10, have become more reliable over time.

To what degree are the manuals valid? Validity is more controversial. Right now the answer is that diagnostic manuals are valid *to some extent*. Horwitz (2005) believes that validity should be valued over reliability, so the class can discuss this view. DSM-I and DSM-II situated a diagnosis within one's life context and were highly valid. The move to symptom-based diagnosis in the DSM-III and IV improved reliability but compromised validity. DSM-5 still focuses on reliability, but includes some attempts to increase validity, such as using severity ratings to help define an individual's experience.

Increasing reliability decreases validity and vise versa. No diagnostic system effectively balances reliability and validity and there is disagreement as to which is more valuable.

A brief history of the DSM and ICD
A brief history of two diagnostic systems, the **DSM-5**, the **ICD-10**, (ICD-11 is due out by 2018) helps students understand why mental disorders are not real things.

Understanding the *assumptions* of diagnostic manuals helps for reflecting on their level of reliability and validity.

DSM-IV-TR (American Psychiatric Association, 2000) included a section outlining its history, claiming that physicians have always needed to classify mental illnesses. The authors included the blunt statement, "There has been little agreement on which disorders should be included and the optimal method for their organization" (p. xxiv).

> **Overlap with classification**
> This material directly relates to validity and reliability. However, it also should be used when discussing classification systems.

The classification of mental disorders had varied purposes and organization over the past two centuries. The number of disorders in each system changes. Sometimes the purpose was to collect statistical data while other times the purpose was to find the right help for patients.

Class activity: Roadmap of the DSM
Diagnosis is abstract so get a piece of computer paper. Title one side "Schematic diagnosis" and draw a winding road showing the journey of the DSM. Start the road with pre-DSM diagnosis and then show DSM-I through 5. Students can include twists and turns representing the changes. At each change, include the assumptions of each manual to increase critical thought. Go ahead and be artistic or goofy with the drawings to highlight the point that many changes have been made as we try to get diagnosis right. Title the other side "The future of diagnosis: non-schematic biomarkers." This seems where we are headed. Include the Gotlib (2015) study about telomeres and depression. Also Google E. Redei from Northwestern University and see her early work on a blood test for depression. This test shows gene expressions in people with depression that differ from people without depression.

The first classification systems

Collecting statistics was the goal of the first US classification systems, starting with the 1840 census report that had just one classification, idiocy/insanity. Seven categories were used in the 1880 census, including mania and melancholia. After 1917, the American Medical Association included psychiatric disorder in its Standard Classified Nomenclature of Disease.

Responding to the needs of World War II Veterans, a broader classification system for mental disorders was developed. At the same time, the World Health Organization (WHO) included mental disorders into the sixth edition of the ICD. Each new edition of the DSM and the ICD was made in collaboration.

DSM I and II

The goal of DSM-I (1952) was to find the right treatment for patients. DSM-I used the term *reaction* throughout the manual to mean mental disorders were a reaction to biological, social, and psychological factors. *This makes etiology, or causes, a primary assumption of DSM-I diagnosis.*

DSM-II (1968) was similar to DSM-I except the term *reaction* was removed. *It was a move away from diagnosing mental illness with causation.*

The first two editions were high in **validity**. Theories of causation help us understand a person's situation. *Highly valid diagnoses have low reliability*, making it hard for different health providers to talk about the same thing. Critics such as David Rosenhan pushed for more reliable systems. Rosenhan (1973) sent seven friends and colleagues to mental hospitals throughout the country, instructing them to complain of hearing voices. All were admitted, and then showed no other signs of mental illness. The pseudopatients stayed in the hospitals from seven to fifty-three days. The study shocked the psychiatric community and was one motivation to create a classification system high in **reliability**.

DSM-III and IV

Unlike the first two editions, DSM-III (1980) was organized in clusters of symptoms where the *context* of the illness was eliminated (Horwitz, 2005). A symptom-based system assumes that causation is unimportant, and that anyone having a certain number of symptoms has a disorder, thus increasing reliability. Clinicians with different theoretical orientations more easily agree on lists of symptoms.

The move away from context ***increased reliability at the expense of validity***. DSM-III was neutral to causation, consisting of specific *descriptions* of disorders (American Psychiatric Association, 2000).

DSM-IV (1994) kept the symptom-based approach. However, the American Psychiatric Association task force for DSM-IV admitted that coming up with "absolute and infallible criteria" (p. xxviii) was impossible.

Disorders added to DSM-IV were based on research, though there was no way to include everything. *The authors of DSM-IV knew there were limits to its categories.* There was no assumption that categories were discrete. In addition, a category system works best if everyone is the same and there are "clear boundaries between cases" (p. xxxi). The obvious problem in applying a categorical system is that the problems of real clients seen in clinical practice do not fit neatly into a discrete category.

Cultural considerations were new to DSM-IV, though *culture was not essential to DSM-IV diagnosis, limiting its **validity***. Cultural considerations were part of an appendix and related to understanding culture-bound disorders.

DSM-5

DSM-5 offers many changes to diagnoses, though it is overall similar to DSM-IV in that it focuses on a symptom-based system high in **reliability**.

DSM-5 changes include the following (Grohol, 2012; Jabr, 2012).

1. Severity ratings are required for each symptom to understand an individual's diagnosis.
2. The bereavement exclusion for diagnosing depression was removed, meaning people grieving the loss of a loved one could qualify for a diagnosis of depression after two weeks.
3. Some disorders were removed, such as Aspergers' Syndrome.
4. DSM-5 contains some new disorders. One is binge eating disorder, defined as lacking control over what to eat and when, and consuming more than a normal person in the same amount of time in the same circumstances.
5. Some disorders are combined into a single diagnosis. For example, substance abuse and dependence are joined under one new disorder, substance use disorder, relevant for students studying health psychology. Internet addiction did not make it into DSM-5, but a disorder called Internet Use Gaming Disorder is identified for further research and possible inclusion later.
6. DSM-5 moves away from the Roman numeral system, motivated by the need to have an online version of the manual that can be frequently changed. In the future, look for DSM-5.1, DSM-5.2 and so on.

Critics attacked DSM-5 from the start, including (a) medicalizing everyday life experiences, (b) inclusiveness was motivated by drug companies seeking patients, and (c) some real problems seen in clinical practice were excluded.

The National Institute of Mental Health declared DSM-5 was reliable, yet invalid (Insel, 2013). DSM-5 is "At best, a dictionary, creating a set of labels and defining each" (p. 1). The NIMH's future research goal is to create a diagnostic system based on biological markers that have specific cognitive and emotional effects similar to physical illnesses. Historically, NIMH research rejected biological markers that were not directly relevant to DSM diagnostic criteria. The split opens the door for new research and perhaps a different type of diagnosis system in the future.

> **Watch Insel's TED Talk**
> It is titled "Toward a new understanding of mental illness." Insel retired from the NIMH in 10/15, but this still is relevant for understanding new NIMH research goals and why new diagnostic tools can help reduce prevalence.

Positive and negative aspects of diagnosis

Diagnostic manuals have both supporters and critics.

Supporters claim that DSM-5 transforms diagnosis in many ways. One example was changing the diagnosis of anorexia by eliminating the symptom about having a fear of getting fat, often called the "fat phobia." The fat phobia made diagnosis difficult cross-culturally.

The US National Institute of Mental Health (NIMH) is one critic. NIMH is unhappy with DSM-5 for using lists of symptoms (schematic) for diagnosis rather than biological markers that can be objectively measured, which compromises **validity** (Insel, 2013). Future NIMH research will not focus on DSM-5 mental disorder categories, but will design studies to identify biological and cognitive markers.

DSM-5 supporters claim the manual is structured to get people the help they need. For example, getting rid of the bereavement exclusion for depression was a good thing because some people were labeled grieving in the past when they were really depressed, missing out on needed treatment for long periods of time. Now psychiatrists have the option to use a depression diagnosis.

Some new research will examine DSM-5 categories while some research will follow revised NIMH goals. Expect to see heated debate and a continued evolving diagnostic system struggling to gain some validity while maintaining its focus on reliability.

Research about diagnosis: Making future diagnosis more valid

Progress has been made since Insel's Ted Talk on finding biological markers for the early detection of risk of mental illness.

One correlation study **aimed to show** that shortened **telomeres** were a risk factor (a biological marker) for **depression** present before the behaviors listed in the DSM-5 category for Major Depressive Disorder were seen (Gotlib, et al., 2015).

Review the material about the hormone **cortisol** and the **HPA axis** in chapter 9 before reading further, and this study can also be used as research support about stress hormones. Telomeres are structures that cap the ends of chromosomes, helping their stability. Telomeres are like the plastic caps at the ends of shoe laces that prevent unraveling. Telomeres naturally shorten with each cell division, so they are damaged over time. The presence of stressors is known to damage telomeres earlier than normal, so understanding cortisol and the HPA axis is important.

Girls with chronically depressed mothers were compared to girls with mothers who were not depressed, the **independent variable** (Gotlib, et al., 2015). There were two predictions. First, daughters with chronically depressed mothers would have shorter telomeres than girls with mothers without depression. Second, shorter telomeres would be correlated with greater cortisol levels, a sign of HPA axis disruption.

> **Thinking skills: Approaches to research and ethics in abnormal psychology**
>
> This is new but promising research and it should be noted in essays. More studies are needed to create a body of research. The sample was girls 10-14, so the research should also use different ages and males.
>
> The girls were in a stress condition, so the informed consent should include it as a risk. Some of the girls were at higher risk for stress reactivity because of their family history of depression, so care was needed to avoid harm, such as providing resilience training at the end of the study.
>
> It is well documented that genetic risks for depression unfold in stress environments, so this study makes sense considering Caspi's research about the **serotonin transporter gene**, detailed in chapter 6 about genetic influences on behavior.

For **procedures**, telomere length and cortisol levels were measured after participating in a stressful activity where the girls had 3 minutes to count backwards from 400 to 7 in increments of 7. They were interrupted if a mistake was made and if good at the task, asked to start again from 4000.

Results showed that girls with chronically depressed mothers had shortened telomeres and higher levels of cortisol. With what scientists know about cortisol, it was assumed that heightened levels damaged telomeres.

The authors **conclude** that shortened telomeres are a risk factor for depression and that it *appears before someone shows the behavioral signs that is diagnosed using DSM-5 classification categories.* People with shortened telomeres are at risk for all diseases associated with aging, so it is important to identify these people and provide early intervention, such as resilience training to reduce stress.

25.5: Role of clinical biases in diagnosis: Overview

We would like to think of ourselves as unbiased, making fair judgments based on evidence. A **clinical bias** is the "tendency toward responding or acting in one way or another, and it is not necessarily negative" (Poland & Caplan, 2004, p. 9). Unfortunately, it is impossible for clinicians to be completely unbiased because of their own gender and culture, plus professional biases from training (such as an MD, a Clinical Social Worker, or an acupuncture physician, all with different assumptions about health). Biases often stem from information processing biases (Poland & Caplan, 2004). These were studied in chapters 11 and 13 and include the following. Students might consider how each can be a problem.

1. Confirmation bias
2. Availability and anchoring heuristics
3. Illusory correlation
4. Stereotyping

Diagnostic labels from manuals such as the DSM may seem scientific and valid to the general public, but they might have effects similar to "name-calling" based on stereotypes, something usually considered negative (Caplan & Cosgrove, 2004)? A psychiatric diagnosis wields a great deal of power, and but if not correct, can cause great harm. Consider what might happen to someone after being labeled with a mental disorder. The goal might be to help someone so they can stay employed and care for a child, but could someone instead lose a job or custody of a child because the diagnosis makes them seem incompetent? Even what happens during a therapy session might be influenced by a diagnosis. Consider that a seemingly harmless bias such as thinking that appearance concerns are a "woman's thing" can cause a man to fail to get a diagnosis of an eating disorder when he has one!

Even if someone means well, gender biases can affect both males and females negatively. Stereotypes, availability, and professional biases are some sources of the problem. It is unlikely someone can recognize and put aside all of their them. This is a good reason to work on objective and measurable diagnoses. Source: pixabay.com

We must remember that all diagnostic categories, such as major depression, are **schemas** and not real things (Caplan & Cosgrove, 2004). We do not yet have a system of objective measurements as we do with diagnosing physical health. These schematic categories can be very subjective and they change over time, and current manuals are more inclusive than ever.

This is potentially a huge problem given our multicultural world (Caplan & Cosgrove, 2004), so *it is important for clinicians to be aware of their biases,* and the two in this book are related to gender and culture.

25.6: Role of clinical biases in diagnosis: Gender

Discuss means to give a considered and balanced review supported by evidence. There is much to consider for a balanced view, and the goal is to see the many concerns that might affect clinical biases related to gender.

An overview of gender differences in diagnosis that can lead to biases

Males and females have similar overall rates of mental illness but differences are seen in specific diagnoses (Lips, 2005). Women are more frequently diagnosed with depression, eating disorders, and specific phobias. Males are more frequently diagnosed with antisocial behavior, substance abuse, and autism.

Three reasons for gender differences in diagnosis should be considered.

Reasons for gender differences in diagnosis that can be biases

Stereotyping and gender role norms	Gender **stereotypes** may affect expectations of how someone should cope with distress (Lips, 2005). Stereotypes can come from ignoring the context of women's lives, such as experiencing more poverty and abuse (McSweeney, 2004). The result is that real societal problems are dismissed as expected feminine behavior, with women seen as weak and emotional, perhaps depressed. In addition, following traditional Western stereotypes for gender roles, called the **masculine hypothesis** and **feminine hypothesis**, are both risk factors for disordered eating, reviewed later in this section (Griffiths, Murray, & Touyz, 2015).
Politics of diagnosis	A "**politics of diagnosis**" reflects gender stereotypes and role expectations, and "sex-biases built into diagnostic categories may well influence perceptions of whether women and men are psychologically healthy" (Lips, 2005, p. 373). Psychiatry is dominated by males, and biases may surround diagnostic categories using male behavior as the "norm." Females behaving in line with their socialization may be diagnosed as abnormal. Do males and females reporting similar symptoms to a doctor get the same diagnosis and treatment?
Males and females experience stress differently	Both males and females experience stressful events, such as accidents or divorce, but *women experience stress differently than men and have more lifelong stressors*, such as poverty and the responsibility for children (Lips, 2005). Questionnaires are popular research tools but some may not accurately estimate male and female experiences. Are lists of stressful events biased toward male experiences? Do men have more positive life changing experiences than women? Could women respond more strongly to stressful events? Sometimes lists of stressful life events fail to include circumstances important to women, such as rape and difficulties managing child care.

Depression: An example of gender differences in diagnosis

Females are three times more likely to be diagnosed with depression than males. What explains the large difference? One issue for consideration is that women experience more stressors and experience stress differently than men (Nolan-Hoeksema, 2004).

Females have more social stressors than males. Two particular life events are correlated with higher rates of depression. First, women experience greater amounts of childhood sexual assault, which is related to developing depression in adulthood. Second, women tend to have lower social status than men and often do not have a voice in decision-making.

Interpersonal orientation is an aspect of one's self-concept relevant to depression rates. Females are more concerned with relationships than males. Females place less emphasis on their own needs and are more vulnerable to depression when relationships are troubled or end.

To complicate matters, females ruminate, meaning to think over problems, more than males. Rumination increases the risk for depression.

Last, females may be more biologically reactive to stress. One theory needing more research is that sex hormones affect the stress system. Sex hormones have not been shown to directly affect mood. Females experience more social stressors and are more prone to disturbances in the HPA axis, referring to the cascade of events that occur in the hypothalamus, pituitary gland, and adrenal cortex after someone experiences a stressor. Are sex hormones part of the puzzle?

Males may be underrepresented in depression statistics because they experience depression differently. Six million men in the US experience depression each year (NIMH, 2008). Men and women show DSM symptoms, but research suggests they experience and cope with depression differently. Females talk more openly about emotions than men and seek health care more frequently. Men report more physical symptoms, such as sleep difficulties and irritability. Some researchers believe the DSM category is inadequate to describe male depression. For example, men are more likely to be diagnosed with substance use disorder. Is substance use really a symptom of depression? In addition, men are more likely to throw themselves into their jobs or engage in reckless behavior than females, perhaps other signs of male depression.

Diagnosing an eating disorder is full of potential clinical biases

Statistics show that females have most of the eating disorders, but a discussion about male disordered eating raises concerns about gender and diagnosis. The DSM-5 categories do not offer insight about gender differences.

Females are diagnosed with anorexia at rates three times greater than males. Males are diagnosed with 10% of the eating disorders, though they are most likely to have binge-eating disorder (BED) when they have one (Keel, 2005). Most of the research on eating disorders uses female samples, so psychologists do not know as much about the male experience. For example, males account for 40% of BED but are generally excluded from samples studying it.

Do the findings from studies using female participants apply to males? Are some risk factors for eating disorders specific to males that are unknown from studying females? Do males show symptoms of eating disorders that differ from those women display? Perhaps males have plenty of disordered eating but are underrepresented in eating disorder statistics.

Diagnosing males with eating disorders is challenging for three reasons (Hildebrandt & Craigen, 2016).
Males show disordered eating in diverse ways.
Motivations behind males disordered eating are different from motivations of females.
Males body image problems are different from those of females.

Male and female disordered eating is different. For example, males can have **muscle dysmorphia**, sometimes called **reverse anorexia**. Muscle dysmorphia is when someone has a compulsion to be lean and fit, sometimes with obsessions with working out to get fit. Males with muscle dysmorphia have the same compulsions, disordered eating, and body image dissatisfaction as girls with anorexia, but male symptoms are expressed mainly through body image dissatisfaction. This contrasts with females who show symptoms related to restricting eating.

Motivations for disordered eating for both males and females surround body image, however males focus on functional demands of the body such as strength and fighting, and girls focus on appearance.

Male body image can fall into two extremes, becoming lean or building muscles. Males wanting to build muscle are more likely to have muscle dysmorphia. Males who use appearance- and performance-enhancing drugs (APEDs) have more risk for disordered eating.

In addition, males face specific **clinical biases** when seeing a clinician that might prevent a correct diagnosis (Hildebrandt & Craigen, 2016). The issues follow and clinicians must examine their beliefs.

1. There is a stereotype that eating disorders and over-focusing on appearance are strictly women's concerns. However, the gender gap is narrowing and males have half of the binge-eating disorders.
2. This leads to a stigma for males seeking help.
3. Men report shame about having and reporting disordered eating and tend to avoid getting help as a result. Males can feel they have let down the traditional male gender role expectations focusing on winning and keeping emotions in check.
4. Gay culture has a tendency toward being concerned with appearance, so clinicians should be aware of this.

Research support: New ideas about male disordered eating that should reduce clinical biases in diagnosis

Two survey studies highlight the need to reflect on male disordered eating more carefully and change diagnostic categories currently in DSM-5 and other manuals.

Male eating disorders can show up as muscle dysphoria, often called reverse anorexia. Some males can become obsessed with weight training. Used with license from megapixl.com.

The **aim of one survey** was to see if male disordered eating was rising. One survey was given to 3000 Australian adults in 1998 and then again in 2008 to see if prevalence rates were changing (Griffiths, Murray, & Touyz, 2015).

Results showed that rates of dieting and purging were growing much faster in males than it was in females. Males also reported they did not have the same thin-ideal as females and rather preferred a body that looked more like a competitive swimmer. Male disordered eating is not being captured with the diagnostic categories currently in manuals and may account for as much of 25% of anorexia.

The **aim of a second survey** was to examine **gender role norms** (Griffiths, Murray, & Touyz, 2014). The **masculinity hypothesis** says that conforming to male norms promotes body dissatisfaction related to muscle size and disordered eating.

For the **procedures**, heterosexual males answered survey questions about body image and dissatisfaction, thinness, and disordered eating. For example, questions about masculine disordered eating assessed feelings about one's body and included questions such as "Have you definitely wanted a 6-pack stomach (p. 3)"? They also were rated themselves on a scale of "never" to "every day" about their use of disordered eating habits.

Participants were characterized as either following the masculine hypothesis, meaning they try to be dominant, strong, and powerful, or the **feminine hypothesis**, meaning they conformed to roles about being nice, passive, and achieving interpersonal dependence with others.

Results showed that participants conforming to male norms had more muscle dissatisfaction and disordered eating to achieve it, but did not report wanting to be thin. The males conforming to a feminine norm reported more muscle dissatisfaction but it was related to wanting to be thinner and included disordered eating to become skinny. It used to be thought that conforming to male gender role norms reduced the risk of eating disorders but this is now challenged. The fact that males with disorder

25.7: Role of clinical biases in diagnosis: Culture

Bias related to **context** is a major source of clinical bias (Poland & Caplan, 2004). Discuss means to give a considered and balanced review supported by evidence, and knowledge of someone's cultural values is essential to avoiding mis-diagnosis, a critical issue in our multicultural world.

Too often, people living in Western cultures are caught up in technology and the scientific method, and believe that the medical view is a solution for all once a diagnosis can be made (Poland & Caplan, 2004). Adding to the problem is the typical insurance company policy that a treatment will be paid for only if someone has a diagnosis! Context is often ignored even by well-meaning clinicians who have professional and cognitive biases that put looking more deeply into someone's situation on the sidelines.

Students must get educated about the many issues that cause a breakdown in diagnosis related to misunderstandings of culture. This section includes things to consider before saying someone has a western mental illness, an example of how DSM-5 now has a more culturally relevant way to diagnosis anorexia so we can lessen clinical bias, an overview of Cultural Syndromes that should be consulted when making a diagnosis, and an interview study about using the label "depression" in the Bagandans of Uganda.

Over and under-diagnosis are the potentially dangerous and unethical results of strictly applying western diagnostic criteria cross-culturally.

Clinicians should avoid judging people from other cultures without investigating their situations with an open mind. Clinicians run the risk of **ethnocentrism** if "variation" is interpreted as deviating from a "real" standard set in a western diagnostic manual. Ethnocentric people treat their own culture as if it was the model by which all cultures should be judged.

What is important to consider about culture and diagnosis before saying someone has a western mental illness?

Cultural psychiatry views behavior within the cultural context (Marsella & Yamada, 2007). Unfortunately, reliable diagnostic manuals do just the opposite, and they *decontextualize* mental illness. Western diagnostic manuals fail to take *situational factors* affecting the person into account, consistent with the conclusion that people have a tendency to make dispositional **attributions** and ignore situational factors shaping behavior. Many mental illnesses actually stem from family and community problems.

Studies investigating culture and mental illness often come from western thinking, even if the studies are meant to be cross-cultural. Psychiatrists practicing in nonwestern countries often are required to use the western standards but find they are not really useful for behaviors in other cultural contexts.

Western diagnostic systems are *dominant* rather than *accurate*. The focus on consistent diagnoses using the DSM and ICD might overshadow local diagnostic systems.

Several situational factors contribute to mental illness across culture, particularly **depression**.

1. Social conditions such as "war, natural disasters, racism, poverty, cultural collapse, aging populations, urbanization, and rapid social and technological changes" (p. 811) are important.
2. Western depression may be linked to an abstract language separating people from daily experiences, emphasizing guilt, and highlighting values related to **individualism**. In contrast, people in nonwestern cultures experience depression primarily through physical symptoms that show a unity of mind and body.
3. Depression and social class are negatively correlated, meaning that as social class lowers, depression rates rise.

Therefore it is important to understand cultural differences in defining normal and abnormal, such as the **element of abnormality of deviancy** (Yamada & Marsella, 2013). For example, health providers should consider what cultures value in conformity. Some cultures require strict conformity and others tolerate a great amount of deviancy. In a culturally pluralistic world it is important to remember that the world population is about 6 billion people but just a small portion of this is of European and North American ancestry, so we cannot apply one universal definition of normal and abnormal.

Culture and diagnosing eating disorders: A specific example of the concern

Norms about food consumption and body shape differ across cultures, so it follows that symptoms of body image and disordered eating differ (Becker, 2007). It is also important to realize that eating disorders are correlated with modernization (Becker, 2016). Although the stereotype exists that eating disorders are most common in Western countries, global statistics show large growth on a global scale. This means that in addition to western countries, middle income and poor nations also have experienced a surge in eating disorders. Reasons for this global increase come from migration, **acculturation**, and media use in a global society.

Ethics groups living in the US even show higher prevalence for eating disorders than once thought (Becker, 2016). For example, the survey study detailed later in this section under research support demonstrates this in Latino groups.

Etics and **emics** are useful for understanding why DSM-5 includes changes to the category for anorexia from DSM-IV for better cross-cultural application. The history of diagnosing eating disorders is worth knowing because it shows the correct use of etics and emics.

Etics/Emics Overview

Etics and emics are research tools that make cultures comparable.

Etics are universal continuums and every culture falls somewhere on the continuum. Examples are marriage and all dimensions of culture, including time orientation and individualism-collectivism.

Emics are specific cultural practices, such as a particular marriage ceremony or being future or present time oriented.

Researchers begin their studies with an etic in mind, or something assumed to be universal, often something observed in the West. An intense fear of fat was a presumed etic from studying some western cases of anorexia.

Over time, researchers see cultural behavior that may suggest an assumed etic is incorrect.

Researchers next redefine the etic to describe all cultures and make adjustments as often as needed, ending in an etic that applies to all.

DSM-5 includes changes to classifying **anorexia** (AN) making future diagnosis more accurate, ethical, and cross-culturally relevant. A DSM-IV diagnosis of AN was not possible without an extreme fear of gaining weight or being fat that has been removed from DSM-5. The consequences of requiring a "fat phobia" resulted in many cases of over and under-diagnosis over the years. Self-starvation cases exist all over the world (Keel, 2005). *The fat phobia was not universal and made international relevance of AN impossible.* "When the fear of fat criteria is removed, AN is seen with equal frequency in Western and nonwestern cultures" (p. 23).

Correct diagnosis involves properly using **etics** and **emics**. Etic approaches apply universal diagnostic systems to everyone, usually based on western classifications. An intense fear of getting fat, the "fat phobia" was an etic seen in many western patients. Assessment tests, such as the Eating Disorders

Attitude Scale (EAT-26) that try to measure the etics, are *intended* to have cross-culturally **reliability** and **validity**.

The etic approach is inadequate, though its intention is to make cross-cultural data comparable.

An emic approach starts with locally meaningful contexts for eating disordered symptoms. An emic approach is a good way to collect data, though it compromises comparability.

Next is examples of over and under-diagnosis from using limited DSM-IV definitions of AN that ignored emic expressions of disordered eating.

Persons from Hong Kong, Japan, Singapore, Malaysia, South Africa, and India can have all the other symptoms of AN except the fat phobia (Becker, 2007). Persons from Hong Kong have been misclassified as non-cases of eating disorders based on the EAT-26 simply because they lacked a fat phobia. Black adolescents from South Africa who tested positively for disordered eating with the EAT-26 clarified in follow-up interviews that they were preoccupied with food because of poverty, hunger, and food shortages. Knowledge of a person's social context is vital.

Cultural differences in attitudes about food consumption complicate the etic approach. During Fijian feasting, local herbal tonics are used for purging after culturally sanctioned overeating. The behavior may look like binging and purging, but traditional Fijian culture does not consider it disordered. A local Fijian diagnosis exists for **macake**, an appetite disorder that is not similar to anything in the West. Persons with macake refuse food and have poor appetites, behaviors that arouse great social concern. The disorder is brief since persons are willing to take herbal supplements to restore their appetite. The behaviors lack meaning unless we are aware of the social context.

The DSM-5 AN category can help people from many cultures get the diagnosis when it is the correct one, which prevents over and under-diagnosis. In addition, emic expressions of body image, norms about food consumption, and local situations are respected. Instead of requiring a fat phobia, DSM-5 uses general language that requires a *continual behavior that prevents weight gain when the person is already at a very low weight*.

Many people from all over the world could be at risk for an eating disorder and it is important for psychiatrists using DSM-5, as is often the case around the world, to use the Cultural Formulation Interview to detect the variety of ways symptoms can present (Becker, 2016). Otherwise people from different ethnic groups suffer from two disadvantages. They suffer the stereotype that eating disorders are most prevalent in Western countries and have to manage stigmas within their cultures about having a disorder.

Cultural syndromes

DSM-5 includes a section about **cultural syndromes** that identifies clusters of symptoms existing in some places that are not recognized outside of the culture that should be considered before giving a diagnosis (American Psychiatric Association, 2013). DSM-5 categories do not use similar symptom clusters and health providers must use caution before applying them to people showing these syndromes. Does the category really fit?

Examples of cultural syndromes in DSM-5 include the following that are similar but not exactly the same as depression.

1. **Susto**, a Hispanic fright illness
2. **Shenjing Shuairu**, a disorder seen in China that focuses on physical complaints
3. **Nervios**, a common way for Latinos to describe general stressful events
4. **Kufungisisa**, or "thinking too much" in the Shona of Zimbabwe

Research support: An interview study about Uganda's Baganda: Are they depressed as defined in the West? What is a western clinical to do?

Class activity

Students can debate if the Bagandan's symptoms should be diagnosed with DSM-5 categories or if illness of thought is a cultural syndrome to be treated by local healers.

This is a chance to learn about another culture and see what a clinician is up against when considering a depression diagnosis for the Bagandans.

What do students think about the statement by Ugandan University academics that depression is high in Uganda? Is it accurate considering the study results? This is difficult because we want people to get treatment when needed, so how should the symptoms be diagnosed.

Does a Western diagnosis of major depression apply to the Bagnadans? The **aim of this interview study** was to explore local perceptions of depressive symptoms in the Baganda of Uganda (Okello & Ekblad, 2006). This is the type of research that can help lessen cultural biases in diagnosis.

Individual and focus group interviews using case vignettes were used to gather data. Vignettes are short stories.

Baganda culture

The clan system dominates the way Bagandans think about others. No one is thought about without reference to patrilineal descent. Clan members are viewed as extended family, even if blood ties are distant. The clan is a hierarchy with the clan leader at the top. All clans have a primary and secondary totem, a symbol for the clan often taking the form of an animal or plant. Everyone introduces themselves to others in the context of the clan.

The Baganda believe in superhuman spirits where a person's spirit remains after death. Many other African cultures share this belief. Several types of spirits are important to the Baganda. One is *mizimu*, ghosts of the dead. These spirits seek people the dead person holds a grudge against.

Misambwa are objects the mizimu has entered. *Balubaale* are spirits that have the talents of outstanding men. All three spirits are called *byekika*, or "the clan things." Spirits are believed to influence health and are divided into two general groups, the family or community spirits that aid in health unless they are upset, and alien or evil spirits causing trouble.

The Baganda connect illnesses with body parts. For example, a cough is labeled "chest." Depressive symptoms stem from thoughts or the heart, so depression is connected to either, such as "illness of thoughts." Illnesses are further broken down into ones treated by traditional healers or folk remedies and ones treated by western doctors.

Depressive symptoms in Uganda are often expressed and referred to as an **"illness of thought"** rather than an emotional illness. Illnesses of thoughts do not require medicine because no medicine exists for thinking. Medical help is required only in cases of constant or recurring illness.

The Bagandan view shows the complexities of diagnosis. If a local population does not recognize a group of symptoms as depression, the diagnosis is unlikely to be accepted. The Bagandans have their own way of thinking about mental illness that matches cultural expectations.

The prevalence of depressive symptoms in Uganda is high (according to researchers), between 10-25%, largely because of its violent history and the large number of HIV/AIDS cases. Although observations made in Ugandan psychiatric clinics suggest depression is common, the people of Uganda rarely recognize it as such. About 70 to 90% of mental health problems in Uganda never reach mental health services.

Procedures are next. The interviews took place in Bajjo, a small semi-rural district close to the capital. Next is some background on the Baganda necessary to interpret the case vignettes.

DSM-IV was used to create the vignettes. A series of stories illustrated different experiences with depression and participants considered if they knew anyone fitting the descriptions.

The researchers used five vignettes for the study. Two examples are next.

One case was a twenty-eight year-old person with major depression symptoms without psychotic features. The symptoms included unhappiness, a lack of enjoyment of usual activities, a closed mind, feelings of emptiness, sleeping difficulties, a change in eating habits, no energy, thoughts that life was no longer worth living, wandering thoughts, and thoughts of death and suicide.

Five individual participants responded to the vignettes, including three traditional healers and one faith healer. Other participants took part in four different focus groups of six each representing different societal layers. The focus groups were secondary school girls, village women, village men, and primary school teachers. Variables such as age and educational level, were controlled.

Results showed that all thirty participants connected the vignette with their own experience or someone they knew. Almost everyone described the symptoms as "too many worrisome thoughts." Participants decided the thoughts were under the person's control and recommended avoiding the thoughts. Few considered the person "mad." While the "illnesses of thought" were identified as a mental illness, most considered treatments by traditional healers more appropriate than western medicine. Traditional healers viewed the symptoms as "mild

Portrait of a Ugandan woman. The 21st Century student is open-minded and wants to learn about the views of people living in other cultures. Knowledge about cultural values is essential to a correct diagnosis that is meaningful to the person.
Used under license from megapixel.com.

madness" resulting from witchcraft. Both the lay participants and traditional healers supported local customs where traditional healers treated all illnesses resulting from community or cultural causes.

Four reasons for people to have mental illnesses came from the interviews.

1. *Psychological,* from thinking too much about things such as relationship problems
2. *Socioeconomic,* such as job loss
3. *Spiritual,* such as witchcraft and angry ancestral gods
4. *Biological,* such as genes or constant physical illness, which was reserved for cases with recurring symptoms

Eighty percent of the participants thought depressive symptoms came from social stress and called the symptoms "illness of thoughts" best treated by spiritual healers. Only chronic symptoms linked to genetics or illness needed western treatment, but even if someone benefited from western medicine, local healers also treated the cases.

Seeking help from family, friends, clan elders, religious leaders and traditional healers was stressed by all participants. Traditional healers were recommended when the illness was caused by witchcraft, angry ancestral gods, or had an unknown cause.

The researchers highlighted some limitations of using focus groups. **Informants** helped the researchers gain access to study participants, and local authorities could have biased the study by recommending particular people as informants. The use of specifically designed vignettes in the individual interviews may have limited the discussion to just those situations.

The authors **concluded** that it if local cultures were unlikely to accept western diagnoses and treatments if they did not perceive the symptoms in the same way as western doctors.

Chapter 26
Abnormal Psychology: Etiology of Abnormal Psychology

Chapter objectives

Students will:
1. Practice thinking strategies related to analysis and synthesis, with discuss demonstrated.
2. Discuss the symptoms and prevalence rates of depression as listed in DSM-5 and the CCMD-3.
3. Discuss the etiologies (causes) of depression from the biological, cognitive, and sociocultural approaches to behavior.
4. Discuss the symptoms and prevalence rates of anorexia as listed in DSM-5 and the CCMD-3.
5. Discuss the etiologies of anorexia from the biological, cognitive, and sociocultural approaches to behavior.
*** IB students are required to study just one disorder, so students can select just one, study both for IB exams, or study both for general knowledge and then prepare one for testing.

26.1 Symptoms and prevalence of depression

Discuss means to give a considered and balanced view supported by evidence. Next is a reflection about major depression and its prevalence. Students should consider why rates of depression are growing.

Inquiry & global/local awareness
Students should become good inquirers and consider **why the rates are so high**. This is a chance for students to think globally yet become locally aware of a problem. Depression rates are growing, especially for adolescents, and it is the #1 mental disorder world (Major Depression Facts, 2016). The risk for depression is estimated to be 10 times greater for people born after 1945 than before.
Photo used with license from megapixl.com.

"Major depressive disorder, also called major depression, is characterized by a combination of symptoms that interfere with a person's ability to work, sleep, study, eat, and enjoy once-pleasurable activities. Major depression is disabling and prevents a person from functioning normally. An episode of major depression may occur only once in a person's lifetime, but more often, it recurs throughout a person's life" (NIMH, 2008, p. 1).

Let's compare **DSM-5** and **CCMD-3** symptoms and prevalence rates for major depression.

DSM-5 diagnosis for major depression and prevalence reports

To receive a diagnosis of major depressive disorder, five symptoms from the list must occur during the same two-week period (American Psychiatric Association, 2013). The symptoms must be very different from a person's normal regular behavior. *One of the symptoms must be depressed mood or loss of interest or pleasure.*

DSM-5 symptoms of depression: 5 symptoms must occur during the same two weeks

Self-reports or information from others show the person has depressed mood most of the day each day.
Self-reports or information from others show the person has a significantly lowered interest and pleasure in activities all day almost every day.
The person experiences changes in appetite and/or weight. This means a 5% weight gain or loss when not dieting occurs or one's appetite increases or decreases almost every day.
Almost every day, the person suffers from insomnia or hypersomnia (extreme sleepiness).
Reports from others show the person is physically too active or not active enough.
The person is tired or has low energy almost every day.
The person feels worthless or shows too much or inappropriate guilt almost every day.
The person cannot concentrate or is indecisive almost every day.
The person has frequent thoughts of dying that are not just fears of dying. The person has thoughts of suicide without a plan, has plans for suicide, or has attempted suicide.

Severity ratings are included for each person, including mild, moderate, severe, and with psychotic features. Severity ratings might help people get the best treatment and track treatment effectiveness.

The next table summarizes depression **prevalence** rates both in the US and cross-culturally.

Depression prevalence rates

Country	Prevalence rates and summary
United States	Prevalence is 7% overall over a 12-month period sampling (American Psychiatric Association, 2013). Females have rates up to 3 times higher than males and the differences show starting in adolescence. People aged eighteen to twenty-nine have depression rates 3 times higher than people over sixty. Depression is the factor carrying the greatest disability, or 3.7% of all disability (NIMH, 2016). A lifetime rate of 16.9% is reported, meaning that one's chances of getting a depression diagnosis over the lifespan is almost 17% (Kessler & Bromet, 2013).
China and India	China and India are the two most populated countries with 32% of the world's disease burden from mental illnesses (Liu & Page, 2016). This is greater than the total of all other developed countries. Rate estimates of depression in China are 17% and 15% in India. This rate seems similar to that of the US. Stigma for having a diagnosed mental disorder and is very high so the impact on social roles and employment is great (Liu & Page, 2016). Even with such high rates, China and India also have lower numbers of western style mental health professionals. It is possible that in addition to western psychiatry, these countries should partner with traditional cultural treatment providers (Thirthalli, et al., 2016).
Generally across culture	The first cross-cultural statistics appeared in 1996 showing depression to be a common disorder with the highest rates in westernized countries (Kessler & Bromet, 2013). A World Health Organization survey found lifetime rates of 1% in the Czech Republic to 16.9% in the US, with mid-range rates of 8.3% in Canada and 9% in Chile. Rates may vary a great deal across cultures but there are still many sociocultural factors that everyone has in common. Females are twice as likely to have depression across culture. In addition, having depression early in life disrupts education and makes it harder to find jobs across cultures and incomes are lower. The highest rates of depression are found in the richest countries, perhaps making depression a disorder of the wealthy far more than others. However, we cannot discount that it still exists across all cultures and low income countries have fewer mental health workers and budgets for services. There is much to reflect on because, for example, not all cultures might think of a set of symptoms as depression. The Baganda of Uganda are one such case to consider from the last chapter.

CCMD-3 diagnosis for depressive episode

The CCMD-3 (Chinese Society of Psychiatry, 2003) contains a disorder called "depressive episode" similar to DSM-5 major depressive disorder but with some differences reflecting its use in Chinese culture. To receive this diagnosis, a person must have a depressed mood different from life circumstances. The depressed mood must include four of the symptoms in the list below. These symptoms refer to a single episode of depression. Separate diagnoses are used for recurrent depression and mild depression. A diagnosis of recurrent depression requires that any type of depression must occur within the past two months. Mild depression is the same as depressive episode but the impairment in social behavior is mild.

CCMD-3 depressive episode symptoms

The person has a loss of interest in or loss of enjoyment.

The person has low energy or fatigue.

The person is either physically agitated or shows little motor activity.

The person has low self-esteem, feels worthless, is self-blaming, or is preoccupied with guilt.

The person is unable to focus thoughts.

The person has tried some kind of self-harm or suicide or has thoughts of doing either.

The person has insomnia, wakes too early in the morning, or has hypersomnia.

The person has little appetite or obvious weight loss.

The person has a decreased libido.

The CCMD-3 includes a separate diagnosis for **Neurasthenia**. Chinese persons often express depressive symptoms as somatic complaints. Neurasthenia is then a more appropriate diagnosis, though it is not used as widely as it once was. Neurasthenia is classified in the group of disorders called Hysteria, stress related disorders, Neurosis.

Neurasthenia is listed as a *neurosis.* It can reduce the stigma of mental illness and can be a better account for symptoms in the Chinese.

CCMD-3 Neurasthenia symptoms

The person meets the criteria for neurosis. Neurosis is classified as a stress related disorder in the CCMD-3, which also includes phobias, panic attacks, and obsessive behavior.

The person has mental and physical weakness, such as a lack of vigor, poor concentration and memory, and physical fatigue that are recovered by rest, along with two of the following.
   a. The person has emotional difficulties, such as tenseness, anxiety and depression that are not the prominent symptoms, irritability and difficulty in coping with daily life.
   b. The person is easily excited, such as difficulty concentrating on one thing at a time.
   c. The person has muscle aches and pains or dizziness.
   d. The person has problems sleeping, such as insomnia.
   e. The person has other psychological or physical problems, such as rapid heartbeat or tinnitus, meaning ringing or roaring noises in the ears.

History of the prevalence of depression in China: Helping students consider why rates are rising

The CCMD-3 does not contain prevalence rates and exact rates probably vary a great deal by region.

Cultural values affect the expression and diagnosis of mental illness. Understanding symptoms and prevalence rates of depression in China requires a history lesson about mental health in China.

The Chinese are the world's largest ethnic group, about 22% of the world's population (Parker, Gladstone, & Chee, 2001). *Many factors make understanding the symptoms and prevalence rates complex.* About fifty-five ethnic groups live in China and some have adopted western psychiatric views, some combine western and traditional Chinese views, and others have kept their beliefs exclusive to Traditional Chinese Medicine.

Depression was rarely diagnosed in China in the 1980s. The lifetime prevalence rate for it was .08% in 1993. Even studies on the prevalence from Taiwan between 1982 and 1986 showed depression was low.

Reasons for the low rate were that the actual was low, that there was low reporting because of social **stigma**, or that other disorders similar to depression but more culturally valid for the Chinese were used.

Chinese psychiatrists have not historically diagnosed depression as often as they have other disorders. For example, in Hunan province, only 1% of the patients were diagnosed with depression while 30% received the diagnosis for neurasthenia. Adding to the complexities is the typical attitude toward doctors. For example, people are more likely to consult a Traditional Chinese Medical (TCM) doctor for problems they consider "illnesses" and a western type doctor for problems they categorize as "diseases." *Chinese persons do not generally consider emotional upset a disease.*

If this man experiences distress and sadness in our modern world, will it be called depression or neurasthenia in China? Source: pixabay.com

Does a true western depression exist in China? It has a CCMD-3 category, but the relevance of depressive symptoms is embedded in the history of how the Chinese think about mental illness. *The Chinese may deemphasize depressive symptoms as defined by western standards, but in turn, depression may be over-emphasized and pathologized in the West.*

TCM was the primary care for mental health problems in China until the beginning of the 1900s (Chinese Society of Psychiatry, 2005). TCM makes no distinction between mental and physical health. All mental and physical health problems are Chi, or energy, imbalances treated with acupuncture, herbs, and lifestyle changes.

In the early 1900s, new ideas came to China and neurasthenia was one of those (Parker, et al., 2001). Neurasthenia was a condition where a person experiences **somatic**, or bodily, symptoms. In China, neurasthenia was called **shenjing shuairuo**, meaning neurological weakness. Shenjing shuairuo was common. About 80% of psychiatric patients in China received the diagnosis of neurasthenia during the 1980s. People without much experience and knowledge of western mental disorders experience distress physically, symptoms less **stigmatizing**.

Another factor is the various translations of the word depression, which can mean "repress," "gloomy," or "disorder," all of which are unpopular with the Chinese. Instead, somatic symptoms are *a cultural preference for showing distress, a "display rule," that dictates what the Chinese report to doctors.*

In the 1980s, China opened to western influence, which included western psychiatric practice. By the time the DSM-III appeared, Chinese psychiatrists thought most neurasthenia cases could be re-diagnosed as depression. Chinese doctors realized the diagnosis of depression gave them a new treatment option, antidepressant drugs. There were no anti-neurasthenia drugs.

Rates of depression in China continued to increase and the diagnosis of neurasthenia continued to decrease over a fairly short time span, so fast that social factors must be the reason for the changes (Lee & Kleinman, 2007). Lee and Kleinman claim that **DSMizing** the world may or may not bring the best treatments to local communities. DSMizing means to export western classification manuals to others.

26.2 Discussion of depression etiologies
A frame of reference for considering major depression
Discuss means to give a considered and balanced view supported by evidence. A balanced view comes from considering etiology all three approaches to behavior. There is much to consider!

A statement from the New England Journal of Medicine is a good place to start. "**Depression** is a heterogeneous disorder with a highly variable course, an inconsistent response to treatment, and no established mechanism" (Belmaker & Agam, 2008, p. 55). This means people diagnosed with depression have many symptoms, have different experiences with it, respond differently to treatments, and there is no agreement among psychologists about the causes.

No simple answers exist in the real world. Discard any preexisting ideas that depression is a specific thing. Any text identifying "causes" in such a way as to make them appear distinct and easy to verify is oversimplified and misleading. *Tolerating uncertainty is the best strategy.*

Although depressive symptoms are universal and rates are increasing, cultural schemas influence how depression is experienced and treated. "The way in which depression is confronted, discussed, and managed varies among social worlds, and cultural meanings and practices shape its course" (Kleinman, 2004, p.1).

The list of reasons (the risks) people have depression, and they come from all three approaches to behavior. This book covers just a few of these reasons.

Depression is often described as a black cloud hanging over one's head. The **film** "Deeply Depressed" talks about depression this way.
Used with license from megapixl.com.

Biological approach to behavior:
Genes, such as 5-HTT, the serotonin transporter gene
Sleep patterns, for example, EEGs show that some depressed persons go into REM sleep rapidly,
    just after 60 minutes, about 20 minutes earlier than non-depressed persons
Hormone or neurotransmitter imbalances
Qi (or Chi, energy) imbalance
Poor diet
Lack of proper exercise
Illness or the presence of another mental disorder
Techno-Brain Burnout
Under-stimulation of the effort reward system

> **Biological, cognitive, and sociocultural factors linked to abnormal psychology**
> The best examples come from studying etiology for each disorder covered in this book. Just remember that the ATBs interact in a multidirectional way. It is unlikely that one factor works alone.
>   Treatment of mental disorder is another place to study factors.

Cognitive approach to behavior:
Cognitive schemas and maladaptive thoughts
Negative attribution style

Sociocultural approach to behavior:
Low self-efficacy
Marital problems
Expected female roles
Parental maltreatment
Neighborhood factors
Poverty
Discrimination and prejudice
War
Social class
Grieving a loss
Aging populations

> **Youtube: Sapolsky on depression**
> Robert Sapolsky from Stanford has many videos about depression on Youtube. Students love Sapolsky and these are recommended.

Natural disasters
Increased urbanization
Media messages
Lack of social support
Witchcraft
Spirits and other culturally based community causes

Thinking skills: Evaluate research methods in abnormal psychology
Correlation studies are the main research method used to study causation in humans. Strict "causation" cannot be inferred from correlation studies. While animal experiments add to our understanding of causation, animal lives and brains are not exactly the same as human lives and brains. Review the section in chapter 10 about the use of animals models.

A *risk model* is the best way to study factors contributing to depression and is important for using the multidirectional model.

If a person has none of the factors, then the risk of depression is low. If a person has the two short alleles of 5-HTT, the risk increases. If the person also has stressful life events, such as parent maltreatment, the risk increases a little more. If the person also lives in poverty, the risk further increases. Add low-self efficacy or a negative cognitive style and the risk increases even more. Many combinations exist and everyone has a risk load from low to high.

No one has all the risk factors, but you see how it works. Explaining depression is complex because so many factors contribute to the total picture. One factor is not enough for someone to become depressed. In addition, culture mediates all factors. *Any answer to exam questions asking for one explanation of mental disorder should include a discussion of how the selected factor interacts with other factors as shown on the multidirectional model.* All mental disorders have the same framework.

It's impossible to know the exact cause of someone's depression. The "causation" pattern is *multidirectional*.

Film
One useful film is "Deeply Depressed" available from the Films for the Humanities and Sciences. It distinguishes ordinary sadness from clinical depression, something hard for students to imagine without meeting some people diagnosed with the disorder. It is a western view of depression but will introduce students to the problem.

The explanations in this book includes genes for the biological approach to behavior, depressive schemas for the cognitive approach to behavior, and Internet overuse for the sociocultural approach to behavior.

Biological approach to behavior: Genes and depression

The material for this section can be found in chapter 6 about genetic influences on behavior. Caspi's research on the **serotonin transporter gene** is highlighted. It helps to review the nature of the gene in chapter 4 along with Caspi.

On the cutting edge: New research on a biological risk for depression: Diet
Diet could be a key part of good mental health. This is a good topic for the class because students struggle with making healthy food choices. Might we eat a better diet if we know our mental health is at stake?

The *Scientific American Mind* article titled 'In search of the optimal brain diet' includes a study called PREDIMED (Prevention with Mediterranean Diet) (Stetka, 2016). This study comes from researcher Almundena Sanchez-Villegas showing that a sample of 12,000 Spaniards following this diet of olive oil, fruits, vegetables, beans, whole grains, and moderate amounts of lean meat and red wine showed a 30% less risk of depression. The diet was low in sugar and processed foods.

This is a new line of research and needs much investigation but looks promising. Students can benefit by reading the article and evaluating their own diet.

Anyone citing this study on an exam must say it is new research. I prefer students to write about genetic risks (Caspi, 2010; 2003) that are well researched and stand the test of time. I teach diet as a general stressor for the body. More research is needed to see how diet interacts with other biological systems to produce low mood.

Cognitive approach to behavior: Cognitive style and depressive schemas

Aaron Beck created the cognitive model of depression (now called the Generic Cognitive Model) and founded cognitive therapy. According to Beck, thoughts are primarily responsible for how we feel and behave (Engler, 2007).

Just how does negative cognitive style become a risk factor?

The **Generic Cognitive Model** (GCM) is a theory explaining the common cognitive processes seen across many mental disorders yet gives specific **modes of thinking** unique to the different disorders (Beck & Haight, 2014).

Every disorder is an exaggeration of normal adaptive functioning. The change from adaptive behavior into mental disorder comes from someone's faulty **information processing**, which is full of attention and memory biases leading to faulty beliefs. People with depression, for example, have biased attention to focus on negative emotional stimuli and biases toward negative memories. People with depressed symptoms also ruminate, meaning someone cannot stop thinking about something.

**Thinking skills:
See how the ATBs interact**
Beck specifically noted the influence of the **serotonin transporter gene** as a way for someone to have sensitivity to the environment, something involved in creating depressive schemas.

Chapter 7 details the ss alleles of the serotonin transporter gene from Caspi's research under the section about genes and behavior. People with the ss alleles are more vulnerable to negative schemas.

Look for ways to see how the ATBs interact.

Beck divides thinking into *automatic* or *controlled* (Engler, 2007). Automatic beliefs occur just below one's surface awareness and are more difficult to change than conscious controlled thoughts. Automatic thoughts of people with mental disorder are full of information processing biases that can be called cognitive distortions. One kind of distortion magnifies problems, making things worse than they are in reality. An example of magnification is "anything less than an A on a test is a failure and I will never go to college and have a good future, and even a B grade is a failure." Another cognitive distortion is **dichotomous thinking**, or thinking in extremes. An example of dichotomous thinking is "I am either a total failure or a complete success."

Information processing biases are stored in memory over someone's lifetime and lead to the formation of **schemas**, which are shaped as we experience the world (Beck & Haight, 2014). Schemas of people with mental disorders contain these information processing biases. Although schemas often stay hidden for a long time, if activated by a stressful event they can increase the risk of mental disorder.

To summarize, schemas are activated during stress, resulting in bias in attention to emotional stimuli, bias in emotional processing, rumination, and bias in memory for negative events.

The GCM uses all the approaches to behavior to detail how someone develops a mental disorder. This diagram shows the many interacting parts leading to negative schema.

Genes ⟷ Sensitivity to ⟷ Attention ⟷ Memory ⟷ Schemas ⟷ Disorder
　　　　　the environment　　 bias　　　 bias

Based on Beck & Haight (2014)

Events from the environment can trigger any part of this model. For example, someone may have to give a speech in front of others and it triggers the model at the sensitivity to the environment section. The resulting fear can trigger the attention biases toward negative emotional stimuli.

Modes are important because they are networks of information processing biases that get activated by schemas.

For example, the depression mode is made up of information processing biases about the self, which Beck called the **self-expansive mode**. People want to enhance the self, and this mode is made of thoughts about someone's value, such as "I must get all A grades to be worthy" or "I must study harder than others to be worthy."

There are different modes for each group of disorders. Disorders related to **anxiety** are unified under a **self-protective mode**. For example, someone with anxiety overestimates threat and will self protect, such as developing a phobia because of maladaptive avoidance of public speaking or spiders.

Changing depressive schemas is challenging. Good reasons for this conclusion come from studying Beck's research detailing how the brains of people caught up in a cycle of depressive schemas operate differently from the brains of people without depression (Disner, Beevers, Haight, & Beck, 2011).

The table below summarizes the cognitions and the related brain activity. Generally, negative cognitive biases start with faulty bottom-up processing from subcortical brain structures combined with faulty top-down processing that is supposed to control cognitions.

Critical thought increases when students see how the ATBs interact

Review brain structures in chapter 4. It is important to explain how the brain is activated during depressive schemas so students realize that the brain has adapted to someone's thinking style.

Cognitive therapy, reviewed in the next chapter, works because these brain pathways are modified through top-down processing.

Learn at least one from the chart below to increase critical thought. There is no need to recall the entire list.

A sampling of the brain activity in someone with depressed schemas
(Disner, et al., 2011)

Cognitive bias	Brain activity
Biased attention for emotional stimuli	Includes **prefrontal cortex** (PFC): People without depression are biased toward positive stimuli and people with depression are biased toward negative stimuli. The PFC helps select between competing stimuli. **Top-down processing** is required to switch one's attention towards positive stimuli and away from the negative. A negative stimulus that stands out to the person with depression blocks out the processing of the anything else. They cannot switch from negative to positive because of impaired top-down processing due to decreased PFC activity.
Biased processing of emotions	Includes **thalamus** and **amygdala**: Emotion stimuli is sent to the amygdala from the thalamus. Amygdala activity increases in people without depression as they process emotions. They also have more activity in regions related to **top-down processing**. Amygdala activity in people with depression is greater and lasts longer, resulting in faster emotion processing, which is correlated with lower levels of well-being. It causes a strong bottom-up signal that is not thought about clearly when using normal top-down processing.
Rumination (can't stop thinking about something)	Includes **amygdala**: Rumination is related to over-activation of the amygdala that allows for over-processing of emotions These people also have faulty top-down processing that should help regulate emotional thoughts.
Biases toward negative memories	Includes **amygdala** and **hippocampus**: Negative memories are related to an overactive amygdala that triggers bottom-up processing into the hippocampus. This allows someone with depression to recall depressive thoughts over and over without the **top-down processing** from the **prefrontal cortex** to regulate and shift thoughts.

Hundreds of studies confirm that cognition is a risk factor correlated with depression. **Cognitive style**, **brooding**, and **rumination** are some of the risk cognitions studied. Rumination means to constantly think about a problem. The pathways are illustrated next.

1. Negative emotions ➔ cognitive style or brooding ➔ depression
2. Life stressors ➔ rumination ➔ depression

   Cognitions are the middle men and are good targets for prevention programs seeking to lower the risk for depression.

Research support: Two correlation studies showing that cognition is a risk factor for depression

The **aim of one correlation study** was to show that cognition plays a clear role in how someone's negative emotions, an inborn temperament, turn into depressive symptoms (Arger, Sanchez, Simonson, & Mezulis, 2012).

For **procedures**, participants filled out questionnaires about negative emotion as well as the **cognitive style**, **brooding**, and **rumination** thought to turn the emotions into depression.

Results showed that participants with negative emotions, who also brooded and had a negative cognitive style, were most vulnerable to depression.

Researchers **concluded** that brooding and negative cognitive style mediated the negative emotion.

The **aim of a second correlation study** clarified the role of **rumination** as a predictor of depressive symptoms (Michl, McLaughlin, Shepherd, & Nolen-Hoeksema, 2013). Rumination was not significant in the Arger, et al. (2012) study and needed investigation.

The authors believed that rumination was important as a specific mediator of stressful events that led to depressive symptoms.

Evaluate research methods and ethics in abnormal psychology
Why are correlations the primary way to study causes of mental illness? The answer has to do with ethics. Researchers never want to put study participants in situations where they are at risk for harm. Experiments investigating causes of disorders would create conditions where someone a disorder is caused in a group. Correlations examine already existing conditions and do not seek to cause an outcome. To what extent are the animal used in studies good models for humans with mental disorder? It is not an easy answer. Make sure to review the monkey experiments in chapter 6 reviewed along with Caspi's correlation study.

For **procedures**, adolescents and adults filled out self-report questionnaires about social stressors, rumination, and depressive symptoms twice over one year.

Results showed that stressful life events were correlated with rumination, and that the greater the rumination, the greater the correlation between rumination and depressive symptoms.

Sociocultural approach to behavior: Internet use and depression

Internet use has positive and negative affects on human behavior and is part of a major cultural shift in human interaction. Internet use increases some skills but it comes with a price— increased stress. Constant stress causes changes in adrenal functioning that affects the brain and increases one's risk for depression.

Theory of Knowledge Link: For the IB Student
A good discussion for TOK reflects on the following questions as the class reads the rest of the material in this section. What is the difference between normal Internet use and excessive use that appears addictive? How has technology affected learning? In what ways does technology contribute to stress and depression? In what ways do people substitute Internet use for real life relationships and what are the consequences? Why is it so hard to be objective about the cell phones and Internet we use each day?

The solution is not to get rid of the Internet. It is, however, a tool that has become a lifestyle for many, with major consequences. Computers can make life easier, such as shopping on Amazon or connecting with out-of-town family members. Students should, however, consider some of the negative effects.

Thinking about technology is challenging because we are living in the midst of it. Imagine what the human mind was like before the written word. Everything had to be remembered. The first printing press probably had critics claiming the written word would end excellent memories.

> **Thinking, social, & communication skills: Be honest about Internet effects**
> The Scientific American article *Generation Z: Online and at Risk?* from Nicholas Kardaras is a good source for class debate.
>   Does the article describe anyone you know? Is there a way to reduce risks?

The concept **neuroplasticity** reminds us that the brain changes in response to the environment. Young developing brains are the most vulnerable to changes, especially changes affecting the thinking parts of the brain. Each era of information ushered in different underlying brain processing. Information sharing started with storytelling, then changed to the written word, to television, and then to the computer and mobile phones. It is safe to say that brains in the computer era are different from brains of the past. Today's students grew up with computers and cell phones and do not know of a world without them.

Even 5 days of Internet exposure for people who had never used it creates neuroplastic changes in the brain similar to expert users (Small & Vorgan, 2008).

Modern adolescents ages eight to eighteen get an average of 8.5 hours of technology stimulation every day, including television, video and DVD movies, video games, mobile phones, and computers (Small & Vorgan, 2008). This is a lot for the brain to manage.

One startling survey result was that 63% of 12-year-olds relied on texting and just 35% communicated with people face-to-face (Kardaras, 2016). Being social is necessary for human culture and essential for good mental health. Even if texting and social media are convenient and fun, the rise of its use is correlated with poor mental health. Depression rates have risen and 74% of adolescents report trouble sleeping and seeing a mental health professional. Large numbers of Facebook friends is correlated with depression this is because these friends do not share your experiences in the real world. Receiving a smiley face from someone in a text is not the same as sitting across from the person who is really smiling.

Technology use starts young and it is important to consider how much is appropriate.
Used with license from megapixl.com.

Constant computer use trains the brain to be in a state of **continuous partial attention** where people are always busy, monitoring the Internet and the phone for bits of information but never really focusing on one task (Small & Vorgan, 2008). Multitasking is different and its purpose is to improve efficiency. Continuous partial attention keeps people alert for *any* contact, such as news alerts, an email, or a text message. Everything is in one's peripheral attention.

Stress increases when someone is in a state of continuous partial attention. People "no longer have time to reflect, contemplate or make thoughtful decisions. Instead they exist in a sense of constant crisis—on alert for a new contact or bit of exciting news or information at any moment" (Small & Vorgan, 2008, p. 47).

Losing a sense of control may be a consequence of long term "continuous partial attention." Fatigue, irritability, and distractedness are reported from heavy technology users. The stress of constant alertness signals the fight and flight system and the adrenal glands continually produce the stress hormone **cortisol**.

Research support: Internet overuse is correlated with depression

A growing body of research correlates Internet overuse and **depression**. Note that this is a new area of study so watch jumping to conclusions that you automatically get a mental disorder from using the Internet. Just so everyone knows, Internet addiction is identified as needing further study by the DSM-5 committee for possible later inclusion into the diagnostic manual but is not an official DSM-5 disorder as of the writing of this book.

Pathological Internet use increases the risk of developing depression (Lam & Peng, 2010). Pathology means "disease causing," and pathological overuse of the Internet means that someone is addicted to its use. Males have the highest rates of Internet addiction, but excessive Internet use by females is increasing. Internet addiction is most studied in East Asian samples, but new research confirms the findings in Western samples.

The **aim of one correlation study** was to show how Internet overuse was linked to depression (Lam and Peng, 2010). Participants were a random sample of students from a database of all Chinese high school students in Guangzhou, China. Data were gathered with questionnaires such as The Internet Addiction Test. One example of a question is "How often do you feel depressed, moody, or nervous when you are off-line, which goes away once you are back online?"

Results follow.

1. Pathological Internet use negatively affects mental health.
2. Students identified as pathological Internet users have a one and a half times greater risk for developing depression than students with normal use.
3. Students starting out free of mental health problems can develop depression after pathological Internet use begins.

Making social comparisons on Facebook and having many online friends are risk factors for depression.
Used under license from megapixel.com.

Lam and Peng were the first to gather data over a long time-period, following up with students for nine months. Similar research has confirmed these findings in the West using UK samples (Morrison & Gore, 2010). These studies do not predict a specific pathway for the correlation. Does the Internet put people at risk for depression, or are depressed people attracted to online lives? Future research should clarify the pathway, but the relationship is alarming.

Approaches to research in abnormal psychology: Evaluations

Even with a large number of new studies correlating Internet overuse and depression, students must step back and ask about its quality.

The research is in its infancy and gathers data mainly through self-report questionnaires, so it may lack enough rigor for sweeping conclusions (Toseeb & Inkster, 2015).

Along with self-reports, research needs to use social networking site (SNS) activity to document individual use, as reporting biases interfere with collecting usage data. SNS leaves behind a digital trace of huge amounts of activity logs that could be used in research. Many existing studies using small samples could be improved with SNS data.

The research mostly uses correlation and this does not show causation. Ethics prevent putting participants in an experimental condition that encourages depression.

Research support: Facebook depression

A new group of studies show that social comparison when on **Facebook** is the reason for people's depression symptoms. Stay open-minded because you might not like hearing this but should know about the research. The class might come up with a profile of the person most likely to be at risk for **Facebook depression**. This is a good chance to apply what you learn to daily life.

Facebook study and aim or important theory	Predictions, procedure, and results
Correlation: The aim was to find the mechanism for the correlation between Facebook overuse and depression (Feinstein, et al., 2013).	The study predicted that college students tended to compare themselves with others in a negative way when on Facebook and ruminated (overthinking) about the comparisons. College students filled out an online survey then again three weeks later to see usage over time. Results supported predictions. Negative social comparison was the context of Facebook use, and this was correlated with greater rumination. Rumination was then linked to greater depression.
Correlation: The aim was to compare active and nonactive Facebook users to see if social comparison was the reason for Facebook depression (Steers, Wickman, & Acitelli, 2014).	The hypothesis was that active Facebook users would have more opportunity to make social comparisons than nonactive users and this was the reason for Facebook depression. Participants filled out an online questionnaire, reporting the time spent on Facebook and responding to questions such as "When I am on Facebook, I always pay a lot of attention to how well I have done something compared to how others do things." Results showed that participants spending more time on Facebook was correlated to depression symptoms but social comparisons were greatest for males.
Correlation: The aim was to see if the amount of Facebook logins was correlated to depression and if these logins were correlated to making social comparisons (Steers, Wickman, & Acitelli, 2014).	Researchers predicted that the amount of logins would be correlated to depression and that depression would be correlated to making social comparisons in both males and females. Participants kept a 14-day dairy of Facebook logins and time spent on the site as well as a record of making social comparisons. Participants rated themselves daily on measures such as feeling less competent and comparing how they did things in relation to others. Results showed that social comparisons were correlated with people spending more time on Facebook and feeling depressed.
Evolutionary Psychology (EP) is a theory explaining our reaction to the Internet (Blease, 2015). **EP was first introduced in chapter 7 so this is another use for the theory.**	EP explains the evolution of human psychological processes. Depression may have been adaptive in our evolutionary past as a way to solve recurring social competition problems. This is because depression gives us the ability to ruminate to find a solution, and it signals others to help. In modern times, prestige has replaced dominance as the way someone judges their self-worth, creating a mismatch between our evolutionary history and modern life. **Facebook** is full of triggering cues for depression. People judge their social standing in comparison to others. In addition, people tend to use the Internet alone, so it provides a context for making more negative comparisons with others. Those most at risk for depression: 1. Have the most online friends 2. Spend great amounts of time reading updates from this friend group 3. Focus on the updates that contain bragging and success stories

26.3 Symptoms and prevalence of Anorexia Nervosa (AN)

Discuss means to give a considered and balanced view supported by evidence.

Eating disorders involve a "persistent disturbance of eating or eating related behavior that results in the altered consumption or absorption of food and that significantly impairs physical health or psychological functioning" (American Psychiatric Association, 2013, p. 329).

DSM-5 *makes fundamental changes to diagnosing* **anorexia nervosa** (AN) that are more cross-culturally friendly, allowing more actual cases to be detected. DSM-5 drops the requirement of an intense fear of fat, the "fat phobia." The ICD-10 still has a requirement for the intense fear of getting fat, which is likely to disappear in its new edition (by 2018). A fear of getting fat has always been *possible but not required* for a CCMD-3 diagnosis. Cultural differences in attitudes about weight account for the CCMD-3 language about fears of fat.

Anorexia nervosa as a medical term first appeared in 1874 as the way William Gull described the symptoms of four girls who deliberately lost weight (Keel, 2005). So eating disorders existed before modern times.

> **Inquiry and global/local awareness**
> Students should collaborate to figure our why rates are rising across culture and why younger and younger children are diagnosed with an eating disorder, particularly anorexia. What are the rates in your area?
> Do not try and learn all the statistics! Make some good generalizations and come up with some plausible reasons.

Historically, AN was not linked to a fear of fat. Instead, AN was self-starvation related to moral beliefs and attention seeking. The DSM-IV diagnosis in for AN changed the historical meaning of AN to include an assumed **etic** based on modern, perhaps western, cultural influences concerning weight and body shape. Research showing **emic** expressions of disordered eating helped create a better universal etic for AN in DSM-5.

In addition, DSM-5 removes the requirement for amenorrhea, or loss of the menstrual cycle, because many girls do not lose it and the requirement is irrelevant for males.

While AN exists historically, there has been a modest increase in its diagnosis over time (Keel, 2005).

DSM-5 diagnosis for anorexia nervosa (AN)

The DSM-5 (American Psychiatric Association, 2013) categorizes AN under the heading of feeding and eating disorders. Eating disorders include AN, bulimia nervosa (BN), and a new category for binge eating disorder (BED).

DSM-5 diagnosis for anorexia

The person restricts energy intake in a way that differs significantly from requirements. The person has a significantly low body weight relative to what is normal or expected for their age and developmental level.

The person has extreme fear of gaining weight or being fat, **or** has a persistent behavior that prevents weight gain, even hough he or she is already at a significantly low weight.

The person denies that his or her weight loss or lack of weight gain is a serious problem, has self-evaluations showing an undue influence of body shape and weight, or persistently denies the seriousness of their low weight.

Severity ratings are mild, moderate, severe, and extreme.

DSM-5 lists two types of AN, restricting type and binge-eating/purging type. Restricting types engage in extreme fasting, dieting or exercising. Binge-eating/purging means large amounts of food are consumed and are followed by self-induced vomiting or the use of laxatives, diuretics, or enemas.

Prevalence rates for anorexia in the US and across cultures

Country	Prevalence
US	**Prevalence** of AN over a twelve-month time-period is 0.4% for females (American Psychiatric Association, 2013). Male prevalence rates are hard to know. Males show AN differently and this is discussed in chapter 25. AN usually starts in adolescence or early adulthood and stressful events often come first. The time someone has AN and the level of recovery varies. Some fully recover after one episode of AN, some have problems with fluctuating weight and then relapse, and some people have constant problems and even die from AN. Sometimes persons with AN are hospitalized in an attempt to stabilize weight. About 5% eventually die of AN. Some ethnic groups living in high socioeconomic nations, such as Latinos in the US, do not seek help as often as Caucasian groups, so exact prevalence rates are hard to know.
Generally across high income countries for all eating disorders	One in every 6-7 people will get an eating disorder, with AN the most prevalent and chronic (Schmidt et al., 2016). Across all eating disorders (AN, bulimia nervosa, and binge eating disorder) rates are rising in high income countries. The peak age for having an eating disorder is 15-25 and it typically lasts for 6 years. The scariest thing is that eating disorders are increasing in younger and younger children. Having bulimia or binge eating disorder gives someone twice the risk of death, and the risk is 6 times greater if someone has AN.
Hong Kong	In 1989 there were just a few cases of AN in Hong Kong. By 1991 there was a small rise of reported AN cases to .46%. In 1996, 6.5% of females in Hong Kong showed disordered eating.
Chinese living in Singapore and mainland China	In 1982, seven cases of AN were reported in Chinese females living in Singapore (Makino, Tsuboi, & Dennerstein, 2004). By 1997, it rose to fifty cases. The prevalence of AN in Asians is correlated with westernization. AN prevalence increased in many Asian countries throughout the 1990s, including Japan, Hong Kong, Taiwan, and the Republic of Korea (Lee, 2000). When Asian governments loosened restrictions on advertising, rates of AN rose in Asian countries such as China, India, and the Philippines. Cases of self-starvation existed in China before westernization, so AN was never exclusive to the West. However, many cases of AN in nonwestern culture involve females with exposure to western culture.
Iran, Malaysia, & Egypt	The lifetime prevalence rate for AN is 0.9% for Iranian schoolgirls (Keel, 2005). Between 0.05% and 0.16% of mental health cases in Malaysia and 0.19% of cases in Egypt are related to AN.

CCMD-3 diagnosis for anorexia nervosa (AN)

Eating disorders are classified as part of a group of disorders called "physiological disorders related to psychological disorders" in the CCMD-3 (Chinese Society of Psychiatry, 2003). Eating disorders include

AN, bulimia nervosa, and disordered vomiting. AN is described as an adolescent female disorder where they deliberately eat less and weigh less than is considered normal. Patients sometimes worry about being fat even when they are already underweight and if a doctor tells them they are not fat. AN patients suffer from the consequences of poor nutrition as well as metabolism and hormone imbalances.

CCMD-3 diagnosis for anorexia

A person shows a large amount of weight loss of at least 15% below the expected weight.

A person deliberately loses weight and has at least one of the following.
    A.   The person avoids fatty foods.
    B.   The person uses self-induced vomiting to purge food.
    C.   The person exercises in the extreme.
    D.   The person uses drugs to lessen appetite and/or diuretics.

The person typically has a fear of getting fat, *but a fear is not required for a diagnosis.*

The person's endocrine system is out of balance. The imbalance can take numerous forms, such as amenorrhea, heightened levels of growth hormone, and high cortisol levels.

The symptoms have lasted for at least three months.

26.4 Discussion of anorexia nervosa (AN) etiologies

Discuss means to give a considered and balanced view supported by evidence. A balanced view comes from considering etiology from all the approaches to behavior.

Use the same **risk model** approach to consider etiologies of **anorexia nervosa** (AN) introduced in the last section about depression. One factor is unlikely to explain AN. The etiologies of AN, bulimia nervosa (BN), and binge-eating disorder (BED) are different, so the following is specific to AN.

A list of factors that increase the risk of AN from all 3 ATB

Genes
Appetite and weight regulation imbalance in the hypothalamus
Neurotransmitters, including serotonin, and dopamine
Temperament
Cognitive factors, such as attentional biases toward food and body related cues, cognitive
    distortions such as dichotomous thinking
Perfectionism
Media portrayals of cultural attitudes toward thinness
Family interaction
Social learning, including modeling from parents and low self-efficacy
Peer groups, such as sororities

Many people with anorexia see themselves as fat even though they are extremely thin, a body-image problem.
Used with license from megapixl.com.

Examples of etiologies discussed in this book are genes, cognitive style, and media. The approaches to behavior interact in complicated ways, so students can use the multidirectional model to explain these interactions.

Film
The Nova film *Dying to be Thin* is available from www.pbs.org or amazon. It is a good summary of anorexia and bulimia, allowing students to meet people with the disorders. The film is popular with students and a good way to start the section about anorexia.

Dancers are at high risk for anorexia because of professional demands that they look a certain way. The film includes examples of dancers struggling with AN.
Used with license from megapixl.com.

Research support: Biological explanations: Genetics

Genes are important risk factors for AN, but they do not work alone (Trace, Baker, Penas-Lledo, & Bulik, 2013). Over forty genes potentially contribute to AN, accounting for approximately 40% to 60% of the risk, and the list is growing. *Genetic risk is complicated by the many pathways genes take to affect behavior, so tolerate uncertainty and avoid oversimplification.*

The exact contribution of genes is hard to pinpoint because genes fit into an interactive model with cognitive and sociocultural factors. Family inheritance is well documented, and first-degree relatives are eleven times more likely to have AN. The challenge is to discover which genes stand out as important. Genes related to serotonin, dopamine, opioids, appetite regulation, food intake, weight regulation, high cholesterol, and early development of synapse and neuronal networks are studied, but so far nothing has surfaced as prominent (Boraska, et al., 2014; Zeeland, et al., 2014; Trace, et, al., 2013). Studies suffer from inconsistency, lack of replication, and small sample sizes, so conclusions are tentative at best.

Scientists have at least concluded that genes related to AN do not work alone, so it is best to study them along with cognitive and sociocultural factors related to gene expression. Genes affect behavior through many pathways and some examples follow.

Thinking skills: How to draw tentative conclusions
Students cannot remember all of these genetic pathways for a test. Do not be afraid of genetic research!

The point is for students to understand the complexities of drawing a conclusion about causation. Practice getting your head around these ideas.

There are many ways to correlate genes with AN, and the rGE correlations are highlighted as the research examples, so perhaps focus on this pathway for a test.

Students can point out on a test that we must avoid oversimplification, and some examples of the rGE are quite interesting.

A good conclusion might say that genes can make us sensitive to the environment but are rarely the determining factor, with two research findings from Mazzeo and Bulik (2009).

Genetic pathway to anorexia	Description
Gene by environment interactions (rGE)	These are correlations showing how a genetic risk influences a person's environment, meaning "environmental exposure is influenced by genetic factors" (p. 605-6). Three ways for genes to affect a person's environment are active, passive, and evocative interactions. A **passive rGE** occurs when a parent contributes both genes and an environment for a child. The child is a passive recipient of both, yet their behavior is affected greatly because they inherit the genetic risk and are exposed to parental behavior. An **active rGE** implies that a child's behavior is important to the correlation. For example, girls with a genetic risk for AN might seek out media about cultural values of thinness, thus actively seeking certain kinds of environments (Mazzeo & Bulik, 2009). An **evocative rGE** also implies a child's behavior is important, and occurs when a genetic risk for a behavior, such as a certain temperament, helps create an environment that evokes, or stirs up, behavior from the parent (Trace, Baker, Penas-Lledo & Bulik, 2013).
Gene X environment interactions (GxE)	These are correlations showing how genes express differently in different environments. Two ways that GxE operate are when an environment enhances or buffers gene expression. For example, most girls viewing thin-ideal media do not develop AN, but the risk is enhanced for those with the risk genes. Stress free environments may buffer, or make someone more resilient, to AN.
Gene X gene interactions (GxG)	These are correlations showing how a gene interacts with other genes to increase the risk of a behavior (Trace, et al., 2013). For example, people with both one short allele of 5-HT and a long allele of MAOA have eight times the risk for AN. The interaction has a greater effect than it does on its own, called a synergistic effect.

The **aim of a body of research** was to show rGE correlations between AN and the environment (Mazzeo & Bulik, 2009). If you know someone with anorexia you might know of examples of these behaviors.

A **passive rGE correlation** exists between parental models and child disordered eating behavior. For example, studies show that mother's *comments and complaints about their own weight* are correlated with the esteem of their fourth and fifth grade children as well as the concern level that their daughters have about their own weight. It is a passive correlation because these parents pass on genes to their children *and* provide an environment. The children get a "double dose" of risk factors for eating disorders without doing anything.

An **evocative rGE correlation** also contributes to AN. **Perfectionism** is one example. Although temperament is influenced by genetic factors, a person's temperament also influences how a person interacts with the environment. Persons with perfectionist temperaments *seek out demanding environments and hold themselves to very high standards.*

> **Ethics in abnormal psychology**
> One good reason to investigate genetic risks is to identify people early so they can get resilience training. However, genotyping has ethical consequences related to privacy, so although attitudes toward finding genetic risk may become more of the norm in the future, we must guarantee confidentiality. This is not as easy as it seems.

These persons seek evaluations from others about their performance. Perfectionist persons "evoke" comments from others, and even positive responses from another reinforces a perfectionist personality.

Media is one factor showing an **active rGE correlation** with AN. All girls do not develop eating disorders, although most are exposed to western media idolizing thinness. Girls with a genetic vulnerability for eating disorders might actively seek out media about thinness that reinforces negative views of their own body shape. One study found that girls whose eating disorder symptoms increased over a sixteen-month time-period also reported reading more fashion magazines during that time. In addition, research suggests that girls with genetic vulnerabilities to eating disorders actively select peer groups with the same ideals. European-American girls in sororities have high rates of eating disorders symptoms. Girls in sororities have significantly greater eating disorder symptoms than girls not in sororities after a three-year period.

Research support: Cognitive explanations: Cognitive flexibility

Two cognitive factors increase the risk for eating disorders, **attentional biases** toward food and body image, and **cognitive styles** that distort reality (Keel, 2005). A growing body of research confirms cognitive style as a risk factor for AN. The **aim of one quasi-experiment** was to investigate **cognitive flexibility** as a specific type of cognitive style (Tchanturia et al., 2011).

Cognitive flexibility refers to adapting to changes, and persons with AN have poor flexibility. One study prediction was that persons with AN would perform more poorly on a task measuring the ability to learn new rules as compared to controls without AN. Adapting to change was operationalized in the experiment as the ability to learn new rules.

For the **procedures**, participants took the Brixton Spatial Anticipation Test, where the position of a blue colored circle changed for each trial. A rule must be anticipated to figure out the next position of the circle. The ability to anticipate the rule was measured by the number of errors on the test.

Results supported the prediction. Persons with AN had significantly more errors, meaning less flexibility, than controls. The authors think poor cognitive flexibility is an enduring trait of persons with AN, and one factor that maintains the disorder.

*Cognitive inflexibility is now considered a **biomarker** for eating disorder, meaning that it is a biologically based temperament predisposing some people to a cognitive style that contributes to eating disorder. This is the kind of thing the National Institute of Mental Health is interested in identifying for earlier diagnoses.*

Research support: Sociocultural explanations: Television

Anyone thinking that media is not a risk factor for developing disordered eating should read Anne Becker's research. Rates of disordered eating and negative body image increased after television came to Fiji in the 1990s (Becker, Burwell, Gillian, Herzog, & Hamberg, 2002).

Isolating the effects of television on behavior is hard because a control group without exposure are rare. Fijian adolescent girls were the perfect solution because television access was limited before 1995.

The **aim of the study** was to see if exposure to western television a risk factor for developing disordered eating behavior despite traditional cultural values.

Quantitative data, using a field experiment, and qualitative data, using an interview, were collected.

Fijians did not have much access to television before 1995, but once they got it, girls showed more disordered eating.
Source: pixabay.com.

Procedures are next.

First, a field experiment tested the incidence of disordered eating in 1995 before exposure to television and again in 1998 after three years of western television. Data for the field experiment were collected through a self-report questionnaire about attitudes toward eating.

Second, semi-structured interviews collected narratives covering a range of eating attitudes from the 1998 sample. The narratives reflected opinions about diet, weight control, and traditional Fijian values. Important themes were identified through content analysis.

All ethnic Fijian adolescent girls from two schools were in the sample.

Results follow.

1. Field experiments showed an increase in disordered eating between the 1995 and 1998 samples. Second, 74% of the 1998 sample said they felt too fat.
2. Interesting themes emerged. The girls admired the television characters and 83% said that television changed the way they felt about their body type. About 40% felt they had a better chance at career advancement if they were slimmer.

The authors **concluded** that television played a large role in changing values toward body shape and eating behaviors. The following excerpt from the narratives is an example: 'When I look at the characters on TV, the way they act on TV and I just look at the body, the figure of that body, so I say "look at them, they are thin and they all have this figure", so I myself want to become like that, to become thin.' (p. 513).

Were the samples comparable? This may be a study limitation. The same girls were not in both samples so it is unknown if the 1998 sample had disordered eating before the arrival of television. The authors feel it was unlikely that these girls had disordered eating before 1995 because there was only one report of AN in Fiji before that time.

Research support: Sociocultural explanations: Facebook

The **aim of the correlation study** was to find out just what was it about **Facebook** (FB) use that increased the risk for disordered eating.

For the **procedures**, college women filled out online questionnaires measuring three behaviors thought to be correlated with disordered eating (Walker, et al., 2015).

1. Facebook intensity, defined as the amount of time spent on the site and the number of friends
2. Online physical comparison to others
3. "Fat talk," defined as negative comments about one's body

An example question was "The best way for a person to know if they are overweight or underweight is to compare their figure to the figure of others in Facebook photographs" (p. 159).

Results are next.

1. Online physical comparison and fat talk are positively correlated with disordered eating.
2. FB intensity is positively correlated with disordered eating only when the person also made many physical comparisons with others.

> **Drawing credible conclusions**
> Could it be that Facebook is a risk mainly for those with genetic risks discussed earlier in this chapter? Remember that genes can influence how one interacts with the environment. Not everyone who uses FB makes too many comparisons and engages in excessive fat talk.

The authors **conclude** that FB is a risk factor for disordered eating but in some cases, when there is no physical comparison, it can act as a buffer against loneliness. Loneliness is a risk factor for mental illness, so FB may also have a positive effect.

Chapter 27
Abnormal Psychology: Treatment of Disorders

Chapter Objectives

Students will:
1. Practice using thinking strategies related to synthesis and evaluation, with discuss, evaluate, and contrast demonstrated.
2. Discuss biological treatments for depression.
3. Evaluate biological treatments for depression.
4. Discuss psychological (cognitive) treatments for depression
5. Evaluate psychological (cognitive) treatments for depression
6. Contrast treatments for depression.
7. Discuss biological treatments for anorexia.
8. Evaluate biological treatments for anorexia.
9. Discuss psychological (cognitive) treatments for anorexia.
10. Evaluate psychological (cognitive) treatments for anorexia.
11. Discuss the role of culture in treatment and evaluate indigenous healing.
12. Discuss how researchers should assess the effectiveness of treatments.
***Again, chose 1 disorder, both disorders, or study both and prepare one for tests.

27.1: Introduction to depression treatments

Many biological and psychological (cognitive) treatments can help depression. It is important to remember that they *all affect neurotransmission and neural circuitry, so treatments end up with the same effects, even if treatment assumptions differ and the pathways to change vary*. Health care providers and patients must decide which approach is the "best fit" or if an **eclectic** approach, meaning a combination of treatments, is needed. Decisions about treatment depend on the situation of the patient as well as the bias of practitioners, which tends to relate to they way they were trained.

The prevalence of depression is increasing and everyone wants to find the best treatments. The most effective treatment is **prevention**, but depression will continue until sources of stress are identified and eliminated.

All the discussed treatments are effective, so selecting the best one depends on many factors that vary by person. Ensuring that everyone has access to treatment is necessary because untreated mental health problems affect all aspects of a person's life, including the ability to work and maintain stable family relationships.

Any source claiming that a particular treatment is best for everyone with a set of symptoms is guilty of *oversimplification*. Treatment choice depends on many factors, such as the severity of the symptoms, a person's culture, the cause of the problem if one can be identified, personal preferences, and the presence of other mental and/or physical health problems.

A cross-cultural list of depression treatments

Depression treatments include, but are not limited to the following.

Drug therapy, such as Prozac
Electroconvulsive therapy
Acupuncture
Herbal medicine, such as St. John's Wort
Diet change
Exercise
Family therapy
Transcranial Magnetic Stimulation
Cognitive therapy (CT)
Mindfulness-based cognitive therapy (MBCT)
Guided mastery therapy to raise self-efficacy
Faith healers and shaman

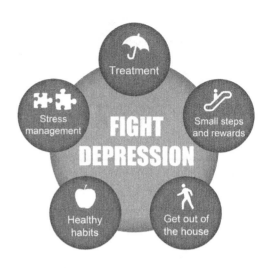

Treating the whole person is best.
Used under license from megapixl.com.

Treatments should have a high degree of **efficacy**, meaning they must be supported by evidence. For western researchers, there is a demand that this evidence comes from randomized controlled experimental evidence. The section about the role of culture and treatment gives a balanced view for deciding what counts as evidence and students must carefully consider if the western demand is appropriate.

Three biological treatments (Prozac, acupuncture, and exercise) and cognitive therapy are discussed and evaluated in this chapter as depression treatments with research support.

27.2: Discuss and evaluate biological treatments for depression: Drug therapy

Drug treatments: Prozac

Discuss means to give a considered and balanced view supported by evidence. Next is the theory and assumptions of drug treatments so students know what they are and why they work.

The main assumption of a Western psychiatric approach to treatment is that mental illnesses as diseases with drugs as a primary treatment. Drugs are assumed to "work" if symptoms are reduced, which is shown in experiments.

Western psychiatrists often prescribe **antidepressants** as the "first line of defense" against depression, though drugs are sometimes combined with other treatments. Many antidepressants are available and they all affect **neurotransmission** in some way. One type is the SSRIs, the selective serotonin reuptake inhibitors, such as **Prozac**.

A good place to start thinking about Prozac is with a case of someone taking it.

Film idea and evaluating ethics in abnormal psychology
Students sometimes have trouble understanding **risk versus benefit** when evaluating
treatments, an important ethical consideration. Avoid extremist views. One place to start
is with the film segment about depression from the PBS series "The Secret Life of the
Brain." Lauren Slater shares the first twelve years of her Prozac use. Lauren's
symptoms were severe. Did the benefits of taking the drug outweigh the risks? The film
sparks good discussion.

Studying any treatment should include a discussion about its risks versus its benefits.

Discuss biological drug treatments: The case of Lauren Slater

Clearly there are people who need drug therapy and benefit from it.

Consider Lauren Slater's case from the impressive PBS series called "The Secret Life of the Brain."
Although the show is older, it is still relevant for introducing students to Prozac's effects on the brain and
someone's experiences with the drug. Lauren Slater is featured in the depression segment. Lauren, author
of the book *The Prozac Diary*, talks candidly about managing severe depression and taking Prozac over
the twelve-year period the film covers. Her experiences might surprise you and elicit your empathy. Those
students who believed that drugs are a simple solution now understand differently and those who spoke
out against prescription drugs see that drugs can be helpful. Prozac helped Lauren, but as the drugs
reduced one set of problems, others emerged.

After five hospitalizations, Lauren started taking Prozac in 1988, the year Eli Lilly released it (Book
Clubs/Reading Guides, 2008). Lauren had an immediate positive benefit and her symptoms melted away
after just five days. Lauren was accepted into Harvard and she earned a doctorate in psychology. Lauren
married, had a child, and became a therapist.

Life is never simple. Lauren experienced what patients call **Prozac Poop-Out**. Poop-Outs mean that
the brain develops a *tolerance* to the drug and its effectiveness diminishes. This is one limitation of
antidepressant drugs, as about one-third of people taking Prozac experience tolerance problems after one
year of taking the drug (Harvard Magazine, 2000).

Along with tolerance, Lauren experienced other side effects of taking Prozac, such as a loss of
creativity (Book Club/Reading Guides, 2008). Over the first twelve years of taking Prozac, Lauren's
doctor raised her dosage from 10 milligrams each day to 80 milligrams, the top limit approved by the US
Food and Drug Administration (FDA). Sometimes Lauren's doctor switched her to other types of
antidepressant drugs when Prozac was not working at all and her symptoms returned.

Lauren raises ethical questions about her use of Prozac in *The Prozac Diary*, such as, "Am I really
myself on the drug?" and "Is taking the drug robbing me of important experiences?"

Lauren continued to take the drug because her symptoms were so bad. The doctor continued to
increase her dosage after the film to levels higher than recommended by the FDA. Lauren says she will
wait and see what happens. She embraces the reduction of depressive symptoms yet fears the potential
increases in side effects, cognitive damage, toxicity, or a time when Prozac does not work at all. Why did
Lauren continue to take Prozac? *Because the benefits outweighed the risks.*

Risk factors, benefits, and the way antidepressants work

Antidepressants have been around for a long time and decisions about taking them are complicated. They
are being used more often and we must consider why. However, any time someone uses these medications
they must consider that benefits must outweigh risks.

Risks of taking antidepressants

Risks	Description
Side effects	Check the side effects of Prozac at PubMedHealth. This is a particular concern given the discovery that drug companies have not published all data showing the full extent of their potential harm (Kwon, 2016). The report claims 70 studies about SSRIs and SNRIs found that the risk for suicidal thoughts and aggression doubled in young people taking the drugs. This information was not included in FDA reports but might make people more careful about using them except when the risk from symptoms is very high.
Tolerance to the drug, called Prozac poop-out	Tolerance means that the brain compensates for the drug's effect. Prozac prevents the reuptake of **serotonin**, making more available at synapses. The brain responds by creating more receptors.
We might not learn new behaviors	Drugs reduce symptoms, which is beneficial, but there is a risk that people do not learn new behaviors without taking action to learn new ways of managing stress.
Placebo effects may be great	Many reports suggest antidepressants may be as effective as **placebos**, plus there are other effective treatments.

Benefit of taking antidepressants

Benefit	Description
Symptom reduction	The primary benefit of taking Prozac is symptom reduction, which makes it possible for people to live more normal day-to-day lives, including working, caring for children, and lessening the risk of suicide (because the symptoms can be quickly reduced).

How do antidepressants work? Many are available, grouped according to how they affect **neurotransmission**. Newer antidepressants are not necessarily more effective than older drugs. Three examples follow.

1. Tricyclics, such as Elavil that prevent serotonin and norepinephrine reuptake
2. SSRIs, such as **Prozac** and Lexapro that prevent serotonin reuptake
3. SNRIs, such as Cymbalta that prevent serotonin and norepinephrine reuptake

Drugs cannot get approval from the Food and Drug Administration (FDA) unless they perform better than **placebos** in randomized placebo-controlled experiments. Some reports suggest that antidepressants lessen depressive symptoms by 65% compared with a 30% reduction with placebos (The Royal College of Psychiatrists, n.d.). Other researchers report that placebos work as well as antidepressants and are effective up to 47% of the time (Lambert, 2008).

Prozac is widely used and our example antidepressant. Many SSRI drugs are on the market and you might recognize some of the others, such as Paxil and Zoloft.

Depression

Healthy Synapse

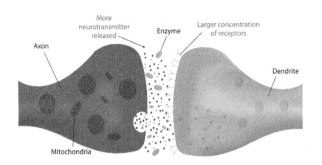

Synapse of a Depressed Person

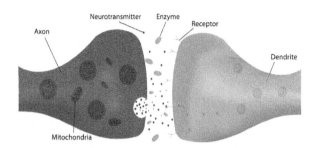

Less serotonin in synapses is a problem for people with depression.
Used with license from megapixl.com.

Prozac is approved for use for adolescents

The FDA approved Prozac in 1987. It is the only SSRI approved by the FDA for use in children 8 and older.

Prozac is used for many reasons, including a low risk for weight gain, mild withdrawal symptoms when someone decides to stop taking the drug, and a lower risk of suicide.

Using antidepressants with children is controversial so let's explore research from 2004 to 2009 investigating the effectiveness of Prozac, including comparisons with cognitive therapy. In addition, research shows that Prozac makes important neuroplastic brain changes in adolescents that account for its effectiveness.

Do not underestimate the risk of suicide in depressed persons. If suicide risk is high, then the fastest treatment is the best.

Evaluate biological treatments for depression: The TADS studies: Prozac and its combination with Cognitive Therapy for adolescents

Evaluate means to make a judgment using evidence. The claim that Prozac is effective is supported by research.

The Treatment for Adolescents with Depression Studies (**TADS**) shows how antidepressant research progresses over time. Each study builds on previous findings. The US National Institute of Health (NIH) funded TADS and aimed to study short- and long-term effects of antidepressants and cognitive therapy alone and in combination for depressed teenagers (NIH, 2012). The studies took place between 2004 and 2009.

TADS study	Aim, IVs, basic procedures, and results
TADS I: Experiment	**TADS I aimed to study** treatments that worked best over a short-term 12 week time period. Participants were randomly assigned to get Prozac alone, cognitive therapy alone, combined cognitive therapy and Prozac, or a placebo (the **independent variable**) (TADS Team, 2004). Depressive symptoms were rated using the Children's Depression Rating Scale. **Results** follow. 1. The combination Prozac and cognitive therapy groups improved more than the placebo group. 2. Combined Prozac and cognitive therapy was better than either treatment alone. 3. Prozac alone was better than cognitive therapy alone. The team **concluded** that combined Prozac and cognitive therapy was the best short-term treatment for adolescent depression. One reason to favor combination treatments is that cognitive therapy helps teenagers learn new ways to manage stress.
TADS II: Experiment	**TADS II aimed to study** longer-term treatment effectiveness and safety over thirty-six weeks (TADS Team, 2007). TADS II used 327 adolescents between the ages of with moderate to severe depression. TADS II used the same conditions as the 2004 research. The placebo group was ended at twelve weeks because researchers could already see its effects. **Results** follow. 1. After twelve weeks, 73% responded positively to combination therapy, 62% to Prozac, and 48% to cognitive therapy. 2. After eighteen weeks, 85% responded positively to combination therapy, 69% to Prozac, and 65% to cognitive therapy. 3. After thirty-six weeks, 86% responded positively to combination therapy, 81% to Prozac, and 81% to cognitive therapy. The fastest response was the combination treatment but the groups responded about the same at the end of thirty-six weeks. The authors **concluded** that taking Prozac or combining it with cognitive therapy gave the fastest response. It took longer for cognitive therapy to work and the authors were concerned that *the risks associated with depression, such as suicide, must be treated quickly.* This is a genuine concern and is one benefit that might outweigh the risks associated with taking the drug.

TADS study	Aim, IVs, basic procedures, and results
TADS III: Naturalistic study using questionnaires for a long-term follow-up	Do the effects of Prozac, cognitive therapy, and their combination last over the long-term? The **aim of TADS III** was to examine effectiveness over a one-year follow-up (TADS Team, 2009). TADS III is not an experiment. Testing treatments over long periods of time are difficult because confounding variables, such as getting a new job, interfere with the study conditions. The follow-up study used the Children's Depression Rating Scale to see how the participants in the 2007 TADS II study were doing after one year. **Results** follow. 1. Participants receiving combined Prozac and cognitive therapy had the fastest recovery and the recovery continued over the one-year follow-up. 2. Long-term treatment is better than short-term treatment. Long-term treatment lessens relapse. 3. Adolescents receiving cognitive therapy along with Prozac reported fewer suicide thoughts. In **conclusion**, Prozac can be an effective treatment for depression in adolescents.

Neuroplasticity research: Prozac normalizes the brain

We studied the Tao et al. (2012) experiment in chapter 5 about neuroplasticity. This is a chance to apply the concept neuroplasticity to studying Prozac.

27.3 Discuss and evaluate biological treatments for depression: Acupuncture

Discuss means to give a considered and balanced view supported by evidence. This discussion includes a consideration of Traditional Chinese Medicine. Evaluate means to make a judgment using evidence. A growing body of research shows that acupuncture is effective in relieving depression.

Acupuncture uses hair-thin needles and it is very relaxing, even if this picture makes you think otherwise! Stay open-minded.
Used with license from megapixl.com.

How does acupuncture work?

Acupuncture, part of **Traditional Chinese Medicine (TCM)**, works differently than drug treatments.

Chinese doctors consider the entire person, both physically and psychologically. Chinese doctors ask questions about things that seem unrelated to a person's complaint, such as diet and exercise. Chinese doctors look for patterns of disharmony in the entire system of a

354

person that show general imbalances (Kaptchuk, 1983). *Finding relationships is far more important than determining cause and effect in TCM.* The pattern of disharmony might be maintained by one fundamental problem that seems unrelated to the symptom. For example, food allergies might play a fundamental role in maintaining a number of interrelated symptoms, including depressed mood.

Chinese medicine views a person's physiology as a series of **meridians**. Meridians are bioelectrical impulses, similar to an electrical system, to put it in western terms. "Meridians are the channels or pathways that carry Qi and Blood through the body" (Kaptchuk, 1983, p. 77). **Qi** (Chi) means "energy," the life force (Hammer, 2005). Energy passes through twelve meridians that keep one's physical system in balance (Kaptchuk, 1983). Blood that flows through the meridians is not real blood but "an invisible network that links together all of the fundamental substances and organs" (p. 77). *Meridians connect this interior flow of Qi and Blood with the outer body. This is why acupuncture works.* **Acupuncture**, **Tai Chi**, and **herbal medicines** unblock stagnated Qi and blood flow and restore balance. Acupuncture points on the exterior body are places along meridians where needles are inserted to stimulate Qi and Blood flow within the interior system and unblock stagnations. Tai Chi practice cultivates Qi within the body. Tai Chi practice does this by facilitating a calm strength in the body through the coordination of hands, feet, head, and breathing. Tai Chi improves circulation, balance, and flexibility. It relaxes and strengthens the nervous system and relieves many medical problems such as hypertension, allergies, arthritis, diabetes, **depression**, aggressive feelings, and anxiety.

The goal of Chinese medicine is to create harmony and reestablish balance within the meridians. *Western medicine has no concept similar to Qi* (Hammer, 2005).

The aim of TCM is to reestablish harmony, a holistic concept not easily demonstrated in experiments. However, in the experiments demanded by western science to show caution, acupuncture is judged effective when symptoms are reduced. It is fine to see acupuncture studied in an experiment as long as you remember that treating the person in a real clinical setting is done more holistically than the experiments imply.

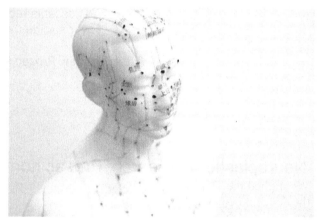

This model shows the location of some meridians and acupuncture points.
Source: pixabay.com.

Evaluate acupuncture research

Evaluate means to make a judgment using evidence. Evidence shows that acupuncture is effective for treating depression and has no side effects, an ethical consideration for selecting a treatment. Modern acupuncture experiments are also better designed than they were in the past, so look for important features of a well controlled experiment as you read.

Acupuncture affects physiology in many ways, such as releasing **neurotransmitters** and reducing pain (Nahas & Sheikh, 2011). Poorly designed studies plagued early acupuncture research. Some studies did not use control groups. In addition, **placebos**, or **sham acupuncture**, have a physical effect that complicates testing the use of real acupuncture points. Previous studies using placebo acupuncture often confused the physiological response from the placebo with the treatment response because the placebo needles were inserted too close to the real acupuncture needles.

New experiments fix the problems and show that both **laser acupuncture** and **electroacupuncture** are effective. Laser acupuncture does not use needles. Instead, a laser device that looks like a pen stimulates acupuncture points. Electroacupuncture uses needles inserted at desired acupuncture points that are attached to a device providing a small and continuous electrical current to all the needles.

Acupuncture does not hurt, contrary to first impressions of people new to TCM. Needles are hair thin and not at all like the needles used for flu shots or sewing. Patients often cannot feel the needles. Laser acupuncture does not use needles and is a good choice for studying placebo effects because the person does not feel any stimulation. Instead, the patient just knows the laser pen is pressing the point but may not get any stimulation in the placebo condition. The electrical current used in electroacupuncture is not a shock. Its purpose is to provide consistent stimulation to acupuncture points. Acupuncture is very relaxing.

Research support: Two acupuncture experiments

Side effects are one reason people stop taking antidepressants, so alternatives that act like antidepressants but do not have the side effects are useful. The **aim of one experiment** was to see brain changes during **laser acupuncture** or a placebo condition using fMRI (Quah-Smith, et al., 2012). The authors predicted that laser acupuncture would cause the same brain changes as antidepressants.

For **procedures**, ten depressed participants received both laser acupuncture and placebo acupuncture (the **independent variable**) while the fMRI watched the brain.

Results showed that laser acupuncture was more effective than a placebo and has the following effects on the brain.

1. Laser acupuncture makes brain regions active similar to the brain activation that occurs after taking antidepressants, such as switching on the medial frontal gyrus that is often deactivated in people with depression.
2. Laser acupuncture creates quiet time in the brain, referred to as **"yoga time for the brain,"** by modifying the resting state activity, or what the brain does when not performing a task. The brain still works in a resting state and acupuncture makes the down time meditative.
3. Laser acupuncture adjusts **cerebellum** activity, which is associated with mood regulation and emotion perception.

Imagine your brain doing yoga while getting acupuncture, getting the rest and relaxation it needs. Try yoga for **CAS** and get all its health benefits.
Used with license from megapixl.com

Ten participants is a small sample, but the data is high quality and part of a growing body of research showing that acupuncture is more effective than placebos in treating depression.

The second experiment **aimed to see** if **electroacupuncture** combined with **Prozac** made the drug work faster (Zhang, et al., 2012). Antidepressants are often ineffective when used alone, so it is important to search for combinations of treatments that include natural remedies without side effects.

For **procedures**, seventy-three patients with major depression were randomly assigned to receive a combination of electroacupuncture/Prozac or placebo acupuncture/ Prozac (the **independent variable**). The electroacupuncture group received treatment to acupuncture points in the forehead.

Results showed that participants receiving electroacupuncture in combination with Prozac had significantly faster improvement than participants in the placebo/Prozac condition. Electroacupuncture appears to enhance Prozac's results.

27.4: Discuss and evaluate biological treatments for depression: Exercise

Discuss means to give a considered and balanced view supported with evidence. This discussion gives a consideration of why exercise works. Evaluate means to make a judgment using evidence. A body of research shows that exercise is an effective depression treatment.

Why does exercise reduce depression?

The reasons why **exercise** as a depression treatment are different from both drug therapies and acupuncture.

Exercise is effective because it alters the brain and many of the changes are similar to brain changes after taking drugs (Nahas & Sheikh, 2011). Exercise releases **neurotransmitters** such as **serotonin**, promotes growth in the **hippocampus**, and lowers **cortisol**, an important human stress hormone. **Endorphins** are released, which are related to enhanced mood and well-being (Craft & Perna, 2004). In addition, exercise provides social connections and helps people feel in control of their health and raises **self-efficacy** (Nahas & Sheikh, 2011; Craft & Perma, 2004). Some doctors hesitate to prescribe exercise because of low patient motivation, but it is recommended as a first line of defense for all patients if doctors provide a structured exercise routine and check on progress with counseling (Nahas & Sheikh, 2011).

Research with mice suggest that exercise increases resilience to stress, thus reducing the risk of depression (Agudelo, et al., 2014). If exercised, skeletal muscles increase production of a protein that reduces kyrurenine. Kyrurenine rises during stress and creates inflammation in the brain that increases the risk of depression. This research is on mice and needs to be studied in humans, but you can see that good reasons for exercising are mounting.

Research support: Exercise is just as effective as drugs

Evaluate means to make a judgment using evidence. Research since 1981 supports the conclusion that exercise is effective (Harvard Medical School, 2009).

The **aim of the experiment** was to show that exercise was just as effective as drug treatments (Babyak et al., 2000).

Researchers recruited participants interested in exercise. All met the DSM-IV requirements for major depression.

For **procedures**, participants were randomly assigned to one of three groups, the **independent variable**. The first group received three aerobic exercise sessions each week for sixteen weeks. The second group took Zoloft, an SSRI. The third group took both the exercise program and Zoloft.

Cycling is a great aerobic sport and it is well known that exercise relieves low mood. The January/February 2017 Scientific American Mind magazine has a new article on depression and exercise that strengthens these study results. This magazine is worth getting. Source: pixabay.com.

Depression symptoms were measured at the start of treatment, at the end of the sixteen-week period, and six months after the end of the experiment, for a total of ten months.

Results showed that all three groups showed similar remission rates at the end of the sixteen week period, 60.4% for the exercise group, 65.5% for the medication group, and 68.8% for the combined group. The most interesting results were those after six months. After the full ten-month period, those who exercised reported lower depression rates than those taking medication, even participants taking medication along with an aerobic program.

Research support: Exercise helps maintain depression treatment

Exercise helps people maintain positive treatment progress over time.

The **aim of this correlation study** was to find out if continued Zoloft use or an exercise program was most effective in maintaining treatment progress (Hoffman, et al., 2011) They used participants from an earlier experiment where they were randomly assigned to receive Zoloft, supervised aerobic exercise, home-based exercise, or a drug placebo. The exercise groups performed as well as the Zoloft group, and 44% of both groups showed significant decreases in depressive symptoms. Participants were free to choose any treatment they wished during a one-year follow-up period.

In the **procedures** for this study, self-reports about exercise routines and continued drug use were collected and correlated with the treatment choice and depressive symptoms after one year. Some participants selected just exercise or a combination of exercise and Zoloft.

Results showed that 66% of participants showed fewer depressive symptoms after one year and it was correlated only to exercise.

The authors **conclude** that continued exercise after initial treatment extends the benefits of primary exercise programs and build on the benefits of taking Zoloft.

27.5: Discuss and evaluate psychological treatments for depression: Cognitive therapy (CT)

Discuss means to give a considered and balanced view supported by evidence. This discussion includes a consideration of what cognitive therapy is and how it works. Evaluate means to make a judgment using evidence. Cognitive therapy is shown to be a highly effective treatment, even for severe cases of depression. Look for the high degree of control in these experiments, including controlled samples and procedures, and consider what must be done to ethically use a placebo control group.

Why is cognitive therapy so effective?

The long-term aim of cognitive therapy is to restructure thinking styles. Cognitive therapists hope for long-term internalization of new behaviors, so reaching the long-term goal may take a longer period of therapy than is measured in most treatment outcome experiments.

Cognitive therapy works even with severe depression cases.
Used with license from megapixel.com.

The **Generic Cognitive Model** (GCM) explained in chapter 26 proposes that maladaptive information processing is the reason for depression, and that modes of thinking organize the destructive thinking behind different disorders (Beck & Haight, 2014).

*Cognitive therapy attempts to bring negative automatic thoughts used with each **mode** to conscious awareness.* Remember from the last chapter that the depressive mode of thinking is related to self-expansion. Applying the GCM involves interacting parts that are **schema** activated.

1. A situation
2. A biased focus
3. A belief
4. A situation
5. The resulting behavior (depression in this case)

Therapists now have a useful tool because each part of the model offers chances for intervention. Even focusing therapy on one part of this model can reduce symptoms. Therapists challenge biased thoughts and help people set reasonable goals.

A large body of research shows that CT is beneficial for persons with depression and is relevant cross-culturally. CT is the most studied psychotherapy and is frequently compared to drug treatments or combined with them.

As you learned in the last chapter, people with depressive schemas have faulty top-down processing and too much subcortical, bottom-up processing. Increasing the skills to use top-down processing is important in making long-term changes to the thinking that keeps someone in the cycle of depressive thoughts. Any part of the model can be a target for increasing top-down processing.

Research support: Cognitive Therapy is effective for severe cases

Evaluate means to make a judgment using evidence. Research supports the conclusion that CT is effective even for severely depressed persons.

Cognitive therapy (CT) is well studied, particularly for people with mild and moderate symptoms. The **aim of the experiment** was to show that cognitive therapy was as effective as an antidepressant for people with severe symptoms (DeRubeis, et al., 2005).

For the **procedures**, participants with depression were randomly assigned to one of three groups, the **independent variable**. Groups received Paxil, a drug placebo, or CT. Treatment lasted for sixteen weeks for the Paxil and CT groups, but for ethical reasons, placebo treatment ended after eight weeks, long enough to see differences between it and Paxil.

> **Excellent film!**
> See **Aaron Beck** use cognitive therapy the way it was meant to be delivered to clients. This is a film from 1977 but Marcia's problems are the same things people complain about today. The value of this film is it clearly highlights the therapist skills that facilitate change.
>
> The film is available from Insight Media on DVD, called a demonstration of cognitive therapy.

The experiment took place at two sites, Vanderbilt University and the University of Pennsylvania.

Data on symptom reduction were gathered at the end of eight weeks for all three groups and then at sixteen weeks for CT and Paxil. **Results** showed that at the end of eight weeks, 50% of the Paxil group, 43% of the CT group, and 25% of the placebo group showed positive symptom reduction. At the end of sixteen weeks, there was no overall significant difference between the Paxil and CT groups but only when looking at data from Pennsylvania.

The authors **conclude** that both moderate and severe cases respond better to drugs and CT than a placebo. The different findings from the Vanderbilt and Pennsylvania sites were probably related to therapist skill. Future research must ensure that all therapists are well trained.

These results do not support American Psychological Association and National Institute of Mental Health (NIMH) recommendations that severely depressed patients automatically need drug treatments (DeRubeis, et al., 2005). The authors believe that when administered by a qualified therapist, CT is just as effective as drugs for severely depressed patients.

Research support: CT is best for certain kinds of symptoms

Modern research clarifies *when to use a treatment*. The **aim of one experiment** was to show that cognitive therapy and antidepressants helped patients in different ways (Fournier, et al., 2013)? Both cognitive therapy and antidepressants can be effective, and now health professionals can match patients with the best treatment.

For the **procedures**, participants with depression were randomly assigned to one of three groups, cognitive therapy, Paxil, or a placebo, the **independent variable**. Comparisons were made within each group to see if the assigned treatment was best based on the following symptom clusters.

1. Anxiety

2. Mood
3. Cognition/suicide
4. Vegetative-atypical
5. Typical-vegetative

Don't get overwhelmed by the psychiatric language. Vegetative symptoms are related to sleeping, eating, weight loss, and experiencing pleasure. Atypical does not mean unusual. Atypical symptoms start early in life, having constant symptoms, over sleeping, and hypersensitivity to interpersonal rejection.
Results follow.

1. Paxil made a faster change in cognitive or suicide symptoms compared to a placebo at four weeks. Both Paxil and CT were effective after eight weeks.
2. Cognitive therapy made a faster change in atypical-vegetative symptoms compared to a placebo.

Drugs and cognitive therapy have different general pathways to help patients and *the future of treatments involves matching patients to the best ones for them*. Drugs and cognitive therapy did not reduce symptoms better than the placebo for the other three clusters.
The authors **concluded** that patients might get treatments tailored to their symptoms in the future.

27.6 Contrast treatments for depression

Contrast means to identify what is different about two or more things. Any essay contrasting treatments should be organized around the points, looking at each separately and making reference to each treatment under each point. Treatments should not be listed separately.

The treatments have more similarities than you might think. They are all effective and are tested the same way in randomized experiments. However, this section focuses on the differences.

	Drug treatments: Biological	Acupuncture: Biological	Exercise: Biological	Cognitive Therapy
Amount of time it takes to reduce symptoms or make other changes in the person	Drugs may work the fastest, after 12 weeks (see TADS studies) but works even faster combined with cognitive therapy or acupuncture.	Acupuncture can work quickly (open Chi flow) but is rarely tested against drug treatments so it is hard to know if it is comparable. Acupuncture combined with drugs can make them work faster and patients can take less of the drug.	Patients show improvement after 16 weeks similar to patients taking Zoloft (Babyak, 2000). Exercise can work as fast as drugs but after 10 months may be a better treatment for maintaining results.	CT takes longer to work (see TADS studies) but is just as effective as drugs after 36 weeks. CT combined with drugs works the fastest. CT can reduce symptoms fairly quickly but there is a longer term goal to change maladaptive thinking. CT can work even on severe cases (DeRubeis, 2005).

	Drug treatments: Biological	Acupuncture: Biological	Exercise: Biological	Cognitive Therapy
Mechanisms making the treatment work	Drugs are a bottom-up approach to targeting brain regions starting with limbic and subcortical regions then moving up to the prefrontal cortex (Goldapple et al., 2004). One effect is increased serotonin at synapses.	Acupuncture unblocks stagnated chi flow to restore balance. Acupuncture needles are inserted into points where meridians come to the surface of the skin. In western terms, one change is increased endorphins and neurotransmitters, similar to the other treatments. The mechanism is different.	Exercise releases neurotransmitters such as serotonin, lowers cortisol, releases endorphins, and promotes hippocampus growth. Note that a similar end effect of increased serotonin occurs but the mechanism promoting change differs from other treatments.	CT is a top-down approach to targeting brain regions starting with brain cortexes and working its way down to the limbic system (Goldapple et al., 2004). It has the same end effect as drugs. Serotonin is also increased at synapses. It may be the same end effect as other treatments but the mechanism differs.
Side effects	Drugs have the worst side effects, including warnings of increased suicidal thoughts. Drug poop-outs are a problem.	No side effects	Exercise has no side effects but the person could get injured. A clear plan should be made and monitored.	No side effects
Ethics of use	If the person's case is severe drugs may be the best choice, especially if the patient is suicidal. The most severe cases may respond fastest to combination therapies, such as with CT or acupuncture. Drugs have side effects and can be harmful so their use must not be taken lightly.	Highly ethical, often less expensive, and culturally relevant for many people. Combining acupuncture with drugs can lessen the risk of drug side effects.	Ethical if the patient is motivated. The physician can provide structure and monitor exercise to increase the chances it is used. Exercise raises someone's self-efficacy, and this may positively influence other aspects of their lives.	Highly ethical because the patient learns new thinking skills and behaviors to manage depressive schemas.

27.7: Discuss and evaluate biological treatments for anorexia

Discuss means to give a considered and balanced view supported by evidence. For a balanced view of anorexia nervosa (AN) treatments, it is important to review more than one. Cognitive therapy and family therapy are probably the best treatments, but a balanced view includes a discussion of **drug therapy** for **anorexia** so students can judge a range of treatments. *Drug therapy for AN is not well supported*, though it is still used. The reasons drug therapies are used and an evaluation, a judgment using evidence, is next.

Clinicians struggling to treat AN are faced with two barriers to getting patients to change their behavior (Steinglass, Mayer, & Attia, 2016).

> **Evaluate ethics in abnormal psychology**
> Is it ethical to prescribe a treatment where the benefit does not outweigh the risk? Consider the evidence presented in this section.

1. No treatment has been shown effective for every AN patient, making it hard for clinicians to know where to start outside of medical stabilization.
2. AN patients are reluctant to get help.

Some AN patients are at such a low weight that they are at great risk of death, and these people may need a hospital-based inpatient treatment first. All AN patients need nutritional plans that include supervision to make sure they eat and education about food (Steinglass, et al., 2016).

After stabilizing and starting a nutritional plan, what should a clinician do? Some try drug therapy, and this could be in part because of **biases** that come from what people are taught in schools.

There are not many experiments testing drug treatment for AN, and as a result, clinicians wanting to use medical management rely on the fact that AN patients tend to also have depressed and anxious symptoms related to disorders that often are treated with drugs (Steinglass, et al., 2016). Case studies showed that drugs might be helpful, but when tested against placebos in experiments, the results were disappointing. Even meta-analysis studies, where a body of research is scrutinized for treatment outcomes, showed drugs are not all that helpful.

Unfortunately, drug therapy is used anyway, increasing the risk for patients that they are not getting the best treatment and since drugs have side effects, might suffer complications. This is an ethical concern that should not be taken lightly as students evaluate drug therapies for AN.

How about antidepressants?

Many AN patients have depressive symptoms and some antidepressants have weight gain as a side effect (Steinglass, et al., 2016). Armed with this information, clinicians sometimes prescribe antidepressants.

Research shows antidepressants are not effective (Steinglass, et al., 2016). For example, The **aim of one experiment** was to compare Prozac with a placebo to treat AN, the **independent variable. Results** showed that AN patients gained some weight, but the Prozac group did no better than the placebo group. Might Prozac work better for AN patients after they finished their nutritional plan and had already gained weight? Results were also disappointing after following these patients for 1 year, and again, the Prozac group did no better than the placebo group.

How about antipsychotic drugs?

The idea behind using an antipsychotic drug comes (Steinglass, et al., 2016).

Few studies have been conducted, but for adults, olanzapine may be helpful in relieving the obsessions. Weight gain is a side effect of taking the drug, so it might have some benefit for the patient.

More research needs to be done though, and considering drug side effects, olanzapine needs more support. Olanzapine has not been shown effective for adolescents.

A better choice?

Psychological treatments such as cognitive therapy and family therapy have research support, so perhaps it is better to start with one of them after medical stabilization and along with a nutritional plan.

Students should understand that both cognitive and family therapy are effective, so the choice is made based on which treatment is the best fit.

27.8: Discuss and evaluate psychological treatments for anorexia: Cognitive therapy

Discuss means to give a considered and balanced view supported by evidence. Next is a considered view of **Cognitive Therapy** (CT) for **anorexia** and an evaluation of the research supporting it. Evaluation means to make a judgment using evidence. The body of research shows that CT is effective for AN in both adults and adolescents (Steinglass, et al., 2016). Just remember that family therapy is also effective, so if CT is the patient's choice, then it should be used.

Cognitive therapy for AN: This is how it works

Anorexia is hard to treat because patients strongly resist it and there are so many medical complications (Dalle Grave, El Ghoch, Sartirana, & Calugi, 2016). Cognitive therapy has been adapted for the specific needs of AN patients, called CBT-E, meaning Cognitive Behavioral Therapy Enhanced.

AN behavior is hard to change because it is sustained by "overvalued ideas about the personal implications of body shape and weight" (Dalle Grave, et al., 2016, p. 2). Beck's **Generic Cognitive Model** describes the eating disorder thinking **mode** as a group of thoughts related to self-worth, such as "I am not a likable person" and "I am dull." (Beck & Haight, 2014, p. 14). The self-worth mode maintains the overvalued ideas about body shape and weight and is the target of therapy.

CBT-E starts with the therapist and patient partnering to identify a personal formulation, which means identifying all the thoughts standing in the way of behavior change (Dalle Grave, et al., 2016). Behavior changes as the patient practices self-monitoring of maladaptive thoughts as "homework." Patients go through three steps in CBT-E.

1. Realizing they need to change their behavior
2. Applying self-monitoring strategies to reduce maladaptive thoughts
3. Maintaining a healthy weight

> **What is a thinking mode?**
> A mode is a group of thoughts central to creating and maintaining a mental disorder. Each disorder has a mode, or way of thinking. Beck's theory is detailed in chapter 26 with the cognitive theory of depression.

Research support: Cognitive therapy is effective for anorexia

A body of research supports a positive evaluation of CBT-E for anorexia. Some of this research is experimental and others are case studies following the progress of patients getting CBT-E. Two examples follow.

The **aim of one experiment** was to see if CBT-E was effective compared to other treatments (Dalle Grave et al., 2016). AN patients were randomly assigned to one of three treatments, CBT-E, treatment as usual where patients went to the doctor of their choice for ongoing care, or non-cognitive therapy combined with hospitalization, the **independent variable**. **Results** showed that all three treatments were equally effective, so patients have the choice of getting CBT-E if it is a good fit.

Another is a case study of AN patients with severe cases getting inpatient CBT-E and the **aim of the study** was to describe 27 AN patients and their CT treatment (Dalle Grave et al., 2016). **Results** showed that all participants finished the treatment and maintained their weight gain even after 12 months.

It is concluded that CBT-E is effective, with about 60 percent of adolescent and 40 percent of adult patients achieving and maintaining weight goals.

You may think that these are fairly low percentages, but remember that it is hard to get AN patients to admit they need to gain weight and change thinking patterns. No treatment for any disorder is 100 percent effective.

27.9: Discuss and evaluate psychological treatments for anorexia: Family therapy

Discuss means to give a considered and balanced view supported by evidence. Next is a considered view of the **Maudsley Family Therapy** approach to treating **anorexia** and an evaluation of the research supporting it. Evaluate means to make a judgment using evidence. A body of research shows the Maudsley approach is effective, and since it is just as effective as cognitive therapy, people wanting family treatment can choose it as the best fit (Steinglass, et al., 2016). This section also includes a case study showing how structural family therapy can be applied cross-culturally.

What is Maudsley Family therapy?

Parents play an active role in the Maudsley approach where they take control of their child's eating behavior, gradually give this control back to the child, and encourage normal development and eating behavior (Le Grange & Lock, n.d.). The hope is to prevent hospitalization and make changes to eating behavior within the normal home environment of the child. Many may think that family approaches blame parents for their child's eating disorder but this is not true of Maudsley. Parents are seen as resources helping to create positive change.

Maudsley family therapy has three phases taking a year to complete.

Phase	Description
Restoring weight	With the help of therapists, parents take control over their child's eating, with the therapist observing parent and child interactions during feeding times and offering help.
Returning control over eating to the patient	The patient has now shown an acceptance of parental rules about eating more food and gaining weight and is ready to self-manage, respecting the demand to eat properly and keep a good weight.
Creating a new healthy identity	This phase starts when the patient maintains at least 95% of their normal weight. Therapy focuses on encouraging a normal adolescent identity and more personal autonomy.

Research support for the Maudsley family therapy for anorexia

Plenty of evidence supports the Maudsley approach (Steinglass, et al., 2016).

The **aim of one experiment** was to evaluate the effectiveness of Maudsley therapy with general medical care. Participants were randomly assigned participants to receive Maudsley family therapy or to a general clinical management condition where the patient is supported by a dietitian and other care providers, the **independent variable** (Schmidt, et al., 2015).

Results showed that both treatments worked and patients gained weight and reported less distress after one year.

The **aim of another experiment** was to compare Maudsley therapy with a second type of family therapy (Agras, et al., 2014). Participants were randomly assigned patients to either Maudsley family therapy or a different kind of family treatment called systemic family therapy, the **independent variable**.

Results showed that both groups gained weight over the 9 months, though participants in the Maudsley condition gained it faster and has significantly fewer days spent in a hospital. The authors **concluded** that the Maudsley approach was the best choice of these two treatments for adolescents.

Case studies show how family therapy works for AN patients and shows cross-cultural application

Students should have a chance to see how qualitative research adds richness to our understanding of someone's experience with therapy. **Case studies** show something controlled experiments cannot— the meaningful experiences of someone while in therapy. On their own we must watch over-interpreting case studies because they do not show causation. But this is in addition to a body of experimental research and together, they have **method triangulation**. This case study also shows that family therapy can be applied successfully across culture, something important for good critical thinking.

This study is not about the Maudsley program, but gives us insight into how powerful family therapy is, and structural family therapy is also well studied and supported.

Ma (2008) studied parent-child conflicts between young people with eating disorders and their parents living in Shenzhen, China. The goal was to analyze the meanings of the conflicts within the sociocultural context of living in Shenzhen. This case shows the importance of understanding a person's culture.

Drug treatment for eating disorders is not very effective, especially if it is the only treatment used. Family therapy is more effective than individual therapy, so this was explored.

Ma created a family therapy treatment based on Salvadore Minuchin's **structural family therapy**. Structural family therapists make changes in the way a family manages stressors by rearranging the boundaries between family members. Sometimes dysfunctional families are too enmeshed, meaning emotionally entangled, and they focus too much on the behavioral problem of the patient instead of ways to resolve

Family therapy can be applied cross-culturally, and can defuse the power struggles between mothers and daughters without damaging cultural values, including how to involve the father. We cannot see the process in an experiment that just shows symptoms are reduced at the end of the study.
Source: pixabay.com

it. Ma's goal was to shift the family focus away from the child's destructive behavior and reframe conflicts that maintained the disordered eating behavior. Reframing means to give people a different perspective on a problem. Ma used *culturally relevant ways to resolve conflict to ensure that the therapy was meaningful to the participating families.*

There are many studies investigating eating disorder treatments in China, but the recommended treatments are fairly ineffective. Some Chinese mental health practitioners think that hospitalization is the best solution. Ma believed that parent-child conflict, particularly the mother-daughter relationship, was a main contributor. It is not helpful to blame the mother for causing her child's eating disorder. Rather, the mother-child interaction is reciprocal, meaning that it is a give-and-take process. It is a vicious cycle where the mother's behavior intensifies the child's behavior and the daughter's behavior also intensifies the mother's reactions.

China has experienced rapid economic growth since the 1980s and one result is that people have more access to Western media, which comes from individualistic countries. As a consequence, intergenerational conflict is rising. The parents grew up in a highly collectivist and conforming China while young people embrace more western standards for beauty (such as slimness). The highest rates of eating disorders in Chinese people are in Hong Kong. Shenzhen has the next highest rate and is an example of a region rapidly transforming from rural farming into a city. Shenzhen does retains most features of traditional Chinese family culture where the family is dominated by the father's wishes. Hunan is still rural and has the lowest rates of eating disorders. Shenzhen was a good place to conduct the study because it was in transition.

This case study used a **multiple case studies design**. The design has **data triangulation** because many cases were used for the data collection. The use of multiple cases also gives the study **analytical generalization** because replicating the findings of each individual case supports the same theory.

Ten families seeking family therapy at a Shenzhen clinic were in the sample. The families were of different ages, from different regions of China, and from different socioeconomic groups, although they were primarily middle and upper socioeconomic families. Ma used an **opportunity sample** made up of families that gave consent for videotaping and had attended at least three previous family therapy sessions.

All treatment sessions lasted about 90 minutes and were transcribed using **verbatim transcription** into Chinese and then into English.

Inductive content analysis (IPA) was used to identify **categories** of parent-child conflicts. The conflicts were originally **coded** into general groups and then major categories representing important **themes** were extracted. Here is how the coding worked. First, Ma (2008) and her research team read through the transcripts and "marked off units that were related to the same thing (e.g. parent-child conflicts), and then divided them into topics (e.g., mother-child conflicts, father-child conflicts) and subtopics (e.g. mother-daughter conflicts in the lunch room, father-son conflicts in the lunch room)..." (p. 805). By the end of data analysis, all the similarities and differences among parent-child interactions were analyzed, and any disagreements were open for discussion until the research team agreed on the final categories.

Three categories emerged.
1. Control issues and power struggles between parents and children.
2. Children's psychological development was growing more slowly than their physical development.
3. The desire of the children to pursue their own life goals within a rapidly developing economic society that was often in contrast to traditional Chinese cultural values.

These Chinese parents had problems with managing their children's disordered eating that were similar to the problems of Western parents. These similarities were seen particularly in the parent-child interactions in the lunchroom. For example, the therapist encouraged Mrs. M. to get her daughter to eat a little food. Patient M responded with screams that she would follow her mother's directions only at home, not in the clinic. The mother then retreated and asked the therapist to hospitalize her daughter. Then the therapist encouraged Mr. M. to try. The father was more patient and slowly was able to get patient M to eat a little food. It is typical for a child with an eating disorder to have a more antagonistic relationship with one parent than the other. Power struggles are typically more intense between mothers and daughters. To defuse and reframe the parent-child interaction, the therapist creates a small struggle between the parents and children in the lunchroom and then empathizes with the pain everyone feels. Then the therapist can help the patient understand the importance of getting assistance from both parents, who are also learning new coping skills. Both parents and children end up viewing each other through a new lens. Parent blaming is avoided, and underlying issues, such as seeking independence, are reframed as developmental issues. The family is no longer focused on the eating behaviors.

27.10: The role of culture in treatment

Discuss means to give a considered and balanced review supported by evidence. Three examples for consideration follow.

1. The use of western treatments with ethnic groups living in western cultures
2. Learning about and respecting **Indigenous Psychology** (IP) healing practices, including a consideration of how research shows treatment effectiveness
3. The effect of exporting western treatments to other cultures.

Failing to take culture into account can have huge consequences for others. Even if mental illness is **universal**, the way in which groups of symptoms are "confronted, discussed, and managed varies among social worlds, and cultural meanings and practices shape its course" (Kleinman, 2004, p. 1). We must be educated about how culture affects treatment to avoid the ethnocentric practice of automatically applying western treatments without considering if they are culturally relevant for others. We must also consider if some people might best be served with indigenous healing.

There is no one set of guidelines to apply but we can come up with a general list of ideas to think about in a discussion about the role of culture in treatment and then get some examples out on the table.

Culture and treatments: Basic principles: Keep these in mind as we go through our three examples

1. Western clinicians may need to consult with family members and local healers to recognize symptoms (Paniagua, 2013).
2. **Clinical biases** need to be examined so they do not affect treating people from a range of cultures (Paniagua, 2013).
3. Culturally acceptable questions to ask must be explored (Paniagua, 2013). For example, we learned about susto in the section about normality and abnormality. The question "Do you really think susto can explain what is going on with your daughter" (Paniagua, 2013, p. 42) will not work well with a Hispanic family thinking susto is the problem.

> **Ethics in abnormal psychology**
> Just as misdiagnosis, under-diagnosis, and over-diagnosis are ethical issues related to diagnosis, so is *incorrectly applying treatment*.
> Watch the tendency to be **ethnocentric** about treatments, such as exporting western treatments. Even when someone means well, it can be damaging to others.

4. Therapists must understand how **schemas** affects beliefs about what should be done to treat a set of symptoms (Angel & Williams, 2013). Schemas help people label and categorize a set of symptoms, which shows someone's **subjective culture**.
5. We cannot assume that people across cultures label emotions such as anger and sadness the same way, even if we all have the same basic emotions (Angel & Williams, 2013).
6. Some groups do not value the independent view of the self that is part of western treatments (Angel & Williams, 2013).
7. **Indigenous Psychology** (IP) may offer the best treatment for many (Sundararajan, Misra, & Marsella, 2013). IP treatments are widely used and include "massage, acupuncture, meditation, Yoga, brain washing, purification, detoxification, fortune telling, needling, burning essences, use of herbs, creative art (music, song, dance, poetry, folktales), worship of gods and goddesses in various forms, bathing, devotion of various kinds, and serving Guru, holy men, and women" (p. 77). IP treatments do not just exist in a nonwestern culture, such as Maori traditional healing, but also can be accessed within the West, such as the increased use of acupuncture.

Next is a chance to apply these ideas to 3 situations.

1. Treating Asian Americans with western treatments
2. IP treatments for the Maori in the Pacific Islands and Maya in Belize
3. Exporting antidepressants to Japan

Example #1: Guidelines for treating Asian Americans with Western therapies

The term Asian American refers to many groups with diverse languages and cultures, as well as different immigration histories into the US (Okazaki & Ling, 2013). The Asian American population is rapidly growing so it is an important example. We should never assume that one kind of mental health treatment works equally well for all the different Asian American groups, but we still can make some general statements.

1. Asian-Americans have stresses related to racism and discrimination. One example is that Asian American adolescents experience daily discrimination and bullying, and this stands out in their minds as important.
2. Families have members at different stages of **acculturation** and this is a source of stress.
3. Asian ethnic groups tend to express stress as a somatic problem, meaning bodily complaints such as fatigue and headaches.
4. Asian Americans can show emotion differently. For example, Caucasian depressed patients often show lowered emotional reactions and Asian-Americans may show greater emotions. This is useful information for a therapist.

> **Evaluate approaches to research methods in abnormal psychology**
> Do not assume that western randomized experiments are always the best way to know if a treatment works. Review Maori IP treatments in the chapter 22 for a working example to discuss.
> Some IP treatments, notably **acupuncture**, have been studied in randomized placebo controlled experiments so they show causation, meeting Western demands for evidence, if you think it is necessary.

There are two ways therapists can prepare to work with Asian-Americans.

1. *Establish credibility*. The first few meetings are critical so clients trust the therapist and perceive him or her as credible. This may involve shared cultural backgrounds and language if the therapist is also of Asian descent but can involve finding similarities in attitudes and values in therapists who are not. Credibility is also strengthened when clients perceive Western therapy as flexible.
2. *Recognize that Western treatments such as Cognitive Therapy can be adapted for Asian-Americans*. Therapists should consider the Chinese view of the **self-concept** when offering CT.

> **Evaluate ethics and research in abnormal psychology: Increase open-mindedness**
> Many think an IP treatment, such as acupuncture or spiritual healing, works *because someone believes in it.*
> Consider that this viewpoint seems condescending to other cultures and is contrary to research findings. For example, we know a great deal about the physiological effects of acupuncture and meditation. The next study about Maya healing shows the mechanisms making it work, a good place to start in demonstrating treatment efficacy.
> Does Prozac or Cognitive Therapy work because just someone believes in them? Avoid ethnocentrism and get the facts. Of course it is helpful if a patient is enthusiastic about a particular treatment and it is culturally relevant. Consider that belief in any treatment could be part of a **placebo** effect, something plaguing all treatments.
> However, is it more scientific to research the mechanisms of how a treatments works.

Example #2: Learning about and respecting Indigenous healing: Maori and Q'eqchi' Maya healers

Students will not just discuss indigenous healing but will evaluate its effectiveness.

Indigenous **Maori healing** is a good place to start a discussion and evaluation, and is detailed with the topic **universalism** and **relativism** in the chapter 22. It includes a consideration of research issues needed in an evaluation. Do not get caught in the trap of thinking that randomized controlled experiments are the only way to know something. This is a western standard, and although experiments are the only (western) research method showing causation, other cultures have ways of knowing that IP healing works.

Twenty-first century psychology students enjoy learning about other cultures and are open-minded enough to consider the validity of different ways to know if a treatment works.

Semi-structured interviews with **Q'eqchi' Maya healers** and a case study about someone with **rahil ch'ool**, similar to **depression**, can help us understand healing (Hatala & Waldram, 2016). How does this healing work?

Sometimes people in the West think that IP healing works only if a patient believes in a practice and consciously knows what is happening during treatment. This does not appear to be the case. Western students must get outside of themselves and consider that someone's physical body can be the site of communication with the healer and transformation away from mental illness. The treatment works through a sensory pathway.

Interviews with healers suggest it is not important to directly talk to a patient (Hatala & Waldram, 2016), something critical to western treatments such as cognitive therapy. Healers do communicate with their

Mayans have beliefs about treating mental disorder that should be respected and researched. TOK students must consider that there are other ways to know that a treatment works.
Used under license from megapixl.com.

patients, but much of this is done with elements of the body, such as blood, the sickness itself, and spiritual forces (Hatala & Waldram, 2016). A patient may not even understand what the healer is saying when chanting or praying. Perhaps we should call IP healing "medicine" because it gets rid of the illness.

More than a decade of interview and case study research has been done through the Maya Healers Association in Belize pointing to the conclusion that treatment can take place at a sensory bodily level, and help us understand healing efficacy.

The **case study of Serena** demonstrates the healing process (Hatala & Waldram, 2016).

Most of the family adjusted in a reasonable amount of time after grieving a grandmother's death, but Serena remained sad and depressed. She became anxious, stopped doing household chores, and avoided socializing. Serena's appetite was poor and she complained of stomach pain. Her healer Emilio diagnosed Serena with rahil ch'ool, a Q'eqchi' disorder related to grieving a loss meaning "sadness of the soul." The real meaning is "often glossed over as depression" when translated (p. 65).

A summary of Serena's healing process

Steps	Description
Step #1	Emilio said a healing prayer for several minutes without an introduction as soon as Serena sat down with him.
Step #2	While praying, Emilio made small gestures toward Serena as if talking with someone else about her.

Steps	Description
Step #3	Emilio dipped his hand into a bucket and flicked a small amount of liquid (medicinal herbal medicine) toward Serena.
Step #4	Emilio read Serena's pulse.
Step #5	Emilio dipped his hand in the bucket again and then grasped Serena's feet. Then he read her pulse again.
Step #6	Emilio again dipped his hand into the bucket and flicked some liquid toward Serena's face.
Step #7	Serena then received a "spiritual massage" where Emilio did not touch her but ran his hands over her head and down around her body to her legs.
Step #8	Emilio then prayed while holding Serena's feet.
Step #9	Emilio flicked the medicinal herbal medicine toward Serena and held her feet twice more and then said this part of her healing was complete.
Step #10	Emilio told Serena to drink the medicine and use it to wash her head and feet over the next two days.
Step #11	Emilio then put more herbs and incense into a pan and put it over a fire, using the smoke to cover Serena. As this was happening, Emilio placed his hand on Serena's forehead and prayed.
Step #12	Emilio continued to fan the smoke into Serena's face and pray.
Step #13	To complete the healing, Emilio sprayed "spirit water" over Serena.

Patients with rahil ch'ool have "too much thinking," which is one of the cultural ways to display distress listed in DSM-5.

Too much thinking is a common way for many people to express their distress in nonwestern cultures and can show up as sad mood. The mind and the heart are closely related in Q'eqchi' culture. Moods and thoughts do not belong to just the person but also an evil spirit in their blood as well as a presence of another spirit that takes over the person. As such, Serena was not in control of her thoughts and mood.

To stabilize Serena's moods, Emilio talked to the spirits and her illness rather than directly to her. The healing involves sensory experiences in the body that included smells of incense.

Smell heals because it triggers a range of bodily sensations resulting in higher self-esteem, confidence, and happiness. Burning incense is just one example of how IP healing engages the entire body in health-improving sensations, quite different from a western treatment focusing on talking. Touch, sound, and sight are also used, with touch critical to creating empathetic communication between patient and healer. Engaging smell and touch heals because the senses bypass conscious thought, stimulating the connection between the senses and mood.

To put it in western terms, the brain is working behind the scenes. The **amygdala** is linked to emotion and mood, and smell calms it (Hatala & Waldram, 2016).

Ritual healing also trains patients in **mindfulness** (Hatala & Waldram, 2016). One goal of Mayan healing is for patients to become mindfully in touch with their physical experiences. Scientists know a great deal about the physical effects of mindfulness, covered in chapter 29 about health psychology.

It is useful to remember that **schemas** are always working in someone's mind. Cultural values link sensory processes and the mind, and healing practices activate narratives that are a "sensation **script**" for the person telling them what they need to do to reenter their cultures (Hatala & Waldram, 2016).

This discussion provides some evidence to make an evaluation of Mayan healing. Students have something specific to say about how the treatment works and how it can be researched. If you think western style randomized experiments are needed, consider how a credible one might be designed that is culturally relevant. Some western experiments assign someone to get a placebo or to sit on a waiting list (get no treatment). What are the ethics of doing this and might it be culturally meaningful to the people in Belize?

Example #3: Exporting western treatments: A lesson about introducing antidepressants to Japan

What happens when **antidepressants** are used in nonwestern cultures? The increasing use of them is a chance to consider in a discussion the positive and the negative aspects of exporting drug treatments.

We want everyone to get the needed treatments, but what is the best way to deliver them? Do not assume that what works in the West works outside the West.

The World Health Organization's Nations for Mental Health Program promotes drug treatments throughout the world, supported by drug companies (Kirmayer, 2002). The consequences can be great for a culture when individuals take antidepressants.

Exporting drug therapy may change **cultural norms**. "The professional culture, driven by the political economy of the pharmaceutical industry, may represent the leading edge of a worldwide shift in norms" (Kleinman, 2004, p. 2).

Latinos living in the US are even reluctant to use antidepressants (Vargas, et al., 2015). Interviews suggest Latinos are reluctant to get help and worry about becoming addicted and being stigmatized.

So what happens when western drugs are exported?

Before 2001 antidepressants were rarely used in Japan, but after that their use dramatically increased (Kirmayer, 2002).

Japan uses drug treatments for physical

The Japanese tend to be collective, so using antidepressants violates cultural meanings of how someone fits in with the group.
Source: pixabay.com.

and mental health other than antidepressants. In addition, Japan offers more mental health services than most Asian countries. So *the reluctance was specific to antidepressants*.

After 2001, SSRI use increased to the equivalent of 25,000,000 US dollars every month.

Depression symptoms exist in Japan but there are many reasons it took so long for antidepressants to become popular.

1. Historically, Japanese psychiatry focused on severe disorders.
2. The Japanese view distress as physical symptoms.
3. The Japanese government requires new efficacy trials using Japanese samples before any drug is approved for use.
4. Cultural variations in the social meaningfulness of a group of symptoms are important.
5. Values related to relationship harmony and conformity define the Japanese view of the self.

Japanese persons with depressive symptoms prefer to see internal medicine doctors for physical complaints to reduce **stigmatization** and conform to social norms. Although 20% of patients seen by clinicians meet the category criteria for depression, Japanese doctors have traditionally prescribed anti-anxiety drugs or just told patients to relax.

Laws about testing drugs in Japan complicate matters. Government policy requires new experiments using Japanese samples before drug approval. Culture affects responses to drug treatments, so it makes sense to require new testing. Studies are hard to conduct in Japan for many reasons, one being the stigma of participation. Zoloft was not approved for use in Japan because efficacy trials were unsuccessful.

Despite these factors, *cultural variation is the key to understanding the reluctance of the Japanese to use antidepressants.* Each culture has a set of socially meaningful values that defines groups of symptoms.

DSM categories reflect socially meaningful ways of classifying a set of symptoms in the West. Is the category "major depression" meaningful to the Japanese? While younger Japanese psychiatrists now promote antidepressants, cultural values keep them from widespread use. Mental disorder is less prevalent in the Japanese than in westerners, perhaps because westerners are more preoccupied with themselves. In contrast, the Japanese focus on interrelatedness and do not want their behavior exaggerated, so sedative drugs are more popular than antidepressants.

Studying the issues *challenges the notion that diagnosing and treating depression is universal.*

Is the reluctance to use antidepressants in Japan simply their failure to adapt to modern times or is it an expression of traditional culture?

Before taking an SSRI, a person in the West may be sad and say, "I am depressed," meaning general unhappiness. Antidepressants make a person more outgoing

> **Ethics in abnormal psychology and global/local awareness**
>
> The class might learn about other cultures, perhaps those of students in the class, and consider how the concerns about using antidepressants in Japan might apply to others. There is plenty of research out there.
>
> For example, interviews with people living in rural India show they agree that some symptoms indicate depression, but think it is caused by personal failure (Nieuwsma, Pepper, Maack, & Birgendeir, 2011). They suggest social support, spiritual practice, and relaxation through yoga and meditation for treatment. These treatments prevent someone getting diagnosed with a mental illness, something bringing stigma to the person.
>
> Scientists know a great deal about how yoga and meditation heal, so be careful about automatically saying people with depressed symptoms need western treatments. Some cultures might reserve western treatments just for certain types of problems or reject them completely.
>
> People from other cultures can even respond differently to drug therapies (Kleinman, 2004).

and extroverted, an **individualist** view of the self. Japan is a **collectivist** culture, and value harmony and conformity. Taking an SSRI might make the individual stand out, something not valued in Japan. In addition, the Japanese tend to view mood disturbance as social or moral problems.

Sri Lanka is another example and many people seem to meet the western diagnostic category of depression. However, the Buddhist point of view prevents disability. To a Buddhist, depressive symptoms can show one's wisdom. Antidepressants interfere with the meditations that transform the self to the ultimate goal of enlightenment.

27.11: Assess (evaluate) the effectiveness of treatments
Some things to consider when evaluating any treatment

Discuss means to give a considered and balanced view supported by evidence. Next is a consideration of many factors used to assess treatment effectiveness, meaning to make a judgment using evidence.

These seven points should be considered when evaluating treatments. Many of these points have already been discussed in this chapter. Use treatment research from this chapter as support.

Points to consider	Description
Point #1: Ethics: Treatment selection should take into account benefits versus risks	No treatment should be used unless its benefits outweigh the risks. This was discussed in the section about Prozac. Drugs can be helpful but they also have side effects, so selecting it should include reflecting on its potential benefits versus potential risks. A clinician's biases toward a treatment should not interfere with this rule. Because drug treatments have many side effects, it is most ethical to consider a broad range of options. Patients must be fully educated about risks versus benefits of a range of options. The 21st Century student enjoys learning about other cultures and is open-minded in understanding that many treatments from around the world can be effective.
Point #2: Culture and treatments	Culture affects the perception and acceptance of treatments, even affecting how drugs alter the brain, so cultural relevance is important for delivering all treatments (Kleinman, 2004).
Point #3: The problem of placebos	Placebos complicate studying treatments, particularly depression. Whether placebos are ethical is debated, but they are useful for acting as a comparison for the treatment and against a no treatment group (which is also an ethics concern). The most ethical experiments using placebos end the placebo control as soon as it is obvious that one or more of the tested treatments work.
Point #4: It is hard to know if any treatment works in the long run.	Treatments are studied in the short run because confounding variables interfere with longer testing. Follow-ups after a year, for example, usually do not use experimental research methods, so it is not known if the treatment is still causing the changes. The TADS experiments about Prozac are an example. Another point is that all treatments seem to do similar things to the brain, even indigenous treatments. Some therapies can take longer to work, such as cognitive therapy, but in the long run many treatments are effective.
Point #5: No one treatment works for everyone.	Some people do not respond to any treatment. Some people get better without any formal treatment. Students should reflect on this issue as well as the fact that many people do not get any treatment.
Point #6: No studies compare all available treatments, making comparisons difficult.	A study comparing all available treatments is not practical. All we can conclude then is that a treatment works better than a placebo, or in comparison with a particular set of other treatments. Scientists are learning more about the mechanisms of change, so it can be helpful to learn that treatments might get to the same place in the end.

Points to consider	Description
Point #7: What counts as evidence: Should all treatment outcome research be from randomized experiments?	Western health providers require evidence from RCTs, or randomized controlled experiments. "Randomized" means that participants are randomly assigned to groups. Randomized experiments show that a treatment caused a change to occur. RCTs are studied over limited time frames, typically eight to sixteen weeks, and symptom reduction is how "working" is defined.
	RCTs have advantages, such as showing cause and effect and using clearly defined samples to control participant variables. This may appear a disadvantage, but everyone knows that the point of the studies is to test the treatments and that real life clients are more complicated.
	Are RCTs are the only way to know if something works? It is discussed in chapter 22 about indigenous psychology and universalism, as well as in this chapter about the role of culture in treatment.
	People can have strong emotions about this topic, so stay open-minded. No one wants to give destructive treatments, but there is not one simple answer to this issue, particularly when considering indigenous treatments. Some of them, such as acupuncture, are studied in RCTs, but does this mean that we need to study all indigenous treatments this way?
	This does not mean to automatically say we should accept case study evidence, which happens to be a typical questions westerners ask. Weigh the evidence. For example, cases might have suggested that drug therapy was beneficial for treating anorexia, but RCTs show they are not.
	How should indigenous treatments be evaluated? Can it be done from a western viewpoint or should it come from within (an emic perspective) a particular culture?

Chapter 28
Health psychology: Health Problems: Introduction and Prevalence Rates of Health Problems

---

Chapter Objectives

Students will:
1. Practice thinking strategies related to evaluation and synthesis, with discuss demonstrated.
2. Consider the extent to which they are healthy.
3. Discuss health trends over time.
4. Discuss cultural views of the term health.
5. Discuss prevalence of general health problems on a global scale.
6. Discuss prevalence of alcoholism.
7. Discuss prevalence of obesity.

Students study health psychology because they want to learn about health problems, so the chapters about health psychology are organized them. These are **stress**, **alcoholism**, and **obesity**. **Pain** is included in chapter 31 with the biopsychosocial model.

An introduction to health psychology and prevalence statistics make up this short chapter before getting to the health problems.

28.1: Introduction: The future of health

Are you healthy? My students say overwhelmingly no! School schedules (our school starts at 7:05 a.m.), homework, jobs, sport practice, clubs, the IB CAS and extended essay projects, social networking websites, texting, and family obligations take up so much time that there is little left for preparing healthy food, exercising, and sleeping. Even regular school sport activities demand extreme training schedules that can over-train and exhaust adolescents

Why does improving one's health take a back seat to all the other activities? Perhaps students feel little control over all the things bombarding them. People have always had a lot to do, but modern technology complicates life. Technology is convenient and expands opportunities, but unlimited choices can be stressful, particularly if teens eat on the run and are sleep deprived.

We have the power to significantly improve our physical health. We are not prisoners of our genetic make-up and can choose healthy diets, get enough sleep, exercise, and manage stress.

Might you live to be 100? According to a Harvard Medical School report (n.d.), the 2000 US census listed 330,000 persons over age 95 and 3.9 million between the ages of 85-94. The report says that people living to 100 enjoy good health. Life expectancy worldwide is increasing little by little so it is important to reflect on the meaning of good health.

Sleep is a topic dear to the hearts of students. How sleepy are the people in your class? Getting enough sleep is a key factor for good health. Used with license from megapixl.com.

The future may seem a long way away, but in all likelihood, unless you get run over by a bus in the near future, you will live a long life. While genes play a role, lifestyle choices are a huge factor determining longevity and quality of life (Harvard Medical School, n.d.).

The report includes some important lifestyle factors related to health.

1. Avoid smoking
2. Increase your exercise
3. Eat a balanced healthy diet
4. Take a daily multivitamin
5. Keep a healthy body weight
6. Keep challenging your mind
7. Increase your social support
8. Adopt an optimistic outlook on life

Decisions about managing health must start early. Many teens are already on the road to poor health but do not realize it because the wear and tear has not yet shown up on medical tests. Some teens already have chronic health problems. Now is the time to learn and make changes. The alternative is low energy and vulnerability to disease. People must answer the question, do we want to treat chronic sickness throughout our lives or take charge of our health while young?

CAS and Health Psychology
Ideas for CAS are included throughout the health chapters, and one place to start is to increase your exercise. Try yoga, Tai Chi, or work with a certified trainer at a gym. Set some goals and document your progress. Working with a yoga or Tai Chi teacher or a trainer can help raise self-efficacy to stick with exercise.

High **self-efficacy** is probably the most important factor in taking charge of one's health, so Albert Bandura's Social Cognitive Theory is important. *Creating and maintaining high self-efficacy to start and follow through with lifelong lifestyle changes related to eating, exercise, and stress management should be the goal of all individuals, parents modeling good health, school education programs, and health promotion campaigns.*

An informal look at our stressors: Something for each student to consider

Consider means to reflect on something, so let's start the health chapters by taking an informal look at our stressors. This is important because stress has so much to do with all health problems and should be considered before studying health problems and promotion.

Make a list of everything you find stressful. It might be long but be honest. Do you find day-to-day life very stressful, somewhat stressful, or not stressful? Are your stressors related to particular things? The class can compare stressors and group them into categories, such as school, relationships, diet, sleep, and stress related to living in a technological world.

Stress is a modern buzzword and it is on everyone's mind so we must consider its meaning and possible solutions. But what is a stressor?

Stressors are "anything that throws your body out of allostatic balance and the stress response is your body's attempt to restore allostasis" (Sapolsky, 2004, p. 8). **Allostasis** means returning to stability. Allostasis is a modern way to view homeostasis, meaning to remain stable, and includes many interacting biological, cognitive, and sociocultural factors.

Humans have many sources of stressors so the next task is to organize them using the approaches to behavior.

The multidirectional model is a useful way to categorize sources of stressors. Stressors are interactive, meaning one stressor usually does not affect someone in isolation from others. Consider all the ways the different stressors coexist and interact! Students should next organize their own stressors using the model to create an individual stores profile. many stressors appear on this list but feel free to add more

Do you ever feel this way? Taking an informal look at our stressors is a place to start taking control of our lives. A **CAS** activity to change your life might be a good idea.
Used with license from megapixl.com.

Sociocultural stressors
Self-efficacy, level of social support, socioeconomic status (SES), noise and overcrowding, work stress, violating cultural norms, school start times, fast food cultures, overuse of cell phones, neighborhood factors, discrimination, living in a war zone, Internet overuse

Cognitive stressors
Cognitive appraisal (when you decide something is stressful), coping style and level of self-management, attribution style

Biological stressors
illness, diet, sleep deprivation, lack of exercise, electromagnetic fields, techno-brain burnout, genetic risks, pesticide exposure

Stressors affect everyone, so take an international perspective. **Culture** shapes the meaning and experience of stress, so perceptions and appropriate ways to display and manage it varies. How might student stressor lists vary between cultures? This is something to explore, especially if the class has already studied the **dimensions of culture**. If not, the dimensions of culture are reviewed in chapter 3. For example, someone with a monochronic time orientation might feel stressed if he or she was late to a meeting and someone with a polychronic time orientation is not as stressed about punctuality. However, all stressors activate the **HPA Axis**, the cascade of events that produce **cortisol**, the main human stress hormone (review chapter 9). The biological response unites us all.

The model shows interplay between stressors and is a rough estimation of the appropriate approach to behavior where each stressor falls.

Most human stressors are man-made and interact with cognitions and biology. For example, optimal teen brain health requires 9 ¼ hours of sleep each night, but early school start times interfere with the biological need. A second example is that while illness affects us on a biological level, poor coping skills, negative cognitive appraisal, and low SES contribute to illness. Last, one reason diet is listed under biological is because poor diet contributes to low levels of **serotonin**, a **neurotransmitter** associated with depression.

Several stressors listed on the model are discussed in more detail in the next chapter, such as activation of the HPA axis and the immune system, cognitive appraisals, and SES.

A **risk model** is a good way to evaluate someone's total stress load. Each person has a total stress load with each stressor adding to health problems. One stressor may not be enough to cause a problem, but each additional stressor contributes to the total risk load. For example, having lots of homework can be stressful, particularly if someone lacks effective coping skills and makes negative appraisals. If this person also fails to get enough exercise and eats an unhealthy diet, then the risk for poor heath increases. If the person has genetic predispositions for disease, then the risk increases further. You see how it works.

Self-management: Health promotion activity: The meal bar challenge

The first health promotion activity is the meal bar challenge. I start with a diet related activity because students so often eat on the run without considering the links between diet and health or between what they eat and feeling stressed.

I bought one bar of each brand available on the meal bar aisle of my local supermarket and then two more from the health food store, since the perception is that something from a health food store is better. I used 12 bars.

Divide students into groups. Each group is responsible for researching the ingredients of one bar. Students list all the different sugars, fats, protein sources, and added chemicals and then conduct an Internet search about any potential health risks. Since some effects are controversial, I ask teams to make tentative conclusions.

Next we compare results as a larger group. Decide the extent to which each bar is healthy.

Most of my students did not read food labels before this assignment and it was a real eye-opener.

This bar might taste good but is it good for you? Might certain foods increase your stress?
Photo used with license from megapixel.com.

What does your personal risk model look like? It may motivate you to learn more about sources of health problems and ways to improve health.

28.2: Health trends and cultural definitions of health

Most deaths in the past were from infectious diseases and accidents. Now death is more often from chronic illness that *develops over time and relates to lifestyle*. This change promoted a **biopsychosocial approach** to thinking about health taking into account biological, psychological (cognitive) and sociocultural factors for prevention, diagnosis and treatment of health problems (Straub,2014).

Overview of Health Trends	The newer focus in healthcare
People live longer	Choose healthy behaviors so a longer life is productive and meaningful
Increase in disease related to lifestyle, such as heart disease, Type 2 diabetes, cancer, and all stress-related illnesses	Educate people on risk factors and ways to reduce their risk
Health care costs are spiraling out of control	Change focus to prevention
Limitations of a strict biomedical model of health	Use a broader biopsychosocial model considering all parts of a person's life

Source: Based on Straub (2014)

Defining health: The meaning differs and culture is an important part of the biopsychosocial approach

The World Health Organization (1948) defines health as "a state of complete physical, mental and social well-being and not merely the absence of disease or infirmity" (p. 100).

The WHO definition may be different from what many students living in western countries experience with medical care. Next is examples of different cultural views of health (Gurung, 2010) showing the importance of the WHO definition. Balance is common across most definitions.

1. Many western cultures define health as the absence of disease.
2. Chinese culture thinks of health as balance between yin/yang and balanced chi (energy).
3. Indian culture views health as a balance between mind, body, and spirit.
4. The Hmong, an Asian ethnic group living in Vietnam and Thailand, view health as the prevention of soul loss.
5. Ethiopians and other African groups, believe health is the prevention of spirit possession.
6. American Indians define health as being in spiritual, mental, and physical harmony with nature.
7. Mexicans define health as a balance of mind, body, and spirit.

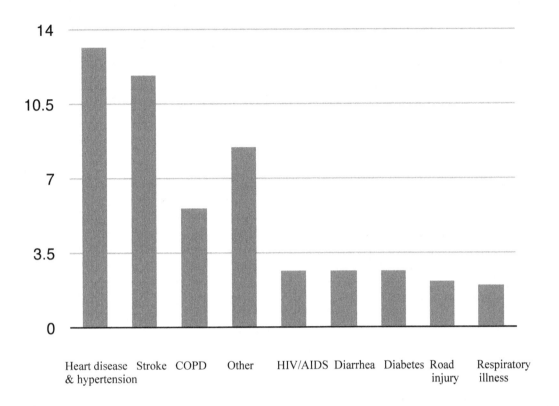

■ Top causes of death globally by percentage (Global Health Observatory, 2012)

Heart disease & hypertension · Stroke · COPD · Other · HIV/AIDS · Diarrhea · Diabetes · Road injury · Respiratory illness

28.3 Prevalence of rates of health problems

Prevalence of health problems on a global scale: Trends and leading causes of death

This section is about health statistics related to health problems. The reasons for these health statistics can be found when students study specific health problems such as alcoholism and obesity. There are many reasons people consume alcohol and eat unhealthy foods, even when it causes them problems. These reasons are complex, and involve biological (genetic), psychological (cognitive), and sociocultural factors. Students should take a **biopsychosocial** approach when giving reasons. This approach simply means that biological, psychological (cognitive), and sociocultural factors are considered any time someone wants to diagnose or treat someone. No one factor explains why people are unhealthy or how to promote health.

Although people say they understand that problem drinking and obesity are problems, why do they still drink and eat too much of the wrong foods? And with all the

---

Thinking skills and conceptual understanding: Considering why

Do not try to memorize all these statistics. Instead, study them and draw some meaningful conclusions. *Why do you think these problems exist?* Since many health problems are rising, why might this be? It is the students task to come up with a considered reflection about issues surrounding prevalence.

Global impact/local awareness: What are the greatest health issues in your area? Are they preventable? How might you get involved to solve these problems?

information available about stress management do people still report high stress levels?

When teaching health it is helpful to start with a global view and then move to statistics specific for local groups. There is no way someone can learn all the prevalence statistics, but what are the most important ideas? Learn a few statistics to support these ideas and perhaps focus just on the health problem(s) the class wills study for exams.

Next is trends in global health (WHO, 2014).

Trends in global health (WHO, 2014)
Life expectancy has increased 6 years since 1990
Heart disease is the leading cause of death
1 in 10 adults has diabetes
Mental health disorders such as depression are in the top 20 causes of death
Tobacco causes or contributes to about 6 million deaths each year
About 3500 people die in car crashes each day

Prevalence of disability on a global scale

Next is the causes of **disability**, important because disability lasts for extended periods, and could even lead to death in the long-run.

Disability for both males and females is increasing because of population growth and aging (Global Burden of Disability Study Collaborators, 2013). Note that Major depression and low back pain are ranked #1 and #2, and both are among the top 10 for most individual countries.

Leading causes of disability worldwide for males and females
Major depression
Low back pain
Substance use disorders
Other mental health problems
Chronic respiratory disease

Mental health and substance abuse disorders are the leading causes of disability in children and adolescents worldwide (Erskine, et al., 2015). Most of these examples are studied in this course, especially if you also study abnormal psychology. Note that alcohol use problems are seen mostly in high income countries, but these problems may grow in teens living in developing countries.

Leading causes of disability in children and youth worldwide
Major depression ranks first
Anxiety disorders rank 5th
Eating disorders rank 6th
Alcohol use disorder ranks 17th

Life expectancy in the US increased about 3 years between 1990 and 2010 and healthy life expectancy (HALE) also increased (US Burden of Disease Collaboration, 2013). However, disability is also a problem, and the leading causes of disability follow.

Leading causes of disability in the US
Dietary risks
Tobacco use
High Body Mass Index (BMI)
Lack of exercise
Alcohol use

These are all preventable, and it is hoped students understand sources of health risk and disability and ways to change them.

Prevalence of alcoholism worldwide

Alcoholism is a good topic for students because so many people drink and there are so many consequences for out of control drinking behavior. Alcohol use is listed as a leading cause of disability in both adults and adolescents, so students should know the scope of the problem, causes, and treatments.

Several important statistics stand out when problem drinking is considered on a global scale (WHO, 2015).

Problem drinking statistics worldwide
3.3 million people die each year from problem drinking.
About 5.1% of the global burden of disability is related to problem drinking.
Problem drinking causes death and disability early in life. About 25% of deaths in people aged 20-39 are because of alcohol use.

Prevalence of alcoholism in the US

About 13.8 million adults in the US abuse alcohol and about 8.1 million are alcoholics (Alcoholism-Statistics.com, 2009). Alcohol is the drug of choice for high school students, with about half reporting drinking in the past month (Gunrung, 2010) and 31% reporting that they have had five or more drinks in a row (binge drinking) sometime in the past two weeks (Alcoholism-Statistics.com, 2009). About 3 million adolescents in the US between the ages of 14-17 are alcoholics. Adolescents that start drinking before the age of 15 have a greater risk of alcoholism than people that wait to start drinking until age 21. Binge drinking at colleges is a big problem and a target for health promotion campaigns. In 2013, 24.6% of people aged 18 or older reported they participated in binge drinking and 6.8% said they were heavy drinkers (NIH, 2015).

Problem drinking, along with other substance abuse, causes more deaths, accidents, and disabilities than any other preventable health problem (Straub, 2014). About 40% of traffic deaths involve alcohol and half of the murders in the US involve some type of substance abuse.

Research support explaining alcoholism prevalence: Socioeconomic status is one reason for drinking patterns in a UK sample

The **aim of the correlation study** was to see if living in lower socioeconomic neighborhoods was related to a type of drinking pattern, either binge drinking or excess drinking (Fone, Farewell, White, Lyons, & Dustan, 2013).

For **procedures**, a large Welsh sample took a survey asking about patterns of drinking, either binge drinking or excess drinking. Participants reported the highest number of drinks they had each day over the last week. Three categories were created for answers. The first was no drinking or drinking small amounts, which for men was no more than 3. The second was excess drinking, defined as drinking 4-8 drinks a day for males. The third was binge drinking, defined as more than 8 drinks a day for males.

Results follow.

1. The lowest SES neighborhoods had the highest amounts of binge drinking.
2. The higher SES neighborhoods had more excess drinking not binge drinking.

> **Explore alternative explanations**
> Many things contribute to problem drinking, so it is important to consider alternative explanations. Chapter 29 details some of these, such as genetic risks and low self-efficacy.
> The authors suggested that social norms and peer influence might be alternative reasons for the patterns of drinking. Do not forget to include genetic risk, explored in chapter 7.

The authors **concluded** that this knowledge could help prevention programs by targeting the type of drinking most prevalent in specific neighborhoods. This is not a causal relationship, but data are from a sample of 58,000 participants, so the target population is large.

Prevalence of obesity worldwide

The World Health Organization (WHO) uses the term **globesity** to describe the pandemic nature of overweight and obesity (McKinley, 2008). The idea that obesity occurs only in high-income nations or just in one nation is incorrect. The US has a high obesity rate but other nations are not too far behind, such as Mexico and the UK. Obesity is usually defined by a BMI of 30 or greater and is calculated by multiplying one's weight by 703 and dividing it by the square of one's height in inches. BMI does not always indicate obesity because, for example, an athlete with high muscle mass might have a large BMI, so it is important to consider individual circumstances. BMI is a general measure of overweight and obesity.

Obesity rates have doubled globally since 1980 (WHO, 2015). Important obesity statistics follow. Obesity contributes to health problems on the top 10 list of deaths, and since it is preventable we must learn about its causes and how to prevent it.

Obesity statistics worldwide
In 2014, more than 1.9 billion people 18 or older were overweight with 600 million of them obese.
39% of adults were overweight and 13% were obese in 2014, with Body Mass Index (BMI) readings over 25
In 2013, 42 million children under age 5 were overweight or obese.
Even lower income nations report increasing rates of overweight and obesity. For example, Indonesia reports a rate of 40% and Middle Eastern countries report a rate of 25%.

Public health costs for managing obesity are great. Between $52 billion and $79 billion is spent annually in the US on medical care associated with obesity, about 12% of the healthcare budget. Other countries have large healthcare costs associated with obesity. For example, the UK spends approximately $232 million each year.

Childhood and adolescent statistics are the most alarming. Children and adolescents tend to carry obesity into adulthood and have a greater risk of a wide range of medical conditions complicated by obesity, such as heart disease, stroke, diabetes, hypertension, and cancer, most of which are listed in the top 10 causes of death worldwide. Rates are rising, so we should care about creating prevention programs to arm young people with tools and high **self-efficacy** to improve their health. This is where we have some control.

Prevalence of obesity in the US

A summary of obesity statistics follow for both adults and children (US Department of Health and Human Services, 2012). Obesity rates have doubled since the 1960s, and although rates have stabilized since 2010, they are still growing among men overall as well as Black women and Mexican American women.

Adults obesity	Childhood obesity
About 2/3 are overweight or obese	31.8% of children age 2-19 are overweight
About 1/3 are obese	16.9% are obese
3 out of 4 men are overweight or obese	18.6% of boys and 15% of girls are obese
Prevalence of obesity for men and women are the same	About 2 in 5 Hispanic and Black youth are overweight or obese

Adults obesity	Childhood obesity
8% of women are morbidly obese	About 2 out of 3 Caucasian children are overweight or obese

Research support explaining obesity prevalence: Socioeconomic status is one reason in a US sample

People are obese for many reasons and one is **socioeconomic status** (SES). Explain includes giving reasons and the **aim of this correlation study** was to see the relationship between income and obesity in US children (Ogden, Lamb, Carroll, & Flegal, 2010).

For the **procedures**, data were collected through surveys, interviews in people's homes, and physical exams that included blood samples.

Results follow.

1. Childhood obesity increased between 1994 and 2008 at all income levels and parent education levels.
2. The only significant relationship between income and obesity was for white males and females. For obese boys, 20.7% were from low income families compared with 10.2% of obese boys living in higher income families. The same thing was found for girls, with 18.3% were from low income families compared to 10.6% from higher income families.

> **Explore alternative explanations**
> Correlations never show causation, so low income is not shown to be a cause of obesity. Consider alternative explanations, including biological factors and food advertising to children, topics explored in chapter 29.
> It is unlikely that one factor can explain any behavior, so draw a multi-directional model to show the different factors.

3. There was no relationship between income and obesity for Hispanic and Non-Hispanic black children.

What can we **conclude**? Income is related to obesity but it is a more complicated problem than it looks on the surface, especially because rates are rising for everyone. Read about the health problem obesity in chapter 29 to see other reasons for rates.

Chapter 29
Health Psychology:
Health Problems of Stress,
Addiction, and Obesity

Chapter Objectives

Students will:
1. Practice thinking strategies related to evaluation and synthesis, with discuss demonstrated.
2. Discuss biological, psychological (cognitive), and sociocultural explanations of stress.
3. Discuss biological (genetic), psychological (cognitive: addictive beliefs), and sociocultural (Bandura's Social Cognitive Theory) explanations of alcoholism.
4. Discuss biological (genes and hormones) and sociocultural (food marketing and media) explanations of obesity.
5. Consider ways to improve our health.

For the IB teacher: Choosing topics

The syllabus allows teachers to select one health problem. There are three choices in this book, stress, alcoholism, and obesity. Teach all three for interest and then study one for the exam or just choose one and skip the rest. The information is here if you want it!

This information is highly relevant to student's lives, so consider teaching all of them if time allows for it. Be mindful that any health problem selected should be woven into the other health topics for simplicity.

It is important for a text to cover more than one topic so students and teachers have some choice, even if it makes the chapter look long!

29.1 Health problem of stress: Biological, cognitive and sociocultural explanations

Discuss means to give a considered and balanced view supported by evidence. Next is a reflection on stress, its origins, and how it affects health. Many factors interact to produce stress and a multidirectional model helps us organize three detailed in this chapter.

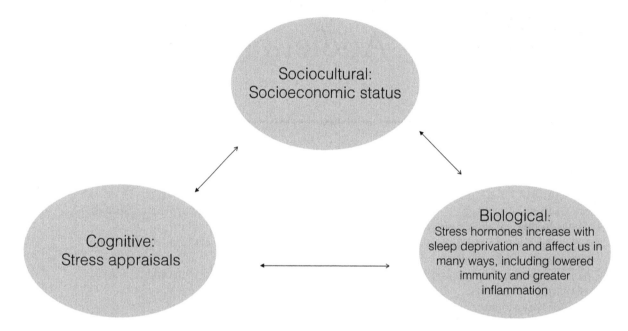

Biological explanations of stress

Film

Consider starting this section with the National Geographic film, *Stress: Portrait of a Killer* (2008) featuring Robert Sapolsky. The film raises some important issues for thinking about factors related to stress. It primarily covers biological factors and SES, including the Whitehall study, reviewed under sociocultural. Sapolsky is funny and popular with students.

Let's start with Hans Selye's theory that humans and animals have a general response to all stressors, called the **general adaptation syndrome**, which Robert Sapolsky (2004) calls the **stress response**.

Selye discovered the general adaptation syndrome while in college (Sapolsky, 2004). Selye intended to study the effects of an isolated ovarian extract on the body using rats. However, research does not always work out as intended. Selye did a poor job of handling the rats. They escaped during the injections and Selye chased them around the lab. Selye discovered that the rats had ulcers, enlarged adrenal glands, and damaged immune system tissue. Selye was perplexed and designed a new experiment with a control group to figure out why. One group was injected with the ovarian extract and the other with saline, and then Selye handled the rats the same way. Again he found that both groups had ulcers, enlarged adrenal glands, and damaged immune system tissue. Selye accidentally discovered something important about stressors.

Selye theorized that all stressors led to the same general stress response.

Researchers now know how the general stress response works. Any stressor activates a cascade of events stimulating the **HPA Axis** and ending with **cortisol** production, an important human stress **hormone**. The HPA axis was introduced in chapter 9, so review it first.

HPA Axis refers to the hypothalamus, pituitary gland, and adrenal cortex (Kalat, 2007). Stressors, such as teacher announcing a test or accidentally stepping out in front of a bus, activate the hypothalamus. The hypothalamus sends a message to the pituitary gland to produce ACTH, a hormone, which sends a message to the adrenal glands to produce **cortisol**, an important stress hormone in humans. Cortisol is often used as a stress measurement by researchers.

Why do we need cortisol? Some cortisol is necessary to respond to emergencies, such as jumping away from the bus. Moderate amounts of cortisol are adaptive (Sapolsky, 2004). The problem is that we do not spend much time jumping out from in front of buses. Most human stressors are man-made, such as worrying about tests. Humans frequently have the stress response turned on most of the time, and scientists know that chronic activation of the HPA Axis is linked to health problems, such as damaged immunity, increased risk of **heart disease**, increased risk of mental illness, and damage to telomeres, which protect chromosomes from damage as they divide.

> **Cortisol review**
> **Cortisol** is a steroid **hormone** produced by the adrenal cortex in response to stress.
> Its job is to increase blood sugar, suppress the immune and reproductive systems, as well as all other primary systems so you can flee a stressor.

STRESS CURVE

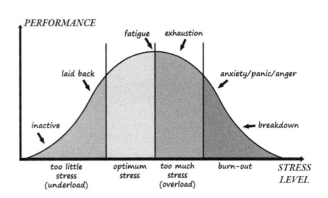

Where do you fit on the stress curve? We need some cortisol for motivation but many people have too much stress. Used with license from megapixl.com.

Self-management: Class activity: Mindfulness Meditation
I teach mindfulness-meditation to students from the beginning of the health psychology unit as a way to promote health (detailed in the next chapter about health promotion). Sapolsky's film introduces the concept telomeres, and under the topic about coping with stress, I discuss how mindfulness-meditation might protect telomeres. Students have a good introduction to meditation before we start the coping with stress material. Developing the patience to sit quietly takes time so we start meditating right away.

Research on three topics show how stress affects health, **immunity (common cold), glucocorticoid receptor resistance**, and **sleep deprivation**.

How stress affects immunity

Chronic stress increases the risk of disease, but we still need to learn about what happens between having chronic stress and getting sick (Cohen, 2005). Robert Sapolsky (2004) has some ideas about the connection.

The **immune system** fights off invaders, such as viruses and bacteria, by identifying foreign substances in the body and creating memories of them so that antibodies can fight off future invaders.

Lymphocytes are immune system cells affected by stress. **T cells** and **B cells** (the white blood cells) are two types of lymphocytes. T cells migrate from bone marrow and mature in the thymus and B cells stay in the bone marrow to mature. T cells are responsible for cell-mediated immunity and spring into action when a virus or bacteria invade the body, sending out an alarm that causes killer cells to grow, attack, and kill the invader. B cells play a different role, called antibody-related immunity. Once the T cells have activated the alarm, the T cells send a message to B cells to grow, seek out, and bind to the infectious substance and create a memory of these substances for future immune resistance.

Stress hormones interfere with immunity in many ways.

1. Stress hormones block the creation of new lymphocytes.
2. Stress hormones interfere with the release of lymphocytes into circulation.
3. New antibodies have difficulty forming in the presence of stress hormones.

Sapolsky speculated about how stress hormones suppressed immunity. When faced with a stressor, immunity is enhanced, probably to help you prepare to fight off a crisis. But after one hour, the presence of stress hormones has the opposite effect. Now immunity is suppressed. The body must have some way of bringing the heightened immunity back into balance. This works well for the example of accidentally stepping out in front of a bus. The crisis is over quickly and you avoid getting smashed. However, after an hour of heightened stress response related rises in immune activation, stress hormones seem to have the opposite effect.

The stress system should reset itself quickly after fleeing the bus. But since most human stress is man-made, stress can last longer than an hour. Stressing over tests, telling the story about jumping away from a bus, or taking care of someone with a long-term illness all last longer than an hour. Now the immune system is over-worked and the result is immune suppression. Sapolsky (2004) says that what goes up must come down, and over-working the immune system plunges it even below normal baselines.

Whatever the pathway is between stress and disease, the two are linked and this is why everyone should learn to cope with stress.

Next is three research examples about physiological aspects of stress. The first is an experiment about stress, immunity, and the common cold. The second is an experiment showing how stress increases inflammation that contributes to health problems. The third is an experiment about sleep deprivation and cognitive skills.

The activation of the stress system

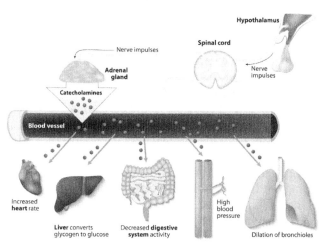

Besides lowering immunity, many other systems are affected by the activation of the HPA axis.
Used with license from megapixl.com.

Research support #1: Types of stressors that increase one's risk for the common cold

The Cohen experiment is detailed in chapter 9 about hormones. This is a chance to reuse research!

Research support #2: Sleep deprivation increases stress hormones and lowers cognitive abilities

If you have not already heard enough bad news about stress, the next example might make you reconsider some bad habits. Many students claim they do not need adequate sleep, which is 9 ¼ optimally, even suggesting they perform best under stress. The research does not support this view.

An experiment using a repeated measures design **aimed to test** the effects of **sleep deprivation** (SD) on stress hormones and cognitive skills (Joo, 2012).

Participants were 6 healthy men between the ages of 23-27 with good health and sleeping habits.

For the **procedures**, measurements were taken before and after SD, the **independent variable**. Participants took the Continuous Performance Test (CPT) first thing in the morning after a normal night of sleep and then again after 24 hours of SD. The CPT measures tasks that require attention and working memory. Blood samples taken before and after SD measured **cortisol** levels.

Nothing good comes from sleep deprivation. Even short amounts of it affect school performance, especially the most challenging tasks.

Used with license from megapixl.com.

Results included the following.

1. Cortisol levels were significantly higher after SD.
2. SD did not affect performance at the easiest level.
3. SD greatly affected performance at the difficult levels.

Joo **concluded** that SD is a cause of stress and that increased stress hormone negatively affects working memory and attention.

A similar finding comes from an experiment showing that sleep deprivation causes heightened HPA axis activity and the resulting cortisol production (Minkel, et al., 2014). Participants were randomly assigned to a good night sleep or one night of sleep deprivation. The next day participants gave a speech and solved hard math problems in front of a panel of three people. The sleep deprived participants had higher levels of cortisol production as measured in saliva samples.

Research example #3: Chronic stress causes inflammation in the body that contributes to health problems

Chronic stress is related to many health problems, such as heart disease, diabetes, depression, and respiratory infection, all health problems listed as leading causes of death or disability. Just what is the mechanism for stress to contribute to these health problems?

The mechanism is **glucocorticoid receptor resistance** (GCR), which means stress causes "a decrease in the sensitivity of immune cells to glucocorticoid hormones that normally terminate the inflammatory response" (Cohen, et al., 2012). This means inflammation runs wild within the body because cortisol interferes with the ability of immune cells to do their job.

Cohen's team ran two experiments using a simple procedure, called the viral-challenge paradigm that you learned about in Cohen's previous experiment **with the aim** to examine the role of stressors on GCR.

For the **procedures**, stress levels and GCR are measured before and after participants are exposed to a virus (the **independent variable**) and quarantined to see who gets sick.

Results showed that participants reporting a recent long-term stressor had GCR.

Cognitive explanations of stress: Cognitive Appraisals

The HPA axis activates when we experience stress, but no direct line exists between a stressor and the stress response unless you really step out in front of a bus and must jump away.

Lazarus (1993) developed the **cognitive appraisal theory**. Appraising means to make judgments about whether or not an event is stressful.

Lazarus noticed that stressors did not directly produce a stress response, so stress reactions were more complicated than simple biological or stimulus-response reactions. Something must happen between a stressor and a response. People go through four steps when faced with judging any type of stressor.

1. An external event happens that might be labeled as a stressor.
2. An appraisal of the stressor is made.
3. Coping skills to manage the stressor are consulted.
4. Some type of reaction to the stressor occurs.

Thoughts contribute to stress. You might appraise something as stressful that someone else does not. How can we learn to tame our stressful thinking?
Source: pixabay.com

People use both **primary appraisals** and **secondary appraisals** as they go through these steps.

Primary appraisals are the first judgments made about an event. Lazarus distinguished three types of psychological stress that influence primary appraisals.

1. Harm, or what someone has lost or might lose
2. Threat, or when someone anticipates a negative outcome
3. Challenge, or feelings of confidence to use effective coping skills to meet a demand

Secondary appraisals are one's ability to cope with a stressor.

This flow chart shows how someone experiences high or low levels of stress after an event. Students might try putting some events they routinely face through the model. For example, the teacher announces a test......

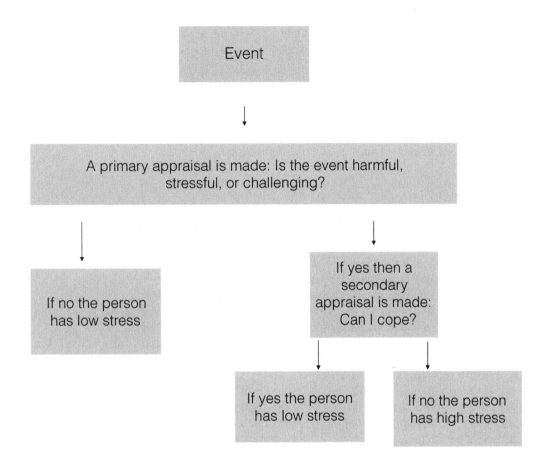

Culture affects all aspects of Lazarus's model (Gurung, 2010). Research on the Lazarus model is not complete without considering culture. Cultural effects include the following.

1. Primary appraisals may be affected by the meaning a cultural group gives to an event.
2. Secondary appraisals may be affected by ethnic beliefs about the group's self-efficacy to manage an event or beliefs about fate.
3. Coping skills may be affected by cultural sanctions against using certain types of coping or having the necessary language skills to negotiate if living within another culture.

Research support: Lazarus's original experiment

Lazarus (1993) designed an experiment **with the aim** to study real experiences with psychological stress in a lab setting as much as possible.

For **procedures**, participants listened to recorded speeches and then watched a series of stressful films. Researchers measured self-reported stress, heart rate, and skin conductance (measures changes in psychological arousal that vary with changes in skin moisture) throughout the experiment.

One of the films showed male rite of passage incisions performed on young Arunta men in Australia. Another was an employee safety training film showing someone getting a finger cut off and someone impaled from a board flying out of a circular saw.

The **independent variable** was the different speeches, with each one using a different cognitive appraisal style, denial, distancing, and threat sources. One recorded speech used *denial*, such as "these accidents didn't really happen but were staged for their effect" (p.6). A second used *distancing*, such as "This is an interesting anthropological study of aboriginal customs" (p. 6). A third focused on *threat* sources, such as "Many of the people you see in this film suffer pain and infection from these rituals" (p. 6).

The three conditions were compared with each other and a control group that saw the films but heard no speeches.

All three speeches influenced participant's stress reactions. **Results** follow.

1. Threat source speeches caused the most distress compared to all the other groups.
2. The denial and distancing speeches caused the least in comparison with controls, even though participants in each condition saw the same films.

Sociocultural explanations of stress: Socioeconomic status (SES): Whitehall II:

If stress is linked to health then it is important to understand how social factors affect stress. Who has the most stress? The answer might surprise you.

One variable studied since the 1960s is **socioeconomic status** (SES).

The goal is to unravel some of the issues linking SES and health. **Whitehall II** is highlighted, but the issues are complicated and students should avoid oversimplification.

Two common ideas about health are that people working in high status jobs have higher rates of heart disease and that health differences between rich and poor people are explained by differences in the quality of health services they receive (CCSU, 2004). The Whitehall II study shows that both ideas are incorrect. If you do not know, Whitehall refers to British civil servants.

Poverty is an important factor related to health (Sapolsky, 2004). The lives of the poor are full of stress, such as jobs requiring manual labor, working more than one low paying job, and living in poor neighborhoods where there is more crime, crowded conditions, and noise. Often there are fewer places to shop because corporations are less likely to maintain stores in poor neighborhoods. There are fewer opportunities to take walks in quiet parks and little money for recreation or gyms. Often diets are poor. As an example, organic vegetables and free-range meats are expensive. Although spending extra money on quality food probably reduces medical expenses over the long run, making it cost effective, the poor do not typically have this option. Many variables are associated with poverty, and while they work together in complex ways, it is safe to assume from the existing research that the poor have high stress levels. Lower SES in early life sets people up for poor health for the rest of their lives.

Research support: The Whitehall II study

Whitehall was the perfect place to study SES and health because of the strict job gradients and salary differences (CCSU, 2004). SES is defined in the study as **job gradient** (or social gradient).

Job gradient and perceived control is negatively correlated with health outcomes such as **heart disease**. This means that as job gradient and control increase, rates of disease decrease.

What accounts for the negative correlation?

Sir Michael Marmot and a team of researchers have collected data since the 1960s (Marmot & Brunner, 2005). The **aim of the correlation study** was to look for relationships between job gradient and health. Questionnaires, hospital records, medical exams, and job records such as sick leave reports were used for data.

British civil servants are a good sample because many confounding variables that might influence the study are controlled. For example, everyone in the sample has access to the same medical care, so quality of medical care is not an alternative explanation.

The target population was all British civil servants working in London government departments between 1985 and 1988. Participants held a variety of government jobs with strict gradients and pay differences, executives as well as clerical and office support jobs.

For the **procedures**, data were gathered 6 times. Every 5 years the sample visited the clinic and filled out questionnaires. Self-report questionnaires were mailed between clinic visits. Hospital and sick leave records verified self-reports.

Data confirms the negative correlation between social rank (defined as job grade in this study) and health. **Results** include the following (Marmot & Brunner, 2005; CCSU, 2004; North, et al., 1996).

One conclusion from Whitehall II is that job stress should not be ignored. Increasing an employee's sense of control is one strategy to improve health. Used with license from megapixl.com.

1. A negative correlation exists between job gradient and diseases such as cardiorespiratory illness and diabetes,
2. The degree to which someone has a sense of control is negatively correlated with cardiovascular illness.
3. People perceiving a clear link between their hard work and their pay is negatively correlated with coronary heart disease.
4. Risky health behavior is negatively correlated with job gradient. For example, the highest smoking rates were from employees with lower job grades.

Marmot and Brunner (2005) identified several strengths and weaknesses of the Whitehall II study.

Strengths include that the study population allows for control of variables that might confound the research if it were conducted in another country. All participants had access to the same medical care.

Weaknesses include that Whitehall's job gradient system is far more rigid than the typical workplace. The results may not apply to conditions in a private corporation.

29.2: Health problem of alcoholism: Biological, cognitive, and sociocultural explanations

Discuss means to give a considered and balanced view supported by evidence. A balanced view considers factors from all three approaches to behavior, with reasons why they contribute to alcoholism. Students cannot call these factors "causes" because cause implies experimental evidence showing causation, and the studies used are correlation.

Since so many people drink, it is important to understand the difference between social use and disordered use.

Some believe that social use is acceptable, and research shows that a small amount may be beneficial. For example, moderate use may increase HDL, the good cholesterol (Gunrung, 2010).

DSM-5 (American Psychiatric Association, 2013) uses the category **alcohol use disorder** to describe problem drinking. The term **alcoholism** is used in this book instead of alcohol use disorder to simplify the language. Problem drinking reaches a certain point where it meets the category for an official diagnosis and students should learn about these symptoms.

DSM-5 Diagnosis for Alcohol Use Disorder: Problematic pattern of use leading to significant impairment with at least 2 of the following behaviors within a 12-month period
1. Alcohol is used in larger amounts and for longer periods than intended.
2. Someone has a persistent desire or unsuccessful attempts to cut down.
3. Much time is spent obtaining and using alcohol and recovering from its effects
4. Cravings for alcohol
5. Using the alcohol so much that someone fails to fulfill obligations at work, home, or school
6. Continued use despite persistent or recurrent social problems caused or made worse by the alcohol use
7. Important social, work, or recreational activities are given up or reduced because of drinking
8. Continues to use alcohol in situations where it is physically hazardous
9. Continues to use alcohol despite knowledge of having a physical or psychological problem related to drinking
10. Tolerance to alcohol, either marked increase in the need for alcohol to feel its effects or diminished need to feel effects

The consequences of alcoholism are high. Alcoholism increases one's risk of a range of medical conditions relating to organ damage, such as the liver (Gunrung, 2010). Doctors do not know how much alcohol a pregnant mother can drink before the child is at risk for fetal alcohol syndrome. In addition, alcoholism increases aggressive behavior and accidents, particularly driving accidents.

The cost of alcoholism to the public is high. Many factors interact to produce alcoholism and a multidirectional model helps us see three detailed in this chapter.

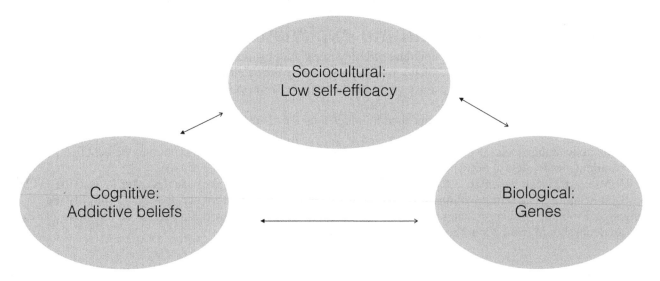

Biological explanations of alcoholism: Genetics

Marc Schuckit's research about **low response to alcohol** (LR) is the example and this is covered in chapter 7 about genetic influences on behavior. LR is the most studied and verified genetic risk for alcoholism (Schuckit, 2013). This is a chance to reuse previously studied material.

A film on the biology of addiction that includes Marc Schuckit

Schuckit is featured in the popular film, *The Hijacked Brain*, available from the Films for the Humanities and Sciences. The film is older but still relevant, as LR has stood the test of time. Students are very interested in Schuckit's research about low response to alcohol (LR).

Many genes may contribute to alcoholism but I focus on one researcher and one research method to keep it simple. Besides, LR is the most studied and verified genetic risk for alcoholism. Students will meet many people with LR in their lives and should be educated about it.

Overall the film is quite good and popular with students.

Cognitive explanations of alcoholism: Addictive beliefs

There are many layers to someone's **addictive beliefs** (Beck, 1993). Social Cognitive Theory concepts of **self-efficacy** and **outcome expectations** probably oversee these addictive beliefs, making them affect behavior most when someone's self-efficacy is low and they have high expectations for getting something positive from drinking. You can see how the approaches to behavior interact. Adding a genetic risk to the equation makes the risk someone becomes an alcoholic even greater.

Addictive beliefs come from **schemas** about how to behave (Beck, 1993). Beliefs shape the way someone interprets an event, and social events can even activate beliefs. For example, someone may hold the general belief that they are unworthy and think they are more likable when drinking at a social event. The social event may even activate these interpretations, such as going to a party, feeling uncomfortable, and then believing that a drink is necessary to fit in with the group.

Next is a four-step process showing addictive belief patterns.

Four-Step process showing addictive beliefs (Beck, 1993)

Core beliefs are fundamental, such as "I am worthless and no one likes me." Core beliefs concern one's survival, achievement, and autonomy.

Automatic thoughts arise from core beliefs, such as "If I use alcohol I will fit in with the group and people will like me."

Emotions are triggered by automatic thoughts or an event, perhaps going to a party and feeling frustration and anxiety over not fitting in with others.

The person draws a conclusion, such as "I need a drink."

Frustrating life problems and anxiety producing situations do not *cause* someone to drink excessively. However, people attach *meanings* to situations that activate the beliefs leading to excessive drinking.

Two other cognitive processes contribute to alcoholism, **attributions** and **decision-making**.

Attributions refer to the way someone explains events. Addicts can use either internal or external attributions. An example of an internal attribution is "I am addicted, so I need the alcohol." An example of an external attribution is "Anyone with the amount of problems I have would drink." Both types of attributions maintain the drinking because the person feels their behavior is out of control.

Decision-making maintains drinking behavior and can promote relapse. A series of decisions seem innocent but are part of a chain of events leading up to more use and then relapse. For example, someone decides to quit drinking. But then a decision is made to go to a bar with friends who drink. Although the original intent is to drink soda, the person is now in a high-risk situation.

Research example: Correlations show predispositions for addictive beliefs

Addictive beliefs contribute to alcoholism and certain character predispositions are correlated with addictive beliefs, *but these predispositions are not likely the determining factor for developing an addiction unless the person also has other vulnerabilities, particularly low self-efficacy and high expectations for positive effects from drinking.* It will not help the situation if the person also is a low responder to alcohol, a genetic risk.

Next is a list of character predispositions that may exist before an addiction belief and are correlated to the addictive beliefs (Beck, 1993). A body of correlation research leads to this conclusion.

1. Hypersensitivity to unpleasant emotions and low tolerance for normal mood changes
2. Instant gratification is valued over control
3. Poor coping skills and low motivation to change
4. A pattern of poor impulse control
5. Low tolerance for frustration
6. Excitement seeking
7. The future is not as important as the present

When someone with these characteristics faces unfulfilled expectations, a **schema** is activated to guide behavior that includes the following cognitions.

1. Exaggerations of pain and suffering
2. Exaggerations of long-term problems associated with delayed gratification
3. Blaming others
4. Heightened anger
5. A tendency to overlook other ways to cope and problem-solve

Beck explains that the result is an angry person ready to fight the world, but in reality, a real outlet does not exist. The person then must reduce tension. Alcohol and drug use is one way to reduce tension, at least for a while. A vicious cycle is created and the person is at risk for developing an addiction.

Sociocultural explanations of alcoholism: Outcome expectancy and self-efficacy

Review Social Cognitive Theory basics in chapter 18. Two **Social Cognitive Theory** concepts interact with and mediate addictive beliefs in problem drinking.

1. **Outcome expectancies** (part of anticipating reinforcement) means to expect a pleasant reinforcement from the substance. One example is anticipating stress relief because of the outcome expectancy that alcohol helps people relax and manage difficult situations.

2. **Self-efficacy** beliefs are judgments relating to one's ability to manage a situation, such as "I can say no if someone offers me a drink."

Bandura has an interesting perspective about problem drinking. He claims that alcohol prevention and treatment is hampered by western medical model beliefs (Bandura, 1997). The medical model includes three parts, that alcoholism is a disease, that cravings directly lead to heavy drinking, and that giving up all alcohol use is the only way to recover.

Bandura makes two important conclusions about problem drinking. One is that many problem drinkers change their behavior in midlife and continue to drink but at less problematic levels. Another is that many alcoholics either stop drinking or revert to controlled drinking without the help of treatment programs.

Self-efficacy and outcome expectancies may be the greatest factors related to why someone starts drinking, even if someone has genetic predispositions and addictive beliefs.

This information has been around for several decades and should be part of comprehensive prevention and treatment programs.

Research support #1: Drinking refusal self-efficacy and problem drinking in college students

Problem drinking is a big problem on college campuses. Drinking remains a problem even though health promotion campaigns target it, especially **binge drinking**.

The **aim of a correlation study** was to examine **alcohol outcome expectancy** and **drinking refusal self-efficacy**, two factors predicting college student drinking (Young, Connor, Ricciardelli, & Saunders, 2006).

Alcohol outcome expectancies usually involve if-then statements that reflect one's association between learning and reinforcement. For example, an alcohol outcome expectancy statement might be "If I drink at the party, then everyone will think I am fun."

Drinking refusal self-efficacy relates to one's confidence in resisting alcohol.

For the **procedures**, students from Australian Universities filled out two questionnaires, the Alcohol Expectancy Questionnaire (AEQ) and the Drinking Expectancy Profile (DEP).

> **Thinking skills: Drawing conclusions from research**
> Many studies with time, observer, and method **triangulation** show that outcome expectancies and self-efficacy are probably the greatest predictors of the actual start of problem drinking, even if someone has a genetic predisposition and addictive beliefs.

The AEQ measures the amount of positive expectancies someone has for drinking. Participants agree or disagree with statements such as "I feel more creative after I've been drinking."

DEP questions include "I have more self-confidence when drinking" and "drinking makes me bad-tempered." The second part measures refusal self-efficacy. Participants respond a statement list about when they are likely to drink including "when I am uptight" and "when I see others drinking."

Participants also reported how often they drank, the amount consumed, and were tested for alcohol abuse or dependence using DSM-IV.

Results showed that positive drinking outcomes expectancies on the AEQ and DEP were correlated with the following.

1. Frequency of drinking
2. Quantity of drinking
3. Severity of someone's problem drinking

The authors **concluded** that drinking refusal self-efficacy is a leading predictor of why someone starts drinking. The results could be helpful in designing health promotion strategies and treatments. *What good* *does it do to educate people about the dangers of drinking if self-efficacy to refuse the drinks is low?* Colleges can raise self-efficacy by providing, for example, alcohol free tailgating sections at football games. Students see other people having fun without alcohol.

Drinking refusal self-efficacy is correlated with drinking in Korean college students, so it has some cross-cultural relevance (Oh & Kim, 2014).

Research support #2: Drinking refusal self-efficacy links low self-awareness and drinking identity to start problem drinking

The **aim of a correlation study** was to show that drinking refusal self-efficacy was the key variable linking someone's self-awareness level and drinking identity to predict who was at risk for problem-drinking (Foster, Neighbors, & Young, 2014).

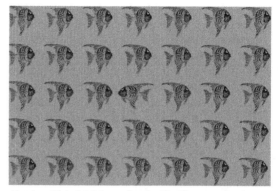

It takes high drinking refusal self-efficacy to be the fish swimming in the opposite direction from others encouraging drinking. Most people are not problem drinkers, so it is possible to raise your self-efficacy. You also do not have to follow a family history of problem drinking and raising self-efficacy is likely the best strategy.
Source: pixabay.com

It was hypothesized that drinking refusal self-efficacy (DRSE) had to be low for someone with a drinking identity and low self-awareness to start on the path to problem drinking.

Self-awareness means someone can direct their attention inward rather than focusing on what is happening in the immediate environment. Drinking identity is defined as "how closely individuals believe that consuming alcohol is a crucial aspect of their identities" (p. 4).

Results showed that drinking was predicted most when someone had the following.

1. Low DRSE
2. High drinking identity
3. Low self-awareness

The authors **concluded** that if DRSE was low, then someone's drinking identity took over and the person was more likely to drink, especially if they had low self-awareness. These findings add to the body of Social Cognitive Theory research helping us understand why people get started with problem-drinking.

29.3: Health problem of obesity: Biological and sociocultural explanations

Discuss means to give a considered and balanced view supported by evidence. Next is material to consider and ample evidence to show that genetics, hormones, and food advertising contribute to obesity.

Cognitive factors are weaker explanations of obesity, so this book focuses on the factors supported by research.

A multidirectional model helps us see the interacting factors. Researchers used to think that dichotomous thinking (thinking in extremes) was part of an explanation, but the research points to biological and sociocultural factors as most important. It is possible that dichotomous thinking does not help the situation, so it is on the model but is not developed in this chapter.

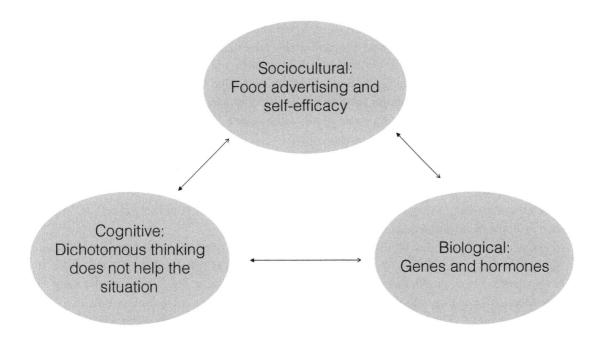

Biological explanation of obesity: The ob gene and the hormone leptin

Leptin and the **ob gene** are covered in chapters 8 and 9 about hormones. This is a chance to reuse previously studied material.

Sociocultural explanation of obesity: Food marketing to children

Childhood obesity rates have dramatically escalated in the past few decades, with some startling statistics (Linn & Novosat, 2008). The number of overweight children ages 6-11 doubled to 15.3 percent and the number of overweight adolescents tripled to 15.5 percent over a few decades. About 30 percent of American children and adolescents are overweight or obese.

The rise in obese children parallels the rise in **food marketing** targeting young people, with food advertisers spending approximately $10 billion to $15 billion each year. About 83 percent of commercials during popular children's television shows are for snacks, fast food, and sweets. It is not surprising that candy and other snacks, cereal, soft drinks, and fast food make up the most frequent purchases of young people. The World Health Organization (WHO) claims that there is a clear link between advertising and increases in child and adolescent obesity.

Marketing tactics make it hard for parents to stay one step ahead of advertisers. The US does not regulate advertising to children as much as other countries, so these examples represent advertising practices in the US For example, Finland bans advertising using children or famous characters as spokespersons. While opinions vary about what degree of regulation is best, the WHO thinks

> **fMRI shows how advertising affects children's brains**
> Refer to chapter 5 about brain imaging technology for more evidence from Amanda Bruce that advertising affects children, especially obese children.
>
> The body of research about food advertising effects on obesity is strong, part of an effective evaluation about the topic.

that advertising should be addressed.

1. *Brand licensing.* One example is Kraft using Spiderman shaped macaroni noodles.
2. *Product placement.* Coca-Cola paid $20 million for advertisements to appear on American Idol, which is a top-rated favorite for children and adolescents.
3. *Contests.* One example is Sunny D's Sunmobile, which toured the US with games and prizes while featuring advertisements for the drink. Although Sunny D contains 100 percent of the vitamin C requirements, a serving contains 120 calories and has 29 grams of sugar. Other company drinks contain up to 43 grams of sugar.
4. *Promotions.* The movie Star Wars: Episode III: Revenge of the Sith contained promotions encouraging children to collect all 72 Stars Wars M&M candy wrappers. Children had to buy 45 pounds of M&Ms to get all the wrappers.
5. *In-school Marketing.* Schools sell many name brand products, such as McDonald's. Companies such as Pepsi make donations and set up vending machines.
6. *Internet advertising* About 34 million children between the ages of 3 and 17 use the Internet. Advertisers have more access to children through sites such as Facebook.
7. *Video games.* For example, Burger King released a video game in 2006 featuring the King character. Children turn into the King character and give hamburgers to hungry people.
8. *Cell phones and iPods.* Text messaging is now part of typical marketing plans. For example, Frito Lay used texting as part of its strategy to sell Black Pepper Jack Doritos.
9. *Social networking sites.* Advertisers have become a part of social networking. One year after Burger King launched a MySpace page for its King character, the King had 120,000 friends.

Even when parents set limits, advertisers work against them in subtle ways. For example, parents are sometimes portrayed as mean or incompetent in commercials.

Self-management and collaboration: Class activity about food advertising
One idea for a class activity is to conduct a content analysis on advertising aimed at children. Divide the class into 9 groups based on categories from the Linn and Novosat article. Each group gathers data and reports to the class with specific examples.
   Students are so used to seeing advertising that they may not notice the effect. Activities such as this one make the issues more salient and create an opportunity for students to consider all the advertising around them. Students might discuss how advertising influences their own food choices.

A large body of research shows a connection between advertising practices, eating behavior, and obesity.

Research support #1: An experiment about food branding and children's food preferences

One experiment **aimed to show** that **food branding** affected children's food preferences (Robinson, Borzekowski, Matheson, & Kraemer, 2007). The research question was "Do children prefer the taste of food and drinks if they think they are from McDonald's?" (p. 795). It appears that even small children recognize and prefer brand name foods.

The sample used 3-5 year-old preschool children and their parents. The children attended Head Start Programs for low-income families in California.

401

This experiment used a repeated measures design where children were exposed to both conditions, seeing foods wrapped in the brand name packaging and seeing foods identically wrapped in plain packaging, the **independent variable**.

For the **procedures**, children sat at a table with a research assistant. The assistant sat behind a screen to lessen the chance of giving off subtle messages about which foods to choose. The assistant told the children they could still talk to her even if she was behind a screen.

Another research assistant brought 2 samples of 5 different foods. Food from a local McDonald's was divided into 2 identical samples, just wrapped differently. The foods were presented in random order and included the following.

1. One quarter of a McDonald's hamburger packaged in either a McDonald's wrapper with the logo showing or in a white wrapper without the logo
2. A Chicken McNugget wrapped in either a McDonald's bag with the logo showing or a similar plain white bag
3. Three McDonald's French fries, either in a McDonald's bag or a similar white bag
4. Three ounces of milk, one in a McDonald's cup with a lid and straw and one identical except that it was a plain white cup
5. Two baby carrots sitting on top of a McDonald's French fries bag or on top of a plain white bag. McDonald's does not sell carrots

Teaching children to garden may be the best strategy to counteract advertising and promote healthy eating. This could be done for **CAS**. Watch the **TED talk** "Teach every child about food" by Jamie Oliver. Used under license from megapixl.com.

but this condition was a control to ensure that the preferences were not based on familiarity or food smell.

Each pair of food items was presented one at a time in random order. No characters such as Ronald McDonald appeared with the food. The children tasted a little of each item and told the researcher which one they preferred.

Results showed that children preferred the food with McDonald's wrappers significantly more than they preferred the plain wrapped food. *This was true even with the carrots.*

The experiment was well controlled. For example, the children were not swayed with characters such as Ronald McDonald and were allowed to say that the food samples tasted the same.

The authors **concluded** that corporations with heavily marketed brands could use the study results as an opportunity to change their menu to include healthier foods.

Research example #2: Food advertising primes children and adults to eat more snack food while watching television

The **aim of two experiments** was to show that food advertising does not just influence brand preference, but also primes people to snack more while watching television (Harris, Bargh, & Brownwell, 2009).

Food advertising contains powerful consumption cues that prime snacking. These cues work outside of someone's conscious awareness by pairing snacking and having fun, for example. Two experiments provide the causal evidence.

For **procedures**, experiment #1 randomly assigned children to watch a 14-minute episode of a Disney cartoon with either 4 snack food commercials or 4 non-food commercials for toys and games, the **independent variable**. Children were given a bowl of cheddar cheese "goldfish" crackers and water to eat during the cartoon. Each child was tested alone to prevent imitation and social desirability.

Results showed that children ate significantly more snack food in the food advertising condition, consuming 8.8 grams of food more during 14 minutes. Considering the average time children watch television each day, that translates into eating an excess of calories each day.

We snack when watching television, especially when seeing food commercials. Used under license from megapixl.com.

Experiment #2 used adults. For **procedures**, college students were randomly assigned to watch a 16 minute comedy show with either two commercial breaks (the **independent variable**) containing 11 short commercials, with one group getting 4 of the 11 as food commercials. Both groups had both healthy foods (carrots and celery), moderately healthy foods (trail mix), and unhealthy foods (chocolate chip cookies and cheesy snacks) available during the 16 minute show.

Results showed that the group seeing food commercials were primed to eat more of all the foods, even participants who rated themselves as restrained eaters or not even hungry before watching the comedy show. This shows that food advertising is a powerful cue to eat, affecting people on an unconscious level.

The authors **concluded** that these results contradicted food advertisers claims that their ads just promote food brands. The ads prime people to eat more food, even when not hungry.

Sociocultural explanations for obesity: Low-self-efficacy to stick to a diet

People do not become overweight or obese unless they eat high calorie foods and lead sedentary lives (Bandura, 1977). Low **self-efficacy** to avoid too many sweets and fatty foods is an explanation for obesity, something that can be changed. High self-efficacy is needed for people to develop **self-regulation**, part of Bandura's Social Cognitive Theory. Promoting high self-efficacy to self-regulate eating is further explored under health promotion in the next chapter.

Research example: Self-efficacy in cookie paradise

This experiment demonstrates how high self-efficacy helps people self-regulate eating behavior.

Who can resist cookies in a cookie paradise? Apparently women with high **self-efficacy** for restrained eating can. A body of research shows that self-efficacy plays a key role in whether someone diets successfully (Bandura, 1997). The **aim of an experiment** by Steven Stotland was to show that falling off the dieting wagon is preventable (as cited in Bandura, 1997)!

Is your self-efficacy high enough to say no to these cookies? It is not a problem to have some now and again for treats as we want to avoid an all or nothing attitude toward eating. Used with license from megapixl.com.

Stotland hypothesized that high self-efficacy was the most important factor predicting whether women could stick to their diets.

For the **procedures**, women took ta Self-Efficacy Scale that measured beliefs about the ability to stick to a diet. The women were categorized as having low or high self-efficacy to regulate eating, the **independent variable**. All the women were on a diet at the start of the experiment.

First, all participants violated their diets by eating a piece of chocolate cake. Next, everyone entered cookie paradise, a room filled with cookies. Participants could eat as many cookies as they wanted.

Results showed that women with high self-efficacy ate fewer cookies in cookie paradise than women with low self-efficacy. Perhaps women with low self-efficacy perceived eating the cake as a sign that they had already ruined their diets.

Raising self-efficacy to self-regulate eating behavior should be part of any health promotion program because it may be one reason people are obese. Newer experiments continue to show that raising self-efficacy enhances the results of weight loss management programs over participants just getting standard weight management training (Burke, et al., 2015).

Ethics in health psychology research and a film

You may wish to be in a cookie paradise, but how ethical is this experiment? The Stotland experiment shows that high self-efficacy is a cause of eating regulation, but do the benefits of the study outweigh the risks to participants?

One thing to consider is the nature of the "cookie lab" that forces someone to go off their diet. This is especially a problem for participants with lower self-efficacy because they might see violating their diets with chocolate cake as ruining their diet and think they may as well go ahead and eat cookies. How do researchers know the long term effects of being in this study? Could it damage someone's ability to stick to a healthy diet in the future?

The informed consent form should include that everyone will violate their diet, and might screen out women with serious health problems that could worsen if they do not lose weight. However, since obesity is related to many health problems, is it possible to screen for all possible risks? There is no easy answer, but students should consider potential harm, what researchers should do for participants after being in the study, and if the overall benefits outweigh the risks.

The Scientific American **film *Losing It*** helps us understand what it is like to try and stick with a diet, helping to explain obesity. The film is hosted by Alan Alda so it is funny as well as educational. This film is available from pbs.org. It includes an interview with Jeff Friedman, a researcher studied in the biological ATB about the hormone leptin. Friedman explains the complicated nature of the decision to eat.

Chapter 30
Health Psychology: Promoting health

Chapter Objectives

Students will:
1. Practice using thinking strategies related to evaluation and synthesis, with discuss and evaluate demonstrated.
2. Discuss ways to promote health and reduce stress.
3. Evaluate ways to promote health and reduce problem drinking.
4. Evaluate ways to promote health and reduce obesity.
5. Discuss and evaluate the Theory of Planned Behavior for promoting health.
6. Discuss and evaluate the Health Belief Model for promoting health.
7. Discuss and evaluate Social Cognitive Theory for promoting health.
8. Discuss and evaluate the effectiveness of Healthy Campus to reduce problem drinking at colleges.
9. Discuss and evaluate the effectiveness of Let's Move to reduce obesity.

Health promotion involves preventing or reducing problem behaviors (stress, problem drinking and obesity as our examples) and/or it involves applying formal health promotion theories (Theory of Planned Behavior, Health Belief Model, and Social Cognitive Theory as our examples).

Students might be interested in studying all of the health promotion topics as a general guide to improving health, but prepare two or three for exams. This information is here if you want it, and it is important to have some choices.

The topic about the **effectiveness of health promotion programs** includes Healthy Campus and Let's Move as examples of specific programs.

30.1: Promoting health: Reducing stress with Tai Chi

Discuss means to give a considered and balanced view supported by evidence. Tai Chi and meditation Are two good ways to reduce stress and promote health. We will reflect on these strategies and consider examples of research from the large body of research supporting both.

Self-management: Class activity or CAS: Practice Tai Chi

One goal for teaching health psychology is to encourage students to apply and internalize what they learn. Internalization promotes understanding, and students do not forget as much about something they understand.

Practicing Tai Chi and mindfulness-meditation throughout the health option promotes internalization. I give a health promotion participation grade each marking period during this time.

Many DVDs demonstrate Tai Chi for beginners. I subscribe to Tai Chi magazine, available through www.tai-chi.com/. Wayfarer catalog is accessible through the Tai Chi magazine website. Learning a short Tai Chi form is a great class activity. Many students might not start a stress management project on their own.

I highly recommend Dr. Yang Yang's website for The Center for Taiji Studies, www.chentaiji.com. Click on "about CTS" to watch a video about Yang Yang's journey and read about Tai Chi basics. Click on "research" and "articles" for evidence that Tai Chi influences many aspects of health. Some of my students study a 108-movement Yang Style Tai Chi form. I teach the form I know but teachers can order DVDs or look for a Tai Chi Society in the community.

I attended Yang Yang's seminar and then selected his work for students because of Dr. Yang's research through the University of Illinois. Dr. Yang's book *Taijiquan: The Art of Nurturing, The Science of Power*, is an excellent introduction to Tai Chi and meditation, plus it reviews some Tai Chi research. Some students read Dr. Yang's book as part of their Tai Chi CAS activity.

CAS activities spring from studying ways to reduce stress.

Tai Chi to reduce stress

A large body of research shows that **Tai Chi** reduces stress and promotes health. It improves many health conditions including viruses, hypertension, diabetes, heart disease, respiratory disease, arthritis, pain, sleep difficulties, multiple sclerosis, anxiety, depression, balance, and muscle strength. Tai Chi even enhances cognition, such as improving attention (Converse, Ahlers, Travers, & Davidson, 2014). It is recommended that Tai Chi be investigated as an ADHD treatment.

The Tai Chi most people practice is a "moving meditation," the Tai Chi dance, so the benefits of meditation probably apply to Tai Chi.

Tai Chi practice promotes balance through slow movements that are coordinated with breath. Tai Chi is a walking meditation and there is something serene and appealing about the slow movements.

Tai Chi is a centuries old discipline for health, relaxation, meditation, self-defense, and self-cultivation. The term Tai Chi Chuan means "supreme ultimate fist" and is a powerful martial art. Many people do not know that Tai Chi first developed as a martial art over 2000 years ago. Most people do not practice Tai Chi as a martial art now, but if you practice Kung Fu, the only way to reach the top level is to practice meditation and Tai Chi, both which emphasize inner calm and strength.

The hardest part of practicing Tai Chi is clearing the mind! Achieving serenity during Tai Chi practice requires effort to focus on one's breathing and take the mind away from all the little things we must do each day. Tai Chi breathing is similar to meditative breathing where the breath is deep and moves slowly through the nose and all the way down into the stomach, then slowly returning out through the nose. Correct breathing is essential for cultivating inner energy.

Tai Chi is an *internal* style of training, meaning that it cultivates inner energy and moves it outward. This is the opposite of *external* styles of training, such as karate, weight lifting, or running. *Tai Chi's focus on developing internal energy is probably responsible for its success in improving health.* Tai Chi requires slow movements that are coordinated with deep breathing, both necessary to develop chi (energy).

Tai Chi emphasizes inner calm rather than physical strength. Unbelievable as it might seem, martial artists who understand the strength of internal calmness are feared fighters. This is because Tai Chi teaches one to create and circulate chi, which promotes the creation of inner calm. Chi can be channeled to different parts of the body to promote healing, such as moving the chi to the knee to reduce pain. Channeling chi takes time and practice. Tai Chi, or any other stress management strategy, should be a lifelong practice.

Tai Chi promotes serenity and positive health. This move is called 'snake creeps down.' Anyone can learn Tai Chi!
Used under license with megapixl.com.

The movements of Tai Chi take place in circular patterns and represent yin and yang, opposite forces that coexist, like day and night. Day turns into night and night turns back into day. Both are necessary and represent balance. Examples of yin and yang are everywhere and relate to all aspects of life. One is that cars are a both a convenience and an inconvenience. We travel faster, but must put up with noise, pollution and the risk of accidents. The Internet is convenient and gives us access to more information, but the overuse of the Internet increases stress and anxiety. People love to build houses next to the ocean because of the view, but then must accept that the ocean can become stormy and dangerous. We cannot fight the yin and the yang and can use it to our advantage if we learn about it.

Individuals living in a modern society can use Tai Chi to cope with a stressful world. We can all benefit from creating balance and calm strength in ourselves. Four styles of Tai Chi are available. Each style is named after the families that developed them for teaching within their Chinese villages. The four families are Yang, Sun, Wu, and Chen.

Research support #1: Tai Chi reduces stress in college students

The **aim of one experiment** was to see if Tai Chi was effective in improving college student's mental and physical health (Wang, Y., 2008)

Thirty college students participated in a 3-month long Tai Chi program. Classes met twice each week for one hour. The experiment used a repeated measures design comparing students to themselves before and after Tai Chi classes, the **independent variable**.

For the **procedures**, Wang used a questionnaire that asked about a person's subjective reports of physical and mental health. Physical health questions included body pain and level of physical ability. Mental health questions included vitality, mental and emotion states, and social relationships.

Results showed significant improvement in both physical and mental health. Wang recommends that colleges consider offering Tai Chi as part of regular campus activities.

One advantage is that repeated measures control for history and researchers know if an individual makes changes after Tai Chi practice.

One drawback is that the experiment does not include objective stress measurements, such as saliva cortisol levels.

Research support #2: Tai Chi increases mindfulness in college students, which is correlated with better mood, sleep, lowered stress, and higher self-efficacy

An experiment **aimed to see** if practicing Tai Chi increased mindfulness more than in a control group assigned to recreation (the **independent variable**), and if mindfulness was correlated to better mood, sleep, lowered stress, and higher **self-efficacy** (Caldwell, Emery, Harrison, & Greeson, 2010).

Participants were randomly assigned to a condition, and were measured for mindfulness, mood, perceived stress, and self-efficacy level before and after the Tai Chi or general recreation with questionnaires.

Experimental **results** showed that mindfulness increased only in the Tai Chi condition. Tai Chi participation was also correlated with better mood and sleep, lower stress, and higher self-efficacy.

Research support #3: Tai Chi helps people cope with stress and raises immunity to viruses

Ethics in health research
Placing participants on a waiting list can put them at potential risk for harm if someone is already feeling stressed.

Wait-list control groups must be monitored for increased stress throughout the study, must be informed of potential risks in an informed consent form, and offered the treatment if it is shown beneficial.

Participants in Irwin's study were offered Tai Chi at the end of the study, but they still must be monitored throughout.

Experiments show that **Tai Chi** increases relaxation, which increases immunity to viruses.

An experiment **aimed to study** two research questions (Irwin, 2003). Does Tai Chi practice increase one's immunity to a virus? Does Tai Chi practice positively affect one's general health status? The answer to both questions is yes.

Doctors know that one's risk of getting the **shingles virus** increases with age. Shingles specific cell-mediated immunity (CMI) decreases with age. Vaccination is one way to increase one's immunity. Tai Chi may also be effective, and regular practice may extend the short-term effectiveness of shingles vaccinations.

For the **procedures**, participants were aged 60 or above and were randomly assigned to the Tai Chi group (45 minutes, three times a week for 15 weeks) or a waiting list, the **independent variable**. Everyone on the waiting list received Tai Chi training at the end of the experiment.

Health measures took place at the start of the study, at weeks 5, 10 and 15 (15 weeks total of Tai Chi training), and then at a 1-week follow-up. Measures included physical activity or limitations, social relationships, and pain levels. Blood samples measured shingles immunity at the start and end of the study.

Results follow.

Tai Chi is based on yin/yang, a symbol of balance.
Used under license from
megapixel.com.

1. Shingles virus immunity increased by 50% in people learning Tai Chi.

2. Tai Chi participants reported great improvement for physical functioning. The level of improvement was equal to what someone would have after getting certain medical procedures, such as the new mobility someone has after hip replacement surgery.
3. Tai Chi participants informally reported overall greater relaxation and flexibility.

30.2: Promoting health: Reducing stress with meditation

Meditation is "a practice in which the individual focuses his or her attention inward to achieve a greater sense of clarity and stillness" (SAGE glossary of the Social and Behavioral Sciences, 2009, p.1).

Mindfulness-Meditation

Mindfulness Meditation is a specific type of meditation supported by a large body of research showing

---

Self-management: A walking meditation activity

A good mindfulness meditation activity is a mindfulness walk around school. Students race through campus many times each day and I wonder if they really notice their surroundings. We walk slowly around campus without talking. Students are instructed to notice everything. I work at a historic school with interesting architecture, courtyards, gardens, and photos from the past. We share our experiences after returning to the classroom. I am afraid that the problem of failing to notice one's surroundings is compounded now in the age of cell phones and texting. Reducing stress requires **quieting the mind**. Kabat-Zinn's (1990) book contains a similar activity where people are instructed to mindfully eat a raisin, another class activity.

---

that regular practice reduces stress and chronic illness, and protects chromosomes from damage.

Kabat-Zinn (1990) created Mindfulness-Meditation and heads the Stress Reduction Clinic at the University of Massachusetts Medical Center. He recommends devoting forty-five minutes each day to quiet the mind, something everyone needs to achieve balance.

Lifestyle choices cause or worsen many chronic illnesses, including heart disease, cancer, and diabetes (Ludwig & Kabat-Zinn, 2008). Mindfulness meditation helps people take control of their lives, whether they need to reduce stress or take an active role in managing chronic conditions, such as diabetes or pain.

Mindfulness-based meditation teaches people to live in a state of "being" (Kabat-Zinn, 1990). Living in a constant state of doing where people try to cram too much into a 24-hour day creates ridiculously high stress levels. The consequences of continual high stress levels are great.

Kabat-Zinn asked, "What if you only had moments to live?" People spend so much time focused on the past or future and are missing out on "being," or what we are doing right now. "We may find that much of the time we are really on 'automatic pilot,' functioning mechanically,

Meditation benefits are fast! Used under license from megapixl.com.

without being fully aware of what we are doing or experiencing. It's as if we are not really at home a lot of the time or, put another way, are half awake." (p. 21). Kabat-Zinn says the past has already happened and the future is not yet here. We only own the present. Focusing on the present is not easy for many people but one's quality of life can improve through learning to live in the simplicity of the moment. This does not mean to ignore future college plans or avoid making up with a friend over a past argument, but we can do these things without the past and future taking over our lives.

Mindfulness-meditation helps us live more fully and in the moment.

Self-management: Learning to focus on the breath when meditating

Breathing is the key to meditation. Breathing is the anchor, something on which to focus one's attention.

Kabat-Zinn's meditation CDs include sitting meditations and lying down meditations. Both involve focusing on the breath and include some type of guided practice. One is a body scan, which is my favorite because it occupies constant thinking more than the others. Another CD has mountain and lake meditations. Others ring bells during silent meditation. Guided practices are the best way for beginners to learn to push away the annoying thoughts that intrude on the quiet mind. Davidji also has many good meditations so look him up as well.

Meditation breathing is a four step process.

1. Sit on a chair or comfortable pillow (or lie down, though the tendency to fall asleep is great).
2. Focus on the breath, the anchor. Perhaps counting to 3 slowly as you breathe in and 4 as you breathe out (the relaxation occurs more on the out-breath) will help you stay focused on the breath.
3. Do not get upset or think you are failure when thoughts intrude. Simply acknowledge the thoughts and push them away, going back to the breath.
4. Start with a few minutes and work up to longer periods. Kabat-Zinn recommends forty-five minutes each day.

Seven pillars, or attitudes, promote successful practice (Kabat-Zinn, 1990).

1. *Non-judging.* Become aware of constant streams of thinking but do not label the thoughts good or bad. Thoughts are just thoughts. Humans are designed to think so acknowledge the thoughts and push them away. Time spent labeling thoughts is wasted time. Getting caught up in unproductive thoughts creates a downward spiral. For example, focusing on the thought "I am failing all my classes and will never be a success" is unproductive and will most likely lead to other unproductive thoughts.
2. *Patience.* Life unfolds in its own way and efforts to control everything usually work against us.
3. *Beginner's mind.* Approach each new experience with a fresh eye.
4. *Trust.* Trust gut feelings when making decisions. If something feels wrong then it probably is wrong.
5. *Non-striving.* Meditate without a set goal. Being and non-doing are enough.
6. *Acceptance.* Things are the way they are no matter how hard we might try to exert control. This attitude helps with every aspect of life. Remember, what is happening right now may not be happening in a little while. As Kabat-Zinn says on his body scan CD, "Let go of the tendency we all have to want things to be different than they really are right now"…
7. *Letting go.* Accept life as you find it.

A summary of some main benefits of meditation.

Used under license of megapixl.com.

Research support #1: Mindfulness Meditation improves the brain and immune system

Does practicing mindful meditation change the brain and immune system (Davidson, et al., 2003)?

This experiment **aimed to show** the pathway linking immunity, meditation, and left-side brain activation.

Forty-one employees from a Wisconsin biotechnology corporation were vaccinated for the influenza virus. The study had two hypotheses.

1. Participants receiving Mindfulness Meditation training will show higher antibody titters after taking the influenza vaccine than a wait-list group.
2. Participants with a larger magnitude of left-sided activation in the brain will have a larger increase in immunity as compared to a wait-list group.

> ### Self-management: Using meditation for a class activity or CAS
> I purchased Jon Kabat-Zinn's mindfulness meditation CD series for my students. We practice regularly throughout the health psychology unit. Some are available through www.amazon.com and some are available through www.mindfulnesstapes.com.
>   Davidji's meditations can be found through davidjn.com and davidjn.com/meditations/.
>   Students have trouble sitting still and focusing on the breath for more than a few minutes the first time. We worked up to 20 minutes with the mountain meditation segment.

For the **procedures**, participants were randomly assigned to receive an eight-week Mindfulness Meditation training program led by Kabat-Zinn or a wait-list control group after vaccination, the **independent variable**. The meditation group met for three hours each week and attended a silent seven-hour retreat during week six.

EEGs were recorded before random assignment, after the eight-weeks, and then four months after training. Blood was drawn at three to five weeks and then again at eight to nine weeks to measure immune responses.

Results showed that meditators had higher immunity and greater left-sided anterior brain activation. Davidson concluded that the greater brain activation was caused by meditation. In addition, Davidson noticed that left-sided brain activation increased with both positive and negative events, suggesting that left-sided activation was correlated with adaptive responses to stress.

This was the first study of its kind and opened the door for other research.

Research support #2: A large number of studies show mindfulness meditation has positive effects on physiology

The research base for Mindfulness Meditation's positive effects keeps growing.

Meditation promotes stress reduction through many pathways
It helps people to cope with pain (Ludwig & Kabat-Zinn, 2008).
It reduces stress and depression (Ludwig & Kabat-Zinn, 2008).
It lessens the need for pain and antidepressant medication (Ludwig & Kabat-Zinn, 2008).
It modifies biological pathways by which stress damages the body and mind, such as changing hormones and raising immunity (Ludwig & Kabat-Zinn, 2008).
It may help treat chronic medical conditions such as obesity, eating disorders, and type 2 diabetes. (Ludwig & Kabat-Zinn, 2008).
Mindfulness-meditation may slow cell aging by protecting **telomeres** (Epel, et al., 2009). Think of telomeres as plastic tips on the end of shoelaces (Siegel, n,d,). Telomeres protect chromosomes from damage as they divide. Stress hormones appear to shorten the length of telomeres, exposing chromosomes to early damage.
EEGs show that mindfulness meditation in long-term meditators, such as Buddhist monks, creates **neuroplastic** brain changes that do not exist in people who do not meditate (Ferrarelli, et al., 2013). Long-term meditators have increased parietal-occipital EEG gamma power, which is related to greater attention, **working memory**, and long-term memory.   Since Buddhist monks have more time to meditate than most people, is it possible to learn enough meditation to improve memory and still live in the real world? Training in breath counting may be the key, as it was found that people trained to focus on their breathing and count 1-9 while breathing in and out had decreased mind-wandering, which should help anyone focus their attention where needed (Levinson, Stoll, Kindy, Merry, & Davidson, 2014).

Just how does meditation make so many physiological changes that end with stress reduction? Technology used to study the brain shows the pathways, and *these are unique to meditators* (Ludwig & Kabat-Zinn, 2008).

1. **fMRI** research shows that mindfulness-meditation stimulates **prefrontal cortex** activity and decreases bilateral **amygdala** activity. The amygdala is related to emotion so meditation may help people to mindfully monitor and push aside harmful emotions.
2. **EEGs** show that experienced meditators have heightened coordination of brain activity.

Research support #3: Using meditation to reduce stress in college students

The **aim of the experiment** was to compare two types of meditation with a wait-list control group and study stress and forgiveness in college students (Oman, et al., 2008).

Stress is named as a primary factor contributing to poor academic performance by students.

Participants from a Catholic university in California were randomly assigned to one of three groups, the **independent variable**. Two groups received meditation for eight weeks and the other was placed on a waiting list. Mindfulness-Meditation and Easwarans Eight-Point Program (EPP) were the two meditation conditions. Both meditative practices share similar fundamental components, such as sitting meditation and motivational support, and just differ in detail.

One hypothesis was that participants in both types of meditation training would report greater stress reduction than participants on a waiting list. Another hypotheses predicted that participants receiving meditation training would show increases in forgiveness.

Creating a peaceful place to meditate can benefit us all. Is there a corner somewhere you can do this?
Used under license from megapixl.com.

For **procedures**, participants received meditation training during ninety minute weekly sessions for eight weeks. The authors measured stress, forgiveness, hope, and rumination with questionnaires before the study, at the end of eight weeks, and then again after an eight-week follow up.

Results follow.

1. Both meditation programs produced the same positive changes for participants.
2. Participants receiving meditation training showed a significant reduction in perceived stress, both after the eight-week training and the eight-week follow up period.
3. Participants receiving training showed significantly higher levels of forgiveness than participants on the waiting list.

The authors **concluded** that meditation was an effective stress management strategy for college health promotion programs. Oman's study is the first of its kind to investigate typical college students.

Strengths of the experiment include the follow-up measurement. Many randomized experiments about meditation do not include a follow-up to see if the effects last.

Two limitations are noteworthy. First, the control group did not do anything. What if the control group received a different type of stress management training? Second, the experiment relied on self-reports. There was no objective assessment of stress, rumination, forgiveness, and hope, such as saliva tests measuring stress hormones.

Research example #4: New research showing that mindfulness training lessens binge drinking in college students

An exciting application for mindfulness is to help lessen a huge problem on college campuses—**binge drinking**. The **aim of the experiment** was to show that meditators binge drink less often. This research is new and needs replication so do not think it is fully verified. It is included to show you the broad applications of mindfulness.

Participants were assigned to one of two groups, mindfulness meditation or a control group, the **independent variable** (Mermelstein & Garske, 2015). Questionnaires were given both before and after treatments. One was the Drinking Refusal Self-Efficacy Questionnaire, used because low **self-efficacy** to refuse drinks is a key component of what makes people start drinking.

Results show that both groups were equal in all measurements before treatment but after 4 weeks, the meditation group reported less binge drinking, higher self-efficacy to refuse drinks, and higher dispositional mindfulness. Students in the meditation condition seemed to like the treatment because they had good attendance and gave high satisfaction ratings to the process.

> **Drawing relationships between ideas**
> Low drinking refusal self-efficacy is one of the causes of alcoholism used in the next section, so file this away in your mind.
>   **Self-efficacy** is a key concept for health psychology and it appears frequently.

30.3: Promoting health and reducing problem drinking

Treating alcoholism is challenging. Perhaps 80% to 90% of recovering alcoholics experience at least one relapse, so a better strategy is prevention so fewer people are problem drinkers in the first place. One successful strategy is to target **outcome expectancies**, a **Social Cognitive Theory** concept meaning that people expect something particular to happen. For example, outcome expectancies for drinking are that it solves people's problems, reduces stress, and increases popularity. All of these expectations are incorrect and contribute to problem drinking.

Programs targeting outcome expectancies are very successful. They are most often used on college campuses and are aimed at younger people before they show the symptoms of alcohol use disorder.

Evaluate means to make a judgment supported by evidence. The research base for Social Cognitive Theory strategies is highly ethical, stands the test of time, and is cross-culturally relevant.

Research support #1: Early findings about the role of expectancy beliefs

Correlation studies already pointed to a relationship between challenging positive alcohol expectations and lessening moderate to heavy drinking in college males (Drakes & Goldman, 1993). The **aim of the experiment** was to confirm that treatment targeting outcome expectancies really caused positive changes.

For the **procedures**, moderate to heavy drinking college males were randomly assigned to one of three conditions, the **independent variable**. One group received an expectancy challenge targeting alcohol outcome expectancies. The second group received general alcohol information. The third group acted as a control.

Results follow.
1. Participants in the challenge condition lowered their alcohol expectancies and reported less drinking.
2. Participants receiving information had more knowledge but no decrease in reported drinking.

The authors **concluded** that college prevention and treatment programs should include strategies to change alcohol expectancies.

Evidence supporting expectancy challenges grew over the next two decades. Two examples are next.

Research support #2: The benefits of just one day of expectancy treatment

The **aim of the experiment** was to see if a one-day **expectancy treatment** is beneficial (Fried & Dunn, 2012)? The Expectancy Challenge Alcohol Literacy Curriculum (ECALC) is a one-session program attempting to change alcohol expectancies and decrease alcohol use. Fried studied the effectiveness of ECALC in college males with a high risk for problem drinking.

Heavy drinking males at a large US University were randomly assigned to the ECALC program or a control group receiving general drinking information, the **independent variable**.

Results showed that students in the ECALC session improved over the control group in all aspects of drinking behaviors that included the following.

1. Decreased blood alcohol content
2. Decrease in the number of days of drinking each week
3. Decrease in binge drinking

Fried **concluded** that colleges had two important reasons for using the strategy.

1. A single-session is beneficial.
2. Changes in expectancies occurred without artificial lab situations. Participants are not exposed to drinking in the study, such as with studies using **bar-labs** where participants can drink (similar to cookie paradise in the last chapter that exposed overweight women to cake and then all the cookies they wanted) so researchers can figure out what helps reduce drinking, increasing the ethics of research.

> **Evaluate ethics in health psychology**
> Treatments targeting outcome expectancies are highly ethical. They are low risk and participants in other conditions can easily be given the expectancy treatments at the end of the study. Everyone learns something important about drinking, so a likely result is higher self-efficacy to refuse drinks.

Research support #3: Culture and outcome expectancy programs

The **aim of a correlation study** was to investigate how culture influenced the effectiveness of outcome expectancy programs (Des Rosiers, Schwartz, Zamboanga, Ham, & Huang, 2012). Outcome expectancies about **acculturation** were examined in 1,527 Hispanic students attending a wide-range of US colleges.

Acculturation means that people's behavior and thinking change when they move into a new culture and absorb its practices. People may adopt the behaviors of their new cultures and/or feel pressure to give up their original cultural values and practices.

For the **procedures**, participants filled out self-reports about their Hispanic and American cultural practices and drinking habits, such as heavy drinking, binge drinking, and drunk driving. Students were divided into two cultural orientation groups. One group had bicultural values, meaning they valued both Hispanic and American cultures. The second group had acculturated values, meaning they primarily valued American culture.

Questionnaire responses were correlated to cultural orientation. Culture matters. **Results** included the following.

1. Hispanic students with bicultural values had negative outcome expectancies for their experience with alcohol, meaning they expected a negative experience and also had high levels of binge drinking and drunk driving.
2. Hispanic students acculturated into American values had negative outcome expectations and less binge drinking and drunk driving, similar to other findings about outcome expectations and drinking behavior.

The authors **concluded** that the link between outcome expectations and behavior is different in students not acculturated into American cultural practices and should be noted by college administrators.

30.4: Promoting health: Reducing obesity

Evaluate means to make a judgment (appraisal) supported by evidence. There is a large body of evidence supporting the use of biological and sociocultural strategies to promote a healthy weight and reduce obesity. Most all of these studies are experiments showing causation. One is a correlation study, and this provides method triangulation for the need to increase self-efficacy when promoting health.

Evaluate research and ethics in health psychology

Do not assume that all levels of a biopsychosocial model are verified as important for promoting health for every health problem.

Targeting cognitive factors is not effective for reducing obesity or helping people maintain weight loss after dieting (Cooper, et al., 2010). Cognitive strategies are at best useful in the short-term.

It is not ethical to use strategies to promote health without long-term evidence, possibly causing potential harm to participants. As a result of this concern, this book focuses on biological and sociocultural strategies to promote a healthy weight and reduce obesity.

Many strategies to promote a healthy weight are available but the most important plan of action is *lifestyle change* related to diet and exercise. All the other strategies are meant to support one's efforts to make lifestyle changes. Efforts to reduce weight without lifestyle changes are unlikely to produce desired long-term effects. A person's **self-efficacy** to make effective changes is probably the most important part of maintaining a healthy weight and is the key element for **health promotion**.

Studying ways to promote a healthy weight may increase your empathy for people trying to lose weight. Sticking with a plan is challenging given what we know about leptin resistance, self-efficacy, and food marketing. There is so much working against someone's attempts to change long-standing habits. The best reason for the 21st Century student to study this topic is to develop good habits when young to reduce the risk of becoming obese in the first place!

Self-management activity: Evaluating media claims about weight reduction
The 21st century student looks for ways to avoid health risks in the future. Why get into a situation where you must diet? Exploring diets advertised in the media can helps students get some perspective.

Educating students about media and behavior is important. One activity is for students to locate online, magazine, and television advertisements for weight loss drugs and evaluate the information. What promises are implied? What pictures make people think that the drugs are a quick fix? What does the small print say? Do advertisers make it clear that diet change and exercise are expected along with taking the drug? What research is cited? How much of the advertisement consists of personal testimony? Students should evaluate the use of personal testimony. I expect to see randomized experiments backing up any causation claims.

Once someone is obese it is hard to lose the weight and stick to a healthy diet. Learn better health habits so this is not you needing help to lose weight!

Promoting health: Reducing and preventing obesity with a high-protein breakfast

High-protein diets (HP), particularly the addition of a **HP breakfast**, have experimental support as an effective strategy to prevent and treat obesity (Leidy, et al., 2015).

Obesity in children and adolescents is of particular interest because eating habits are formed early and evidence shows young people are greatly affected by our modern food environment (Leidy, Ortunau, Douglas, & Hoertel, 2013). Adolescents eat most of their calories between 4 p.m. and midnight, resulting in food cravings throughout the day. Most of the snacking consists of great tasting but calorie packed foods such as candy, cookies, soda, and chips. Breakfast skipping is common and worsens the problem because it increases cravings for snacks throughout the day. This pattern of eating contributes to the shift away from eating for physiological reasons in favor of eating for reward-driven reasons, habits hard to break later in life.

HP diets work best when people eat protein throughout the day, with breakfast having the greatest effect (Leidy, et al., 2015). It is recommended that each meal contain at least 25-30 grams of protein.

The two studies reviewed will help students understand how a HP breakfast changes physiology. A body of research supports HP breakfast as a way to reduce and prevent obesity and increase health.

Research example #1: No more breakfast skipping: A high-protein breakfast helps control appetite throughout the day

The **aim of the experiment** was to show that adding more protein to a teenager's breakfast influenced feelings of hunger and fullness, hormone levels, and eating later in the day (Leidy & Racki, 2010).

Why do so many adolescents skip breakfast? Perhaps they are not hungry, have little time to cook, or think that breakfast skipping is a good way to lose weight. The problem is worsened when teens do not get enough sleep and rush to school, leaving no time for breakfast.

Breakfast skipping is associated with overeating during the day, weight gain, and **obesity** (Leidy & Racki, 2010). Fewer people eat breakfast compared with twenty years ago and the decline mirrors increasing obesity rates. Currently, about 75% of older and overweight adolescents regularly skip breakfast.

Thirteen normal weight and overweight breakfast skipping teenagers were in the sample. For the **procedures**, they were randomly assigned to one of three groups, the **independent variable**. One group continued to skip breakfast. The second group ate a protein normal breakfast. The third group ate a protein rich breakfast.

Participants went to a lab on three different days and spent five hours eating required foods, giving blood tests, and filling out questionnaires. A seven-day interval occurred between each testing day. Participants were paid $120.

Each session required the teenagers to do the following.

1. Provide a blood sample after fasting overnight. One **hormone** tested was **Peptide YY** (PYY). PYY decreases the time it takes for one's stomach to empty after a meal, increases the efficiency of digestion, and increases nutrient absorption.

2. Complete a questionnaire about hunger and fullness.

3. Eat an assigned meal, either a protein-normal breakfast, a protein-rich breakfast, or water (the breakfast skipping group). The breakfast groups were similar except for changes related to protein. *Pancakes for the protein–rich group contained ½ cup of whey powder.* Overall, the protein-normal breakfast contained *14% protein*, 73% carbohydrates, and 13% fat. The protein-rich breakfast contained *38% protein*, 49% carbohydrates, and 13% fat. The meals included the following.

A high-protein breakfast similar to the one in the experiment. You do not have to eat the meat to get enough protein, as the study used Whey protein. Vegetarians and vegans can substitute vegetable-based protein powder. Vegans can also use an egg substitute.
Used under license from megapixl.com.

A. Three buttermilk pancakes with butter and syrup
B. Scrambled eggs (1/4 cup eggbeaters and 1 and 2/3 Tsp cheese)
C. Water

4. Eat the assigned breakfast within 20 minutes.

5. Take more blood samples and fill out more questionnaires during the rest of the five-hour testing period.

6. Everyone ate a buffet lunch at the end of testing that included crackers, fruits, vegetables, meats, cheeses, and water.

7. Keep a record of all food eaten until the next morning.

Results follow.

1. There were no appetite differences between the breakfast skipping group and the protein-normal group.

2. The protein-rich breakfast group experienced the greatest feelings of fullness between meals.

3. Adolescents eating a protein-rich breakfast consumed fewer calories throughout the rest of the day.

4. PYY concentrations increased after eating either type of breakfast.

Self-management activity
Try a **breakfast challenge**. Ask students to create healthy breakfast menus that can be prepared ahead of time.

The authors **concluded** that while eating any kind of breakfast is important, eating a protein-rich breakfast helps adolescents control their appetite throughout the day. The recommended daily allowance

418

of protein for adolescents is between 10% and 30% of total food intake. Do you think most adolescents eat enough protein?

One limitation of the study is that it examined food intake over the short-term. Future studies should examine the effects of eating a protein rich breakfast on long-term appetite.

CAS ideas

One idea for **CAS** is for students to revamp their diets. I like CAS activities that start with something on a personal level that then moves out to the community level and also has global implications. Students frequently eat on the run, skip meals, and consume large amounts of caffeine, sugar and fats. In addition, they eat large amounts of grain products that turn into sugar quickly in the bloodstream.

One place to start is with *Food and Mood* by Elizabeth Somers. Somers discusses how diet affects health in a way that anyone can understand. Somers asks readers to take many questionnaires, which we know students love, and then suggests alternatives foods, including easy recipes. Somers discusses the **glycemic index**, which everyone should understand.

After making personal changes, students could design a CAS project that includes educating others at school about foods and encouraging schools to include healthy foods for purchase. To increase internationalism and ethics in CAS activities, students can trace the food sources from a favorite fast-food restaurant or start a school garden. Look at the website turninggreen.org to see what your school might participate in a global effort.

Research example #2: More evidence about the physical benefits of a HP breakfast

The **aim of the experiment** was to show that a HP breakfast caused reward stimulation in the brain and reduce snaking through the day (Hoertel, Will, & Leidy, 2014). For **procedures**, twenty adolescent girls were in the sample and were randomly assigned to one of three groups, the **independent variable**. One group continued to skip breakfast, one group ate a 350 calorie breakfast with 13 grams of protein, and one group ate a 350 calorie breakfast with 35 grams of protein.

Participants ate their assigned breakfast for 7 days and then went into the lab for tests that included giving a blood sample and taking questionnaires about their feelings of fullness and what they ate throughout the rest of the day.

Results showed that both breakfast groups had fewer food cravings throughout the day than the breakfast skippers, and increased HVA concentrations in the blood, which is correlated with **dopamine** activity in the brain.

Dopamine is a **neurotransmitter** that stimulates reward centers in the brain. This is important because if people crave snacks throughout the day to get this reward stimulation, then it would be helpful to know if dopamine activity is increased by eating a HP diet. Stimulating dopamine activity through a HP breakfast is then helpful in reducing obesity because people are less likely to snack throughout the day.

Promoting health: Reducing and preventing obesity: Traditional Chinese Medicine

Herbs and **acupuncture** are effective for reducing **obesity** and promoting the natural balance in one's body that promotes health. Just remember that herbs and acupuncture are meant to support lifestyle changes. You cannot eat a terrible diet and then expect a Doctor of Oriental Medicine to fix the problem.

Doctors practicing **Traditional Chinese Medicine** (TCM) view all health problems as imbalances in five areas, poor diet, emotions, the external environment, lifestyle habits such as lack of exercise, and genetics (Helmer, 2006). Diet, lifestyle, and genes are the most important for obesity, but diet and lifestyle are the only things people can control. *Herbs and acupuncture create physiological changes that support a person's efforts to make lifestyle changes.* Research shows that diet and exercise are often not enough to reduce or someone's weight or keep someone at an ideal weight.

Ears, hands and feet contain links to all other areas of the body and are common sites for acupuncture needles. *Acupuncture is very relaxing and the needles are hair thin so they do not hurt the way a needle used to give a shot might hurt!*

Acupuncture points on the ear

You would never get needles in all of the points at the same time, just those related to opening up you chi!
Used under license from megapixl.com.

Acupuncture is inexpensive in comparison to costs for Western medical care and has no adverse side effects.

Acupuncture affects an obese person's physiology in a number of ways (Cabyoglu, Ergene, & Tan, 2006).

1. It increases stomach muscle tone, which helps suppress appetite.
2. It stimulates the satiety center in the **hypothalamus**.
3. It stimulates the vagal nerve, which then increases **serotonin** and helps to suppress appetite. Serotonin increases intestinal movement.
4. It reduces **stress** and **depression** by stimulating the production of serotonin and **endorphins**.

Before we examine the evidence, it is helpful to get an overview of Chinese medicine.

Traditional Chinese Medicine Overview

Western and Traditional Chinese Medicine (TCM) differ radically.

- ❖ Western medicine focuses on identifying symptoms, finding causes of the symptoms, and then eliminating the cause or at least the symptoms (Kaptchuk, 1983). TCM doctors focus on the entire person both physically and psychologically, look for relationships between seemingly unrelated things, such as your diet, low mood, sinus problems, and digestive problems, and then treat the entire person.
- ❖ TCM seeks to restore balance in the entire system.
- ❖ TCM views the human body as a series of 12 meridians, bioelectrical impulses that can be viewed as an electrical system throughout the human body. Meridians circulate energy, or Qi (you may see this word as chi), throughout one's system and then connect the energy to the outer body.
- ❖ Acupuncture points are the places where the meridians connect Qi with the outer body. Acupuncture needles unblock stagnant energy flow through a specific meridian. **Tai Chi** and **herbs** also unblock stagnant energy flow.
- ❖ Western medicine has no concept similar to Qi (Hammer, 2005).
- ❖ Unblocking stagnant energy has its theoretical roots in the concepts of **yin and yang**. Yin and yang represent balance, opposites that co-exist, like night and day, good fortune and bad fortune. One cannot exist without the other and both are necessary for a balanced life. For example, everything comes with a convenience and an inconvenience. Cars make travel easier, but we have the danger for accidents and the annoyance of traffic jams. But the two opposites are inevitable. Westerners often try to fight inevitable yin and yang opposites and have trouble finding balance.
- ❖ Acupuncture and Tai Chi are studied in the same way as western treatments. The best experiments randomly assign people to groups. Over time, TCM treatments have come under the same demands for evidence-based treatments as western treatments. Some TCM experiments do not use randomization, so those studies have weaknesses. Case studies are frequently used to study herbs and obesity and cannot stand alone for claims that herbs cause a change. Look for more experimental studies as the entire field of TCM research develops.

A body of randomized experiments shows the effectiveness of acupuncture in reducing obesity and promoting overall chi balance in the body. The research has **observer triangulation**, meaning that independent researchers find the same thing.

Research example #1: Acupuncture reduces weight, bad cholesterol, and triglycerides

One experiment **aimed to study** the effects of acupuncture on weight loss and randomly assigned women to receive acupuncture for 20 days, a 1425-calorie diet for 20 days, or to act as a control, the **independent variable** (Cabyoglu, Ergene, & Tan, 2006). Twenty-two women received acupuncture and 21 received the diet. Weight, total serum cholesterol, HDL (good cholesterol), LDL (bad cholesterol), and triglycerides (fat in the body that is linked to heart disease) were measured before and after the study. **Results** showed that the women receiving acupuncture lost more weight (a 4.8% reduction) than the diet group (a 2.5% weight reduction). The acupuncture group also showed significant reductions in total cholesterol, triglycerides, and LDL.

The physiological changes listed on the previous page are stated in terms that everyone in western countries can understand. Studying a little TCM philosophy related to obesity helps students to understand why herbs and acupuncture are useful and increases **intercultural understanding**, an important mission for a program taking an international approach to learning.

TCM doctors view obesity as a weakened digestive system and seek to strengthen it (Helmer, 2006). TCM doctors believe that a series of **meridians** run through the body like an electrical system. Each meridian line is related to an organ. The spleen is the organ related to obesity. A weak spleen is related to build-ups of phlegm in the digestive system. Phlegm is turbid, meaning it is muddy and dense. Phlegm keeps **Qi** (energy) from freely flowing throughout the body. Someone with phlegm build-up has excessive heat and dampness in their digestive system. *Herbs and acupuncture reduce dampness and heat.* Once heat and dampness are reduced, Qi flows more freely, clears out the turbid phlegm, and the spleen is stronger. Patients must make fundamental lifestyle changes to support the weight loss.

Research example #2: Acupuncture combined with diet and exercise is more effective than diet and exercise changes alone

An experiment **aimed to show** that acupuncture assists efforts to change diet and increase exercise (El-Mekawy, ElDeeb, & Ghareib, 2014). Obese participants were randomly assigned to either laser acupuncture along with diet and exercise changes or diet and exercise changes alone for 12 weeks, the **independent variable**.

Results showed that the acupuncture group lost the most fat in their waist and hips, along with lowered cholesterol and insulin levels than the control group.

This study is important because the experimental evidence for acupuncture to help someone maintain a normal weigh has grown significantly since 2010 using randomized controlled experiments, something required to demonstrate causation. Students can look up acupuncture and obesity studies at pubmed.gov if they would like to see a list of all that has been published.

Promoting health: Reducing and preventing obesity by raising self-efficacy

No anti-obesity strategy is successful in the long run without lifestyle change (Bandura, 1997). Perceived **self-efficacy** to make effective life change is fundamental to maintaining a healthy weight. Bandura believes that self-efficacy mediates cognitive factors, such as dichotomous thinking (thinking in extremes, such as "I had one cookie so my diet is a total failure") and is the most important predictor of behavior.

How do people sustain a pattern of choosing healthy foods? How do people stick with a regular exercise routine? Can you say no to the cookies someone brings to class? Can you find another way to vent frustration besides eating potato chips or ice cream? Do you schedule and then respect the time set aside for regular exercise?

People become overweight only after overeating high-calorie foods and leading sedentary lifestyles; genetics is not a direct cause (Bandura, 1997). People often eat when stressed, even though they are not hungry and especially after seeing food advertisements. When stressed, we tend to crave sweet and fatty foods, adding to the frustrations of sticking with a healthy diet. People try to manage weight problems by going on and off diets, which works against them in the long run (Bandura, 1997). The body adapts to low calorie diets by reducing metabolism, one factor related to weight regain.

Weight loss programs must help people manage stressors related to emotional overeating and sporadic dieting. Forming new habits requires **self-regulation** skills to raise one's self-efficacy.

Bandura outlines 6 strategies for keeping a healthy weight.

1. Self-monitor eating and exercise behaviors.

2. Create a series of realistic short-term goals, such as losing one pound a week and eating fast food 3 times a week instead of every day. Goals such as losing 20 pounds in 2 weeks and never eating snacks are unrealistic. Modify goals after each small success.

3. Plan rewards for achieving goals and learning new thinking styles that maintain realistic short-term goals.

4. Find new activities to replace the time spent eating. Taking a walk or playing with a pet are better ideas.

5. Create an environment that supports realistic goals. Perhaps you can eat a meal before going to the grocery store. Do not buy a bag of cookies, thinking that you can avoid the cookies once at home. The cookie bag sitting on the counter is too tempting. The decision to stay away from high-risk situations is similar to the decisions alcoholics must make. Just as an alcoholic may make a poor decision to go to the bar and just drink soda when surrounded by drinkers, the dieter may make a poor decision to keep sweets and fatty comfort foods at home where they are too tempting.

6. Plan strategies for getting yourself back on track after little slips. For example, eating one cookie does not destroy the entire diet.

Planning activities that can be done in place of sitting and eating raises self-efficacy. Walking your dog is a great choice.
Source: pixabay.com

Besides the experiment in the last chapter about self-efficacy to say no to cookies in cookie paradise, next is a correlation study showing the use of health coaches to promote self-regulation for starting and continuing healthy diets and lifestyles. Bandura loves the idea of health coaches and thinks they can lessen the cost of health care. Some people need regular coaching, some need it now and then, and others need just a little help. Bandura aims to promote health rather than treat the problem once someone is obese.

Research support: Self-regulation training raises self-efficacy to exercise and change eating habits

The **aim of a correlation study** was to show the relationship between **self-regulation** training, **self-efficacy** to exercise and eat healthy foods, and changes in BMI (Annesi & Gorjala, 2010).

Weight loss program results are disappointing. People have trouble getting past all the barriers to weight loss, such as lack of time and social pressure to eat unhealthy foods. It is no surprise that most people regain lost weight.

Men and women with an average BMI of 40.5 were in the sample. For **procedures**, the study measured exercise self-efficacy, eating self-efficacy, mood, and BMI before and after treatment. All wellness specialists were blind to the purpose of the study.

The exercise part of the study consisted of 6 one-hour long meetings with a wellness specialist over 6 months. Computer programs assisted participants between sessions. The self-regulation training covered goal setting, negative thought-stopping, cognitive restructuring, self-reward, and how to overcome barriers to change.

The diet part of the program consisted of 6 one-hour sessions over 3 months led by a wellness specialist. Instruction covered nutrition, using the US Food Pyramid, meal and snack planning, and self-regulation strategies.

Results showed improvements on all measures.

1. BMI was lower.
2. Self-regulation for exercising increased.
3. Self-regulation for choosing healthy foods increased.
4. Self-efficacy was higher.

The authors **concluded** that self-regulation training correlated with higher self-efficacy to exercise, choose healthy diets, and lower one's BMI. This study was conducted in the field rather than a lab setting, and offers **method triangulation** to experiments about self-efficacy and obesity.

30.5: Health Promotion: Theory of Planned Behavior

Chapters 11 (Described the theory) and 12 (Evaluated the theory and gave you much to consider for a balanced view) included the **Theory of Planned** Behavior. One application was about eating a healthier diet. Students can reuse what they learned about **decision-making** for exam questions about promoting health.

30.6: Health Promotion: Health Belief Model

Discuss means to give a considered and balanced view supported by evidence. This section is a consideration of the **Health Belief Model** along with an evaluation of research supporting it. Evaluate means to make a judgment using evidence. Research supports the Health Belief Model, but it has criticism from Albert Bandura's Social Cognitive Theory.

Model of health promotion: Health Belief Model

The **Health Belief Model** is popular and the basis for many promotion programs so it is important to know if it is a good predictor of health behavior.

The Health Belief Model is one of the oldest health models focusing on social cognition and health behavior (Gurung, 2010). The model was created after surveys sponsored by the US Public Health Service showed that people were not taking advantage of public health screenings.

The Health Belief Model started with the following four components relating to someone's perceptions about disease prevention and treatment (Hayden, 2009).

1. *Perceived seriousness*
2. *Perceived susceptibility*
3. *Perceived benefits*
4. *Perceived barriers*

Each component influences the others. Over time several other components were added.

1. *Cues of action*
2. *Motivating factors*. **Cultural practices** are examples.
3. *Self-efficacy*. Self-efficacy is an additional factor that is tested alongside of the basic Health Belief Model components. Self-efficacy may be fundamental to predicting actual behavior stemming from health beliefs.

The Health Belief Model has had some success as a tool for conducting research about why people take or fail to take positive action for their health.

Research supporting the Health Belief Model: Time Orientation and hypertension management

Let's review the **dimensions of culture** before discussing the Brown and Segal (1996) experiment showing that **time orientation** affects hypertension management. This is a chance to apply cultural dimensions to health promotion.

This experiment doubles as evidence for the cultural dimension time orientation.

Dimensions of culture overview

❖ The dimensions of culture are research tools that help psychologists compare cultures.

❖ The dimensions are **etics**, meaning that they are pan-cultural groups of continuums and every culture falls on these continuums in some way (Hank Davis, personal communication, June, 2008).

❖ Anything that is an etic can be a dimension of culture. Examples of dimensions include but are not limited to the following.
   a. Individualism- Collectivism
   b. Masculinity- Femininity
   c. Power distance
   d. Uncertainty avoidance
   e. Time orientation
   f. Context
   g. Tightness-Looseness

❖ A dimension of culture must be backed up with research showing that it really is universal. Watch making a generality that a dimension of culture automatically explains any cross-cultural behavior difference. Evidence must show that the behavior is actually connected to a dimension through correlations or experiments.

❖ The dimensions are abstractions, tendencies to behave.

❖ Geert Hofstede studied the dimensions in terms of countries, which is valuable, but the work coming out of his analysis of IBM surveys is not as relevant for understanding everyday individual behavior, such as how someone might use a compliance technique or manage hypertension. Harry Triandis studied individualism-collectivism and applied it to individuals so his theoretical perspective is more relevant to the IB learning outcomes. Edward T. Hall studied time orientation, another popular dimension with many applications to individual behavior.

❖ Experiments and correlation studies are two ways to study how the dimensions of culture affect behavior. Questionnaires separate participants into groups for quasi-experiments. A behavior can be correlated to each end of the dimension continuum to show relationships.

Time orientation affects people's motivation to manage **hypertension** (Brown & Segal, 1996). This study shows that culture is a fundamental factor in predicting health behavior and demonstrates how the **dimensions of culture** are used as research tools.

The **aim of the quasi-experiment** was to see if differences in beliefs about hypertension and its treatment existed between White Americans and African Americans. Brown and Segal write that successfully managing hypertension requires future oriented thinking, so differences in time orientation affect medical treatment plans.

The four main factors of the **Health Belief Model** were used as a basis for designing the study along with ethnic group, the degree of poverty, and hypertension time orientation were important modifying factors for the study, the many **independent variables**.

Time orientation is the dimension of culture related to how people use time (Hall, 1959). Hall thought about time orientation as a continuum with two opposite poles, **monochronic** and **polychronic** (Hank Davis, personal communication, June, 2008). People with a monochronic time orientation do one thing at a time, like to be on time, stick to plans, meet deadlines, and value promptness. People with a polychronic time orientation do many things at once, are easily distracted, and put relationships before deadlines.

The sample consisted of African and White Americans living in north and central Florida and the Southeast area referred to as the "stroke belt" (Brown & Segal, 1996). A random sample of participants with hypertension for at least one year and taking pharmaceutical medications was studied.

For the **procedures**, the Hypertension Temporal Orientation Scale questionnaire was developed by the researchers and administered through telephone interviews. The **dependent variables** included the following.

1. Beliefs about a person's view of the severity of their hypertension
2. Beliefs about a person's susceptibility for experiencing the consequences of hypertension
3. Beliefs about the benefits of taking medication and/or home remedies

Many people living in the "stroke belt" have a cultural tradition of eating fried foods, potatoes, and biscuits with butter. Cultural traditions are hard to change, and this study finds that people with polychronic time orientation are less likely to follow through with medical advice.
Used with license from megapixl.com.

Results showed that African American participants were more present oriented than White Americans, particularly in response to questions about day-to-day hypertension management. African Americans were more likely to use home remedies and be non-compliant about taking pharmaceutical medications according to doctor's directions.

The authors **concluded** that health promotion campaigns and medical advice about treating hypertension on a day-to-day basis *must consider time orientation for success*. Health care providers should become educated about time orientation because it is so fundamental to people's beliefs. It does not do any good to give someone directions about managing chronic health problems unless the advice is culturally relevant. For example, the most present oriented participants thought they were the least susceptible to long-term consequences of hypertension such as stroke and heart attack (Brown & Segal, 1996).

The next section about self-efficacy and self-management is important in light of the Brown and Segal study. Perhaps Albert Bandura is right in suggesting that health coaches can help people gain control over chronic disease by offering individualized self-management training aiming to raise self-efficacy.

30.7: Health promotion: Social Cognitive Theory of self-efficacy and self-management

Discuss means to give a considered and balanced view supported by evidence. This section gives a balanced view of health promotion by offering Social Cognitive Theory as an alternative to the Health Belief Model. Evaluate means to make a judgment using evidence. Plenty of evidence exists to support Social Cognitive Theory as an alternative to the Health Belief Model.

Bandura (2004, 2005) wants to help people make long lasting health behavior changes but criticizes the existing western medical care system. Present western medical care philosophy aims to fix chronic diseases after they develop.

The strategy of fixing chronic disease is financially unsustainable. As people live longer, the demand for "fixes" will exceed the supply of available expensive medical treatment. Those currently making all the health decisions (Bandura calls them the gatekeepers) realize that many people have low self-efficacy to change their lifestyles. At the same time these gatekeepers are poorly equipped to handle people's low self-efficacy and the problems are either ignored or the patient receives a pill. When will medical systems provide people with the skills to manage diet, exercise, and stress that are important to the newest health promotion campaigns?

Bandura recommends ways to make the transition, suggesting, "self-management is good medicine" (2005, p. 245). One good reason to study health psychology is for students to learn effective tools to manage their health before traveling too far down the road to chronic disease. Many students report eating too much junk food, failing to get enough sleep, and feeling stressed and where might these behaviors lead? Taking care of any chronic health problem after it develops is expensive and time consuming, plus it limits life's enjoyments.

Self-management uses all the Social Cognitive Theory concepts, including **modeling** and **self-efficacy**. How do self-management health programs change behavior?

Social cognitive theory includes four factors that determine health behavior (Bandura, 2004).

1. Knowledge of risks and benefits of change.
2. Self-efficacy
3. Outcome expectations
4. Perceived impediments

Self-efficacy is the most important and affects the others. People must feel capable to learn about the risks involved in avoiding change, view the benefits as positive even though change requires effort, create positive goals for the outcome of their efforts, and feel competent to overcome impediments.

Bandura (2004) criticizes other health promotion theories and models, including the **Health Belief Model**. Other theories and models are similar to Social Cognitive Theory and just different ways of describing **outcome expectations**. Perceived susceptibility and benefits are really just negative and positive outcome expectations. In addition, other theories and models are not very good at educating people about making positive behavior change. It does little good to predict behavior if the theory does not also include how to change habits. For example, the Brown and Segal (1996) study about time orientation and hypertension management predicts behavior but does not offer specific ways to make changes, other than suggesting that we take time orientation into account. This is a valuable piece of advice but how might we promote change?

Bandura supports self-management strategies such as one called the **self-management model** in an experiment evaluating the success of a program to increase exercise and reduce smoking in heart patients (DeBusk, et al., 1994). The program offered nursing support while patients were still in the hospital and continued support after release. The hope was to reduce the future heart disease. The self-management training was successful.

Self-management programs are most effective when they offer support to varying degrees depending on needs (Bandura, 2005). People with high self-efficacy to make changes receive some training and support, people with moderate self-efficacy receive a little more help, and people with low-self-efficacy start with daily coaches. Self-management programs should be tailored to individual needs. Everyone needs support but at different levels. **Computer assisted self-management programs** should be used whenever possible.

Research support for Self-management: A culturally based self-management program for diabetes care

A large body of research shows the effectiveness of self-management programs for a variety of chronic health conditions.

The **aim of one experiment** was to show that Mexican-Americans living on the Texas-Mexico border receiving a culturally based education program about **diabetes** management would show increased self-management and better health (Brown, Garcia, Kouzekanani, & Hanis, 2002). Many of the participants were obese as well as diabetic.

Film support

I recommended films about obesity called *The Science of Fat*, available free from www.biointeractive.org earlier in the book. Ronald Evans discusses research about the rapid weight gain of Mexican Pima Indians coming to live in the US in one segment. The Sharon Brown experiment is a natural extension of the film material.

Approximately 50% of Mexican-Americans living on the Mexico-Texas border have type 2 diabetes and this group has the highest rate of diabetes related deaths in Texas. Genetic predispositions account for about 40% of the diabetes risk so environmental factors are a primary reason why so many young Mexican-Americans have type 2 diabetes. Environmental factors include poor diet, lack of exercise, lack of education, poverty, and barriers to receiving medical treatment. The right support might improve health.

Starr County, Texas was the research site, a place with low income, high unemployment, and shortages of health care practitioners.

The sample included 265 people with type 2 diabetes. For the **procedures**, half were randomly assigned to receive self-management education and the others were assigned to a waiting list, the **independent variable**.

The education program used bilingual health practitioners and culturally relevant activities.

Participants received 52 hours of instruction over 12 months in weekly educational meetings and support groups. Sessions for the first three months targeted nutrition, self-blood glucose checks, and exercise. The rest of the sessions were support groups to maintain progress.

BMI was calculated and blood samples taken before participation and then at 3,6, and 12 months. **Results** included the following.

1. Fasting Blood Glucose levels decreased.
2. BMI improved at first in the education group but returned to pre-education levels after 12 months. This is a typical and problematic finding in most weight loss studies. Many barriers interfere with exercising, such as high temperatures in south Texas, no access to gyms, neighborhoods without sidewalks for walking, medical complications related to diabetes, and cultural barriers such as the inappropriateness of women walking alone.

The challenge for future self-management programs is to reduce barriers to healthy lifestyles. The authors believe that culturally based self-management education is beneficial and should be the focus of future health promotion campaigns.

30.8: The effectiveness of health promotion programs: Healthy Campus with a focus on problem drinking

Discuss means to give a considered and balanced view supported by evidence. This section provides a consideration of Healthy Campus, one part of **Healthy People**, and an evaluation of the research suggesting Healthy Campus is beneficial to college students.

Healthy People is a national health promotion program that started in the 1970s aiming to improve the health of all Americans. The website www.HealthyPeople.gov outlines program objectives.

Healthy People is planned and studied in chunks of 10-year goals, with each decade's goals building on previous ones. Most of the research measures short-term effectiveness throughout each decade.

Healthy People aims to create a society where people are healthy and live long lives (About Healthy People, 2020). Examples of the general goals give you an idea of Healthy People's scope.

1. Improving general health status such as increasing life expectancy and health during a longer life
2. Studying determinants of health such as genetic, economic, and social factors
3. Reducing health-related disparities related to race and gender

The goals are broad and appear vague. In reality, the general goals are divided into much smaller units with very specific goals. These smaller goals are implemented and studied separately. ***Surveys using random samples are the primary research method used to evaluate Healthy People***. Data for each specific goal are collected at numerous sites and drawn together in a national database, so we have national and local data.

New goals for each decade evolve from previous Healthy People survey data and from new problems.

Healthy Campus 2010-2020: Florida State University's program to reduce problem drinking

Healthy Campus is part of Healthy People and aims to achieve its goals at the college level.

The American College Health Association (ACHA) sponsors Healthy Campus and coordinates much of the research on its effectiveness. Healthy Campus general goals include the following (American College Health Association, 2010).

1. Reduce substance abuse
2. Reduce obesity
3. Increase physical activity
4. Reduce mental health problems
5. Reduce injuries and violence

Many colleges participate in Healthy Campus and each school selects aspects relevant to local student needs.

Class activity

Students can look up colleges they wish to attend to see how Healthy Campus is implemented.

Florida State University (FSU) is one school participating in Healthy Campus. FSU promoted many aspects of Healthy Campus, but the **alcohol prevention program** was considered a priority with the goal to decrease problem drinking and drunk driving (Thagard Student Health Center, 2011).

How successful are FSU efforts? One problem plaguing FSU administration was that the school was routinely listed on the Princeton Review's top party schools roster for so many years (Rockler-Gladen, 2010). FSU was #9 in 2009, #11 for 2010-2011, #8 for 2012, and #12 for 2014-2015, although surveys showed less problem drinking on campus over time. Perhaps a party image is harder to change than anticipated or school administrators must manage risky drinking from specific groups that have not yet been addressed.

University administrators do not like this type of image. The Princeton Review ranking is mentioned not because it is a credible academic information source, but because it is mentioned in college discussions as one reason to spotlight problem drinking.

FSU's top goal was to reduce high-risk drinking (Grizzell, 2003). Administration, teaching staff, health staff, students, and university business partners came together under a promotion campaign that included the following goals.

1. Increase FSU staff involvement with surrounding neighborhoods where students live
2. Enforce laws requiring all beverage servers to learn more about alcohol and alcohol abuse
3. Create an alcohol and tobacco free tailgate area at the FSU stadium
4. Distribute information to students to establish new **social norms**. One example is a blood alcohol content card (BAC) that can be kept in one's wallet or pocket detailing blood alcohol content levels and information about behavior associated with drinking different amounts of alcohol.

Research supporting Healthy Campus: Surveys testing perceptions about drinking on the Florida State University campus

The first task FSU tackled was investigating *perceptions* of student drinking (US Department of Education, n.d). The **aim of the survey study** was to see if actual drinking behavior was the same as perceptions about it. Surveys given in 2002 at FSU to 4500 randomly selected undergraduates included the following **results**.

1. 49.4% of students drank four or fewer drinks at their last social event. Student perceptions were different. They thought that just 24.7% of students were drinking four or fewer drinks.
2. 17.3% said they did not drink at all. Students perceived that just 1% of students did not drink.

The authors **concluded** that student perceptions of drinking at FSU were different from actual reported behavior. Changing the school's future image to fit actual behavior was a goal.

Research supporting Healthy Campus: Survey follow-ups about risky drinking at Florida State University

The **aim of the next survey study** was to compare rates of high risk drinking at FSU between 2002 and 2004 (The Real Project, 2010). **Results** showed an overall decline of 13.8%. Male rates declined 15% and female rates declined 5%.

Conclusions include the following.
1. Perceptions about drinking at FSU are distorted.
2. High-risk drinking decreased between 2002 and 2004.

FSU Healthy Campus administrators realize that health promotion campaigns may not be the only factor in behavior change.

FSU continued to track survey data in 2010 (The Real Project, 2010). Encouraging results show that perceptions and social norms may be changing. Survey **results** between 2000 and 2010 showed the following.
1. 12.6% increase in students who do not drink
2. 25.9% increase in moderate drinking (1-4 drinks at the last social event)
3. 25.3% decrease in risky drinking (5 or more drinks at the last social event)

Although progress has been made, 37% of females and 49% of males are still binge drinking, meaning they drink 5 or more drinks at one time (Florida State University, 2013). The 2020 goal is to reduce this figure to less than 32% of females and 44% of males.

FSU was not listed on the Princeton Review of top party schools for 2015-16. It cannot be known for certain if this was a result of the school's efforts, so students can speculate about the reasons. However, the school administration was probably happy to see this.

An idea that might aid Health Campus success: Matching alcohol prevention to genetic vulnerabilities

Matching alcohol interventions to specific **phenotypes** may be the key to improving college prevention programs (Schuckit, Kalmijin, Smith, Saunders, & Fromme, 2012). The **aim of one experiment** was to test this idea.

Review the section about genetic risks for alcoholism in chapter 7. Schuckit (2009, 2008) identifies the phenotype **low response to alcohol** (LR), meaning it takes more drinks for someone to feel the effects, as one risk factor for alcoholism. Genetics account for about 50% of problem drinking so some people have a risk that colleges might be able to change.

The strategy is called a *phenotype approach to individualizing prevention programs* (Schuckit, et al., 2012). LR phenotypes exist before someone develops an addiction, and it may be easier to address LR before it develops into alcoholism.

LR contributes to drinking more each occasion to feel the effects. Three factors contribute to LR, heavy-drinking peers, the belief that drinking will result in a good experience (**alcohol expectancies**) and poor stress management. Prevention programs can target all three.

The two hypotheses follow.

1. Both general and LR specific prevention strategies will reduce overall drinking.
2. College students with LR will show the greatest decreases in drinking with the strategy aimed at LR associated behaviors.

For the **procedures**, participants were assigned to attend either a general alcohol prevention program or a program targeting LR behaviors, the **independent variable**. LR was determined through self-report questionnaires. Participants in the LR condition received extra training about heavy drinking peers, such as understanding moderate drinking habits of most college students, and skills to help students say no to drinks and avoid the habit of matching drinks with the heaviest drinker.

Results supported both hypotheses. LR and non-LR students reported less drinking. In addition, LR participants showed the greatest decrease in the LR training condition.

Schuckit **concluded** that the phenotype approach was the first practical application of 30 years of research about LR. He realizes that this first study matching prevention and genetic inheritance needs replication.

30.9: A prevention program to reduce obesity: Let's Move: America's plan to raise a healthier generation of children

Discuss means to give a considered and balanced view supported by evidence. This section provides a consideration of **Let's Move** (www.letsmove.gov/), a **prevention program** in the US designed to end childhood **obesity**. It also includes an evaluation of research supporting it. Evaluate means to make a judgment (appraisal) using evidence. Research shows that Let's Move has had some success.

The website www.letsmove.gov/ has information about the prevention program plus valuable links to details of each component and research on its effectiveness. This site may give your students ideas for health promotion strategies at your school.

Let's Move has four components.

1. Healthy choices
2. Healthy schools
3. Physical activities
4. Access to affordable healthy food

Our discussion focuses on strategies to create healthier school meals. **Surveys** are a preferred research method for evaluating health promotion campaigns so this is a good time to review the method in chapter 35.

Survey results never show that a prevention program causes behavior change so discussions about prevention program effectiveness should remain tentative. Surveys show that percentages may change over time, but factors other than the prevention program contribute to changes.

Research supporting Let's Move: Survey results about school meals

Evaluate means to make a judgment using evidence. There is plenty of research evidence to support the conclusion that Let's Move has been successful.

What's for lunch at your school? Get educated and get involved. A **CAS** project might be to make progress in getting healthier food on campus.
Used under license from megapixl.com.

The White House Task Force on Childhood Obesity (www.letsmove.gov/ taskforce_childhoodobesityrpt.html) reports that about 55 million American children spend an average of 6 hours at school every day. Most children eat at least one meal each day at school, both in official meal programs and at snack bars where food is available between classes and at breaks. Most schools also offer a federally funded meal plan. Children's food choices depend on what is available, so it is important to take a close look at school food practices and suggest improvements.

The Task Force concluded that many school meal policies contributed to obesity.

Summary of Task Force findings and recommendations

The quality of school meals often does not meet federal standards.	While all schools met the guidelines for providing adequate amounts of protein, 73% of schools included enough vitamin C and 71% included enough iron. Most schools had a range of food options for children, but whole grains made up few of these choices. French fries and other potato dishes made up too much of the vegetable requirement. While schools offered healthy low-fat meals, most of the meals children actually selected were high in fat. The challenge for schools is to educate children so they make better selections. Task Force findings represent the average, so it is unfair to suggest that no one is making strides. For example, Chef Tony Geraci of the Baltimore school district heads a program called "No thank you bites" where children are encouraged to expand their palate by trying bite-sized portions of different foods. Stickers are awarded for each new food sampled. Anyone can taste and then say no thanks. One reason children may make poor food selections is that they have never tried different foods.
Food sold in addition to meal plans is often exempt from Federal regulation.	Snack bars outside the cafeteria, a la carte lines in the cafeteria, and vending machines all contribute to unhealthy eating. For example, a la carte lines in the cafeteria may be part of federally funded meal programs, but children select less healthy foods when individual items are available. Snack bars and vending machines are loaded with cookies, sodas, and pastries, even if there are other healthier choices. Schools face a dilemma. Often sales from snack bars and vending machines fund school activities, so popular items must be available. The typical snack item at schools undermines parent attempts to teach healthy eating habits. But there is evidence that offering healthy foods at snack bars and in vending machines can become popular.
Food-related factors in the school environment contribute directly or indirectly to obesity.	Nutrition education is a main contributor to healthy food choice but poor funding and lack of staff training are problems. Subtle influences from the school environment include the display, pricing, payment methods, and the length of breaks and lunch periods. For example, some cafeterias have separate lines for snack foods and meals. This discourages low-income students from getting the meals as it draws attention to their socioeconomic status. Some schools allow students to leave campus during lunch. If fast food restaurants surround schools then district meal policies have little impact. Recommendations include making sure that getting a healthy meal does not have a social cost for children, making changes to cafeteria environments, and using gardens at school to teach children about healthy foods.

Research supporting Let's Move: Surveys documenting school meal changes between 2000 and 2012

The United States Center for Disease Control regularly monitors the effectiveness of Let's Move with the **School Health Policies and Programs Study** (SHPPS), a national survey given at regular intervals to a representative sample of schools (CDC, 2012, 2006). Baseline figures are from 2000. It is interesting to compare changes between 2006 and 2012 with baseline 2000 statistics.

Results from the 2006 and 2012 surveys include the following. The statistics are rounded up.

1. Fewer schools offer deep-fried potatoes, with a drop from 40% in 2000 to 19% in 2006.
2. The number of districts allowing soft drink companies to advertise on campus decreased from 47% in 2006 to 34% in 2012.
3. Some states and school districts no longer offer junk food on campus. For example, in 2000 20% of states banned a la carte breakfast and lunches. By 2006, the rate increased to 39% and by 2012, 42%.
4. More schools offer bottled water in vending machines. The rate climbed from 30% in 2000 to 46% in 2006.

Schools have made some positive changes but still have room for many improvements (O'Toole, et al., 2007).

Inconsistent messages sent to students about proper nutrition are still a problem. While healthier cafeteria meals are available, students still can buy snack foods from snack bars and vending machines. *What good does it do to offer nutrition education if schools also offer junk food in snack bars and vending machines?* About one-third of elementary school students have access to snack bars and vending machines. These foods are high in fat, sodium, and added sugars. Snack bars and vending machines are often available to children before school, during lunch, after school, or sometimes all day. Soft drinks are heavily advertised and widely available throughout the school day.

Self-management Activity and CAS: What is served for breakfast and lunch at your school?
Assign students to look up cafeteria and snack bar menus on your school district's website. School districts provide menus and ingredients. Students should consider the quality of available foods and look up any unidentifiable ingredients. Examine fats, proteins, carbohydrates, sugars, and preservatives for each item. Form conclusions about the healthiness of available food. What are the favorite restaurants for students allowed to go off campus for lunch? Look up the ingredients for favorite food items from local fast food restaurants and draw conclusions about the quality.

Can students create meals staying within recommended guidelines for daily recommended intake of calorie, sugar, and sodium? Look up these recommended values online.

CAS activities emerge. How does the your school's food service compare to the research? Where does your school district get its food? Trace the sources. What kinds of contracts does the school district have with food vendors? Does your school district get any of its food from local farmers? Can students initiate improvements?

I highly recommend Barbara Kingsolver's book *Animal, Vegetable, Miracle*. Kingsolver tells the story of her family's quest to eat local and seasonal foods throughout a year and frankly discusses issues related to the food industry. Students wanting to increase the ethics portion of CAS will find Kingsolver's book enlightening. Kingsolver's book can change your life! Students might also look into **super foods**, lists of the most nutritious foods that include leafy green vegetables, blueberries, flaxseeds, honey, bee pollen, mushrooms, and salmon.

Two other favorite books related to urban farming and making positive changes in our world are *Farmer Jane: Women Changing the Way we Eat* by Temra Costa and *Urban Farming: Sustainable City Living in Your Backyard, in the Community, and in the World* by Thomas J. Fox.

Prevention programs document success, so why are people still obese?

This is a good question to ask. A qualitative study about children's understanding of obesity gives us some insight.

The **aim of the interview study** was to see the reasons children thought people were overweight and if they applied what was learned to personal diet and exercise habits (Fielden, Sillence, & Little, 2011).

The 2009 Health Survey for England found that about 66% of men and 57% of women were overweight. Childhood obesity is of particular concern because being overweight when young is likely to be carried over into adulthood. These statistics were compiled after anti-obesity campaigns were implemented, making it clear that prevention programs failed to go far enough for people to internalize and apply what they learned to everyday life. Without doing more, health promotion campaigns are undermined by advertising and social/cultural norms. Might getting children's point of view help us learn the prevention program weaknesses?

For **procedures**, 12 children at high risk for obesity because of their socioeconomic status were interviewed in small **focus groups** of friends. Questions included how to make a healthy meal using food models and explaining why it was healthy, the food they liked, what they ate at home, and if they perceived a relationship between diet, exercise, and health.

Results showed 4 important themes.

The tendency to carry over obesity from childhood into adulthood is great so it is important to find out how to get children to apply what they learn about healthy habits. Source: pixabay.com

1. *Knowledge from education programs.* This theme showed if children understood the importance of diet and exercise for good health. The children knew how to make a healthy meal using the food models, but at the same time defined eating healthy foods for themselves simply as food they liked, even if it was not always healthy.
2. *Role models.* This theme showed if children perceived the most important people in their lives as models for health. Boys said that fathers had healthy behavior, such as exercise. In contrast, females tended to look up to women who wanted to be skinny. All the children looked up to celebrities, even if they were not always healthy.
3. *Fat is bad.* Children thought fat should not be eaten and that being fat was bad, even fearing overweight people. Most of the children had these misconceptions.
4. *Mixed messages.* Comments indicated that information meant to educate was often met with contradictory information, such as television advertising and programming. Some children said that what happened at home was different from what they learned at school about diet and exercise.

The authors **concluded** that the children had knowledge, but that the knowledge was not always applied to behavior. Role models are important, but they cannot be passive models, such as seen on television, but need to be actively engaged with the child at home in healthy behaviors. The most important obstacle was the mixed messages that can be hard to combat. The best strategy is probably for role models at home to demonstrate healthy lifestyles and have the children actively participate.

CAS and authentic learning

The results of this interview should be of no surprise, and it seems children need more **authentic learning**, introduced in chapter 1. **CAS** is a good way for students to have authentic learning if they wish to tackle improving their health. One project is to design a way for elementary school students to learn about health and include home applications. For example, children might grow vegetable gardens at school and even eat some of those foods, but if they do not also eat those foods at home, the children might not fully transfer the learning. Designing exercise programs that can be applied at home is another idea. This is not an easy task, but the study shows the disconnect between what is taught in prevention programs and what is actually done. Consider how Bandura's self-management ideas might help with authentic learning.

Chapter 31
Health Psychology: Determinants of health

Chapter Objectives

Students will:
1. Practice using the thinking strategies related to evaluation and synthesis, with discuss, evaluate, and to what extent demonstrated.
2. Evaluate the biopsychosocial model of health and well-being, and consider to what extent it is used in health care.
3. Discuss dispositional factors and health beliefs.
4. Discuss risk and protective factors related to health.
5. Consider how they might improve their own health by studying these topics, potentially creating balance in their own lives.

31.1: Biopsychosocial Model of health

Model overview

Evaluate means to make a judgment using evidence. Questions to ask when reading this section are, what is the biopsychosocial model, how is it used, and is it well studied?

The **biopsychosocial model of health** is a mind-body approach with interacting biological, psychological (cognitive) and sociocultural factors for prevention, diagnosis, and treatment. It is the dominant health model today as we now see the limitations of a strict biomedical approach (Straub, 2014). Key elements of the approach include but are not limited to the following. Each factor interacts with the others in complex ways.

Biological	Psychological	Sociocultural
Genetic risk and epigenetic factors	Coping skills	Self-efficacy
Hormones	Cognitive appraisals	Socioeconomic status

Biological	Psychological	Sociocultural
Evolved behaviors, such as sensitivity to food cues to be hungry when food is abundant	Attribution style	Cultural values and the violation of them
The stress response		Level of social support
Nutrition		Work stress
Sleep quality		Fast food cultures
Exercise		Overuse of cell phones and Internet
Electromagnetic fields		Discrimination and stereotyping
Chronic illness		Neighborhood quality
		Gender: Males are more likely to eat more unhealthy foods, be overweight, and drink more alcohol

Source: Based on Straub (2014)

US Psychiatrist George Engel proposed the **biopsychosocial model of health** in 1977 as a challenge to the traditional western biomedical approach defining health as the absence of disease. Engel (1977) challenged the biomedical model's assumption that only somatic (bodily) complaints were important for diagnosis and treatment. The biomedical approach is **reductionist**, a view going against modern psychology's approaches to behavior focus to understanding behavior, and claimed physicians were molded in school to believe it early in training.

A biopsychosocial approach considers the whole person, viewing health as an interconnectedness of biological, psychological (cognitive), and sociocultural factors.

How physicians approach patients matters a great deal, and they are greatly influenced by the conceptual models they are exposed to in medical school (Engel, 1980). Unfortunately, physicians are often not aware of the power these models (often biomedical) have over their diagnoses and treatment plans for patients. This is because a specific model is taught without it being openly said that it just one way to look at health, although it makes up most of what is taught to physicians. Any model comes with certain values, and these values are reinforced by teachers, textbooks, and general societal ideals.

Diagnosis and treatment must take into account all aspects of the biopsychosocial model. Engel (1977, 1980) envisioned a hierarchy of interrelated systems, sometimes called an **ecological-systems approach** (Straub, 2014). Each part of the system affects and is affected by the other parts, a model for considering the whole person.

Hierarchy from top to bottom
of interrelated systems

Social systems: Culture,
community, school, work, family,
neighborhood

Biological
systems: Immune, endocrine,
cardiovascular, nervous

Biological systems: Cells and
genes

Psychological systems:
Coping, appraising, attributions

The person

Diabetes is a good example of how a biopsychosocial approach works. When a doctor suspects someone has diabetes they must consider each part of the model (Engel, 1977). One factor alone is never enough for a diagnosis or treatment plan.

Biopsychosocial diagnosis and treatment for diabetes (Engel, 1977)

Biological	Psychological (cognitive)	Social and cultural
Laboratory tests such as blood tests	Emotions and thoughts related to how the person views the self or is viewed as sick by others	Life conditions, such as socioeconomic status or living and work conditions
Treatment with medication and nutrition	The person gives a verbal account of their circumstances, emotions, thoughts, and experience of symptoms and distress important for treatment	The relationship between the physician and patient is a powerful influence on treatment success

To what extent is the biopsychosocial model integrated into health care?

The biopsychosocial model has promoted many advances in health care and has some research support, with examples about pain and alcoholism later in this section. To what extent means to consider the merits of an argument supported by evidence. The biopsyhcolocial model has only been integrated into health care to some extent. So the model has some merit. It is not fully used because more multidisciplinary research needs to clarify how this should be done. Then all health providers must buy into using it, something that has not happened.

Surveys conducted several decades after the model was created showed its integration into mainstream medicine to some extent but not as much as hoped (Suls & Rothman, 2004). As of 2004, medical schools gave less than 40 hours of training in its use to students. Medical journals increasingly used the term biopsychosocial in articles, from 6 articles during the time when Engel introduced the model to 350 by 2001. The biopsychosocial model was concluded to be a "work in progress" (p 121). Currently most research focuses on one aspect of the model at a time.

Challenges to a full integration of the biopsychosocial model continued, particularly with advances in molecular biology that influenced physician's beliefs about diagnosis and treatment (Suls, Krantz, & Williams, 2013), at least those practicing traditional western medicine.

> **An example of the problem and evaluating research in health psychology**
>
> Chapter 29 includes the health problem **alcoholism**. There are many health promotion programs for alcoholism. However, most all of the time they are studied individually, such as outcome expectations or Healthy Campus. Treatments for alcoholism, which also includes drugs to reduce cravings and Alcoholics Anonymous, are studied individually or at most compared to other specific treatments.
>
> Unfortunately, *treatments and promotion programs are usually studied individually rather than in the multidisciplinary approach suggested by the biopsychosocial model.* Does someone recover more when all parts of the model are used? It might be hard to say unless a body of multidisciplinary research exists.

One example can be seen with advances in **alcoholism** treatment (Suls, Krantz, & Williams, 2013). The idea is to match someone's genotype with specific medications. Gene-drug matching is expensive and it is not certain that the practice can be widely applied to everyone, so the strictly biomedical view has limitations. In addition, drugs work only if taken as prescribed, and compliance with doctor's instructions is a big problem. Taking drugs as directed is affected by a number of factors, such as someone's emotions, self-efficacy, and the ability to pay for the drugs, all things that would be taken into account if a physician used a biopsychosocial model.

The solution to the problem is again to encourage more multidisciplinary research and to make the research clinically relevant so health practitioners can easily apply it to their real life patients.

Even if the biopsychosocial model has not been fully integrated into all physician's practices, when used it works well and is supported by research. The model has some merit but needs more research for great merit.

Research support: Biopsychosocial chronic pain treatment

Chronic pain affects millions of people and is increasing (Gatchel, McGeary, McGeary, & Lippe, 2014). Medical costs and lost productivity related to pain in the US alone total $560-635 billion each year. About 100 million people in the US have chronic pain, a much larger number than people with diabetes, heart disease and cancer put together. With the graying of our populations, the need for pain management will rise, as it is projected that about 20 percent of the US population by 2030 will be over 65.

Surgery and pain medication have been the most popular biomedical treatments, but both have great risks. Long-term use of pain medication increases the risk for psychological distress and misuse. Spinal fusion surgery increases the risk of disability, but its use grew over a 10-year period between 1998 and 2008.

Luckily, this is one place where the biopsychosocial model is now widely accepted as an alternative, replacing an outdated biomedical approach for pain treatment. Pain has complex causes and effects, and even biological causes can stem from cognitions and emotions that worsens with stress. People attach meaning to cognitions, which affect emotions and the total experience of pain. It is easy to get into a vicious cycle of injury, thoughts, emotions, and disability. In addition, poor coping skills adds to the problem. If someone with chronic pain adopts a "sick role" then this worsens the situation further.

The best pain treatments involve many care providers, and it is important that everyone clearly communicates. The diagram below shows some of the key elements of a biopsychosocial model for pain treatment.

Biological

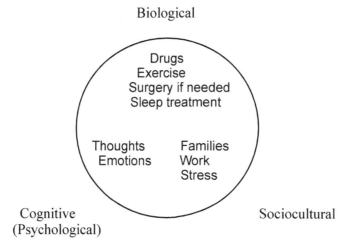

Interactive parts of a biopsychosocial model for treating pain. Based on Gatchel, et al., 2014.

Research **results** for the success of pain treatment using a multidisciplinary approach across many studies follow.

1. Long-term effectiveness of interdisciplinary treatment is successful (Gatchel, McGeary, McGeary, & Lippe, 2014). Patients rated the effects positive across many categories when given questionnaires,

such pain severity and the level of interference the pain had with regular life activities. These gains were still there after a one-year follow-up.
2. Cognitive therapy is reported across a number of studies to be a critical part of a biopsychosocial model of pain treatment (Gatchel, et al., 2014). Cognitive therapy changes negative thoughts and emotions into those that would help someone learn effective coping skills. After cognitive therapy, patients are more accepting of the pain, less likely to use catastrophic thinking, and less likely to avoid activities for fear of pain.
3. A daily SWEM is effective, where pain patients socialize, work, exercise, and meditate each day (Collen, 2015). These self-management strategies decrease pain and the need for pain medication.

Research support: Biopsychosocial alcoholism treatment: Outpatient long-term intensive Therapy for Alcoholics (OLITA)

This is one example where alcoholism treatment is studied as with **biopsychosocial** approach. Appreciating the biological mechanisms as well as the social contexts in which they express are important for recovery (Wallace, 1990). Even if there are clear genetic risks and brain effects, alcoholism must be seen as a human problem related to mind, body and society.

The **aim of one pilot study** was to get research support for **OLITA**, a program from Germany (Krampe, Stawicki, Hoehe, & Ehrenreich, 2007).

Data about the long-term outcome of alcoholism are alarming and signal the need for a multidisciplinary treatment approach. This is because:

1. Only a small percentage of alcoholics maintain sobriety after treatment, with up to 60% relapsing.
2. Many alcoholics are likely to have a poor chance at recovery because of the chronic nature of their drinking, a history of excessive drinking, loss of family and friends, loss of jobs, and having many physical consequences.
3. Treatment takes about 10 years and people are not stable until about 3 years into it.

OLITA aims to socially reintegrate severe alcoholics into a social group with access to talking therapy and medical care.

For the **procedures**, the pilot study for OLITA took place for 10 years with 180 alcoholics. OLITA uses a biopsychosocial approach where the two-year treatment program includes the following.

1. Therapists always available in case of emergencies.
2. Use of alcohol deterrent medications such as Antabuse to show there is no tolerance of alcohol use
3. Regular urine and blood screenings and supervision of taking Antabuse
4. Aggressive aftercare to disrupt the start of relapse, where patients are called if they do not show up for therapy sessions and therapists randomly showing up at home or work

Evaluate research methods
OLITA's pilot study is not an experiment so be careful. Call it an uncontrolled pilot study. OLITA is compared to case controls, meaning its successes are compared to people getting other treatment.
Participants of OLITA had far fewer relapses than participants in other studies.
There is little research about alcoholism treatment using the biopsychosocial approach.

The program consists of:

1. Detoxification, taking about 2-3 weeks
2. Outpatient period I, intensive daily sessions for 15 minutes each for about 3 months
3. Outpatient period II, stabilization for 3-4 months with therapy session at least 3 times a week

4. Outpatient period III for 6 months where patients are weened off therapy and now go twice a week and take Antabuse twice a week
5. Outpatient period IV for 12 months of aftercare, where therapy session are less frequent and the patient takes less Antabuse

Results showed a 9-year abstinence rate of 50%, which is excellent, and a reemployment rate of 60%. Participants also showed a significant drop in physical problems related to alcoholism and lessened symptoms of depression and anxiety.

Challenges to studying the biopsychosocial model for alcoholism

Most people with alcoholism do not get formal treatment and many do not get any treatment, so most alcoholics are not represented in study samples. Formal treatment is most likely to use treatments from various parts of the biopsychosocial model, but even these are most studied separately, such as attending Alcoholics Anonymous (AA) or using drug treatment to reduce cravings such as Naltrexone, even if someone uses both strategies.

More multidisciplinary approaches such as OLITA need investigation because they do not make up most of what is available.

31.2: Dispositional factors and health beliefs
Genetics, Dispositional optimism, and hostility (the worst part of Type A personalities)

A **dispositional factor** is anything internal to the person that affects health beliefs and the resulting behavior. Examples of dispositional factors are genetics and personality traits.

Three dispositional factors

Factor	Description
Genetics	Alcoholism and obesity are the examples and this material is located under the section about health problems. Just remember from studying the biological approach to behavior that genes cannot affect behavior unless they are expressed, so genes are rarely the determining factor for a health problem.
Personality: Dispositional optimism	This is a personality trait positively affecting many health measures and is described in the next section.
Personality: The hostile personality	This is the "toxic core of Type A personalities" (Straub, 2014, p. 381) affecting cardiovascular disease (CVD).

Dispositional factors are important for figuring out why some people get sick and some stay healthy (Adler & Matthews, 1994). Just remember that dispositional factors do not work alone. They interact with social factors to create any health behavior

Dispositional optimism

Optimism versus pessimism is a personality dimension related to what people expect for the future (Carver & Scheier, 2014). Dispositional optimism is a cognitive construct affecting motivation, where optimistic people put effort into their health and pessimistic people disengage from health.

Optimism is a marker for good health, including better outcomes for many health problems including pain, stress, immunity, and heart health (Carver & Scheier, 2014). Optimism is closely related to high **self-efficacy** and hope, things you would expect to increase health.

Optimism-pessimism was first studied in the 1980s, so it was not part of the **five-factor model of personality** (neuroticism, extraversion, openness,

Optimistic people are healthier. Spending time doing something for others might increase your optimism. Used with license from megapixel.com.

agreeableness, and conscientiousness) (Carver & Scheier, 2014). Perhaps it is helpful to think of the five-factor model as traits making up the "what" of personality and optimism as the "how" of personality, or how goals become behavior. Optimism consists of a person's expectancies for the future, their **self-regulation** (which requires high self-efficacy), and the effort exerted to reach health goals.

Consider how important optimistic expectations are when someone faces an obstacle to a goal. For example, following a doctor's advice to quit smoking, to start exercising, or to take steps to reduce stress comes with potential obstacles. The optimistic person has a better chance to meeting the goals because they have enough confidence to look past obstacles.

Characteristics of optimistic people (Carver & Schemer, 2014)

They are more likely to exercise and have healthy diets.
They easily make friends.
They perform better at school.
They have lower **cortisol** levels, an important stress hormone in humans.

It is well known that genes contribute to all behavior but it has been hard to conduct genetic research on optimism that has been replicated enough for acceptance (Carver & Scheier, 2014). Two social factors related to optimism as an adult are parent modeling of effective coping skills and socioeconomic status (SES).

Research support: Dispositional optimism is a buffer against stress hormone production

A correlation study **aimed to show** that **dispositional optimism** was a buffer against **cortisol** production even when people perceived they had high levels of **stress** (Jobin, Wrosch & Scheier, 2014). Cortisol is an important stress hormone in humans and is secreted in a biological process when the HPA axis is activated. The HPA axis was reviewed in chapter 9 so remind yourself before reading the study details.

Participants were all over 60. The **procedures** follow.

1. Everyone filled out a questionnaire for three nights to rate how stressed they felt throughout that day.

2. Saliva samples taken several times throughout each of the three days to measure cortisol levels.
3. Dispositional optimism was measured with the Life Orientation Test-Revised. Participants rated themselves as to how much they agreed with statements such as "I am always optimistic about my future" and "if something can go wrong for me, it will" (p. 6).

Results follow.

1. Optimists who reported higher levels of stress had lower levels of cortisol.
2. Pessimists who reported higher levels of stress had higher levels of cortisol on those days.

The authors **concluded** that dispositional optimism was a buffer against cortisol production. The results need to be replicated on younger samples. As this is a correlation study, it is not evidence that optimism causes lower cortisol levels.

> **A benefit of optimism**
> Optimistic people are not necessarily more capable than pessimistic people but are more willing to persevere when faced with an obstacle (Carver & Scheier, 2014).

Research support: Dispositional optimism protects women from heart disease and hostility is related to greater risk

This correlation study **aimed to see** the relationship between **optimism** and **heart disease** and also between **hostility** and heart disease in both white and black females (Tindle, et al., 2009).

For the **procedures**, participants filled out two questionnaires at the start of the study, one measuring optimism (the same one as the previous study) and the other measuring hostility. Questions about hostility included agreeing or disagreeing with statements such as "It is safer to trust nobody" and "I have often had to take orders from someone who did not know as much as I did" (p. 3).

All the women were free of heart disease at the start of the study and were studied for 8 years.

Results follow.

1. Optimism is correlated with lower amounts of heart disease in both white and black women.
2. Optimistic women reported better health habits than hostile women at the start of the study. These include less smoking and alcohol consumption.

The authors **concluded** that optimism was related to better heart health over time and that the lifestyle of optimists promoted better health. This is an all female sample, so the same research should be done on males.

> **Can someone become more optimistic?**
> Dispositional optimism is a personality trait and as such is internal to the person. However, don't give up. Practicing **mindfulness meditation** might create more hope and forgiveness in someone. This research is detailed in chapter 30 about health promotion.

Hostile personality: The part of Type A personalities increasing the risk for heart disease

The term **Type A personality** was coined in the 1950s as a general description of a disposition explaining why some people had more heart disease, with Type B as the opposite (Straub, 2014). The following chart summarizes the main traits of Type A and Type B.

Type A	Type B
Hostile and aggressive	Easy-going and relaxed
Competitive	Do not mind losing sometimes and enjoy the game
Sense of time urgency	Less time urgent
Rigid achievement goals	Work steadily but do not get upset if a goal is not achieved

Type A was eventually decided to be too broad of a description of the risk personality. Researchers started investigating if any of the Type A components were at the core of the problem such as anger, hostility, time urgency, or competitiveness. It was discovered that **hostility** was the primary reason why some people had a higher risk for heart disease (Straub, 2014). Hostility has even emerged in some research independent of the more general Type A personality label.

Research support: The hostile reaction is a problem for "Type A personalities"

Hostility is "a chronic negative outlook that encompasses feelings (anger), thoughts (cynicism and mistrust of others), and overt action (aggression)" (Straub, 2014, p. 381). Hostility is a long lasting attitude.

The **aim of a correlation study** was to show that men with prehypertension and high levels of hostility were more likely to develop hypertension and heart disease (Player, King, Mainous, & Geesey, 2007).

Males and females aged 45-64 were participants. All had prehypertension readings before the study but were free of hypertension or heart disease.

For the **procedures**, readings of hypertension and heart disease and a questionnaires were taken over several years to measure levels of anger and hostility.

Results showed a correlation between men with high trait anger and hostility and the development of hypertension or heart disease. This was not found for women.

> **Reusing previous studies**
> Use the Tindle et al., 2009 study as a second study for hostility. Students should work on seeing patterns in research so they know when to reuse research.

The authors **concluded** that "sympathetic hyperactivity and arousal associated with anger and physiological stress" (p. 408) explained the correlation. They suggest an exercise program to reduce the effects of the prolonged stress on the body, a treatment with some success.

31.3: Risk and protective factors in health

Discuss means to give a considered and balanced view supported by evidence. A balanced view is shown on the table listing both risk and protective factors. Use the research in the book as support for a factor as either being a risk or protection.

A list of risk and protective factors

Risk factors	Protective factors
Genetics, such as low response to alcohol (LR) or the ob gene mutation related to obesity (affecting the hormone leptin)	Genetics can act as a buffer if you have the right ones, such as the l allele of the serotonin transporter gene acting a buffer against stress reactivity: Stress reactivity is a risk factor for many problems such as depression, which is related to health problems such as heart disease
Personality dispositions, such as trait anger and hostility	Dispositional optimism
Lifestyle: Poor diet, sleep deprivation, lack of exercise	Lifestyle: Good diet, proper sleep, regular exercise
Cognitive factors, such as negative cognitive appraisals (Lazarus) and addictive beliefs (Beck)	Cognitive factors, such as positive cognitive appraisals (Lazarus)
Poor coping skills to manage stress	Good coping skills to manage stress, such as regular practice of mindfulness meditation or Tai Chi
Low self-efficacy and unrealistic outcome expectancies	High self-efficacy and realistic outcome expectancies
Low socioeconomic status (SES)	Higher SES
Work stress	Low work stress
Lack of social support	Good social support
Monochronic time orientation	Polychronic time orientation
Media exposure (such as food advertisements)	Regulated use of television and computers

Chapter 32
Developmental Psychology: Influences on Development

Chapter objectives

Students will:
1. Practice thinking strategies related to evaluation and synthesis, with discuss, evaluate, and contrast demonstrated.
2. Evaluate research methods in developmental psychology.
3. Discuss play and development with a cultural point of view and evaluate research, including a contrast of play across cultures.
4. Discuss the role of peers in development and evaluate research.
5. Discuss how childhood trauma affects development and evaluate research.
6. Discuss resilience and evaluate research.
7. Discuss how poverty and socioeconomic status (SES) affect development and evaluate research.

Class activity: Road map of your life: Remembering childhood

A fun way to get students thinking about development is to make a "life road map" before starting the developmental chapters. Each student gets a piece of construction paper. Draw a roadmap of your childhood, starting with where you were born and your first memory. It does not have to look exactly like a road (though it can) but the map can be anything a student wants (it should be creative). Include important events and people, and anything else a student recalls as an important development milestone. It is fun to reminisce and the project stimulates storytelling (these are usually like Bruner's narratives from chapter 18). Students can draw pictures or paste photos and words.

Play, friendships, relationships, gender roles and identity, and important school and learning experiences, and even traumas might be on the map (perhaps not brain development). Students can even write some narratives about the most important events. The purpose is to stimulate thinking about what has happened. Students might also have a part of the map called the future, which might reflect a great deal on how they developed. It is fun to share stories about the past. Picture: pixabay.com

32.1 Let's start with critical thinking: Evaluating approaches to research in developmental psychology

When evaluating developmental psychology, students should pay special attention to its cultural relevance. Cross-cultural support is often missing and this is acknowledged by researchers. We learned from studying Harry Triandis in chapter 3 that if theories originating in the West have not been studied cross-culturally, then the research is incomplete. Unfortunately, many developmental theories and studies are still incomplete and students can show high critical thought by keeping an eye on this concern.

The core theories in developmental psychology *may aim to be universal but they assume children will follow a developmental pathway leading to an independent self seen in individualistic societies* (Greenfield, Keller, Fuligni, & Maynard, 2003). The authors refer to the **independent-interdependent self** and **individualism-collectivism**, two **cultural dimensions**.

The available research about culture and development leads to the judgment that many core developmental theories must expand to take into account the interdependent and collective nature of relationships that many people around the world value.

For a theory to have global application it should take three ideas about development into account (Greenfield, et al., 2003).

3 things needed for a developmental theory to have global application
Many people around the world have a collective, interdependent view of relationships. Interdependent groups value relationship harmony through maintaining obligations and responsibilities. This is different from an independent view of relationships where individual rights and choice are prominent, meaning a child develops into an independent person.
A child's development is greatly influenced by the physical environment, economic status, and the larger community.
A child's development of cognitive processes, such as memory, is constructed within the context of the culture. Memory is a tool for learning expected cultural norms.

People have much in common but also have some different ways to express behaviors. For example, all cultures might value **sharing**, but value different things about it (Greenfield, et al., 2003). Sharing in the US is valued, but it is a personal choice. In Mexico sharing is also valued, but it is a priority and children are expected to conform to the expectation. Both individualist and collectivist cultures teach sharing but it is applied differently.

Another example comes from studying **attachment theory**. The Strange Situations Paradigm used to study attachment assumes children will develop into independent adults. You will read more about this topic and the concern when studying attachment, with cultural psychology evidence about the Efe society in Africa as an example showing the need to expand the original theory.

There are many chances to learn about different cultures in the chapters about developmental psychology and apply critical thinking.

32.2: The role of play in development

The role of play in development: A cultural perspective

Discuss means to give a considered and balanced view supported by evidence. This section includes many culture's views about **play in development** for a balanced view. Evaluate means to make a judgment using evidence. Students must avoid ethnocentrism because although play is universally recognized as a childhood activity, it has different expressions and meaning across cultures (Roopnarine, 2015). A great deal of the play theory comes from research using European and US middle-class samples and is incorrectly generalized to everyone, referred to as **WEIRD**: Western, educated, industrialized, rich, and democratic (Gaskins, 2015). In evaluating play theory and research, the final judgment might be that *all play is culturally motivated* so we can value many types of **enculturation** and **socialization** practices. There is a growing trend to emphasize play so it is important that this is done with respect to cultural values, which requires theories to provide balance between a universal goal for children to play and local cultural values (Roopnarine, 2015).

The biggest problem for studying play is that there is so much disagreement about how to define it and to what extent play has benefits (Pellegrini, 2013). Some view play as essential for development and others think it is less important.

Students must consider that in some cultures, play is valued and cultivated by adults, and in other cultures, working is valued as a childhood activity more than playing, even though all children still play (Gaskins, 2015). In yet other cultures, academics are favored over play in some places the adults are not as involved. Several factors involved for contrasting play across cultures are the relative value placed on play and work, on adult participation, its relationship with education, and if the final product of development across culture is similar or different.

If our study of play is going to have global relevance, then students must challenge themselves to see which childhood activities are valued across cultures. Deciding which childhood activities matter the most for development is critical in evaluating the role of play.

Keep in mind that each culture has **schemas** for what is valued in behavior, and this is reflected in one's **subjective culture**. We cannot simply say western and nonwestern when discussing play because there is great variability in what is valued about children's activities. We can scratch the surface of the issues with some examples.

Next is descriptions of play in various cultures. Keep track of what is different about them. Play is seen in all cultures and can have various benefits, but its value, purpose, and priority vary. It might become easy to guess which culture a child is from once you learn about their play.

Critical thinking: Challenge assumptions
Students might go into this topic assuming that everyone thinks play is essential in a particular way to development, especially if they studied Vygotsky, Bruner, or Piaget, for example.

Students must ask if these theories have full cultural relevance, and although Vygotsky and Bruner are used in this book, the field of developmental psychology often lacks cultural relevance.

Study **Vygotsky** and **Bruner** to have some play theory background before reading further. Vygotsky is often cited as relevant, even outside of western societies. These theories are described in chapter 18.

Pretending to be an animal is highly valued in European American culture. Would all cultures value this as a way for children to spend their time?

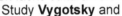

Photo used with license from megapixel.com.

Inquiry: Group collaboration to practice contrasting
Divide the class into groups and use these topic areas. You can add more topics if desired.
1. Parent role
2. Emphasis of play
3. Child-centered versus family centered
4. Play as important for educating children

Each group should compile a list of contrasts from reading the 5 cases of play. Then groups compare what they find. Contrasting is a high level critical thinking skill so identify each group's strengths and also what needs improvement.

Students can also find similarities, but for it should be framed as how the universal behavior is expressed differently because for IB students, the command term is contrast.

Case #1: United States	Play description
Play creates a Zone of Proximal Development (ZPD) and is the most important vehicle for learning	Many western parents, especially European Americans, value play as a developmental tool and create a child-centered world that is highly verbal, full of negotiation between parent and child where the child asserts his or her opinion, is concerned about self-esteem, and where narratives (stories) help the child see their behavior as positive (Gaskins, 2015). Play is valued because it allows children to get rid of energy, practice cognitive skills and social roles, and learn about themselves. Play is the primary "job" of the child as the best way to accomplish these things. Parents cultivate play activities and get involved. Any work a child does is assigned to them as a way to learn a social lesson of responsibility, though much of the time it would easier for the parent to do the task themselves. Western families are child-centered. The following game from Vygotsky's widely respected cognitive theory of play would be valued and encouraged.

Two sisters ages 5 and 7 decide to play being sisters (Vygotsky, 1978). In real life the girls behave as sisters naturally. In the game they carefully display their sisterhood and are obligated to show they know the correct rules for being sisters. The rules of sisterhood dictate which behaviors they can show. In the game they dress the same, talk in ways sisters talk, and emphasize what they do alone as sisters and what they do when they are with strangers. The 7 year-old takes her sister by the hand and teaches her about other people, such as saying "that is theirs, not ours" to help define roles. Vygotsky reflects, "what passes unnoticed by the child in real life becomes the rule of behavior in play" (p. 95) and that play creates a ZPD, where " in play a child always behaves beyond his average age, above his daily behavior; in play it is as though he were a head taller than himself" (p. 102).

Vygotsky claimed that imaginary situations in play always involve rules, and this helps children develop. Vygotsky believed the first signs of higher mental processes emerged during the preschool ages first in play (Bodrova & Leong, 2003). Language was important for development and was part of all children's real play. Children, for example, might talk out loud as they play at being sisters to emphasize rules and important actions. Play also facilitated the development of self-regulation, something needed to enter adult culture. Vygotsky saw **language** as the primary cultural tool for development during play. This has been criticized by some, who think nonverbal modeling of others is also an important activity for preschool children. This nonverbal modeling is a way for children to construct general cognitive competencies they will use as adults.

Both Vygotsky and Bruner have western developmental theories that include play and view culture as tools for development. Burner's theory of narratives has been tested cross-culturally and yes, all cultures narrate. But narrating is not just used in play. The challenge is to figure out if both theories adequately explain how children might spend more time working than playing if they are applied outside of western culture. Vygotsky is cited as important in some writings about nonwestern cultures, so it may have more widespread appeal as a play theory than some others.

Case #2: Yucatec Mayan village in Mexico	Play description
Working and playing	Children naturally play and Yucatec Mayan parents are happy to see their children getting pleasure from it but this is only as long as play does not interfere with family responsibilities to help with work (Gaskins, 2015b). This is one example of cultural values that children can learn through play but they also learn a lot from participating in family work. This is an example of a culture valuing tasks other than play for children's learning. *Two sisters aged 7 and 9 describe what they do after school (Gaskins, 2015a). They list chores and speak proudly about washing their clothes, with the oldest announcing that she now also gets to wash her baby brother's clothes and when her laundry skills get better she will add washing her older brother's clothes. When the researcher asked if they would prefer to play or watch television the girls said no, their mother had many chores to do and they wanted to help. These children were happy being judged competent at helping with adult work.* 　　*The girls also played, and for example, played house with their younger siblings when chores were complete, but still played the role of a worker because they were caring for their brothers and sisters. They enjoyed pretending and even taking physical risks in games, but rarely left the primary role as a caregiver (worker).* Yucatec Mayan parents view play as normal but curtail it when there is something else to do that is more valuable, such as contributing to the family by helping with chores (Gaskins, 2015a). Play is something children can do when there is nothing more important for them to do. Mayan parents do not cultivate play or get involved. Yucatec Mayan parents believe young children need protection, but they expect them to take on work responsibilities early and show understanding, taking a family-centered view. As such, these parents do not spend much time and resources on children's play (Gaskins, 2015b). 　　Yucatec Mayan children play most with relatives rather than friends and these playmates are of many ages and are often the same children (Gaskins, 2015b). Toys are rarely used and objects in nature can become something else when pretending.

This child might spend much of her time working to help the family. She plays, but only after work is complete.
Source: pixabay.com

Case #3: Turkana communities in Kenya	Play description
Play integrates children into culture and community but parents take a more passive role	Play helps children become integrated into their culture and community but parents take a more passive role (Ng'asike, 2015). Children play independently but the youngest stay close to mothers and grandparents while older children often go off on their own. Parents do not create play areas for children or make toys available. The following game is typical. *Children play a fantasy game at a dry river bed. Sand is made into homes and animal shelters. Dry camel dung becomes camels and the children pretend to be herders, imitating what the adults do in real life. Children take their play camels to get water and are branded and then killed for the family to have meat. They pretend to milk the camels and calm them the way adults do, even treating sick pretend camels with herbs from a nearby medicinal tree.* Parents often told children to go out and play, but this was mostly used when children were hanging around adults without having anything to do. However, children were not sent to play just to have an enjoyable experience. Play was expected to teach children social skills and competence. Parents in Africa frequently think that children are responsible for their own learning and development. Parents are not active in play but create cultural expectations about what is important to learn when playing and do monitor children. Peers and siblings are valued in helping to socialize younger children in play and this frees parents to work. Sometimes parents are models for play during celebrations, where they dance and play games related to community activities such as herding, weddings, hunting, and fighting. Children are expected to be part of regular work and as they get older, play cannot interfere with family and community responsibilities, such as herding. They often ran errands for their families, and when finished, started playing until they were called back to help. The African cultural views of play are important for education and play is used to promote values and social competence to one day take on adult roles. Children make their own toys at school and create the play areas. **Vygotsky** is useful for thinking about Turkana play because play is a cultural activity (Ng'asike, 2015). The emphasis on pretend play and the **zone of proximal development** are two key ideas meaningful to the Turkana.

These children play to learn about social skills and community responsibilities, and they make more decisions without parent involvement.
Source: pixabay.com

Case #4: Taiwan	Play description
Academics over play	Scholars were always highly valued and respected in traditional Chinese societies so it is easy to understand why even today Chinese parents see education as a route to social status and prosperity (Chang, 2015). Emphasizing education starts early, and parents can put more pressure on children to perform in school than teachers, sometimes called "tiger moms." Parents focus on their children's test scores and rank, and enroll them in cramming sessions to prepare for exams. Even activities after school reflect these demands, with young children in lessons for singing, dancing, music, and sport teams. Hard work is therefore valued over play, which is often viewed as physical training rather than intellectual preparation. Parents and teachers believe children best learn through memorization, which comes from Confuscian philosophy, and teachers value compliance, conformity, and politeness in students. Education is adult-centered and children are expected to conform. Children play in Taiwan, but play is usually allowed only when studies are complete. Historically, children played during festivals but views of play changed along with Taiwanese economic development and lifestyles. During the agricultural phase from 1945 to 1960, children made their own toys, such as a stone for a marble. Households were large and children had many siblings and children in the village as playmates. During the industrial period from 1960 to 1980, Taiwan expanded economically and children had access to mass produced toys. Government policy limited the number of children for population control and children started playing in smaller groups. After 1980 Taiwan became a large producer of toys for export and also imported toys used indoors, such as television related toys, board games, and stuffed animals. Children had fewer playmates, often playing alone as play moved inside the house. Since children were sent to so many extracurricular activities, they had less time for it anyway. Even with special development centers to encourage more play, children often did not even see the same children each visit. Today's kindergarten teachers do not value play for learning and there is not much child-initiated play at school. Parents of pre-school children are focused on getting their children into elementary school. Government efforts to integrate play into learning have increased, but so far the value is still on academics.

Many Asian cultures value academics over play.
Source: pixabay.com

Case #5: India	Play description

Play is unstructured and contains important themes related to family and expected social behavior, with marginal adult supervision	Children"s play in India is informal and unstructured and is part fantasy and part reality (Chaudhary & Shula, 2015). The following description of play is typical.
	
	"Two girls had kitchen-set toys spread out before them: a cooking range, some utensils, cutlery and cups made of brightly colored plastic. Taking a fork and spoon, Anita deftly lifted some make-believe food and tossed it around in a pan placed carefully on the cooking range as if to mix the ingredients. The younger Dina watched with fascination and then picked up the green plastic fork, following the same action with another pan" (p. 146).
	
	Vygotsky is listed as an important theorist explaining Indian children's play. Play helps children learn the rules guiding cultural and social norms. The **zone of proximal development** provides structure for play, allowing children to move to the top of their zone. Children express themselves in play more maturely than they do in normal life, learning things that might go unnoticed outside of the play setting where rules are not as exaggerated.
	    Childhood is thought of as one continuous developmental phase from birth into adulthood. Because of this, children are part of every aspect of adult life and social events. Family relationships are important in India and one goal of play is to learn about these expected roles. Therefore, play is more about relationships than learning. Indians are concerned with social status and children must learn these social rules early. Play is one place to practice these roles, and even the language used shows expected behavior. Older children act as mentors of younger children's play to aid in learning about responsibilities.
	    Parents believe it is a child's job to play, something they do naturally at home. As a result, parents often believe that when children go to school they should be taught to sit still and do academic work. Academic success is believed the key to better themselves, so play can be downplayed in favor of academics as children grow older.
	    Adults can get involved in play but it is usually to say it is time for a meal or give special instructions. For the most part, children are left to play uninterrupted.

For these children, play is unstructured and full of fantasy.
Source; pixabay.com

Developmental benefits of play

Students should consider both sides of the issue, that **play** can have benefits but it is also might not have as much benefit as is often assumed (Pellegrini, 2013). Considering that *play is culturally motivated* allows us to see how play can have benefits, though other cultures value different kinds of childhood activities.

Play has both immediate and delayed benefits (Pellegrini, 2013). There are many definitions of play but one suggesting a wide range of benefits best serves this discussion. Play has a number of characteristics and all should be there.

1. It is voluntary and in a relaxed environment
2. It does not have an immediate purpose or intention
3. Behavior is exaggerated
4. It is repetitive and does not have to occur in a logical order

---

Critical thought: Drawing relationships between ideas

Pretend play develops hand-in-hand with other developmental milestones, such as the **theory of mind** and **language**.

Recall from studying Vygotsky and Bruner that language is thought to advance cognitive development, and the play situation promotes language use.

Pellegrini's definition is general enough to include a variety of developmental theories about play, including Vygotsky and Bruner, and can be seen in four types of play, all of which can help children develop.

1. Locomotor play
2. Object play
3. Social play
4. Pretend play

It is not possible to review all of the types, so pretend play and social play are examples for our discussion.

Pretend play and development

Pretend play is the most studied type and can also be called symbolic play or fantasy play (Pellegrini, 2013). In pretend play, a child's behavior is taken out of its real context, and one thing can become something else.

Pretend play has to develop, and becomes more complex and social over time. It starts out as an imitation of adult actions without understanding someone else's intentions. Children must be 4 or 5 for their fantasy play to show an understanding of another's mental state (this is when children show a developed **theory of mind**).

Pretend play starts as solitary and moves to **social pretend play** mainly with the help of an adult. Both pretend play and **language** are aided as children come to realize they can solve social problems by imitating adults. It is a milestone in development when children understand that an adult's gestures and speech are aimed at getting a task completed.

Pretending to be a doctor helps children develop a theory of mind and social roles.
Used under license from megapixl.com.

By 2 years of age, pretend play starts to include peers and this behavior peaks at about 5.

Last, pretend play aids children in understanding that a statement can be false, a step toward developing a **theory of mind**.

Research support #1: Pretend play helps a child understand that some statements can be false

Can pretend play help a child learn that a statement can be false? If so, then play may help a child develop the skills needed to pass false beliefs tests for **theory of mind**.

The **aim of the experiment** was to see if creating **pretend play** using toys and dolls would aid children in judging that a statement different from their experience was false (Dias & Harris, 1988).

Children aged 5 and 6 were participants. The hypothesis was that children in the play condition would be better at judging a statement as false and would give a justification (an abstract reason that reflects good judgment) than children in the verbal condition. Judging a statement as false and giving a justification were the **dependent variables**.

Procedures involved giving children were given 24 syllogisms, which varied between containing facts consistent with a child's experience, containing unknown facts, and containing facts different from a child's experience.

Example syllogisms

Type of facts	Syllogism (Dias & Harris, 1988, p. 221)
Facts consistent with a child's experience	All cats meow. Rex is a cat. Does Rex meow?
Unknown facts (These children were not familiar with a hyena.)	All hyenas laugh. Rex is a hyena. Does Rex laugh?
Facts different from a child's experience	All cats bark. Rex is a cat. Does Rex bark?

Children were randomly assigned to the verbal or play condition, the **independent variable**. Both groups had the same instructions that they would hear some stories, some might sound funny, but they should pretend all the stories were true. The difference between the two groups was that the experimenter used toys in the play condition during each syllogism that represented the story. For example, a toy cat was made to meow. After hearing the syllogisms all children answered yes or no to the last question. Children were also asked why they said yes or no. The purpose of asking why was to see if the children used a plausible theoretical reason or something arbitrary.

Results showed that children in the play condition were more accurate than the verbal condition and their reasons were more theoretical and less arbitrary.

The authors **concluded** that pretend play helped children reason, especially when the information was different from their experiences. Other experiments support this conclusion.

Research support #2: Social pretend play develops when a child realizes that an adult's gestures are meant to solve problems

Children have to develop the ability to use objects as symbols in **pretend play**. It is already known that adults help children advance this skill by acting as a scaffold, but can a child imitate an adult and use objects as symbols on their own (Tomasello, Striano, & Rochat, 1999)?

The **aim of the experiment** was to see when children could use objects to represent something else when an adult's help was absent and they could not act as scaffolds.

Children aged 18, 26, and 35 months were participants. It was hypothesized that 18 month-old children would show little evidence of symbolic abilities, that 35 month-old children would do well in all three phases, and that the researchers did not know how the 26-month old children would perform.

Procedures are next. First, children practiced the task and they learned to play the game by putting an object down a chute.

The experimental conditions took place in 3 phases, with each more complex. Each phase had 2 conditions, gestures or objects, the **independent variable**.

In phase 1 an experimenter asked the children to push one of four objects down a chute. The adult either gestured toward the object or held up a toy that looked like the object (gesture or object condition). The objects included a bottle and a book.

> **A film and application to theory**
> Pretend play is something children do that takes them to the to top of their **zone of development**.
> Vygotsky is important to know as a theory about play benefits. One good film is *Play: A Vygotskian Approach.* It is available from Davidson Films.

In phase 2 an experimenter and the child pretended without using language that the object was something else, such as a box being a shoe. Then the child was asked to select the correct object (the box in this case). In the gesture condition the experimenter pretended to put the box on her foot before asking the child to select it. In the object condition the experimenter held up an object the child had never seen similar to the target object (box). Then the child was asked to push the box down the chute.

In phase 3, an experimenter and the child also pretended without using language that an object was something else, such as a wadded up piece of paper being a ball. However, in both the gesture and object condition, the child was asked to select the pretended object, the wadded up paper in this instance.

Results showed that overall, children performed best in the gesture condition and specifically:

1. 18 month-olds performed well with gestures but not objects in phase 1 but failed both phase 2 and 3.
2. 26 month-olds passed all of phase 1 and just gestures in phase 2, failing phase 3.
3. 35 month-olds passed all of phase 1 and 2 but just gestures in phase 3.

Conclusions include the following.

1. Children start to understand symbols and engage in pretend situations sometime before they turn 2, showing they are developing symbolic abilities that are useful as play develops.
2. Social interaction seems important to a child's emerging symbolic skills needed in pretend play, and it is possible they need a **zone of development** provided through interaction with an adult or more capable peer as Vygotsky theorized. The child may only be able to do so much on their own without the scaffold. This emphasizes the need for social interaction in play.

Social play and development

Social play involves a child interacting with an adult or with a peer (Pellegrini, 2013).

Social play starts with parent-child play and one example seen across all cultures is the **peekaboo** game (Pellegrini, 2013). This game is unpredictable for the baby and the adult uses exaggerated facial expression, emotions, and language. One feature of **adult-child social play** is that adults make themselves seem weaker to keep the child engaged so he or she can try out different social roles and become socially capable. This type of social

Peekaboo is seen in all cultures.
Used under license from <u>megapixel.com</u>.

play is highlighted in Bruner's observations of peekaboo games and Vygotsky's zone of proximal development.

Peer social play can involve **rough and tumble play**, not to be confused with aggression (Pellegrini, 2013). Peer social play seems to have two goals in childhood. If aggression occurs it could be part of group bonding and we should not automatically assume there are intentions to hurt others.

1. A competitive goal where children practice fighting skills
2. A cooperative goal where children learn social skills for group bonding

Research support: Social play has benefits: Peekaboo

Peekaboo is rich in what it offers babies and the game is seen universally (Bruner & Sherwood, 1976). Babies must show many skills to play peekaboo, such as having object permanence and understanding rules. Even if a baby can start playing because of biologically programmed behaviors, such as smiling and babbling, as the mind develops so does the cognition needed to follow rules.

The **aim of the observation study** was to examine the peekaboo game rule structures. Six babies and their mothers were observed once every 2 weeks for 10 months as the baby grew from 7 months to 17 months of age. Sessions were videotaped and later analyzed. The results reported in this article focus on one female baby and her mother to illustrate the study findings.

Procedures are next. Peekaboo always starts off with the mother and baby looking at each other at the same time, and if this does not happen the mother speaks to the child to get his or her attention. Sometimes the game starts when a child is fretting, such as getting dried after a bath and the mother used the towel as a prop.

Example behaviors to get peekaboo started (Bruner & Sherwood, 1976, p. 218)

Examples of opening moves	Frequency of the most used behaviors to get peekaboo started
Face-to-face contact	16 (from 21 observations)
Vocalizing	9 (from 22 observations)

The next step in peekaboo is hiding. All of the observations of a child starting the game come once she is 15 months old, a time when the child is also making other milestones in language, theory of mind, and cognitive development.

Example alternatives and frequencies (Bruner & Sherwood, 1976, p. 219)

The possible hiding behaviors	Frequency of the hiding, including who started the game
Mother (M) starts and M is hidden	8
Child (C) starts and C is hidden	2
M starts and C is hidden	11
C starts and M hidden	0

These details give you an idea of how important peekaboo is, and although the mother starts the game, eventually children become self-directed and initiates it on their own.

One interesting **result** is that all observed children and their mothers followed the same set of rules. Language is important when establishing rules and maintaining the game, consistent with Vygotskian theory suggesting that language is part of all aspects of play. The child learns that variations in the game are permitted, such as who initiates and who hides, but that the general pattern remains.

1. Beginning contact
2. Someone disappears
3. Someone reappears
4. Contact is reestablished

The authors **concluded** that peekaboo was a useful tool for developing child competencies such as learning rules.

32.3: The role of peers in development

Peers and development: Peers are important but let's not forget to have a global perspective

Discuss means to give a considered and balanced view supported by evidence. This section focuses on **peers and development**, particularly considering **friendships**. Characteristics of peer friendships are explored, including the benefits of friends. To give a balanced view, cultural variations and online peer friendships are considered.

Evaluate means to make a judgment using evidence. Research on peer friendships is extensive and shows peer relationships are important. To have a culturally relevant framework, students should realize that this conclusion comes from studies using mostly western samples. There is a growing yet still sparse body of research showing that the meaning and value of peer relationships can vary a great deal (Rubin, Bowker, McDonald, & Menzer, 2013). The newer field of online peer friendship research is intriguing and continues to grow.

Some key ideas about peers and development

It helps to start with general statements about peer relationships, though just some of these areas can be discussed in this chapter. Key ideas follow (Rubin, et al., 2013).

1. Friendships are voluntary, and are made based on similar interests and affection. Friendships grow throughout childhood, starting with mutual interests and becoming more intimate and influential in the teen years.
2. Starting and keeping friends is a milestone in development.
3. Aggressive children are often rejected by peers, and then the rejection can worsen the behavior.
4. Same-sex groups are the most important peer relationships in childhood and the

Children tend to play with same-sex friends until they are older.
Used under license with megapixl.com.

early teen years but switches to mixed-gender groups by the end of high school.
5. Boys have more group-oriented peer friendships and girls tend to have dyadic (a group of two) friendships.
6. Cross-cultural research shows both similarities and variations in friendships. The definition of a friend can differ between cultures, with some groups placing less emphasis on the intimate nature of friendships.

Friendship functions throughout development (#1 of key concepts)

Children connect with peers on several levels, interactions (social exchanges between two children), **relationships** (**friendships**), and in groups (a collection of interacting children) (Rubin, Bulowski, & Parker, 2006). Friendship is the most studied level and is considered in this discussion as one example of the role of peers in development.

Function of friendships (Rubin, et al., 2006)

Developmental level	Friendship functions
Infants & toddlers	Relationships provide play opportunities and lay the foundation for later stronger friendships. When toddlers begin playing they show more positive emotions, and have more complex interactions when someone is familiar. Is familiarity equal to having a friend? Reciprocal relationships have been seen in studies. However, these early relationships are unlikely to have the same important meaning as later friendships.
Early childhood, ages 2-5	Relationships continue to provide enjoyable play but now children show preferences for peers, especially to those with gender and age similarities, called behavioral homophily. Children's behavior toward preferred peers is distinct from their behavior toward nonfriends, and includes supportiveness and exclusiveness. Even 3 1/2 year olds have more complex play and more social interactions with friends. About 75% of children have a best friend.
Middle childhood and early adolescence	Friendships change dramatically. Peers are 30% of social interaction as opposed to 10% for children aged 2-5. The size of the peer group is larger and socializing is less adult supervised. An understanding of friendships becomes focused on rewards versus costs. Children 7-8 prefer to be with interesting friends who have great toys and are fun rather than difficult children. Children 10-11 want friends with shared values and know they should stick up for each other. Children 11-13 want shared interests, are willing to self-disclose, and behave more positively when with friends. Sharper differences exist between friends and nonfriends, and friend relationships are more stable. Children without a good friend can be lonely, may be picked on, and often lack social skills. Children with aggressive friends tend to solve social problems with aggression, the opposite from children with nonaggressive friends. Gender differences are seen, and girl best friends are more intimate and caring, which can cause more tension. Boys have friends in a larger network and girls have my dyadic relationships.

Developmental level	Friendship functions
Later adolescence	Children spend larger amounts of time with friends and it continues to be less supervised. Friendships are not as exclusive because adolescents want to grow and develop with many experiences. Friends with similar attitudes, future goals, and intellects are the most stable. Adolescents see big differences between romantic and friend relationships.

Research support #1:Early childhood friendships: Friends share pretend play, have lower conflict, and communicate well

The **aim of one correlation study** was to study the relationship between social, cognitive, and temperament of children and friends and their interactions in play (Dunn & Cutting, 1999). Two predictions follow.

1. The level of **theory of mind** skill and emotional understanding skills of both a child and friend would be related to the children's engagement in pretend play and successful communication.
2. Specific temperament characteristics, such as shyness and hyperactivity, would be related to higher conflict in interactions.

Participants were 4 years old and attended nursery school in the UK. Everyone on the study had a friend. **Procedures** include the following.

1. Tests for theory of mind (such as an **unexpected location test**, see theory of mind section for more on this topic), language skills (such as being able to retell *The Bus Story*), and emotion understanding were given to all children.
2. Two 20-minutes videos of the child and friend playing together unsupervised were made and observed later by researchers.
3. Information about each child's temperament came from teachers and parents.

> **Vygotsky is a good choice for a theorist**
> The **zone of proximal development** helps us evaluate the usefulness of friendships. Not only does play move children to the top of their current ZPD, so does social interaction (Vygotsky, 1978). A peer, especially one with more experience co-constructs with another child during play (Rubin, et al., 2006).
>
> Vygotsky emphasized cooperation in play and externalized speech, meaning that preschool children used **language** while playing to help them figure out a task.

Two of the many **results** follow.

1. The first prediction was supported. A child's level of theory of mind and language abilities were related to the level and quality of **pretend play**.
2. Less conflict was seen between friends with greater emotional understanding while higher levels of conflict were seen between hyperactive children and friends.

The authors **concluded** that a child's social and cognitive skills contribute to friend's pretend play, low conflict and good communication.

This study is part of a large body of friendship research using western samples showing the functions of play.

Research support #2: Children from all cultures value friendships but there are some differences (key concept #7)

Few cross-cultural studies have been conducted about friendships, but although friendship exists in all cultures, children's peer relationships can vary a great deal (Rubin, et al., 2013). Particularly, the meaning and function of friendships differ (Keller, 2010).

The **aim of the interview study** was to see if the emotional intimacy of adolescent friendships was similar in other cultures. **Procedures** involved interviews conducted with children 7-9, adolescents 12-15, and young adults aged 19 from western cultures and China (Keller, 2010). Participants reasoned about a moral dilemma on four different levels about keeping a promise to a best friend or choosing to spend time with a third child new in school. Level one was to define the problem, level two was defining the choices, level three was reasoning about the possible consequences of either choice, and level four was about ways to fix any negative consequences of the choices.

Results showed both similarities and differences.

1. All participants considered playing and sharing at level one, helping at level two, trusting at level 3, and friendships as part of a larger relationship group at level 4.
2. There were cultural differences within the reasoning. Chinese children were most concerned about the morality of their decision, altruism, and maintaining relationships while western participants thought most about keeping a promise.

It was **concluded** that all participants valued friendships and the differences in decision-making showed differences in cultural values. More research is needed to clarify the nature of relationships and test each function of friendship as a child develops.

What about online friends? Study results can conflict

A survey of US youth aged 13-17 shows that especially for older adolescents, friendships can start online (Lenhart, 2015). The statistics about **online peer relationships** are interesting and students should realize that they have both positive and negative aspects.

1. 57% said they made a friend online, with boys more likely than girls to do this.
2. Playing video games or meeting through Facebook and Instagram are the most frequent places to meet friends.
3. Texting is the most common way for adolescents to communicate with friends, with 88% saying they text friends each day.
4. For boys, video games are most important for starting and keeping friendships.
5. Online gaming can build friendships, and 78% of boys felt more connected to friends and relaxed during games with few feelings of anger and frustration.
6. Adolescent friendships are both strengthened and challenged on social media. 83% say they feel more connected to others and 68% say they have been helped through tough times. However, social media is also a platform for negative interactions. 68% thought too much drama was started, 42% said other people posted things about them they could not control, and 21% said they felt worse about themselves from reading other's postings.

Online friendships have both positive and negative aspects

This table summarizes research results every student should know about and is followed with two studies detailed in-depth. Withhold judgment until you read this entire section.

Issue	Description
Online communication and friendship is a benefit but only under certain circumstances	A survey explored the relationship between **online communication and friendship** closeness (Valkenburg & Peters, 2007). Results showed that both early teens and adolescents used online communication and rated their friendships as closer when using it, but *only with an already existing friend.*
Bullying and harassment are risks	The Youth Internet Safety Survey aimed to study harassment, such as feeling threatened or making rude or nasty comments toward another (Jones, Mitchell, & Finkelhor, 2013). Results showed that online harassment increased between 2000 and 2010, and that girls were most often victims. The authors concluded that friends communicate more than ever through the Internet, and it provides a place to bring face-to-face conflict online.
Internet addiction is a risk	A survey of Czech teens aimed to study the correlation between online friendships and Internet addiction (Smahel, Brown, & Blinka, 2012). Results showed that participants having more online friends, preferring online communication, and spending extra time online had a greater risk of Internet addiction.

Research support #1: People can make life-long friends through online gaming

It is widely believed that video games are completely harmful, and the American Psychological Association published a 2015 account of the problem, a conclusion made from reviewing 18 studies, many with questionable designs, and ignoring those finding no effect (Lorentz, Ferguson, & Schott, 2015). Can online gaming be just for fun? Students might access the APA report (APA, 2015), consider its merits with an open mind, and look deeper into the topic.

Perhaps video games and online games can have negative effects, especially if someone becomes addicted to them or if the child is at risk before playing the games. As for making friends, some research shows that online gaming can have benefits. One study is next, but it needs replication now that time has passed and the Internet has continued to evolve with social media use.

> **Inquiry: Class activity**
> Students might look more deeply into online peer relationships by searching journals, particularly journals about cyberspace, and consider how friendships online are similar and different from those off-line.
>
> In addition, what are the benefits versus the risks of online gaming? Students should keep an open mind and make a judgment supported by evidence. Chapter 17 can help answer these questions.

The **aim of this online questionnaire study** was to investigate social interaction when playing **online games** and also outside of gaming (Cole & Griffiths, 2007). Participants were from 45 countries and most were male. Some were adolescents, and these are the participants we are most interested in for our discussion.

Procedures involved asking questions about topics such as friends within online games, attraction to other players, the effect of games on online and offline relationships, motivations for playing, and the number of hours spent playing.

Results follow.

1. Participants played online games an average of 23 hours each week and most were male.
2. Most made good friends through playing, suggesting they were highly sociable.
3. About half met their online friends face-to-face and female players were more likely to do this.
4. The worst consequence from playing was addiction and teens may have the greatest risk.

The authors **concluded** that online gaming allowed many people to make life-long friends and is a comfortable place for people to express themselves.

Research support #2: Social well-being may suffer with online relationships

For a balanced view, consider this finding. The **aim of the survey study** was to see the correlation between girl's use of media, media multitasking, and quality of face-to-face relationships with social well-being (Pea, et al., 2012). Well-being is defined as social success, acceptance, and feeling normal.

For the **procedures**, girls aged 8-12 filled out a survey. Questions about social success included "I feel like I'm important to my friends." Sources of positive feelings came from questions such as "I feel more comfortable with….," with the response of online or face-to-face friends. Sources of negative feelings came from questions such as "I feel more judged by…." The girls reported their hours of sleep and what media sources they used.

Results follow.

1. Face-to-face friends and communication were related to positive well being.
2. Online communicating, media multitasking, and video use were related to negative well being.
3. You may know people who use media while at the supper table or when talking face-to-face. It was found that those who used online media the most also said they used media while talking face-to-face with others. In contrast, those with more face-to-face communications reported less use of media when with others.
4. Online communication and media multitasking were negatively correlated with adequate sleep. Those with more face-to-face communication got more sleep.

Will this child have more online friends than face-to-face friends? It is hard to know because children of this age have not been fully studied. The Pea survey shows that well-being can be damaged for children who do not also have strong face-to-face friendships. We may not be able to fully answer this question for some time.
Used with license from megapixel.com.

The authors **concluded** that even online media meant to encourage interaction did not produce well-being. This study *cannot show causation* so be careful about thinking that online media use causes lowered well being, and the reason for the correlations must be further researched. Digital children are growing up in a different world with a major shift in the way we communicate. We must find out how it affects development and be open-minded to the results. An evaluation must include lack of causation and the fact that we have not studied the youngest digital natives over time.

Evaluate approaches to research and ethics in developmental psychology

Research about online friendships often uses surveys and questionnaires, many accessed online by participants. Chapter 35 details surveys and questionnaires. This type of research counts on participant honesty.

Ethical considerations involve the use of participants under 18. Parents should give consent. If the research is conducted online, how do researchers know participants understand the directions and are really who they say they are? Look for consistency of findings as a buffer against these difficulties in conducting online research.

32.4: Childhood trauma

Childhood trauma refers to deeply disturbing experiences that happen to children ages 0-6. This age group is particularly vulnerable because the **HPA axis** is developing during this time and is strongly influenced by the social environment (Tarullo & Gunnar, 2006). Traumas can be intentional, such as child abuse, or unintentional and/or indirect, such as witnessing domestic violence, experiencing natural disasters, learning about a terrorist act, or living in the midst of war (NCTSN, n.d.).

Discuss means to give a considered and balanced view supported by evidence. Topics for consideration are the extent of the problem, the neurobiology of stress, and research documenting damaged cortisol systems in abused/maltreated children. A balanced view comes with the material in the next section about resilience, because there are ways to keep trauma from having such terrible effects. Evaluate means to make a judgment using evidence. A strong and large body of research exists demonstrating the consequences to children's biological systems and negative psychological and physical health problems.

Trauma	Statistics and description
Abuse, neglect, exposure to violence, and accidents	Abuse, neglect, exposure to violence, and accidents are the most frequent traumas for children (NCTSN, n.d.). Twenty-seven percent of children under 3 are victims of maltreatment and about 2/3 of children in Head Start programs either witness violence or are direct victims.
Terrorism	People do not need to be at the scene of a terrorist attack to experience trauma (Schuster, et al., 2001). Eighty-four percent of parents from a random telephone interview after the 9/11 terrorist attacks on New York said they talked to their children about the situation for at least an hour, and 34% felt they needed to end children's viewing of televised reports about the attack. About 35% of the children had stress symptoms and 47% said their children feared for their safety.
Natural disasters: Hurricanes	Living through a natural disaster is a source of trauma. About 9% of the children who lived through Hurricane Katrina in 2005 suffered from Serious Emotional Disturbance (SED) and showed symptoms for up to two years (Seawel, 2010). SED is similar to Post-traumatic Stress Disorder (PTSD) and is used to describe children's symptoms of incorrect beliefs, high anxiety, and mood swings.

Early trauma negatively affects the developing HPA axis and brain: The problem of risky families

Review chapter 9 about the HPA axis and cortisol before reading further. Early trauma is of particular concern because traumatic experiences affect the developing brain far more than a developed brain (Gunnar & Quevedo, 2007). People vary in both the amount of stressors they must manage and in their sensitivity to them. Frequent stress can negatively affect future psychological and physical health and is even harder to manage if someone has a genetic sensitivity to it.

Two related biological systems are involved (Gunnar & Quevedo, 2007). The first is the SAM (sympathetic-adrenomedullary) that releases epinephrine (adrenaline) to quickly mobilize someone for the fight/flight response. The other is the **HPA axis** that produces glucocorticoids (**cortisol** is the most important). This takes time, about 25 minutes, and also mobilizes us to fight stressors. The problem is that cortisol crosses the blood-brain barrier and affects the brain. Epinephrine does not cross it as much, so cortisol is the culprit because it can damage the brain. To sum up what happens in the end, too much cortisol production over extended periods of time affects **gene expression** by getting inside cells and altering gene transcription. Cortisol also affects the **hippocampus** by binding to receptors on hippocampal neurons, interfering with the **neuroplasticity** of learning.

Learning a little about what happens to the developing cortisol system can help us have some empathy for childhood trauma victims.

In a newborn, cortisol is not bound to proteins the way it is in adults, although it will become more bound to proteins over 6 months (Gunnar & Quevedo, 2007). As a result, newborns have lower levels of cortisol overall, but the free cortisol they do have more easily binds to cell receptors and affects behavior. Researchers have documented that newborns through age 2 month have higher cortisol levels during medical exams. By 3 months, babies are still upset during medical exams but their cortisol levels are not as high and by 1 year there is no evidence of elevated cortisol levels in response to stressors.

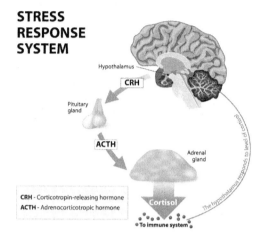

STRESS RESPONSE SYSTEM

CRH - Corticotropin-releasing hormone
ACTH - Adrenocorticotropic hormone

The stress response system is supposed to sense when to shut down via a feedback loop (Sapolsky, 2004). Stress from trauma interferes with normal feedback.
Used with license from megapixel.com.

This change comes from both a maturing HPA system and sensitive parental care acting as a stress buffer. *The role of a supportive caregiver is a vital factor in either a child having elevated or lower cortisol levels. It is not the show of distress itself that is related to high cortisol levels but rather good caregiving.*

It is known that children with **secure attachment** might cry when distressed, but they do not have elevated cortisol levels. In contrast, **insecurely attached** children have elevated cortisol levels when distressed. One lesson here is that supportive parents or caregivers helping a child in any traumatic situation increases **resilience** to HPA over-activation and reduces the damaging effects of chronic cortisol production.

This means *parents and adult caregivers are "powerful regulators of the HPA system"* (Gunnar & Quevedo, 2007, p. 157) and can help prevent a child from having elevated cortisol levels during trauma. It cannot be emphasized more that sensitive and comforting adult caregivers are needed for proper development and **if a parent is a source of trauma and abuse**, one result is likely to be elevated cortisol and the resulting harm. Damage to genes and the brain are carried throughout life, increasing the risk of physical and mental health problems, cognitive deficits, and poor emotional regulation.

Much of the time when discussing abuse and its consequences the person has greater HPA activity and elevated cortisol levels, but sometimes blunted cortisol levels are seen. Why might this happen? This is one finding from the Flinn (2006) study on the next page so we need to know what it means. Let's contrast the higher and lower cortisol production.

Higher cortisol levels are usually caused by "feedback resistance" in the HPA axis, meaning the brain is ineffective in shutting down cortisol production (Sapolsky, 2004). Normally the HPA system is tightly regulated and senses when cortisol needs to be shut down via a feedback loop. Scientists do not fully understand what happens when people have blunted cortisol, but it is hypothesized that at first, trauma victims have higher cortisol levels (hyperactivity) (Carpenter, et al., 2007). However, for some people, the chronic activation of the HPA axis in the face of long-term stress eventually leads to producing less cortisol (hypoactivity). There is much left to learn about the

Abuse and witnessing family violence are probably the worst traumas a child can face. Parents and adult caregivers are "powerful regulators of the HPA system" (Gunnar & Quevedo, 2007, p. 157).
Source: pixabay.com

process but both cortisol hyperactivity and hypoactivity have developmental consequences for the child. We must have the right amount of cortisol production to be normal, and too much to too little of it is serious.

Genes complicate the problem even more (Gunnar & Quevedo, 2007). If, for example, someone has the ss alleles of the **serotonin transporter gene**, they are genetically sensitive to stress. The gene itself is not a reliable predictor of behavior, such as depression, but when combined with experiencing stressors can heighten one's risk for many life problems. Chapter 7 about genes and behavior details this topic.

Research support #1: An 18-year study documents cortisol levels in a variety of situations and family trauma has the worst effect

The **aim of one 18-year correlation study** was to document cortisol levels of children and relate them to a variety of social situations and traumas as they occurred (Flinn, 2006). This is perhaps the only study available tracking the many different stressors children face, including real-time stress readings during traumatic family situations.

For **procedures**, children from 84 households representing the entire village of Bwa Mawego on an isolated side of the island Dominica were tested for saliva cortisol levels each day. Cortisol levels were correlated with everyday events and traumatic challenges in each child's life. Data was collected about both short-term (hourly and daily) and long-term (as long as 10 years) events.

A sample of the **results** follow.

Dominica is in the Caribbean Islands. It was a great place to conduct this research because Bwa Mawego was a fairly isolated village and the people were open to being studied for such a long time.
Source: pixabay.com

1. The highest cortisol elevations (from 100 to 2000%) were related to trauma from family conflict, such as punishment, arguing, fighting, and moving.
2. Children living with a stepparent had higher cortisol levels than their half-siblings.
3. Children living with 2 parents had moderate cortisol levels.
4. Long-term chronic stressors from family trauma often resulted in lowered (blunted) cortisol levels by children when in physical activities that usually were related to higher cortisol levels. These children had blunted cortisol levels even when in activities that were not stressful.
5. Children exposed to natural disasters such as hurricanes and political change had normal cortisol levels at age 10 similar to children who did not experience these events.
6. Children exposed to family stress had higher cortisol levels at age 10 as compared with children who did not experience family problems.

Flinn **concluded** that family trauma was the greatest source of elevated cortisol levels in children. Family trauma was also the greatest source of diminished cortisol levels in children when stressors were long-term.

Research support #2: Reuse Caspi's correlation study because genes can impact HPA activity when people face stressors

Having certain polymorphisms of genes can impact HPA activity because they create a sensitivity to the environment for people making it even harder to manage the stress from childhood maltreatment (Gunnar & Herrera, 2013).

Reuse the Caspi et al. (2003) correlation study from chapter 7 about genes and behavior for this section. The genes alone are not reliable predictors of depression, but in the presence of stress, such as childhood maltreatment, the risk is greater.

Plenty of research backs up the idea that genetic risk makes it harder for people who are abused as children. For example, Gotlib, Joorman, Minor, and Hallmayer found that girls at risk for depression because of the ss alleles had higher cortisol levels when faced with stressors (as cited in Gunnar & Herrera, 2013). Caspi et al. (2010) reported that stressful childrearing environments for Rhesus monkeys is related to higher HPA activity along with the report in chapter 7 about their greater risk for "monkey" depression.

This line of research then has both observer and method **triangulation**, so it is a strong conclusion.

CAS or class activity: Think globally, act locally

Early trauma presents so many risks for children all over the world that it seems one of the most important social issues needing attention. The class can look up statistics about trauma worldwide. Include child abuse, but also look into terrorism, war, natural disaster, political upheaval, and any other events students think should be researched. Consider how these traumas are addressed and judge if the interventions or preventions are successful.

On a local level, what traumas do children face? In my area (Florida, US) it is not just child abuse but hurricanes. What is done to prevent traumas or intervene once they are experienced? Might students get involved through **CAS** to do something positive for these children?

32.5: Resilience

YouTube: Ann Masten: Inside Resilient Children
Ann Masten is an important resilience researcher and the video is an overview of the topic.

Resilience means positively adapting to life's challenges and continuing to develop normally. When we think of resilience we can find examples of people who seem to function well even when living in a difficult situation (stress resistance) or who can recover from trauma (bouncing-back) (Masten, 2013).

Five resilience factors are identified that help children adapt and overcome challenges (Masten, 2013).

Resilience factor	Description (Masten, 2013)
Attachment and supportive, comforting caregivers	Comforting, supportive, and available caregivers are the most important ingredient of resilience. This is discussed by John Bowlby when studying attachment and is reviewed in chapter 33. Protection and security from a caregiver promotes normal development and a child lacking this is at great risk. A parent or caregiver protects children from harm and socializes them in ways that promote resilience, such as modeling self-regulation skills or the skills needed for positive school experiences, such as reading. Parents and caregivers model stress management skills and good health habits, helping the child's own adaptive systems to flourish.

Resilience factor	Description (Masten, 2013)
High self-efficacy	Children are pleased when they act on the environment and find they are successful (I can do it myself!). Resilient people have high self-efficacy to start and follow through with a goal. Children learn to be agents of their own behavior early from parent and caregiver models. Difficulties can be overcome, as in the examples of late bloomers and turnaround kids who find they too can follow through with a goal.
Self-regulation	Children who are good self-regulators have developed executive control, meaning they have control over their attention and behavior and can concentrate on what is important. Self-regulation is really a set of tools children apply to behavior and emotion, helping them direct attention to positive goals.
Learning and intelligence	Problem-solving skills, good judgment, and high intelligence are resilience tools because they direct children's activities into purposeful action. A good educational environment helps develop these skills so children can adapt when needed.
Faith, religion, and other sociocultural factors	Across a wide group of studies, resilient people say their religious or spiritual community played a protective and supportive role when faced with challenges. Other sociocultural factors, such as cultural rituals and group interdependence can aid resilience.

Plenty of research supports these resilience strategies. The first study examines the first factor about a supportive and comforting attachment figure and the fourth factor about learning and intelligence. It is about children exposed to domestic violence as a logical extension of the trauma research suggesting that abuse and witnessing violence is probably the greatest stressor for children.

The second study is support for the last factor about sociocultural factors. It is about **Indigenous Psychology** (IP) and highlights the need to expand our views of resilience to get a global perspective.

Discuss means to make a considered and balanced view supported by evidence. A balanced view shows that parents are important but on a global scale, there is more to the story as we expand our understanding of resilience to add specific cultural practices important to interdependent communities.

Research support #1: Positive parenting and high cognitive ability aids resilience for maltreated children

The **aim of the correlation study** was to see which individual, family, and neighborhood factors were correlated to resilience in maltreated children (Jaffee, Caspi, Moffitt, Polo-Tomas, & Taylor, 2007).

For **procedures**, the participants were children and parents from high risk families in England and Wales, and all the children experienced maltreatment before age 5. Individual characteristics included intelligence, reading ability, and temperament. Family characteristics included maternal warmth, if the mother was depressed or a substance abuse, the extent of deprivation the family faced, and level of adult violence. Neighborhood characteristics included crime level.

Learning and intelligence are resilience factors, so a quality education is vital for high risk children. To what extent do you think they get what they need?
Source: pixabay.com

Results follow, highlighting the greatest resilience factors.

1. Both boys and girls showed resilience, but boys with high intelligence showed the most.
2. Non-substance abusing parents are correlated to resilience in their children.
3. Living in lower crime areas was important because there was more social bonding among families.

Other studies also show that good mental health is important in a supportive parent or caregiver. Similar research has specifically identified having a mother free of depression as important (Martinez-Torteya, von Eye, & Levendosky, 2009). Unfortunately, both of these studies failed to show maternal warmth as important. Perhaps being a supportive parent is related to being mentally healthy in general, something future research should examine. Also unfortunately, children showed less resilience as the number of stressors increased, meaning their adaptiveness broke down with larger stress burdens (Jaffee, et al., 2009).

Research support #2: Global perspectives on resilience: The importance of sociocultural factors

The 21st century is already full of highly publicized traumatizing events, including violence, terrorism, war, natural disaster, and pandemics, and we should be concerned about the effects on children and our lack of readiness to manage the impact (Masten, 2014). Students might revisit the discussion about cortisol and trauma to understand the need to promote resilience on a global scale.

The past two decades saw a rise in the number of psychological studies examining cultural practices that increase resilience for individuals and communities (Masten, 2014). The hope is to expand resilience theories for global application.

Too often, resilience is oversimplified, defined as an individual characteristic outside of someone's larger cultural context (Kirmayer, Dandeneau, Marshall, Phillips, & Williamson, 2011). Individual characteristics are important, but when considering resilience across culture, theory should also include the traditional knowledge and practices of indigenous collective groups. Studying indigenous cultures is best done through **narratives**, special cultural stories that help people make meaning of the self.

Many cultures value interdependence (interdependent self, one pole of the self **cultural dimension)** and collectiveness (one pole of the individualism-collectivism cultural dimension) and this is explored in the following study so students get an idea of how important sociocultural factors are to resilience.

Promoting resilience on a global scale means to include studies of cultural practices from indigenous groups at a collective level, adding to what we know about increasing resilience cross-culturally.
Source: pixabay.com

The **aim of one interview study** was to examine cultural and collective features of resilience in the Mi'kmaq, an indigenous group in Eastern Canada, through stories of identity and change (Kirmayer, et al., 2011).

For **procedures**, researchers used focus group interviews and also interviewed key informants. Participants told stories (narratives) about important cultural values aiding individuals to make meaning of the self when faced with difficulties. In addition, the stories helped participants consider their identity, core cultural values, and creative ways to solve problems. Storytelling is a good way to collect data because it is part of traditional culture and a primary way to transmit culture to children (**enculturation** and **socialization**).

Results revealed an important community level process for restoring harmony and this was a source of resilience for individuals.

1. The Mi'kmaq find the treaties with Canada to be a source of resilience because they represent a partnership. These treaties have a broader role to play in self-understanding because traditional culture values peace and friendship.
2. The Mi'kmaq language has a word *apisiktuagn*, roughly translated into English as forgiveness. There is a ritual for this forgiveness. Historically, when there was a dispute, everyone involved sat around a fire with the Kineup, the group's holy man. A prayer to the wise counsel opened the ceremony and the offender asked the people offended for *apisiktuagn* in a 4-step ritual. The ritual concluded with a summary from the Kineup ending in harmony between all.
3. The Mi'kmaq currently use this old cultural ritual mostly between individuals rather than in a formal gathering, but the spirit of *apisiktuagn* is alive and well, a source of resilience to have a ritual for reinstating harmony.

The authors **concluded** that indigenous research allows us see that resilience often comes from outside the individual, something embedded in cultural rituals passed down through history.

32.6 Poverty and socioeconomic status (SES) effects on cognitive and social development

Let's take a moment to consider **poverty** rates globally, in the US, and in the EU and UK. Poverty rates are most often defined as income, but in reality, poverty also includes less access to quality education and health care, adequate housing, employment, and personal security (International Bank for Reconstruction and Development/The World Bank, 2016). These problems are intertwined and add up to many developmental risks for children.

Poverty on a global scale (International Bank for Reconstruction and Development/The World Bank, 2016)
Globally, 9.6% of people lived in poverty in 2016, defined as living on $1.90 a day or less, or about 700 million people.
The 2016 statistics are less than the 2012 rate of 12.2%, or about 900 million people. The 2011 statistic was 14.1%, so poverty rates are decreasing overall globally.
Poverty rates are still great, with the highest rates concentrated in South Asia and Sub-Sahara Africa. It has also reduced over time in these two areas, but is still very high compared to others. In 1990, the South Asia poverty rate was 50.6% and in 2015 it was 13.5. In Sub-Sahara Africa, the 1990 rate was 56.8%, and in 2015 it was 35.2%. For comparison, East Asia rates were 60.6% in 1990 and 4.1% in 2015.
South Asia and Sub-Sahara Africa have lagged behind other regions in reducing poverty.

What about the United States?

Poverty in the United States (US Census Bureau, 2016)
The 2015 poverty rate was 13.5%, down from 14.8% in 2014.
In 2015, 43.1 million people lived in poverty, 3.5 million less than in 2014.

Poverty in the United States (US Census Bureau, 2016)

Poverty rates are decreasing over time.

What about the European Union and the United Kingdom?

Poverty statistics for the European Union and United Kingdom
(Office for National Statistics, 2014)

The overall poverty rate for the UK in 2014 was 16.8%. About 6.5% of these people were in persistent poverty, meaning they experienced it over a number of years.

The overall poverty rate for the EU in 2014 was about 17%. This varied by country.

Students might also read a little of the report titled Europe 2020 Indicators- Poverty and Social Exclusion, available from http://ec.europa.eu because it says the percentage of the population at risk for poverty and social exclusion is rising in many, but not all, of its member countries. Check to see the different countries and read the explanations.

Even if overall rates of poverty are dropping globally, this is unlikely consolation to those still living in it. The consequences are high for children living in poverty, affecting academic, psychological, and health outcomes.

Poverty affects development in many ways.

1. Families living in poverty have fewer choices about where to live and often end up in crowded and noisy places without quality child care (Blair & Raver, 2012).
2. Parents struggling to make ends meet are at higher risk for depression and emotional problems. They can show anger and aggression out of frustration, placing the child at risk.
3. Children living in poverty are exposed to more environmental hazards such as lead, and have fewer safe places to play.

> **Conceptual understanding:**
> **Executive function**
> Executive function (EF) is the self-regulation skills that include all the cognitive processes meant to give us top-down control over learning and behavior. EF includes working memory, attention control, and cognitive flexibility.

4. Lower SES is correlated with poor health (Sapolsky, 2004).
5. SES is a predictor of academic achievement, affecting the **executive function** needed to learn (Lawson & Farah, 2015).
6. Children living in poverty can lack the necessary environmental stimulation needed for brain maturity, such as lacking the thinning of the cortex that is a sign of a maturing brain (Avants et al., 2015).

> **Inquiry and conceptual understanding**
> It might be helpful to have used **cortisol** as an example hormone and to thoroughly understand the **HPA axis**, both reviewed in chapter 9. **Neuroplasticity** is also important because this is a good example of the brain changing in response to environmental demands. This is a chance to thread ideas through the course so students highlight what is important to know in the biological material that is applied to developmental psychology.

A model for poverty effects on development: The biological pathway

Many people assume that if a poor child has problems with school or health that it is because of some lack of needed "input" from the environment, such as poor parenting or the wrong genes (Blair & Raver, 2012). This is an oversimplified view that must be corrected so we have empathy for what really happens to some children when they grow up in a family with low SES.

Our approaches to behavior framework and the concept **neuroplasticity** help us see the pathway for developmental risk.

The model explains what researchers call **experiential canalization**, a fancy way to say the channel for development. Researchers have uncovered a specific pathway for this channel that revolves around the **stress response**. If you understand how stress works then it makes sense that growing up with more of it changes the brain, and then behavior also changes. Review the HPA axis and cortisol in chapter 9 before going further.

The model below shows the canalization pathway, meaning stressful experiences like the ones described above make changes to the stress response system and the brain that help the child best survive in the environment where they must live (Blair & Raven, 2012). Evolution gives us the ability to survive in different environments and this is done by making adaptive trade-offs. It may seem odd at first thought, but we all adapt to our environment, and our biology "decides" to choose a short-or long-term trade-off, whatever is best for the child at the time.

If someone must adapt to an environment with few resources, crowding and noise, low quality child care, and all the risks described above, they make a short-term adaptive trade-off (not consciously but biologically) so they can better survive. This often means producing more of the stress hormone **cortisol** so the fight and flight system is on heightened alert for survival in unsafe environments. The long-term trade-offs then create developmental problems such as poor mental and physical health and lower executive function needed to do well in school. Think of it this way—*someone's system decides to help the child survive in the short-run but in the long run, the constant activation of the HPA axis damages them in many ways.* This is very different from the experiences of middle-class children whose biological systems can focus on long-term needs such as developing strong executive functions (Blair and Raver, 2012).

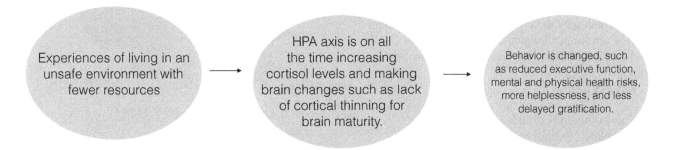

Research support #1: Cognitive development: Executive function is the link between low SES and academic achievement

The **aim of the correlation study** was to see if executive function (EF) acted as a middle man between SES and lower academic achievement, meaning to see if EF was the reason poor children often had lower academic performance (Lawson & Farah, 2015). EF was suspected because it takes a long time to develop and is quite vulnerable due to the experiences children from low SES families face.

For the **procedures**, children aged 6-15 were tested on tasks related to EF, such as spatial working memory and spatial memory tests. For example, the spatial working memory test required children to look at a series of boxes and find blue tokens hidden under some of them. Children could not search under the same box twice. SES was measured by parent income and education. Reading and math achievement was measured during this first testing and then again 2 years later so the researchers could document either positive or negative changes.

Results follow.

1. EF was correlated with SES and reading achievement over 2 years.
2. EF (except for verbal memory) was correlated with SES math achievement over 2 years.

The authors **concluded** that EF was the reason children from lower SES families had lower academic achievement. It is important to consider the sample because it was selected to make sure all the children were healthy and did not have the worst behavior problems. This was a control to make sure it was EF that was correlated to academic changes. Interviews with potential sample members excluded unhealthy participants with more behavior problems. This resulted in fewer of the lowest SES children from the sample. However, the authors feel the differences in EF even in a smaller range of SES difference is evidence of how SES is linked to EF over time, much to the detriment of children's development.

Research support #2: Cognitive development: Stimulating environments at age 4 predict normal cortical thinning in late adolescence

The **aim of the correlation study** was to see the link between childhood experiences at ages 4 and 8 with cortical thickness in late adolescence (Avants, et al., 2015).

Researchers wanted to know which brain regions were affected by experience, if nurturing parents and/or stimulating environments were important, and if it mattered when the parent behavior and/or stimulating environments occurred.

For the **procedures**, only healthy parents and children were participants to keep health from confounding the study. The sample had been studied throughout their lives, with home experiences collected at ages 4 and 8. Children's exposure to books, trips, and music were used to measure the level of stimulating environment. Parent nurturance was evaluated by asking about parent involvement and the amount of language use. During late adolescence, **MRI** scans were taken of the entire cortex.

Results follow.

The prefrontal cortex is the front part of the frontal lobe and is associated with executive function cognitive. Thinning of the prefrontal cortex is a sign of brain maturity. Used with license from megapixl.com.

1. Environmental stimulation at age 4 was correlated to thickness in the right inferior **prefrontal cortex**, and the greater the stimulation, the thinner the region.
2. Environmental stimulation at age 4 was correlated most with cortical thinning in late adolescence.
3. Thinning of the cortex over time is a sign of brain maturity. As a comparison, children with developmental challenges, such as ADHD or autism, have thicker cortexes.

The authors **concluded** that a correlation exists between environmental stimulation at age 4 and normal brain development later in life. Nurturing parents are important for development, but this was not linked to cortical thickness in this study.

Research support #3: Social development: Friendships, externalizing behavior, and challenges for acculturating immigrants

This is a good link to the earlier topic about the role of peers in development, specifically **friendships**. Children experiencing poverty can have more difficulties with friendships (National Children's Bureau, 2016).

The study findings come from parent, children, and teacher reports in the UK. The key findings show that children living in poverty are more likely to:

1. Be bullied
2. Fight with friends
3. Communicate less with friends

The problem is worse if a child suffers from persistent poverty. These children are:

1. More likely to play alone (1/3 of time as compared to 1/4 of the time in children who were never poor)
2. Three times more likely to fall out with friends
3. Four times more likely to fight with friends and bully others (16% versus 9% of children who were never poor)

The authors note that most of the poor children said they were happy, so the statistics represent a social risk and not a guaranteed outcome. Keep in mind that social desirability could affect the answers to a great extent when conducting this research. The resilience topic highlighted the benefit of a supportive caregiver, so being poor is not a straight line to difficult friendships.

The class might speculate about why friendships can be more difficult for children living in poverty. Perhaps one consequence of the biological trade-off made to enhance short-term survival is greater **externalizing behavior**, meaning the child is more likely to destroy things and have a bad temper. Research correlates family income to both lower IQ and greater externalizing behavior (Duncan, Brooks-Gunn, & Klebanov, 1994) and although these authors did not discuss friendships, externalizing is a plausible risk to any relationship. Research about friendship shows that aggressive children tend to be rejected by peers (Rubin, et al., 2013).

Poverty effects on both cognitive and social behavior may also be an added challenge for immigrant children who are in the **acculturation** process (Suarez-Orozco, 2015). In the US, about 21% of immigrant children live in impoverished families as compared with 14% of those born to US parents. It is quite possible that acculturation strategies are even more challenging for these children, as financial insecurity increases stress, which we know negatively affects the developing brain.

Chapter 33
Developmental Psychology: Developing an Identity

33.1 Attachment theory

Discuss means to give a considered and balanced view supported by evidence. This section is a consideration of the parent-child relationship and its lifelong impact on the child.

Attachment theory is supported by a body of research using Ainsworth's Strange Situations Paradigm, but has more recent criticisms from Indigenous Psychology (IP) researchers that the theory must expand to be universal. Remember what you learned from studying Harry Triandis in chapter 3, that the research on a topic is incomplete unless it is studied cross-culturally. Do not assume that Ainsworth's Strange Situations Paradigm is the best way to study attachment cross-culturally, even if it has been declared in the West as being the "gold standard" for conducting research.

Attachment refers to an enduring emotional tie linking one person to another over time and space (Ainsworth, 1973). There is a tremendous amount to know about attachment theory, so next is a list of general research findings (Thompson, 2013).

1. Infant motivation to attach to caregivers is adaptive and has an evolutionary basis. Caregivers nurture and protect children, increasing survival.
2. Different ways to attach to caregivers include secure and insecure attachment. These styles of attachment become a mental representation for the child about the self and what relationships with others should be like.

3. Researchers have developed a way to study attachment, with Ainsworth's Strange Situations paradigm as the main format (at least in the West).
4. A caregiver's sensitivity toward the child forms the basis of an attachment.
5. Secure attachments produce the best outcomes for children. It fosters future healthy relationships, positive personality and self-concept, and emotion regulation.
6. Attachment predicts how children will behave and creates cognitions about the self and others.
7. Attachment research helps us understand what puts a child at risk and what promotes resilience.

YouTube: Case of Beth Thomas

Beth Thomas was diagnosed with Reactive Attachment Disorder, an extreme form of insecure attachment. It is a sad story and one the class might watch and discuss.

However, this film requires great maturity from students and teachers should preview it for suitability before showing it to their classes.

There was a movie made about this case called Child Of Rage. There are many YouTube versions of the film and most include the actual interview with Beth and her adoptive parents. Find one with the ending showing Beth playing with animals and singing in church, as she did improve.

What happened to Beth as she grew up? The class might try to find out. This is a poignant story that reminds us about the traumas abused children face.

John Bowlby's Attachment Theory

Attaching, or making emotional bonds with another person, is a basic part of human nature (Bowlby, 1989). Attachment theory includes three main ideas.

Attachment theory main ideas	Details of Attachment theory
The way a child is treated by the caregiver, particularly the mother, is a major influence on the child's development (Bowlby, 1989).	A caregiver's treatment of a child influences the child's pattern of attachment. Three patterns of attachment come from Mary Ainsworth's research. These are secure and insecure (anxious resistant type and anxious avoidant). These patterns tend to persist over time but can change. Patterns of attachment are not part of a child's inborn temperament but eventually become a blueprint for future behavior and internal cognitions of self and relationships with others. A third insecure type, insecure disorganized/disoriented, was later identified (Thompson, 2013)

Attachment theory main ideas	Details of Attachment theory
The biologically based emotional bond between the child and caregiver gets primary status as a feature of human nature. Attachment has a homeostatic function within the central nervous system and provides the child with a working model of the self and caregiver in relation to each other (Bowlby, 1989).	The attachment relationship is based on emotion between an infant and a caregiver. Making enduring emotional bonds with others is the foundation for stable and positive personalities and good mental health. The child seeks attachment and stays within a close range of a caregiver who is easily accessible for support and protection. Both care-seeking by a child and caregiving by an adult is in human nature. Attachment allows the child freedom to explore and become a competent infant. The more secure the attachment, the more a child feels competent and safe in moving away from the caregiver who can be counted on to be accessible and responsible when needed. In contrast, feeling insecure leads a child to stay close to the caregiver. Children come into the world with evolved behaviors that form the foundation of attachment, such as crying at birth and then socially smiling by 2 months. Children show organized attachment behavior after 6 months of age. The attachment system has a homeostatic function within the central nervous system, seen in a child's use of distance and accessibility with the caregiver. The child uses more sophisticated levels of communication to explore wider ranges over time. Attachment is represented in the mind as a working model of the self and relationships that are held throughout life.
Attachment theory updates psychodynamic theories that focused on stages where a child could fixate or regress (Bowlby, 1989).	Attachment theory uses a theory of motivation replacing theories emphasizing drives and built-up energy and/or stages. The mother-child relationships goes far beyond the need to provide the child with food and focuses instead on providing comfort. Harry Harlow's research with monkeys supports this idea.

Mary Ainsworth's Patterns of attachment

Ainsworth identified three patterns of attachment in her studies and these patterns have shown up consistently in research (Bowlby, 1989), with a third insecure type later seen (Thompson, 2013).

1. **Secure attachment**. These children are confident in exploring their surroundings knowing that the caregiver will be available and responsive if the child becomes frightened or has difficulty managing a situation (Bowlby, 1989). The caregiver shows sensitivity to the child's needs and provides comfort and protection when needed.
2. **Insecure attachment: Anxious resistant type**. These children are uncertain that the parent will be available or willing to provide comfort, and as a result, are anxious about exploring their surroundings (Bowlby, 1989). They can be clingy and experience separation anxiety. Inconsistent parent behavior, such as being available and helpful sometimes but not others, encourages this pattern of attachment.
3. **Insecure attachment: Anxious avoidant type**. These children expect to be rejected by the caregiver and have no confidence that comfort or help will be provided (Bowlby, 1989). Parents who continually rebuff the child encourage this pattern, and the result can be a person who lives their life without love and support of other people.

4. **Insecure attachment: Disorganized/disoriented type**. This was the last type of attachment identified. These children do not show a distinct pattern of behavior with the caregiver and instead act confused, dazed, or disoriented when approaching the caregiver, even walking toward the adult but with head averted (Thompson, 2013).

TOK Link for the IB Student

Is what we know in psychology limited by ethics? What does the Strange Situations Paradigm really tell us about attachment? Because of ethics, the time apart from the parent was short, so researchers did not look at the long-term effects of separation. Harlow gives us some animal research using more extreme deprivation, but you must consider if the monkeys are good models for humans.

The class might consider how other topics studied in psychology are influenced by ethical constraints on research. To what extent is the field of psychology able to tell us what we want to know about humans?

Ainsworth developed the **Strange Situations Paradigm** to use in studies, a way to study attachment that is now the "gold standard" for research (Thompson, 2013). The Strange Situations Paradigm is conducted in a laboratory setting and researchers gather data through observations, parent reports, and interviews with caregivers.

Here is how the Strange Situations Paradigm works. There are eight conditions with a standard order for all mother and child participants (Ainsworth & Bell, 1970). The original study took place in a 9X9 room with the researcher sitting behind a one-way mirror. One end of the room had a child-size chair surrounded by toys, one side had a chair for the mother, and another side had a chair for the stranger.

> **Youtube: Strange Situations Paradigm**
> See how attachment is studied on youtube videos.

The eight conditions take about 3 minutes each.

1. The researcher and the mother carrying the child comes into the room, and then the researcher leaves.
2. The mother puts the child down in the middle of the room and sits, interacting wth the child only if the child asks.
3. A stranger comes into the room, sits quietly, talks with the mother for a minute, and then approaches the child with a toy. The stranger leaves.
4. The mother leaves the child alone to play as long as the child is content and engaged with the toys. If not content, the mother tries to get the child interested in the toys. If upset, the mother offers comfort.
5. Mother enters the room and the stranger leaves. The mother waits until the child is settled and then leaves.
6. The child is left alone.
7. The stranger comes into the room and acts the same way as in #4.
8. The mother returns, the stranger leaves, and the reunion between other and child is observed.

Sensitive and supportive parenting creates children who feel secure to explore their environment. They know mom is there to help. Used with license from megapixl.com

Attachment behaviors are scored with categories showing how the child organizes their responses to the mother, such as behaviors demonstrating "warmth" (Thompson, 2013).

A body of research **concludes** that about 62% of middle class children are securely attached, 15% insecure avoidant, 9-10% insecure resistant, and 14-15% insecure disorganized (Thompson, 2013). The percentage of insecurely attached children is larger in lower socioeconomic families and families with mental health problems, something to consider in light of what you learned about poverty and trauma.

Much of the research is correlation and does not show causation. However, there are some experiments from van den Boom showing that mothers trained to use behaviors related to secure attachment have less irritable babies than the other group (as cited in Ziv, 2005). These babies were naturally irritable, and ethically, the other mothers needed to also receive the secure attachment training.

Correlation research from Ainsworth demonstrates the theory

The **aims of the correlation study** were to see how one-year-olds used their mothers as a secure base when a stranger entered the room and to see if attachment behavior was shown more often than exploring when a stranger entered the room and also when the mother left (Ainsworth & Bell, 1970).

Participants were white middle-class infants and their mothers. **Procedures** used the 8 conditions outlined above, with observers coding behaviors. Three of the behaviors follow.

1. Exploratory behaviors such as visual and locomotor exploration
2. Crying
3. Proximity and either contact seeking, contact avoiding, and contact resistant

Results showed correlations between the behaviors and attachment behavior. These findings are characteristics of the entire sample.

> **Approaches to research in developmental psychology: Evaluations**
> The Strange Situations Paradigm may be the gold standard for studying attachment and has even been adapted for cross-cultural settings, but it is not without criticism. Some suggest it cannot capture the variety of life situations and number of caregivers involved with some children. This can be seen in the example about Efe children living in hunter-gatherer societies (Morelli, 2015).

1. A decline in exploration was correlated with the stranger coming into the room. Visual exploration recovered first.
2. Crying was correlated with the stranger appearing and declined when the mother returned.
3. Contact behavior was correlated with each reunion with the mother.

The authors **concluded** that specific events were correlated with a child's exploratory and attachment behavior. Going back to the aims, children used their mother as a secure base before continuing to explore. Second, attachment behavior was more important than exploring when a stranger entered the room and also when separated from the mother.

Genes contribute to insecure attachment: Serotonin transporter gene

Genetic research suggests a reason why some children have more risk for developing **insecure attachment** (Thompson, 2013).

We have studied the **serotonin transporter gene** before in chapter 7 and

> **Thinking skills: Using the approaches to behavior**
> This research about **genetics** and attachment can be used as an example of genetic influences on behavior in the biological ATB.
> It helps to know some modern research about attachment so students can see how the knowledge base has evolved over time.

here is another risk for the ss alleles.

The **aim of the correlation study** was to see the influence of the ss alleles of the serotonin transporter gene on insecure attachment. **Procedures** involved genotyping parents and children and evaluating children for attachment behaviors at 7 and 15 months based on Ainsworth's patterns of attachment (Barry, Kochanska, & Philbert, 2008).

Results were clear. Infants with the ss alleles of the serotonin transporter gene had a greater risk for developing insecure attachment by 15 months if the mother was also unresponsive to their needs. Infants with the ss alleles with responsive, comforting mothers did not have a greater risk for developing insecure attachment.

This is a called a *passive gene-environment correlation* where the child inherits a genetic risk and also lives in an environment supporting insecure attachment. We know that genes can make people sensitive to the environment and the s allele makes people more reactive to stress.

The authors **concluded** that a child's development was the result of complex interplay between many factors. This is another place to use the multidirectional model as we learn more about how specific genes interact with environmental situations to affect behavior.

The Strange Situations Paradigm has been used to test attachment cross-culturally

Bowlby and Ainsworth knew attachment developed within a cultural context so the Strange Situations Paradigm has been used to test cross-cultural samples.

Generally, research shows that children in Africa, China, Japan, Israel, Indonesia, Chile, and Europe demonstrate similar patterns of attachment, with secure attachment the most common (Thompson, 2013). These findings are cited as evidence that secure attachment is demonstrated across culture.

Insecure patterns can vary and sometimes children are hard to classify, so findings from one group to another do not always generalize well. For example, adult personality and social development after growing up in an Israeli Kibbutz is not correlated with an attachment style with the mother and father. This is because there is great variation in cultural values about raising children. So even though children in Israel show secure attachment, if raised in a Kibbutz the attachment to a biological parent is not as influential.

More accurate research results might be achieved if the Strange Situations Paradigm is carefully adapted to the many cultural variations in raising children. Let's get a test example for discussion.

Efe child rearing

This excerpt helps students get some context for considering the extent to which Attachment Theory applies cross-culturally.

"Efe forest camp. Eighteen-month old Maua sits in her Aunt's lap focused intently on the families streaming from the forest into the bright light of the freshly cleared camp. Cheerful greetings and songs meet the newcomers as they are helped to ease baskets and infants to the ground. Babies are cuddled by people they do not know or do not remember, and, with a bit of coaxing, toddlers shake hands, and older children bring water to the travelers. In time, they sit and share news, and voices blend with the sound of honeybees circling overhead" (Morelli, 2015, p. 149).

The class might look into Efe culture to understand more about the cultural circumstances under which adult-child relationships develop. Students can Google Efe, and one site with good descriptions is www.culturalsurvival.com.

Including all cultures in attachment research

A balanced view of attachment theory includes criticisms. Studying attachment cross-culturally is challenging because we need to "develop assessments informed by cultural standards of good care, competent children, and close relationships" (Morelli, 2015, p. 160).

Ainsworth and Bowlby considered culture important and Ainsworth even tested the Strange Situations Paradigm using US and Ugandan mothers and children in one study, but accommodating the cultural contexts did not go far enough. Although Bowlby knew culture variations in attachment existed, he did not see the need to modify the basic theory to make sure it applied to all.

Considering the **Efe**, a foraging society living in the forests of the Democratic Republic of Congo, provides a balanced view of how attachment theory needs modification to fit the requirements of **universalism**. Efe infants are cared for by many individuals and by the time they are toddlers, and children develop close relationships with them all rather than just particular caregivers (Morelli, 2015).

Ideas for class discussion come from ethnography research (Morelli, 2015). Students can research other cultures to see how these ideas might apply.

1. Bowlby's original theory said that attachment was an adaptive way to evade predators, balancing a child's need to explore and seek protection from a primary caregiver. Newer research expands the evolutionary basis of attachment to include psychological and social development helping people get access to scarce resources. Specifically, the context of harmonious relationships helps people survive and find food.

2. Resource insecurity shaped the values used to raise Efe children. People depend on others to help get scarce resources and a child's mother cannot do this alone in a foraging society. The person available to help the child might vary day to day.

3. Efe children are very social and form relationships with a large number of adults as a result.

4. Researchers are documenting the different aspects of children's lives across culture that shape attachment. One aspect is how people represent the self as separate or different from others. Chapter 20 details the **independent self** and **interdependent self**. Cultures with interdependent self concepts value harmony in relationships. The distinction between the two types of self-concept helps us understand the difference between what Bowlby proposed for sensitive care from mothers in Western societies and what it means to be a **competent child** receiving **good care** within harmonious relationships.

In Efe society children have secure relationships with many adults.
Curtsey of G. Morelli

5. Bowlby's term "sensitive care" should be changed to "good care." Good care can refer to how children are raised to fit into a group's social harmony. For example, parents might control children by requiring that they conform with the goal to increase social harmony. Controlling children is a widely held chid care value outside of Western cultures. Good care outside of the West also can include reducing extreme emotions, both positive and negative. The goal is for emotional expressions to increase social harmony so no one stands out from the others.

6. Exploring is even different in cultures valuing social harmony. Children may stay closer to an adult who controls the child's activities. This should not be called insecure attachment.

483

This is an overview of concerns about applying Bowlby's original theory and Ainsworth's Strange Situation Paradigm to all cultures.

Attachment theory still has a ways to go before it applies to everyone. The proper use of **etics** and **emics** is needed to create a universal attachment theory. Rich ethnographic research can point out variables moving us toward a true etic. Students might wish to review John Berry's description of etics and emics in chapter 3 to help with a discussion.

Monkey with surrogate mother

© Harlow Primate Laboratory
Used with permission

Harry Harlow's research supports Bowlby's theory that children use caregivers for comfort

Research using rhesus monkeys confirms Bowlby's theory that an infant does not simply use the mother for food, but relies on it for comfort and support (Harlow & Zimmerman, 1959).

Motherless infant monkeys living in isolated cages were given two "mothers," a wire mother surrogate with a food bottle and a cloth covered comfortable mother surrogate, the **independent variable**. The **aim of the experiment** was to see if the infants would attach to either one.

Procedures were observations of the monkeys with their assigned mothers. **Results** showed that the monkeys went to the wire "mother" for food but spent most of their time with the cloth mother, especially running to it and clinging when Harlow put a novel object into the cage. Harlow **concluded** that comfort was most important for making an attachment and that there was no substitute for good parenting and positive early experience.

Evaluate ethics in developmental psychology

All monkeys living at the Harlow primate laboratory are now raised with their mothers (Personal communication with C. Coe, Director, Harlow Center for Biological Psychology, 3/2/16). Many lessons have been learned about the need for quality parenting as a result of Harlow's research.

Animals should be used in experiments only if the benefit to science outweighs the risk to the animal. The monkeys in this Harlow experiment were taken from their mothers and given a surrogate.

Review chapter 10 about the use of animal models to draw conclusions about humans. Rhesus monkeys are one of the **model animals used in research** (MOP animals) and students should not automatically conclude that findings can be generalized to humans.

Harlow exposed monkeys to great stress in his research, and experimenters are required to avoid harm when possible and give good quality medical care.

Harlow did reverse the effects of deprivation for some monkey participants by using monkey therapists a few months younger who followed the abused monkeys and hugged them until they acted normally (Suomi & Harlow, 1972). However, not all the monkeys could be rehabilitated so the benefits to humans must be substantial and the monkeys must be good models for humans.

33.2: Gender identity and social roles

Discuss means to give a considered and balanced view supported by evidence. Since people have so many stereotypes about why male and female behavior seems to be different from reading popular media, we must get a balanced view of just how great the differences are and if these are seen cross-culturally and in animals. Evaluate means to make a judgment using evidence. Gender identity and social roles have a large research base but some it is inconclusive, so this is a place to tolerate uncertainty.

Inquiry: Class activity

Since the number one reason students give for taking psychology is to understand why people do things, before starting this unit the class can look up some opinions explaining gender behavior in popular media. Is it true that males and female behavior is different and if so why? For example, books such as *Men are from Mars and Women are from Venus* are widespread, and the Internet and social media also contains much information. Have students compile a list of reasons as a frame of reference to study the scientific research on the topic. How do they compare?

Students should next review **schema** in chapters 11 and 12 because gender schema is one of the topics.

Important definitions: Use the terms correctly!

A person's sexual identity has three parts. The definitions are next and this chapter focuses on gender identity and gender role behavior (the social roles).

1. **Gender identity** (also known as core gender identity). This is the sense people have of being male or female (Hines, 2004). **Gender dysphoria** is "a marked incongruence between one's experienced/expressed gender and assigned gender" (APA, 2013, p. 452). Assigned gender is the gender category you have at birth.
2. **Gender role behavior** (the social roles). These are behaviors reflecting social and cultural norms for what people are expected to do (Hines, 2004).
3. **Sexual orientation**. This means a preference for sexual partners (Hines, 2004).

Gender identity is where most differences between males and females are seen.
pixabay.com

Students have many questions about what role biology and environment play in shaping each aspect of sexual identity, so it is best to begin with some general statements about it (Hines, 2013).

1. Males and females are more similar than most people think even though there are some average differences in each area of sexual identity.
2. Factors from each approach to behavior contribute to the differences, such as genes, hormones, gender socialization and cultural expectations, schemas, and peer interaction.
3. Each aspect of sexual identity develops from different combinations of these factors. One example is that prenatal hormones give children a predisposition for **toy preference** (gender social roles), and this may be different from beliefs many students may have about toys at the start of the course. On

the other hand, **stereotype threat** is a reason why females do not test as well on high level mathematics skills, especially if the test items require **spatial rotation**.
4. The early hormone environment is related to **sexual orientation**, and even if people think social and cultural norms shape it, the research has not identified them. Although we will not develop the topic in this course, students have many questions and might look into it if they wish.
5. Do not automatically assume that finding brain structure differences between males and females means those differences are innate. **Neuroplasticity** means the brain can change with experience, so some differences can be acquired.

Gender Identity: The basics

Gender identity is the part of sexual identity showing the greatest differences between males and females (Hines, 2013). Most men have a gender identity as a male and most females have a gender identity as female. There is a tiny overlap where a small group of people with physical male characteristics (Y chromosome attributes) have a gender identity as female and a group of people with female characteristics (X chromosome attributes) have a gender identity as male. These are the people with **gender dysphoria**, though it is rare that people surgically change their sex.

> **Inquiry: Class discussion**
> **Gender dysphoria** is a DSM-5 disorder category so students may want to look into it. Scientific American Mind has an article in the Jan/Feb 2016 edition about transgender kids.

Gender identity development takes place in stages and once a child has achieved gender constancy then gender identity is stable (Hines, 2013).

Stage	Description
#1: **Basic gender identity**	Children can match a picture with the label boy or girl at about 30 months and can sort pictures into male and female groups at about 36 months.
#2: **Gender stability**	This develops between 3 and 5 in US samples. Gender stability means knowing that a girl will not change into a boy and a boy will not change into a girl with time.
#3: **Gender consistency (constancy)**	This develops between 5 and 7. This means a child knows a boy will not become a girl just by wearing a barrette and a girl will not change into a boy by wearing boy typed clothes, getting a boy typed haircut, or through any other surface change.

Researching the causes of gender identity

Studying the causes of gender identity involve fleshing out the contribution of prenatal genetic and hormonal influences and postnatal socialization (Hines, 2013; Hines, 2004). Case studies and correlation studies about people whose gender identity does not match their assigned gender are the main ways to study the topic and this is where our discussion starts.

Gender identity research focuses on three types of situations.

1. Female reassignment cases of XY infants
2. Congenital adrenal hyperplasia (CAH)
3. Persons without the necessary enzyme 5 α-reductase to produce androgen

Gender identity research #1: A follow-up look at a case study of female reassignment for an XY infant

One line of research about origins of gender identity come from studying **XY persons reassigned to be raised as females** because the penis is poorly formed, absent, or is damaged during surgery. There is conflicting evidence from studying these cases as some results find severe gender identity problems but other cases find the reassignment is not a problem (Hines, 2013, Hines, 2004).

One case is of a boy reassigned to be a female after his penis was destroyed by cutting during surgery (Diamond, Sigmundson, & Keith, 1997).

This is a case of normal XY twins, and one had his penis damaged during surgery at 8 months. This child was called John/Joan for the study and John was reassigned to physically be a girl afterwards. This case was originally reported by Money and colleagues in 1972 and they concluded that Joan had no problems adjusting to a female identity. Money's original conclusions were that the re-assignment was successful, Joan was happy with a female identity, and that gender identity stays open for change for at least the first year of life.

The aim of Diamond's case study was to challenge this conclusion with a follow-up investigation. Many things were uncovered in the follow-up leading to an alternative explanation. **Results** showed that it was disastrous to even dress Joan as a girl, as the child tried to pull off frilly clothes. Joan was reported to have many feminine behaviors up to age 6 but more often was reported to play male-typed games and even imitated her father shaving instead of her mother applying make-up. Joan even saved her own money to buy a toy truck. By 11 Joan knew she was not a girl, saying for example, "I began to see how different I felt and was, from what I was supposed to be. But I did not know what it meant…I looked at myself and said I don't like this type of clothing. I don't like the type of toys I was always given" (p. 4). Joan even had suicidal thoughts brought on by her **cognitive dissonance**. She rebelled against her estrogen treatments at age 12 and at 14 decided to live as a male, requesting male hormones and surgery to be a male by age 16. The authors **concluded** that John was happy with his male identity and even married at 25.

Are these cases good evidence that gender identity is hormone driven? Watch jumping to this conclusion because John/Joan was raised as a male for the first 8 months and we know there is tremendous cognitive and brain development during this time (Hines, 2013, Hines, 2004). There is also little information about how John/Joan was raised after reassignment or how the parents adjusted to raising a genetically male child as a girl. There is research showing that re-assignment was not a problem in several other cases, so conclusions differ. We do not have experiments to show causation, so evaluate the case carefully.

Gender identity research #2: Congenital adrenal hyperplasia (CAH)

Girls with **CAH** are prenatally exposed to abnormally high levels of androgens and they

---

Conceptual understanding: Don't worry if research is complex or still developing
Causes of gender identity are hard to know so students should cultivate an attitude of humbleness about the research. Students must still make an evaluation but must do so tentatively, knowing the topic is *hard to study outside of persons with abnormal circumstances*.

For example, male and female brains are different in many ways that may be related to gender identity (Hines, 2013). Researchers study the hypothalamic/preoptic area and the corpus collosum, but you cannot assume any differences are innate and irreversible (Hines, 2013).

Neuroplasticity can make the brain change in response to the environment, the brain changes at puberty, and sometimes men and women use the brain differently to get to the same goal (Hines, 2013)!

Fleshing out the contributions of biology and environment is hard. Although older research points to more biological factors for identity, some newer research challenges this conclusion, claiming that **schema** and family/medical support is very important.

have masculine role behaviors, such as in play. This is another case where the research is inconclusive because plenty of older research supports the **hormone** argument but newer research is leaning more toward **schema** as the basis of gender identity.

Research between 1968 and 2005 concludes that hormones account for gender identity. It was found that 2-5% of CAH girls want to live as men and this is a large percentage compared with the .001% of girls without CAH (Hines, 2013). In addition, research showed less satisfaction with a female gender role identity in girls with CAH.

Newer research challenges the conclusions and two correlation studies are highlighted.

Study aim	Procedures, results, and conclusions
The aim was to show that good family and medical support was correlated with happiness with a female gender identity in CAH girls (Kanhere et al., 2015).	Data were gathered with questionnaires asking about childhood experiences, family support, and medical support. **Results** showed that high quality medical care and family support were correlated with better childhood experiences and reports from CAH girls that they were happy with a female gender identity. This is different from early findings suggesting hormones are responsible for gender identity. The authors **concluded** that good support systems were a large factor for CAH girls to have a successful female identity.
The aim was to compare girls with classic CAH (prenatal exposure to high levels of androgens) and non-classical CAH (postnatal exposure to high levels of androgens) to see if abnormal exposure to androgens was related to gender identity (Endendijk, Beltz, McHale, Bryk, & Berenbaum, 2016) .	Data were gathered with questionnaires and interviews. Participants took several questionnaires about activities, interests, and attitudes about being a girl. Interviews measured comfort or distress about female gender identity, such as asking how they would feel if they woke up one morning and discovered they were a boy. Hormone exposure was known through their diagnosis as classical or non-classical CAH. **Results** showed that prenatal androgen exposure was correlated with interests and activities but was not correlated with gender identity. Gender identity was similar in both classic and non-classic CAH girls. The authors **concluded** this was evidence that hormones were not responsible for gender identity.

Students must decide how to draw conclusions from this body of research. As time passed research showed that hormones are not necessarily the greatest influence on gender identity. However, the newer research needs some development because data uses self-reports and the 2015 study had no control group.

Gender identity research #3: Persons without the necessary enzyme 5 α-reductase to produce androgen

Cases of persons born with ambiguous sexual organs at birth provides more evidence. However, these cases are not proof that gender identity comes from hormones, because other evidence from cases in the West where the child is usually raised as a female and stays with this gender identity contradicts it (Hines, 2013).

One set of cases worth considering comes from Papua New Guinea, where 17 babies born with ambiguous sexual organs were raised as girls but then changed to a male identity at puberty (Imperato-McGinley, et al., 1991). These cases were similar in outcome to those observed in the Dominican Republic and Turkey.

The **aim of the study** was to observe cases of **5 α-reductase deficiency** over 3 decades where the children lacked the enzyme needed to produce androgen. **Results** showed that at puberty, these children switched to a male gender identity and lived as men. Blood samples taken at puberty showed an increase in male hormones that enlarged the penis and started facial hair growth, although the hair growth was less than that seen in normal males.

The authors noted that Papua New Guinea culture was highly sex segregated after puberty, "one of the most strongly dichotomous cultures known" (p. 294). Gender segregation was so great that females might be killed if they knew information about male right of passage rituals.

What conclusions can be drawn from these cases? Conclusions should remain tentative because on one hand hormones made the children physically male at puberty, but at the same time it was a cultural advantage to be male in Papua New Guinea, the Dominican Republic, and Turkey. It is likely a combination of hormones and cultural pressure to adopt a male identity.

Social roles (gender role behavior): Play is the example
One of the many **social role behaviors** is **play** behavior.

Differences between male and female play behavior can be great (Hines, 2013, Hines, 2004). Although students can probably think of individuals who do not fit the profiles, remember that conclusions from study results reflect averages.

1. Boys like to play with vehicles and guns and girls like to play with feminine toys such as dolls and houses.
2. Differences in toy preferences show up by 12 months.
3. Boys play more rough and tumble games and are more physically active than girls.
4. Animals show similar play differences.

Both **hormones** and **socialization** influence play behavior and a balanced view looks at both lines of evidence. Even if there is a large research base supporting hormones as a primary factor for toy preference, socialization also plays a role, particularly through building on innate predispositions. There are some good socialization theories, such as **Social Cognitive Theory** and **Schema Theory**, both detailed in the sociocultural and cognitive approaches to behavior.

Boys like to play with vehicles and this is not simply because of socialization.
Used under license with megapixl.com.

Social role research #1: Hormones are a primary influence on toy preferences in humans
Prenatal hormone exposure is an influence and much of the evidence comes from studying abnormalities such as **CAH** (Hines, 2013, 2004). A group of independently run studies show that CAH girls have preferences for male-typed toys. Another group of studies examined children with **androgen insensitivity syndrome**, which means there is a problem where androgen receptors do not respond to androgen. These children appear female from birth and are raised as such because the disorder is not discovered until puberty. These children prefer female-typed toys. The reason hormones are suggested as the greatest influencing factor in these abnormal cases is that even in situations where the physical appearance of a baby is ambiguous, the hormone exposure is the winning factor explaining toy preference.

Even normal variations in prenatal hormone environments contribute to toy preference (Hines, 2013). For example, longitudinal research shows that mothers with higher levels of testosterone during pregnancy have girls with more male-typed play.

Play studies on normal children support the conclusion that the prenatal hormone environment is a primary influence on toy preference.

The **aim of one experiment** was to investigate through eye-tracking technology if male and female babies had a visual preference for a gender-typed toy (Alexander, Wilcox, & Woods, 2009).

Two of the hypotheses follow.

1. Girls would have more visual fixations on female-typed toys.
2. Boys would have more visual fixations on male-typed toys.

Infants aged 3-8 months sat in car seats and were randomly shown 10 trials of a doll or a truck, the **independent variable**, while researchers tracked their eye movements. Visual preference was the **dependent variable**.

Results showed that girls preferred the doll over the truck more than the boys. Boys had more visual preference for the truck than the girls, however they also looked some at the doll.

The authors **concluded** that toy preferences emerge in babies before cognitive schemas develop for gender-typed toys and are better explained by innate differences, though these innate differences are enhanced by **socialization**. It is possible that prenatal hormonal differences are adaptive, a tendency to react to cultural cues for accepted behavior (Alexander, et al., 2009; Hines, 2004).

Research into the topic has continued because boys seem to develop gender-typed toy preferences a little later than girls, between 12-18 months (Alexander & Saenz, 2012). This shift in boys to a strong preference for non-social toys such as vehicles was again thought to be the result of early hormones predispositions shaped by socialization.

Social role research #2: Even monkeys shows preferences for gender-typed toys

Vervet monkeys show similar preferences for gender-typed toys as human children (Alexander & Hines, 2002). These monkeys have no cultural socialization so it is an intriguing finding.

The **aim of the experiment** was to see if monkeys showed the same gender-typed toy preferences as children. Hypotheses were that female monkeys would prefer female-typed toys, that male monkeys would prefer male-typed toys, and that there would be no favoritism for the gender neutral toys.

Groups of monkeys were tested three times over about 6 months, with the first trial as a way to get familiar with the task and the researchers. This is a quasi-experiment comparing males and females. Gender was the **independent variable** and toy preference was the **dependent variable**.

Six toys, a ball, a police car, a doll, a cooking pot, a picture book, and a stuffed dog were individually placed in the group cage for 5 minutes. Videos were made and observers coded just the actual contact with the toys. It was not coded if a monkey simply approached a toy, as the goal was to see which toy the monkeys actually handled.

Monkeys have preferences for gender-typed toys similar to human children.
Curtsey of G. Alexander

Results showed that female monkeys had more contact with female-typed toys and male monkeys had more contact with male-typed toys. Females had more contact with the doll and cooking pot and the males had more contact with the ball and truck, though males also handled the female typed toys. There was no difference in contact for the picture book, a gender-neutral toy.

The authors **concluded** that gender-preferences for toys probably started early in evolutionary history before hominid lines clearly developed. There may have been a survival advantage to those developing male and female behaviors.

One interesting difference was found between the monkeys and the children. Male monkeys did not shy away from female-typed toys the way human male children do, and this may be because male children are strongly socialized to stay away from female toys. So even if hormones are a primary influence on toy preference, socialization plays a role in shaping behavior over time.

This conclusion is supported and expanded on by an experiment comparing male and female rhesus monkey's preferences for either wheeled vehicles or plush toys (Hassett, Siebert, & Wallen, 2008). Male monkeys preferred the vehicles and female monkeys preferred the plush toys. This study builds on the Alexander and Hines study because it required the monkeys to choose between masculine and feminine toys *presented at the same time*. The findings are a little different, in that in this study, the males interacted with male toys and females interacted with female toys, wherein the study above showed that females interacted with female toys and males interacted with all the toys. However, when given a choice of male or female toys simultaneously, the male monkeys showed a clear preference. This is an interesting study because so many people assume toy preference and play behavior come mostly from socialization. The authors concluded that "toy preferences reflect hormonally influenced behavioral and cognitive biases which are sculpted by social processes into the sex differences seen in monkeys and humans" (p. 359).

Social roles research #3: Parents play a role in socializing children's toy preference

Evidence over many decades points to a secondary but important role for socialization in toy preference.

The **aim of the field experiment** was to examine a parent's positive and negative reactions to children's play preferences, and whether their responses were based on the toy choices or on the sex of the child (Fagot, 1978). This study is not as controlled as lab experiments so keep this in mind.

One hypotheses was that parent ratings of the appropriateness of a child's would be sex-typed.

For **procedures**, observations were first made at the participant's home. Parents and children were told to behave normally and researchers coded the play behavior as male or female-typed, the **independent variable**. Researchers also coded the parental reactions, the **dependent variable**. Afterward, parents filled out a questionnaire about child-rearing practices and their views of appropriate behavior for boys and girls.

Some of the behaviors coded from the 46-item checklist as children played follow.

1. Playing with blocks (male-typed)
2. Manipulates an object (male-typed)
3. Vehicle toys (male-typed)
4. Dancing (female-typed)
5. Asks for help (female-typed)
6. Dresses up (female-typed)

Conceptual understanding: Alternative explanations for theories of gender identity and social roles
Gender identity research is inconclusive because there are many alternative explanations for study results. It can be hard to decide which position to defend.

Socialization theories for play behavior are alternative theories, but students should avoid taking an extreme position choosing one or the other. Instead, it may be more reasonable to conclude that socialization builds on innate factors, consistent with our interacting approaches to behavior framework.

Even the researchers supporting hormones as a primary influence for toy choice still see the importance of socialization building on innate factors, especially for boys.

Results showed differences in parental reactions to play. Parents reacted most favorably when their child behaved in line with gender role expectations and were more negative when their child played in non-gender typed ways.

It is interesting that parents reported on the post-observation questionnaire that they did not treat their children differently or in sex-typed ways.

The authors **concluded** that parents have subtle **stereotypes** and seem unaware of giving off these messages to their children.

Social roles research #4: Parent reactions socialize children's play

Another **field experiment aimed** to investigate the differences between the way mothers and fathers reacted to male and female children play at 12 months, 18 months, and 5 years old (Fagot & Hagan, 1991).

One hypothesis was that parents would react to male and female children's play differently at each age. The study focused on parental reactions rather than attitudes reported on questionnaires, so it is the actual parental behavior being studied. The **independent variables** were being a male or female parent and the ages of the child.

For **procedures**, observations took place during 4 one-hour long sessions. Clusters of gender-typed behaviors were used for coding. For example, the female-typed play included dolls, puppets, and art activities. Male-typed play included building and transportation toys. Other clusters were made for positive and negative parental responses.

Results include the following.

1. Mothers gave children more instructions and fathers engaged in more positive play.
2. The most significant differences were found for 18-month-olds. Fathers showed more negative reactions when boys played with female-typed toys and mothers gave girls more instructions when they tried to communicate. Parents did not show these same behaviors for 12-month and 5 year-olds.
3. Parents reacted more negatively when boys tried to communicate and more positively when girls did.

The authors **concluded** that 18 months was a critical time for gender-typed socialization.

This conclusion supports the Alexander & Saenz (2012) finding that socialization fine-tunes a boy's strong preference for male-typed toys by 18 months.

33.3: Development of empathy in children

Discuss means to give a considered and balanced view supported by research. This section is a consideration of empathy-driven behavior needed to be prosocial and interact successfully with others, including Hoffman's theory of empathy development. This section also includes an evaluation of research

---

Inquiry: Class activity

Students can observe children in natural settings and see how they display empathy at any or all of Hoffman's stages. Students can find children at playgrounds, at the beach, and at parks.

Students must decide how to code behaviors, become accurate at noticing behaviors, and figure out how they fit into categories. The class might brainstorm categories and all use the same ones.

Informed consent is not required as long as students do not introduce anything into the situations and the people are not identifiable.

Students might work in pairs so no one is alone and should have written parent permission to conduct the study.

Students can compare their findings and even pool them for writing a report.

supporting Hoffman's theory. There is a body of research supporting theories of empathy development and the claim that it is the basis for prosocial behavior. It is important to note that most of the research on empathy development theory uses Western samples (Eisenberg, Spinrad, & Morris, 2013), so it cannot be assumed that conclusions from Hoffman's theory apply to everyone.

The evaluation of empathy development is therefore that the research is incomplete because it is not well studied cross-culturally. Keep this concern in mind as you read so critical thinking is highlighted.

Key concepts for understanding empathy theory and research
A discussion of empathy begins with an overview of research and the resulting prosocial behavior (Eisenberg, Spinrad, & Morris, 2013).

1. Empathy is an emotional response when the person seeing someone else feels similar. Sympathy is a feeling of concern for another. Both encourage prosocial behavior.
2. Babies are born with evolved behaviors that are the start of empathy. Sympathy appears later and increases with age as the child develops cognitively.
3. Prosocial behaviors are stable over time, with girls testing as more sympathetic than boys.
4. Sympathy and empathy are motivations for prosocial behavior.
5. Children who show empathy and prosocial behavior are less aggressive and have higher grades.
6. Empathetic and prosocial children tend to have supportive authoritative parents and are **securely attached**.
7. Both genes and the environment contribute to empathy and prosocial development. This is demonstrated in twin studies.

Developing empathy: Hoffman's theory
"Empathy is the spark of human concern for others, the glue that makes social life possible" (Hoffman, 2000, p. 7). **Empathy** is the ability to understand and share the feelings of another. Studying empathy helps us understand the development of prosocial behavior, something innate in children that develops in stages.

The case of David
How do we know when children have made a milestone in empathy development? At age 2 David comforted a crying friend by bringing him his own teddy bear (Hoffman, 2007). This did not work and David stopped for a minute and then ran into another room, and came back with his friend's teddy bear. The friend hugged the bear and stopped crying.

David showed he had developed from egocentric (where the child cannot tell the difference between some else's distress and their own) to veridical (means to behave according to reality) empathetic distress.

David had cognitively advanced enough to think about why giving the friend his own teddy bear did not stop his distress. He started off showing egocentric empathy with bringing his own bear but could process feedback to show this did not work and then showed a developed empathy. Memories of his friend playing happily with his own bear might have sparked the idea to find it. Sometime soon David will start to show sympathetic empathy, and show fully developed prosocial behavior.

Empathy is the root of **moral behavior** (Hoffman, 2007). Empathy develops along with a child's cognitive sense of self as different from others, and as **language** and the **theory of mind** develop.

Hoffman (2007) considered empathy the motive for moral behavior and claimed that children went through 5 stages to develop the "empathetic distress" needed to assist others. The theory is that people are more likely to help others if they feel empathy for them and children must develop this ability. Helping others has evolutionary roots increasing survival.

Hoffman's empathy development stages

Approximate age	Empathetic stage
Newborns	Global empathetic distress: Reactive crying
11-12 months	Egocentric empathetic distress
After 1 year	Quasi-ecocentric empathetic distress
End of age 2 and the start of age 3	Veridical (corresponds with reality) empathy
By age 4 or 5	Sympathetic distress

1. *Global empathetic distress.* A newborn's cry is the root of empathy development and not just a signal for someone to care for it. They cry in response to other's crying and imitate the sound of a human cry. A baby becomes distressed at hearing its own cry and moving his or her face muscles that go with it. Newborns can respond to a distress cue by showing their own distress. An infant does not know what it is responding to, so the crying is called "global." By 6 months the cry is not automatic and is directed at specific people.

2. *Egocentric empathetic distress.* By 11-12 months, babies still cry, but also start to whimper and watch quietly when witnessing distress. Any helping actions observed in babies this age are directed at reducing their own distress instead of another's. Hoffman gives the example of a child seeing someone fall and cry. The child stared, cried, and put her head in her mother's lap, the same thing she did when she was hurt. Children's behavior at this stage shows they have trouble telling the difference between what happens to others and what happens to the self, showing they have not yet developed the necessary cognitions to separate self from others. Children reduce their own distress, yet are prosocial, because the behavior begins with seeing another's anguish.

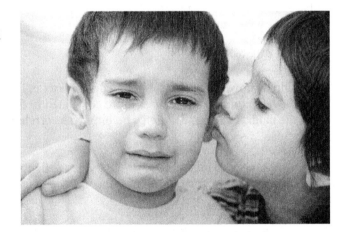

Comforting another and showing empathy must be developed. Used with license from megapixel.com.

3. *Quasi-egocentric empathetic distress.* Now children help others showing distress. Children approach others and pat, touch, kiss, hug, and reassure. These helping behaviors are mostly nonverbal. It is an advance, but the child still does not know that another person has their own independent view, meaning they lack a **theory of mind**. Children respond to others as if the person experiences things the same way they do. Hoffman gives the example of a 14 month old boy who saw another child crying and led him to his own mother, something the boy would do for himself.

4. *Veridical empathy (empathy that corresponds with reality).* Children this age know themselves when looking in a mirror, and have a clear idea that their body is separate from a sense of self that others can see. David's case is a good example. A child's aid to another is now more effective.

5. *Sympathetic distress.* Children are accurate with **theory of mind** tests by age 4, so they can respond to stress with the highest prosocial behavior, sympathy. A child's behavior has a motive to help.

Sympathy and prosocial behavior require the child to have a cognitive sense that others are separate and a sense that it is the moral thing to do to help others. Children no longer help and forget about what happened, but remember and internalize the experience as part of a moral framework guiding future behavior.

Research support #1: When children have a sense of self they can help others in distress

Hoffman's theory that a sense of self separate from others is required for prosocial behavior has support.

One correlation study tested children aged 18-24 months in both a lab setting and with observations recorded by mothers in a variety of places for two weeks afterwards (Johnson, 1992). The **aim of the study** was to see the relationship between a child's self-recognition and the use of altruistic behavior toward both simulated and natural distress in others.

Procedures are next. In the lab portion of the study, children were assessed for self-recognition through a mirror test and a picture recognition test. For example, one way to know if children have a sense of self separate is to put rouge on their noses and see if they point to themselves when looking in a mirror. To test for behavior showing the child is aiding another, a mother and a stranger both pretended to be distressed when an object was taken away.

In the natural setting phase of the study, mothers recorded children's natural responses to distress in a wide range of setting, such as at home and at a park.

Results follow.

> **Evaluate ethics in developmental psychology**
> Special rules apply for using children in research.
> Parents must give consent but children should also be asked and be allowed to stop if they want. Special care must be given to potential harm, so in the case of Johnson's study, the simulated distress must be something the child might normally experience.
> It is more ethical to test altruistic behavior in a correlation study rather than place children in experimental conditions promoting distress.

1. Children showed a variety of helping behaviors in both the lab and natural setting.
2. In the lab, children's responses more correlated to the mother's distress.
3. In the natural setting, children's helping was correlated to distress form other children, siblings and parents.

Johnson **concluded** that there is strong evidence that young children are capable of giving empathetic help to others, and supports Hoffman's theory.

Research support #2: A mother's display of empathetic help to others is correlated to the behavior in their child

The **aim of this correlation study** was to see if a mother's empathetic helping of others in distress was correlated with a child's empathetic helping of another (Zahn-Waxler, Radke-Yarrow, & King, 1979).

Children aged 1 1/2 and 2 1/2 and their mothers were participants. As this is the age when children show the roots of empathetic helping, it was thought that child-rearing might be important in influencing the child's behavior.

Procedures are next. Mothers were trained to observe and then recorded their child's reactions to helping others when encountering natural instances of distress. Mothers and the researchers also simulated distress to see how the children would behave.

Results follow.

1. The mother's explanations for their actions about responding to distress in others was positively correlated with children's helping behavior when they were a bystander.
2. The mother's empathetic caregiving to another in distress was also positively correlated with the way the children responded to others.

This study helps to demonstrate how children advance in developing empathy.

33.4: Developing a theory of mind (ToM)

Discuss means to give a considered and balanced view supported by evidence. This section is a consideration of how children develop a **theory of mind** (ToM), which seems fundamental to all aspects of normal development.

Evaluate means to make a judgment using evidence. There is a tremendous body of research on theory of mind development that spans decades. This research is strong, with consistent replicated findings showing that false belief tasks needed for a developed ToM occurs by ages 4-5, that ToM development takes place in distinct phases, and that the conclusions apply cross-culturally. Developmental pathways can vary cross-culturally, but the end result is the same.

The biological ATB includes the theory of mind in chapter 7 about **evolutionary explanations of behavior**. Students can use the ToM as a behavior for that topic.

Consider the interaction between the theory of mind, **empathy**, and **language**. These have evolutionary roots and seem to develop hand in hand. Each is a separate function, but all are fundamental to children entering the social world. The section about the evolutionary explanation of behavior reflects on the biological roots of language and how children come to learn the language(s) they will speak, something important to decoding other's mental states. Jerome Bruner's cognitive development theory, detailed in chapter 18 under socialization, also referred to children as developing within intersubjective relationships with others where there is an intention to know another's mental state. There are many places to use information about the ToM in a psychology course.

Games such as Peek-a-boo are practice for understanding the intentions of others. This child will pass a false belief test by age 4.
Used under license from megapixl.com

Key concepts about theory of mind

A discussion of theory of mind begins with an overview of important research conclusions. This is a point of departure for considering all the many things that happen in children's minds to give them the ability to engage in social interactions and prosocial behavior (Astington & Hughes, 2013).

1. A theory of mind means that someone can read the mental states of others and infer their beliefs, desires, and intentions. A theory of mind allows people to live in a social world and to explain and predict other's behavior. A child has a ToM when he or she can pass a **false belief test**.
2. Infants have an innate understanding that actions have something to do with another person's intentions and these behaviors will later develop into a full ToM.
3. Babies and toddlers have the beginnings of a ToM measurable with tests such as the violation-of-expectations.
4. By age 4 children show a more developed ToM as evidenced in false belief tests.

5. Children aged 6 understand second-order false beliefs and that others can interpret things differently, allowing them to understand irony, metaphors, white lies, and faux pas.
6. There are distinct phases for developing a ToM seen in all children.
7. The neural basis for the ToM includes **mirror neurons** and activity in the **frontal cortex**. Mirror neurons might be the neural basis for **empathy**.

A review of the evolutionary basis of the Theory of Mind

The evolution of the human brain required a social environment (Baron-Cohen, 1995). Social intelligence was a primary adaptive problem driving the human brain's evolution of cognitive skills. Remember from chapter 7 that Evolutionary Psychology (EP) explains the evolution of human cognitive processes. The ToM is needed for human cognitions.

Social behavior is complex. Remember how hard it was for Temple Grandin, a high functioning autistic person, to manage social interactions? The most adaptive way to manage social behavior was for humans to develop a mechanism allowing humans to decode the intentions of others, the ToM.

Mind reading is universal and people in all cultures have a ToM (Baron-Cohen, 1995). Humans are born with innate *skills* that form the basis of a ToM.

Phases of developing the Theory of Mind

Children go through 4 phases of ToM development (Astington & Hughes, 2013).

ToM development
Based on Astington & Hughes (2013)

Age	Goal for the developmental phase
From birth to about 18 months	Children begin to understand another's goals using innate intuitive skills. Children gaze at the caregiver's eyes, follow another's pointing, point things out to others (requires the shared attention Vygotsky considered in chapter 18), and give objects to others.
From 18 months to 3 years	Children know the difference between someone's belief about something versus the reality. Children start pretend play at this time and know that another's desires might be different from their desires. They have some understanding of false beliefs and realize that someone's actions can be different from their intentions. They can pass violation-of-expectation tests. For example, children watching an animated show about caterpillars looking for food showed surprise when one of the uninformed caterpillars was successful but were not surprised when the informed caterpillars found the food. By 18 months a child can tell the difference between what they desire and what someone else might desire, such as which food is preferred, but only as long as the child can see all the objects used in the test and can use nonverbal communication.

Age	Goal for the developmental phase
4 years to 5 years	Children show a clear understanding of false beliefs. They know the difference between how something appears and what is reality. They can even tell the difference between someone's apparent emotions (seems real but is not necessarily so) and true emotion.
	They can pass a **false belief test** such as an **unexpected contents test** where they first experience their own false belief before thinking about another person's beliefs. A box of crayons, for example, has candy in it instead of crayons. Children know that someone who has never looked inside will guess that crayons are in the box although they know it really contains candy.
	They also pass **first order false belief tests** involving a story about dolls such as the Sally-Ann task, where the child must infer beliefs of a doll. Sally and Ann are dolls. Sally has a basket and Ann has a box. A child watches as Sally puts her marble in the basket and leaves. Ann moves the marble to her box. The child is asked where Sally will look for her marble when she returns.
6 years onward	Children understand second-order mental states. Children can pass **second order false belief tests** where they are asked extra questions on false belief tests such as why Sally would think to look in her basket upon returning and could Sally have peeked. Children also understand different interpretations, irony, white lies, and faux pas.
	The ToM continues to develop through adolescence into adulthood.

Research support #1: By 18 months children know another person's desires are different from their desires

How do we know when a child reaches an early milestone of development where they start to understand that someone may have desires different from their desires? The **aim of this experiment** was to demonstrate when children start to reason about other's desires. It was predicted that children aged 14 months would not know that someone had a different desire but by 18 months they did know (Repacholi & Gopnik, 1997). This is a quasi-experiment with age as the **independent variable**.

The **procedure** was a nonverbal task with two types of food. One was crackers, something children like a great deal, and broccoli, something children at this age tend to dislike. Bowls of each were placed in front of children and the researcher pointed out what each contained while the children watched. Children were asked to select a food for themselves and most preferred the crackers. Then the researcher tasted both and said, "yum, broccoli" and "yuck,

---

Film about the ToM

Alison Gopnik demonstrates this experiment about understanding other's desires in the film *The Impact of Disorders and Trauma in the Social Brain,* available from Films for the Humanities and Sciences.

The film discusses autism and other traumas, but also details the ToM, including a demonstration of a first order false belief test, the Sally-Ann task.

Students can meet Temple Grandin, a famous and high-functioning autistic. It is theorized that autistics lack a developed theory of mind. If you go back to the start of this book you are reminded that humans evolved to live in cultures, and living together required the development of sophisticated cognitive skills, including the ability to read another's mental states.

crackers" making faces and expressing clear emotions toward each food. Then the researcher asked the child to give them some food.

Results showed that 68% of the 14-month old children choose the crackers for the researcher, the food they liked. The 18-month olds were more likely to give the researcher the broccoli, the food different from what the children liked but what was preferred by the researcher.

The authors **concluded** that children aged 14 months still showed egocentric thinking. By 18-months children were less egocentric, reaching a milestone where they can distinguish other's desires from their own. This study supports the theory that by 18 months children have a psychological representation in their mind of another person's desires and understand that another person's desires caused him or her to make a specific request.

Research support #2: False belief tests: 3-year-olds cannot pass an unexpected contents test but 4-5 year olds can

The **aim of the experiment** was to show that 3 year olds have trouble telling the difference between their own experience with a false belief and someone else's point of view but by 4 and 5, children have no trouble (Perner, Leekam, & Wimmer, 1987). A **false contents task** was used.

A **procedure** was designed so children experienced their own false belief and then had to decide what another might think when that person did not have the same amount of information. A box of candy was shown to the each child and they were asked what was in it. Children said it contained candy. Next the researcher opened the box and pencils were inside instead of the candy. The children saw what was really in the box and then the researcher put them back inside and closed it. Next children were asked what was really in the box and they said pencils. The critical test phase asks children what their friend, who hasn't seen what is inside the box, would think is in it. And last, children were asked what they thought was originally inside the box.

Results showed that 3-year-olds thought the friend would think pencils were in the box, and this was based on what they knew was inside. Most of the 4-5 year olds knew the friend would think candy was inside the box. This is a quasi-experiment with age as the **independent variable**.

False belief test **conclusions** *are greatly replicated*, so it is important to consider why 3 year olds fail these tests and 4-5 year olds easily pass them (Astington & Hughes, 2013).

Between 2 and 3 children's language grows tremendously, giving them the representational thought to talk about things they cannot see (Astington & Hughes, 2013). When a child infers another's inner state, such as in the food preference desire experiment, the tasks are nonverbal and the objects in sight, so the skill needed for a false belief test is much greater.

Three-year olds also have difficulty understanding **representational change** (that things can change shape and still be the same), which interferes with their ability to pass false belief tests (Gopnik & Astington, 1988). Representational change is needed to pass a false belief test.

A False Contents Test

The child is shown the first picture and asked "what is in the box?" The answer should be "crayons." Then the child is shown that candy is really inside the crayon box. Next they are shown the first picture again and asked "if your mother comes into the room and sees this box, what will she think is inside?" The answer should be crayons, although the child knows that candy is really inside.

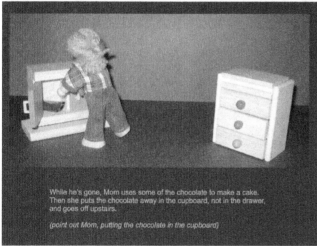
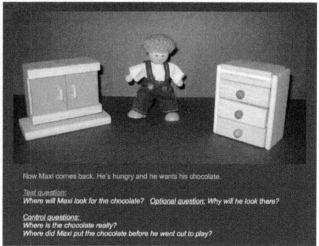

First order false belief test: Children should be able to pass this by age 5
Curtsey of J. Astington

Research support #3: Theory of mind continues to develop through later childhood and adolescence into adulthood

An experiment **aimed to show** that children, adolescents, and adults use the ToM differently and that executive functioning development accounted for some of the age differences in getting a task correct (Symeonidou, Dumontheil, Chow, & Breheny, 2015). The study had two **independent variables**, age and the director or no director condition.

Executive function is a set of skills that aid people in tasks. One executive function is inhibitory control, meaning to focus on what is relevant even when irrelevant things are present. It was thought that inhibitory control was not fully developed until adulthood.

Participants were children aged 9-13, adolescents aged 14-18, and adults aged 19-29.

The **procedure** used a director's paradigm. Participants interact with a director about a group of objects placed on a series of shelves that are to be moved according to the director's instructions.

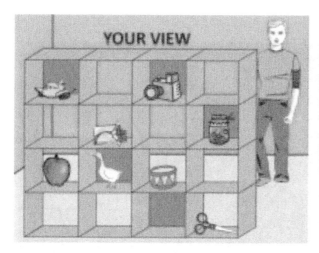
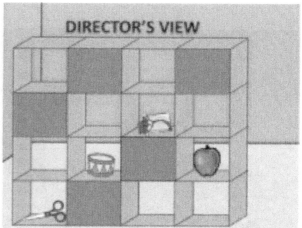

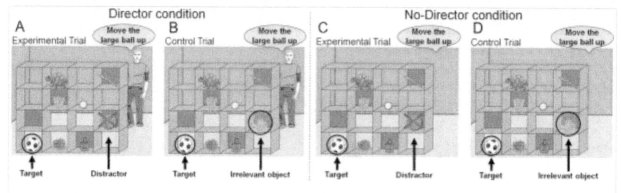

Source: Symeonidou, Dumontheil, Chow, & Breheny, 2015

Stimuli of the perspective-taking task. (A and B) Director condition. The participant heard the instruction "Move the large ball up" from the director. In an Experimental trial (A), if the participant did not take the director's perspective into account, he or she would move the basketball instead of the football, which is the second largest and can be seen by both the participant and the director. In a Control trial (B), the distractor is replaced by an irrelevant object. (C and D) No-Director condition. The participant is told that instructions do not refer to items in slots with a gray background; therefore, the correct responses are the same as in the Director condition. Used with permission.

Some of the objects are hidden from the director's view with gray paper but can be seen by participants, who could see that some of the shelf slots were clear and some blocked with gray paper from their side. So when the director asks participants to "move the large ball up," they must ignore any object that is not seem by the director and instead move an object that is common to both. Participants must infer the mental state of the director and consider what the director is thinking.

In the no-director condition, participants heard a recording with instructions to move objects that were only in shelf slots that were clear rather than those with gray background blocking view from the other side.

Inhibitory control was measured with a colored square presented to the left or right side of the screen displaying the shelves with objects. Participants marked if they saw a blue or yellow square but were told to ignore a red square.

Results follow.

1. Children and adolescents performed worse in the director condition.
2. There was no age performance difference in the no-director condition.
3. Children had the poorest inhibitory control.
4. Eye-tracking showed that all participants used the same process of elimination strategy. Differences in performance had to come from how participants inferred the beliefs of the director.

The authors **concluded** that there are age differences in their use of the ToM, and it is only into adulthood that the executive function is fully developed to aid people to read other's mental states.

Research support #4: Theory of mind is universal, an etic

Cross-cultural research supports the conclusion that theory of mind is **universal**, an **etic**.

One quasi-experiment **aimed to test** Australian and Iranian children (the **independent variable**) on 5 skills showing ToM development (Shahaeian, Peterson, Slaughter, & Wellman, 2011).

1. Others have different desires
2. Others have different beliefs
3. Seeing provides a person with knowledge and not seeing something makes the person ignorant
4. People can have false beliefs
5. People can have an emotion but hide it

Children aged 3-6 were individually tested for each skill using ToM tests.

Results showed clear differences between the two groups.

1. Iranian children understood that people could become knowledgable before they understood that people could have different beliefs.

Apply universalism, etics, and collectivism from SCATB

Etics and collectivism were introduced in chapter 3 and universalism was introduced in chapter 22. A good critical thinker uses the terms correctly and looks for cultural verification.

Students should always to look to see if cross-cultural research verifies research originating in the West, otherwise, it is incomplete. We learned this from studying Harry Triandis. ToM is an example of a developmental topic with cross-cultural support.

---

2. Australian children were the opposite and knew others had different beliefs before they knew people could become knowledgable.
3. There was no difference between Iranian and Australian children in showing the end product of a ToM.

The authors **concluded** that children living in a culture valuing **collectivism** grew up in families where children were expected to conform to beliefs of adults without showing their own opinion. They also witness fewer examples of diverse opinions between adults. In contrast, children in western cultures are encouraged to express their own views. Regardless of culture, all children have a developed ToM in the end.

This conclusion is supported by correlation research about children's development of a ToM comparing Chinese children with North American samples (Liu, Wellman, Tardif, & Sabbath, 2008). The Chinese children understood that someone else could have knowledge about something before they understood others could have a different opinion about it, but had the same ToM skills as the western children in the end. This gives **method triangulation** to the experiments.

Neuroscience and the theory of mind

Mirror neurons may be the neural basis of understanding another's goal-directed behavior (Astington & Hughes, 2013). Mirror neurons were discovered in 1996 in monkeys when researchers picked up a peanut to hand to the monkey and found the monkey's brain registered activity as if the monkey was really doing the action. This is probably why you cry at sad movies, because your brain is acting as if the event is happening to you. Mirror neuron activity overlaps language systems and some believe that since imitation is linked to showing **empathy**, mirror neurons may be responsible for it (Astington & Hughes, 2013).

The class might investigate mirror neuron research more fully, including evaluating the claim that autism involves a deficit in mirror neuron functioning. It has been claimed that autistics lack a developed ToM, and the extent to which this is related to mirror neurons is unclear.

What might **fMRI** studies add to our understanding of neural circuitry of the ToM? Two brain areas are found repeatedly in research about the brain and reading another's mental state, the **right temporoparietal junction** (TPJ) and the **medial prefrontal cortex** (mPFC) (Astington & Hughes, 2013). The TPJ is consistently active in research where participants must identify other's goals and intentions, and is also active when mirror neurons fire. The mPFC is active when people must integrate social information over time.

Studies using **EEG,** specifically **event-related potentials** (ERP), show the prefrontal cortex is critical for development and use of the ToM (Astington & Hughes, 2013). ERPs showed late slow wave (LSW) activity in the left frontal cortex for children who could pass a false belief test. Even though both children and adults show this LSW activity, it is spread out more in children's brains and becomes less so later in life.

Thinking skills: Is theory of mind without criticism?

Avoid thinking that because theory of mind research is strong with cross-cultural validation that it is without room to grow. There are some things that must be clarified in future research.

For example, we know that the stages and end product of ToM are consistent in western samples, but it is unclear why it takes some children much longer within a developmental phase to reach the milestone (Astington & Hughes, 2013).

We need more research about mirror neurons and the ToM before drawing too many conclusions.

One other point about designing experiments is to make sure a child's lack of language skills is not confounded with the conclusion that a child lacks a milestone such as understanding false belief tests. Tasks such as Sally-Ann require the child to think about what a doll might be thinking, something requiring fairly sophisticated cognitions and language. An unexpected contents test might be a better choice because the first situation is their own false belief. Be careful when reading studies using tests of thinking about dolls not to jump to the conclusion that a child cannot pass the false belief test because they do not have a ToM. To **confound** means to confuse an outcome with a variable that is not accounted for in a study, and in this case it might be language ability.

Chapter 34
Developmental Psychology: Developing as a Learner

Chapter Objectives

Students will:
1. Practice thinking strategies (command terms) related to evaluation and synthesis with discuss and evaluate demonstrated.
2. Discuss cognitive development and evaluate research.
3. Discuss brain development, with an emphasis on the milestones of brains development that are related to cognitive development, and evaluate research.

34.1: Cognitive Development

Discuss means to give a considered and balanced view supported by evidence. Next is a reflection about cognitive development that includes language, ToM, and the mind's executive function. Evaluate means to make a judgment using evidence. The body of research supporting cognitive development is strong and it includes cross-cultural validation. Some of the research is older, but that does not mean it is out of date. This was *just when the research was done.*

Key concepts about cognitive development

Five key concepts about cognitive development stand out from studying modern theory and research (Bjorklund, 2013). They are good generalizations to guide our discussion. Cognitive development:

1. Is the result of interaction between internal and external factors
2. Is a combination of stability and **neuroplasticity**
3. Involves knowledge representation changes over time and children can represent knowledge in many ways
4. Matures as children gains more control over behavior and cognition
5. Unfolds in the social and cultural context

Cognitive development has a strong evolutionary basis, detailed in chapter 7 under the topic **evolutionary explanations of behavior**. Review **Evolutionary Psychology** (EP), the theory about the evolution of human cognitive processes. Children come into the world with evolved potentials that grow into sophisticated cognitions through infancy, childhood, and adolescence as they interact with and adapt to cultures (Bjorklund, 2013).

Humans have developed the highest intellectual skills of all the species, so learning about cognitive development helps us understand people (Bjorklund, 2013).

Details for considering each key concept are next, including research support.

Getting children to the point where they can participate in Kindergarten lessons is a huge cognitive and brain developmental process!
Used with license from megapixl.com.

Key concept #1 (Bjorklund, 2013)	Details for consideration in a discussion
Interaction between internal and external factors	Development is a complex interplay between internal factors, such as genes, and the social and cultural context. It is nature and nurture. Children come into the world with *core knowledge* or *skeletal competencies* that unfold as they interact with environmental input. **Language** is an example. Evolutionary psychology is a good explanation for language as an evolved potential. Communicating with others and transmitting practices to the next generation were adaptive problems humans had to solve, and language was a good solution. However, although children come into the world with the potential to learn language, input from caregivers is essential for development.

Research support: Language development experiments from Patricia Kuhl and Janet Werker

Students can find this material in chapter 7 under the topic evolutionary explanations for behavior. Patricia Kuhl and Janet Werker demonstrate how language develops and both provide specific examples of internal and external factors coming together to produce language. They demonstrate that children come into the world ready to hear all sounds produced by languages but by 10 months, a child's sound perception is pruned so they hear just those sounds of the language they will speak. Input from caregivers is essential.

Key concept #2 (Bjorklund, 2013)	Details for consideration in a discussion
Cognition is both stable and the result of neuroplasticity	Some basic cognitions seem stable over time, such as **visual memory**. For example, babies with good visual memory at 7 months also had good perceptual speed at 11 years. This does not mean that all cognition is permanent from babyhood into childhood. Much human cognitive development requires **neuroplastic** changes, such as the **language** example used in key concept #1. Humans have to adapt to a wide range of environmental situations. Children's brains are slow-developing in comparison to other species because we must adapt to complex cultural environments.

Research support: Reuse language research

Reuse the research from Janet Werker and Patricia Kuhl about language if you wish to illustrate this key concept for exams.

Remember from studying Werker and Kuhl that this baby may still be able to hear the sounds of all languages, but the brain fine tunes itself via neuroplasticity to hear the sounds of the language(s) she will speak. This is called perceptual pruning of sounds in the brain. Source: pixabay.com

---

Learn a modern cognitive development theory

Lev Vygotsky and Jerome Bruner have credible and well-supported theories of cognitive development. Both believe language builds cognition and both believe that children have *prelinguistic behaviors that development within social and cultural contexts*.

These theories are detailed in the chapter 18 and are better choices than Piaget.

Both theories illustrate the 5 generalizations about cognitive development. Although Vygotsky's theory is older, it still supports what we know today about development.

Students of developmental psychology might also study language theories because so much development relates to using language. As Vygotsky stressed, all other human cognitive processes, such as memory and attention, are removed from actions and made are represented in the mind through language.

Key concept #3 (Bjorklund, 2013)	Details for consideration in a discussion

Knowledge representation development occurs as children cognitively develop, and there are many ways to represent knowledge (ToM and imitation are the two ways used as examples in this section)	Children make advances in how they are able to represent knowledge as they pass from babyhood to childhood. Representing knowledge is necessary for participating in human cultures.
	
	    Lev Vygotsky and **Jerome Bruner** have the two language and cognitive development theories detailed in chapter 18 and are highly recommended as background for this section. Both theories are well supported and offer insight into representational changes. Vygotsky and Bruner have better supported theories than **Jean Piaget**.
	
	    Piaget was wrong in thinking that sensorimotor was a distinct stage, with symbolic thought emerging when children were able to use language (Bjorklund, 2013). Modern research supports the conclusion that babies have the beginnings of representational thought far earlier, and that it does not suddenly appear when children are able to use language.
	
	    One thread of studies demonstrating knowledge representation changes is **theory of mind** research, discussed in the last chapter. One necessary cognitive skill is **shared attention**, something Vygotsky said was important that set humans apart from animals. Babies without language can even demonstrate they have shared attention. Bruner also considered knowledge representation, and said babies come into the world with prelinguistic skills that unfold in 3 phases through **intersubjective** experiences with adults. Intersubjective experiences start long before a child has language and is a give-and-take relationship with the parent where each has the **intention** to decode the mental state of someone else. Animals do not have a fully developed ToM.
	
	    Another aspect of representational changes comes with a baby's ability to **imitate**. Even Albert Bandura's Social Cognitive Theory accounts for a baby's ability to imitate long before he or she has the verbal language needed to model (Bandura, 1977). A baby develops imitation early, and by 14 months can imitate what adults intended rather than their mistakes or if they did not finish a task (Bjorklund, 2013). Imitation is not done just for the sake of copying but because it is meaningful for belonging to a social group. At 6 months a baby can copy another's actions but it is not until 14 months that the "copying" is real imitation showing an understanding of another's intentions (Carpenter, Akhtar, & Tomasello, 1998).

Research support #1: Theory of mind studies

Theory of mind research from the previous chapter can be used to illustrate how children go through phases of representational change. Passing a false belief test is a huge milestone in representational thinking.

Research support #2: Imitating the intentions of others

Imitation to show representation change development is well studied, and the **aim of one experiment** was to investigate if babies could tell the difference between and then imitate intentional or accidental actions of adults (Carpenter, et al., 1998).

The hypothesis was that children as young as 14 months would imitate an adult's intentional actions over accidental actions. This would show that children know the difference between what someone intended to do and what was an accident, showing advances in representations in the mind.

Babies ages 14 to 18 months were participants. For **procedures**, babies saw adults handle six objects. Each object, such as a bird feeder, had two moving parts and an end result, such as colorful lights or a toy that popped up. The **independent variables** were age and the two conditions (intentional acts and accidental acts).

Each baby saw an intentional act and an accidental act with each of the six objects. Babies were **randomly assigned** to see one or the other first, called **counterbalancing** that is used to avoid **order effects** in experiments. The order of presentation of the six objects was also random, as was the order the researcher pulled one or other of the object's parts, once again to prevent the order shown to be the reason for a child's response.

In the intentional condition, the researcher pulled a moving part of an object on the structure, got the end result, and said "there" as emphasis that this was an intentional act.

In the accidental condition, the researcher pulled the same moving part of an object on the structure, got the end result, but said "woops" as emphasis that this was accidental.

This sequence was repeated until each child saw each object, both intentional and accidental acts.

Results showed that all the babies imitated significantly more actions in the intentional conditions than the accidental conditions, suggesting they understood the difference between an action someone meant to do and something they did not intend.

The authors **concluded** that 14 months marked a milestone in cognitive development with a change in being able to mentally represent others.

Evaluate approaches to research used in developmental psychology

Randomization and **counterbalancing** are important in experiments and this one about imitation uses them extensively.

Randomization and counterbalancing mean there is an equal chance that children see an object, intentional act or the accidental act, or which moving part was pulled first or second. This ensures it is the baby's ability to tell the difference between an intention and an accident that is measured and not some property of the object or the order of the sequence.

Randomization is important for **control** in experiments.

Children imitate adults more often when they are old enough to recognize the action as intentional. Fourteen months is the milestone.
Used with license from megapixl.com.

Key concept #4 (Bjorklund, 2013)	Details for consideration in a discussion
Development occurs as children gain control over behavior and cognition	Cognition abilities evolved to help us solve problems and children get better at problem-solving as they get older. Developmental psychologists study how children gain the **self-regulation** needed to have intentional control to problem-solve. Children develop self-regulation as their **executive function** develops. Executive function refers to children regulating their attention and being able to process information from long-term memory. **Working memory**, **inhibition**, and **cognitive flexibility** are part of a child's executive function and each must develop. Review working memory from chapters 11 and 12. A child's progress in cognitive development is measured through his or her working memory span, specifically with processing speed, such as how many words children can remember that increases with age. Developmental age differences with verbal working memory are due to development in the articulacy loop. The outer limit for working memory span seems to be 7 plus or minus 2 items but this takes time for children to master. There are some cultural differences in working memory span development, though the general process is the same. For example, Chinese children have faster working memory spans for counting than English speaking children because digits 1-9 are more easily communicated in Chinese. Inhibition means a child can prevent a response. Resisting something that interferes with another is one example, such as when the television is on while a child is also reading a story. Can the child resist attending to the television and concentrate on the story? Children are tested for inhibition through tasks such as a **day-night task**, where they must say night when they see a picture of a sun and day when they see a picture of a moon. They are also tested with a **tapping task**, where the child taps once when the researcher taps twice and twice when the researcher taps once. High level cognitive abilities help with inhibition, such as passing a false-belief test that shows a maturing **theory of mind**. Cognitive flexibility means a child can switch between two tasks or rules when solving problems. Executive function development goes hand-in-hand with brain development. For example, the development of **frontal lobes** is needed for executive function to mature. The next section about brain development discusses the brain side of things in more depth.

Research support: A tapping experiment demonstrating that inhibition develops by age 6-7

Researchers **aimed to see** how children develop executive function through **inhibition** of behavior and remembering rules using a **tapping task** (Diamond & Taylor, 1996). This experiment is an example from a large body of research about **executive function** development.

Researchers hypothesized that "the percentage of correct responses would increase over age, and that response latency would decrease over age" (p. 320). Response latency means the amount of time between the researchers behavior and the child's behavior. Researchers believed that the tapping task required children to show inhibition and to remember two rules.

Two of the **dependent variables** follow.

1. If the response was correct or incorrect
2. Response latency for each the 16 trials (the time it took children to do their task after the experimenter handed them the dowel)

Two of the **independent variables** follow.

1. Between subject age differences
2. Within subject differences in the trials

For **procedures**, children between ages 3 1/2 and 7 were given the rule to tap once with a dowel immediately after the experimenter tapped twice and to tap twice with a dowel immediately after the researcher tapped once. The experimenter tapped and then handed the dowel to the child to tap and then the child gave the dowel back. Three year olds could not manage the practice trials so they were not included. The experiment used 16 trials varying the tapping sequence between 1 and 2 taps.

Results showed that children's accuracy and speed (lower latency response times) improved with age, with most of the improvements starting at age 6. The youngest participants made the most mistakes and had the longest latency response times. The most common mistake when younger was to tap once or twice no matter what the experimenter did, which might reflect immaturity in **working memory** and lack of ability to judge the context (3 year olds have trouble with **theory of mind** tests).

The authors **concluded** that their results were similar to other studies about the inhibition development needed for executive function, strengthening the finding that executive function matures by age 6-7.

Key concept #5 (Bjorklund, 2013)	Details for consideration in a discussion
Cognitive development unfolds within the social and cultural context	A good reason to study Vygotsky and Bruner is they both discuss development within the social and cultural context. Children develop their thinking as they interact with their social and cultural environment. Vygotsky's **zone of proximal development** (ZPD) and Bruner's **scaffolding** explain how parents and other caregivers assist children in their development. Even if all parents assist children in their development, cultures provide different contexts for this help and create cultural differences in the expression of cognitions. For example, the work of Richard Nisbett is detailed in chapter 21 showing how East Asian cultures are more holistic in their attention and Westerners are more analytical. Review this material and look at the example picture of the fish tank. Kitayama's research about culture and the brain (object perception) is detailed in chapter 4, another example of differences during a cognitive task.

Students can use research from Bruner, Nisbett, or Kitayama discussed earlier in this book and use the following example about mathematics to demonstrate how the cultural context affects cognitive development.

Cognition unfolds in a cultural context: Chinese speaking children can count to 20 before English speaking children

Lev Vygotsky (1978) wrote that cultures provide *tools for intellectual adaptation* for learning to think and problem-solve. Vygotsky considered **language** the most important of the cognitive processes so for example, the way a culture's language expresses numbers affects a child's mathematical thinking.

Although there are no cultural differences in counting to 10 or to 100 once the first twenty are mastered, the cultural tools differ.

Consider how Chinese and English languages express numbers (Bjorklund, 2013). Both English and Chinese speaking children must memorize the base numbers 1 to 10, (one, two, three or yee, uhr, shan). After that it gets tricky for the English speakers. Chinese children have a fairly easy rule to follow because they have a word for ten (shi) and then count "ten one" (shi yee) "ten two" (shi uhr), etc. English speaking children must remember arbitrary words after 10, such as eleven and twelve until they get to twenty and then can count twenty-one, twenty-two, etc. Chinese children learn to count to twenty faster as a result.

Other cultures show similar language differences. In studies of Amazonia cultures, the Piraha and Munduruku languages do not have words for a quantity more than 5 (Bjorklund, 2013). People speaking these languages show mastery of managing small quantities early in life but struggle with larger amounts. Some of the people who grew up with Piraha as their first language learned Portuguese as well, and then had no trouble with large amounts.

Researchers conclude that language creates the mathematics differences. We all come into the world with physiology that adapts to cultural expectations. However, resist the urge to conclude that culture is the only thing that shapes cognitive development. Cognition is the result of the interaction of biology and the social and cultural environment.

The next section is a discussion of the specific brain development milestones that relate to cognitive development so children can flourish as learners within human culture.

34.2: Brain development

Discuss means to give a considered and balanced view supported by evidence. This section considers the brain growth milestones related to the cognitive development necessary for children to flourish as learners within human culture. Brain and cognitive development go hand-in-hand.

Evaluate means to make a judgment using evidence. Research shows that the prefrontal cortex develops when babies aged 8 months start mastering cognitive tasks. On the other hand, there is just indirect evidence that the prefrontal cortex is developing as older children cognitively develop.

The focus of this section is on **cortex** development because it is related to cognitive development studied in the last section.

Key concepts of cortex development

Cognitive development is an interplay between environmental experience and brain development. **Neuroplasticity** is the concept allowing the brain to change as the child interacts with their social and cultural world.

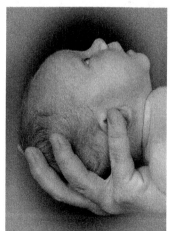

This baby's brain is already pretty complex at birth but must grow within a cultural context so the child develops as a learner.
Source: pixabay.com

1. *At birth a baby's brain is already complex*, with cortical layers, neuron connections, and myelination (Gazzaniga, et al., 2014). It is however, not fully developed, because the human brain is designed to mature within the social and cultural context. It might be best if babies came into the world with the instructions "some assembly required" (Kalat, 2007, p. 121). Although some important aspects of brain development occur prenatally, development continues postnatally and into adulthood (Markant & Thomas, 2013).
2. *Brain growth is not always preprogramed* (Markant & Thomas, 2013). Instead, there is a dynamic interplay between brain and environment where a baby's brain needs to grow before he or she gains new cognitive skills, and at the same time brain growth can be dependent

on experience (Kalat, 2007). The distinction can get blurred about what comes first, brain or experience. One example is when babies do not know a toy they just saw is still there when blocked from view (**A-not-B task**, illustrated in this section). Babies will know to look for the toy in the correct place as their **prefrontal cortex** matures, and there is tremendous growth in it between 7 and 12 months. On the other hand, if students review Patricia Kuhl's research in chapter 7 under the topic evolutionary explanations of behavior, they will know that children come into the world able to hear the sounds of all languages. It takes experience hearing the primary one(s) they will speak for the brain to fine-tune itself to hear just the sounds they need to speak a primary language. Bilinguals and trilingual from birth must learn the sounds of all the primary languages they will use.

3. *Postnatal brain growth does not go in straight line and different parts develop at different rates* (Markant & Thomas, 2013). For example, the **prefrontal cortex** takes a long time to develop as the baby interacts with a complex world because there is so much for humans to learn.
4. *Neurons can grow throughout the lifespan* and this has been shown in the **hippocampus**.
5. *A baby's brain has more neurons than will really survive* as they interact with the world (Kalat, 2007). Some will prune off and some axons will attach to other cells through synaptic connections (Markant & Thomas, 2013).
6. *The human **prefrontal cortex** continues to be fine-tuned throughout postnatal development* (Markant & Thomas, 2013).
7. ***Enriched environments*** *cause greater dendrite and axon branching*. Review the section in chapter 5 about **neuroplasticity** for specifics.

Details about brain development for our discussion

Focusing on **neocortex** development is important because it is most related to cognitive development and preparing the child to develop as a learner.

The neocortex is the largest part of the human brain and makes us different from other species. It contains the various lobes detailed in chapter 4, including the frontal lobes needed for **executive function** during cognitive development.

A summary of **prenatal** brain development follows (Gazzaniga, Mangun, & Ivry, 2014; Markant & Thomas, 2013; Kalat, 2007). Remember that the fetal brain is already complex, though by no means fully developed.

Conceptual understanding and **collaboration**: Students should first skim through all of this brain development information, looking for ways to categorize it (create a schema) so it can be remembered. Then get into groups and brainstorm the key trends in brain development, making sure to align them with other skills children must develop, such as a theory of mind and empathy. The brain information is important because it supports children's cognitive and behavior development. Source: pixabay.com

1. Each fertilized egg is made up of billions of cells and these cells will have specialized functions as they develop. This specialization is greatest in the brain.
2. The nervous system forms 2 to 3 weeks after fertilization. A transformation occurs where some of the tissue becomes the **ectoderm**, an outside layer of the embryo that develops into the nervous system, among other things.
3. The ectoderm grows into a neural tube at about 18 days and contains a fluid-filled cavity. This tube sinks under the skin and starts to differentiate into a hindbrain, midbrain, and forebrain. The fluid-filled cavity grows into the central nervous system that includes the brain and spinal cord. At birth the brain weights about 350 grams. By age 1, the brain weights about 1000 grams. A mature brain weight 1200 to 1400 grams.
4. Five processes take place to produce and mature neuron functions of the brain, proliferation, migration, differentiation, myelination, and synaptogenesis.

5. **Proliferation** means to make new cells. Early on, some brain cells stay where they are and continue to divide. Others become neurons and glia that migrate to other places. Although all species have cell proliferation, human cells take longer to complete the process.
6. **Migration** means to move to a new location. Each cell must follow a specific path to its ultimate destination and it can be a long journey. Chemicals guide migration, and if there is not enough of any of the chemicals, cells can have impaired migration and decreased size.
7. **Differentiation** means to give a cell its correct shape. Neurons differ from each other both in shape and chemical make-up depending on where they are in the brain.
8. **Myelination** (white matter) grows when glia produce insulating fatty sheaths that insulates axons, increasing transmission speed.
9. **Synaptogenesis** is the formation of new synapses. This happens throughout life as neurons create new synapses and lose others.
10. At the same time as synaptogenesis, neurons increase their dendritic connections and extend axons. Synapse pruning happens after synaptogenesis, meaning the nervous system fine-tunes itself to keep only the connections it really needs and sheds the excess.
11. Synaptogenesis and pruning happens differently in humans and primates. In primates, both happen at about the same rate throughout the brain. In humans, it occurs at different speeds in different places, probably reflecting the need for some parts of the human brain to interact more complexly with the social and cultural context.

A summary of **postnatal** brain development follows (Markant & Thomas, 2013).

1. **Axon** and **dendrite** growth continue making more connections between neurons. Although a general pattern of axons is in place at birth, axon length grows tremendously until about 12 months. Axon growth continues between ages 1 and 5 but the rate slows.
2. **Synaptogenesis** continues in postnatal development and parallels dendrite growth. The child's brain reaches its peak synapse density by age 12 months. Synapse density peaks in the **frontal cortex** at 15 months. If you go back and read about cognitive development there are many skills a child cannot do until they are about 14-15 months when the cortex has matured a little.
3. Synaptic transmission (neurotransmission) requires **neurotransmitters** such as serotonin and dopamine for normal behavior. Neurotransmitters are active early on in the prenatal brain and play a big role in brain development, but continue to develop postnatally and into adolescence. Dopamine is one example and it grows in the adolescent **prefrontal cortex** as thinking matures.
4. The brain as a whole takes a long time to develop and reminds us that the human brain is complex and must interact with the environment. Babies are born with about 100 billion neurons but their brains are still only about 1/3 the volume of an adult brain. By age 5-6, children's brains are about 95% of the weight of an adult brain.

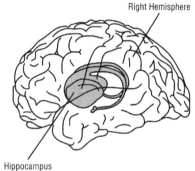

This is a reminder that the **hippocampus** can grow with enriched environments or can be damaged with stress. It helps us understand what happens when children experience traumas.
Source: pixabay.com

5. In terms of functional brain development (behaviors seen in cognitive processes such as language and memory) there are a couple of important trends. First, children have more subcortical brain activity when cognitive processing while adults use more cortical activity. Children must develop the cortical focus. Second, children show more diffuse brain activity when cognitive processing, such as in trying to represent others mental states, while adults show activity that is more focused. Again, this is something children must develop.
6. **Neurogenesis**, generating new neurons, takes place throughout life. Neurogenesis in a child's **hippocampus** is one example related to cognitive processing. **Enriched environments** promote neurogenesis and **stress** damages the brain, such as killing cells in the hippocampus.

Research support #1: EEG shows brain development in 8-month-old babies during the A-not-B task

One way to demonstrate when a child's brain has developed is to test it with EEG while doing a cognitive task where children use both **working memory** and inhibitions. This does not mean that brain development *causes* cognitive advancements, but just demonstrates the milestones.

The **aim of one experiment** was to show electrical activity changes in 8- month-old babies while doing the **A-not-B task** (Bell, Wolfe, & Adkins, 2007). This type of task is often used to measure **prefrontal cortex** functioning.

The **procedures** required a baby to look for a hidden toy by moving his or her eyes to one of the two possible locations. To correctly find the toy, the baby must keep updating working memory and inhibit looking back to a place the toy was previously hidden. The baby sits on the parent's lap as a researcher shows him or her a toy and then hides it under one of two plastic tubs. After the toy is hidden, the researcher breaks the baby's concentration on where the toy is hidden by calling their name and saying, "Where is the toy?" This brings the baby's eye movement back to the midline between the two tubs. Hidden cameras record the baby's eye movement for each trial and **EEG** measured brain electrical activity. The study uses a **repeated measures design** where each baby's responses are compared over trials. The **independent variable** was the baby's EEG readings before and after their concentration was broken. Where the toy is hidden in each trial changes after any two back-to-back correct responses.

At 8 months this baby has the brain activity to pass the A-not-B task.
Source: pixabay.com

Results show that by 8 months, babies have significant increases in electrical activity from baseline to experimental readings in both the front and back of the brain.

The authors **concluded** that changes in EEG activity from baseline to task showed the prefrontal cortex was developing.

This study was replicated by the same researchers and other experimenters.

Evaluate approaches to research used in developmental psychology

When drawing conclusions it is important to remember that recorded brain activity does not show the brain *causes* cognitive development. Brain activity changes when cognitive advancements occurs but it is not a causal pathway.

One other thing is to ask if a study has been **replicated**. If not, then withhold judgment until it has. The most solid evidence has many replications, even if they are not strict replications. It can be hard to do the same experiment exactly, but the point is to get a body of evidence pointing in the same direction.

Research support #2: EEG examines brain development in 4 year olds during a day-night task

The **day-night task** was introduced in the last section about cognitive development, where children are tested for working memory and inhibition. In the day-night task a child must say night when they see a picture of a sun and day when they see a picture of a moon. It is a modification of the **Stroop test** so a child does not have to read.

There may be clear evidence that the cortex grows as 8 month-olds develop cognitively, but we do not find the cortex growing as 4 year-olds cognitively develop.

The **aim of the experiment** was to use the day-night cognitive task along with **EEG** to see if there were measurable electrical brain changes similar to those found in the A-not-B task (Bell, et al., 2007).

Children aged 4.5 took the day-night test while EEG was recorded in both left and right hemispheres at 8 locations. Baseline EEG recordings were made while children watched a video and then when a child did the day-night task. The **independent variable** was watching a video or doing the day-might task. The **dependent variable** was the EEG readings.

4 year-olds must say night when they see the sun and day when they see the moon, a modified Stroop test.
Used with license from megapixl.com.

Results showed that just one brain region, the medial frontal region, had significant EEG changes from the baseline video. This region is located above the prefrontal cortex and helps with memory and decision-making, two cognitive processes needed for the day-night task.

However, the authors **concluded** that their research provided more indirect evidence for the role of the prefrontal cortex in working memory and inhibition tasks rather than direct evidence of prefrontal cortex development. Even if this is indirect evidence, it is consistent with other studies showing brain development occurs when cognitive development occurs.

Researchers pointed out that not all children improve their cognitive skills at the same rate, and this might be a reason that just one brain region was important when taking the day-night task (Bell, et al., 2007).

Chapter 35
Evaluating the Approaches to Research

Chapter objectives

This chapter covers the IB **Paper 3**. Students will:
1. Learn what is on Paper 3 for IB HL students and understand that the information is useful for Paper 1 & 2 and the internal assessment for both SL and HL IB students
2. Outline characteristics of quantitative and qualitative research methods
3. Describe sampling in quantitative and qualitative research
4. Suggest alternative research methods for qualitative, quantitative, and mixed method studies
5. Describe and explain ethical considerations in quantitative and qualitative research
6. Discuss generalizing from quantitative and qualitative research
7. Discuss how to avoid personal and methodological bias in quantitative and qualitative research
8. Discuss how to increase credibility in quantitative and qualitative studies

Paper 3 is for HL students, but all students need to evaluate research methods and ethics for Papers 1 and 2, and prepare for the IA, so everyone should study this material. When preparing summative assessments, it is recommended that all students apply the Paper 3 static questions to a variety of studies in this book.

35.1 What is on Paper 3 for IB HL students and how is it useful for Paper 1 & 2 and the internal assessment (IA)?

Paper 3 requires students to evaluate the different approaches to researching behavior.

The best way to prepare for **Paper 3** is to create a sample mock test for each method that can be stimulus material using the questions in the guide. This book has examples of all of the methods, and the studies are detailed in enough depth to be useful as sample stimulus material.

Stimulus material for Paper 3 can come from the following types of research.

1. Experiments (classic lab experiments, quasi, field, natural)
2. Correlation studies (data usually comes from questionnaires)
3. Surveys (data is often reported as percentages but can be data for correlation studies)
4. Qualitative studies (interviews, observation, case studies)
5. Mixed methods (two qualitative methods in the same study or a mix of qualitative and quantitative in the same study)

Both the quantitative (experiments, correlation studies, surveys) and qualitative methods are useful and are selected based on what the research wants to know.

There is no hierarchy of best to worst methods as all of them have strengths and limitations. The research aim influences whether a psychologist uses quantitative or qualitative research methods, as well as which one. Researchers using **quantitative methods** seek objective knowledge and gather data with numbers. In contrast, researchers using **qualitative methods** seek meaning and context, and do not quantify human characteristics.

Ethics and research methods are at the center of the IB course, so it is expected that students use critical thought related to them in Paper 1 and 2 essays, particularly extended responses. In addition, knowledge about experiments helps students prepare for the IA.

First it is helpful to see two examples of mixed methods studies because students do not study as many of these in the course.

Which research method should I use? It all depends on what a scientist wants to know so look at the aim of the study. Source: pixabay.com

Mixed methods qualitative study: Participant-observation about addiction recovery combined with semi-structured interviews

Ehrmin (2002) studied the recovery of substance-dependent African-American women through observation and semi-structured interviews. The aims of the study were to explore the recovery care needs of the women living in an inner-city transitional home for substance abusers and help them successfully complete treatment.

Three aspects of these women's recovery require research methods focused on an individual's life context. First, substance-abusing women frequently experience abuse and rape before they start using the substances. Second, many women report using drugs and alcohol to numb emotional pain. Third, little research has explored other factors that contribute to these women's substance abuse, particularly racism and the early death of their mothers.

Ehrmin took the role of **participant-**observer and the study used **overt observation**, meaning that participants knew they were being observed.

The study took place over three years in a transitional home in a large United States midwestern city. Ehrmin attended the Friday afternoon "house meeting" and then gradually lengthened her stay to include supper. Eventually she worked her way into participating in many of the woman's activities, such as attending AA meetings, cooking meals, having meals with the women and their children, and celebrating birthdays.

Ehrmin called her level of participation that of a "**moderate participant observer**," meaning that she kept a balance between participation as an insider and participation as an outsider. Along with taking observation notes, she kept a **reflexive journal** to document her own feelings and biases.

The study used an **opportunity sample** of twelve key and eighteen general participants for the participant-observation portion of the study. The key participants were the most knowledgeable. The rest included staff and other women recovering from substance abuse who lived in the community but had not stayed at the transitional home.

Three to five interviews were next conducted with eleven of the twelve key participants. This part of the study used a **purposive sample** of the most knowledgeable women.

Guaranteeing **confidentiality** was of particular importance because of the potential legal consequences from the substance use. Ehrmin assigned participants numbers and used these in the coding phase of data analysis to prevent anyone from being identified.

This study has a high level of **credibility**. Ehrmin did three things to increase the credibility in her study.

1. She increased the certainty of the findings by observing participants over a three-year period and documenting the important context issues throughout the study.

2. She increased the ability to **generalize** findings with a **purposive sample** that met specific guidelines and gathered rich detailed data, creating over 1,000 pages of transcripts just for the interviews.
3. She kept a **reflexive journal**.

The results included two main **themes** and numerous sub-themes, some of which are listed here.

1. One main theme was that the women needed to work through the emotional pain of their abuses and losses.
2. A second main theme was that working through emotional pain gave the women an understanding of the context for their use of drugs and alcohol.
3. One sub-theme was the death of loved ones.
4. A second sub-theme was racism.
5. A third sub-theme was rejection.

Ehrmin concluded that working through emotional pain was a key factor for the recovery of African-American substance abusers because of their high rates of using drugs and alcohol to escape from difficult life situations. The women needed treatment helping them experience pain rather than numb it. These women also faced "cultural pain" associated with racism and discrimination that is critical to understanding the context of their recovery.

Mixed methods qualitative and quantitative study: Field experiment and semi-structured interview

This is reprinted from chapter 26 about the etiologies of anorexia nervosa. Rates of disordered eating and negative body image increased after television came to Fiji in the 1990s (Becker, Burwell, Gillian, Herzog, & Hamberg, 2002).

Isolating the effects of television on behavior is hard because a control group without exposure are rare. Fijian adolescent girls were the perfect solution because television access was limited before 1995.

The **aim of the study** was to see if exposure to western television a risk factor for developing disordered eating behavior despite traditional cultural values.

Quantitative data, using a field experiment, and qualitative data, using an interview, were collected. **Procedures** are next.

First, a field experiment tested the incidence of disordered eating in 1995 before exposure to television and again in 1998 after three years of western television. Data for the field experiment were collected through a self-report questionnaire about attitudes toward eating. All ethnic Fijian adolescent girls from two schools were in the sample.

Second, semi-structured interviews collected narratives covering a range of eating attitudes with a **purposive sample** selected from the girls in the field experiment. The narratives reflected opinions about diet, weight control, and traditional Fijian values. Important themes were identified through content analysis.

Fijians did not have much access to television before 1995, but once they got it, girls showed more disordered eating.
Source: pixabay.com.

Results follow.

1. Field experiments showed an increase in disordered eating between the 1995 and 1998 samples. Second, 74% of the 1998 sample said they felt too fat.
2. Interesting themes emerged. The girls admired the television characters and 83% said that television changed the way they felt about their body type. About 40% felt they had a better chance at career advancement if they were slimmer.

The authors **concluded** that television played a large role in changing values toward body shape and eating behaviors. The following excerpt from the narratives is an example: "When I look at the characters on TV, the way they act on TV and I just look at the body, the figure of that body, so I say, look at them, they are thin and they all have this figure, so I myself want to become like that, to become thin." (p. 513).

Were the samples comparable? This may be a study limitation. The same girls were not in both samples so it is unknown if the 1998 sample had disordered eating before the arrival of television. The authors feel it was unlikely that these girls had disordered eating before 1995 because there was only one report of AN in Fiji before that time.

35.2: Outline characteristics of quantitative and qualitative research methods

Outline means to give a brief summary. The following tables contain what is needed to briefly summarize the characteristics. These tables identify what is important about the categories of quantitative and qualitative methods and then the individual methods.

Characteristics of all quantitative research methods (experiments, correlation studies, and surveys)

Characteristics of all quantitative research methods (Coolican, 2004)
They are narrow and focused.
They are objective.
They are meant to be artificial.
They are structured and controlled.
They are not meant to show the context of life and as such have low ecological validity. Avoid criticizing a study for doing what it is supposed to do.
They are low in reflexivity, meaning the researcher intends to stay objective and does not reflect on how he or she might influence the results.

Characteristics of experiments: Quantitative methods

Experiments have the following characteristics (Schumacher and McMillan, 1984).

Characteristics of experiments

Characteristic	Description
Experiments compare at least two groups or two conditions. It is the only method showing causation.	The goal of an experiment is to see if an independent variable (IV) *caused* changes to a dependent variable (DV). Because of this goal, researchers must create a study with at least 2 groups or conditions, with one serving as a control or getting something different from the other group or condition.
At least one **independent variable** (IV) is manipulated.	The independent variable is defined as what the researcher changes, or makes different, between the two groups or conditions. The IV must be something that can be manipulated in a a classic lab experiment, such as learning alone or learning in groups. Human features such as gender or age cannot be used as independent variables in classic controlled lab experiments. Gender and age cannot really be manipulated, even if they are differences between groups. If an IV is not manipulated, the study is a **quasi-experiment**. In a quasi-experiment, one does not know what causes the change in the dependent variable. Participants are not randomly assigned to conditions in quasi-experiments. Rather, quasi-experiments just test the boys versus the girls, for example. Many published experiments are quasi-designs and they are quite valuable. **Field experiments** are uncontrolled and take place in the real world. Field experiments still have IVs and DVs, but they are not isolated from all the confounding variables that could interfere with them. **Natural experiments** are when a situation occurs that was not planned, but an IV and DV are identifiable and it is a chance for the researcher to study behavior.
At least one **dependent variable** (DV) is measured.	The DV is what the researcher wants to find out, such as the number of math problems solved correctly after training.
They use **inferential statistics**.	Inferential statistics show if a **significant difference** between the groups or conditions exists. Sometimes it appears that there is a difference between the raw scores or the means of the groups or conditions, but it is unknown if these differences are *significant* until an inferential statistical test is calculated. A significant difference means that within a stated probability, such as 5%, it is the IV rather than chance that causes the change in the DV.

Characteristic	Description
They are designed for maximum **control**.	The IV is isolated from all extraneous variables that may influence the change. ***Control is the greatest strength of experiments***, and this is important to remember when evaluating strengths of a study. Because control is high, experiments by their nature are artificial. Avoid criticizing experiments for being artificial. They are supposed to be artificial. Because there are so many internal controls, meaning the experiment has high internal validity, any individual experiment has low ecological validity and typically does not generalize well. **Triangulation** ensures that the results of experiments fit in with a larger body of research and have meaning outside study conditions.

Characteristics of correlation studies (and the questionnaires frequently used to gather data)

Questionnaires are commonly used in research, but students do not always realize how often they come across them because introductory texts seldom identify all the details about the methods used in studies.

Genetic research frequently uses questionnaires, including twin, adoption, and gene-environment correlation studies where one's genotype is correlated with environmental factors. For example, questionnaires ask people about their alcohol use, aggressive behavior, or depressive symptoms and correlate the responses to having a specific polymorphism. Genetic research, however, is just one place to find questionnaires.

Research about the **dimensions of culture** also use questionnaires. People are classified on the dimension continuums such as individualism and collectivism. These questionnaire responses can be correlated with another variable.

Questionnaires gather data about many human characteristics (Neuman, 2006). They tend to have a limited focus, making them different from surveys.

1. *One's behavior*, such as will you comply with a request or whether you voted
2. *Attitudes/beliefs/opinions*, such as do you eat diet foods or whether you think that bullying is a big problem on campus
3. *Characteristics*, such as marital status, educational level, and self-construal (meaning self-understanding)
4. *Expectations*, such as what kind of education you expect your children will receive
5. *Frequencies*, such as how many stressful events you have had in the last two years

Characteristics of correlation studies

Characteristic of correlation studies	Description
They show relationships	Correlation research examines the extent to which two variables occur together and how they occur together. Correlation studies show a **positive correlation, negative correlation,** or **no pattern of correlation.** *A correlation really refers to the straightness of a line on a graph, so try not to give a correlation more meaning than it really has.*
They can be useful when ethics are a concern	Sometimes a topic is unethical to study in an experiment. However, designing a correlation study is not without ethical considerations, and two that are important are confidentiality and how the data might be used.
They analyze data most frequently from questionnaires	Correlations are statistics used to analyze data, frequently from questionnaires. Sometimes books use the term "correlation study," but the data are always gathered another way, such as with a questionnaire.
They never show causation no matter how many correlation studies say the same thing, plus they can be over interpreted	For example, if you read the Caspi study about genes and depression, you discovered that 40 independent replications show the same thing. However, this still does not mean causation. Caspi was not trying to show that genes caused behavior anyway, and wanted to see if several variables were related. There is a tendency to over interpret the meaning of correlations (personal communication with John Brooks, May, 2007). For a correlation to have meaning it should be strong. The term "significant" correlation is frequently used, but what does it mean? The word *significance* has a particular meaning in experiments, which is the probability that the independent variable caused the change in the dependent variable. The term *significance* is used rather loosely outside of experiments, so check the strength of the correlation rather than checking for the word *significant*. The term *significance* in correlation studies is used differently than it is in experiments. For example, when experimental data are analyzed with a t-test, they are tested directly against a level of significance, something that is not available in correlation studies.

Let's use examples about television viewing and aggression to see how to interpret correlations.

Many studies show a positive relationship, or correlation, between the amount of violent television viewed and levels of aggressive behavior. This means that viewing violent television and aggressive behavior positively **co-vary**— as one variable increases, so does the other. *It does not mean that one variable caused the other to do anything.* Correlation studies are uncontrolled. It is not known whether television violence caused aggressive behavior, whether violent people watch violent television, or whether other unaccounted for variables, such as parenting, contribute to aggression. For example, as the number of hours spent viewing television increases, so does the amount of aggressive behavior, perhaps measured by the number of aggressive acts children perform on the playground.

A negative correlation means that as one variable goes up, the other goes down. An example of this is the relationship between viewing violent television and creativity scores. As children's viewing of violent TV increases, creativity test scores decrease.

No pattern of correlation means no relationship exists between the variables.

There are two ways to analyze correlations.

One is a **scatterplot**. Researchers plot points on a graph and look for patterns. Each point on a graph represents the two scores for a participant. In the example of a positive correlation, a child may watch 8 hours of television each day and show 15 incidences of aggression on the playground. A point on the graph is made where 8 and 15 meet. In the example of a negative correlation, a person may watch 7 hours of television each day and have a creativity score of 20. A point on the graph is made where 7 and 20 meet. Points are placed for the scores of each participant until everyone's scores are plotted. The rule is this—the straighter the line, the stronger the correlation.

No pattern of correlation means that no line or pattern forms when the points are plotted on the graph.

Another way to analyze data with correlation is to use a formula to get a correlation coefficient. *This is how most published studies report correlations.* **Correlation coefficients** range from -1.0 to 1.0. The coefficients are not percentages and are interpreted as **weak, moderate,** or **strong**. Weak coefficients are from .01 to about .40, moderate coefficients are from .40 to about .80, and strong coefficients are from about .80 to 1.0. A coefficient of 1 is a perfect correlation. Positive correlations are expressed as +.70, for example, and negative correlations are expressed as -.70, for example. The interpretation is based on the absolute value of the coefficient.

Square the coefficient to get the percentage of the characteristics the two variables have in common, A correlation of .70 has only 49% of it variation accounted for, having much to chance.

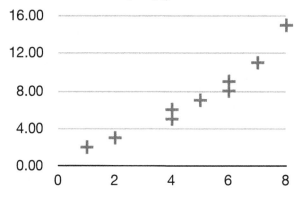

Number of hours watching television each day

Positive correlation between viewing television and aggressive acts on the playground and the number of hours of television watched each day.

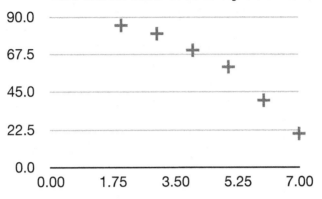

Negative relationship between the hours spent watching television and creativity scores

Number of hours watching television each day

Negative correlation between the number of hours spent watching television and creativity scores.

Think of it this way— correlations can be strong and useful to psychologists, but they do not suggest causation.

Characteristics of surveys

Surveys aim to make statistical inferences about a larger population. Surveys are a preferred research method for public opinion polling and evaluating large-scale health promotion campaigns.

Characteristics of surveys

Characteristic of surveys	Description
They make statistical inferences about a larger population	Surveys are meant to generalize to a larger target population, such as gathering statistics about US colleges in the Healthy Campus health promotion campaign.
They contain a broad range of goals	*Surveys are different from questionnaires* so use the terms properly. Questionnaires usually concentrate on one behavior that is the focus of a study, such as questionnaires gathering self-reported work stress. In contrast, surveys contain a broad range of goals and are useful for evaluating progress of large-scale campaigns with large numbers of goals, such as the US national Let's Move campaign to end obesity or the US national Healthy Campus campaign to increase college student health.

Characteristic of surveys	Description
They often use random samples	Surveys use **random samples** because the goal is to generalize findings from a smaller sample to a larger group, called the **target population**. For example, universities implementing Healthy Campus, a health promotion program in the US, send out surveys to randomly selected students that represent the larger campus.
Data are often reported as percentages, but data can also be correlated	Survey results never show that a prevention program causes behavior change so discussions about prevention program effectiveness should remain tentative. Surveys show that percentages may change over time, but factors other than the prevention program contribute to changes. When correlations are used, there is also no causation demonstrated.

General characteristics of all qualitative research: Interviews, observations, and case studies

Qualitative research differs from quantitative research and does not use numerical values other than percentages or frequencies that are used to generate themes.

General characteristics of all qualitative studies (Coolican, 2004; Snape & Spencer, 2003)
They provide a rich range of information rather than narrowly focused information.
They are subjective and data collection is sensitive to the context of the person.
They reflect the natural environment of behavior, the opposite of artificiality. They are meant to study the contexts, meanings, and processes of behavior.
They are loosely structured and sometimes unstructured.
They have high ecological validity.
They have low reliability.
They are high in reflexivity.
They are an **emic** approach to understanding behavior and investigate the unique perspective of people, sometimes challenging assumed **etics** researchers can have at the beginning of research.
Research strategies are flexible and are conducted in the real world.
Close contact between researchers and participants is useful for understanding meaning and context.
Data analysis is aimed at identifying themes that emerge from the data.

Several objections to quantitative research led to the development and growing acceptance of qualitative methods (Coolican, 2004).

1. Quantitative methods ignore the context of the person and often separate out a section of behavior, such as "memory," from the rest of the person.
2. Even if researchers try to be objective, their impersonal relationship with study participants *is* a relationship with them that might influence study outcomes.
3. Experiments and questionnaires gather superficial information and context is ignored. For example, the EAT-26, a commonly used questionnaire to assess one's level of disordered eating, does not gather information about the person's social context. The answers to the questions may be the result of social conditions or cultural rules, and the risk to the participant is that they are wrongly categorized as "at high risk for developing an eating disorder," when perhaps the preoccupation with food is simply the result of living in an impoverished country.

Sometimes qualitative research is the *only* way that a topic can be studied. For example, someone's unique life challenges would be ignored during addiction recovery in an experiment.

Since the 1990s, qualitative methods have seen an "explosion of interest" and are now accepted as valid research (Snape & Spencer, 2003, p. 10). Before the mid-1990s, there was some use of qualitative methods. Cultural psychology is a good example. Cultural psychologists had a tradition of using ethnography, meaning observations of cultural practices, which was borrowed from Anthropology. Now qualitative methods are used to study a wide range of behaviors.

Next is characteristics specific to interviews, observations, and case studies that are in addition to the general list.

Characteristics of interviews: The semi-structured interview

The purpose of an interview is to ask questions to get someone's point of view. Many interviewing styles are available but the semi-structured interview is most used. It allows an interviewer to identify themes from interview transcripts, where the goal is to understand how someone makes meaning of their particular life circumstances.

The semi-structured interview is popular with researchers taking a qualitative approach where the goal is to identify important themes (Coolican, 2004).

Characteristics of semi-structured interviews (Coolican, 2004; Legard, Keegan, and Ward, 2003)
They ask questions to get someone's point of view.
Researchers conducting semi-structured interviews have a specific topic to investigate but questions are not asked in the same way to all participants. The goal is to understand the person's way of making meaning in a particular context.
The researcher is free to engage in a conversation with the participant who might automatically cover the topics the interviewer is investigating. The interviewer will go back and ask anything the participant did not answer spontaneously.
They are flexible, interactive, and probe beyond the surface level.
Semi-structured interviews can be **one-to-one interviews**, where the interviewer talks with one person at a time, or **focus groups**, where people with a particular expertise are interviewed together.

Characteristics of semi-structured interviews (Coolican, 2004; Legard, Keegan, and Ward, 2003)

Some semi-structured interviews use **narratives**, a type of story that helps people make meaning of their culture. Narratives focus on **context** and increase **richness**. Narrative style interviews encourage participants to tell their story when answering questions. Sometimes narrative interviews use **vignettes**. Vignettes are "hypothetical examples" that give focus group studies consistency (Arthur & Nazroo, 2003, p. 129). The vignette represents a typical case that someone might come across. Focus group participants then narrate, meaning to tell a story, about the vignette. Vignettes are useful for making sure that everyone in the focus group is familiar with the examples for discussion.

Characteristics of observation research

Observation studies examine participants within their real life contexts.

Characteristics of observation studies (Neuman, 2006)

Observers view people in natural settings and interact with participants personally, getting an insider's view while still using rigorous methods.

An observer views participants holistically, showing empathy for someone's circumstances.

An observer collects data that goes beyond objective facts.

An observer records participant remarks and also unspoken but observed aspects of a situation or culture.

The researcher's role is either participant-observer or nonparticipant observer (observer-participant).

The participant-observer style has high **ecological validity** and reduces problems associated with **participant expectancy**, especially if the observation is covert (means the participant does not know he or she is being observed). Covert participant-observation increases the **reliability** and **validity** of the observations because it captures real life experiences. However, **ethics** are a concern when using **covert observations** and researchers cannot assume that they blend in with the observed group well enough to eliminate **participant expectancy**.

The role of **nonparticipant-observer** style increases the trust between researcher and participants but the researcher's presence may increase participant **expectancy effects** and cause participants to alter natural behavior, especially if the study uses **overt observation.**

Characteristics of case studies

Case studies examine an individual or group within their unique situation. Examples include an individual or family's progress in therapy or relationships within organizations, such as a corporation or a school. The case study method is a good choice for research questions that ask "how" or "why" something occurs (Yin, 2009). The goal is to get a complete picture of behavior, so many data sources are tapped.

Case study is a good choice when a researcher wants to understand a real-life situation in depth, something that requires studying people in their everyday context (Yin, 2009). Researchers frequently use **multiple sources of evidence** to make sure they study all aspects of a situation. The data triangulate as all the different sources come together.

Case studies are popular with psychologists because they are a good way to understand individuals, groups, and organizations. Selecting the case study allows researchers to "retain the holistic and meaningful characteristics of real-life events-such as individual life cycles, small group behavior, organizational and managerial processes, neighborhood change, school performance, international relations, and the maturation of industries" (Yin, 2009, p. 4).

Characteristics of case studies (Yin, 2009; Willig, 2001)
Case studies are **idiographic** because they concentrate on unique traits of people. If the situation is unique, case study may be the only way to research behavior.
Multiple sources of evidence are appropriate for gathering case study data, including the following.   1. Documentation, such as letters, email, diaries, minutes of meetings, or mass media articles   2. Archival records, including US census data, budget or personnel records, maps, and survey data   3. Interviews   4. Observations
The best case studies use multiple sources for good **data triangulation**. Multiple data sources merge for a greater understanding of a situation. However, even if triangulation from multiple sources is an advantage of case studies, it can also be a weakness if the researcher emphasizes the multiple perspectives over context.
Potential **ethical** problems can plague case studies. Confidentiality and anonymity are important, particularly if the situation is unique enough that someone is easily identified.
Poor **population validity** is the greatest weakness of case studies because data comes from specific individuals or groups. However, if the case is instrumental and data is gathered from multiple sources, the case has more **generalizability**.
Researcher bias is a potential problem. Consider all the possible sources of data for a case study. Could researcher selectivity become a problem?
Cases are **intrinsic** or **instrumental**. **Intrinsic case studies** are unusual or interesting and are not easily **generalized.** Cases of feral children who never hear human language are good examples of intrinsic cases. Feral cases are interesting, but they are difficult to generalize from because there are so few examples and so many confounding variables could explain the brain damage to these children's language centers. **Instrumental case studies** examine how individual or group experiences fit with larger theory. Cases of children with **leptin** deficiency (they do not produce the hormone leptin) are instrumental, and even if they are rare, illustrate the cause and treatment of similar people, and are more easily generalized.

35.3: Describe sampling in quantitative and qualitative research

Describe means to give a detailed account. Two types of sampling, **representative** (probability sampling) and **non-representative** (non-probability sampling) are used in psychology research and the important details follow. Quantitative studies can use either representative or non-representative sampling. Qualitative methods use non-representative sampling, meaning the sample does not necessarily represent a target population.

Representative sampling: Best for most surveys but rarely used for experiments and correlation studies

A representative sample is selected so it generalizes to (or represents) a larger group, a target population. **Simple random sampling** is an easy way to get a representative sample. Random sampling means that *everyone in the population to which researchers wish to generalize has an equal opportunity of being in the sample*. Random sampling provides the researcher with a representative sample of a larger target population. To obtain a random sample, suppose a researcher wants to conclude something about a target population of all 11th graders at St Petersburg High School. Luckily researchers do not have to study all of the students but can take a representative sample of them, say 30 participants. Do two things to select the sample.

1. Suppose there are 400 11th graders. Assign each student a number from 1 to 400.
2. A computer or a calculator can generate random numbers. For example, program a calculator to generate random numbers between 1 and 400. We just want 30 for the sample, so the first number might be 15. That student is now selected. The next number might be 375, and that student is selected. Continue until you have 30 students.

Which type of sampling should I use? It depends on which research method is selected, as the goals of sampling methods aids with the overall needs of the study.
Source: pixabay.com

Another form of random sampling is **stratified random sampling**. A study with the target population of the entire student body of St. Petersburg High may have a selection bias without a stratified sample. Stratified sampling ensures that all age groups, cultural groups, grade levels, ability levels, and both genders are represented in the sample according to the percentage the group represents. If 12th graders represent 20% of St Petersburg High School, then 20% of the sample is seniors. This is time consuming and not usually done for most studies, but it is an option.

Researchers conducting surveys use random sampling. In contrast, researchers conducting experiments and correlations studies most often use **opportunity sampling**, described under the heading about non-representative sampling. Most experiments and correlation studies reported in textbooks use opportunity samples of volunteer college students. One correlation study cited in this book used a random sample, and this is the Caspi study about genes and depression. However, it is not usually the case to use random sampling. An opportunity sample means a researcher uses participants based on the convenience and opportunity to use them, such as college students taking a psychology course or at Mrs. Smith's 4th period English class at a high school.

Regardless of how samples are selected, researchers should use **random allocation** to assign participants to the groups or conditions in experiments. Random allocation controls for participant variables and means that *everyone in the sample has an equal chance of being in either condition or group*. Follow the guidelines for getting a simple random sample when randomly allocating.

Non-representative sampling

Three types of non-representative sampling are **opportunity sampling**, **purposive sampling**, and **theoretical sampling**.

Experiments and correlation studies most often use opportunity samples. Qualitative studies use purposive sampling when possible, but sometimes use opportunity sampling because of the study circumstances, such as Ehrmin (2002) faced when studying addiction recovery in women. Theoretical sampling is particularly useful for observation studies when it can be done.

Non-representative samples are generalizable only to the individuals studied, if you view generalizing in a strict sense. However, qualitative studies *can* have **symbolic generalization**, something possible to do from non-representative samples. Symbolic representative means the sample is well selected to include a range of views that symbolize the larger group.

529

It can be argued that *qualitative research is not meant to be representative of a larger target population, though it can represent it. Representative means something a little different for qualitative research.* When using a non-representative sample, "Units (participants) are deliberately selected to reflect particular features of or groups within the sampled population" (Ritchie, Lewis, & Elam, 2003, p. 78). This is usually done with a purposive sample and if selected with rigor, can have some generalization outside the study.

Avoid criticizing the studies for doing what they are supposed to do, including using sampling techniques that meet specific research goals. When considering **generalization** from a qualitative study make sure to include these insights.

Opportunity sampling

Opportunity sampling is useful for most experiments and correlations studies and sometimes when conducting qualitative research, but an opportunity sample is not rigorously selected. Purposive sampling is far more rigorous and a better choice!

Sometimes opportunity sampling is the best choice for a qualitative study. As an example of a study described under observations, Ehrmin (2002) used opportunity sampling in her combination observation or interview study to investigate the process of recovery from substance abuse in African-American women because these were the only participants available.

The main strength of opportunity sampling is its ease. Its main limitation is that participants are not selected with any rigor. They have no specific characteristics making them representative of a larger group. The sample *may* represent a larger group but you cannot be sure. This is important to know when considering generalizing from a study.

Purposive sampling in qualitative research

Purposive sampling is more rigorous than opportunity sampling and is frequently used for qualitative research. Purposive sampling means the researcher selects a sample for a particular purpose and the participants have specific characteristics. The term **symbolic representation** is used when referring to purposive samples (Ritchie, et al., 2003). *A purposive sample is meant to symbolize a larger group,* so it allows for some generalization.

As an example, Ehrmin (2002) used a purposive sample of the most knowledgeable participants when conducting the interview portion of her addiction recovery study.

Researchers should do two things when choosing a good purposive sample (Ritchie, et al., 2003).

1. Use a small sample that can demonstrate all the different points of view, called **sample coverage**. Small samples are typical in qualitative research for two reasons. First, there quickly comes a point in conducting qualitative research when the use of more participants adds nothing new to the analysis because *the study becomes saturated.* One notation of an opinion or attitude is enough to make a point of view part of the analysis. Second, qualitative studies are rich in detail, and too many participants make the study unmanageable. How can a researcher provide a rich view of meaning and context if there are large numbers of participants?
2. Th **sample frame**, or information source, should be well selected. Sample frames come from different kinds of sources, such as administrative records, previously surveyed samples, a household screen, where interviews are conducted with all households in a study area, or from **snowball samples**.

Several types of purposive sampling fit the needs of qualitative research (Coolican, 2004). Knowing details of the participants in a purposive sample make it easier for independent critics to examine the proper **generalizing** from the study sample.

Type of purposive sampling	Description
Focus groups	Focus groups are experts on a topic or people selected because they have certain experiences in common.
Snowball sampling	Snowball sampling means to ask one expert for an interview, and then that person suggests the next expert participant, and so on. Rosenthal (1993) used snowball sampling to study homeless people living in Santa Barbara, California. He did not have any contacts of his own to start the interviewing process, so he attended a meeting for the homeless. There he met a woman who introduced him to other homeless people. This is how Rosenthal gained entry into the lives of the homeless. However, Rosenthal experienced one limitation of snowball sampling. When one person suggests the next person for the sample, those suggested might represent only the point of view of the original interviewee. Rosenthal noticed that many of the tougher homeless people did not socialize with this woman and wondered if he had sampled the full range of opinion. Researchers using snowball samples should be aware of this potential problem and try to get a variety of opinions and circumstances.
Critical cases	Critical cases have characteristics similar enough to others that just a small number need to be studied (Coolican, 2004).

Theoretical sampling in observation research

Theoretical sampling is one way to get a sample for observation studies (Neuman, 2006). Theoretical sampling is a type of purposive sampling where decisions about what to sample are guided as the study develops.

The sampling evolves with the interpretation of field notes. For example, one sampling of a particular location might lead the researcher to ask questions that lead to new ideas about other locations and people to sample. Theoretical sampling is related to the term **grounded theory**, meaning that theory is created from interpreting each new set of data collected in a study. If a researcher is in the field and has the opportunity to study a variety of data, then theoretical sampling is a good choice.

35.4 Suggesting alternative research methods

Conceptual understanding: Alternative research methods?

When asked to suggest an alternative research method to investigate a topic, avoid automatically thinking, "Run an experiment" for a qualitative study or "Run an interview study" for an experiment. Instead, suggest a different method that will help achieve the original study aim or clarify our understanding of the topic in a specific way.

For example, an experiment looks for causation, so an interview or correlation

Can I find an alternative to the method used in any study? Asking for an alternative research method is a tall order for someone new to psychology. Suggest something that will help achieve the original study aim or clarify our understanding of the topic in a specific way. Source: pixabay.com

study will not help this goal. However, these methods might triangulate the results or lead to new experimental variables.

In contrast, qualitative study research questions require the person to be studied in their context. If you look at the aim of any qualitative study it will not ask about causation, so consider if an experiment is a productive alternative.

If you do suggest quantitative methods as an alternative to qualitative studies and vis versa, then it should help with triangulation or clarify something about the topic.

Practical examples are a good model for learning how to suggest alternatives and all of the example studies cited in the charts are detailed in the book. Many alternatives can be suggested, but make sure you have a good reason. Developing reasons is a sophisticated skill, so the examples here are meant to introduce you to how it might be done.

The original qualitative study	Alternative research method	Reason for the alternative
Interview study: Diagnosing depression in the Baganda of Uganda (Okello & Ekblad, 2006) in chapter 25	Case study	A good alternative is to document a particular participant's unique experience. Multiple sources of evidence (such as observations, diaries, and a personal interview) increase data triangulation.
Observation study: Addiction recovery (Ehrmin, 2002) at the beginning of this chapter	Case study	Same reason as above. The researcher already used observation and interviewed some critical participants, so it makes sense to include an in-depth case of an individual using multiple sources of evidence.
Case study: Treating anorexia patients with family therapy (Ma, 2008) in chapter 27	Interview	The purpose of an interview is to get someone's opinion and point of view. A semi-structured interview using a vignette (narrative) is a nice compliment to the case study, uncovering themes that might increase therapy success. Richness of data is increased. A focus group might also be a good choice to let participants hear other's experiences with family therapy.

The original mixed method study	Alternative research method	Reason for the alternative
Mixed observation and interview (Ehrmin, 2002) from this chapter	Case study and correlation	A case study would allow one participant to be followed in depth using multiple sources of evidence. The correlation part of the study could use a questionnaire to ask specific questions related to themes found in the original study and correlate these answers to level of addiction recovery.
Mixed field experiment and interview (Becker, Burwell, Gillian, Herzog, & Hamberg, 2002) from this chapter and from chapter 26 about etiologies of mental disorder	Correlation study and case study	The correlation study could use a questionnaire to explore the relationship between the hours of television watched before and after it came to Fiji and symptoms of disordered eating. The case study might follow several girls who serve as critical cases for understanding the context of developing disordered eating greater exposure to western television.

The original quantitative study	Alternative research method	Reason for the alternative
Experiment: Eyewitness memory (Loftus & Palmer, 1974) from chapter 14	Correlation study or interview	A correlation study is helpful because a questionnaire can ask people about things such as their confidence level, what they perceive as their strengths and limitations in recalling an event, etc. These can be correlated to memory accuracy. A semi-structured interview might help us understand the reasoning behind someone's beliefs in their confidence of memories.

The original quantitative study	Alternative research method	Reason for the alternative
Correlation study: Foot-in-the-door compliance study (Petrova, et al., 2007) from chapter 3	Experiment	The goal of Petrova's study was to see if individualism and collectivism predicted compliance. To run a quasi-experiment, participants could be placed in groups based on being collectivist or individualist, and then tested on compliance to a request.
Survey: Healthy campus health promotion campaign at Florida State University (The Real Project, 2010) from chapter 31	Correlation study or interview	A correlation study can gather data using a questionnaire to target a specific aspect of the original survey, such as asking about drinking habits and correlating this to participation in programs such as alcohol free tailgating at football games. A semi-structured interview can get someone's specific opinions about various aspects of the health promotion campaign.

35.5: Describe and explain ethical considerations in quantitative and qualitative research

Describe means to give a detailed account and explain means to include a reason. Students need to give important details about ethical principles for conducting research and then give reasons for what should be included when conducting the study or when applying the results.

It is expected that all ethical issues be resolved before research begins. One source for information is the American Psychological Association (APA) ethical guidelines, available from www.apa.org but each region has their own, and these are all fairly similar.

Many ethical rules apply to both quantitative and qualitative studies but there are some specific to each.

Ethical guidelines most important for quantitative studies

1. Participants must give their **informed consent**. An informed consent form must tell participants the nature of the study. Participants must be informed about what they are expected to do in the study and any risks they might face. Participants must be guaranteed **anonymity** and that data are **confidential**.
2. Deception cannot be used unless there is no other way to gather the data, the risk for harm is not great, and participants are debriefed as soon as possible, hopefully right after participation. The

use of deception is a violation of the requirement to get informed consent, and should not be done without careful consideration.

3. There should be no **potential harm** to participants. Professionals must show that the scientific benefit of the study outweighs the rights of participants, and must include details about any potential harm in the informed consent form.
4. Participants are volunteers and have the **right to withdraw** from the study at any time or withdraw their data from experimental results. This must be stated in the informed consent form. Any limitations should be clearly stated, such as the process that is expected for someone to leave a study testing the effectiveness of a drug, where it might be harmful for someone to simply walk away.
5. Participants have the right to a **briefing** and **debriefing** statement and must have a way to find out their results, which should be stated in the informed consent form.
6. An **inducement** is something given to participants, such as money or medical care, for being in the study. Inducements should never be so much that someone would participate in the study just to get them.
7. **Animals** can be used in research that benefits humans but the benefits must be great, and they must be treated humanely and given medical care. Students might want to consider the material in chapter 10 about the use of animals in research because a consideration of their ethical use includes deciding if they are good models for humans.

How can I be ethical and respect all study participants? Many ethical rules apply to both quantitative and qualitative studies but there are some specific to each.
Source: pixabay.com

Ethical guidelines most important for qualitative research

Six ethical concerns are particularly important for the unstructured features of qualitative research (Webster, Lewis & Brown, 2013; Lewis, 2003).

1. Research needs a clear purpose and should not impose unreasonable demands.
2. **Informed consent** from all participants is required.
3. **Anonymity** and **confidentiality** are guaranteed.
4. Participation is **voluntary** and no one should feel coerced or pressured to participate.
5. Participants are protected from **potential harm**.
6. Researchers are protected from potential harm.

Three additional ethical issues are specific to observation studies.

1. Psychologists using participation-observation may not want participants to know about the study (Gillham, 2008). This means that careful thought must go into the planning stages. The debate is complicated because of the difference between **covert observations**, meaning people do not know they are being observed, and **overt observations**, meaning people know they are being observed. In addition, some observations take place in open, or public settings, and some take place in closed settings, such as a classroom. Considering the ethics of an observation study requires knowledge of all four types, covert, overt, open, and closed. For example, a study could be overt and in a closed setting. On the other hand, a study could be covert and in a closed setting. The way a study is set up drives the discussion about getting or not getting informed consent.
2. Who owns the observations (Gillham, 2008)? Do **ethnography** participants have the right to go back and challenge what is recorded and how their behavior is interpreted?
3. Participant-observation studies have two other potential ethical considerations. These are involvement with deviants and problems with 'the powerful' (Neuman, 2006).

Each rule for qualitative studies is detailed next.

Research needs a clear purpose and should not impose unreasonable demands

Three practices reduce the chance of imposing unreasonable demands on participants (Webster, Lewis & Brown, 2013).

1. The research must be perceived as valuable and it must add something relevant to science. This value must be clearly communicated to participants.
2. Participants might feel the demands of the study are unreasonable if they have to sit through lengthy or multiple interview sessions. This can be tricky for researchers because they want to do a thorough job, so what is needed to get the job done must be carefully considered.
3. Qualitative data collection is by nature somewhat intrusive, such as sharing personal circumstances in interviews. Topics can be sensitive and difficult for participants, so a balance must be found between achieving research goals and avoiding unreasonable demands.

Informed consent and confidentiality

An **informed consent** form should include the following (Lewis, 2003, APA, 2002).

1. Purpose of the study
2. Everything that the participant is required to do
3. Potential risks and benefits from participation
4. Any situation where participants might be identified or quoted
5. Voluntary participation
6. Any anticipated factors that might influence a person's decision to participate
7. Any possible consequences of leaving the study before its end
8. Any inducements for participation, such as payment
9. How the data will be used
10. How to contact someone to find out the results of the study

The informed consent form should include a statement that data are **confidential** and the identity of the person is **anonymous**. Confidential data includes data from all stages of the study, including collection and storage. The informed consent form should outline any conditions in which anonymity or confidentiality might not be honored. For example, if a participant in an interview reveals something potentially damaging, such as a plan to harm another person, should the researcher keep this confidential? One solution is to outline any conditions where the person will not remain anonymous or the data will not remain confidential in the informed consent form.

Consent when working through a **gatekeeper** requires extra care (Webster, Lewis & Brown, 2013). A gatekeeper is someone in charge of organizing participants and is the person who interacts with researchers. Gatekeepers might be used, for example, when a supervisor arranges for employees to be part of an interview or where language barriers require an interpreter for a larger group. Steps must be taken to ensure gatekeepers are not selective about who participates and do not pressure some people to be in the study.

Consent from **online research** can present problems (Webster, Lewis & Brown, 2013) Online data collection requires researchers to consider the difference between public information that can be collected without consent and collecting data from private online groups that must have consent. Just what online information must remain private without getting consent is constantly being challenged, so do not assume that any information is necessarily public.

Potential harm of the participant

The participant should be informed of all expectations for the study, including any **potential harm**. Participants should feel comfortable with all aspects of the study and understand that they may withdraw at any time. Interview research requires particular consideration (Lewis, 2003). For example, a person may seem comfortable during the interview but later have regrets about revealing sensitive or personal information. Participants should have the opportunity to withdraw anything in the interview making them uncomfortable. In addition, someone may reveal something potentially harmful to them in an interview. An interviewer should respond to these comments by encouraging the participant to seek appropriate help. If no disclaimer is made in the informed consent form, this is all an interviewer can do. Disclaimers protect both the researcher and the participant.

Potential harm for the researcher

Fieldwork is potentially dangerous to the researcher, so it is important to consider **potential harm** again. If the study takes place in a public place, the researcher should have clear directions to the site and a clear plan for quickly leaving if necessary (Lewis, 2003). If the study takes place in a private place, such as an interview in an individual's home, others should know where the researcher is and when he or she is expected to return. Researchers should plan a strategy in advance for possible angry feelings that might be displayed during an interview. The researcher should respond to anger with empathy and perhaps move on to another question, but must also know when to end the interview. Neuman (2006) adds that the researcher should not dress and act too much as an outsider, should create a safety zone of comfortable companions when conducting field research, and perhaps even find a protector if the field research is in a dangerous place.

Observation studies have some special ethical concerns

Participant-observation studies present some special ethical concerns. First, it might not be possible to get the informed consent of everyone observed. Participants may be those who come in and out of a courtyard over the course of a day. In addition, since one goal of participant-observation is to view people in their natural setting, getting informed consent can interfere with the study.

This is a contentious point. Some feel conducting observation studies without the consent of participants is ethical as long as the researcher does not manipulate anything in the environment and participants cannot be identified in the report. Others feel that the deception is difficult to justify. After participant-observers disclose and tell others about the study, many people cannot recall what they said, when they said it, and what they did during the project (Coolican, 2004). Thus, some participants cannot withdraw their data even if they wish to do so.

Researchers using observer-participant usually conduct **overt observation**. In this case, the consent of participants is required. Ehrmin's (2002) study of women recovering from addictions used overt observation and she had consent. She paid close attention to the anonymity and confidentiality rule, as some of her participants had broken the law.

It is important to consider **who owns the observations** (Gillham, 2008). If the ownership is a partnership between the researcher and the observed group, then researchers should check to see if the observed participants agree with the quality of the observations and interpretations. Then participants have the right to challenge selections for recordings and the interpretations. Viewing the participants as partners in ownership strengthens the **credibility** and validity of the study.

One thing Ehrmin (2002) experienced was the ethical issue of observing and interviewing participants who had broken the law, what Neuman (2006) called "**involvement with deviants**" (p. 413). Of the twelve women interviewed, eight used crack, one used cocaine, one used heroin, and one used combinations of alcohol and cocaine. In addition, these women may have had knowledge about crimes. Thus, the interviewees had broken the law and Ehrmin knew about it. Special considerations apply for researchers studying people who engage in illegal, immoral, or unethical activity (Neuman, 2006). These researchers might know about illegal activity, might have information of interest to the police, and sometimes might engage in illegal activity to gain access to the study group. Neuman calls it "**guilty**

knowledge" (p. 413). The researcher must balance gaining participant trust with keeping enough distance so they do not violate their personal moral standards.

Last, Neuman (2006) discusses "**the powerful**". Many qualitative studies are done on participants without power, such as Rosenthal's (1993) study of the homeless. Researchers sometimes come across the "hierarchy of credibility" when conducting a study. This is when people in powerful positions feel they have the right to create the rules of society, such as with the homeless or in organizations. When giving a voice to groups that are not usually heard, researchers must be careful of accusations of bias from those with power. It is an ethical dilemma because the researcher wants to give specific groups a voice, but must balance this intention with the knowledge that powerful persons who may have something to lose can block access to participants or even discredit the researcher.

35.6: Discuss generalizing from quantitative and qualitative research

Discuss means to give a considered and balanced view supported by evidence. There is much to reflect on when considering how and when quantitative qualitative research can be generalized. A balanced view comes from understanding when results generalize and when they do not.

To what extent can findings be generalized from quantitative studies?

Students should read the section generalizing from an experiment in chapter 36. Most experiments use opportunity sampling and artificial conditions, so the results cannot be generalized outside of the sample (population validity) or setting (ecological validity).

I want so much to generalize my study findings! Is there a way to do this correctly? Yes, but some guidelines should be followed. Source: pixabay.com

Students tend to use a formula when writing and tack onto the end of an experiment description, "And a weakness of the experiment is that it has low ecological validity." Be care with this statement, as it shows a lack of understanding of the purpose of an experiment and is far too vague. Students might read Albert Bandura's comments about studying aggression in the lab with the Bobo experiments in chapter 19 as he has a nice way of educating us about the purpose of an experiment.

Surveys can be generalized to the target population sampled during random sampling, but not to everyone in the world!

Correlation studies usually use opportunity studies and cannot be generalized outside of those participants. If a random sample is used, then the study can be generalized to the target population, but not to everyone!

How might findings be generalized (transferability) from qualitative studies?

Two types of generalizing from qualitative studies are useful (Lewis & Ritchie, 2003).

Type of generalization	Definition and benefits
Representational generalization	This means generalizing outside of the sample, which is related to **population validity.** The concept "representational" has a strict statistical meaning in quantitative research. However, things work differently in qualitative studies because, "Sampling in qualitative studies is not statistical. Rather, representation is not a statistical match but one of inclusivity" (Lewis & Ritchie, 2003, p. 269). Instead of using the word *representative*, perhaps we should call it **symbolic representation**. The best way to get symbolic representation is to select a high quality **purposive sample** including a range of views.
Inferential generalization	This means generalizing outside of the study conditions to other settings, which is related to **ecological validity**. A researcher increases the inferential generalization of a study by providing **thick descriptions** of the study setting, the observations, and participant responses (Lewis & Ritchie, 2003). Thick descriptions help a reader consider the extent to which the conditions of data collection are similar to other settings. Ehrmin (2002) devoted a large amount of her research report to describing details about the transitional house and the circumstances of participants in her observation/interview study of women recovering from addictions. The report is thick with descriptions allowing a reader to imagine how women living in other transitional homes might have similar experiences.

It is also important to also consider the **reliability** and **validity** of studies when generalizing findings from qualitative studies.

Reliability and validity in qualitative studies involve two factors (Lewis & Ritchie, 2003).

1. Could the same interpretations made about someone's experience in one context ever be exactly the same for someone's similar experience in a different context? Rather than expecting strict **replication**, qualitative researchers consider the **trustworthiness** of a study. Can we trust that experiences are fairly similar from one context to another?
2. How does the researcher interpret data? Researcher interpretations are an internal validity concern. Internal validity is increased through **reflexivity**, where all procedures are clearly outlined with **thick descriptions** and a researcher's personal involvement is detailed. Reflexivity "enables readers imaginatively to replicate studies" (p. 271), increasing the generalizibility of qualitative studies.

Let's use observation research to illustrate how to *increase* the reliability and validity of qualitative research.

Reliability means to have both internal and external consistency (Neuman, 2006). Internal consistency means that the interpretations make sense, given what is known about the sampled data. External consistency means to verify interpretations by checking and cross-checking with other sources and researchers. Reliability of observed data depends on a number of factors, such as the researcher's awareness of the subjectivity and context of the observations that may interfere with it. For example, data from group members is always influenced by context, so good researchers recognize that someone may say one thing in public and behave differently in private. Misinformation and even lies from participants must be considered. It is important to sample different angles of the research site to get a clear picture, such as a variety of locations, a variety of people, and a variety of contexts.

539

It is almost impossible to replicate field observation research (Neuman, 2006). However, **validity** can be increased with careful interpretation. Consider the extent to which the observed events are undisturbed by the presence of the researcher. Then get some **member validation**— that is, ask key participants whether the observed data are accurate. If participants agree that the selected data represents their real-life experiences and agrees with interpretations, validity is increased.

An example of generalizing: Is it possible from a single case study?

Generalizing refers to the extent to which the findings of a study apply to similar situations or people outside of the study. Case studies have the potential for generalization outside of the study (Willig, 2001). However, we must distinguish **intrinsic** and **instrumental** studies.

As an example, although students are fascinated by feral children when studying language or attachment theories, there really are few feral children, too few to make good generalizations about normal human behavior from them. The feral cases available are indeed fascinating and unique in their own right, but are **intrinsic cases**. Just watch the tendency to want to make general statements about human behavior from them. Evaluating cases of feral children is difficult for many reasons. For example, any one feral child case could be confounded by diet, abuse, or exposure. Any of these factors could contribute to brain damage to language centers, poor language skills, or insecure attachment.

On the other hand, **instrumental cases** have more potential for generalizing. Case studies such as Ma (2008) about therapy for eating disorders is instrumental because it is typifies the treatment and others have similar experiences. Ma used multiple cases, so there was more **data triangulation**.

There is more chance for generalization if enough cases show the same thing (Willig, 2001).

Yin (2009) agrees and believes feels there is more chance for generalizing from case studies if the concept generalization is closely examined. Generalizing from a single case study is questionable. Think about it a different way. What if we were to ask the same question about generalizing from a single experiment? In reality, no one should generalize from a single experiment. Good generalizations from experiments are made only from those that have been replicated numerous times. The same approach is useful for thinking about generalizing from case studies, "The short answer is that case studies, like experiments, are generalizable to theoretical propositions and not to populations or universes" (p. 15).

35.7: Discuss how to avoid personal and methodological bias in quantitative and qualitative studies

Discuss means to give a considered and balanced view supported by evidence. Reflecting on this topic shows that scientists can never completely be free of bias. We can become aware of biases and reduce them, but must also consider that some bias may also be there.

Quantitative studies: Avoiding personal and methodological bias

Sometimes students think that the structured and artificial nature of quantitative research prevents bias, but it does not always do this.

Personal bias in experiments can be reduced by making it double-blind, where the researcher does not know the aim (in addition to the participants being blind to it). This ensures the researcher does not give off subtle clues that are perceived by participants as something demanded of them (demand characteristics).

Reducing methodological bias includes controlling for the Hawthorne effect. Participants have expectations and often want to please the researcher. This can be avoided by running blind experiments, though it requires deception or at least a filler activity.

Independent replications can reduce any concerns that results are because of personal bias.

Mixed designs can be helpful because findings from each part can be compared to see if they lead in a similar direction.

Researchers should follow guidelines for question writing when creating surveys and questionnaires. For example, removing gender-biased language can help participants can remove subtle cues representing researcher beliefs (personal bias) and reduce stereotyped answers based on a participant's beliefs (methodological bias). Remember this when designing questions or even choosing word lists for your internal assessment experiment!

Qualitative studies: Participant expectations and researcher bias (personal bias)

Participant expectations and **researcher bias** (personal bias) are familiar terms from quantitative research. Both are also potential challenges for qualitative studies and require special consideration.

Because the purpose of qualitative research is to discover the richness and complexities of real-life situations, the researcher's role is more subjective. *Greater subjectivity might increase researcher bias.* For example, interviewers using a semi-structured approach might have a general list of topics to ask, but are open to the direction taken by the participant. Interviewers frequently use their intuition to probe participants for more detailed information and context. Because of this more subjective role, researchers should include a detailed statement of **reflexivity** to reduce personal bias.

Researcher bias can be reduced in observation studies, for example, with the use of **thick descriptions**. Thick descriptions are detailed descriptions telling the reader exactly what happened at the research site.

Participant expectations should be considered in the planning stages of any study, something that can cause methodological bias. Although qualitative studies are meant to be more subjective, at what point do participant expectations interfere with gathering credible data? For example, researchers writing interview questions should consider if questions might trigger **demand characteristics**. Researchers must write questions that invite genuine responses without making participants feel they must give a particular type of answer.

Is it possible to remove all the biases in my study? Researchers can never be completely free of bias, but must examine their interests and make it clear when writing a study report how they lessened personal and method bias. Qualitative researchers can keep a reflexive journal and quantitative researchers can add controls to the study.
Source: pixabay.com

One way to minimize participant expectations in observation research is to conduct a covert observation study. However, the use of covert observing comes with special ethical considerations, so sometimes solving one problem creates another. Considering benefits versus risks is critical for making a choice when considering participant expectations.

The best way to avoid **methodological bias** is to increase **data triangulation** by using multiple sources of evidence. Otherwise, any weakness of a particular method can overshadow study results. For example, Ermin (2002) used observation and interviews in her study about addiction recovery. The results of each method can be checked against the other.

35.8 Discuss how to increase credibility in quantitative and qualitative research

Discuss means to give a considered and balanced view supported by evidence. Reflecting on credibility is important because it helps us understand all that goes into designing, running, and analyzing data. Researchers should openly state what they do to increase credibility. Do not assume anything! One reason the Ehrmin (2002) observation/interview mixed methods study is included in this chapter is that she went to great lengths to include what was done to achieve high credibility.

Credibility in quantitative studies: Control is the best bet

Experiments are credible if they have good **internal validity** (internal control), something covered in depth in chapter 36. Quasi, field, and natural experiments are less controlled because the researcher does not have control over the IV and does not use random assignment to groups or condition, but these studies must be designed with as much rigor as possible. *Without good internal validity, an experiment has little chance of high credibility outside of the study as part of a body of evidence.* The terms population validity and ecological validity are reviewed in chapter 36. Samples should be narrow and controlled and study results correctly generalized.

Surveys and correlation studies using questionnaires can have increased credibility when the question writers follow a set of rules outlined in chapter 36. Samples should be well selected, and the results correctly generalized.

How do I judge a study's credibility? This section gives us some guidelines to look for in study reports.
Source: pixabay.com

The importance of credibility in qualitative research

High **credibility** is demanded of any qualitative study, meaning it is trusted and believable. Many strategies are available to increase credibility.

Credibility is increased a number of ways.

1. Using **reflexive** statements (reflexivity)
2. Doing things that increase the generalizibility of the study
3. Using **triangulation** that is appropriate for qualitative research
4. Providing **thick descriptions** of the data interpretation process (Willig, 2001)
5. Describing the life circumstances of the sample (Willig, 2001)
6. Checking interpretations against those of other researchers for consistency (Willig, 2001)
7. Exploring the extent to which the study results are **transferable** to other people and contexts (Willig, 2001)
8. Identifying all rival interpretations for the data and showing how they are not plausible (Yin, 2009)

Reflexivity increases credibility and lessens researcher bias

Credibility of qualitative studies is increased through **reflexivity,** anything done to increase the **generalizing** of studies, and **triangulation.**

Reflexivity means that a researcher is aware how his or her personal biases and feelings affect the construction of meanings throughout the research process and acknowledges that it is impossible to remain objective while conducting research (Nightingale & Cromby, 1999). The researcher knows their bases affect both data collection and analysis. Willig (2001) identified two kinds of reflexivity, **personal reflexivity** and **epistemological reflexivity**.

Type of reflexivity	Description
Personal reflexivity	Researchers are aware that their own values, experiences, political beliefs, and social identities influence the study.

Type of reflexivity	Description
Epistemological reflexivity	Researchers have considered their assumptions about the nature of the world and the nature of knowledge that relates to a study.

Quantitative research is low in reflexivity. Scientists conducting experiments want an objective role and studies are designed so that the researcher has little affect on participant behavior and data analysis.

In contrast, qualitative research is high in reflexivity. For example, Ehrmin (2002) included a detailed reflexive statement in her observation study on women recovering from addictions. "Criteria for evaluation of qualitative research were used to assure trustworthiness of the data, including......
confirmability, established with a reflexive journal demonstrating underlying processes, philosophical orientation, and the decision-making process in determining codes, categories, and themes" (p. 783).

Reflexivity aids in **generalizing** from the original research setting and population.

The effect of triangulation on the credibility and trustworthiness of qualitative research

Triangulation is important for qualitative studies, but researchers apply a set of standards best for them. This section is also important for considering **credibility** and **generalizing** of qualitative research.

Many qualitative researchers caution against holding qualitative research to a strict requirement that triangulation be used to validate research (the goal of triangulation in quantitative research).

Some believe the real value of triangulation for qualitative research is not in creating more certainty, as it is for quantitative research, but in giving the results of qualitative research more depth, credibility, and trustworthiness. With this in mind, let's look at how triangulation can do these things

Two examples of triangulation used to increase one's confidence in data gathered with qualitative methods follow (Yin, 2009; Lewis & Ritchie 2003).

Triangulation for qualitative studies	Description
Data triangulation	Collecting data from multiple sources (interviews, observations, documents, archival records)
Member triangulation	Checking with the participants to ensure the interpretations are consistent with what participants meant in their original responses

Let's use **case studies** as an example of how triangulation for qualitative research is applied. **Data triangulation** increases the strength of case studies (Yin, 2009). The need to use multiple sources in **case studies** is much greater than it is in other kinds of research.

Case studies paint a rich picture of behavior. Richness implies that researchers examine multiple data sources. For example, documents, archival records, interviews, and observations can each add something to increase the richness and depth. If these sources *converge*, meaning have similar findings, then researchers have a high degree of triangulation for their interpretations, far more evidence than using data from just one source. The use of multiple sources increases the **credibility** and **trustworthiness** of a case study and gives the researcher more confidence in **generalizing**.

On the other hand, using multiple sources has some limitations. It is time consuming, expensive, and case study researchers must have extensive training to be knowledgeable about a variety of research methods.

Chapter 36
Designing experiments for the IB Internal Assessment

One goal of this chapter is to demonstrate how to design a simple experiment that manipulates *one* independent variable and measures *one* dependent variable. Another goal is to learn about analyzing data and evaluating findings.

Experimentation is the only research method that answers research questions about the *causes* of behavior, so it is the best choice for research questions wanting to know the cause of something.

Suppose a researcher is interested in investigating gender differences in math performance. Learning style is probably part of the explanation. Might specific learning conditions be one cause of female math performance? Since experiment terms are abstract for beginners, a sample experiment in this chapter investigates

Thinking skills: Getting the language straight!
1. Experiment is the **research** method. A research method offers a systematic and organized way to collect and analyze data.
2. **Design** refers to the way an experiment is structured to compare groups or conditions, usually independent samples, repeated measures, or matched pairs.
3. **Data collection** refers to how an experimenter gathers data, such as timing a task, a questionnaire, or with observation. For example, Bandura's Bobo studies used experiment as the method, independent samples as the design, and observation for data collection. The Bobo studies are experiments, not observation studies. Avoid confusing data collection as the research method.

whether different learning conditions cause females to perform better in math. Decisions are explained at each step.

36.1 Characteristics of experiments

This table is reprinted from chapter 35 so students can start the IA with a review of an experiment's purpose.

***** Please note: A **field experiment** is allowed for the IA, but it is not recommended by the author. A student's first experience designing an experiment should be a classic lab experiment. Field experiments are difficult for many reasons. Often they are just poorly implemented lab experiments done in a hallway or crowded library or lunchroom rather than a real field experiment. Students can read a field experiment in chapter 14 with the topic eyewitness memory. Note that all field experiments require deception, something contrary to the ethical need to get informed consent. The decision not to get informed consent is complicated and not something recommended for high school students. In addition, field experiments lack the control we want students to learn about and use in their studies.

Characteristics of experiments

Characteristic	Description
Experiments compare at least two groups or two conditions. It is the only method showing causation.	The goal of an experiment is to see if and independent variable (IV) caused changes to the dependent variable (DV). Because of this goal, researchers must create at least 2 groups or conditions, with one of them serving as a control or getting something different.
At least one **independent variable** (IV) is manipulated.	The independent variable is defined as what the researcher changes, or makes different, between the two groups or conditions. The IV must be something that can be manipulated in a a classic lab experiment, such as learning alone or learning in groups. Human features such as gender or age cannot be used as independent variables in classic controlled lab experiments. Gender and age cannot really be manipulated, even if they are differences between groups. If an IV is not manipulated, the study is a **quasi-experiment**. In a quasi-experiment, one does not know what causes the change in the dependent variable. Participants are not randomly assigned to conditions in quasi-experiments. Rather, quasi-experiments just test the boys versus the girls, for example. Many published experiments are quasi-designs and they are quite valuable. For the high school student who is a beginner, it is important to know what a classic lab experiment is first. **Field experiments** are uncontrolled and take place in the real world. Field experiments still have IVs and DVs, but they are not isolated from all the confounding variables that could interfere with the IV. **Natural experiments** are when a situation occurs that was not planned, but an IV and DV are identifiable and it is a chance for the researcher to study behavior.
At least one **dependent variable** (DV) is measured.	The DV is what the researcher wants to find out, such as the number of math problems correctly solved after training.

Characteristic	Description
They use **inferential statistics**.	Inferential statistics show if a **significant difference** between the groups or conditions exists. Sometimes it appears that there is a difference between the raw scores or the means of the groups or conditions, but it is unknown if these differences are *significant* until an inferential statistical test is applied. A significant difference means that within a stated probability, such as 5%, it was the IV rather than chance that caused the change in the DV. If a significant difference exists between the learning styles, researchers know it is probably, with 5% chance of error, learning style causing the amount of math problems solved correctly, and not something else, such as teacher attitude.
They are designed for maximum **control**.	The IV is isolated from all extraneous variables that may influence the change. In the example experiment developed in this chapter, it must be the learning conditions that influence the ability to complete math problems, and not another feature of the group, such as self-efficacy level or the number of math courses taken by the girls. ***Control is the greatest strength of experiments***, and this is important to remember when evaluating strengths of a study. Because control is high, experiments by their nature are artificial. Avoid criticizing experiments for being artificial. They are supposed to be artificial. Because there are so many internal controls, meaning the experiment has high internal validity, any individual experiment has low ecological validity and typically does not generalize well. **Triangulation** ensures that the results of experiments fit in with a larger body of research and have meaning outside study conditions.

36.2: Conducting Experimental Research: Topic choice

The next part of this chapter is about conducting a classic lab experiment where one independent variable is manipulated, one dependent variable is measured, and two groups or conditions are used. Even if the original study to replicate has more than two conditions of the IV, choose just two. If the study measures more than one dependent variable, choose one.

The sample experiment investigates the best way for girls to learn mathematics. This idea comes from reviewing literature on the general topic of gender differences in cognitive abilities. How do I get from studying general theory to a well-defined hypothesis?

Topic choice

Appendix 3 has a list of cognitive topics along with references for published studies recommended for the IA.

It is suggested that topics are simple and from the cognitive ATB. There is a good reason for this. The goal of the IB internal assessment project is for students to learn the basics of study design, data collection and analysis, and data evaluation. It is not the goal for students to manage complex designs or to venture into topics that may become ethically contentious.

It is the recommendation of this author that social psychology topics be avoided, as even topics that seem innocent on the surface, such as stereotyping, can cause long term harm and it could be hard to know just what that might be.

In addition, it is recommended that no student use deception, as it involves the complicated process of justification and goes against the need for informed consent.

Students wanting to use ethically contentious or complicated topics might wait until college or their professional career. Also, *students are too concerned with keeping participants blind to the hypothesis*. If the experiment is about memory it should be stated as such on the informed consent form. Participants do not need to know the exact hypothesis but need a reasonable account of what they are expected to do. Why complicate the project? Students can use filler activities within the study that are not considered deception but distract participants from doing things like rehearsing or spending time guessing.

The Internal Assessment for IB students or a class project for any psychology student
This section includes directions for the IB **Internal Assessment** project, something required for IB SL and HL students.

Any student in a psychology course should design and analyze a simple experiment in their course.

IB students must **collaborate**, one of the approaches to learning. They should work in teams of 2 to a maximum of 4. Some parts of the report will be similar, including the appendices, the hypothesis and null, and how the IV and DV are operationalized. However, once data is collected, each students must analyze and evaluate data independently without talking to other group members. SL and HL students may work together.

36.3: Introduction
The introduction of an experiment contains the aim of the study, the theory and research used as background, a research hypothesis, and a null hypothesis. The independent and dependent variables are clearly operationalized within the hypothesis and null.

Students should replicate a study, and this often means a partial replication. Students can make the study their own by creating new word lists or other materials, but must make sure that these changes are relevant to the study aim and clearly state this.

IB Introduction rubric:
For the highest marks of 5-6 points:
1. The aim is stated and its relevance fully explained.
2. The background theory/model and study is clearly described and explicitly linked to the experiment aim.
3. The IV and DV are operationalized to be easily identified in the research hypothesis and null hypothesis.

Notice that you cannot simply give a list of details. A reason the aim is relevant must be stated, the description of theory/model and study must have a stated link to the aim, and the reader should not have to hunt for the IV and DV.

The IA rubrics reflect an overall impression of the work and are not a checklist of what must be included. This chapter tells students what they should include.

Aim of the study
The aim explains the purpose of the study. For the sample experiment, "The aim of the study is to investigate whether girls will perform better on the XYZ mathematics test after studying in groups or

studying alone." A clear statement of the aim orients the reader to the experiment. The aim must be operationalized so that the independent and dependent variables are easily identified.

The relevance of the aim must be explained, meaning a reason must also be included about why the topic is worthy of investigation.

Background theory and research

IB students must include a description of the theory or model used as the basis for the experiment. This means to give a detailed account and it should be from a reliable source. Students are discouraged from using blogs or generalized texts as a source because the tendency is for them to be vague and even sometimes incorrect, sometimes incorrectly referenced, or lacking a reference. Primary sources are a better choice or a high quality cognitive psychology text, such as Robert Sternberg's *Cognitive Psychology*, the book used for some of the background theory by students in the author's class. However, students should use primary sources for the background study for the greatest accuracy and depth of detail.

Students may have read literature reviews in published studies and will see them in the primary sources. A literature review is an evaluative discussion of the existing published literature on the experiment topic. The purpose of reviewing literature is to justify a hypothesis.

IB students are not asked to produce a literature review and instead must replicate an experiment published in a peer reviewed journal, with the leeway to narrow down the sometimes numerous independent variables to two and to adapt the dependent variable to just one if more are measured. IB students must do the following.

1. *Detail the background* theory and study.
2. *Explain its link to the aim* of the experiment. Explain includes giving reasons, and a good one is to show that the theory and research are highly representative of the aim, such as a prominent researcher on the topic and possibly a classic study demonstrating an effect on behavior.
3. *Explain the relevance of the study*, meaning why it should be run. Explain includes giving reasons, so avoid superficial ones, such as "students need to

---

How many sources?
Become educated on the topic before starting the experiment so the introduction is meaningful, well detailed, clearly linked to the aim, and is important to run.

This does not mean to include a long list of references. IB does not require a specific number of references, so a good theory source and one research studies is enough, given that students must link them to the aim, etc.

---

learn how to study" or "we need to know more about the topic." Better reasons are the need to replicate the study on a different type of sample or follow the authors's recommendations for making, for examples, a particular small change in a word list or the time needed to complete a task. One good reason to read the primary source is to see the discussion. Authors include strengths and limitations of their experiment and students who want to adapt it can find ideas there. IB students should make only small changes, such as a different word list or altering the time allotted. Students choosing to alter the study should state a clear reason and not make changes arbitrarily.

Background theory for the sample experiment about girls learning math takes into account that numerous theories compete for a prominent role on the topic of gender and cognitive abilities. Some theorists argue that hormones are the dominant causal factor. Others argue that causal factors related to culture, stereotyping, the school environment, gender schema development, self-efficacy, and parental behavior are dominant and exacerbate any inherited gender differences. A modern view is that all of these contribute to mathematical ability. However, *even if all these factors work together, researchers can only focus on one aspect of the issues at a time.* The sample experiment in this book looks for an experimental problem simple enough for a high school student to manage, while at the same time allowing students to adapt it if desired, advancing the existing literature. A well-focused hypothesis is required that examines one small aspect of the theory. Gender is inappropriate as an independent variable because we do not want a quasi-experiment to limit our ability to show cause and effect. It is better to focus on one aspect of the problem such as specific learning difficulties that girls face. There is a debate on what factors are involved in the learning situation for girls, suggesting this as a possible causal factor, making the link to the aim clearly focused.

Research Hypothesis (alternative hypothesis)

The research hypothesis is a statement of the predicted outcome and can be called the **alternative hypothesis** because it is accepted only if the null can be rejected statistically (Coolican, 2014). It is either a **one-tailed hypothesis** or a **two-tailed hypothesis**, depending on whether the researcher can make a prediction or not. The independent and dependent variables are easily identified in the hypothesis.

A one–tailed hypothesis is a **directional hypothesis**: it makes a specific prediction that one group or condition will perform better than the other group or condition. According to some research on gender and math abilities, girls and boys learn differently. Boys may learn best working alone because girls may learn more effectively in groups. A one-tailed hypothesis for the sample experiment might be "girls learning mathematics material in groups will perform better on the XYZ math test than girls learning mathematics material alone." The IV is learning alone or in a group. The DV is the performance on the XYZ math test.

A two-tailed hypothesis is a **nondirectional hypothesis**: it does not make a specific prediction about which group or condition will perform better. A two-tailed hypothesis states that there will be *a* difference. Two-tailed hypotheses are useful when it is hard to make a prediction. A two-tailed hypothesis for the sample experiment might be "girls learning new math material in groups and girls learning new math material alone will perform differently on the XYZ math test."

Warning!
Many students *incorrectly* identify the **independent variable**. Avoid identifying the independent variable as "the learning condition". Rather, the IV is learning alone or in a group, an operationalized and complete description.

Regardless of whether a researcher uses a one or two-tailed hypothesis, it is crucial that the hypothesis contains **operationally defined variables**: the IV and the DV must be stated in clear and well-defined behavioral terms. Experiments are designed for **replication**. Researchers must be able to repeat the experiment to verify the original results.

A one-tailed hypothesis is used in the sample experiment.

Null Hypothesis

Experiments state a null hypothesis, which is the experimental hypothesis.

The null hypothesis is a statement that there is no significant difference between the two conditions, that the probability of either occurring is the same (Coolican, 2014). A null for the sample experiment is "there is no difference in the scores on the XYZ test between the girls learning mathematics in groups or the girls learning mathematics alone." Notice the null is also operationalized.

The null is the experimental hypothesis because all science experiments work on probability. Researchers try to reject the null within a reasonable margin of error. There is no proof that scientific theories are 100% true. The largest level of acceptable error in the social sciences is 5%. Inferential tests examine if the null can be rejected, not if the research (or alternative) hypothesis is true.

The null hypothesis is *not* the opposite of the research hypothesis.

36.4: Ethics in experiments

Experiments must be ethical and it is assumed that all potential ethical problems are considered before running the experiment.

All participants must give written informed consent before participation, and if under 16, must have parental consent. Children under 12 should not be used at all as there are too many special features of the consent.

Specific to the sample math experiment is protecting girls from potential harm to self-efficacy, since girls may be "at risk" for low math self-efficacy. The sample experiment is designed to minimize this risk. The experiment has potential benefits, such as learning new study strategies. No situation should arise where participants feel less competent because of the experimental tasks.

It all boils down to considering **risks versus benefits**. There should be no risk to the participants in a student's first experiment for a class project because this is when students learn to design studies and analyze data. Professional psychologists understand that the benefit to science must be great for any the experiment to place a participant at risk for harm.

All student researchers should write a **briefing statement** that orients participants to the nature of the study before their participation. Participants should hear a **debriefing statement** at the end of data gathering that includes what the researchers expected to find. Participants should have access to the results after statistical tests are applied.

The APA guidelines are available at www.apa.org.

The ethical considerations that come up in simple studies are next.

1. Participants must give their **informed consent**. An informed consent form must orient participants to the nature of the study. Participants must be informed about what they are expected to do in the study and any risks they might face. If the study investigates memory, then tell participants the study is about memory. Informed consent forms asking participants to take part in "a psychology study" are inappropriate and deceptive. Participants must be guaranteed **anonymity** and that their data are **confidential**.

2. The use of **deception** must be justified and because this is hard to do, deception is not recommended. The author's students are not allowed to use deception because doing away with informed consent is complicated. 'Clean' studies on cognitive psychology topics are preferred. Students love social psychology, but many social psychology experiments involve deception. *It is not sufficient to justify deception by saying that it must be used to keep participants from guessing the research hypothesis.*

3. There should be no **potential harm** to participants. Student researchers should leave potential harm issues to professional researchers who have the experience to weigh risks versus benefits.

4. Participants are volunteers and have the **right to withdraw** from the study at any time or withdraw their data from experimental results. This must be stated in the informed consent form.

5. Participants have the right to a **briefing** and **debriefing** statement and must have a way to find out their results, which should also be stated in the informed consent form.

36.5: Exploration

The exploration section of the experimental report contains the design, participants, materials, and procedures. Procedures do not explicitly gain students marks, mostly because these are created in collaboration with others and it can be hard to know an individual's contribution. However, materials and procedures are part of any experiment report and key to ensuring that the study is well controlled and can be replicated.

IA rubrics: Exploration
Students must explain (give details and reasons) a research design, sampling technique, choice of participants, controlled variables, and choice of materials. Students might specifically include the word "reason" when writing to draw the examiner's eye to the fact that they are giving a reason. This will help students focus on the command term.

Research Design

Experimental design refers to the way groups or conditions are compared. Three designs for simple experiments follow.

1. Independent Samples (between group designs)
2. Repeated Measures (within group designs)
3. Matched pairs

Design is an art form and there are many ways to construct any experiment. The best experiments creatively address concerns about control and data collection.

A table of the three designs follows this paragraph (Goodwin, 1998; Schumacher and McMillan, 1984). First there are a few things you need to know about selecting a design. A design needs to be explained as the best one for the experiment. *This reason comes primarily from the* **control** *offered by each design.* Sometimes students are vague about explaining the design. Clearly use research design language about control in experiments. Each design controls specific **internal validity** concerns. A characteristic of experiments is the isolation of the IV from all extraneous variables. Internal validity refers to the control *within* an experiment. Just understand that selecting one design to control for threats to interval validity leaves other threats uncontrolled. There is no way to change this problem. Accept it as a limitation of experiments because there is no way to control for everything. The best you can do is control the internal validity threats that are the worst ones for your particular study by choosing the best research design.

> **Explaining a design: It is about control!**
> Avoid vague and superficial reasons such as "Researchers used an independent samples design because there are two groups" or "Researchers used a repeated measures design because the sample is small."
>
> The best reasons are the control each design offers. The table below gives definitions and the best reasons. Students must refer to strengths of the study in the evaluation section and these are some of those strengths. In fact, a potential limitation of the study is the design, that it did not offer the best control, even after considering it carefully. **Experiments are all about control and you must give reasons for selecting particular controls**. Anything not controlled by the design can be controlled in procedures, such as counterbalancing for repeated measures selected to control for history.

Design	Description
Independent samples	Independent samples designs compare two different groups. This is the best one for the sample math study because we want to investigate the effects of two different learning methods. *Independent samples designs are explained as the best way to control for testing and progressive errors, order effects, maturation, and mortality.* However, independent samples designs leave history uncontrolled.

Design	Description
Repeated measures	Repeated measures designs compare the participant to himself or herself before and after the independent variable is introduced. This design could be used for the sample math experiment. One group of girls could be tested in the alone condition and then in the group condition. Repeated-measures designs work well for some experiments, such as those testing attitude change. However, the problem with testing errors is too great for the sample math study. *The main explanation for selecting repeated-measures designs is to control history.* However, order effects, maturation, mortality, and testing are left uncontrolled.
Matched pairs	Matched pairs is more complicated and not something the author recommends, but it is listed as a choice in the IB guide, so here goes. This is when participants with something in common, such as being a twin, need to be paired so that one is in one condition and the other is in the other condition. The twin pair is randomly assigned to one of the two conditions. It is recommended that students use one of the first two as they are less complicated designs. *The main explanation for using a matched pair design is to reduce participant history.*

You are now aware that different designs are selected to control threats to internal validity. Next is a list of ten **internal validity** concerns (Goodwin, 1998; Schumacher and McMillan, 1984), some of which are controlled by selecting a particular design. Internal validity refers to the control a researcher applies to the experiment, such as making sure that participants do not have a chance to share information during the study. **The different designs offer control for varying aspects of these internal validity errors.** Decide which ones are most important and choose a design that maximizes the control of these threats. As designs control only some things important to the study, *you may also have to put some control into your procedures.* It is impossible to control everything in an experiment. Sometimes one control choice causes another problem. For example, repeated-measures designs control for history but introduce order effects into experiments. Researchers should then control for order effects in their procedures by counterbalancing. Control issues are something all researchers face. Make the best choices to control as many variables as possible.

**Explaining the controls and finding
limitations of the study**

This list includes all the control factors needed for a good experiment with high internal validity. Learn the terms and use them when writing, both in the exploration section and in the evaluation section.

Carefully consider this list before running the study, because IB students should not expect credit for saying, "We should have counterbalanced" in the evaluation. It is assumed you would with a little planning. But some of these are hard to control and still might be a problem, though some prescreening of participants can help you attempt to add controls. The section about evaluation builds on this idea.

It is a poor plan to make an obvious mistake and just later say, "oops," as if saving the mistake for the limitations section of the evaluation!

This does place the burden on teachers to supervise students so they have a controlled sample and a place to run the study where they can implement control factors. *Do not run studies in the hall or in the lunch room.*

Some internal validity errors are **random errors**. Random errors are characteristics participants bring with them to the study. Identifying and controlling random errors is not always possible, even if you try. Controlling the sample and prescreening for participant variables that may **confound** the experiment is recommended. **Systematic errors** are mistakes made by the researcher.

Random and systematic errors should be anticipated and accounted for before the experiment is run.

Internal Validity Errors

Internal validity errors	Description
History	History refers to participant variables that confound the experiment. Some random history errors always exist, even when control is attempted. Prescreening for unwanted participant variables is one action to take. There are going to be differences in prior math success regardless of what is found in a prescreening in the sample study. These differences may relate to the participant's history of parental reinforcement, early childhood play, or experiences with teachers.
Mortality	Mortality is a systematic or a random error depending on the situation. Mortality refers to participants dropping out of the experiment before its completion. It does not mean dying! It is a systematic error if the researcher makes the experiment too long or difficult for participants. It is a random error if the experiment is well designed with appropriate tasks and a participant leaves the study anyway. Participants have the ethical right to leave the study anytime they wish. Researchers may never know the reason.
Maturation	Maturation is a systematic or a random error depending on the situation. Maturation is when participants change after the study begins. Researchers avoid maturation errors by anticipating all potential possibilities. Experiments taking place over numerous days run the risk that participants learn something new on the topic, such as watching a documentary. Researchers cannot control every random instance of maturing. Maturation is best avoided by gathering data at one point, a practice that is adequate for our simple study.
Diffusion of treatment	This systematic error occurs when participants share information about the study. Diffusion might occur in the sample math experiment if participants from each group have a chance to compare experiences outside of the study before its completion. Two ways to control diffusion are to prevent participant interaction during the experiment and collect data all at one time, such as within one class period. Sometimes students want to design an experiment in which they compare memory after a short time, such as 30 minutes, with memory after a long time, such as after a week. Waiting a week introduces the possibility of a diffusion-of-treatment error into the study, so you must decide which is more important, seeing how memory works over time or controlling diffusion of treatment.
Order effect	Order effects are systematic errors in which the order of the tasks, rather than the IV, causes the responses of participants. If a researcher shows participants a series of pictures, the participants tend to remember the first or the last one. **Counterbalancing** controls order effects. Half of the participants are shown the pictures in one order, and the other half are shown the pictures in another order. Counterbalancing ensures the experiment measures what it claims to measure. Repeated-measures designs should always use counterbalancing.

Internal validity errors	Description
Hawthorne Effect	The Hawthorne effect occurs when participants alter their behavior to try to please the researcher by anticipating the correct answers. It is a systematic error if the researcher fails to consider how the Hawthorne effect influences the study. A **single blind study**, where subjects are deceived about the real nature of the study, controls the Hawthorne effect. However, the use of deception requires justification, and there are ways to control for the Hawthorne effect without deceiving participants. A **filler activity** is a good idea. At appropriate times, researchers distract participants with tasks having no relationship to the hypothesis. An example of a filler activity in a memory experiment is when participants read an article on another topic during the interval between the first exposure to words and the measurement of the DV to prevent rehearsal. In addition, students do not need to tell participants their exact hypothesis to gain informed consent, and just tell them that it is a memory study, for example. Thus, participants are informed about the nature of the study, but the exact hypothesis has not been revealed.
Experimenter bias	A systematic error occurs when researcher behaviors influence participant behavior. **Demand characteristics** may exist, meaning participants find out the true purpose of the study and think that certain behavior is "demanded" from them by the researcher. The researcher may not be aware that he or she is giving off subtle clues about the true nature of the study. Experimenter bias can be controlled. One way to control for experimenter bias is to use **standardized instructions**, which keeps researchers from accidentally adding anything into the predetermined instructions.
Instrumentation	Instrumentation is a systematic error leading to unanticipated changes in the results because of inconsistencies in data collection. In the sample experiment, the math material for the two groups is exactly the same. Instrumentation can also occur when observation is used to collect data. If the observer becomes tired or there is a great deal happening at once, the checks on an observation grid may be inaccurate.
Constancy of condition	Conditions must be the same for all participants or it is a systematic error. If the two groups of girls are tested in separate rooms, then conditions are not the same. The best way to avoid this error is to test participants in one place at the same place. If one group is tested at 8:00 a.m. and the other at 1:00 p.m. or if you use two separate classrooms, you have constancy of condition errors.
Testing errors and progressive errors	Testing and progressive errors are systematic errors. Testing errors are the effects of pretesting on the posttest, the final measurement of the DV. Pretesting in independent-samples designs sometimes controls for history errors. However, the pretest may have an unwanted learning effect. Repeated-measures designs may contain testing errors. Progressive errors occur when participants practice the experimental skill before the experiment begins. Practice tests help make baseline skills equivalent, such as allowing participants practice at putting together a difficult puzzle. Practice tests control history, but create a progressive error.

This is a long but important list. If an experiment has poor internal validity, the chances of having **external validity** is remote. External validity refers to the extent to which the results of the study can be generalized outside the study. There are two types, **population external validity** and **ecological external validity**.

Population validity refers to generalizing the results to a larger population. It is limited to people from a target population with the same characteristics as those in the sample or just the opportunity sample if this was used. Samples must be controlled so that researchers can say it was the IV that caused the changes in the DV. Uncontrolled samples might introduce history errors into the study.

Ecological validity involves generalizing based on experimental conditions, such as time of day, temperature, and the setting. If the experiment is run in a well-lighted, soundproof room at 9:00 a.m., this is the extent of its ecological validity. The conditions are artificial, but researchers know that lab conditions are necessary to test the effects of an IV on a DV.

An independent-samples design is best for the sample experiment. The testing error from the first trial would still exist after counterbalancing in a repeated-measures design. History random errors are not as much of a threat to the validity of the experiment. Participant variables are controllable in other ways, such as in the selection of the sample. Variables in the history of individual participants can **confound** the experiment. This means that characteristics of participants that are not measured in the experiment, such as prior learning or differences in intellectual level, might interfere with measuring the change in the DV. Confounding variables are easily controlled by selecting a controlled sample.

The decisions made for exploration require collaboration and teamwork. The reward is that as a freshman in college, you are ready to work as a research assistant. This is in addition to having a good IA score! Source: pixabay.com

The math experiment controls for participant variables in sample selection. The participant variables follow:

1. Math level. Choosing only honors level trigonometry math students controls this variable.
2. Number of math courses taken. Selecting students in honors-level trigonometry with approximately equal numbers of courses in their histories controls this variable.
3. Sports history. Girls with a history of playing sports may have an advantage on spatial skills. Control is achieved by selecting participants with approximately the same sports background.
4. Age. All participants are 16 years old.
5. Cultural expectations. Different cultures may have different performance expectations, different self-efficacy levels for performance, or different ways of problem solving or using memory. The experiment is limited to one culture.
6. Attribution style, or what people say is responsible for a success or failure. Girls generally have more internal attributions than males, blaming themselves for failure rather than an outside factor. It is safe to assume this is fairly constant among all girls.
7. Self-efficacy level, or the belief in one's ability to master a skill. Bandura (1997) thinks math self-efficacy in girls can come from adult female models, among other things. Self-efficacy levels are difficult to examine in experiments because of ethical considerations. Separating girls by self-efficacy level is an ethical risk of harm to one's self motivation. This experiment does not control for self-efficacy differences. It adds a history risk, but the results can be triangulated with other methods.

Sampling

Experiment reports give details about characteristics of the sample and how the sample is selected. This is important information for evaluating or replicating the study.

The sample must be controlled and should be small. Twenty to thirty participants is sufficient, randomly allocated into two groups. If you have fewer than twenty then that is fine too, but do not fall into the trap of selecting repeated measures designs simply because of a smaller sample. Repeated measures studies control for history, so choose it only if this is important control needed for your study.

Students typically want to use samples that are too large and varied. Control the sample to the extent possible. Get participants all the same age, all the same grade, all males or females if needed, and all the same intellectual level. Large and varied samples run the risk of introducing **confounding variables** into the study, which becomes a control problem.

Students often think they need a **representative** sample that is described in chapter 35 so students know what this means. However, an **opportunity sample** is fine, which is what most published studies use anyway! Getting a representative sample through random sampling can be complex and time consuming, and might be impossible given the limitations we have to give students access to participants in a high school setting.

Students can get frustrated at this point. They want to select a sample that represents a large group so that they can generalize their results outside of the experiment. Just remember that experiments— including the samples— are supposed to be tightly controlled. Any one experiment does not generalize well. If an experiment is part of a larger body of research with similar conclusions, then the study has more chances for generalization. So don't worry so much about getting a random sample. Just interpret the study correctly when you get to the discussion.

Sometimes students insist on getting a random sample, so then make sure the sample really is randomly selected and follow the directions in chapter 35.

Researchers most often use **opportunity sampling**. Opportunity sampling is explained because students working within the confines of a school schedule have limited chances to get a sample and must select participants based on the convenience and opportunity to use them. For example, all the students in Mrs. Smith's 4th period English class might be the opportunity sample.

Regardless of how samples are selected, researchers should use **random allocation** to assign participants to the groups or conditions. Random allocation controls for participant variables and means that *everyone in the sample has an equal chance of being in either condition or group*.

An opportunity sample of 20 girls from an 11th grade honors-level trigonometry class is used in the experiment. They are all 16 years old and have about the same math ability.

> **Explaining the sampling technique and participant choice**
> Opportunity sampling is explained because students working within the confines of a school schedule have limited chances to get a sample and must select participants based on the convenience and opportunity to use them. Do not spend the time random sampling.
>
> Explaining the sample choice means to give details about their characteristics and that they are a *controlled* sample, all very similar (age, grade, intellectual level). Do not get a large and varied sample, which adds to **confounding variables** in experiments, lessening the control. Students can cite the controlled sample as part of their controls section. Internal validity comes first!

Materials: Data collection ideas

A decision about **level of measurement** (defined in section 36.6) is the next step. *Level of measurement refers to how data are collected*. As explained in the side box, certain materials go best with the different levels measurement.

Figure out the correct level of measurement for your experiment and then choices for materials and descriptive and inferential statistics are easy because they all match.

Even if IB students are not required to name the level of measurement in the

> **Explaining material choices**
> One of the best reasons for choosing a particular material is that it fits with the study level of measurement. This just means that the materials are the best for measuring the dependent variable as it is operationally defined. For example, if eyewitnesses rate their confidence level on a Likert Scale, it is the best material for the ordinal level of measurement. A yes/no questionnaire can be the best material to measure a nominal scale.

report, using the level of measurement as a starting point for designing materials and selecting statistics keeps things consistent and *gives you a reason for using materials and statistics.*

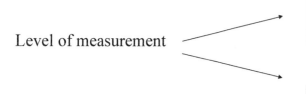

Level of measurement

Materials: Make sure they reflect the level of measurement.

Statistics: Specific descriptive and inferential statistics are the best choices for your level of measurement.

The sample experiment uses two groups of materials. The first are materials for new trigonometry problems. The materials must be relevant for the trigonometry course and new to all participants. The second group is the XYZ math test to measure the DV. The XYZ test has a sample of problems that represent all facets of the new material. The XYZ tests must accurately measure the DV. Scoring procedures must be explained. One point is awarded for each correct problem. A copy of all materials is included in the appendix at the end of the experiment. The details of material development and scoring is provided for replication purposes.

An ordinal level of measurement is best for the sample experiment. It may seem that an interval level of measurement is appropriate. Although scores can be ranked it cannot be assumed that the rankings represent specific intervals. One reason is that all the math problems on the test cannot be assumed to be equivalent. A related issue is when students count the number of words recalled by participants. While it appears to be an interval, it may not really be an interval. Students can rank the scores, but do not assume that all the words are of equal difficulty. You can better ensure the words better fit an interval scale if they are selected to be similar.

Pilot the materials on a group similar to the participants in the real study before running the experiment. Student researchers might use students in their class for the pilot to make sure all materials and conditions for the real study are appropriate. For example, might participants have too little time or too much time to learn a word list?

> **The value of piloting: Important for explaining materials**
> This is all about getting more **control** into an experiment.
>   Avoid making mistakes that could easily be foreseen during the real experiment by running a pilot to see if your materials are easy to understand, can be done in a particular time frame, or are too easy or hard. For example, how long should you give participants to learn a word list? One minute? Thirty seconds? It is not sufficient to say in the discussion that you would give less time to learn the words. Find it out ahead of time and avoid costly mistakes. Piloting helps reduce **type II errors** as well.

There are many ways to design materials to collect data. A list of popular data collection methods opens the next section. Materials used to collect data should reflect the study's level of measurement.

There is one last thing to consider about data collection. Researchers are concerned with designing materials and procedures that minimize the chances of making a **type II error**, or the chance that the hypothesis is correct but the study is unable to show it, and inferential testing accepts the null hypothesis. Students can easily try to maximize the chance that the IV has a chance of causing the difference in the DV by making sure that what is different about the two groups or conditions is *very* different (Coolican, 2004). If you do not find significance with an inferential test, and the study is well controlled, the reason might be that you did not create enough of a difference between the groups or conditions. Students often think that if there is no significance between groups or conditions that a future study should be run using a larger and more varied group. Student perceptions make it seem as if a larger and more varied sample is needed, but the problem is more likely to be that the difference between the groups or conditions was not sufficiently great.

Ideas for materials: Data collection
Many choices are available for simple experiments.

a. Time participants on a task.
b. Count the number of items someone answers correctly.
c. Ask participants questions that can be answered with yes or no.
d. Observe participants. Many researchers collect experimental data with an observation grid. Make sure that items on the grid measure only the dependent variable. The grid contains items fitting the operational definitions for behaviors representing the DV.
e. Construct a questionnaire. Questionnaires for experiments can be used in two ways. First the questionnaire can contain the IV, such as in the Loftus (1975) experiment. Loftus changed one word in one question on each questionnaire, called the critical question. All the other questions were filler questions. Second, questions can measure the DV, such as a Likert Scale measuring the degree of likability after reading different adjectives to describe a job candidate. Make sure that all questions measure the dependent variable and nothing else. Follow these guidelines for writing good questions (McMillan & Schumacher, 1984). *All mistakes in question writing are instrumentation errors, a failure to use proper control in the study.*

> **Increase control in materials**
> When using word lists, the words can be put in random order to make sure no one can guess what comes next, especially if the words represent categories that aid memory (Coolican, 2014).
> Assign each word a number and use them in the order selected by a calculator or computer.

1. *Clearly state items*. There is a difference between a questionnaire asking general questions and those asking clear and specific questions. "I feel angry at my parents" is too general. Break it down into several questions containing specific behaviors, such as "My parents make fair rules about curfews."

2. *Ask one question at a time*. Asking more than one item in a question is **double-barreled**. "Do you approve of the tardy policy and the dress code?" is double-barreled. If the participant answers yes, to which item is the participant responding? Break this question down into two separate questions.

3. *Keep questions simple*. The longer and more complex a question, the greater the chance that it is misunderstood or skipped.

4. *Eliminate all negative questions*. Negative questions are misunderstood more than positive statements. Say, "The cafeteria staff does a good job" rather than "The cafeteria staff is not doing a good job."

5. *Edit the questions for biased language*. The Hawthorne effect is sometimes prompted by the way in which items are phrased. Gender stereotyped language is an example. Sometimes students are not actively aware of cultural biases in language and should get advice on word choice. Slang is never appropriate.

Structured questionnaires use an accepted response format. Every question uses the same scale. Here is an example.

a. **Likert scales**. Likert scales rank-order responses. This format is for experiments gathering data with ordinal levels of measurement. Here are two examples of scales.

1. I approve of the dress code.

| strongly agree | agree | neither agree or | disagree | strongly disagree |

b. **Semantic differential scales**. This format uses adjective pairs. Participants rate their opinions by marking somewhere on the scale between the opposing adjectives. Semantic differential scales are used with the ordinal level of measurement.
   1. My parents are:
      fair _____ _____ _____ _____ unfair
      trusting _____ _____ _____ untrusting

   Make as many adjective pairs as necessary to measure the DV.

c. **YES or NO QUESTIONS**. This format is for experiments using nominal levels of measurement. Yes or no formats do not supply much information about opinions. A response style systematic error may exist if a nominal scale is used in an experiment that is really appropriate for ordinal or interval levels of measurement.

d. **CHECKLISTS**. A checklist is appropriate for gathering data in experiments such as female career choices after an IV is introduced. Participants place a mark beside all the relevant items on the checklist.

Procedures: Helps to show controls used, helps others replicate the study, and helps others see how you applied ethics

The research design offers the experiment control, but the design never controls everything. It is likely you will include more **control in the procedures**, such as counterbalancing. These extra control features of your study are part of the procedures, something that is done so others can **replicate** the study.

Besides the steps followed when running the experiment, *include how participants are randomly allocated and the control used in the procedures that the design does not control.*

What is random allocation? Increasing control in your experiment.
Random allocation increases *control*, and means every participant has an equal chance to be in either group or condition. This is done by giving each participant a number. Next use a random number generator (computer or calculator) or a random number chart to select participants for group A. Last, select the other group.

   Practices that are not random:
1. Dividing the room in half
2. Putting surnames in alphabetical order, and selecting the first 10 for one condition and the last 10 for the second condition.
3. Participant self-selection to a condition

   Practices that do not necessarily guarantee randomness:
1. Drawing names out of a hat, unless the hat is large, the papers are folded exactly the same and cannot be seen by the selector, and is shuffled each time (Coolican, 2014). Why bother when it is so easy to use a calculator or computer? And what is meant by shuffling?
2. Shuffling, which is vague. What is meant by shuffling and how would someone else do it exactly in the same way?

Control features in the procedures make up for the threats to internal validity that the design leaves vulnerable. Here are three common examples: (1) Counterbalancing is important for all repeated-measures designs. (2) Screen participants for unwanted variables for independent-samples designs, such as an experiment on the Mozart Effect screening out the few potential participants who are accomplished musicians. (3) Develop **standardized instructions** to be read to participants that guide the entire experiment and reduce experimenter bias. Include these instructions in an appendix.

Procedures are also the place to control potential internal validity threats such as diffusion of treatment. It is common for students to come up with a way to keep participants from talking to each other during the experiment. Since this is a big problem for students, make a clear plan on how to manage it.

Last, describe how you applied ethical guidelines during the experiment. Include the briefing, the informed consent, the participants rights, and the debriefing.

36.6: Analyzing data from an experiment: Approaches to analysis

IA rubrics: Analysis

Students must:
1. Choose and apply appropriate descriptive and inferential statistics. Do not use all the available choices, but know which are the best choices for your study. For descriptive statistics, choose one measure of central tendency and one measure of dispersion. For inferential statistics, choose the most appropriate one. Students must show their work for the inferential test in the appendices.
2. Include one graph that shows the measure of central tendency and perhaps dispersion if desired.
3. Interpret the findings so data are clearly linked to the hypothesis. Link the statistical findings to the hypothesis.

This section is about selecting the correct descriptive and inferential statistics for analyzing raw data. The material is limited to analyzing experiments where one independent variable (IV) is manipulated and one dependent variable (DV) is measured. This book does not demonstrate calculations or discuss the statistical analysis for experiments manipulating more than one IV and/or measuring more than one DV. Calculations for descriptive and inferential statistics are easily found on the Internet or in texts such as Coolican (2014).

Raw data are the data collected from participants during the experiment. This is the score given to each participant representing the dependent variable, such as the number of items recalled or the number of math problems solved. Each participant gets an overall raw score.

The following chart shows raw data for the sample experiment. This chart should appear in the appendix of a research report and *should never appear in the body of the report*. The raw data are used only to figure appropriate descriptive and inferential statistics.

Raw data mean little until they are interpreted. It is necessary to know the level of measurement of the data before relevant statistics are applied. The level of measurement guides decisions about selecting relevant statistical tests.

Raw data: Number of Math Problems Completed either Alone or in a Group

Alone Condition   Group Condition

Participant #1	5	Participant #11	12
Participant # 2	3	Participant #12	8
Participant #3	8	Participant #13	8
Participant #4	7	Participant #14	13
Participant #5	2	Participant #15	14
Participant #6	3	Participant #16	12
Participant #7	8	Participant #17	13
Participant #8	4	Participant #18	12
Participant #9	4	Participant #19	11
Participant #10	5	Participant #20	11

Level of Measurement: This will help you choose appropriate descriptive and inferential statistics

The level of measurement refers to how data are collected. Choosing a level of measurement is a decision about how to measure the DV, something that all experimenters must consider. Developing materials, collecting data, and analyzing data flows smoothly once you understand level of measurement. Most topics can be studied at any of the levels of measurement so use the one that best fits what you want to know about behavior.

Sometimes students think they can tell a study's level of measurement by looking at a chart or seeing if numbers are used. Both ideas are incorrect. The reasoning is faulty and based on appearances. All experiments quantify data, meaning they use numbers to represent human characteristics.

The four levels of measurement are **nominal, ordinal, interval** and **ratio** (Coolican, 2014; Goodwin, 1998; Schumacher & McMillan, 1984). The first two are **nonparametric**, meaning data are not normally distributed and do not necessarily fall on a bell curve. The last two are **parametric**, meaning data are normally distributed and fall on a bell curve. The best way to identify the level of measurement is to ask, "How did I collect data?"

Nonparametric levels of measurement	Description
Nominal data	Nominal data are the most crude of all the measurements and give the researcher the least amount of information. Nominal data are collected in mutually exclusive categories. The categories do not overlap and cannot be ranked. Asking for yes or no responses or categorizing subject by hair color groups of blond, brunette, or redhead are examples. The Loftus (1975) eyewitness testimony experiment where participants are asked if they see a barn is an example of a nominal-level experiment.

Nonparametric levels of measurement	Description
Ordinal data	Ordinal data are also considered crude, but they give the researcher more information than nominal data do. Ordinal data are collected in such a way that they are ranked, and the rankings may overlap, meaning they are not mutually exclusive. Most human characteristics are ordinal. **Likert scales** ranking participants from the most to the least confident about an answer or the most to the least attractive are ordinal scales. There may be some overlap between participant ratings, such as very confident and somewhat confident. The overlap is unknown. Ordinal scales are not designed to pick up small differences between responses, which is why they are considered crude. Ordinal data are collected in numbers artificially applied to human behaviors, such as 5 points for very attractive.

There is no inherent (natural) meaning to the numbers assigned to nominal or ordinal scales and the numbers simply identify separations in the groups. Ordinal scales are not as precise as the parametric scales and they are not necessarily normally distributed. A **normal curve** is a theoretical curve standardizing scores. A normal distribution is not assumed for confidence, creativity, or any other data examining a non-standardized rating of human behavior. Many student researchers use the ordinal level. Nonparametric statistics allow researchers to have small samples, use levels of measurement that are simple rankings or exclusive categories, and do not require a normal distribution.

Parametric levels of measurement fall on a normal distribution and must be collected by interval or ratio levels of measurement.

Parametric levels of measurement	Description
Interval data	Interval scales rank data, and the exact differences between the rankings are known. Interval scales are things such as the time it takes to complete a task or standardized measurements such as SAT scores. *The numbers are not arbitrarily assigned.* Interval levels of measurement for human characteristics require that the characteristics be standardized, meaning converted into a score that falls into percentile rankings on a normal curve, or require data to be collected in naturally occurring intervals, such as time. For example, temperature is an interval measurement and the 0 is a changing point rather than an absence of temperature (Goodwin, 1998). *Sometimes it is hard for students to tell the difference between interval and ordinal levels of measurement.* If you are not sure, treat the data as ordinal. For example, is the number of words recalled really an interval? Is it possible that the words are not equivalent? This means that some words may be easier to recall than others. If the might be easier to remember than others, then treat the data as ordinal. Some words might even be easier for females or males to remember. This way you do not make a mistake in applying statistical tests for interval data that assume a normal distribution.

Parametric levels of measurement	Description
Ratio data	*Ratio data are interval scales that have a real 0 point and are expressed as a ratio*, meaning that one measurement in a category—such as weight or speed—can be twice as large as another measurement in that category. The 0 in ratio data represents a true zero point (Coolican, 2014; Goodwin, 1998), an absence of something. Zero weight or speed means the absence of weight or length. Because of the way in which ratio data uses a "real" 0 point, it is the only data that are really expressed as a ratio. For example, 40 degrees C is not twice as warm as 20 degrees C, it is just warmer, but 4 pounds is twice as heavy as 2 pounds. Interval and ratio data use the same statistics, so you get the same result in the end!

Why care about levels of measurement? It sounds dull but it is important. All social and natural science experiments *require the researcher to make a choice on how to represent the DV*. The choice of measurement level is important for **ecological validity**, meaning **generalizing** the results outside of experimental conditions. Consider that most topics can be operationally defined so they fit on several levels of measurement and the researcher makes a choice based on what they wish to know.

Let's use **eyewitness memory** as an example.

Eyewitness memory data can be collected at any level of measurement: Get the right one for your aim and hypothesis and to apply statistics!

Eyewitness data on the different levels of measurement	Description
Nominal	You have a nominal scale by asking participants to check yes or no, did you see the broken headlight?
Ordinal	You get an ordinal level by asking participants to rate the confidence of their memory for seeing or not seeing a broken headlight by rating themselves on a Likert Scale from 1, no confidence to 5, great confidence.
Interval	Speed estimation is an interval but see below as it is an example of an interval *that is also* a ratio since it meets the definition. So call speed estimation a ratio. Time is an interval that does not meet the definition of ratio data, so if you run the Stroop test and time participants, call it interval.
Ratio	Last, we can study it at a ratio level by asking participants to estimate the speed of a car. This is also an interval but speed starts from an absolute 0.

Knowing how eyewitness memory is operationalized helps the reader understand the strengths and weaknesses of the research.

Choose the best level of measurement for your research goals.

What is the level of measurement of the sample experiment? The DV is measured as the correct number of math problems solved, which appears to be an interval scale. However, consider whether the interval scale is a true interval scale. It may be more appropriate to think about the collected data as ordinal. Why? Many interval scales are arbitrary. GPA is an example. Grades vary from teacher to teacher, though the 4.0 scale seems uniform. Time is a better example of a true interval scale. The sample experiment really examines learning style. Data is collected as the number of math problems solved and trigonometry covers a variety of material. Each teacher selects different problems for different tests. The option was available to have participants rate their learning experience on an ordinal scale from 'learning a great deal' to 'learning a little.' However the number of math problems was the choice. Either is appropriate but gives us different interpretations of learning.

You must figure your results without the help of the group. It may seem like entering a huge maze, but statistics have rules for you to follow, so finding your way is manageable. Never give up!
Source; pixabay.com

Results

The results section includes descriptive and inferential statistics. The task is to explain in a short amount of space *why* certain descriptive and inferential statistics are used in data analysis so you will choose the best ones. Calculations are the easy part and formulas are easily accessed on the Internet or from Coolican (2014).

Descriptive Statistics

After raw data are collected, researchers make choices about describing data in a way that makes sense to others. Descriptive statistics organize raw data and are useful tools in the beginning stages of organizing and interpreting it. However, descriptive statistics cannot tell you whether to reject a null hypothesis. An apparent large difference in the scores of the two groups shows *a* difference, not a significant one.

Students are frequently apprehensive about statistics. However, statistics are the easy part as the real challenge is designing a well-controlled study. The experiment's level of measurement guides the choices for descriptive statistics. It is unnecessary and inappropriate to simply calculate all available descriptive statistics. Each measure of central tendency and dispersion has a specific purpose, and you should use the one that best represents your data.

Choosing appropriate descriptive statistics

It is incorrect to litter the results section with mean, median, and mode. The same goes for using range and standard deviation. Choose ONE measure of central tendency and ONE measure of dispersion and learn why they are the best choices. The statistics must be appropriate. Using all three measures of central tendency means the student does not know what they are and when they are appropriate to use.

Each descriptive statistic has a specific purpose and works with the assumptions of a level of measurement. For example, the mean should be used only if you have a normal distribution. Students can easily figure if they have normally distributed data, and even collecting data with an interval level of measurement does not guarantee that it is normally distributed.

The IB rubric says statistics must be "appropriate," so even if you do not have to explain or justify their use, the examiner looks for them to be appropriate. Therefore students must know why the statistics are the right choices. This goes for inferential statistics as well.

Students should report a correct **measure of central tendency**. Measures of central tendency show the central point of a data set. Choose between the **mean, median,** or **mode** depending on the level of measurement. All three are averages, so avoid using the word *average* in a general way. *The mean is best for interval data, the median for ordinal data, and the mode for nominal data.* When students use all three, it is clear that they do not understand the purpose of each. *Littering the results section with irrelevant statistics is incorrect and inappropriate.*

Measure of central tendency	Description
Mean: Interval and ratio data	The mean is the sum of all scores in a data set divided by the number of scores. It is easily affected by extreme scores (the outliers).
Median: Ordinal data	The median is the midpoint and is not affected by extreme scores.
Mode: Nominal data	The mode is the most frequently occurring score. Think of the mode this way: It is the number of people who said yes, said no, or fall into some other category. Most of the nominal data experiments students run contain more than one measure. For example, group A might have eight people who said yes and six people who said no. Group B might have ten people who said yes and four people who said no. The graph shows the yes and no responses from both groups, meaning it has four bars.

Students should include a **graph** representing the appropriate descriptive statistic, such as a bar graph of the median or mean. Graphs should not include raw data or more than one measure of central tendency. You may include the measure of dispersion as well. A sample bar graph is at the end of this section.

Report a correct **measure of dispersion** for the level of measurement. Measures of dispersion show "the degree to which individual scores differ from one another in a data set" (Runyon, et al., 1996, p. 142). If you find level of measurement hard to understand, just follow the chart.

Measure of dispersion	Description
Variation ratio: Nominal	Experiments using nominal levels of measurement have no real measure of dispersion because data are collected in categories, such as the number of people saying yes or no. Dispersion is not something useful for nominal level studies because the categories are not really related to each other (Coolican, 2014). Measures of dispersion are more useful for experiments using ordinal, interval, and ratio levels of measurement where data is really related. However, students can use the **variation ratio** with nominal data to get an idea of how "cases spread across categories" (Coolican, 2014, p. 357). Check Youtube for calculating the VR. Most students want to report dispersion.
Range: Ordinal but it may not the best choice. It is described here so you know why it may not best represent data. Be careful when using the range.	The **range** can be used for experiments using an ordinal level of measurement, meaning the distance between the lowest and highest score, but it is limited because it is easily affected by extreme scores. Just one extreme score can distort the range (Runyon, 1996).

Measure of dispersion	Description
Interquartile range and semi-interquartile range: Ordinal data, especially when there are outliers.	The **interquartile range** and the **semi-interquartile range** are more stable than the range, and are better choices for ordinal levels of measurement where the median is reported (Coolican, 2014). One reason to use these measures is because they are not distorted by extreme scores. Students should not use standard deviation with ordinal level studies! The interquartile range is the range of the middle 50% of scores. The semi-interquartile range is half of the interquartile range. Even if a distribution is skewed, and **skew** refers to whether the distribution is symmetrical, the middle 50% of scores will fall into the semi-interquartile range (Runyon, 1996).
Standard deviation: Interval and ration data	**Standard deviation** is meant for normally distributed data and is best for interval and ratio levels of measurement. The standard deviation represents the "average deviation between the mean and the observed score" (Runyon, 1996, p. 148) and is the square root of the **variance,** or how dispersed scores are from the mean. Accurate use of the mean and the standard deviation requires that data fall on a normal distribution.

Graph showing the medians of the alone and group conditions

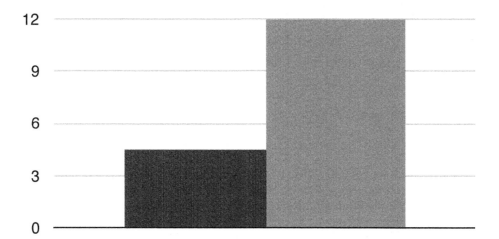

Graph of the medians of the two groups in the sample experiment.

Inferential Statistics:They must be appropriate so students should understand their assumptions

Inferential statistics go beyond describing data. They tell us if there is a **significant difference** between groups or conditions. A noticeable difference between the medians or means of two groups or conditions does not automatically imply that the difference is significant.

An inferential statistics test is the only way to know if a **null hypothesis** can be rejected. Students are interested in whether their hypotheses are correct or not, but there is really no direct way to test them. Instead, inferential statistics test null hypotheses. It may seem strange, but we must assume that the groups or conditions are very similar, the null hypothesis, unless we can show through an inferential test that they are not. Even if you reject the null hypothesis *it does not prove that the hypothesis is correct*. This is consistent with the reality of **probability**. Random errors exist in all social science experiments. It is impossible to be 100% sure that the independent variable (IV) caused change in the dependent variable (DV). Errors are part of all experiments to some degree. Errors might be related to the history of participants. Studying in groups *probably* caused the change in the independent variable in the sample experiment. It is impossible to *prove* that studying in groups caused the change.

Calculating an inferential test provides a **level of significance**. A level of significance is the probability that it was the independent variable, and not chance, that caused the change in the dependent variable. Social science research allows a maximum of 5% error for experiments. Significance levels are reported, for example, as $p < .05$, representing 5% error, or $p < .01$, representing 1% error.

While there are many inferential tests, the following chart identifies the best tests for the types of designs and levels of measurement in experiments manipulating one IV and measuring one DV. Experiment reports include a written summary of inferential test results.

Level of Measurement	Independent Samples	Repeated Measures
Nominal	Chi Square	N/A
Ordinal	Mann-Whitney U	Wilcoxon
Interval/Ratio	T-test for independent groups (unrelated t-test)	T-test for dependent groups (related t-test)

Inferential tests that go with different designs and levels of measurement.

Students think inferential statistics are difficult, but these tests are easy to select and calculate. The choice for an inferential test is determined by the design and level of measurement. Students already have experience using formulas. Some inferential tests can be calculated without a formula, requiring only that data can be ranked and counted. The most difficult part of running an experiment is the design. Once the design is solid, everything falls into place behind it.

The sample experiment uses the Mann-Whitney U test. It is the best choice for small samples, and there is no assumption of a normal distribution. It is a systematic error to choose incorrect statistical tests. Why do I choose the Mann-Whitney U test over the unrelated t test? It has to do with my ultimate choice for level of measurement. This is why it is so important to understand level of measurement and get it right. The choice of an inferential test is easy after you are sure of how you want to define the level of measurement.

Using the t-test: Yes, it is robust but it does have some assumptions that are best not violated!

It is possible to use the t-test even with ordinal level data because it is quite robust, however, students might want to consider if they really want to do this because of the actual assumptions of the t-test. Remember that statistics must be appropriate, so the author's students will not use the t-test unless they fully meet its assumptions.

Using a t-test can be complicated because researchers should not violate any of its assumptions. There is an extra step to complete before calculating a t-test. Data must meet three requirements (Coolican, 2014). If the data does not meet the requirements, go down to an ordinal level test, but remember to say why in your report. Using the t-test inappropriately is an error on the researcher's part and the conclusions may be incorrect.

> **How to decide if an inferential test is appropriate**
> Inferential tests are selected based on the design and level of measurement. In addition, using the t-test requires more information. T-test use is not usually the best choice unless it meets the three assumptions listed in this chapter. If you read on, there are some guidelines that must be explicitly stated if the student wants to use the t-test even if all the assumptions are not met.
>
> ***Do not make the examiner try to guess if your t-test use is appropriate as he or she cannot read your mind.*** Be explicit about choosing an inferential test and letting the reader know why you did so. Note that the novice psychology student should probably avoid problems and not use a t-test without clearly showing it is correct to use.

1. *Data are really at the interval level of measurement.*
2. *Data are from a normal distribution.* If there are extreme scores, then the data are skewed and are unlikely to be normally distributed, and in this case a t test might not be the best choice. The made-made scales used in ordinal level studies present the biggest problem for this assumption (Coolican, 2014), so make sure data are normally distributed or use an ordinal level test.
3. *Check for the homogeneity of variance*, that the variance in different samples coming from the same population is similar. This step is only necessary in experiments using an independent-samples design. Coolican (2014) writes that the homogeneity of variance has the most chance of being a problem if the number of participants in the two groups is very different, such as 5 in one group and 20 in another. Usually students randomly allocate participants evenly to groups, so this third requirement is typically not a problem. One way to see if your data meets this requirement is what Coolican (2014) refers to as a "rough guide," where "one variance is more than four times the value of the other (for small N, i.e.: 10 or fewer) or more than twice the value for larger N" (p. 454). Using this rough guide keeps students from going through lengthy statistical calculations.

When students want to use the t test but their data violates an assumption a little bit, but like the robustness of the t-test, it is possible to use it anyway and just report to readers what the issues are with your data (Coolican, 2014). However, there is nothing wrong with choosing an ordinal level test with what appears to be interval level data, if for example, it is not normally distributed. This is perhaps better suited to students new to psychology. However, using the test when data violates some assumptions requires you to have a very high significance level so others do not criticize you for using the test incorrectly, a choice that may not the best choice for students new to psychology.

36.7: Evaluation of results

All researchers offer evaluations of studies in a discussion. Next is what to include.

Relating findings back to the theory and research in the introduction

How do your findings fit in with the theory and research used in the introduction? This *must be a discussion*, meaning a considered and balanced view. Go beyond saying the findings are similar or different and reflect on why they are similar or different. Differences could relate to characteristics of the sample, the way the IV and DV were operationalized, procedural mistakes, or internal validity threats (go back to the list of 10 threats).

Explain strengths

Explain means to give reasons, so *focus on why* something is a strength. Strengths are best related to the study's control. Review the controls you used when choosing a design and participants, operationalizing the IV and DV, creating materials, running a pilot, and standardizing procedures. This includes running the study in a controlled environment and using standardized instructions. Avoid superficial strengths, such as "we were ethical." It is assumed the study is ethical.

You are almost finished this climb, so persevere and follow these guidelines for considering what your findings mean.
Source: pixabay.com

Explain limitations

Explain limitations next, focusing on why something is a limitation. The best limitations come from design and procedural mistakes that are hard to control or from decisions about design, operationalized definitions, and level of measurement.

The following examples are superficial and could have been avoided with a little foresight and planning. Avoid:

1. Blaming participants, such as saying, "they did not pay attention or care" or "they talked to each other." These are things the researchers should have considered before running the study to control for maturation and diffusion of treatment errors. Errors are more likely to be Type 2 errors anyway, those errors made by the researcher in designing the experiment.
2. Saying, "I wish I had counterbalanced" when using repeated measures as it is expected this is done with good planning and foresight.
3. Saying, "I wish I had not run my study in the school hallway where so many people walked by" or "I wish I had not used two classrooms and tested at different times of the day" because these are poor choices for setting up the study in the first place and should have been considered as a constancy of condition error.

4. The most superficial of all by suggesting a limitation of the study is the lack of a varied and large sample (greater population validity) and the need to have more chances for generalization outside of the setting (greater ecological validity). Both are superficial because the purpose of an experiment is to test theories and not the real world. Read the section about generalizing from studies for greater understanding. Both the sample and the setting should be tightly controlled for maximum internal validity when running a credible experiment.

> **Thinking skills: Experiments do not prove anything**
> Get rid of the word 'prove' from reports! Experiments suggest conclusions but never prove anything. There is always the chance for errors in experiments.

Better limitations follow.
1. Random participant variables that are hard to detect and control could be in the study, even if you find significance. Consider what these might be.
2. If you do not find significance the errors are most likely Type 2 errors and not because of participant behavior.
3. The design itself could be a limitation as each controls just for certain things. A different design might have led to a different outcome.
4. The way the IV and DV are operationalized could be a limitation.
5. The level of measurement used in the study is another potential limitation as each level of measurement means collecting data differently and using different types of statistics.
6. Although all students should pilot their materials and procedures before running the experiment, a pilot does not always eliminate all the errors, partially because they are run on different participants. For example, many of the author's students ran several pilots and still found errors in the amount of time given to the real participants. These are errors that students worked hard to eliminate, but are still Type 2 errors in the study. This is the reality of designing experiments that professionals must manage all the time.

Credible modifications

Modifications should be linked to the limitations and are clearly justified, meaning reasons are given for them. If students use examples from the list of better limitations above, modifications are credible and meaningful.

Resist the urge to include greater ecological or population validity as modifications as these are superficial and never belong in an evaluation. Just do not mention either.

Example evaluations for the sample study

There are numerous relevant evaluations for the sample experiment. Significance was found with the pretend data using the Mann-Whitney U test.

1. "The results are consistent with the existing body of research on gender differences in mathematics education". Students are expected to relate their findings back to the studies in the introduction. Are the findings similar or different from the reviewed studies? If different, why do you think you found something dissimilar? This is a good place to analyze the descriptive and inferential statistics.
2. "Even with a significance level of .001, there is still a small probability that chance caused the change in the dependent variable." This may be due to random participant variables. Are

participant variables left uncontrolled? One participant variable left uncontrolled in the sample study is self-efficacy level. It is possible that girls with low self-efficacy levels learn differently than those with high self-efficacy levels. Ethical concerns make it difficult to separate girls based on efficacy level or to test efficacy level after the introduction of an IV. However, it is a potential issue for studying this topic and should be researched in the future.

3. Are there any problems with the design of the experiment? Selecting any design has limitations. Researchers choose a design because it offers them the most control, noting that the design left other things uncontrolled. It is hoped that the researcher's procedures addressed any weaknesses.

For example, selecting a repeated measures design controls for history, but then adds a potential order effect. A careful researcher counterbalances to reduce chances of order effects. Research design is an art form and it is impossible to design an experiment that controls everything. For example, the sample study does not fully control for history. Consider the list of threats to interval validity.

> **Alternative conclusions**
> There are always **alternative conclusions** for any study, and these might come from random participant variables or any unaccounted for variable, such as low self-efficacy from viewing parent models related to math competence in the case of the sample study.

4. If there is not a significant difference between the two groups or conditions and the null hypothesis is accepted, it is likely because of design mistakes, the type 2 errors.

It is unlikely that the sample is at fault. Participant behavior during the experiment is an unlikely reason for insignificance. Perhaps what was different about the two groups or conditions was not different enough. Did the researcher control all threats to internal validity, such as diffusion of treatment? Suggesting that a larger sample be used in future research will not necessarily correct the problem. Instead, large and varied samples can introduce unwanted confounding variables into the study.

5. What about the design or level of measurement? Would using different ones change the outcome? It is possible to use a repeated measures design as long as it is counterbalanced because then participant variables might bot have interfered with the study. This level of measurement was ordinal, but what if data were collected at an interval level?

Appendices: What to include?
Label each appendix starting with Appendix A: Informed consent, and make sure the labels are marked within the report when writing about materials and procedures. This way an examiner can easily follow your work.
1. Informed consent form
2. Parent consent if using participants under 16
3. Briefing statement
4. Debriefing statement
5. Standardized instructions
6. Materials: Include slideshows, pictures, a questionnaire, link to a video, or anything else used. Include the answer keys and a note about how materials are scored.
7. Raw data charts
8. Calculations of inferential statistics (perhaps include calculations of descriptive statistics just to make sure an examiner does not get upset if they are missing)

36.8: Generalizing from Experiments

Because generalization is a difficult but important topic, next is a list of points to consider as you examine the meaning of an experiment's results. Avoid wanting to generalize the results of any single study.

1. Students frequently overgeneralize the results of experiments.
2. Students must accept that any single experiment has limited generalizibility.
3. Generalization is affected by the conditions of the study, meaning ecological validity, the characteristics of the sample, meaning population validity, and the way that the independent and dependent variables are operationalized.
4. Ecological validity of experiments is typically low. This is because experiments are artificial. Experiments test theories, not the real world. Artificiality is not a valid criticism of experiments. Watch criticizing a study for doing what it is supposed to do.
5. Experiment is the only method that tests cause and effect. To see if one variable (the IV) causes another to change (the DV), all the other variables that might affect the DV must be controlled.
6. Control in experiments is a strength. If an experiment is not well controlled, meaning it has poor internal validity, it will *never* have any external validity.
7. The population validity of experiments is also generally low. Samples must be tightly controlled so that participant variables do not confound the study. Since most experiments use opportunity samples, we cannot be sure that they represent a larger target population. These non-representative samples *may* represent a larger population, but it is not certain. In a strictly statistical sense, only samples selected through representative samples really represent a larger target population. However, these target populations are usually fairly narrow, as it is difficult to get a sample that represents too large of a group.
8. Check to see how the IV and the DV are operationalized. Any generalization outside of the study is limited to situations with the same definitions.
9. Researchers realize that experiments are artificial and use controlled samples. They are not making errors when they create artificial research situations.

So then what conclusions can we draw about experiments?

10. It is inappropriate to make too many generalizations based on one experiment.
11. Instead, experiments should be **replicated** by others using different samples. If the results are similar, then we can make more generalizations. Is the experiment part of a larger body of research that points in the same direction? Observer and method triangulation are important. Perhaps independent researchers replicate the experiment and find the same thing, called **observer triangulation**. Perhaps independent researchers design studies using other research methods, sometimes following successful experiments, and find the same thing, called **method triangulation**. Triangulation takes care of the limitations of any single experiment.
12. Ultimately, researchers hope to generalize their findings because constructing theories that explain behavior are the whole point of conducting psychological research.
13. A good way to evaluate a single study is to ask: "Is the experiment well controlled?" It is not appropriate to evaluate an experiment by suggesting that it get greater ecological or population validity. In effect, you are then suggesting that the experiment become uncontrolled, defeating the purpose of experiments.

36.9: Triangulation in Experiments

Triangulation ensures there is enough evidence to make valid claims. Triangulation shows the richness and complexity of behavior by studying theories from more than one viewpoint. Psychologists have greater certainty about their findings if similar findings emerge from research using other methods, different samples, or different data sources.

Triangulation was first considered for use in studies using quantitative methods, so separate triangulation appropriate for experiments from triangulation appropriate for qualitative studies.

Triangulation is "the use of two or more methods of data collection in the study of some aspect of human behavior" (Cohen, Marion, & Morrison, 2000, p. 233). Five types of interest to this course follow.

Type of triangulation	Description
Method triangulation	This means that a theory is investigated using a variety of experimental and nonexperimental methods. The multimethod approach stands in contrast to the single-method approaches of some historical theorists. Single-method verification is limited. The works of Freud, Skinner, and Piaget are examples. Much of their work is outdated because of mistakes with single-method verification strategies, called being method bound. Freud incorrectly generalized his findings to all people from case studies of Victorian females with mental disorders. Skinner incorrectly made generalizations about human complex behavior from simple animal experiments. Piaget observed his three children and came up with a general cognitive development theory. Modern psychology validates theory through a variety of research strategies, including experiments, ethnographies, and correlation studies. Research about the causes of aggression is an example of a topic with a large amount of method triangulation. For some types of research questions, such as those asking for specific causes, psychologists believe that experiments must be done first and then validated through non-experimental methods. For example, Bandura (1973) writes that researchers cannot claim to know anything about the causes of aggression without first isolating potential causal variables in tightly controlled lab experiments. Experiment results should be confirmed through other types of research, such as ethnographies studying aggression in the natural environment.
Time triangulation	Sometimes research is gathered during one specific time in history or certain topics are popular only for specific time periods. Time triangulation ensures that the time is not the reason for research results. Using both **cross-sectional data**, meaning data gathered at one time, and **longitudinal** data, meaning data gathered over time, increases time triangulation. Examples of topics with high levels of time triangulation are aggression, language, and genetic studies of low response to alcohol and depression.
Observer triangulation, or investigator triangulation	Examples of topics with a high level of observer triangulation include narratives, a special kind of story that helps children learn about their culture that is part of the research on language, and the contribution of the serotonin transporter gene (5-HTT) to depression. When research is **replicated** by an independent researcher, observer triangulation is increased.

Type of triangulation	Description
Theory triangulation	Theory triangulation is increased when two similar theories have support or when two or more theories are sometimes combined to create a more comprehensive theory. Lev Vygotsky's and Jerome Bruner's language theories are similar and are backed up by a large amount of research. The General Aggression Model (GAM) (Anderson and Bushman, 2002) combines social cognitive theory with other theories to create a more complex account of aggression.
Space triangulation	If a theory is studied in only one culture it lacks space triangulation. Culture is an important determinant of behavior. Look for cross-cultural verification of a theory. Cross-cultural psychology has made many concepts conceived and studied in the West relevant for everyone. Conformity and Social Identity Theory are examples. Look to see if a psychological concept has been studied cross culturally.

Advantages of triangulation follows.

1. Triangulation reduces experimenter bias.
2. Triangulation gives a broader and complex causation model of behavior.
3. Triangulation reduces **method-bound theories**.
4. Triangulation reduces **culture-bound theories**, meaning that some entire theories are based on the observation of one culture.

TOK Link: For the IB Student

Triangulation is important because it helps researchers avoid incorrect conclusions from using just one research method to study behavior. Too often important details that cannot be studied with one method can be seen in another for a complete understanding. Triangulation also allows results to be conformed.

Appendices

Appendix #1: Self-management: The sleep challenge

The sleep challenge can be done as a class activity or for **CAS** (IB). Students sometime scoff at the suggestion they get more sleep as a way to get better grades, perform better at sport competitions, and remain healthy, but should think twice about ignoring the facts.

Before tackling this project students might become inquirers and look into the research for themselves. They might look up researchers such as William Dement and Mary Carskadon, and also look into research about the effect of having electronics in the bedroom on adolescent sleep. Avoid reading blogs and social media because these are not credible sources for information. Look at pubmed.gov for published research. Type in Mary Carskadon's name for free articles.

Background and guidelines follow.

It is clearly documented that adolescents need eight or more hours of sleep each night, with nine and a quarter as the ideal. Sleep deprivation effects include lowered immunity, irritability, decreased attention, and decreased memory consolidation. People often say sleep deprivation does not affect them but the research shows otherwise.

Students should document 8 hours of sleep each night, including weekends. Depending on your current level of deprivation, you may feel drowsy until your sleep debt is paid back, a term used by William Dement. "We discovered that the effect of each successive night of partial sleep carried over, and the effects appeared to accumulate in a precisely additive fashion" (Dement, 1999, p. 60). This means that if you sleep six hours each night, you will feel progressively tired each day, even with the same six hours of sleep. To feel normal again you must make up the lost hours of sleep. Although you might feel a little better after catching up on some sleep, the rest of the debt is still there and must be paid. You will know when it is paid and this varies by individual.

Dement recommends keeping a sleep diary. Document your sleep and wake times for a week and how you felt throughout the day for a week before starting the challenge. Judge your progress against this baseline data during the challenge. After paying back the sleep debt you will feel more alert in the morning, more relaxed, and better able to manage stress.

You may have to reorganize your life to get enough sleep but this is a good self-management exercise promoting good time management and study habits. This is good practice for a balanced life.

During the challenge keep a log with the sleep and wake times and how you feel throughout the day. Students and parents should sign the log each day. *Naps do not count toward the eight hours*. You should not need a nap and it might interfere with going to bed at a decent time.

There are cases where entire families have taken the sleep challenge together!

Appendix #2: The psychology of terrorism

This lesson is a logical extension of studying **Social Identity Theory** and **Social Cognitive Theory**. Students have a chance to apply their knowledge to a troubling and growing global problem.

Albert Bandura on Terrorism: Agency and moral disengagement to use the highest forms of aggression

One must **morally disengage** to commit a **terrorist act** (Bandura, 2001).

Humans are agents of their behavior, meaning people judge their actions as right or wrong against certain standards and self-regulate behavior accordingly. These standards come from a variety of sources.

1. Personal ideals
2. Situational circumstances
3. The anticipation of reinforcement from others viewed as more capable. Sometimes we give **proxy control** for our behavior standards to another. Leaders determine accepted behavior in terrorist groups.
4. The anticipation of reinforcement from the larger cultural group. Bandura believes that a group's ideology maintains behavior far more than biology. Adults teach accepted standards to children early.

Humans are self-directed and make choices to meet goals. Persons in both **individualistic** and **collectivistic** cultures are self-directed, though the standards for choices vary. Moral standards mostly come from childhood teachings.

Morals are fairly stable over time. Core moral values do not change on a regular basis. This is why moral disengagement is required for someone to commit a terrorist act.

Most of the research on moral disengagement examines military and political aggression (Bandura, 2004). Because of this limited focus, it may appear that moral disengagement happens only in extreme circumstances. In reality, moral disengagement is part of everyday life. Think of moral disengagement in terms of *degrees*. Terrorism is extreme disengagement, but moral disengagement also takes place in corporate misbehavior, politics, and personal relationships. There are plenty of examples where typically honest people further their own interests at the expense of others. Telling a lie to a friend, cheating on one's income taxes, or giving and accepting insider information about a company stock all require disengagement from moral beliefs against lying and cheating. Disengaging requires justifying the behavior, which Bandura calls **self-exonerations**.

People can choose humane behavior or inhumane behavior, even in the face of extreme circumstances (Bandura, 2001). There are many examples where even under severe pressure, many choose strongly held moral convictions to behave humanely, even receiving punishment for these actions. Deviating from core moral standards requires mental disengagement.

Committing terrorist acts killing many people by blowing up buses or flying planes into buildings need special training that builds on childhood modeling. Terrorist training includes morally justifying these actions (Bandura, 2004). For example, Bin Laden portrayed the attacks on the U.S. as a religious duty, a defensive jihad.

There are many ways to psychologically disengage (Bandura, 2001). They are part of everyday life as well as terrorist training. Again, these take place in *degrees*.

1. The behavior is cognitively restructured. Here are three examples of the process.
    A. The behavior is framed as socially or morally worthy.
    B. Euphemistic language makes the behavior seem appropriate. This means that words making an action seem inoffensive are substituted for distasteful words. Bandura (2004) uses the example of bombs being called "vertically deployed anti-personal devices." People are more likely to commit aggressive acts if the acts are called something else.
    C. **Advantageous comparisons** justify behavior by making a comparison with worse behavior. Here is an everyday example you might use with your parents. If you do something wrong it is easy to say, "Mom, be happy I am not a drug dealer." It might defuse the situation but is still an advantageous comparison. At an extreme level, some terrorist groups feel they are less of a problem than other groups because they attack only military targets. Terrorists sometimes minimize their cruelty by saying it is a way to end the worse cruelty of the existing government (Bandura, 2004). Counterterrorist activities are often justified by claims that they must use violence to end the attacks of terrorists. Each side minimizes their cruelty and condemns the other side, citing their "just causes". It is a dilemma for groups wanting to use military retaliation against a terrorist act. Moral disengagement must be high for citizens to support the policies.

2. A person lessens their personal responsibility for an action by displacing the responsibility.
3. A person minimizes or challenges the effects of their behavior on others.
4. The victim is dehumanized. Dehumanizing another involves giving them animal qualities or blaming them for bringing on their own suffering.
5. Terrorist activities sometimes have the support from legitimate organizations that may provide indirect support for the violence, such as providing financial assistance.

No quick fixes exist for terrorism. Solutions include addressing social situations that drive people to commit terrorist acts. For example, "Islamic terrorists come mainly from populations living in an environment of poverty, political oppression, gross inequities, illiteracy, and a paucity (means a lack of) of opportunities to improve their lives" (Bandura, 2004, p. 150). Islamic terrorists learned to value suicide bombing from early childhood. It is not easy to reverse values instilled in childhood.

Appendix #3: Internal Assessment: Experiment topic recommendations

All of my students use the following text for background theory. Background theory can also be found in the primary sources listed. The 7th edition was published by Sternberg in 2016.

Sternberg, R. J. & Sternberg, K. (2012). *Cognitive psychology* (6th Ed.). Belmont, CA: Wadsworth.

Topic#1 Eyewitness memory

Foster, J. F., Huthwaite, T., Yesberg, J. A., Garry, M., & Loftus, E. F. (2012). Repetition, not the number of sources, increases both susceptibility to misinformation and confidence in the accuracy of eyewitnesses. *ACTA Psychologica,* 139, 320-326.

Loftus, E. F., Burns, H. J., & Miller, D. G. (1978). Semantic integration of verbal information into a visual memory. *Journal of Experimental Psychology,* 4(1), 19-31.

Loftus, E. F. & Palmer, J. C. (1974). Reconstruction of an automobile destruction: an example of the interaction between language and memory. *Journal of Verbal Learning and Memory,* 13, 585-589.

Topic #2 Short-term memory store: storage of visual memory

Lee, D. & Chun, M. M. (2001). What are the units of visual short-term memory for objects or spatial locations? *Perception and Psychophysics,* 63(2), 253-257.

Luck, S. J.& Vogel, E. K. (1997). The capacity of visual working memory for features and conjunctions. *Nature,* 390, 279-281.

Vogel, E. K., Woodman, G. F., & Luck, S. J. (2001). Storage of features, conjunctions, and objects in visual working memory, *Journal of Experimental Psychology,* 27(1), 92-114.

Topic #3: Ambiguous figures

Chambers, D. & Reisberg, D. (1985). Can mental images be ambiguous? *Journal of Experimental Psychology: Human Perception and Performance,* 11(3), 317-328.

Goolkasian, P. & Woodberry, C. (2010). Priming effects with ambiguous figures. *Attention, Perception, & Psychophysics,* 72(1), 168-178.

Peterson, M. A., Kihlstrom, J. F., & Glisky, M. L. (1992). Mental images can be ambiguous: reconstruals and reference-frame reversals. *Memory and Cognition,* 20(2), 107-123.

Topic #4: Heuristics

Epley, N. & Gilovich, T. (2006). The anchoring and adjustment heuristic. *Psychological Science,* 17(4), 311-318.

Strack, F. & Mussweiler, T. (1997). Explaining the enigmatic anchoring effect: mechanisms of selective accessibility. *Attitudes and Social Cognition,* 73(3), 437-446.

Tversky, A. & Kahneman, D. (1974). Judgment under uncertainty: heuristics and biases. *Science: New Series,* 185(4157), 1124-1131.

Tversky, A. & Kahneman, D. (1973). Availability: a heuristic for judging frequency and probability. *Cognitive Psychology,* 207-232.

Topic #5: Stroop Effect

Algom, D., Dekel, A., & Pansky, A. (1996). The perception of number from the separability of the stimulus: the Stroop effect revisited. *Memory and Cognition,* 24(5), 557-572.

Bugg, J. M. & Jacoby, L. L. (2008). Multiple levels of control in the Stroop task. *Memory and Cognition,* 36(8),1485-1494.

MacLeod, C. M. (1991). Half a century of research on the Stroop effect: An integrative review. *Psychological Bulletin,* 109(2), 163-203.

Stroop, J. R. (1935). Studies of interference in serial verbal reactions. *Journal of Experimental Psychology,* 18, 643-662.

Topic #6: Some great memory studies
Baddeley, A. D. (1966). Short-term memory for word sequences as a function of acoustic, semantic, and formal similarity. *Quarterly Journal of Experimental Psychology,* 362-365.

Craig, F. I. M. & Tulving, E. (1975). Depth of processing and the retention of words in episodic memory. *Journal of Experimental Psychology: General,* 103(3), 268-294. (make sure to manipulate an IV!)

Kahana, M. J. & Howard, M. W. (2005). Spacing and lag effects in free recall of pure lists. *Psychonomic Bulletin and Review,* 12(1), 159-164.

Roedier, H. L. (1980). The effectiveness of four mnemonics in ordering recall. *Journal of Experimental Psychology,* 6(5), 558-567.

Tulving, E. & Osler, S. (1968). Effectiveness of retrieval cues in memory for words. *Journal of Experimental Psychology,* 77(4), 593-601.

Tulving, E. (1962). Subjective organization in free recall of unrelated words. *Psychological Review,* 69(4), 344-354.

Topic #7: Top-down processing and schema
Bransford, J. D. & Johnson, M. K. (1972) Contextual prerequisites for understanding: some investigations of comprehensions and recall. *Journal of Verbal Learning and Memory,* 11, 717-726.

Palmer, S. E. (1975). The effects of contextual scenes on the identification of objects. *Memory and Cognition,* 3(5), 519-526.

Appendix #4: Extended Essay (EE) in Psychology

This section is about writing good research questions (RQ), the key to starting an extended essay.

Too often students assume that psychology EEs are easy and are attracted to vague and exotic topics. Examples of vague RQs include:

1. What are the biological causes of depression?
2. Why do we dream?

Dreaming is one of those exotic topics attracting students that are hard to narrow and perhaps impossible to answer. I recommend staying away from such topics. The one about biological causes of depression is so vague and broad that it cannot be managed in 4000 words. Abnormal psychology topics are not recommended as they are very complex and require more time and effort than a student has. This is stated in the EE guide, so please have students read it carefully.

Good RQs have the following qualities.

1. They are narrow.
2. They are operationalized.
3. They are worthy of study, are timely, and have great significance.
4. The student can show that at least 10 primary sources are available on the topic that are credible and manageable for the student.
5. They are of great interest to the student.
6. The topic is doable, meaning the student can tackle the topic with a reasonable amount of research.

I recommend that teachers avoid trying to find topics for students as the EE is the student's investigation. Teachers act as guides and are not partners on the project. After hearing a good general topic idea I often refer students to an article to get their research started but they must follow through with finding appropriate sources. I approve all the sources before students start writing.

Examples of excellent EE research questions
What are the merits of the claim that transcendental meditation positively impacts student grades and stress reduction in US middle school students?
To what extent does playing chess improve cognitive abilities?
To what extent should parents raise their children to be gender aschematic?
What is the role of prenatal nutrition in breaking the cycle of bad eating choices over a lifespan?
To what extent is athlete burnout caused by internal cognitions?
To what extent does education affect memory decline in aging adults?
How does the cultural dimension individualism-collectivism impact corporate success?
To what extent are the imagery techniques used by elite athletes effective?
What is the relationship between juror attributes and their verdicts?
What are the merits of the claim that eating a healthy breakfast improves standardized testing in elementary students?
What is the relationship between women's breast cancer progression and their personality?
What are the risks versus the benefits of using pharmaceutical cognitive enhancements Adderall and Ritalin in healthy individuals?
What are the merits of the claim that the interests of males and females contribute to the amount of female STEM professionals in the workplace?
What is the relationship between social acceptance and belonging as a result of transracial adoption?
How are adolescent sleep patterns disturbed by the use of electronics during evening hours prior to sleep?
To what extent is Melodic Intonation Therapy effective in helping Aphasia patients recover language?
How do children and adolescents who experience forced-migration use acculturation strategies to adapt to new cultural norms?

Appendix #5: Replication in studies

To increase thinking skills and conceptual understanding, students should critically consider the term **replication**. This section is a broad summary of the replicability project and a challenge to it. Students should read the article or at least the summary attached to it as well as the challenge to its conclusions.

Replication is a critical feature of science. It means that different scientists use the same procedures with a different sample in a different setting to see if the same outcome is found.

Replication makes a study credible rather than the authority of a researcher (Open Science Collaboration, 2015). Replication creates a body of research that increases reliability, the consistency between study findings that lets us know if a theory can be supported and if a study conclusion is generalizable.

The **aim of the replicability project** was to estimate the number of psychology studies that were reproducible using a sample of 100 experiments and correlations (Open Science Collaboration, 2015). The team was intrigued with why many attempted replications fail and set out to see for themselves just how many claims about replication were accurate.

Results showed that although 97% of the original studies reported significance, just 36% of the attempted replications did. The weaker findings existed even when using strict replications using materials from the original author, exact procedures, and robust statistical analysis.

Questions for reflection

If students take the replicability project at face value and accept it, the conclusions challenge the assumption that psychologists have a credible scientific understanding of human behavior! Do most psychology studies really have little ability to support a theory or generalize as part of a reported body of research? This is an extreme position and good critical thinkers know that extreme positions are hard to defend.

Inquiry: Examples in this book

1. Chapter 7 includes Caspi's correlation between the ss alleles and reactivity to stress, something that is a risk for depression. Caspi claims to have about 40 independent replications. Do some research and see for yourself. You can start with his website moffittcaspi.com.
2. For the topic in-groups and out-groups, chapter 18 includes the original Asch conformity study. It also includes a replication that is similar but not a strict replication from Matsuda and then a strict replication from Takano. Consider these three studies in light of the replicability project. The chapter has enough detail so you can see the original procedures and, for example, how Matsuda changed them.

A challenge to the replicability project

An examination of the methods and statistics used in the replicability project finds that the Open Science Collaboration got it wrong and psychology studies are highly reproducible (Gilbert, King, Pettigrew, & Wilson, 2016).

Again, students can read this article or can read a summary from an article titled *"Study that undercut psych research got it wrong" from the Harvard Gazette*. Google the title as this summary is more student friendly.

The authors uncovered numerous flaws in the replicability project and examples are next.

1. Participants were typically not new samples from the same population, and were different from the original in many ways.
2. Procedures often differed in ways that introduced confounding subject variables into the studies. For example, one original study used Stanford University students in the US discussing admission policy and the replication used Dutch students watching US student speaking in English far away from their culture. It is puzzling that the Open Science Collaboration seemed to know that running the study with

Dutch students might be a problem and ran another study using US students that replicated the original. However, the one showing replication was not used in the estimation of reproducibility!

3. Many of the attempted replication used procedures that failed to be identical to the original studies and these were 4 times more likely to fail.

The article is worth reading simply because it helps students get some perspective about attacks on psychology and what is involved in replicating research. We must have a healthy skepticism and realize that a body of research does not always include exact replications.

Ending comments

High schools students cannot get bogged down in all the statistical errors reported in both the Open Science Collaboration or in the challenge study (unless you want a big challenge). Just realize that psychology studies never prove anything, they can contain error, and a body of research can be created even if they are not all strict replications.

Psychology theories and studies show us tendencies about human behavior, not truths. Psychology theories evolve over time and change with new research building on previous studies. Some topics studied in this book represent about 30 years of research to understand the topic, such as Marc Schuckit's work on genetic risk for alcoholism, so careful replications and extensions are part of the process.

From the start of this book I emphasize the need to create a global psychology, and this means to make sure that theories and studies created and studied in the West also apply to others. Research about conformity is a good example. Doing this increases the credibility of psychology theory.

Come away from this discussion with a healthier and more realistic view of science. There is no need to throw psychology out of the window because of the replicability project!

TOK link for the IB student

The replicability project is a good topic to discuss in a TOK class. Replication is a cornerstone of science, and if we cannot replicate, how can we have a credible science? An extension is to discuss how replication is done within the natural sciences and compare it with psychology.

Appendix #6: Developing critical thinking and reading

The new IB psychology syllabus focuses on critical thought and developing a course to meet these needs can be challenging.

Many students focus their attention on telling you everything they know, concerned at getting all the facts down on paper, and then feel frustrated when this approach produces mediocre marks. When writing, student can feel pressured to get something tacked onto the end of an essay or at the end of study facts that might count as critical thought.

The end result can be students developing "**formulas**" to use with all answers, such as saying something general about ethics or pointing out that an experiment has low ecological validity. Unfortunately, these formulas are easily spotted by examiners and contribute to mediocre marks, frustrating students and their teachers. It is perhaps a developmental issue with this age group to focus on facts and to feel uneasy at moving past their comfort zone into higher levels of critical thinking.

Regardless of what students present to us at the start of the course, it is our job as teachers to gently push students to new levels of critical thought that will lead to higher marks and higher levels of learning.

A useful strategy is to use Vygotsky's **zone of proximal development** in the classroom. Students can memorize and regurgitate facts on their own, but the teacher can create new zones of development, constantly shifting students to higher levels.

One way to do this is to focus on critical reading. The author's students read everything in class the first time to ensure that it is done slowly and deliberately rather than hastily and skimmed late at night. There is plenty of time to get through the material while doing this. Three ideas come to mind.

1. Read with your students, particularly with the more difficult parts of the syllabus. For example, sometimes we do large group read-alouds, where each student reads a paragraph and the teacher comments on the finer points that students might miss on their own. The teacher is a model for learning to pick out and focus on important points. As students develop they can take turns leading the large group reading.

2. Read in small groups of three. The first student reads a paragraph, the second student says what he or she heard and thought was important, and the third student decides what they should takes notes on. Shift the roles with each paragraph. It slows down the reading and forces students to concentrate on thinking about it.

3. Use a critical thinking jigsaw. Small groups can be assigned a command term, and they process the material with that term. Students then jigsaw with others to get ideas about how to use other command terms with the same material. Last, students meet back with their original group to put everything together. Many other jigsaws can be done.

> **Choosing what to read**
> The teacher should be selective about what to read in this book. It is designed to have detailed depth and for students to see how critical thought and activities emerge from the content.
>
> Choose your option(s) first and then as you read, focus on the choices related to the options when choices are available.
>
> All the chapters titled knowledge and understanding contain background material that is not directly tested, but is there so students have the information needed for the testable topics. You may not need all of this background material so choose wisely. The material is here if you want it, and it keeps teachers and students from having to seek out relevant background material.

A huge benefit of class critical reading is that besides ensuring it is done, the practice allows the critical thought to emerge and be noticed as such. **The best critical thought emerges from in-depth content, so consider teaching a content rich class.** I frequently hear teachers say they have to sacrifice content to teach skills, and I wonder why they think this. The two really go together. When reading content rich materials, *relevant* critical thought emerges naturally, and it differs from topic to topic and study to study.

Students might learn something general about ethics and research methods at the start of the course (in chapter one) so they can read knowing to look for these things. As students read, the relevant evaluations of ethics and research methods emerge. For example, sometimes authors highlight particular ethical concerns with a study or say that alternative explanations keep us from having a particular view about a topic. Sometimes researchers highlight special controls they played on the studies or highlight replication in their work.

This book takes a content rich approach and helps students develop real critical thought so a general formula is then seen as superficial by students. Practice drawing multidirectional models to show the interactions between the approaches to behavior to reduce oversimplification.

If students want any hint of a formula from studying this book, it **should be to ask if a topic has cross-cultural relevance**. To what extent are we moving to a more developed and culturally relevant global psychology that applies to all?

References

Abbo, C. (2010). *Traditional Healers and Mental Health Problems in Uganda.* Saarbrucken, Germany: Lambert Academic Publishing.

Abbo, C, Okello, E. S., Musisi, S., Waako, P., & Ekbad, E. (2012). Naturalistic outcome of treatment of psychosis by traditional healers in Jinga and Iganga districts, Eastern Uganda- a 3 and 6 months follow up. *International Journal of Mental health Systems,* 6: 13, 1-11.

Abbo, C., Ekbad, E., Waako, P., Okello, E. S., & Musisi, S. (2009). The prevalence and severity of mental illnesses handled by traditional healers in two districts in Uganda. *African Health Sciences,* 9 (1), 16-22.

About Healthy People (2010). Available from www.healthypeople.gov/2020/about/default.aspx.

Adelson, R. (2005). Lessons from H.M. *American Psychological Association: Monitor on Psychology,* 36(8), 1.

Agudelo, L. Z., Femenia, T., Ohran, F., Porsmyr-Palmertz, M., Goiny, M., Martinez-Redondo, V. . . . & Ruas, J. L. (2014). Skeletal muscle PGC-1∝1 modulates kynurenine metabolism and mediates resilience to depression to stress-induced depression. *Cell,* 159, 33-45.

Ainsworth, M. D. S. (1973). The development of infant-mother attachment. In. B. Caldwell & H. Ricciuti (Eds.), *Review of Child Development Research,* Vol. 3, 1-94. Chicago: University of Chicago Press.

Ainsworth, M.D. & Bell, S. M. (1970). Attachment, exploration, and separation: illustrated by the behavior of one-year-olds in a strange situation. *Child Development,* 41, 49-677.

Alcololism-Statistics.com. (2009). Alcoholism and teen statistics. www.alcoholism-statistics.com/teend.php.

Alexander, G. M. & Saenz, J. (2012). Early androgens, activity levels and toy choices of children in the second year of life. *Hormones and Behavior,* 62, 500-504.

Alexander, G. M., Wilcox, T., & Woods, R. (2009). Sex differences in infant's visual interest in toys. *Archives of Sexual Behavior,* 38, 427-433.

Alexander, G. M. & Hines, M. (2002). Sex differences in response to children's toys in nonhuman primates. *Evolution and Human Behavior,* 23, 467-479.

Advameg, Inc, (2015). Epinephrine. Retrieved from www.medicaldiscoveries.com.

Ajzen, I. (2013). Consumer attitudes and behavior: the theory of planned behavior applied to food consumption decisions. *Rivista di Economia Agraria, Anno LXX,* 2, 121-138.

Ajzen, I. (2012). The theory of planned behavior. In P. A. M. Lange, A. W. Kruglanski, & E. T. Higgins, (Eds.). *Handbook of Theories of Social Psychology, Vol. 1,* p. 438-459. London: Sage Publications.

Alcoholism-Statistics.com. (2009). Alcoholism in the population. alcoholstatistics.com/facts.php.

Ambady, N. & Freeman, J. B. (2014). The cultural neuroscience of human perception. In M. S. Gazzaniga & G. R. Mangun, Eds. *The Cognitive Neurosciences,* 5th Ed. Cambridge, MA: MIT Press.

American College Health Association (2010). Available from http://www.acha.org/info_resources/hc2010.cfm.

American Academy of Pediatrics (2016). Media and children. Retrieved from www.aap.org/en-us/advocacy-and-policy/aap-health-initiatives/Pages/Media-and-child.

American Psychiatric Association. (2013). Diagnostic and Statistical Manual of Mental Disorders, Fifth Edition. Washington, D.C., American Psychiatric Publishing.

American Psychiatric Association, (2000). Diagnostic and Statistical Manual of Mental Disorders, Fourth Edition, Text Revision. Washington, D.C., American Psychiatric Association.

American Psychological Association (2015). Ethical principles of psychologists and code of conduct. Available from www.apa.org/ethics/code/.

American Psychological Association (2015). APA review confirms link between playing violent video games and aggression. Available from www.pa.org.

Anderson, C. A., & Bushman, B. J. (2002). Human aggression. *Annual Review of Psychology.* 53. 27-51.

Anderson, C.A. & Anderson, K. B. (1996). Violent crime rate studies in philosophical context: a destructive testing approach to heat and Southern culture of violent effects. *Journal of Personality and Social Psychology,* 70, 740-756.

Angel, R. J. & Williams, K. (2013). Cultural models of health and illness. In Paniagua, F. A. & Yamada, A. M., (Eds.), *Handbook of Multicultural Mental Health,* 2nd Ed., Amsterdam, Elsevier.

Annesi, J. J. & Gorjala, S. (2010). Relationship of self-regulation and self-efficacy for exercise and eating and BMI change: A field investigation. *BioPsychoSocial Medicine*, 4: 10, 1-6.

Argas, W. S., Lock, J., Brandt, H., Bryson, S. W., Dodge, E., Halmi, K. A.,…& Woodside, B. (2014). Comparison of 2 family therapies for adolescent anorexia nervosa: a randomized trial. *JAMA Psychiatry,* 71 (11), 1279-86.

Arthur, S. & Nazroo, J. (2003). Designing fieldwork strategies and materials. In J. Ritchie & J. Lewis, Eds. *Qualitative Research Practice.* London: Sage Publications.

Arger, C., Sanchez, O., Simonson, J., & Mezulis, A. (2012). Pathways to depressive symptoms in young adults: examining affective, self-regulatory, and cognitive vulnerability factors. *Psychological Report,* 111(2): 335-348.

Aronson, E., Wilson, T. D., & Akert, R. M. (2007). *Social Psychology,* 6th edition. Upper Saddle River, NJ: Pearson Prentice Hall.

Asch, S. E. (1956). Studies of independence and conformity: I. A minority of one against a unanimous majority. *Psychological Monographs: General and Applied.* 70 (9), Whole No. 416), 1-70.

Astington, J. W. & Hughes, C. (2013). Theory of mind: self-reflection and social understanding. In P. D. Zelazo, (Ed.), *The Oxford Handbook of Developmental Psychology.* Oxford: Oxford University Press.

Atkinson, R. C. & Shiffrin, R. M. (1968). Human memory: a proposed system and its control processes. In K. W. Spence & J. T. Spence, (Eds.). *The Psychology of Learning and Motivation, Vol. 2., Advances in Research and Theory.* New York: Academic Press.

Australian Academy of Science (2006). Epigenetics— beyond genes. *Nova Science in the News.*   www.scienceorg.au/nova/098/098key.htm.

Avants, B. B., Hackman, D. A., Betancourt, L. M., Lawson, G. M., Hurt, H. & Farah, M. J. (2015). Relation of childhood home environment to cortical thickness in late adolescence: Specificity of experience and timing. *PLOS ONE,* 1-10.

Azar, B. (2000, April). Online experiments: ethically foul or fair? *Monitor on Psychology.* 31(4).

Baddeley, A. (2009). Working memory. In A. Baddeley, M. W. Eysenck, & M. C. Anderson (Eds.), *Memory.* New York: Psychology Press, p. 41-68.

Baddeley, A. (2002). Is working memory still working? *European Psychologist,* 7(2), 85-87.

Baddeley, A. (2000). The episodic buffer: A new component of working memory? *Trends in Cognitive Science,* 4(11).

Baddeley, A. D. & Hitch, G. (1993). The recency effect: implicit learning with explicit retrieval? *Memory and Cognition,* 21(2), 146-155.

Baddeley, A. D. & Hitch, G. (1974). Working memory. In G. H, Bower, (Ed.). *The Psychology of Learning and Motivation: Advances in Research and Theory* (Vol. 8, p. 47-89). New York: Academic Press.

Babyek, M., Blumenthal, J. A., Herman, S., Khatri, P., Doraiswamy, et, al. (2000). Exercise treatment for major depression: maintenance of therapeutic benefit at 10 months. *Psychosomatic Medicine,* 62, 633-638.

Bahrick, H. P. & Hall, L. K. (1991). Lifetime maintenance of high school mathematics content. *Journal of Experimental Psychology,* 120(1), 20-33.

Baily, K., West, R., & Anderson, C. A. (2011). The influence of video games on social, cognitive, and affective information processing. In J. Decety & J. T. Cacioppo, (Eds.). *The Oxford Handbook of Social Neuroscience.* Oxford: Oxford University Press.

Bandura, A. (2005). The primacy of self-regulation in health promotion. *Applied Psychology: An International Review*, 54(2): 245-254.

Bandura, A, (2004). Health promotion by social cognitive means. *Health Education & Behavior*, 31, 143-164.

Bandura, A. (2004). The role of selective moral disengagement in terrorism and counterterrorism. In F. M Mogahaddam & A. J. Marsella (Eds.), *Understanding Terrorism: Psychological Roots, Consequences and Interventions.* Washington, D.C.: American Psychological Association Press. 121-150.

Bandura, A. (2002). Social cognitive theory in cultural context. *Applied Psychology: An International Review*, 51: 2, 269-290.

Bandura, A. (2001). Social cognitive theory: an agentic perspective. *Annual Review of Psychology.* 52, 1-26.

Bandura, A. (1997). *Self-Efficacy: The Exercise of Control.* New York: W. H. Freeman.

Bandura, A. (1977). *Social Learning Theory.* Englewood Cliffs, NJ: Prentice-Hall.

Bandura, A, Taylor, C. B., Williams, S. L., Mefford, I. N., & Barchas, J. D. (1985). CatchATBmine secretion as a function of perceived coping self-efficacy. Journal of Consulting and Clinical Psychology, Vol. 53, No. 3, 406-414.

Bandura, A. (1973). *Aggression: A Social Learning Analysis.* Englewood Cliffs, NJ: Prentice-Hall.

Bandura, A. (1965). Influence of models' reinforcement contingencies on the acquisition of imitative responses. *Journal of Personality and Social Psychology,* 1: 6.

Bandura, A., Ross, D., & Ross, S. (1963). Imitation of film-mediated aggressive models. *Journal of Abnormal and Social Psychology,* 66: 1, 3-11.

Bar, M. (2004). Visual objects in context. *Nature Reviews Neuroscience,* 5, 617-629.

Baron-Cohen, S. (1995). *Mindblindness: An Essay on Autism and Theory of Mind.* Cambridge, MA: The MIT Press.

Barry, R. A., Kochanska, G., & Philbert, R. A. (2008). G X E interaction int he organization of attachment: mother's responsiveness as a moderator of children's genotypes. *Journal of Child Psychology and Psychiatry,* 49(12), 1313-1320.

Bartlett, F. (1932). Remembering: A study in experimental and social psychology. Cambridge: Cambridge University Press.

Bazaragan-Hejazi, S., Teruya, S., Pan, D., Lin, J., Gordon, D., Krochalk, P. C., & Bazargan, M. (2016). The theory of planned behavior (TPB) ad texting while driving behavior in college students. *Traffic Injury Prevention,* [Epub ahead of print].

Beck, A. T. & Haight, E. A. P. (2014). Advances in cognitive theory and therapy: The generic cognitive model. *Annual Review of Clinical Psychology,* 10, 1-24.

Beck, A. T., Wright, F. D., Newman, C. F., & Liese, B.S. (1993). *Cognitive Therapy of Substance Abuse.* New York: The Guilford Press.

Becker, A. E. (2016). Eating problems in special populations: Cultural considerations. In Walsh, B. Y., Attia, E., Glassier, D. R., & Sysco, R., (Eds.), *Handbook of Assessment and Treatment of Eating Disorders.* Arlington, VA: American Psychiatric Association.

Becker, A. E., (2007), Culture and eating disorders classification. *International Journal of Eating Disorders,* 40, S111-S116.

Becker, A.E., Burwell, R.A., Gilman, S.E., Herzog, D.B., & Hamburg, P. (2002).Eating behaviors and attitudes following prolonged exposure to television among ethnic Fijian adolescent girls. *British journal of Psychiatry,* 180, 509-514.

Bell, M. A., Wolfe, C. D., & Adkins, D. R. (2007). Frontal lobe development during infancy and childhood: contributions of brain electrical activity, temperament, and language to individual differences in working memory and inhibition control. In D. Coch, K. W. Fischer, & G. Dawson (Eds.), *Human Behavior, Learning, and the Developing Brain: Typical Development,* 247-276. New York: Guilford.

Belmaker. R. H. & Agam, G. (January 3, 2008). Mechanisms of disease: major depressive disorder. In *The New England Journal of Medicine.* 358, 55-68.

Beltz, N. E. & Hackett, G. (1981). The relationship of career-related self-efficacy expectations to perceived career options in college women and men. *Journal of Counseling Psychology,* 28(5), 399-410.

Bem, S. (1998). Gender schema theory and its implications for child development: raising gender-aschematic children in a gender-schematic society. In D. Anselmi & A. Law, (Eds). *Questions of Gender: Perspectives and Paradoxes.* New York: McGraw-Hill.

Bem, S. L. (1981). Gender schema theory: A cognitive account of sex typing. *Psychological Review,* 88(4), 354-364.

Bennett, C. M. & Miller, M. B. (2010). How reliable are the results from functional magnetic resonance imaging? *Annals of the New York Academy of Sciences,* 133-155.

Berry, J. W. & Sam, D. L. (in press). Theoretical perspectives. In J. W. Berry & D. L. Sam, (Eds). *Handbook of Acculturation Psychology.* Cambridge: Cambridge University Press.

Berry, J. W. (2013). Achieving a global psychology. *Canadian Psychology,* 54 (1), 55-61.

Berry, J. W., Poortinga, Y. H., Breugelmans, S. M., Chasiotis, A., & Sam, D. L. (2011). *Cross-Cultural Psychology: Research and Applications* (3rd ed.). Cambridge: Cambridge University Press.

Berry, J. W. (2008). Globalization and acculturation. *International Journal of Intercultural Relations.* 32(4), 328-336.

Berry, J. W. (2005). Acculturation: Living successfully in two cultures. *International Journal of Intercultural Relations.* 29, 697-712.

Berry, J. (1997). Immigration, acculturation, and adaptation. *Applied Psychology: An International Review.* 46(1), 5-68.

Berry, J. (1969). On cross-cultural comparability. *International Journal of Psychology,* 4: 2, 119-128.

Bhawuk, D. P. (2008). Globalization and indigenous cultures: Homogenization or differentiation? *International Journal of Intercultural Relations.* 32, 305-317.

Bjorklund, D. F. (2013). Cognitive development: an overview. In P. D. Zelazo (Ed.), *The Oxford Handbook of Developmental Psychology, Vol. 1.* Oxford: Oxford University Press.

Blacker, K. J., Curby, K. M., Klobusicky, E., & Chein, J. M. (2014). Effects of video game training on visual working memory. *Journal of Experimental Psychology,* 40 (5), 1992-2004.

Blackwell, N. J., Bentall, R. P., ffytche, D. H., Simmons, A., Murray, R. M., & Howard, R. J. (2003). Self-responsibility and the self-serving bias: an fMRI investigation of causal attributions. *NeuroImage,* 20, 1076-1085.

Blair, C. & Raver, C. C. (2012). Child development in the context of adversity. *American Psychologist,* 67 (4), 309-318.

Blease, C. R. (2015). Too many 'friends,' too few 'likes'? Evolutionary psychology and 'Facebook depression.' *Review of General Psychology,* 19 (1), 1-13.

Bodrova, E. & Leong, D. (2003). Learning and development of preschool children from a Vygotskian perspective. In A. Kozulin, B. Gindis, V. S. Ageyev, & S. M. Miller (Eds.), *Vygotskian Theory in Cultural Context. Cambridge: Cambridge University Press.*

Book Club/Reading Guides- The Prozac Diary by Lauren Slater. (2008). Retrieved 10/21/08 from www.us.penguingroup.com/static/rguides/us/prozac_diary.html

Boot, W. R., Blakeley, D. P., & Simons, D. J. (2011). Do action video games improve perception and cognition? *Frontiers in Psychology,* 2 (226), 1-6.

Bond, M. H. (1991). *Beyond the Chinese Face: Insights from Psychology.* Oxford: Oxford University Press.Bond. M. H., & Smith, P. B. (1996). Cross-cultural social and organizational psychology.*Annual Review of Psychology.*

Bond, M. H. (2002). Reclaiming the individual from Hofstede's ecological analysis- a 20-year odyssey: comment on Oyserman et. al. (2002). *Psychological Bulletin,*128: 1, 73-77.

Bond R., & Smith P. H. (1996). Culture and conformity: A meta-analysis of studies using Asch's (1952b, 1956) line judgment task. *Psychological Bulletin,* 119:1, 111- 137.

Boraska, V., Frankin, C. S., Floyd, J. A. B., Thornton, L. M., Huckins, L. M.,Southam, L. ... & Bulik, C. M. (2014). A genome-wide association study of anorexia nervosa. *Molecular Psychiatry,* 19 (10), 1085-1094.

Bower, G. H., Black, J. B., & Turner, T. J. (1979). Scripts in memory for text. *Cognitive Psychology,* 11, 177-220.

Bowes, L., Maughan, B., Ball, H., Shakoor, S., Quellet-Morin, I., Caspi, A., ... Arseneault, L. (2013). Chronic bullying victimization across school transitions: The role of genetic and environmental influences. *Developmental Psychopathology,* 25(2), 1-26.

Bowlby, J. (1989). *A Secure Base: Parent-Child Attachment and Healthy Human Development.* New York: Basic Books.

Bransford, J. D. & Johnson, M. K. (1972). Contextual prerequisites for understanding: some investigations of comprehension and recall. *Journal of Verbal Learning and Verbal Behavior,* 11, 717-726.

Brewer, M. B., & Yuki, M. (2007). Culture and social identity. In Kitayama, S., & Cohen, D., (Eds.). *Handbook of Cultural Psychology.* New York: The Guilford Press.

Brown, C. M. & Segal, R. (1996). Ethnic differences in temporal orientation and its implications for hypertension management. *Journal of Health and Social Behavior,* 37, 350-361.

Brown, S. A., Garcia, A. A., Kouzekanani, K., & Hanis, C. L. (2002). Culturally competent diabetes self-management education for Mexican Americans. *Diabetes Care,* 25(2), 259-268.

Brown, R. & Kulik, J. (1977) Flashbulb memories. In Neisser, U. & Hyman, I. E., Eds. *Memory Observed: Remembering in Natural Contexts, 2nd Ed.* New York, Worth.

Bruce. A. S., Lepping, R. J., Bruce, J. M., Cherry, B.C., Martin, L. E., Davis, A. M., ... Savage, C. R. (2013). Brain responses to food logos in obese and healthy weight children. *The Journal of Pediatrics.* 162(4), 759-764.

Bruner, J. (1996). *The Culture of Education.* Cambridge, MA: Harvard University Press.

Bruner, J. (1990). *Acts of Meaning.* Cambridge, MA: Harvard University Press.

Bruner, J. (1978). Learning to do things with words. In Bruner, J. & Garton, A. (Eds.) *Human Growth and Development.* Oxford: Clarendon Press.

Bruner, J. (1977). *The Process of Education.* Cambridge, MA: Harvard University Press.

Bruner, J. S. & Sherwood, V. (1976) Peekaboo and the learning of rule structures. In J. Bruner, A. Jolly, & K. Sylva (Eds.), *Play: Its Role in Development and Evolution.* New York: Basic Books.

Buller, D. J. (2009). Four fallacies of pop evolutionary psychology. *Scientific American*

Burke, L. E., Ewing, L. J., Ye, L., Styn, M., Zheng, Y., Music, E. . . . & Sereika, S. M. (2015). The SELF trial: A self-efficacy based behavioral intervention trial for weight loss maintenance. *Obesity,* 11, 2175-82.

Busy, K. & Bandura, A. (1999) Social cognitive theory of gender development and differentiation. *Psychological Review,* 106, 676-713.

Butcher, J. N., Mineka, S. I., Hooley, J. M. (2007), *Abnormal Psychology and Modern Life,* 13th edition. Boston: Pearson Education, Inc.

Butler, T., Imperato-McGinley, J., Pan, H., Voyer, D., Cordero, J. Zhu, Y.......Silberzweig, D. (2006). Sex differences in mental rotation: Top-down versus bottom-up processing. *NeuroImage,* 32, 445-456.

Byrne, S. M., Cooper, Z., & Fairburn, C. G. (2004). Psychological predictors of weight gain in obesity. *Behavior Research and Therapy, 42,* 1341-1356.

Cabyoglu, M. T., Ergene, N., & Tan, U. (2006). The treatment of obesity by acupuncture. *International Journal of Neuroscience, 116,* 165-175.

Cadoret, R. J., Yates, W. R., Troughton, E., Woodsworth, G., & Stewart, M. A. (1995). Adoption study demonstrating 2 genetic pathways to drug abuse. *Archives of General Psychiatry,* 52 (1), 42-52.

Call, J. & Tomasello, M. (2008). Does the chimpanzee have a theory of mind? 30 years later. *Trends in Cognitive Science,* 12: 5, 187-192.

Caldwell, K., Emery, L., Harrison, M., & Greeson, J. (2010). Changes in mindfulness, well-being, and sleep quality in college students through Taijiquan courses: A cohort control study. *The Journal of Alternative and Complementary Medicine,* 17 (10), 931-938.

Caplan,P. J. & Cosgrove, L. (2004). Is this really necessary? In P. J. Kaplan & L. Cosgrove, (Eds.). *Biases in Psychiatric Diagnosis.* Latham, MD: Rowman & Littlefield.

Carey, G. (2003). *Human Genetics for the Social Sciences.* Thousand Oaks, CA: Sage Publications.

Carnagey, N. L. & Anderson, C. A. (2005). The effects of reward and punishment in violent video games on aggressive affect, cognition, and behavior. *Psychological Science,* 16 (11), 882- 889.

Carpenter, L. L., Carvalho, J. P., Tyra, A. R., Wier, L. M., Mello, A. F., Mello, M. F....& Price, L. H. (2007). Decreased ACTH and cortisol responses in healthy adults reporting significant childhood maltreatment. *Biological Psychiatry,* 62 (10), 1080-1087.

Carpenter, M., Akhtar, N. & Tomasello, M. (1998). Fourteen- through 18-month old infants differentially imitate intentional and accidental actions. *Infant Behavior and Development,* 21(2), 315-330.

Carreiras, M., Lopez, J., Rivero, F., & Corina, D. (January 6, 2005). Neural processing of a whistled language. *Nature,* 433, 31-32.

Carskadon, M. A. (2004). Sleep deprivation: health consequences and social impact. *Med Clin N Am,* 88:767-776.

Carver, C. S. & Scheier, M. F. (2014). Dispositional optimism. *Trends in Cognitive Science,* 18 (6), 293-299.

Casali, M. E., Borsari, L., Marchesi, I., Borella, P. & Bargelli, A. (2015). Lifestyle and food habits changes after migration: a focus on immigrant women in Modena (Italy). *Annali di giene,* 27(5), 748-759.

Caspi, A., Hariri, A. R., Holmes, A., Uher, R., & Moffitt, T. E. (2010). Genetic sensitivity to the environment: The case of the serotonin transporter gene and its implications for studying complex diseases and traits. *American Journal of Psychiatry,* 167(5): 509-527.

Caspi. A. & Moffitt, T. E. (July, 2006). Gene-environment interactions in psychiatry: joining forces with neuroscience. *Neuroscience,* 7.

Caspi, A, Sugden, K, Moffitt, T. E., Taylor, A., Craig, I. W., Harrington, H.,..... Poulton, R. (July 18, 2003).Influence of life stress on depression: moderation by a polymorphism in the 5-HTT gene. *Science,* 301, 386-389.

Castano, E. & Giner-Sorolla, R. (2006). Not quite human: infrahumanization in response to collective responsibility for intergroup killing. *Journal of Personality and Social Psychology,* 90: 5, 804-818.

Castillo. R. J. (1997). *Culture and Mental Health: A Client-Centered Approach.* Belmont, CA: Brooks/Cole.

Ceci, S. J, Ginther, D. K., Kahn, S., & Williams, W. M. (2014). Women in academic science: A changing landscape. *Psychological Science in the Public Interest,* 15(3), 75-141.

Center for Disease Control (2013). Distracted driving. Atlanta.

Center for Disease Control (2006). School Health Policies and Programs Study (SHPPS).

Center for Disease Control (2012). School Health Policies and Practices Study (SHPPS).

Chang, P. (2015). Understanding Taiwanese children's play via constructing and reconstructing: a prospective vision. In J. L. Roopnarine, M. M. Patte, J. E Johnson, & D. Kuschner, (Eds.). *International Perspectives on children's play.* Berkshire: England: Open University Press: McGraw-Hill Education.

Chaudhry, N. & Shukla, S. (2015). "Children's work is to play": beliefs and practices related to childhood play among Indians. In J. L. Roopnarine, M. M. Patte, J. E. Johnson, & D. Kuschner (Eds.). *International Perspectives on Children's Play.* Berkshire, England: Open University Press: McGraw-Hill Education.

Cheryan, S., Master, A. & Meltzoff, A. N. (2015). Cultural stereotypes as gatekeepers: Increasing girls' interest in computer science and engineering by diversifying stereotypes. *Frontiers in Psychology,* 6(49), 1-8.

Chiao, J. Y. & Blizinsky, K. D. (2010). Gene-Culture coevolution of individualism-collectivism and the serotonin transporter gene. *Proceedings of the Royal Society,* 277, 529-537.

Chiao, J. Y., Harada, T., Komeda, H., Li, Z., Mano, Y., Saito, D…& Iiaka, T. (2009). Neural basis of individualistic and collectivistic views of the self. *Human Brain Mapping,* 00:000, 1-8.

Chiao, J. Y. & Ambady, N. (2007). Cultural neuroscience: parsing universality and diversity across levels of analysis. In Kitayama, S. & Cohen, D., (Eds.). *Handbook of Cultural Psychology.* New York: The Guilford Press.

Chinese Society of Psychiatry (2005). History of Chinese Psychiatry. Retrieved from www.cma-mh.org/English/.

Chinese Society of Psychiatry (2003). CCMD-3. Retrieved from www.cma-mh.org/English/.

Chen, S. X., Chan, W., Bond, M. H., Stewart, S. M. (2006). The effects of self-efficacy and relationship harmony on depression across cultures: applying level-oriented and structure-oriented analyses. *Journal of Cross-Cultural Psychology,* 37, 643.

Chen, X., Bian, Y., Xin, T., Wang, L.,. & Silbereisen, R. K. (2010). Perceived social change and childrearing attitudes in China. *European Psychologist,* 15, 260-270.

Cialdini, R. B, & Sagarin, B. J. (2005). Principles of interpersonal influence. In Brock, T. C., & Green, M. C., (Eds.). *Persuasion: Psychological Insights and Perspectives,* 2nd ed. Thousand Oaks, CA: Sage Publications.

Cialdini, R. B, Vincent, J. E., Lewis, S. K., Catalan, J., Wheeler, D. & Darby, B. L. (1975). Reciprocal concessions procedure for inducing compliance: the door-in-the-face technique. *Journal of Personality and Social Psychology.* 31(2), 206-215.

Comer, R. (2013). *Abnormal Psychology,* 8th Ed. New York: Worth.

Cohen, D. (2007). Methods in cultural research. In Kitayama, S. & Cohen, D., Eds. *Handbook of Cultural Psychology.* New York: The Guilford Press.

Cohen, L., & Marion, L. (2000). Triangulation. *Research Methods in Education.* London: Routledge.

Cohen, S., Janicki-Deverts, D., Doyle, W. J., Miller, G. E., Frank, E., Rabin, B.S., & Turner, R. B. (2012). Chronic stress, glucocorticoid receptor resistance, inflammation, and disease risk. *PNAS,* 109 (6), 5995-5999.

Cohen, S. (2005). Psychological stress, immunity, and upper respiratory infection. In Miller, G & Chen, E., Eds. *Current Directions in Health Psychology.* Upper Saddle River, N.J.: Pearson Prentice Hall.

Cohen, S., Frank, E., Doyle, W. J., Skoner, D. P., Rabin, B. S., Gwaltney, J. M. (1998). Types of stressors that increase susceptibility to the common cold in healthy adults. *Health Psychology,* 17:3, 214-223.

Cole, H. & Griffiths, M. D. (2007). Social interactions in massively multiplayer online role-playing games. *Cybersychology and Behavior,* 10(4), 575-583.

Cole, M. (2003). Vygotsky and context: Where did the connection come from and what difference does it make? Paper prepared for the biennial conferences of the International Society for Theoretical Psychology, Istanbul, Turkey, June 22-27, 2003.

Cole, M. (1996). *Cultural Psychology: A Once and Future Discipline.* Cambridge, MA and London, England: The Belknap Press of Harvard University Press.

Cole, M. & Gay, J. (1972). Culture and memory. *American Anthropologist,* 74(5), 1066-1084.

Colegrove, F. W. (1899). Individual memories. In U. Neisser & I. E. Harsch, (Eds.), *Memory Observed: Remembering in Natural Contexts, 2nd ed.* New York: Worth. (Reprinted from *American Journal of Psychology, 10, 228-255*).

Collen, M. (2015). Operationalizing pain treatment in the biopsychosocial model: Take a daily "SWEM"- socialize, work, exercise, meditate. *Journal of Pain and Palliative Pharmacotherapy,* 3, 290-299.

Converse, A. K., Ahlers, E. O., Travers, B.G., & Davidson, R. J. (2014). Tai Chi training reduces self-report of inattention in healthy adults. *Frontiers in Human Neuroscience,* 8 (13), 1-7.

Coolican, H. (2014). *Research Methods and Statistics in Psychology,* 6th edition. London: Psychology Press.

Coolican, H. (2004). *Research Methods and Statistics in Psychology.* 4th edition. London: Hodder & Stoughton.

Cooper, Z., Coll, H.A., Hawker, D. M., Byrne, S., Bonner, G. ... & Fairburn, C. G. (2010). Testing a new cognitive behavioral treatment for obesity: A randomized trail with three-year follow-up. *Behavioral Research Therapy,* 48 (8), 706-713.

Cosmides, L. & Tooby, J. (1997). *Evolutionary Psychology: A Primer.* University of California Santa Barbara Center for Evolutionary Psychology.

Council of Civil Service Unions/Cabinet Office (CCSU). (2004). Work stress and health: The Whitehall II study. London: Public and Commercial Services Union.

Craft, L. L. & Perna, F. M. (2004). The benefits of exercise for the clinically depressed. *Pain Care Companion to the Journal of Clinical Psychiatry.* 6 (3), 104-111.

Craik, F. I. M. & Tulving, E. (1975). Depth of processing and the retention of words in episodic memory. *Journal of Experimental Psychology: General.* 104(3), 268-294.

Cross, S. E. & Madson, L. (1997). Models of the self: Self-construals and gender. *Psychological Bulletin,* (122) 1, 5-37.

Crowley, P. (2015). Long-term drug treatment of patients with alcohol dependence. *Australian Prescriber,* 38 (2), 41-43.

Curci, A, Lancing, T., Maddalena, C., Maddalena, S. & Sartori, G. (2015). Flashbulb memories of the Pope's resignation: explicit and implicit measures across differing religious groups. *Memory,* 23(4), 529-544.

Curci, A., & Luminet, O. (2006). Follow-up of a cross-national comparison on flashbulb and event memory for the September 11th attacks. *Memory,* 14: 3, 329-344.

Davidson, R. J., Kabat-Zinn, J., Schumacher, J., Rosenkratz, M., Muller, D., Santorelli, S. F., ... & Sheridan, J. F. (2003). Alterations in brain and immune function produced by Mindfulness Meditation. *Psychosomatic Medicine,* 65: 564-570.

DeBusk, R.F., Miller, N. H., Superko, R., Dennis, C.A., Thomas, R. J., Lew, H. T., Berger, W. E., . . . & Taylor, B. (1994). A Case-management system for coronary risk factor modification after acute myocardial infarction. *Annals of Internal Medicine,* 120(9), 721-729.

Dalle Grave, R., El Ghoch, M., Sartirana, M., & Calugi, S. (2016). Cognitive-behavioral therapy for anorexia nervosa: An update. *Current Psychiatry Rep,* 18 (2), 1-8.

Devlin, A. M., Brain, U., Austin, J., & Oberlander, T. F. (2010). Prenatal exposure to maternal depressed mood and the MTHFR C677T variant affect SLC6A4 methylation in infants at birth. *PLoS ONE* 5(8) e12201.

DeRubeis, R. J., Hollon, S. D., Amsterdam, J. D., Shelton, R. C., Young, P. R., et al. (April, 2005). Cognitive therapy vs. medications in the treatment of moderate to severe depression. *Archives of General Psychiatry,* 62.

Des Rosiers, S. E., Schwartz, S. J., Zamboanga, Ham, L. S., & Huang, S. (2012). A cultural and social cognitive model of differences in acculturation orientations, alcohol expectancies, and alcohol-related risk behaviors among Hispanic college students. *Journal of Clinical Psychology,* (Epub ahead of print).

Diamond, M., Sigmundson, H., & Keith, H. (1997). Sex reassignment at birth: long-term review and clinical implications. *Archives of Pediatrics and Adolescent Medicine,* 151(3), 298-304.

Diamond, A. & Taylor, C. (1996). Development of an aspect of executive control: development of the abilities to remember what I said to do and to "do as I say, not as I do." *Developmental Psychobiology,* 29(4), 315-334.

Dias, M. G. & Harris, P. L. (1988). The effect of make-believe play on deductive reasoning. *British Journal of Developmental Psychology,* 6, 207-221.

Disner, S. G., Beevers, C. G., Haight, E. A. P., & Beck, A. T. (2011). Neural mechanisms of the cognitive model of depression. *Nature Reviews Neuroscience,* 1-11.

Dobbs, D. (March 24, 2005). Fact or phrenology? The growing controversy over fMRI scans is forcing us to confront whether brain equals mind. *Scientific American Mind.*

Dobbs, D. (April/May, 2006). A revealing reflection. *Scientific American Mind,* 17(2).

Domingos. A. I., Vaynshteyn, J., Sordillo, A., & Friedman, J. M. (2014). The reward value of sucrose in leptin-deficient obese mice. *Molecular Metabolism,* 3, 73-80.

Doty, R. L. (2014). Human pheromones: do they exist? In C. C. Mucignat-Caretta, (Ed.). *Neurobiology of Chemical Communication.* Boca Raton, FL: CRC Press/Taylor & Francis.

Drakes, J. & Goldman, M. S. (1993). Expectancy challenge and drinking reduction: Experimental evidence for a meditational process. *Journal of Consulting Clinical Psychology,* 61(2): 344-53.

Duncan, G. J., Brooks-Gunn, J., & Klebanov, P. K. (1994). Economic deprivation and early childhood development. *Child Development,* 65 (2), 296-318.

Dunn, J. & Cutting, A. L. (1999). Understanding others, and individual differences in friendship interactions in young children. *Social Development,* 8(2), 201-219.

Durie, M. (2009). Maori knowledge and medical science. In M. Incayawar, R. Wintrob, & L. Bouchard, (Eds.). *Psychiatrists and Traditional Healers: Unwitting Partners in Global Mental Health.* Oxford: Wiley-Blackwell.

Duval, T. S. & Silvia, P. J. (2002). Self-awareness, probability of improvement, and the self-serving bias. *Journal of Personality and Social Psychology.* 82(1), 49-61.

Ehrmin, J. T. (2002). "That feeling of not feeling": numbing the pain for substance abuse-dependent African American women. *Qualitative Health Research;* 12, 780-791.

Eisenberg, N., Spinrad, T. L., & Morris, A. S. (2013). Prosocial development. In P. D. Zelazo, (Ed.). *The Oxford Handbook of Developmental Psychology, Vol. 2.* Oxford: Oxford University Press.

Ekman, P, Davidson, R.J., Ricard, M., & Wallace, B.A. (2005). Buddhist and psychological perspectives on emotions and well-being. *Current Directions in Psychological Science.* American Psychological Society.

Ekman, P. (2003). *Emotions Revealed.* New York: An Owl Book, Henry Holt.

Ekuni, R., Vaz, L. J., & Bueno, F. A., (2011). Levels of processing: the evolution of a framework. *Psychology and Neuroscience,* 4(3), 333-339.

El-Mekawy, H. S., ElDeeb,A. M. & Ghareib, H. O. (2014). Effect of laser acupuncture combined with a diet-exercise intervention on metabolic syndrome in post-menopausal women. *Journal of Advanced Research,* 6, 757-763.

Endendijk, J. J., Beltz, A. M., McHale, S. M., Bryk, K., & Berenbaum, S. A. (2016). Linking prenatal androgens to gender-related attitudes, identity, and activities: evidence from girls with congenital adrenal hyperplasia. *Archives of Sexual Behavior,* 1-9.

Engel, G. L. (1980). The clinical application of the biopsychosocial model. *The American Journal of Psychiatry,* 131 (5), 535-544.

Engel, G. L. (1977). The need for a new medical model: A challenge for biomedicine. *Science,* New Series, 96 (4286), 129-136.

Engler, B. (2007). *Personality Theories: An Introduction,* 7th edition. Boston: Houghton-Mifflin.

Epel, E., Daubenmier, J., Moskowitz, J. T., Folkman, S., & Blackburn, E. (2009). Can meditation slow rate of cellular aging? Cognitive stress, mindfulness, and telomeres. *Annals of the New York Academy of Sciences,* 1172, 34-53.

Erskine, H.E., Moffitt, T. E., Copeland, W. E., Costello, E. J., ...& Scott, J. G. (2015). A heavy burden on young minds: The global burden of mental and substance use disorders in children and youth. *Psychological Medicine,* 45, 1551-1563.

Fagan, G., Wilkinson, D. L., & Davies, G. (2007). Social contagion of violence. In Flannery, D. J., Vazsonyo, A. T., & Walkman, I. D., (Eds.). *The Cambridge Handbook Of Violent Behavior and Aggression.* Cambridge: Cambridge University Press.

Fagot, B. & Hagan, R. (1991). Observations of parent reactions to sex-stereotyped behaviors: age and sex differences. *Child Development,* 62(3), 617-628.

Fagot, B. I, Leinbach, M. D., & Hagan, R. (1986). Gender labeling and the adoption of sex-typed behaviors. *Developmental Psychology,* (22) 4, 440-443.

Fagot, B. (1978). The influence of sex of child on parental reactions to toddler children. *Child Development,* 49(2), 459-465.

Farah, M. J., Hutchinson, J. B., Phelps, E. A., & Wagner, A. D. (2014). Functional MRI-based lie detection: scientific and societal challenges. *Nature Reviews/Neuroscience,* 15:123-131.

Farah, M. J. (2010). Animal neuroethics and the problem of other minds. In M. J. Farah, (Ed.). *Neuroethics: An Introduction with readings.* Cambridge, MA.: The MIT Press.

Farah, M. J., Ed. (2008). *Neuroethics.* www.neuroethics.upenn.edu/.

Feinstein, B. A., Hershenberg, R., Bhatia, V., Latack, J. A., Meuwly, N., & Davila, J. (2013). Negative social comparison on Facebook and depressive symptoms: Rumination as a mechanism. *Psychology of Popular Media Culture,* 2 (3), 161-170.

Feng, J., Spence, I., & Pratt, J. (2007). Playing an action video game reduces gender differences in spatial cognition. *Psychological Report,* 18 (10). 850-855.

Ferrarelli, F., Smith, R., Dentico, D., Rieder, B.A., Zennig, C., Benca, R. M.....& Tononi, G. (2013). Experienced mindfulness meditators exhibit higher parietal-occipital EEG gamma activit during NREM sleep. *PLOS ONE,* 8 (8), 1-9.

591

Ferguson, G. M., Iturbide, M. I., & Gordon, B. P. (2013). Tridimensional (3D) acculturation: Ethnic identity and psychological functioning of tricultural Jamaican immigrants. *International Perspectives in Psychology: Research, Practice, Consultation.* 3(4), 238-251.

Festinger, L. (1957). *A Theory of Cognitive Dissonance.* Stanford, CA: Stanford University Press.

Festinger, L. & Carlsmith, J. M. (1959). Cognitive consequences of forced compliance. *Journal of Abnormal and Social Psychology,* 58(2), 203-210.

Fielden, A. L., Sillence, E., & Little, L. (2011). Children's 'understandings' of obesity, a thematic analysis. *International Journal of Student Health and Well-being,* 6(7170), 1-14.

Finucane, M. L., Peters, E., & Slovic, P. (2003). Judgment and decision making: the dance of affect and reason. In S. L. Schneider & J. Shantey (Eds.). *Emerging Perspectives on Judgment and Decision Making Research,* p. 327-364. Cambridge: Cambridge University Press.

Finucane, M. L., Alhakami, A., Slovic, P. & Johnson, S. M. (2000). The affect heuristic in judgments of risk and benefit. *Journal of Behavioral Decision making,* 13, 1-17.

Finkenauer, C., Luminet, O., Gisle, L., El-Ahmadi, A., van der Linder, M., & Philippot, P. (1998). Flashbulb memories and the underlying mechanisms of their formation: towards an emotional-integrative model.

Finkenauer, C., Gisle, L., & Luminet, O. (1997). Flashbulb memory: a special case of memory as an individual and social faculty. In Pennebaker, J.W., Paez, D. & Rime, B., Eds., *Collective Memories of Political Events: Social and Psychological Perspectives.* Mahwah, N. J., Erlbaum. p. 191-208.

Fiske, S. T. & Taylor, S. E. (2008). *Social Cognition: From Brains to Culture.* Boston: Mc-Graw-Hill.

Fiske, A. P. & Fiske, S. T. (2007). Social relationships in our species and cultures. In Kitayama, S. & Cohen, D., Eds. *Handbook of Cultural Psychology.* New York: The Guilford Press.

Fiske, S. (2004). *Social Beings: A Core Motives Approach to Social Psychology.* Hoboken, NJ: John Wiley & Sons.

Flegal, K. M., Carroll, M.D., Ogden, C. L., & Curtin, L.R. (2010). Prevalence and trends in obesity among US adults, 1999-2008. *JAMA, 303* (3), 235-241.

Flinn, M. V. (2006). Evolution and ontogeny of stress response to social challenges in the human child. *Developmental Review,* 26, 138-174.

Florida State University (2013). Healthy Campus 2020: Executive summary. www.healthycampus.fsu.com.

Fone, D. L., Farewell, D. M., White, J., Lyons, R. A., & Dunstan, F. D. (2013). Socioeconomic patterning of excess alcohol consumption and binge drinking: a cross-sectional study of multilevel associations with neighborhood deprivation. *BMJ Open Access,* 1-9.

Forwood, S. E., Ahern, A., Hollands, G. J., Fletcher, P. C., & Marteau, T. M. (2013). Underestimating calorie content when healthy foods are present: an averaging effect or a reference-dependent anchoring effect? *PLOS ONE,* 8(8), e71475.

Foster, D. W., Neighbors, C. & Young, C. M. (2014). Drink refusal self-efficacy and implicit drinking identity: An evaluation of moderators of the relationship between self-awareness and drinking behavior. *Addictive Behavior,* 39 (1), 196-204.

Foster, J. L., Huthwaite, T., Yesberg, J. A., Garry, M., & Loftus, E. F. (2012). Repetition, not number of sources, increases both susceptibility to misinformation and confidence in the accuracy of eyewitnesses. *Acta Psychologica,* 139, 320-326.

Fournier, J. C., DeRubeis, R. J., Hollon, S. D., Gallop, R., Shelton, R. C….& Amsterdam, J. D. (2013). Differential change in specific depressive symptoms during antidepressant medication or cognitive therapy. *Behavior Research and Therapy,* 51: 392-398.

Fried, A. B., & Dunn, M. E. (2012). The expectancy challenge alcohol literacy curriculum (ECALC): A single session group intervention to reduce alcohol use. *Psychology of Addictive Behavior,* (Epub ahead of print).

Friedman, J. M. & Mantzoros, C. S. (2015). 20 years of leptin: From the discovery of the leptin gene to leptin in our therapeutic armamentarium. *Metabolism,* 64, 1-4.

Friedman, J. (2014). Leptin at 20: An overview. *Journal of Endocrinology,* 223, T1-T8.

Friedman, J. M. (2011). Leptin and the regulation of body weight. *Keio Journal Of Medicine,* 60 (1): 1-9.

Frontline: Inside the Teenage Brain: Interview with Mary Carskadon. (1999). Retrieved from www.pbs.org, 12/30/2007.

Garmy, P., Nyberg, P, & Jakobsson, U. (2012). Sleep and television and computer habits of Swedish school-age students. *The Journal of School Nursing,* 28 (6), 469-476.

Gaskins, S. (2015a). Childhood practices across cultures: play and household work. In L. A. Jenson, (Ed.), *The Oxford Handbook of Human Development and Culture.* Oxford: Oxford University Press.

Gaskins, S. (2015b). Yucatec Mayan children's play. In J. L. Roopnarine, M.M. Patte, J. E. Johnson, & D. Kushner, D. (Eds.), *International Perspectives on Children's Play. Berkshire, England:* Open University Press: McGraw-Hill Education.

Gatchel, R. J., McGeary, D. D., McGeary, C. A., & Lippe, B. (2014). Interdisciplinary chronic pain management. *American Psychologist, 69* (2), 119-130.

Gay, J. & Cole, M. (1967). *The New Mathematics and an Old Culture: A Study of Learning among the Kpelle of Liberia.* New York: Holt, Reinhart, & Winston.

Gazzaniga, M. S., Ivry, R. B., & Mangun, G. R. (2014). *Cognitive Neuroscience: The Biology of the Mind,* 4th Ed. New York: Norton & Norton.

Geertz, C. (1979). From the native's point of view: On the nature of anthological understanding. In P. Rabinow & W. Sullivan, *Interpretative Social Science: A Reader., 225-242, Berkeley, CA: University of California Press.*

Gazzaniga, M. S., Ivry, R. B., & Mangun, G. R. (2008). *Cognitive Neuroscience: The Biology of the Mind,* 3rd Ed. New York, Norton & Norton.

Gilbert, D. T., King, G., Pettigrew, S., & Wilson, T. D. (2016). Comment on "Estimating the reproducibility of psychological science." *Science,* 351 (6277), 1037a.

Gibson, R., Knight, A., Asante, M., Thomas, J., Goff, L. M. (2016). Comparing dietary macronutrient composition and food sources between native and diasporic Ghanaian adults. *Food and Nutrition Research,* 59, 1-9.

Gibson, J. J. & Gibson, E. J. (1955). Perceptual learning: Differentiation or enrichment? *Psychological Review.* 62(1), 32-41.

Gibson, W. T., Farooqi, S., Moreau, M., DePaoli, A. M., Lawrence, E., O'Rahilly, S., & Trusswll, R. A. (2004). Congenital leptin deficiency due to homozygosity for the A133G mutation: Report of another case and evaluation of response to four years of leptin therapy. *The Journal of Clinical Endocrinology and Metabolism,* 89 (10): 4821-4826.

Glanzer, G. & Cunitz, A. R. (1966). Two storage mechanisms in free recall. *Journal of Learning and Verbal Behavior,* 5, 351-360.

Gillham, B. (2008). *Observation Techniques: Structured to Unstructured.* London: Continuum.

Global Burden of Disease Study Collaboration Group (2015). Global, regional, and national incidence, prevalence, and years lived with disability for 301 acute and chronic diseases and injuries in 188 countries, 1990-2013. *The Lancet,* 386 (9995).

Godin, G. & Kok, G. (1996) The theory of planned behavior: a review of its applications to health-related behaviors. *American Journal of Health Promotion,* 11(2), 87-98.

Goldapple, K., Segal, Z., Garson, C., Lau, M., Bieling, P., Kennedy, P, & Mayberg, H. (2004). Modulation of corticol-limbic pathways in major depression. *Archives of General Psychiatry,* 61, 34-41.

Goodwin, C.J. (1999). *A History of Modern Psychology.* New York: John Wiley.

Goodwin, C. J. (1998). *Research in Psychology,* 2nd Ed. New York: John Wiley.

Gopnik, A. & Astington, J. W. (1988). Children's understanding of representational change and its relation to the understanding of false beliefs and the appearance-reality distortion. *Child Development,* 59(1), 26-37.

Gotlib, I. H., LeMoult, N. L., Colich, N. L., Foland-Ross, L. C., Hallmayer, J., Joorman, J., . . . Wolkowitz, O. M. (2015). Teolmere length and cortisol activity in children of depressed mothers. *Molecular Psychiatry,* 20, 615-620.

Gould, E. & Gross, C. G. (Feb 1, 2002). Neurogenesis in adult mammals: some progress and problems. *The Journal of Neuroscience,* 22: 3, 619-623.

Grandin, T. (Feb., 1999). Social problems: Understanding emotions and developing talents. Retrieved 1/11/2008 from www.autism.org/temple/social.html.

Granic, I., Lobel, A., & Engels, R. C. M. E. (2014). The benefits of playing video games. *American Psychologist,* 69 (1), 66-78.

Gray, P. & Bjorklund, D. F. (2014). *Psychology,* (7th ed.). New York: Worth.

Gray, P. (2011). *Psychology,* 6th Edition. New York, NY: Worth.

Greenfield, P. M., Keller, H., Fuligni, A., & Maynard, A. (2003). Cultural pathways through universal development. *Annual Review of Psychology,* 54, 461-490.

Greenberg, M. S., Westcott, D. R., & Baily, S. E. (1998). When believing is seeing: The effect of scripts on eyewitness memory. *Law and Human Behavior.* 22(6), 685-694.

Gresson, J. M. (2008). Mindfulness research update: 2008. *Complementary Health Practice Review,* 14(10), 10-18.

Griffiths, S., Murray, S. B., & Touyz, S. (2015). Keeping pace with the growing problem of male eating disorders. *Medicine Today,* 16, 63-65.

Griffiths, S., Murray, S. B., & Touyz, S. (2014). Extending the masculinity hypothesis: An investigation of gender role conformity, body dissatisfaction, and disordered eating in young heterosexual men. *Psychology of Men and Masculinity,* 16(1), 108-114.

Grizzell, J. (November, 2003). Healthy Campus 2010 addresses high-priority college public health issues. *Spectrum,* 21-24.

Grohol, J. M. (2012, Dec. 14). Final DSM 5 approved by American Psychiatric Association. Retrieved from http://psychcentral.com.

Grubin, D. (Executive Produce). (2001). The teenage brain: a world of their own. *The Secret Life of the Brain* [PBS DVD Video]. (Available from Time Warner Company, 4000 Warner Blvd., Burbank, CA 91522).

Gunnar, M. R. & Herrera, A. M. (2013). The development of stress reactivity: a neurobiological perspective. In Zelazo, P. D., (Ed.). *The Oxford Handbook of Developmental Psychology, Vol. 2.* Oxford: Oxford University Press.

Gunnar, M. & Quevedo, K. (2007). The neurobiology of stress and development. *Annual Review of Psychology,* 58, 145-173.

Gunrung, R.A.R. (2010). *Health Psychology: A Cultural Approach* (2nd ed.). Belmont, CA: Wadsworth.

Guo, Q., Johnson, C. A., Unger, J. B., Lee, L, Xie, B., Chou, C….& Pentz, M. (2007). Utility of the theory of reasoned action and theory of planned behavior for predicting Chinese adolescent smoking. *Addictive Behaviors,* 32, 1066-1081.

Gureckis, T. M. & Gladstone, R. L. (2010). Schema: The history of schemas. Retrieved from www.cognitrn.indianna.edu…/schema for language.pdf.

HHS News (2010). HHS announces the nation's new health promotion and disease prevention agenda. Available from HealthyPeople.gov.

Hall, E. T. (1959). *The Silent Language.* New York, NY: Anchor.

Hamilton, D. L., Dugan, P. M., & Trolier, T. K. (1983). The formation of stereotypic beliefs: Further evidence foe the distinctiveness-based illusory correlation. *Journal of Personality and Social Psychology.* 48(1), 5-17.

Hamilton, D. L. & Rose, T. L. (1980). Illusory correlation and the maintenance of stereotypic beliefs. *Journal of Personality and Social Psychology.* 39(5), 832-845.

Hammer, L. (2005). *Dragon Rises, Red Bird Flies: Psychology and Chinese Medicine,* Revised edition. Seattle, WA: Eastland Press.

Hannon, E. E. & Trainor, L. J. (2007). Music acquisition: effects of enculturation and formal training on development. *Trends in Cognitive Sciences,* 11(11), 466-472.

Hannon, E. E. & Trehub, S. E. (2005). Metrical categories in infancy and adulthood. *Psychological Science,* 16(1), 48-55.

Harlow, H. F. & Zimmerman, R. (1959). Affectional responses in the infant monkey. *Science,* 130, 421-432.

Harris, J. L., Bargh, J. A., & Brownell, K. D. (2009). Priming effects of television food advertising on eating behavior. *Health Psychology,* 28 (4), 404-413.

Hassett, J. M., Siebert, E. R., & Wallen, K. (2008). Sex differences in rhesus monkey toy preferences parallel those of children. *Hormones and Behavior,* 54(3), 359-364.

Hatala, A. R. & Waldram, J. B. (2016). The role of sensorial processes in Q'eqchi' Maya healing: a case study of depression and bereavement. *Transcultural Psychiatry,* 53 (1), 60-80.

Harvard Magazine (2000). Worse living through chemistry: the downsides of Prozac. Retrieved 10/23/08 from http://harvardmagazine.com/2000/05/p-the-downsides-of-prozac.html

Harvard Medical School (2009). Exercise and depression. Retrieved from www.health.harvard.edu/mind-and-exercise-and-depression-report-excerpt.

Harvard Mental Health Letter, (July, 2005). The adolescent brain: beyond raging Hormones, 22: 1.

Harvard Medical School (n.d). *Living to 100: What's the secret?* Komoaroff, A. L., editor in Chief, Boston, MA: Harvard Health Publications.

Hayden, J, (2009). Health Belief Model. *Introduction to Health Behavior and Theory.* Jones & Bartlett.

Heath, A. C. (1995). Genetic influences on alcoholism risk: a review of adoption and twin studies. *Alcohol Health & Research World,* 19 (3), 166-171.

Hecker, J.E. & Thorpe, G.L. (2005). *Introduction to Clinical Psychology.* Boston: Pearson.

Heider, K. (2003). *Seeing Anthropology: Cultural Anthropology Through Film,* 3rd ed. Boston: Allyn & Bacon.

Heilman, M. E., Wallen, A. S., Fuchs, D., & Tamkins, M. M. (2004). Penalties for success: Reactions to women who succeed at male gender-typed tasks. *Journal of Applied Psychology,* 89:3, 416-427.

Heinz, A., Beck, A., Grusser, S. M., Grace, A. A., & Wrase, J. (2008). Identifying the neural circuitry of alcohol craving and relapse vulnerability. *Addiction Biology, 14,* 108-118.

Helmer, R. (2006). Pediatric obesity. www.bluepoppy.com.

Herbert, J. & Stipek, D. (2005). The emergence of gender differences in children's perceptions of their academic performance. *Applied Developmental Psychology,* 26, 276-295.

Higgins, E. S. (2008). The new genetics of mental illness. *Scientific American Mind,* 19: 3, 40-47.

Higgins, N. C., & Bhatt, G. (2001). Culture moderates the self-serving bias: etic and emic features of causal attributions in India and Canada. *Social Behavior and Personality.*

Hilderbrandt, T. & Craigen, K. (2016). Eating-related pathology in men and boys. In Walsh, B. T., Attia, E, Glassier, D. R., & Sysco, R, Eds. *Handbook of Assessment and Treatment of Eating Disorders.* Arlington, VA: American Psychiatric Association Publishing.

Hines, M. (2013). Sex and sex differences. In P. D. Zelazo, (Ed.). *The Oxford Handbook of Developmental Psychology, Vol. 1.* Oxford: Oxford University Press.

Hines, M. (2004). *Brain Gender.* Oxford: Oxford University Press.

Hirst, W. & Phelps, E. A. (2016). Flashbulb memories. *Current Directions in Psychological Science,* 25(1), 36-41.

Hock, R. R. (2005). *Forty Studies that Changed Psychology,* 5th Ed. Upper Saddle River, N.J.: Pearson.

Hoertel, H. A., Will, M. J., & Leidy, H. J. (2014). A randomized crossover, pilot study examining the effects of a normal protein vs. high protein breakfast on food cravings and reward signals in overweight/obese "breakfast skipping", late-adolescent girls. *Nutrition Journal,* 13 (80), 1-8.

Hoffman, B. M., Babyak, M. A., Craighead, E., Sherwood, A., Doraiswamy, et al. (2011). Exercise and pharmacotherapy in patients with major depression: One-year follow up of SMILE study. *Psychosomatic Medicine,* 73: 127-133.

Hoffman, M. L. (2007). The origins of empathetic morality in toddlerhood. In C. A. Brownell & C. B. Kopp, (Eds.), *Socioemotional Development in the Toddler years: Transitions and Transformations.* New York, N.Y.: Guilford.

Hoffman, M. L. (2000). *Empathy and Moral Development: Implications for caring and justice.* Cambridge: Cambridge University Press.

Hofstede, G. (no date). Dimensionalizing cultures: the Hofstede model in context.Retrieved 6/29/08 from www.ac.wwu.edu/~culture/hofstede.htm.

Hofstede, G. & Hofstede, G.J. (2005). *Cultures and Organizations: Software of the Mind,* (2nd ed.). New York: McGraw-Hill.

Hofstede, G. (2001). *Cultures Consequences,* (2nd ed.). Thousand Oaks, CA. Sage   Publications.

Hogg, M. A., Terry, D. J., & White, K. M. (1995). A tale of two theories: a critical comparison of identity theory with social identity theory. *Social Psychology Quarterly,* 58: 4, 255-269.

Hong, Y., Wan, C., No, S. & Chiu, C. (2007). Multicultural identities. In Kitayama, S. & Cohen, D., (Eds.), *Handbook of Cultural Psychology.* New York: The Guilford Press.

Horvath, J., Perez, J., Forrow, L., Fregni, F., & Pascual-Leone, A. (2013). Transcranial magnetic stimulation: Future prospects and ethical concerns in treatment and research. In *Neuroethics in Practice,* A. Chatterjee & M. Farah, (Eds.), New York: Oxford University Press.

Horwitz, A. (2005). The age of depression. *Public Interest.* Retrieved 12/8/08 from http://findarticles.com.

Hoshino-Browne, E., Spencer, S. J, Zanna, M. P., Zanna, A. S., Kitayama, S. & Lackenbauer, S. (2005). On the cultural guises of cognitive dissonance: The case of Easterners and Westerners. *Journal of Personality and Social Psychology,* Vol. 89, No. 2, 294-310.

Howard Hughes Medical Institute (2005). Science of fat. Segment: Deconstructing obesity by Jeffrey Friedman. Available from www.biointeractive.org.

Huesmann, L. R., & Kirwil, L. (2007). Why observing media violence increases the risk of violent behavior by the observer. In D. J. Flannery, A. T. Vazsonyi, & I.D. Waldman, (Eds.), *The Cambridge Handbook of Violent Behavior and Aggression.* Cambridge: Cambridge University Press.

Hull, R., & Vaid, J. (2006). Laterality and language experience. *Laterality,* 11: 5, 436-464.

Hurley, D. (Jan/Feb 2011). Obesity reaches epidemic proportions. *Discover.*

Iacoboni, M, Molar-Szakacs, I, Gallese, V., Mazziotta, J. C., & Rizzolatti, G. (2005). Grasping the intentions of others with one's own mirror neuron system. *PLoS Biology*, 3: 3, e79.

Imbo, I. & LeFevre, J. (2010). The role of phonological and visual working memory in complex arithmetic for Chinese- and Canadian-educated adults. *Memory and Cognition*, 38(2), 176-185.

Imperato-McGinley, J., Miller, M., Wilson, J. D., Peterson, R. E., Shackleton, C., & Gajdusek, D. C. (1991). A cluster of male pseudohermaprodites with 5 α reductase deficiency in Papua New Guinea. *Clinical Endocrinology*, 34, 293-298.

Insel, T. (2013, April 29). Transforming diagnosis. National Institute of Mental Health. Retrieved 5/8/13 from www.nimh.nih.gov/about/director/2013/transforming-diagnosis.shtml.

International Bank for Reconstruction and Development/The World Bank (2016). Global monitoring report 2015/2016: development goals in an era of demographic change. Retrieved from http://pubdocs.worldbank.org.

Irwin, M. R., Pike, J. L., Cole, J. C., Oxman, M. N. (2003). Effects of a behavioral intervention, Tai Chi Chih, on Varicella-Zoster virus specific immunity and health functioning in older adults. *Psychosomatic Medicine*, 65: 824-830.

Ismatullina, V, Voronin, I., Shelemetieva, A., & Malykh, S. (2014). Cross-cultural study of working memory in adolescents. *Procedia- Social and Behavioral Sciences*, 146-353-357.

Jabr, F. (2012). Redefining mental illness: Psychiatry's diagnostic guidebook gets its first major update in 30 years. The changes may surprise you. *Scientific American Mind*, Vol. 23, Number 2.

Jaffee S. R., Caspi, A., Moffitt, T. E., Polo-Tomas, M., & Taylor, A. (2007). Individual, family, and neighborhood factors distinguish resilient from nonresident maltreated children: a cumulative stressors model. *Child Abuse and Neglect*, 31 (3), 231-253.

Jarvis, M., Russell, J., & Gorman, P. (2004). *Angles on Psychology*, 2nd edition. Cheltenham, UK: Nelson Thomas.

Jobin, J., Wrosch, C., & Scheier, M. F. (2014). Associations between dispositional optimism and diurnal cortisol in a community sample: When stress is perceived as higher than normal. *Health Psychology*, 33 (4), 382-391.

Jones, E. E. & Harris, V.A. (1967). The attribution of attitudes. *Journal of Experimental Social Psychology*. 3, 1-24.

Jones, L. M., Mitchell, K. J., & Finkelhor, D. (2013). Online harassment in context: trends from three youth Internet safety surveys (2000, 2005, 2010). *Psychology of Violence*, 3(1), 53-69.

Jones, O. D., Marois, R., Farah, M. J., & Greely, H. T. (2013). Law and neuroscience. *The Journal of Neuroscience*, 33(45): 17624-17630.

Jones, J. (2005). Any time is Trinidad time! Cultural variations in the value and function of time. In Strathman, A. & Joireman, J., (Eds), *Understanding behavior in the Context of Time*. Mahwah, NJ: Lawrence Erlbaum Associates.

Johnson, D. B. (1992). Altruistic behavior and the development of self in infants. *Merrill-Palmer Quarterly*, 28, 379-388.

Johnson, R. E. (1969). Smoking and the reduction of cognitive dissonance. *Journal of Personality and Social Psychology*, 9(3), 260-265.

Joo, E. Y., Yoon, C. W., Koo, D. L., Kim, D., & Hong, S. B. (2012). Adverse effects of 24 hours of sleep on cognition and stress hormones. *Journal of Clinical Neurology*, 8: 146-150.

Kabat-Zinn, J. (1990). *Full Catastrophe Living: Using the Wisdom of Your Body and Mind to Face Stress, Pain, and Illness*. New York: Delta.

Kagan, J. (2007). A trio of concerns. *Perspectives on Psychological Science*, 2: 4, 361- 376.

Kahneman, D. & Frederick, S. (2002). Representativeness revisited: attribute substitute in intuitive judgment. In T. D. Gilovich, D. W. Griffin, & D. Kahneman, (Eds.). *Heuristics and Biases*, 49-81. New York: Cambridge University Press.

Kalat, J. (2006). *Biological Psychology* ((9th Edition). Belmont, CA: Wadsworth.

Kanahere, M., Fugua, J., Rink, R., Houk, C., Mauger, D., & Lee, P. A. (2015). Psychosexual development and quality of life outcomes in females with congenital adrenal hyperplasia. *International Journal of Pediatric Endocrinology*, 21, 1-9.

Kapadia, S. & Gala, J. (2015). Gender across cultures: Sex and socialization in childhood. In L. A. Jensen, (Ed.), *The Oxford Handbook of Human Development and Culture: An Interdisciplinary Perspective*. Oxford: Oxford University Press.

Kaptchuk, T. (1983). *The Web That Has No Weaver: Understanding Chinese Medicine*. Chicago: Congdon & Weed.

Kardaras, N.(2016). Generation Z: online and at risk? *Scientific American Mind*, 27 (5), 64-69.

Kaufman, S. B. (May 16, 2013). Gorillas agree: Human frontal cortex is nothing special. *Scientific American Blogs*. Retrieved from www.blogs.scientificamerican.com.

Keel, P. (2005). *Eating Disorders.* Upper Saddle River, N.J.: Pearson Prentice Hall.

Keller, M. (2010). A cross-cultural perspective on friendship research. *ISBBD Newsletter,* 46(2), 10-11, 14. Available from www.mpid-berlin.mpg.de/.../ISBBD.pd.

Kemmer, S. (February/March, 2007). Sticking point. *Scientific American Mind,* 18: 1, 65-69.

Kessler, R. C. & Bromet, E. J. (2013). The epidemiology of depression across cultures. *Annual Review of Public Health,* 34, 119-138.

Kim, J., Suh, W., Kim, S., & Gopalan, H. (2012). Coping strategies to manage acculturative stress: meaningful activity participation, social support, and positive emotion among Korean immigrant adolescents in the USA. *International Journal of Studies in Health and Well-being,* 7, 1-10.

Kirmayer, L. J., Dandeneau, S., Marshall, E., Phillips, M. K., & Williamson, K. J. (2011). Rethinking resilience from indigenous perspectives. *La Revue canadienne de psychiatrie,* 56 (2), 84-91.

Kirmayer, L. J. (2002). Psychopharmacology in a globalizing world: the use of antidepressants in Japan. *Transcultural Psychiatry,* 39, 295.

Kissileff, H. R., Thornton, J. C., Torres, M. I., Pavlovich, K., Mayer, L. S., Leibel, R. L., & Rosenbaum, M. (2012). Leptin reverses declines in satiation in weight-reduced obese humans. *American Journal of Clinical Nutrition,* 95, 309-317.

Kitayama, S., Duffy, S, & Uchida, Y. (2009). Self as a cultural mode of being. In S. Kitayama & D. Cohen, (Eds.), *Handbook of Cultural Psychology.* New York: The Guilford Press.

Kitayama, S., Duffy, S., Kawamura, T., & Larsen, J. T. (2003). Perceiving an object and its context in different cultures: a cultural look at a new look. *Psychological Science,* 14(3), 201-206.

Kitayama, S., Markus, H. R., Matsumoto, H., & Norasakkunkit, V. (1997). Individual and collective processes in the construction of self: Self-enhancement in the United States and self-criticism in Japan. *Journal of Personality and Social Psychology.* 72(6), 1245-1267.

Kleinman, A. (2012, April 18). The art of medicine: Culture, bereavement, and psychiatry. *The Lancet,* Vol. 379 p. 608-9.

Kleinman, A. (September 2, 2004). Culture and depression. *The New England Journal of Medicine,* 31: 10.

Kneer, J., Glock, S., & Rieger, D. (2012). Fast and not furious? Reduction of cognitive dissonance in smokers. *Social Psychology,* 43(2): 81-91.

Knight, Z. A., Hannan, K. S., Greenberg, M. L., & Friedman, J. M. (2010). Hyperleptinemia is required for the development of leptin resistance. *PLoS ONE,* 5:6, 1-8.

Kolb, B. (1999). Toward an ecology of cortical organization: experience and the changing brain. In Grafman, J. & Christen, Y., Eds. *Neuronal Plasticity: Building A Bridge from the Laboratory to the Clinic.* New York: Springer.

Kolb, B., Gibb, R., & Robinson, T. E. (2004). Neuroplasticity and behavior. In Lerner, J, & Alberts, A. E., (Eds.), *Current Directions in Developmental Psychology.* Upper Saddle River, NJ: Pearson Prentice Hall.

Kolb, B. & Robinson, R. (2011). Brain plasticity and behavior in the developing brain. *Journal of Canadian Academic Child and Adolescent Psychiatry,* 20 (4): 265-276.

Konner, M. (2007). Evolutionary foundations of cultural psychology. In Kitayama, S. & Cohen, D., (Eds.), *Handbook of Cultural Psychology.* New York: The Guilford Press.

Krampe, H., Stawicki, S., Hoehe, M. R., & Ehreneich, H. (2007). Outpatient long-term intensive therapy for Alcoholics (OLITA): A successful biopsychosocial approach to the treatment of alcoholism. *Dialogues in Clinical Neuroscience,* 9 (4), 399-412.

Kuhl, P. K. (2010). Brain mechanisms in early language acquisition. *Neuron,* 67, 713-727,

Kuhl, P. K. & Gaxiola, M. (2008). Neural substrates of language acquisition. *Annual Review of Neuroscience,* 31:511-534.

Kuhl, P. (2000). A new view of language acquisition. *PNAS,* 97: 22.

Kulkofsky, S., Wang, Q., Conway, M. A., Hou, Y., Aydin, C., Mueller-Johnson, K., & Williams, H. (2011). Cultural variation in the correlates of flashbulb memory memories: an investigation in five countries. *Memory,* 19(3), 2330-240.

Kunst, J. R. & Sam, D. L. (2013). Expanding the margins of identity: A critique of marginalization in a globalized world. *International Perspectives in Psychology: Research, Practice, Consultation.* 2(4), 225-241.

Kwon, D. (2016). The hidden harms of antidepressants. *Scientific American Mind,* 27(3), 12.

LaBar, K. S. & Cabeza, R. (2006). Cognitive neuroscience of emotional memory. *Nature Reviews Neuroscience,* 7: 54-64.

Lahey, B. (2008). New developments in behavior genetics for introductory and developmental psychology. NITOP, St. Pete Beach, FL.

LeGrange, D. & Lock, J. (n.d.) Family-based treatment of adolescent anorexia nervosa: The Maudsley Approach. www.maudsleyparents.org.

Lam, L. T., & Peng, Z. (2010). Effect of pathological use of the Internet on adolescent mental health. *Archives of Pediatric Adolescent Medicine.* 164 (10): 901-906.

Lambert, K. (2008). Depressingly easy. *Scientific American Mind*, 19(4), 31-37.

Law, B. M. (2011). Seared in our memories. *American Psychological Association Monitor on Psychology,* 42(8), 1-2. Retrieved from www.apa.org/monitor/2011/09/memories.aspx.

Lawson, G. M. & Farah, M. J. (2015). Executive function as a mediator between SES and academic achievement throughout childhood. *International Journal of Behavioral Development,* 1-11.

Lazarus, R. (1993) From psychological stress to the emotions: A history of changing outlooks. *Annual Review of Psychology,* 44: 1-21.

Leaper, C. (2013). Gender development during childhood. In P. D. Zelazo, (Ed.), *The Oxford Handbook of Developmental Psychology, Volume 2.* Oxford: Oxford University Press.

Lebow, J. L. (2003). Integrative approaches to couple and family therapy. In Sexton, T. L., Weeks, G. R., & Robbins, M. S., Eds. *Handbook of Family Therapy.* New York: Routledge.

Lenhart, A. (2015). Teens, technology, and friendships. *Pew Research Center: Internet, Science, & Tech.* available at www.pewinternet.org.

Lee, S. & Kleinman, A. (2007). Are somatoform disorders changing with time? The case of neurasthenia. *Psychosomatic Medicine*, 69: 846-849.

Lee, S. (2000). Eating disorders are becoming more common in the East too. *British Medical Journal*, 321, 10-23.

Lee, S., Ho, T.P., & Hsu, L.K. (1993). Fat phobia and non-fat phobic anorexia nervosa: a comparative study of 70 Chinese patients in Hong Kong. *Psychological Medicine*, 23, 999-1017.

Legard, R., Keegan, J., & Ward, K. (2003). In-depth interviews. In J. Ritchie & J. Lewis, (Eds.), *Qualitative Research Practice.* London: Sage Publications.

Leidy, H. J., Clifton, P. M., Astrup, A., Wycherly, T. P., Westerterp-Plantenga, M. S., Luscombe-Marsch, N. D. ... & Mattes, R. D. (2015). The role of protein in weight loss and maintenance. *American Journal of Clinical Nutrition,* 101, 1320S-9S.

Leidy, H. J., Ortinau, L. C., Douglas, S. M., & Hoertel, H. A. (2013). Beneficial effects of a higher-protein breakfast on the appetitive, hormonal, and neural signals controlling energy intake regulation in overweight/obese, "breakfast skipping," late-adolescent girls. *American Journal of Clinical Nutrition,* 97, 677-688.

Leidy, H. J., & Racki, E. M. (2010). The addition of a protein-rich breakfast and its effects on acute appetite control and food intake in 'breakfast-skipping' adolescents. *International Journal of Obesity, Epub ahead of publication.*

Let's Move: America's move to raise a healthier generation of kids. Retrieved from www.letsmove.gov/.

Let's Move: Whitehouse Task Force on Childhood Obesity report to the president: Solving the problem of childhood obesity in one generation. Retrieved from www.letsmove.gov/taskforce_childhoodobesityreport.html.

Lewis, J. (2003). Design issues. In, J. Ritchie and J. Lewis, (Eds.), *Qualitative Research Practice: A Guide for Social Science Students and Researchers.* London: Sage Publications.

Lewis, J & Ritchie, J. (2003). Generalizing from qualitative research. *Qualitative Research Practice: A Guide for Social Science Students and Researchers.* London: Sage Publications.

Levinson, D. B., Stoll, E. L., Kindy, H. L., & Davidson, R. J. (2014). A mind you can count on: Validating breath counting as a behavioral measure of mindfulness. *Frontiers in Psychology,* 5 (1202), 1-10.

Lips, H.M. (2005). *Sex & Gender: An Introduction.* Boston: McGraw-Hill.

Linn, S. & Novosat, C. L. (2008). Calories for sale: Food marketing to children in the twenty-first century. *The ANNALS of the American Academy of Political Social Science, 615,* 133-155.

Liu, D., Wellman, H. W., Tardif, T., & Sabbath, M. A. (2008). Theory of mind development in Chinese children: a meta-analysis of false-belief understanding across cultures and languages. *Developmental Psychology,* 2, 523-531.

Liu, S. & Page, A. (2016) Reforming mental health in China and India. *The Lancet,* 1-2.

Lobstein, T. & Jackson-Leach, R. (2008). Prevalence of childhood obesity worldwide. *Encyclopedia of obesity.* SAGE Publications, 5, April, 2010.

Lockhart, R. S. (2002). Levels of processing, transfer-appropriate processing, and the concept of robust encoding. *Memory.* 10(516), 397-403.

Loftus, E. F., Miller, D. G., & Burns, H. J. (1978). Semantic integration of verbal information into a visual memory. *Journal of Experimental Psychology: Human Language and Memory,* 4(1), 19-31.

Loftus, E. F. (1975). Leading questions and the eyewitness report. *Cognitive Psychology,* 7, 550-572.

Loftus, E. F. & Palmer, J. C. (1974). Reconstruction of automobile destruction: An example of the interaction between language and memory. *Journal of Verbal Learning and Verbal Behavior,* 13, 585-589.

Logie, R. H., Zucco, G. M., & Baddeley, A. D. (1990). Interference with visual short-term memory. *Acts Psychologica,* 75, 55-74.

Lopez, E. B. & Yamashita, T. (2016). Acculturation, income, and vegetable consumption behaviors among Latino adults in the US: a mediation analysis with the bootstrapping technique. *Journal of Immigrant Minor Health,* Epub ahead of print.

Lombardi, M. M. (2007). Authentic learning for the 21st century: an overview. D. G. Oblinger, (Ed.). *Educause Learning Initiative.*

Lorentz, P., Ferguson, C. J., & Schott, G. (2015). Editorial: The experience and benefits of game playing. *Cyberpsychology: Journal of Psychological Research on Cyberspace,* 9(3), article 1.

Ludwig, D. S. & Kabat-Zinn, J. (2008). Mindfulness in medicine. *Journal of the American Medical Association,* 300:11, 1350-1352.

Luminet, O. & Curci, A. (2009). The 9/11 attacks inside and outside the US: testing four models of flashbulb memory formation across groups and the specific effects of social identity. *Memory,* 17(7), 742-759.

Lutz, T. A. & Woods, S. C. (2013). Overview of animal models of obesity. *Curr Protoc Pharmacol.,* Chapter: Unit 5:61.

Ma, J. L. (2008). Eating disorders, parent-child conflicts, and family therapy in Shenzhen, China. *Qualitative Health Research,* 18, 6, 803-810.

Ma, V. & Shoeneman, T. J. (1997). Individualism versus collectivism: A comparison of Kenyan and American self-concepts. *Basic and Applied Social Psychology,* 19, 261-273.

Major Depression Facts (2016) Retrieved from www.clinical-depression.co.uk.

Makino, M., Tsuboi, K., & Dennerstein, L. (2004). Prevalence of eating disorders: a comparison of western and non-western countries. MedGenMed: *Medscape General Medicine,* 6: 3.

Manuck, S. B., Kaplan, J. R., & Lotrich, F. E. (2006). Brain serotonin and aggressive disposition in humans and nonhuman primates. In Nelson, R. J., (Ed.), *Biology of Aggression.* Oxford: Oxford University Press.

Marchiori, D., Papies, E. K., & Klein, O. (2014). The portion size effect on food intake: an anchoring and adjustment process? *Appetite,* 81, 108-115.

Markant, J. C. & Thomas, K. M. (2013). Postnatal brain development. In P. D. Zelazo, (Ed.). *The Oxford Handbook of Developmental Psychology, Vol. 1.* Oxford: Oxford University Press.

Markus, H. R. & Hamedani, M. G. (2007). Sociocultural psychology: The dynamic interdependence among self systems and social systems. In Kitayama, S., & Cohen, D., (Eds.). *Handbook of Cross-Cultural Psychology.* York: The Guilford Press.

Markus, H. R. & Kitayama, S. (1991). Culture and self: Implications for cognition, emotion, and motivation. *Psychological Review.* 98: 2, 224-253.

Markus, H. R. (1977). Self-schemata and processing information about the self. *Journal of Personality and Social Psychology.* 35, 63-78.

Marmot, M. & Brunner, E. (2005). Cohort profile: The Whitehall II study. *International Journal of Epidemiology,* 34, 251-256.

Meditation. (2009). *The SAGE Glossary of the Social and behavioral Sciences.* SAGE Publications. 5 April 2010.

Marsella, A. J., & Yamada, A. M. (2007). Culture and psychopathology: foundations, issues, and directions. In, Kitayama, S. & Cohen, D., (Eds.), *Handbook of Cultural Psychology.* New York: The Guilford Press.

Marsh, E. J. & Butler, A. C. (2013). Memory in educational settings. In D. Reisberg, (Ed.), *The Oxford Handbook of Cognitive Psychology.* Oxford, Oxford University Press.

Martinez-Torteya, C., Bogat, A., von Eye, A., & Levendosky, A. A. (2009). Resilience among children exposed to domestic violence: the role of risk and protective factors. *Child Development,* 80 (2), 562-577.

Masten, A. S. (2014). Global Perspectives on resilience in children and youth. *Child Development,* 85 (1), 6-20.

Masten, A. S. (2013). Risk and resilience in development. In P. D. Zalazo, (Ed.), *The Oxford Handbook of Developmental Psychology, Vol. 2.* Oxford: Oxford University Press.

Masuda, T. & Kitayama, S. (2004). Perceiver-induced constraint and attitude attribution in Japan and the US: a case for the cultural dependence of the correspondence bias. *Journal of Experimental Psychology.* 40(3), 09-416.

Matsuda, N. (1985). Strong, quasi-, and weak conformity among Japanese in the modified Asch procedure. *Journal of Cross-Cultural Psychology*, 16: 1, 83-97.

Matsumoto, D. (1996). Interpersonal Assessment Inventory (ICIAI): A Domain-Specific Measure of Individualistic and Collectivistic Values Related to Social Interaction.

Matsumoto, D. (2008). Culture and the teaching of psychology. NITOP. St Pete Beach, FL.

Matsumoto, D.& Juang, L. (2008). *Culture and Psychology,* (4th ed.). Belmont, CA: Wadsworth/Thomson Learning.

Matsumoto, D. (2002). *The New Japan: Debunking Seven Cultural Stereotypes.* London: Intercultural Press, Nicholas Brealey Publishing.

Matsumoto, D, (1996). *Unmasking Japan: Myths and Realities about the Emotions of The Japanese.* Stanford, CA: Stanford University Press.

Mazzeo, S. E., & Bulik, C.M. (2009). Environmental and genetic risk factors for eating disorders: what the clinician needs to know. *Child & Adolescent Psychiatric Clinics North America*, 18: 1, 67-82.

McDermott, A. F., Bavelier, D. & Green, C. S. (2014). Memory abilities in action video game players. *Computers in Human Behavior,* 34, 69-78.

McKinley, T. (2008). World patterns. *Encyclopedia of Obesity.* SAGE Publications 5, April, 2010. www.sage-ereference.com/obesity/Article_n486.html.

McMillan, J. & Schumacher, S. (1984). *Research in Education.* Boston: Little, Brown & Co.

McSweeney, S. (2004). Depression in women. In P. J. Caplan & L. Cosgrove (Eds.). *Bias in Psychiatric Diagnosis.* Latham, MD: Littlefield Publishers.

MedlinePlus (2012). Hormones. Available from www.nim.nih.gov/medlineplus/hormones.html.

Mercurio, M. K. & Mercurio, S. B. (2008). Alcoholics Anonymous. *Encyclopedia of Counseling.*
SAGE Publications. 5 April, 2010. www.sage-ereference.com/counseling/Article_n6.html.

Mermelstein, L.C. & Garske, J. P. (2014). A brief mindfulness intervention for college student binge drinkers: A pilot study. *Psychology of Addictive Behaviors,* 29 (2), 259-269.

Merabet, L. B, Hamilton, R., Schlaug, G., Swisher, J. D., Kirakopoulos, E. T., Pitskel, N. B., . . . Pascual-Leone, A. (2008). Rapid and reversible recruitment of early visual cortex for touch. PLoS ONE 3(8): e3046.

Meyer, M., Cimpian, A., & Leslie, S. (2015). Women are underrepresented in fields where success is believed to require brilliance. *Frontiers in Psychology*, 6 (235) 1-12.

Michl, L. C., McLaughlin, K. A., Shepherd, K., & Nolen-Hoeksema, S. (2013). Rumination as a mechanism linking stressful life events to symptoms of depression and anxiety: Longitudinal evidence in early adolescents and adults. *Journal of Abnormal Psychology,* 122 (2): 339-352.

Miller, C. M. (March, 2003). Are antidepressants placebos? *Harvard Mental Health Letter,* 19: 9.

Miller, G. (2003, March). The cognitive revolution: a historical perspective. *Trends in Cognitive Sciences,* 17: 3, 141-144.

Miller, G. A. (1956). The magical number seven, plus or minus two: some limits on our capacity for processing information. *Psychological Review,* 63, 81-97.

Miller, P., Fung, H., & Koven, M. (2007). Narrative reverberations: how participation in narrative practices co-creates persons and cultures. In Kitayama, S. & Cohen, D., Eds. *Handbook of Cultural Psychology.* New York: The Guilford Press.

Minkel, J., Moreta, M., Muto, J., Htaik, O., Jones, C., Basner, M., & Dinges, D. (2014). Sleep deprivation potentiates HPA axis stress reactivity in healthy adults. *Health Psychology,* 33 (11), 1430-1434.

Moll, H. & Tomasello, M. (2007). Cooperation and human cognition: the Vygotskian intelligence hypothesis. *Philosophical Transactions of the Royal Society.*

Moore, D. S. (2013). Behavioral genetics, genetics, and epigenetics. In P. D. Zelazo, (Ed.), *The Oxford Handbook of Developmental Psychology, Vol. 1: Body and Mind. Oxford: Oxford University Press.*

Morelli, G. (2015). The evolution of attachment theory and cultures of human attachment in infancy and early childhood. In Jensen, L. A., (Ed.), *The Oxford Handbook of Human Development and Culture.* Oxford: Oxford University Press.

Morrison, C. M. & Gore, H. (2010). The relationship between excessive Internet use and depression: a questionnaire-based study of 1319 young people and adults. *Psychopathology.* 43 (2): 121-6.

Morrison, S. J., Demorest, S. M., & Stambaugh, L. A. (2008). Enculturation effects in music cognition: the role of age and music complexity. *Journal of Research in Music Education,* 56, 118-128.

Murdock, B.B. (1962). The serial position effect of free recall. *Journal of Experimental Psychology,* 5, 482-488.

Nahas, R. & Sheikh, O. (2011). Complementary and alternative medicine for the treatment of major depressive disorder. *Canadian Family Physician.* 57: 659-663.

National Child Traumatic Stress Network (2015). Early childhood trauma. www.nctsn.org.

National Children's Bureau (2016). Growing up in poverty detrimental to children's friendships and family life. www.ncb.org.uk.

National Heart Lung and Blood Institute Diseases and Conditions Index (n.d.). What causes overweight and obesity? www.nhlbi.nih.gov/health/dci/Diseases/obe/obe_causes.html.

National Institute of Health (2015) Alcohol Facts and Statistics. www.niaaa.nih.gov.

National Institute of Health (2010). Fact sheet: self-management. Available from http://report.nih.gov/nihfactsheet/Pdfs/self-management(NINR).pdf.

National Institute of Mental Health (2016). Major depression among adults. www.nimh.nih.gov.

National Institute of Mental Health (2008). Depression. www.nimh.nih.gov/.

National Institute of Mental Health (1997). The Diagnostic Interview Schedule (DIS-IV).

National Sleep Foundation (2014). What happens when you sleep? Retrieved 1/10/2015 from http://sleepfoundation.org/how-sleep-works/what-happens-when-you-sleep.com

Neisser, U. (2000). Snapshots or benchmarks? In Neisser, U. & Hyman, I. E., (Eds.), *Memory Observed: Remembering in Natural Contexts,* 2nd Ed. New York: Worth.

Neisser, U. & Harsch, N. (2000). Phantom flashbulbs. In Neisser, U. & Hyman, I. E., (Eds.), *Memory Observed: Remembering in Natural Contexts,* 2nd Ed. New York: Worth.

Neuman. W. L. (2006). *Social Research Methods: Qualitative and Quantitative Approaches,* 6th ed. Boston: Pearson.

Newell, B. R. (2013). Judgment under uncertainty. In D. Reisberg (Ed.). *The Oxford Handbook of Cognitive Psychology.* Oxford: Oxford University Press.

Ng'asike, J. T. (2015). Take me to the (dry) river: children's play in Turkana pastoralist communities of Kenya. In J. L. Roopnarine, M. M. Patte, J. E. Johnson, & D. Kuschner (Eds.). *International Perspectives on Children's Play.* Berkshire, England: Open University Press: McGraw-Hill Education.

Nickerson, R. S. (1998). Confirmation bias: A ubiquitous phenomenon in many guises. *Review of General Psychology.* 2(2), 175-220.

Nieuwsma, J. A., Pepper, C. M., Maack, D. J., & Birgenheir, D. G. (2011). Indigenous perspectives on depression in rural regions of India and the United States. *Transcultural Psychiatry,* 48 (5), 539-568.

Nightingale, D. J. & Cromby, J. (1999). *Social Constructionist Psychology: A Critical Analysis of Theory and Practice.* Berkshire, UK: Open University Press.

Nisbett, R. E. & Masuda, T. (2003). Culture and point of view. *PNAS.* 100 (19), 11163-11170.

Nisbett, R. E., & Norenzayan, A. (2002). Culture and cognition. In D. L. Medin (Ed.). *Stevens' Handbook of Experimental Psychology, 3rd Edition.* New York: Wiley & Sons, Inc.

Nolan-Hoeksema, S. (2004). Gender differences in depression. In T. F. Oltmanns & R. E. Emery, (Eds.), *Current Directions in Abnormal Psychology.* Upper Saddle River, NJ: Pearson Prentice Hall.

Norenzayan, A., Choi, I., & Peng, K. (2007). Perception and cognition. In S. Kitayama & D. Cohen, (Eds.). *Handbook of Cultural Psychology.* New York: The Guilford Press.

North, F. M., Syme, S. L., Feeney, A., Shipley, M. & Marmot, M. (1996). Psychosocial work environment and sickness absence among British civil servants: the Whitehall II study. *American Journal of Public Health, 83,* 3, 332-340.

Nuutinen, T, Ray, C., & Roos, E. (2013). Do computer use, TV viewing, and the presence of the media in the bedroom predict school-aged children's sleep habits in a longitudinal study? *BMC Public Health,* 13 (684), 1-8.

Office for National Statistics (2014). Persistent poverty in the UK and EU. Retrieved from www.ons.gov.uk.

Ogden, C. L., Lamb, M.M., Carroll, M. D., & Flegal, K. M. (2010). Obesity and socioeconomic status in children and adolescents: United States, 2005-2008. *NCHS data brief #51.* Hyattsville, MD: National Center for Health Statistics.

Oh, H. & Kim, Y. (2014). Drinking behavior and drinking refusal self-efficacy in Korean college students. *Psychological Reports,* 115 (3), 872-873.

Okazaki, S. & Ling, A. (2013). Assessing and treating Asian Americans: Recent advances in mental health research. In F. A. Paniagua & A. M. Yamada, (Eds.), *Handbook of Multicultural Mental Health,* 2nd Ed. Amsterdam, Elsevier.

Okello, E. S. & Ekblad, S. (2006) Lay concepts of depression among the Baganda of Uganda: a pilot study. *Transcultural Psychiatry,* 43: 2, 287-313.

Okello, E.S. & Musisi, S. (2006). Depression as a clan illness (eByekika): an indigenous model of psychotic depression among the Baganda of Uganda. *World Cultural Psychiatry Research Review,* 1 (2): 60-73.

Oman, D., Shapiro, S. L., Thorensen, C. E., Plante, T. G., & Flinders, T. (2008). Meditation lowers stress and supports forgiveness among college students: A randomized controlled trial. *Journal of American College Health, 56,* 5, 569-578.

Open Science Collaboration (2015). Estimating the reproducibility of psychological science. *Science, 349* (6251), aac4716-1- 8.

Opportunities in the pharmacotherapy of addiction. (2008). The SAGE Handbook of Healthcare.
SAGE Publications. 5 April, 2010. www.sage-ereference.com/healthcare?Article_n30.html.

O'Rahilly, S. (2002). Insights into obesity and insulin resistance from the study of extreme human phenotypes. *European Journal of Endocrinology,* 147: 435-441.

O'Toole, T. P., Anderson, S., Miller, C., & Guthrie, J. (2007). Nutrition services and foods and beverages available at school: Results from the school health policies and programs study 2006. *Journal of School Health, 77* (8) 500-521.

Ostrov, J. M. & Godleski, S. A. (2010). Toward a gender-linked model of aggression subtypes in early and middle childhood. *Psychological Review,* (117) 1, 233-242.

Pajares, F. & Miller, D. M. (1994). Role of self-efficacy and self-concept beliefs in mathematical problem-solving: a path analysis. *Journal of Educational Psychology,* 86(2), 193-203.

Palmer, S. E. (1975). The effects of contextual scenes on the identification of objects. *Memory and Cognition,* 3(5), 519-526.

Paniagua, F. A. (2013). Culture-bound syndromes, cultural variations, and psychopathology. In F. A. Paniagua & A. M. Yamada, (Eds.), *Handbook of Multicultural Mental Health,* 2nd Ed. Amsterdam, Elsevier.

Papagno, C., Valentine, T., & Baddeley, A. (1991). Pholological short-term memory and foreign language vocabulary learning. *Journal of Memory and Language.* 30(3), 331-347.

Parker, G., Gladstone, G., & Chee, Q. T. (2001). Depression in the planet's largest ethnic group: the Chinese. *American Journal of Psychiatry,* 158:857-864.

Pascual-Leone, A. (2009). Characterizing and modulating neuroplasticity of the adult human brain. In *The Cognitive Neurosciences,* 4th Edition, M. S. Gazzaniga (Ed.), Cambridge, MA: Bradford Book, MIT Press.

Passingham, R. E. & Smaers, J. B. (2014). Is the prefrontal cortex especially enlarged in the human brain? Allometric relations and remapping factors. *Brain, Behavior and Evolution,* 84: 156-166.

Patel, D. (2015). Pharmacotherapy for the management of obesity. *Metabolism: Clinical and Experimental,* 64, 1376-1385.

Patel, V., Flisher, A. J., Hetrick, S., & McGorry, P. (2007). Mental health of young people: A global public-health challenge. *Lancet,* 369: 1302-13.

Pea, R., Nass, C., Meheula, L., Rance, M., Kumar, A., Bamford, H. . . . & Zhou, M. (2012). Media use, face-to-face communication, media multitasking, and social well-being among 8- to 12-year-old girls. *Developmental Psychology,* 48 (2), 327-336.

Pe-Pua, R. (2006). From decolonizing psychology to the development of a cross-indigenous perspective in methodology: The Philippine experience. In U. Kim, K. Yang, & K. Hwang, (Eds.), *Indigenous and Cultural Psychology: Understanding People in Context.* New York: Springer.

Peele, S. & DeGrandpre, R. (1995, July). My genes made me do it. *Psychology Today.*

Pellegrini, A. D. (2013). Play. In P. D. Zelazo (Ed.), *The Oxford Handbook of Developmental Psychology, Vol. 2.* Oxford: Oxford University Press.

Pergolizzi, J., Ahlbeck, K., Aldington, D., Alon, E., Coluzzi, F. .....& Sichere, P. (2013). The development of chronic pain: Physiological CHANGE necessitates a multidisciplinary approach to treatment. *Current Medical Research and Opinion, 29* (9), 1127-1135.

Perner, J., Leekman, S. & Wimmer, H. (1987). Three-year-olds difficulty with false belief: The case for a conceptual deficit. *British Journal of Developmental Psychology,* 5, 125-137.

Peters, R. D., Wagner, E., Alicandri, E., Fox, J. E., Thomas, M. L......& Balwinski, S. M. (1999). Effects of partial and total sleep deprivation on driving performance. Retrieved from http://www.fhwa.dot.gov/publicaccess.gov.

Peterson, T. J. (2006). Enhancing the effects of antidepressants with psychotherapy. *Journal of Psychopharmacology,* 20 (3), 19-28.

Petrova, P. K., Cialdini, R. B., & Sills, S. J. (2007). Consistency-based compliance across cultures. *Journal of Experimental Social Psychology,* 43, 104-111.

Phang, S. H., Ravani, P., Schaefer, J., Wright, B., & McLaughlin, K. (2015). Internal medicine residents use heuristics to estimate disease probability. *Canadian Medical Education Journal,* 6(2), e71-e77.

Phelps, E. A. & Sharot, T. (2008). How (and why) emotion enhances the subjective sense of recollection. *Current Directions in Psychological Science,* 17(2), 147-152.

Phelps, E. A. (2002). Human emotion and memory: interactions of the amygdala and hippocampal complex. *Current Opinion in Neurobiology,* 14, 198-202.

Phelps, E. A., O'Connor, K. J., Gatenby, C., Grillon, C., & Davis, M. (2001). Activation of the left amygdala to a cognitive representation of fear. *Neuroscience,* 4: 4.

Phillips, T. (2002). Animal models for the genetic study of human alcohol phenotypes. *Alcohol Research and Health,* 26(3), 202-207.

Pinker, S. (2002). *The Blank Slate: The Modern Denial of Human Nature.* New York: Penguin Books.

Pinker, S. (1994). *The language Instinct: How the Mind Creates Language.* New York: HarperCollins.

Player, M.S., King, D. E., Mainius, A. G., & Geesey, M. E. (2007). Psychosocial factors and progression from prehypertension to hypertension or coronary heart disease. *Annals of Family Medicine,* 5 (5), 403-411.

Poland, J. & Caplan, P. J. (2004). The deep structure of bias in psychiatric diagnosis. In P. J. Kaplan & L. Cosgrove, (Eds.). *Biases in Psychiatric Diagnosis.* Latham, MD: Rowman & Littlefield.

Porvinelli, D. J. & O'Neill, D. K. (2000). Do chimpanzees use their gestures to instruct each other? In S. Baron-Cohen, H. Tager-Flushberg, & D. J. Cohen, (Eds.), *Understanding Other Minds: Perspectives from Developmental Cognitive Neuroscience* (2nd ed.). Oxford: Oxford University Press.

Preuss, T. M. & Robert, J. S. (2014). Animal models of the human brain: Repairing the paradigm. In M. S. Gazzaniga & G. R. Mangun (Eds.), *The Cognitive Neurosciences,* 5th ed., Cambridge, MA: MIT Press, 59-66.

Preuss, T. M. (2009). The cognitive neuroscience of human uniqueness. In M. S. Gazzaniga (Ed.), *The Cognitive Neurosciences,* 4th ed., Cambridge, MA: MIT Press, 49-64.

Princeton Review (2011). Available from www.thebestcolleges.org/2012-princeton-review- party-school-rankings/.

PubMed Health (2010). Orlistat. Retrieved from www.ncbi.nlm.gov/pubmedhealth/PMH0000175.

Quah-Smith, I., Wei Wen, B. E., Chen, X., M., et al, (2012). The brain effects of laser acupuncture in depressed individuals: An fMRI investigation. *Medical Acupuncture,* 24 (3): 161-171.

Ramachandran, (no date). Mirror neurons and imitation learning as the driving force behind "the great leap forward" in human evolution. Retrieved from www.edge.org/3rd_culture/ramachandran/ramachandran_p1.html.

Ramachandran, V. S. (1998). *Phantoms in the Brain.* New York: HarperCollins.

Raza, Q., Nicolaou, M., Snijder, MB., Stronks, K., & Seidell, J. C. (2016). Dietary acculturation among the South-Asian Surinamese population int he NetherlandsL the HELIUS study. *Public Health and Nutrition,* Epub ahead of print.

Redelmeier, M. D. & Tibshirani, R. J. (1997). Association between cellular-telephone calls and motor vehicle collisions. *New England Journal of Medicine,* 336, 453-458.

Reedy, S. (2015). Pediatricians rethink screen time policy for children. *Wall Street Journal.* Retrieved from www.wsj.com/articles/pediatricians-rethink-screen-time-policy-for-children-14446711636.

Repacholi, B. M. & Gopnik, A. (1997). Early reasoning about desires: Evidence from 14- and 18-month olds. *Developmental Psychology,* 1, 12-21.

Ribeiro, A. C., Ceccarini, G., Dupre, C., Friedman, J. M., Pfaff, D. W., & Mark, A. L. (2011). Contrasting effects of leptin on food anticipatory and total locomotor activity. *PLoS One,* 6(8), e23364.

Riebl, S. K, MacDougal, C., Hill, C., Dunsmore, J. C., Salva, J. ...& Davy, B. M. (2016). Beverage choices of adolescents and their parents using the theory of planned behavior: a mixed methods analysis. *Journal of the Academy of Nutrition and Diet,* 16(2), 226-239.

Rilling, J. K. & Stout, D. (2014). Evolution of the neural bases of higher cognitive function in humans. In M. S. Gazzaniga & G. R. Mangun (Eds.), *The Cognitive Neurosciences,* 5th ed., Cambridge, MA: MIT Press, 41-49.

Ritchie, J. (2003). The applications of qualitative research. In J. Ritchie & J. Lewis, (Eds.), *Qualitative Research Methods: A guide for Social Science Students and Researchers.* London: Sage Publications.

Ritchie, J, Lewis, J. & Elam, G. (2003). Designing and selecting samples. In J. Ritchie & J. Lewis, (Eds.), *Qualitative Research Methods: A guide for Social Science Students and Researchers.* London: Sage Publications.

Robinson, T. N., Borzekowski, D. L. G., Matheson, D. M., Kraemer, H.C. (2007). Effects of fast food branding on young children's taste preferences. *Archives of Pediatric and Adolescent Medicine, 161* (8), 792-797.

Rockler-Glashen, N. (2010). Top party schools 2010-2011: Princeton Review rankings. Available from www.suite101.com/content/top-american-party-schools-2010-2011-princeton-review-rankings.

Roediger, H. L. & DeSoto, K. A. (n.d.). Psychology of reconstructive memory. Retrieved from www.psych.wustl.edu.

Romero, A. J., Martinez, D., & Caravajal, S.C. (2007). Bicultural stress and adolescent risk behaviors in a community sample of Latinos and non-Latino European Americans. *Ethnicity and Health,* 12 (5), 443-63.

Roopnarine, J. L. (2015). Play as culturally situated: diverse perspectives on its meaning and significance. In J. L. Roopnarine, M.M. Patte, J. E. Johnson, & D. Kushner, (Eds.), *International Perspectives on Children's Play. Berkshire, England: Open University Press, McGraw-Hill Education.*

Rose, A. J. & Rudolph, K. D. (2006). A review of sex differences in peer relationship processes: Potential trade-offs for the emotional and behavioral development of girls and boys. *Psychological Bulletin,* (132) 1, 98-131.

Rosenthal, R. (1993). *Homeless in Paradise.* Philadelphia, PA: Temple University Press.

Rubin, K. H., Bowker, J. C., McDonald, K. L., Menzer, M. (2013). Peer relationships in childhood. In P. D. Zelazo (Ed.), *The Oxford Handbook of Developmental Psychology, Vol. 2.* Oxford: Oxford University Press.

Rubin, K., Bukowski, W., & Parker, J. (2006). Peer interactions, relationships, and groups. In W. Damon, R. Lerner, & N. Eisenberg, (Eds.), *Handbook of Child Psychology, Vol. 3. Social, Emotional, and Personality Development* (6th Ed., 571-645). New York: Wiley.

Runyon, R. P., Haber, A., Pittenger, D. J., & Coleman, K. A. (1996). *Fundamentals of Behavioral Statistics,* 8th ed. New York: McGraw-Hill.

Russell, M. J. (1976). Human olfactory communication. *Nature,* 260(5551), 520-522.

Sabbagh, L. (2006, August/September). The teenage brain hard at work: no, really. Scientific American Mind, 17: 4, 20-25.

Sage Publications. (no date). Acculturation. Retrieved from http.//www.sagepub.com/upm-data/30900_chapter4.pdf.

Samuel, D. Brown, B.B., & Blinka, L. (2012). Associations between online friendships and Internet addiction among adolescents and emerging adults. *Developmental Psychology,* 48(2), 381-388.

Sapolsky, R. M. (2004). *Why Zebras Don't Get Ulcers, 3rd edition.* New York: Henry Holt.

Saxe, R. & Wexler, A. (2005). Making sense of another mind: the role of the right temporo-parietal junction. *Neuropsychologia.*

Schank, R. C. (2010). Scripts. Retrieved from www.cognitrn.psych.indianna.edu/.../schemaforlanguage.pdf.

Schmidt, U., Adan, R., Bohm, I., Campbell, I. C., Dingemans, A. Ehrlich, S....& Zipfel, S. (2016). Eating disorders: the big issue. *The Lancet,* 3(4), 313-315.

Schmidt, U., Magill, N., Renwick, B., Keyes, A., Kenyon, M. Delong, H....& Beecham, J. (2015). The Maudsley outpatient study of treatments for anorexia nervosa and related conditions (MOSAIC): Comparison of the Maudsley model of anorexia nervosa treatment for adults (MANTRA) with specialist supportive clinical management (SSCM) in outpatients with broadly defined anorexia nervosa: A randomized controlled trial. *Journal of Counseling and Clinical Psychology,* 83 (4), 796-807.

Schuckit, M.A., Smith, T. L., & Kalmijn, J. A. (2014). The pattern of drug and alcohol use and associated problems over 30 years in 397 men. *Alcohol Clinical Experimental Research,* 38(1): 227-234.

Schuckit, M. A. (2013). A brief history of research on the genetics of alcohol and other drug use disorders. *Journal of Studies on Alcohol and Drugs,* 17, 59-67.

Schuckit, M., Kalmijn, J. A., Smith, T. L., Saunders, G., & Fromme, K. (2012). Structuring a college alcohol prevention program on the low level of response to alcohol model: A pilot study. *Alcoholism: Clinical and Experimental Research*, Vol **, No. **, 1-9. In press.

Schuckit, M. (2008a). An overview of genetic influences in alcoholism. *Journal of Substance Abuse Treatment, 36* (2) 5-14.

Schuckit, M. (2008b). Alcohol-use disorders. *The Lancet, 372*, 1-10.

Schuster, M. A., Stein, B. D., Jaycox, L. H., Collins, R. L., Marshall, G. N., Elliot, M. N….& Berry, S. H. (2001). A national survey of stress reactions after the September 11, 2001 terrorist attacks. *New England Journal of Medicine, 345* (20), 1507-1512.

Seawall, J. T. (2010). Hurricane Katrina: psychological. hurricanekatrina.web.unc.edu.

Shahaeian, A., Peterson, C. C., Slaughter, V. & Wellman, H. M. (2011). Culture and the sequence of steps in theory of mind development. *Developmental Psychology, 47*(5), 1239-1247.

Siegel, L. J. (n.d.) Are telomeres the key to aging and cancer? Available from http://learn.genetics.utah.edu/content/begin/traits/telomeres/.

Singelis, T. (1999). Singelis Self-Construal Scale. Retrieved from www.psychology.ucdavis.edu/acrdr/meausres/singelisscs.doc.

Sleep Health (2010). Available from HealthyPeople.gov.

Slovak, P., Finucane, M. L., Peters, E., & MacGregor, D. G. (2004). Risk as analysis and risk as feelings: some thoughts about affect, reason, risk, and rationality. *Risk Analysis*, 24(2), 311-322.

Small, G, & Vorgan, G. (2008). Meet your iBrain: how the technologies that have become part of our daily lives are changing the way we think. *Scientific American Mind*, 19: 5, 42-49.

Snape, D. & Spencer, L. (2003). The foundations of qualitative research. In Ritchie, J. & Lewis, J., Eds. *Qualitative Research Practice*. London: Sage Publications.

Somer, E. (1999). *Food & Mood*, 2nd ed. New York: Henry Holt & Co.

Sparrow, B, Liu, J., & Wegner, D. M. (2011). Google effects on memory: cognitive consequences of having information at our fingertips. *Science*, 333, 776-778.

Sperling, G. (1960). The information available in brief visual presentations. *Psychological Monographs: General and Applied*, 74(11, Whole No. 498), 1-29.

Stanovich, K. E. (2007). *How to Think Straight about Psychology*, (8th Ed.). New York: Longman.

Steers, M. N., Wickham, R. E., & Acitelli, L. K. (2014). Seeing everyone else's highlight reels: how Facebook usage is linked to depression. *Journal of Social and Clinical Psychology*, 33 (8), 701-731.

Steinberg, L. (Jan, 2008). Inside the adolescent brain. NITOP. St. Pete Beach, FL.

Steinglass, J., Mayer, L., & Attia, E. (2016). Treatment of restrictive eating and low-weight conditions, including anorexia nervosa and avoidant/restrictive food intake disorder. In B. T. Walsh, E. Attia, D. R. Glasofer, & R. Sysko, (Eds.), *Handbook of Assessment and Treatment of Eating Disorders*. Arlington, VA: American Psychiatric Association Publishing.

Sternberg, R. J. & Sternberg, K. (2012). *Cognitive Psychology*, (6th ed.). Belmont, CA: Wadsworth/Cengage Learning.

Sternberg, R. (2006). *Cognitive Psychology*, (4th ed). Belmont, CA: Wadsworth/Thomson Learning.

Stetka, B. (2016, March/April)). In search of the optimal brain diet. *Scientific American Mind*, 27 (2), 26-33.

Stickgold, R. & Ellenbogen, J. M. (2008, August/September). Quiet! Sleeping brain at work. *Scientific American Mind*, 19:4, 23-29.

Straub, R. O. (2014). *Health Psychology: A Biopsychosocial Approach*, 4th edition. New York: Worth.

Strayer, D. L. & Drews, F. A. (2007). Cell-phone-induced driver distraction. *Current Directions in Psychological Science*. 10(3), 128-131.

Stroop, J. R. (1935). Studies of interference in serial verbal reactions. *Journal of Experimental Psychology*. 18, 624-643.

Suarez-Orozco, C. (2015). Migration between and within countries: implications for families and acculturation. In L. A. Jensen, (Ed.). *The Oxford Handbook of Human Development and Culture*. Oxford: Oxford University Press.

Suls, J., Krantz, D. S., & Williams, G.C. (2013). Three strategies for bridging different levels of analysis and embracing the biopsychosocial model. *Health Psychology*, 22 (5), 597-601.

Suls, J. & Rothman, A. (2004). Evolution of the biopsychosocial model: Prospects and challenges for health psychology. *Health Psychology*, 23 (2), 119-125.

Suomi, S. J. & Harlow, H. F. (1972). Social rehabilitation of isolate-reared monkeys. *Developmental Psychology,* 3, 487-496.

Sundararajan, L., Misra, G., & Marsella, A. J. (2013). Indigenous approaches to assessment, diagnosis, and treatment of mental disorders. In F. A. Paniagua & A. M. Yamada, (Eds.), *Handbook of Multicultural Mental Health,* 2nd edition. Amsterdam, Elsevier.

Sussner, K. M., Lindsay, A. C., Greaney, M., & peterson, K. E. (2008). The influence of immigrant status and acculturation on the development of overweight in Latino families: a qualitative study. *Journal of Immigrant Minor Health,* 10(6), 497-505.

Symeonidou, I., Dumentheil, I., Chow, W., & Breheny, R. (2015). Development of online use of theory of mind during adolescence: An eye-tracking study. *Journal of Experimental Child Psychology,* [epub ahead of print].

Tabassum, R., Macaskill, A., &Ahmad, I. (2000). Attitudes toward mental health in an urban Pakistani community in the United Kingdom. *International Journal of Social Psychiatry,* 46: 3, 170-181.

Tajfel, H. & Turner, J. C. (1986). The Social Identity Theory of in-group behavior. In S. Worchel & W. G. Austin, Eds. *Psychology of Intergroup Relations,* (2nd ed.). Burnham, Inc.

Tan, R. & Goldman, M. S. (2015). Exposure to female fertility pheromones influences men's drinking. *Experimental Clinical Psychopharmacology,* 23(3), 139-146.

Takano, Y. & Sogon, S. (2008). Are Japanese more collectivist than Americans? examining conformity in in-groups and the reference group effect. *Journal of Cross-Cultural Psychology,* 30: 3, 237-250.

Talarico, J. M. & Rubin, D. C. (2007). Flashbulb memories are special after all; in phenomenology, not accuracy. *Applied Cognitive Psychology,* 21, 557-578.

Tao, R., Calley, C. S., Hart, J., Mayes, T. L., Nakonezny, P. A., Lu, H….& Emslie, G. J. (2012). Brain activity in adolescent major depressive disorder before and after fluoxetine treatment. *American Journal of Psychiatry,* 169: 381-388.

Tarullo, A. R. & Gunnar, M. R. (2006). Child maltreatment and the developing HPA axis. *Hormones and Behavior,* 50, 632-639.

Tavris, C., & Wade, C. (2001). *Psychology in Perspective,* 3rd edition. Upper Saddle River, NJ: Prentice-Hall.

Tchanturia, K., Harrison, A., Davies, H., Roberts, M., Oldershaw, Nakazato, M….& Treasure, J. (2011). Cognitive flexibility and clinical severity in eating disorders. *PLoS One* 6 (6): e20462.

Tengku, A., Tengku, I., Muda, W. A. M. W., & Bakar, M. I. (2016). The extended theory of planned behavior in explaining exclusive breastfeeding and behavior among women in Kelantan, Malaysia. *Nutrition Research and Practice,* 10(1), 49-55.

Thagard Student Health Center (2011). Healthy Campus 2010. Available from www.tshc.fsu.edu/about/hc2010.htm.

Thirthalli, J., Zhou, L., Kumar, K, Gao, J., Vaid, H., Liu, H…. & NIcher, M. (2016). traditional, complementary, and alternative medicine approaches to mental health care and psychological wellbeing in India and China. *The Lancet,* 1-13.

Thompson, R. A. (2013). Attachment theory and research: precis and prospect. In P. D. Zelazo, (Ed.), *The Oxford Handbook of Developmental Psychology.* Oxford: Oxford University Press.

Thompson, R. A. (2012). Changing societies, changing childhood: studying the impact of globalization on child development. *Child Development Perspectives,* 6 (2), 187-192.

Terra, M. B., Barros, H. M. T., Stein, A. T., Figueria, I., Athayde, L. D., Ott, D. R., De Azambuja, R., & Da Silveria, D. X. (2008). Predictors of relapse in 300 Brazilian alcoholic patients: A 6-month follow-up study. *Substance Use and Misuse,* 43(3-4), 403-411.

The Real Project (2010). How we do it. Available from http://fsureal.com/how-we-do-it/.

The Rockefeller University (n.d.) Topic: Leptin. Retrieved 11/11/10 from http://newswire.rockefeller.edu/topics/leptin/.

Thornton, B., Faires, A., Robbins, M., & Rollins, E. (2014). The mere presence of a cell phone may be distracting: implication for attention and task performance. *Social Psychology,* 1-10.

Tindle, H. A., Chang, Y., Kuller, L. H., Manson, J. E., Robinson, J. G......& Matthews, K. A. (2009). Optimism, cynical hostility, and incident coronary disease and mortality in the women's health initiative. *Circulation,* 120 (8), 656-662.

Tomasello, M. (2004). Culture and cognitive development. In Lerner, J & Alberts, A. E., Eds. *Current Directions in Developmental Psychology.* Upper Saddle River, NJ: Pearson Prentice Hall.

Tomasello, M., Striano, T., & Rochat, P. (1999). Do young children use objects as symbols? *British Journal of Developmental Psychology,* 17, 563-584.

Tonigan, J. S. & Rice, S. L. (2010). Is it beneficial to have an alcoholics anonymous sponsor? *Psychology of Addictive Behaviors,* 24 (3),397-403.

Torgovnick, K. (2012, Sept. 11). TED Blog: Some stats on the devastating impact of mental illness worldwide followed by some reasons for hope. Retrieved from http://blog.ted.com/2012/09/11/some-stats-on.

Toseeb, U. & Inkster, B. (2015). Online social networking sites and mental health research. *Frontiers in Psychiatry,* 6 (36), 1-4.

Trace, S. E., Baker, J. H., Penas-Lledo, E., & Bulik, C. M. (2013). The genetics of eating disorders. *Annual Review of Clinical Psychology,* 9: 589-620.

Triandis, H. C. & Gelfand, M. (2012). A theory of individualism and collectivism. In P.A.M. Van Lange, A. Kruglanski & E. Higgins (Eds.), *Handbook of Social Psychological Theories,* (Vol. 2, 498-520). Los Angeles. CA: Sage.

Triandis, H. (2007). Culture and psychology: a history of the study of their relationship. In S. Kitayama & D. Cohen, (Eds.), *Handbook of Cross-Cultural Psychology.* New York: The Guilford Press.

Triandis, H. C. (1999). Cross-cultural psychology. *Asian Journal of Social Psychology,* Vol. 2, 127-143.

Triandis, H.C. (1995). *Individualism and Collectivism.* Boulder, CO: Westview Press.

Triandis, H. (1994). *Culture and Social Behavior.* New York: McGraw-Hill.

Triandis, H.C. (1989). The self and social behavior in differing cultural contexts. *Psychological Review.* 96(3), 506-520.

Tversky, A. & Kahneman, D. (1974). Judgment under uncertainty: heuristics and biases. *Science, New Series,* 185(4157), 1124-1131.

Tversky, A. & Kahneman, D. (1973). Availability: a heuristic for judging frequency and probability. *Cognitive Psychology,* 5, 207-232.

US Burden of Disease Collaborators (2013). The state of US health, 1990-2010: Burden of diseases, injuries, and risk factors. *JAMA,* 6, 591-608.

US Census Bureau (2016). Income and poverty in the United States. Retrieved from www.census.org.

US Department of Education (n.d.). Florida State University: An integrated approach to reduce high-risk drinking. Available from www.higheredcenter.org/prevention/examples/florida-state-university.

US Department of Health and Human Services (2012). *Overweight and Obesity Statistics.* National Institute of Health.

Uttal, D. H., Meadow, N. G., Tipton, E., Hand, L. L., Alden, A. R., Warren, C., & Newcombe, N. S. (2013). The malleability of spatial skills: a meta-analysis of training studies. *Psychological Bulletin,* 139 (2), 352-402.

Valian, V. (2009). Women at the top of science—and elsewhere. In S. J. Ceci & W. M. Williams, (Eds.), *Why Aren't More Women in Science? Top Researchers Debate the Evidence.* Washington, D.C.: American Psychological Association.
Valkenburg, P. M. & Peter, J. (2007). Preadolescents' and adolescents' online communication and their closeness to friends. *Developmental Psychology,* 43(2), 267-277.

van den Hurk, P.A.M., Janssen, B. F., Batendregt, H. P., & Gielen, S. C. (2010). Mindfulness meditation is associated with alterations in bottom-up processing: Psychophysiological evidence for reduced reactivity. *International Journal of Psychophysiology,* 78, 151-157.

Vargas, P. & Jurado, L. (2016) Dietary acculturation among Filipino Americans. *International Journal of Environmental Research and Public Health,* 13(16), 1-11.

Vargas, S. M., Cabassa, L. J., Nicasio, A., De La Cruz, A. A., Jackson, E., Rosario, M. ... & Lewis-Fernandez, R. (2015). Toward a cultural adaptation of pharmacotherapy: Latino views of depression and antidepressant therapy. *Transcultural Psychiatry,* 52 (2), 244-273.

Verbeke, W. & Vackier, I. (2005). Individual determinants of fish consumption: application of the theory of planned behavior. *Appetite,* 44, 67-82.

Viceroy, B. G., Samuels, M. A., & Ropper, A. H. (2010). How neurologists think: a cognitive perspective on missed diagnoses. *Annals of Neurology,* 67(4), 425-433.

Vucetic, Z., Kimmel, J., Totoki, K., Hollenbeck, E., and Reyes, T. M. (2010). Maternal high-fat diet alters methylation and gene expression of dopamine and opioid-related genes. *Endocrinology,* 151:10, 4756-64.

Vygotsky, L. (1978). *Mind and Society.* Cambridge: Harvard University Press.

Vygotsky, L. (1934). *Thought and Language.* Cambridge: The MIT Press.

Wabitsch, M., Funcke, J., Lennerz, B., Kuhnle-Krahl, U., Lahr, G., Debatin, K., Vatter, P. . . . Fischer-Posovszky, P. (2015). Biologically inactive leptin and early-onset extreme obesity. *The New England Journal of Medicine,* 372, 48-54.

Wagner, D. A. (1975). The effects of verbal labeling on short-term and incidental memory: a cross-cultural and developmental study. *Memory and Cognition,* 3(6), 595-598.

Wagner, D. A. (1973). The development of short-term and incidental memory: a cross-cultural study. *National Institute of Child Health and Human Development, Report #31.*

Walcutt, D. (2009). Stages of Sleep. *Psych Central.* Retrieved 1/9/2015 from http://psychcentral.com/lib/stages-of-sleep/0002073.

Wallace, J. (1990). The new disease model of alcoholism. *Western Journal of Medicine, Addiction Medicine* [Special Issue], 152, 502-505.

Wallace, P. (2016). *The Psychology of the Internet, 2nd Edition.* Cambridge: Cambridge University Press.

Walker, M., Thornton, L., De Choudhury, M., Teevan, J., Bulik, C. M., Levinson, C. A., & Zerwas, S. (2015). Facebook use and disordered eating in college-aged women. *Journal of Adolescent Health.* 57, 157-163.

Wang, Y. (2008). Tai Chi exercise and the improvement of mental and physical health among college students. *Medical Sport Science*, 52, 135-145.

Wang, Q. (2007). "Remember when you got the big, big bulldozer?" Mother-child reminiscing over time and across cultures. *Social Cognition*, 25: 4, 455-471.

Wang, Q. & Aydin, C. (2009). Cultural issues in flashbulb memory. In O. Luminet & A. Curci, (Eds.), *Flashbulb Memories: New Issues and Perspectives.* Hove and New York: Psychology Press.

Washington University in St. Louis (n.d.). C DIS-IV Description. Retrieved from http://epi.wustl.edu/DIS/disdescription.htm.

WebMD (2010). Orlistat, Xenical, alli. Available from www.Medicinenet.com/Orlistat/article.htm.

Webster, S., Lewis, J, & Brown, A. (2013). Ethical considerations in qualitative research. In J. Ritchie, J. Lewis, C. McNaughton Nicholls, & R. Ormston, (Eds.), *Qualitative Research Practice, 2nd Edition.* Los Angeles, CA: Sage.

Werker, J. F. & Lalonde, C. F. (1988). Cross-language speech perception: Initial capabilities and developmental change. *Developmental Psychology,* Vol. 24, No. 5, 672-683.

Werner, E.E. (2005). Resilience in development. In Morf, C.L. & Ayduk, O. (Eds.), *Current Directions in Personality Psychology.* Upper Saddle River, NJ: Pearson Prentice Hall.

Wilhelm, I., Diekelmann, S. & Born, J. (2008). Sleep in children improves memory performance on declarative but nor procedural tasks. *Learning & Memory*, 15, 373-377.

Williams, J. E. & Best, D. L. (1994). Cross-cultural views of women and men. In W. Lonner & R. Malpass (Eds.), *Psychology and Culture.* Boston: Allyn & Bacon.

Williams, T. M. (1986). *The Impact of Television: A Natural Experiment in Three Communities.* London: Academic Press.

Willig, C. (2001). *Introducing Qualitative Research in Psychology: Adventures in Theory and Method.* New York: Open University Press.

Wolfson, A. R. & Carskadon, M. A. (1998). Sleep schedules and daytime functioning in adolescents. *Child Development*, 69: 4, 875-887.

Wong, P. C. M., Roy, A. K., & Margulis, E. H. (2009). Bimusicalism: the implicit dual enculturation of cognitive and affective systems. *Music Perception*, 27(2), 81-88.

Wood, E., Zivvcakova, L., Gentile, P., Archer, K.,De Pasquale, D., & Nosko, A. (2011). Examining the impact of off-task multitasking with technology on real-time classroom learning. *Computers and Education,* 58, 365-374.

World Health Organization (2015). *Alcohol Fact Sheet.* www.who.org.

World Health Organization (2015). *Obesity and overweight, Fact sheet No.311.* www.who.org.

World Health Organization (2014). *10 Facts on the State of Global Health.* www.who.org.

World Health Organization (2012). *Global Health Observatory Data: 10 leading causes of death.* www.who.org.

World Health Organization (2004). Prevalence, severity, and unmet needs for treatment of mental disorders in the World Health Organization world mental health surveys. *Journal of the American Medical Association, 291*(21).

World Health Organization (2001). *World Health Report, 2001.* www.who.org.

World Health Organization (1948). WHO definition of health. Preamble to the constitution of the World Health Organization as adopted by the International Health Conference, New York, 19-22, June, 1946; signed on 22, July 1946 by the representatives of the 61 States (Official Records of the World Health Organization, no. 2, p. 100) and entered into force on 7 April 1948.

Wright, D. B., Boyd, C. E., & Tredoux, C. G. (2001). A field study of own-race bias in South Africa and England. *Psychology, Public Policy, and Law*, 7: 1, 119-133.

Wrightsman, L. S., Greene, E., Nietzel, M. T., & Fortune, W. H. (2002). *Psychology and The Legal System*, 5th Ed. Belmont, CA: Wadsworth.

Wu, B. & Smith, C. Acculturation and environmental factors influencing dietary behaviors and body mass index of Chinese students in the United States. *Appetite*, Epub ahead of print.

Wyatt, T. D. (2015). The search for human pheromones: the lost decades and the necessity of returning to first principles. *Proceedings of the Royal Society B*, 282, 1-9.

Yamada, A. M. & Marsella, A. J. (2013). The study of culture and psychopathology: Fundamental concepts and historic forces. In F. A. Paniagua & A. M. Yamada, (Eds.), *Handbook of Multicultural Mental Health: Assessment and Treatment of Diverse Populations, 2nd Ed.* Amsterdam: Elsevier.

Yin, R. (2009). *Case Study Research: Design and Methods*, 4th Ed. Los Angeles: Sage Publications.

Yoon, E. Chang, C., Kim, S., Clawson, A., Cleary, S. E., Hansen, M.....Gomes, A. M. (2013). A meta-analysis of acculturation/enculturation and mental health. *Journal of Counseling Psychology*, 60(1), 15-30.

Young, R. McD., Connor, J. P., Ricciardelli, L. A., & Saunders, J. B. (2006). The role of alcohol expectancies and drinking refusal self-efficacy beliefs in university drinking students. *Alcohol and Alcoholism*, 41(1) 70-75.

Yuki, M, Maddux, W. W., Brewer, M. B, & Takemura, K. (2005). Cross-cultural differences in relationship- and group-based trust. *Personality and Social Psychology Bulletin*, 31: 1, 48-62.

Yuki, M. (2003). Intergroup comparison versus intragroup relationships: a cross-cultural examination of social identity theory in North America and East Asian cultural contexts. *Social Psychology Quarterly*, 66: 2, 166-183.

Xu, F., Wu, Q., Xie, L., Gong, W., Zhang, J., Zheng, P......Xie, P. (2015). Macaques exhibit a naturally-occurring depression similar to humans. *Scientific Reports*, 5:1-10.

Zahn-Waxler, C., Radke-Yarrow, M. & King, R. (1979). Childrearing and children's prosocial initiations toward victims in distress. *Child Development*, 50, 319-330.

Zeeland, A.A., Bloss, C. S., Tewhwy, R., Bansal, V., Torkamani, A., Libiger, O. ... & Schork, N. J. (2014). Evidence for the role of *EPHX2* gene variants in anorexia nervosa. *Molecular Psychiatry*, 19, 724-732.

Zemore, S. E. & Ajzen, I. (2014) Predicting substance abuse treatment completion using a new scale based on the theory of planned behavior. *Journal of Substance Abuse Treatment*, 46, 174-182.

Zhang, Z., Man, S. C., Li, T. Y. J., Wong, W., et al. (2012). Dense cranial electroacupuncture stimulation for major depression- A single-blind, randomized, controlled study. *PLoS ONE*, 7 (1). e29651.

Zimbardo, P. (2007). *The Lucifer Effect*. New York: Random House.

Zimmerman, P, Bruckl, T., Nocon, A., Pfister, H., Binder, E. B...........Ising, M. (2011). Interaction of FKBP5 Gene variants and adverse life events in predicting depression onset: Results from a 10-year prospective community study. *American Journal of Psychiatry*, 168(10), 1-18.

Zinbarg, R. E., & Mineka, S. (Jan, 2000). Animal models of anxiety disorders. NITOP. St. Pete Beach, FL.

Ziv, Y. (2005). Attachment-based intervention programs. In L. J. Berlin, Y. Ziv, L. Amaya-Jackson, & Greenberg, M. T. (Eds.). *Enhancing Early Attachments*, New York: Guilford Press.

Index

CPSIA information can be obtained
at www.ICGtesting.com
Printed in the USA
LVOW05s1700250417

532120LV00007B/285/P

9 781530 993345